TRIPWIRE 30

ENOUGH.

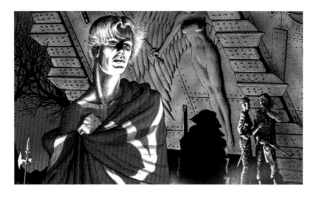

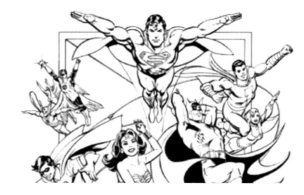

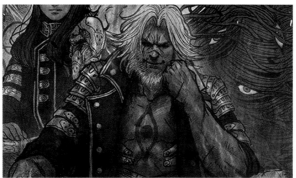

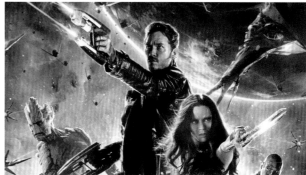

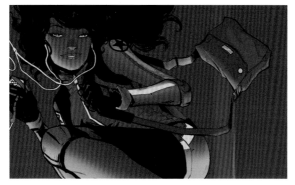

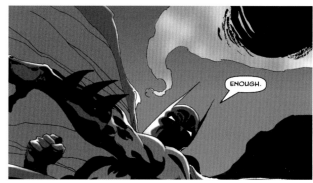

CONTENTS

CONTENTS

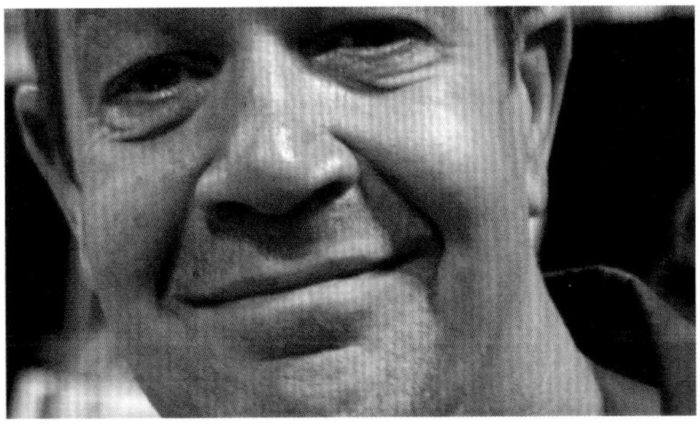

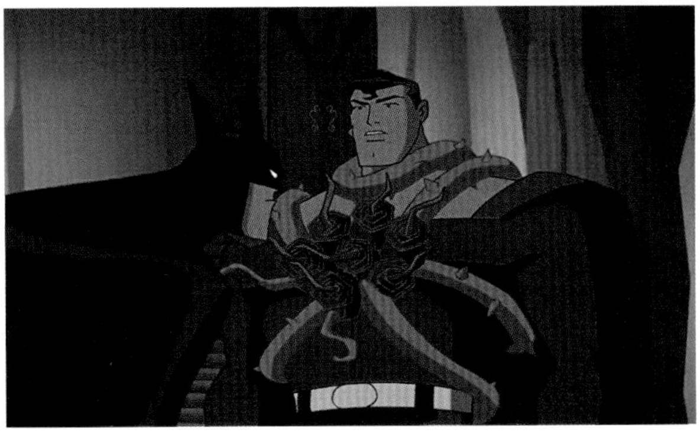

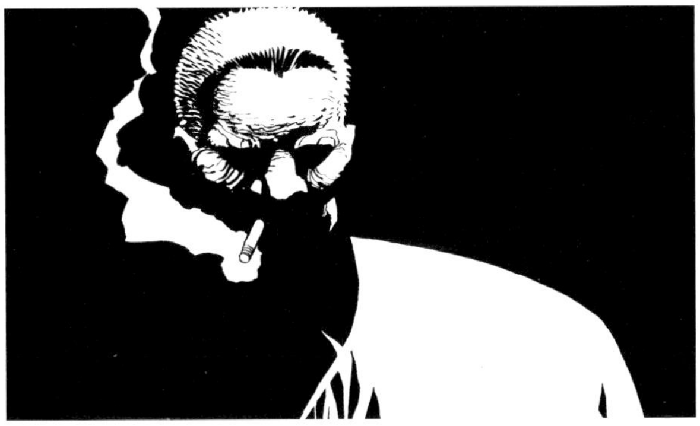

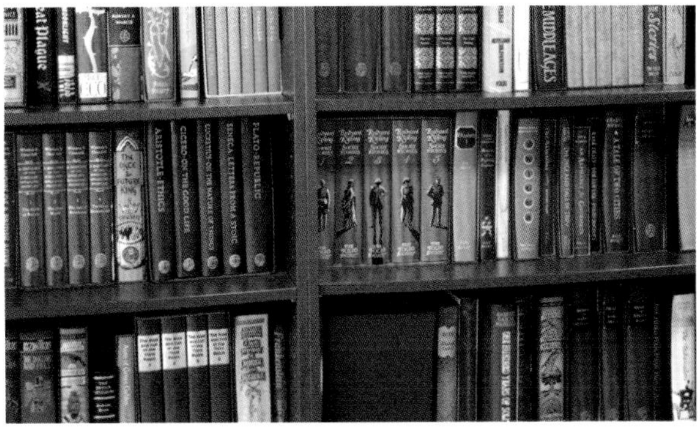

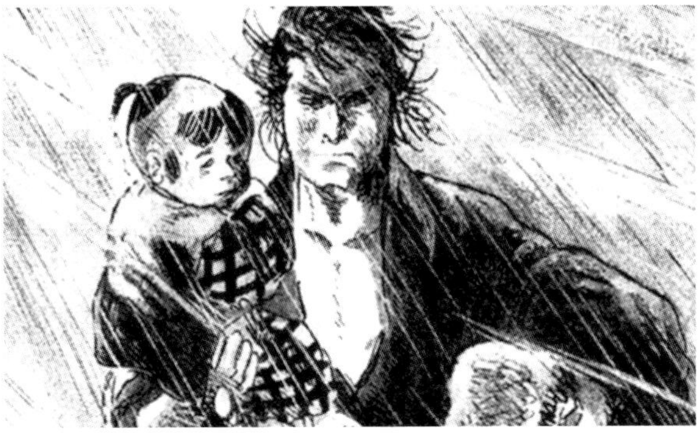

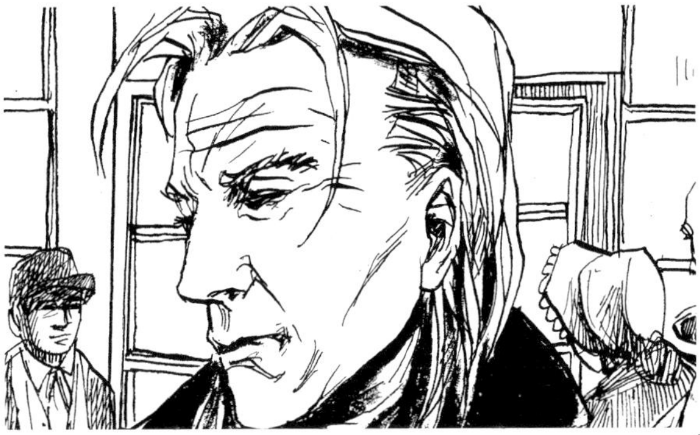

THE TEAM

Joel Meadows
editor-in-chief/ design and layout

Andrew Colman
senior editor/ proofreading and copy editing

Scott Braden
consulting editor

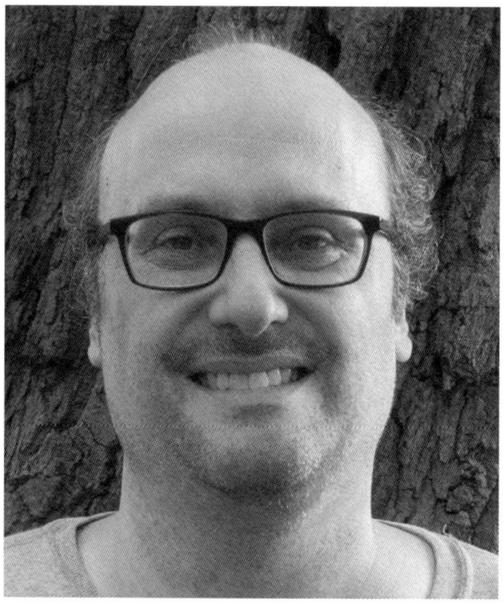

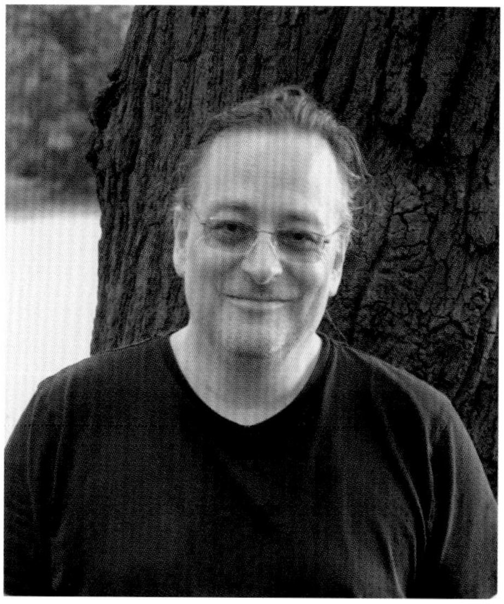

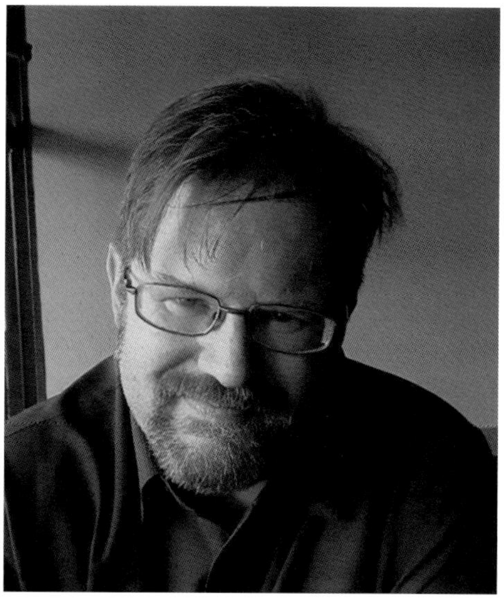

Cover design: Kit Caoagas
Contributing writers: Robert Cave, Tim Hayes, Roger Langridge
Contributing artists: Andy Bennett, Laurence Campbell, Amanda Conner, Simon Davis, Frazer Irving, Jock, Roger Langridge, Shawn Martinbrough, Frank Miller, Frank Quitely, Dan Schaffer, Martin Simmonds, Drew Struzan, Bill Sienkiewicz, Walter Simonson, Bryan Talbot
Special thanks to: Joseph Illidge, Kris Longo, Cat Nuwer, James Killen and Martin Wendel at Heavy Metal, Dirk Wood, Eric Stephenson and Kat Salazar at Image, Amy Huey at Dark Horse, Allison Pond at Mad Cave, Rich Young at Ablaze, Tom Walker at The Folio Society, Silenn Thomas, Ryn Gardner at Prestel Publishing, Stuart Ng, Strange Adventures, Greg Preston, Biff at Ace Comics, Andy Bennett, all of the artists who have given us pieces for this book, design advice from Mark Chiarello, Leonard Sultana and anyone else we have forgotten. Thanks also to our writers on the Tripwire website like Paul N Neal and Stephen Dalton who contribute a great deal to our online presence.

ISBN13: 9781955537391 (softcover)
ISBN13: 9781399933469 (hardcover)

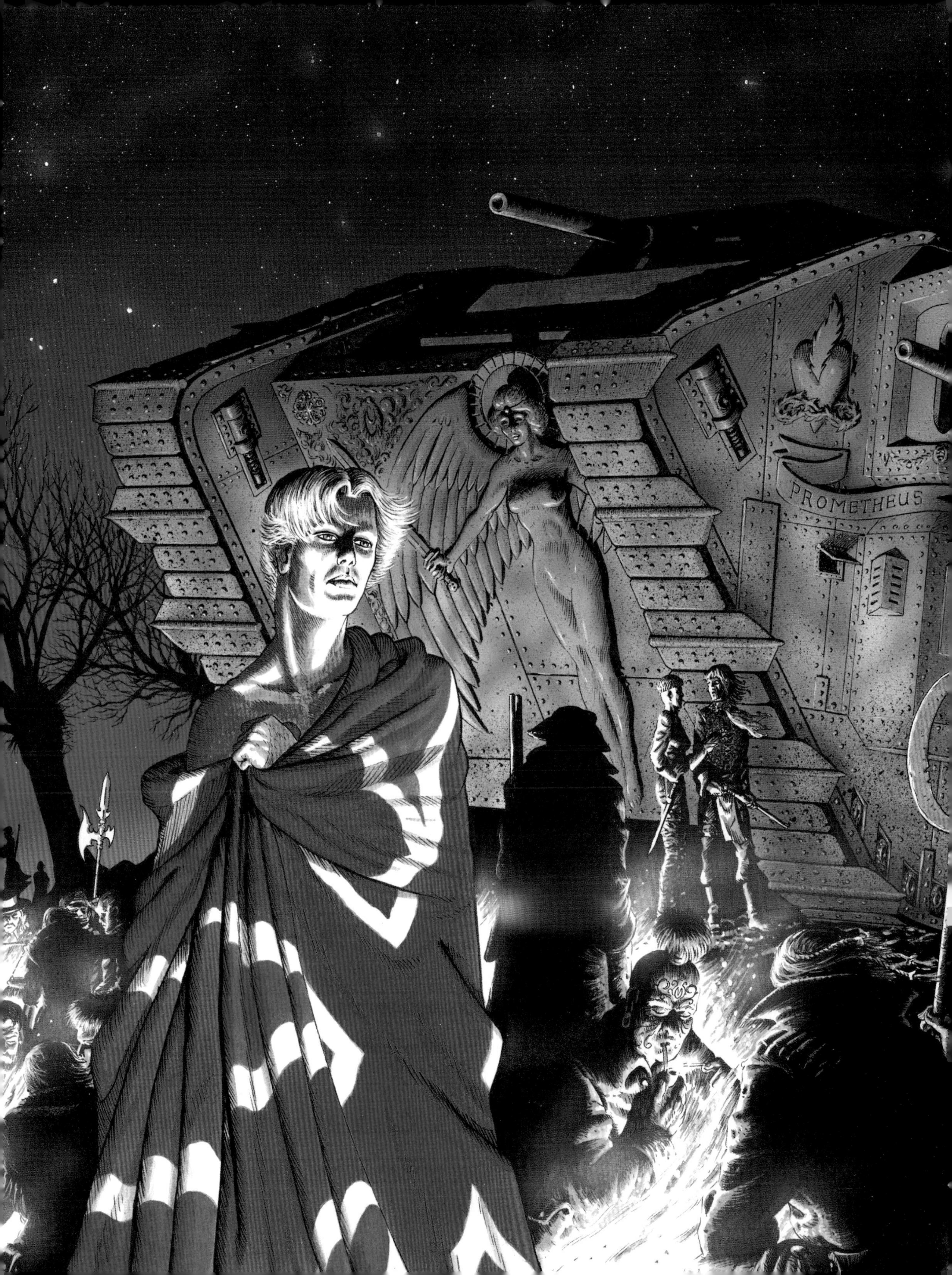
PROMETHEUS

A TRIP THROUGH THE WIRES

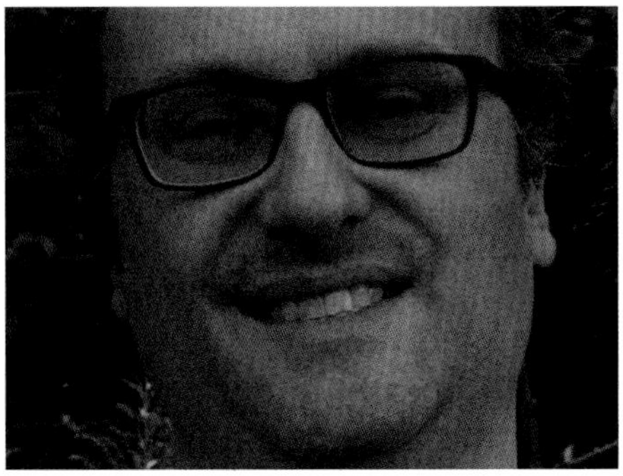

The last time we did one of these anniversary celebrations, it was for our 21st birthday. This time around it is the bigger milestone of 30 years. I never imagined when I was 19 and started the magazine just as a fanzine and a bit of fun to be honest that thirty years later, I would still be talking about it and it would still be a major part of my life.

This book is intended to celebrate thirty years of the magazine and also act as a snapshot for three decades of the changes in the comics industry as well. We have gathered our best current and historical crop of writers like Tim Hayes, Robert Cave, Scott Braden plus the magazine's number two Andrew Colman to document the last thirty years. Braden has contributed quite a bit to this anniversary book but Colman has also done a lot of work on the book too, making certain that it is proofread and copy edited before it goes to press. There have been a huge amount of changes since *Tripwire*'s rather primitive first issue which came out at the very end of February 1992. Vertigo hadn't even really started, Image had just launched and the market was still dominated by superheroes from the big two. Comic book movies were out there but they were not a major part of popular culture.

It wasn't always easy for us either. Between 2003 and 2007 we suspended publishing but we came back stronger with our first print annual which was 124 pages thick. We did stop publishing in print once again in 2011 but we switched to a website in 2015. Then because we missed publishing hard copies, our Tripwire winter 2020 special came out, a print magazine that we are very proud of because it had been a decade since the last one. 2021 saw another print edition and this year will see the third one since we returned to producing magazines.

This book is a mix of classic reprints and a lot of new material plus a selection of pieces of art peppered throughout by the likes of Frank Miller, Walter Simonson, Bill Sienkiewicz, Drew Struzan, Jock, Laurence Campbell, Frazer Irving and many more. It also features the debut of the third *Sherlock Holmes and The Empire Builders* comic strip, The Secret Files of Oswald Mosley, written by me and again drawn by my very talented collaborator, artist and co-creator Andy Bennett. The book also includes a brand new two page *Fred The Clown* strip written and drawn by its creator Roger Langridge.

It has been a challenge to try to boil down thirty years of our history into 224 pages but I think we have done it justice. I do want to thank Kris Longo and Joe Illidge at Heavy Metal for acting as joint supervisors for this project as they have been very generous with their time. Of course we also have to thank Heavy Metal for publishing this too. I'd also like to thank the companies who have kindly advertised in our section at the back of the book as well as the two kind gentlemen who have provided a foreword and an introduction here: Dirk Wood from Image Comics and Marty Grosser, editor of Diamond's *Previews* magazine.

Tripwire 30 is a look back but also a look forward, offering a few clues as to what we have planned for the future. The strip section at the back may offer a few pointers as to what we have coming up over the next couple of years. Thanks for reading, thanks for supporting us over the past thirty years and here's to what's next.

Joel Meadows
Editor-in-chief
Tripwire Magazine and tripwiremagazine.co.uk

INTRODUCTION

Most of you will have no idea who I am, but I've worked in the Comics industry for over 40 years. In my earliest days, I worked at the retail level at my local comic shop, Comics & Comix, at the Birdcage Walk outdoor mall in Citrus Heights, California. After five years with C&C, I was hired by Northern California comics distributor, Bud Plant, Inc., as a customer service agent and, in the second year of my time with BPI, as the head writer for Bud Plant's Quicklist catalog. It was this final role that led me to where I am today in my role as the managing editor of Diamond Comic Distributor's *PREVIEWS* catalog (since 1988).

When I started my long career with Comics, my experience with the British comics scene (and Brit fandom) was fairly limited. *Doctor Who* episodes on the local public TV channel, early issues of the *2000AD* weekly magazine, *Starburst* (the UK's answer to our Starlog), and the material to be found in the *Warrior* comics magazine including Alan Moore's *Marvelman* reboot and *V for Vendetta*, among others. And every once in a while, the odd copy of the UK comics and entertainment magazine, Tripwire.

Over the years, I had encountered the odd copy of *Tripwire* here and there. I wasn't much of a 'zine reader – when it came to the comics, I preferred to let the comics do the talking. But *Tripwire* was different. It was, to me, a "foreign" voice, speaking to me about the comics and entertainment that I knew well, but also the UK releases and creators that I had never heard of. It would take years and the help of a good friend for me to finally catch up with Tripwire... and appreciate it for what it was.

That good friend is my "brother from another mother", Scott Braden, co-creator of *Kent Menace*, which I have proudly supported with my editor's eye, and my late-in-life emerging writing skills. Over the years that I have known Scott, he has always been a major promoter (and contributor) to *Tripwire*. And many is the time that Scott has spoken highly of his friend Joel, and about Joel's labour of love, *Tripwire*. These were the first times that I finally connected the magazine with a name... with a guiding force. Just as *Famous Monsters of Filmland* had its Forrest J Ackerman, *Tripwire* had its Joel Meadows.

Joel obviously loves comics and entertainment. One doesn't associate themselves with something for so long if they don't have a deeply felt appreciation for the subject matter. And I guess Joel really does give a damn. I've spoken to Joel over the phone before, but aside from that, we've never met in-person. I hope to remedy that this fall at the New York Comic Con, whereat Mr. Meadows will be in attendance. Along with my pal Scott, we'll hopefully meet up with Joel in the Big Apple, discuss Joel's latest contribution to the Kent Menace mythos (his story, "Down by the River" in *KM #1: Dangers from the Depths* is simply fantastic!), and will sink a pint or two, have a few laughs, and best of all, just talk comics. It's something that Tripwire has done masterfully for the past 30 years.

So, I tip my hat (figuratively) to Joel Meadows and *Tripwire*! I wasn't "with it" enough to fully appreciate you and your message years ago, but with maturity comes clarity, understanding and appreciation for the better things. Thanks for waiting for me to catch up, mate. And here's to 30 more years!

Marty Grosser
Editor *PREVIEWS*; *Kent Menace* Series
August 2022

Has it really been 30 years since the launch of TRIPWIRE?!?!

Sigh, of course it has. It shouldn't surprise me at this rate. I saw recently that it was the 30th anniversary of the soundtrack to the movie *Singles*. And while that movie was forgettable, the soundtrack... well it was the soundtrack to my early twenties. I was an adult when it came out. I've reached the point in my life where things that are thirty years old... I was an adult when they arrived. Those are my movies, my music... my magazines.

Which brings me to *Tripwire*.

I was born in 1970. As I write this, it's 2022. I could do a bunch of painful math concerning the difference between being 22 years old in 1992, and being 22 years old NOW, but suffice to say -- *Tripwire* was born into a very different world than the one we live in. And so was I, and we've both had a few changes over the years, but (I like to think) we've both stayed pretty true to who we are.

In the early to mid-nineties I was in comics retail, and it was a bit of a golden age for comic-related magazines. They were everywhere. There were plenty that had larger print runs, covering pretty mainstream topics, with price guides on "hot" issues, funny or controversial features about notable young creators, and so on. There were others that took a more academic approach, and dove deep into the careers of Winsor McCay et al. But it was during this time I first laid eyes on a copy of *Tripwire*, and it immediately struck me as different, and made for the likes of me.

Tripwire celebrated the art form of comics (and beyond) in a way I found completely unspoiled by bias. It didn't shy away from the mainstream. It didn't skewer it, either. In fact, it seemed to exist solely to point out the beauty of art, from a true fan's perspective. And that's not to say it didn't seem smart. It did. It dissected things as well as anyone. It just had, I thought, a pure mission statement: "Look at this stuff. Look at this art. Look at these people. Look how these people make this art and why they do it. Isn't it, and aren't they, GREAT?"

I'm not sure if Joel and his stalwart crew, who've soldiered on making *Tripwire* all these years, will agree with my assessment there. I certainly don't mean it to dumb down what I know is an incredibly complicated and nuanced business, that of putting together a thoughtful and long-running magazine, as they obviously have. But that's how it has always felt to me. *Tripwire* felt and still feels like a sincere tribute to art, along with being a nice enough artifact to be art itself.

And that's a bit of the power and magic of print to me, and why I think it's so fitting for *Tripwire* to have returned to the printed page after a few years of being digital only. It's easy to see now, deep in the digital age, that the act of reading print ITSELF is in some way trafficking in instant nostalgia. The global age of immediate news makes the printed word seem obsolete. Old. Just like me. And it makes those of us who work in print, read print, celebrate print... Rebels. Just like the artists that *Tripwire* celebrates. I like the sound of that.

Dirk

Dirk Wood
Image Comics
Live from the Pine Street Theater
August 2022

FOREWORD

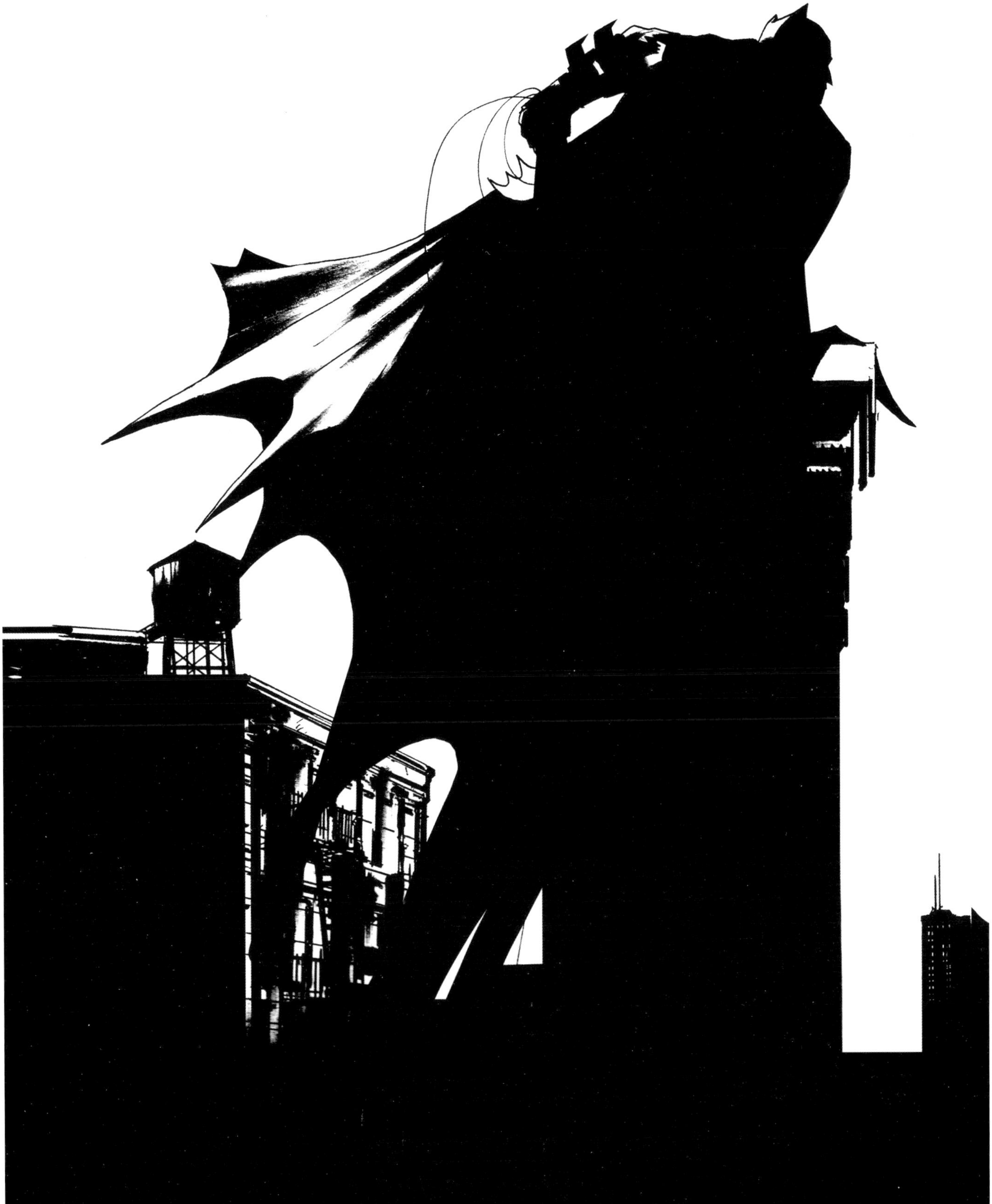

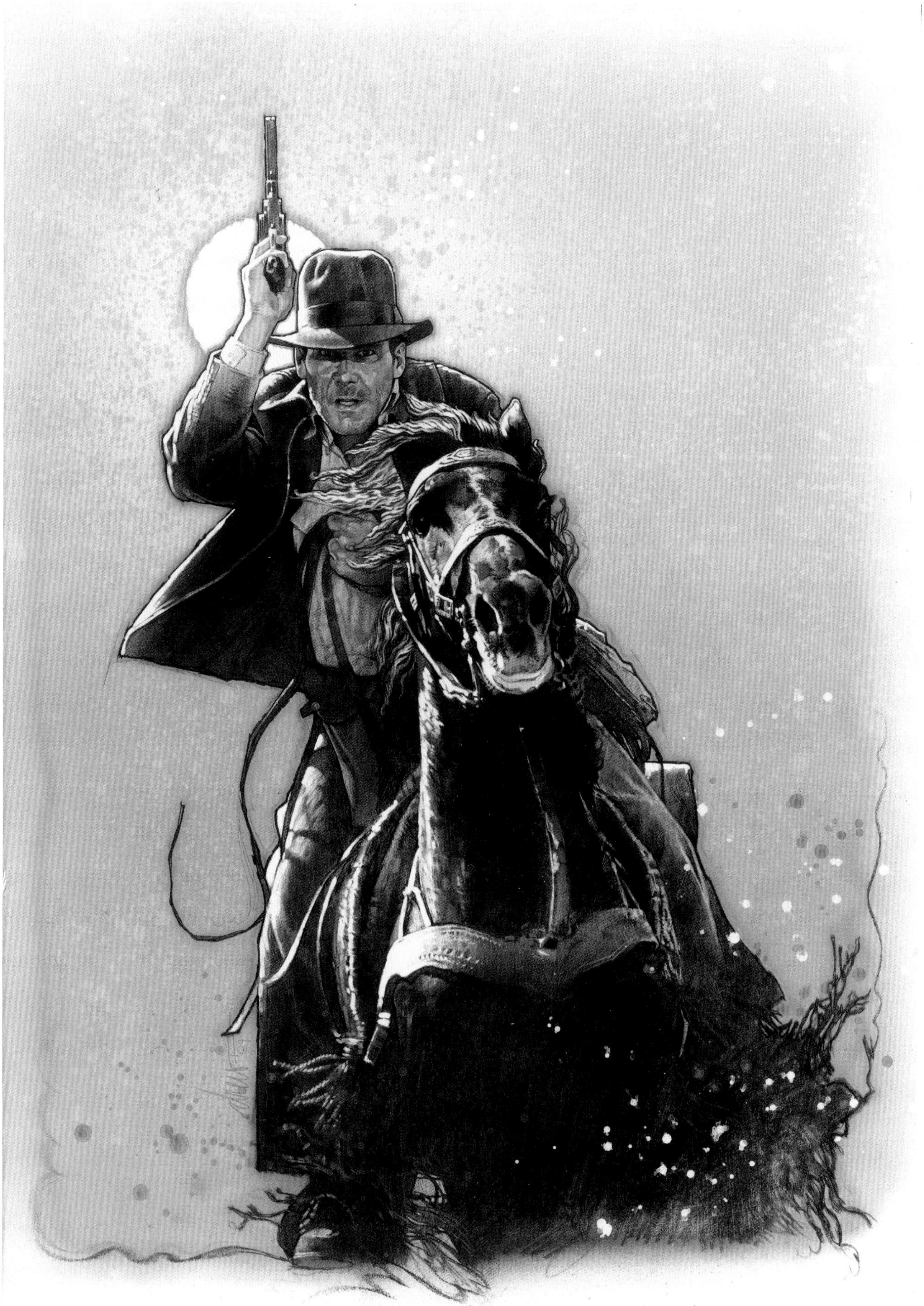

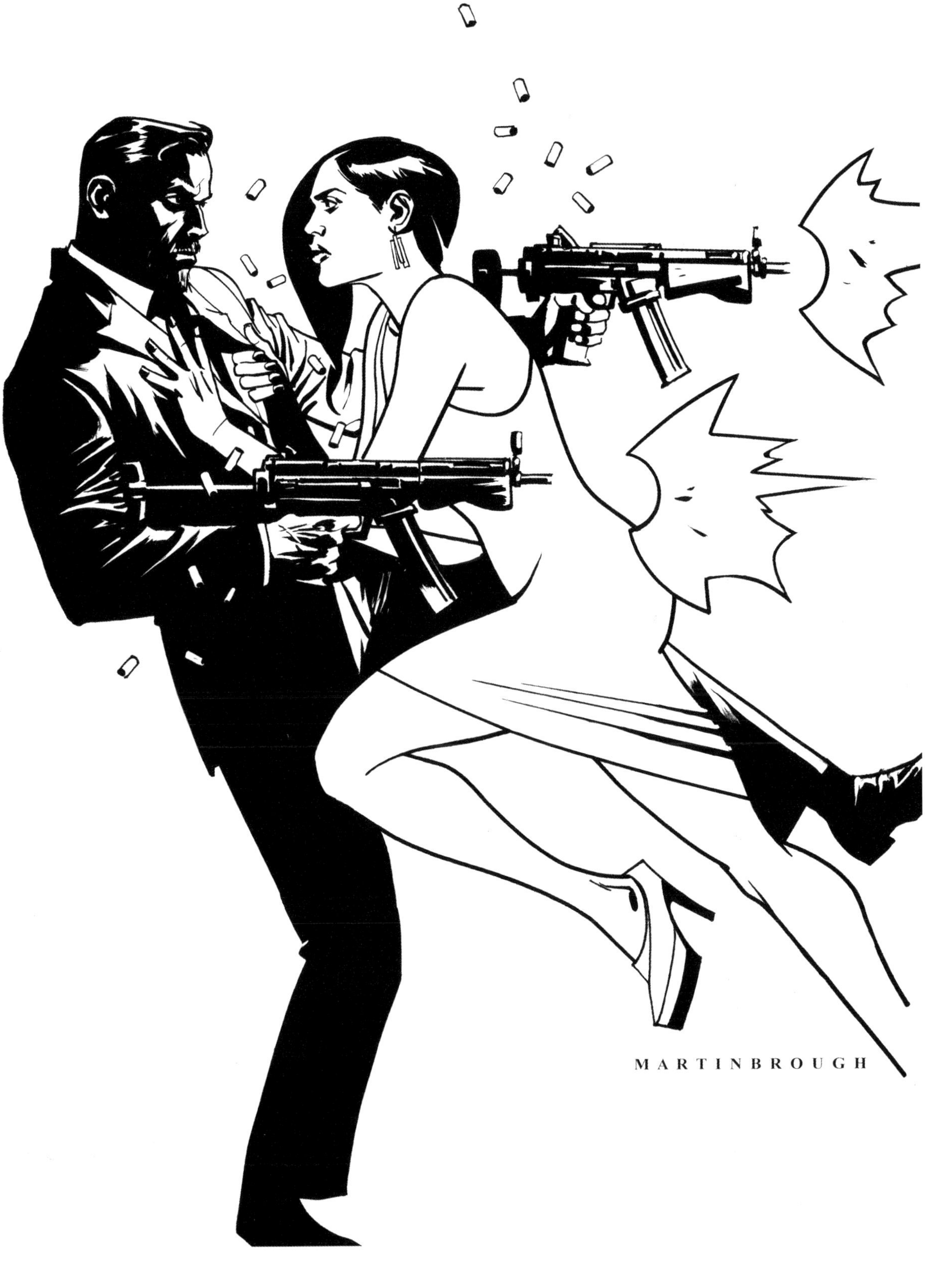
MARTINBROUGH

SCOTT BRADEN'S LOST TALES:
A LIBRARY OF DREAMS AND LONG-LOST STORIES

Scott Braden's Lost Tales has run in Tripwire since the late nineties and here's a few choice tales that remained lost and some that became found...

In his award-winning, critically acclaimed, and best-selling comic book series, *Sandman*, Neil Gaiman envisioned a library of dreams – a repository for all the wonderful ideas and marvelous stories that never came to pass.

Take a moment and imagine it. Imagine its musky smell, its elegant woodworking, and marble floors shining under pale lamplight. Imagine, if you will, its long, narrow halls filled to capacity with undiscovered works by Shakespeare, Dickens, Longfellow and Joyce. Books, billions and billions of books,

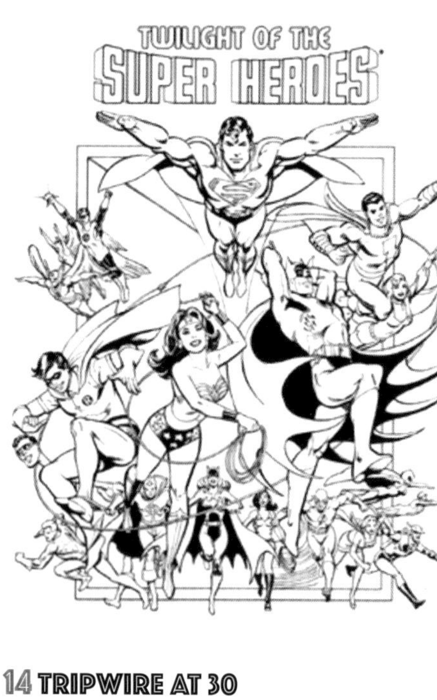
TWILIGHT OF THE
SUPER HEROES

THE BEAUTY OF ARTICLES SUCH AS THESE IS THAT THEY GIVE YOU A GLIMPSE INTO THE AUTHOR'S GREATNESS – A CHANCE TO EXAMINE INSPIRATION AND DREAMSTUFF IN THEIR MOST PRIMORDIAL FORMS.

by whomever you wanted to read at the time – anytime. Now, imagine if such a place existed.

I did.

In discussing his now-legendary untold comic book epic, *Twilight of the Super-Heroes*, Alan Moore referred to the lost tale as a "virtual comic" – reasoning that should it fail to meet the expectations of readers, that the idea was good enough.

Well, that's bullshit. I know I'm playing the ugly American here, but his story would have been friggin' amazing.

Complete with a marketing plan (buttons and T-shirts that would have warned pedestrians that we all were "Waiting for Twilight"), Moore's Twilight of the Super-Heroes would have injected a tangible sense of wonder into DC Comics' then lackluster titles, as well as laid the groundwork for countless stories to come.

Now, all that exists of this lost tale is his initial proposal – published by the "Distinguished Competition" in a 2021-cover dated hardcover collection full of '80s nostalgia, as well as drifting on the internet like a long-lost dream.

Still, can you imagine going to your comic book shop in 1988 and picking up Alan Moore and John Totleben's Twilight of the Super-Heroes #1 off the stands?

I could. And, I did something about it.

For those of you who care, I created Untold Tales for the dearly departed *Overstreet's FAN* magazine. Being in a position where I could ask creators about their unfinished works, I took advantage of that. In fact, those of you who picked up the magazine a quarter century ago can still find stories by such talented creators as Moore, Grant Morrison & Mark Millar, James Robinson, Rick Veitch, Bryan Talbot, Kurt Busiek, Chuck Dixon and John Byrne.

The beauty of articles such as these is that they give you a glimpse into the author's greatness – a chance to examine inspiration and dreamstuff in their most primordial forms. And, perhaps, once you've read these long lost tales, you'll find yourself holding them to your heart and mind, never letting go.

Now, imagine if you weren't given the opportunity to experience these untold stories for yourself.

Well, imagine no more, because that's where Scott Braden's Lost Tales came in three decades ago.

This column is my chance to shed some light on these amazing stories that never were, as well as an honest attempt to answer age-old questions like "What was this project about?" and "Why did this project never come out?" It's a library of dreams, containing stories that exist only in the author's imagination, waiting for their chance to come to light. And, like all true comic book fans know, it's not just the stories that we have in our hands that are cool – it's also those long lost tales that have gotten away from us.

Well, boys and girls, it's time we got those stories back.

Lost tales such as these:

THE KINGDOM

It was a dream project come true . . . almost.

After the phenomenal success of their best-selling *Kingdom Come* prestige format series for DC Comics, the dynamite creative team of Alex Ross and Mark Waid wanted to examine the events foreshadowing their apocalyptic story with the proposed ongoing series originally entitled Godhood – later changed to *The Kingdom*.

To chronicle what could have been a grand project, Ross enlisted a then-new talent by the name of Gene Ha to draw the proposed series; the same man who would go on to work with comic book grandmaster Alan Moore on the beloved super-heroic police drama, *Top 10*.

"Alex picked m-e," Ha said about his joining the proposed series as its artist. "He entered comics before I did, but we're about the same age and met at comic conventions. He liked my art, and obviously I liked his. Annoyingly, he's an even better and faster caricaturist than me!"

According to Ha, the would-be creators of *The Kingdom* met once in New York City to discuss the proposed series. The artist admitted that although they were together in the same room, very little had been decided there.

"Instead of creating a framework," Ha confessed, "we ended up just planting ideas that we developed later by phone and fax."

The original iteration of The Kingdom would have focused on the early days of *Kingdom Come*'s Magog, a complex character Waid referred to in the preliminary series bible (dated November 8, 1996) as "gullible" and "a villain who thinks he's a hero." And although not privy to the first conversations between Waid and Ross concerning Magog, Ha came to understand the "anti-hero" – and calling him that is just us being nice – from viewing Ross' initial designs

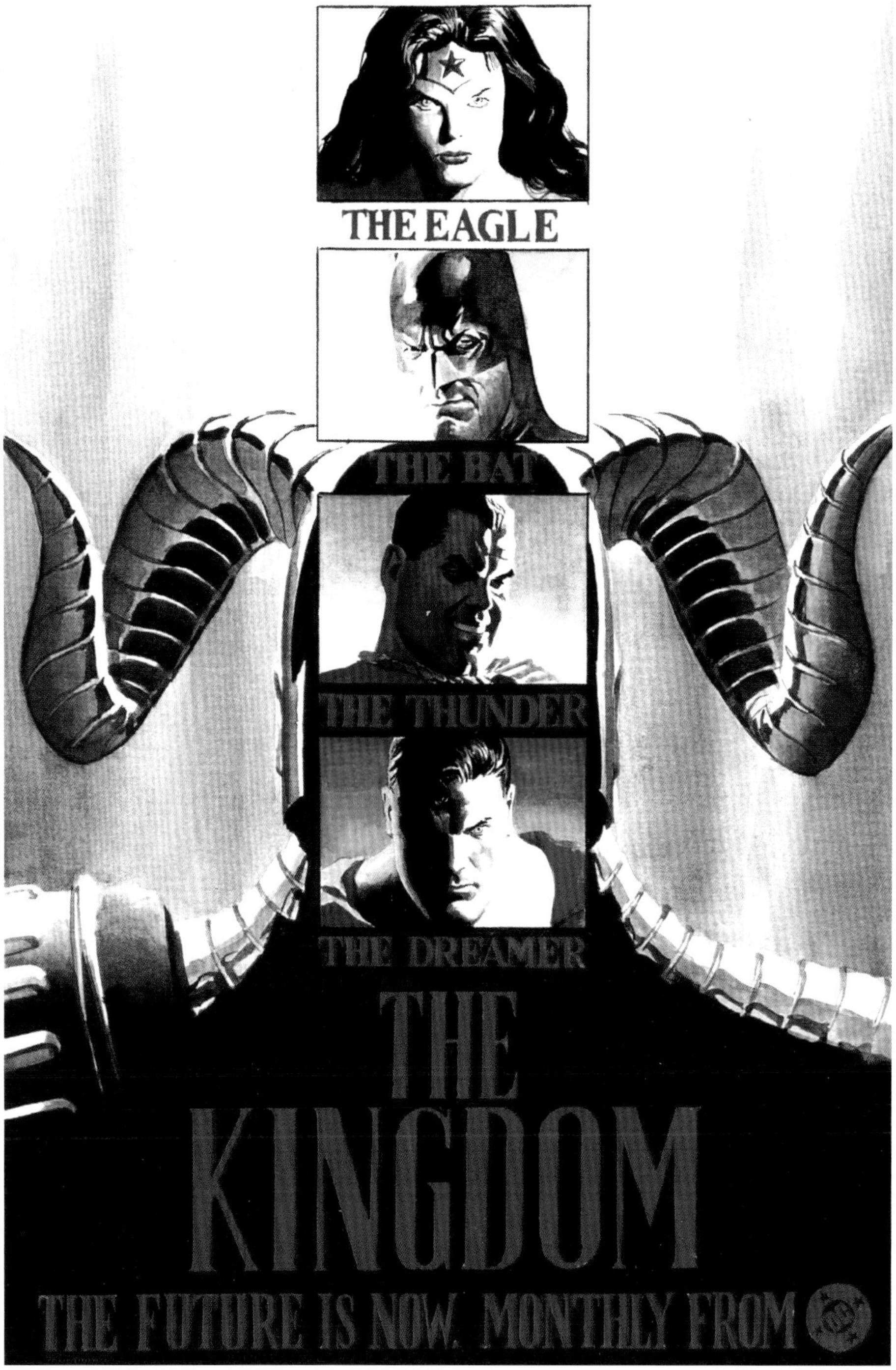
THE EAGLE
THE BAT
THE THUNDER
THE DREAMER
THE KINGDOM
THE FUTURE IS NOW. MONTHLY FROM

and notes on the role he would play in the series during its preliminary stages.

"Magog is younger and unscarred [than what we saw in *Kingdom Come*]," Ha said, "and still brimming with optimism."

The series would have also introduced an all-new Fourth World character named Gog. Gog, as revealed in Waid's preliminary bible, is "impossibly powerful" and would have been from the original world of the Old Gods; the massive planet that had split in two to become Apokolips and New Genesis. He is also the sole survivor of the original pantheon of divine giants. This enormous Fourth World spin-off character has seen many things in his many days, and supposedly, doesn't want Earth to follow in the same manner as his once great world did.

As far as the two, I asked Ha what was Magog's relationship with this mysterious, Kirbyesque "hero?"

"Gog is definitely the senior partner," revealed Ha. "I think it would be fair to call young Magog the sidekick to Gog. I think

"MAGOG IS YOUNGER AND UNSCARRED [THAN WHAT WE SAW IN KINGDOM COME] AND STILL BRIMMING WITH OPTIMISM."–GENE HA

copyright©DC Comics

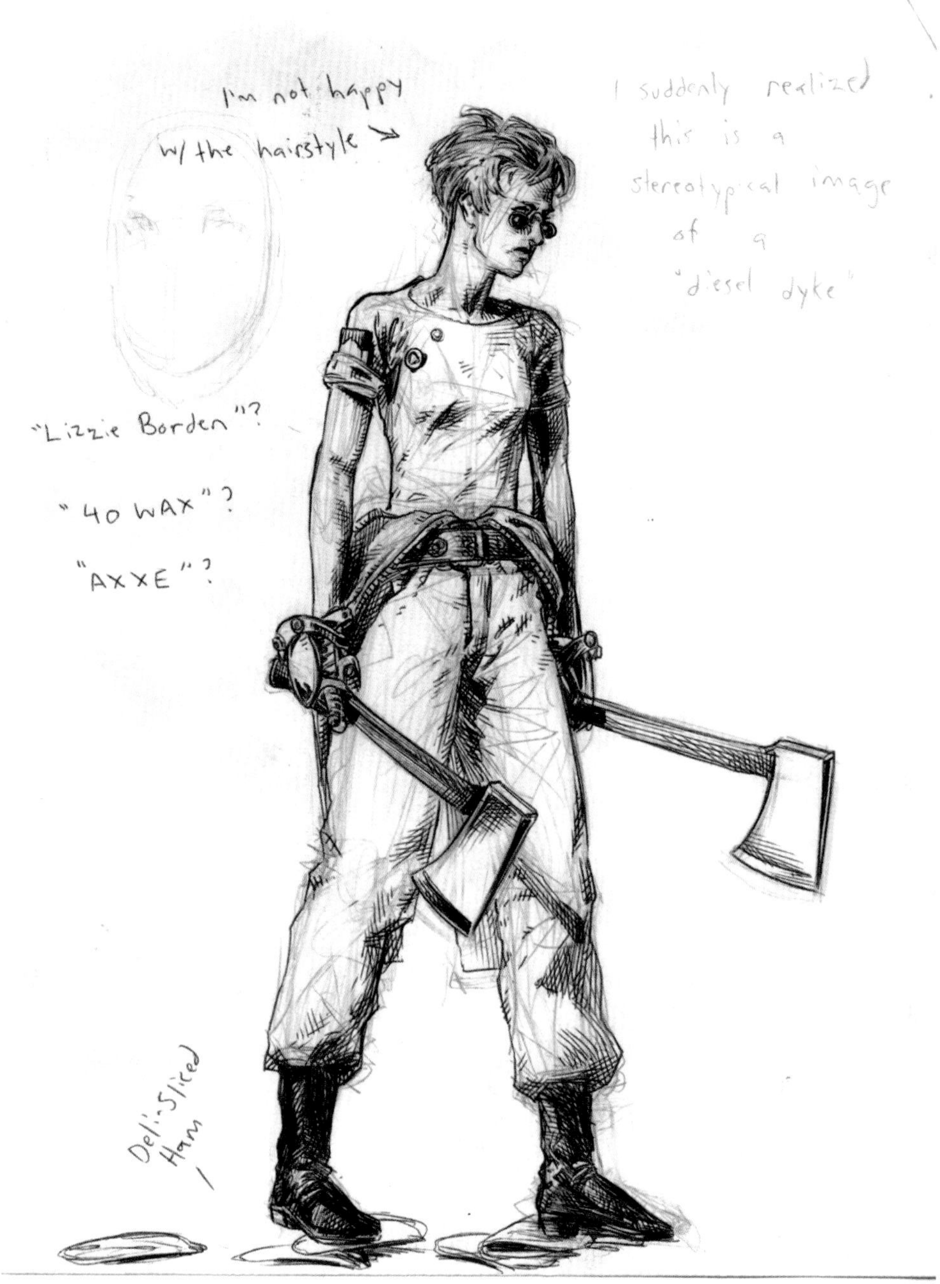
I'm not happy w/ the hairstyle →
I suddenly realized this is a stereotypical image of a "diesel dyke"
"Lizzie Borden"?
"40 WAX"?
"AXXE"?
Deli-Sliced Ham

"JUST AS KINGDOM COME WAS ABOUT WHAT HAPPENS WHEN SUPERMAN'S INFLUENCE IS ABSENT, THERE IS SOMETHING THEMATICALLY FULFILLING ABOUT THE KINGDOM ULTIMATELY REVOLVING AROUND SUPERMAN'S DIRECT INFLUENCE ON THE NEXT GENERATION OF SUPER-HUMANS. "–MARK WAID

Alex planned Gog to be a messianic revolutionary – full of good intentions, but ruthless in achieving them."

Those good intentions would turn out to be a lie, though. Yes, according to Waid's preliminary bible, Gog – who had told Magog that he didn't want *Kingdom Come* to come to pass 20 years in the future – was telling the truth about his motivations . . . in a sense. Instead, though, the Fourth Worlder wanted Kingdom Come to come to pass right now – in all its apocalyptic glory. And for his treachery, Gog would eventually be murdered by Magog who, according to Ross, was not happy with the future role he was fated to play in *Kingdom Come*. Their climatic battle would leave Magog scarred – physically, mentally, and emotionally.

The creators also tossed out a wealth of potential storylines in their initial series notes. Among these was having DC Comics' Man of Steel somehow involved with overpopulating The Kingdom with super-heroes.

"Both Alex and Mark have a profound love and understanding of Superman," Ha said unequivocally, "even deeper than my own. I can't really predict what those two would have come up with, as I learned by exchanging ideas with them and getting patiently schooled on Clark Kent. Waid and Ross' understanding of Clark Kent is truly epic."

Waid's preliminary bible once again clarifies this while shedding some light on some of the motivations behind the lost tale. According to the document, a "forbidden fruit" was to be devised out of Supes' molecular code – creating darker "heroes" like Manotaur, Nuculoid, Phoebus, Trix, Von Bach, and legions of others seen in the pages of the critically acclaimed Kingdom Come story. As Waid once again states in the bible, Superman's DNA "is the original sin that each day continues to spread and infect the world."

"Just as *Kingdom Come* was about what happens when Superman's influence is absent, there is something thematically fulfilling and thematically right about The Kingdom ultimately revolving around Superman's direct and active influence on the next generation of super-humans," Waid wrote.

Another concept that was thrown out there involving Superman – or rather iterations of him – was Ross' idea of having the Man of Tomorrow literally confronting his future self. Ross followed this up by writing, "Superman only truly makes sense at times of ongoing crisis. It doesn't have to be a 'comic book combat crisis.' After all, he was born during the Depression, an economic crisis."

Waid also suggested that readers could discover the transformations of their favorite heroes into their Kingdom Come personas through stand-alone issues peppered throughout the series. These "Untold Tales of Kingdom Come," as Waid coined the special done-in-one issues in his story bible, would be similar to James Robinson's "Times Past" episodes from his fan-favourite Starman title. The proposed "Untold Tales of Kingdom Come" would have allowed high-profile guest artists to contribute their talent to what ended up being a never-released series of stories.

What happened to The Kingdom then as it was described above? Funny you should ask.

The project – which never happened in its original form due to creative differences – did not totally die on the vine. Sans Ross and Ha,

The Kingdom instead evolved into a special comic book event that found Gog, a vindictive survivor of the holocaust that consumed the farmlands of Kansas, working his way back through time in an attempt to wipe Superman out of existence. The future heroes of *Kingdom Come* find themselves joining forces with the super-powered denizens of the current DC Universe (or at least as it stood circa 1999) to save the Man of Steel from this driven madman.

Later collected in a trade paperback, the superstar event of the late '90s featured Waid joining such talented artists as Jerry Ordway, Ariel Olivetti, Frank Quitely, Barry Kitson, and Mike Zeck, among others, to tell stories that broadened the *Kingdom Come* mythos. However enjoyable it was, though, the project as it was released was arguably not as ambitious as what Ross, Waid, and Ha had originally planned. After reviewing their hard work in building the original concept – while also considering what was ultimately released to readers – the original Godhood or The Kingdom, however you want to identify the project, was nothing less than divine.

BATMAN 33 AD

Comic book grandmaster Alan Weiss has worked with everyone from Steve Gerber to Alan Moore to Jim Shooter. He created fan-favorite characters Steelgrip Starkey and War Dancer, among others; was one of the artists who brought rock phenomenon KISS to the four-color page; and provided a more realistic look to DC Comics' Captain Marvel in the publisher's *Shazam!* series in 1978 at the behest of writer E. Nelson Bridwell. He also worked up a "Lost Tale" regarding

copyright © DC Comics

a never-finished Warlock story for Marvel Comics, which if completed would have been reminiscent of the Jonathan Swift novel *Gulliver's Travels*.

While we are on the subject of "Lost Tales," Weiss – one of comicdom's true rare geniuses – was going to have the Distinguished Competition's Dark Knight defending Christianity's Son of God within the pages of the lost "Elseworlds" graphic novel, *Batman 33 A.D.*

What is it about the character of DC Comics' Batman that inspired Weiss as a comic book creator? What do you propose is responsible for the dark hero's amazing 80 year-plus run in comics?

"Well, Batman's a good character," Weiss said. "We all grew up with him. Who doesn't love the Batman? If anything about him inspires me it's the quality of so much of the artwork associated with the guy. Also, at the time, he was DC's best seller. That fact afforded some inspiration as well."

How did Weiss come up with his idea for the Dark Knight meeting Jesus Christ in Ancient Rome? And, what year did he come up with this extraordinary story idea?

"I believe it was 1992 that I had the idea, just after I'd finished drawing another Batman graphic novel. I was considering the fundamental motivation of the character, and how elements of achieving the goals of that motivation might conflict with some of his most basic beliefs. That is, Bruce Wayne must be a Christian, most likely a well-to-do W.A.S.P. So, the simple question becomes, how does he reconcile the violence required by his Dark Knight night job in light of the dictates of the religion his mother and father brought him up in? The same could be posed for anyone who must utilize violence while facing life and death situations almost constantly."

What was Weiss' basic story? Was this to be a standalone graphic novel or a limited series?

"Given the above premise, I decided to take that question, and the main character, all the way back to the beginning of Christianity. And so the Roman-born aristocrat Brucius becomes the Vespirtilio, The Bat, the Masked Gladiator, protector of Jerusalem, in Palestine. As this graphic novel was to be an "Elseworlds" project, setting the story in 33 AD was not an obstacle. With that, what I thought a very intriguing and hopefully commercially successful title: *Batman 33 AD* (or, as I referred to it – Batman meets Jesus) was born."

--MR. PRESIDENT.

Was Weiss going to write and draw the series – or was someone else supposed to be brought in as the project's artist?

"As it was my concept, I intended to write the story as well, but not to do the art on this one. I had just finished another Batman "Elseworlds" graphic novel, a western version taking place during the Civil War, called *The Blue, The Grey, and the Bat*. In it, Batman was done as homage to one of his two original inspirational forbears, Zorro. That story was also my idea, and I drew the story, with Jose Luis Garcia inking and Elliot S! Maggin scripting. But for *Batman 33*, I had Michael Nasser (now Netzer) in mind as the artist. He was a friend, and coincidentally was going through a spiritual/religious "reconstruction" at the time, and was very passionate about Christianity at its core. So, in one way, his spiritual struggle inspired the original concept. As I couldn't draw the story due to other commitments, Michael was therefore the perfect choice. He was, and is, a terrific artist."

Did he have an editor for the project – or had he submitted the idea to anyone at DC Comics at the time?

"Yes, I submitted the idea and a story synopsis to Dick Giordano at DC. After expressing concerns and cautioning me as to what could and couldn't be done storywise concerning Jesus, he ran it past the brass, and to my surprise, they gave it the green light! Denny O'Neil was set to be the editor. I felt the ending of the story would step on no spiritual toes and would serve the character and original concept very well. In addition, I felt the book would have to be a big seller, even if only based upon curiosity and potential controversy. But actually, in the story itself, there is no real controversy."

Did he think of using the idea in another comic late on, or would he like to revisit this idea with the Caped Crusader someday?

"Sure, I've considered doing the original "Elseworlds" story elsewhere. Of course creating a new parallel character would never have the impact of doing the story with the super well-established Batman. If DC Comics were ever to get the gumption some sunny day to do this story . . . fine. I'm ready. But let us not hold our breath."

How was the story going to end?

"About the time the project was coming together, I was relating the idea to some folks. As I was heading in to the climactic scene, I said, "So the story comes down to whether Batman can save J C from crucifixion. How do you think it ends?" One guy immediately spoke up, "Don't tell me! I wanna read the book!" I felt that was the perfect response. Which book did he mean? *Batman 33*? Or that other one, I forget what it's called – but I think it has Testament somewhere in the title. No, I can assure you nothing historical was adjusted or changed. But then, the Bible, the New Testament, isn't historical."

FIREARM ANNUAL

Cable. Deadpool. Punisher. You know the type. Tough guys with bad attitudes and big guns. At first glance, James Robinson's Firearm may have been associated with this none-too-exclusive "super hero" group. But someone coming to that arguable conclusion would be mistaken.

It happens. Carry on.

Published by Malibu Comics for its Ultraverse imprint, *Firearm* was something very special coming out of the barrage of "shoot-em up" comics in the early 1990s. This early masterpiece by Robinson was a very character-driven book, where the story mattered as much as the action – and let me tell you, Firearm wasn't short on action.

Robinson's Firearm was Alec Swan, a non-powered, ex-operative for a covert branch of the British secret service called The Lodge. Sent primarily on missions against "Ultras" (the

Ultraverse term for the super-powered) who posed a threat against the British crown, Swan eventually left both his spymasters and England after some dark and unspeakable acts committed in the name of Queen and Country. Pulling up stakes for Pasadena, CA, and work as a private investigator, the well-read Swan quickly found that most of his cases dealt with Ultras anyway. Thus, making his life and livelihood "interesting" to say the least, as a "Touchstone guy in a Disney-coloured world."

Throughout this critically acclaimed 18-issue series, Robinson presented Swan's story in a way that lets readers get bits and pieces of Swan's and The Lodge's pasts. Even though it was never released, the *Firearm* Annual would have continued that trip down memory lane. Robinson told me in a 1996 interview for Overstreet's FAN that he was writing a story – entitled "Now and Then" – that was going to be done by two artists. Half of the story was going to be drawn by the very-talented Cully Hamner, while the other half was going to be done by the extraordinary Gary Erskine. And, in a spark of brilliance, the two stories were going to intercut with each other.

According to Robinson, the first story, drawn by Hamner, was going to be about one of the Hardcase villains, Headknocker: "a big rampaging guy who was going to be running rampant through Pasadena." With all the cops on full alert to deal with this guy, Swan's African-American detective/friend, Ben Travers asks that the hardboiled Britisher look after his 14-year-old daughter, Sarah, while he's away taking care of business. Swan agrees, since he's not a super-hero and has no reason to go out and after the villain himself.

With his four-color action hero playing babysitter, Robinson took the opportunity to clue the reader in on who Travers is: detailing his friendship with Swan; revealing the relationship this black L.A. cop has with his daughter; and exploring a more sensitive side of his Swan character. Robinson would have created a very personal story full of meaningful moments. At the end of the day, Swan would have shown what a really good guy Travers is and how Sarah should give her widower father a chance. Robinson explained that since Sarah's always liked Swan and can talk to him like an uncle, she ultimately listens to what he has to say. Especially after witnessing (on the telly) her father pulling off some crazy stunt to apprehend the rampaging Ultra – something we readers, as well as those in the story, would expect from Swan himself.

The Erskine-illustrated story, on the other hand, would have provided readers with the long-awaited history of The Lodge. Founded by Arthurian scholar Percival Wentworth during the end of World War II, The Lodge started with five "knights" – agents called "The Advanced" by the good professor, but later known as Ultras. The covert organization's first knights were as follows:

* Lancelot: Endowed with super-strength and nigh-invulnerability;

* Kay: Endowed with advanced strength and flight;

* Guinevere: Possessed the ability to levitate things, start fires, and emanate static bolts;

* Gwaine: Could change physical size at will;

* Morganna: Could read a person's mind during sexual congress; and

* Parsival: Possessed combustible abilities.

Utilised as cold warriors, Wentworth's knights were kept secret from the world – fighting a shadow war on the side of Britain against the "Merlins" of communism and beyond. To aid in keeping Britain's first Ultras a secret, the spymasters of The Lodge enlisted a small number of non-powered agents to serve as "squires" – highly trained individuals who would assist and act as cover for the organization's super-powered knights.

Robinson also pointed out that besides revealing the formation of the highly secretive [group] during the twilight days of the Second War to End All Wars, the unpublished annual would also detail the mission where Swan – a squire -- was betrayed by his keepers and forced to leave the shadow world that this organisation was built around.

"This story was going to list all the original British Ultras that the Lodge fought and all that went on back then," Robinson first said in my 1996 article for *Overstreet's FAN*. "One of them took over running The Lodge and one defected to Russia, like Burgess and Philby. It was going to be The Lodge's history told in a very sort of documentational way, but showing the flaws and the weird, interesting dynamics within this bizarre cell of the British secret service."

Robinson also explained that he was going to use the *Firearm* Annual to set up future stories apt for further exploration in the

ROBINSON · CARR · CHRISTIAN
ULTRAVERSE
MALIBU COMICS
#13 $1.95
FIREARM
#1

ULTRAVERSE
FIREARM
#16 $1.95
#4
THE RAFFERTY SAGA
PRIME
ROBINSON
JORGENSON
CHRISTIAN

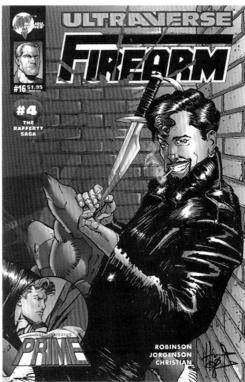

THE FIRST STORY, DRAWN BY HAMNER, WAS GOING TO BE ABOUT ONE OF THE HARDCASE VILLAINS, HEADKNOCKER: THE ERSKINE-ILLUSTRATED STORY, ON THE OTHER HAND, WOULD HAVE PROVIDED READERS WITH THE LONG-AWAITED HISTORY OF THE LODGE.

unlikely hero's monthly book.

"When I first wrote it," Robinson told me in 1996," I had no intention of leaving the book, so it was also going to highlight one time when Swan was in the Special Boat Service, and he was sent to Gibraltar to take out a group of Irish Republican Army (IRA) terrorists.

"It ends up that Swan eventually takes out all but one of them, but then, after one thing or another, he and the surviving terrorist get caught up in this supernatural menace while they're trying to kill each other."

According to Robinson, what results is that the surviving IRA terrorist ends up saving Swan's life, forcing our hero to let the man go with the knowledge that he is indebted to the Irishman.

"In the monthly comic," Robinson revealed to me, "I intended that the debt would finally come in and Swan would have to go and help this guy in a bad situation. What I was then going to try and do was spend a few issues with Alec Swan

and this guy arguing and debating the various sides of the whole Irish problem; the trouble within Ireland. So anyway, the Gibraltar affair was in a little flashback as part of what Alec is going to tell the daughter, and that would have been a set up for another story arc in the future."

Unfortunately, there wasn't much of a future left for *Firearm*. Although Robinson came back to Malibu to write a back-up story in the *Codename: Firearm* limited series, he ended the regular book with issue #18.

Robinson explained the contracts that the Ultraverse's chief creators all originally signed were only for 12 issues. After that, the superstar scribe said it was up to the "discretion of the talent" whether they wanted to continue or not.

"I don't know what it was," Robinson said in 1996, "but I just had this bad feeling about Malibu when I was setting up the whole 'Rafferty Saga' at the time. I just decided that would be

it – that would be where it ended."

AVENGERS ASSEMBLE

"When (Marvel Comics editor) Ralph Macchio first approached me in 1992 to do an Avengers graphic novel, well, I had real reservations," award-winning storyteller George Perez confessed. "I had not read the title in almost a decade, and I certainly didn't consider myself qualified to do an Avengers story – since I had no idea who was on the current team. And, to tell you the truth, I had no real interest in having to read all of the books necessary to find out."

But, all of that would change. Perez – who is probably one of the few creators truly qualified to discuss the best the super-hero genre has to offer – would find himself inspired, not by the future of the House of Ideas' premier super-team, but instead by its humble beginnings.

"(Former Marvel Comics editor-in-chief) Tom DeFalco suggested I do a 'retro' story," Perez continued, "which led Ralph and myself to come up with the beginnings of an Avengers 'Year One' story. Still, I needed a hook that would make it stand out from the rest."

The "hook" Perez would eventually come up with was to tell the story from the point of view of the heroes' supporting cast: Namely, Jarvis, Jane Foster from Thor, and Happy Hogan and Pepper Potts from Iron Man; for Giant Man, Perez found a little-known FBI agent by the name of Lee Kearns.

"(Lee Kearns) appeared once or twice in the entire history of Marvel Comics," Perez said. "But that's Giant-Man for you, though. He barely had a supporting cast.

"It was (the late *Comics Buyer's Guide* editor) Don Thompson who made the comment, 'Super-heroes are never as interesting as the people they affect.' That's

what makes these modern gods so interesting – how people react to them. And, when I set out to write this story, I wondered how I would feel knowing someone with super-powers. So, through Jarvis, Jane, Pepper and the rest – they were my proxies. Their first reactions to these heroes were similar to my reaction to these characters when I was introduced to them in the pages of Avengers and their own books."

"I also wanted to do what Kurt (Busiek) eventually did with *Marvels*, in that I wanted to show how people reacted when they first saw these heroes – that first palpable sense of wonder mixed in with a sense of duty, since the supporting cast was actually involved with the super-heroes. They were the hired help. In order for the super-heroes to be super, these characters had to take care of the mundane, everyday activities."

"Another angle I had," Perez remembered, "was centring the story in the Stark Mansion. I basically started calling it, 'Backstairs at Avengers Mansion,' was transformed from a public domicile – a haven, as it were – into the fortress that would become the headquarters of the mighty Avengers."

Deciding where he wanted to go with the story, Perez changed the format of the project from a graphic novel into a two-issue mini-series, while Macchio assigned artist Angel Medina to illustrate the epic tale that would've been *Avengers Assemble*. In short, the term "epic" was an understatement for what Perez had planned..

Perez wanted to document the Avengers' early days, while also portraying the supporting characters' real sense of horror from being in such close proximity to what – at the time – were strange and fantastic super-humans with powers far beyond those of mortal men.

"Something I wanted to get across was that the Avengers were originally something new and unknown to the populace at large. The Hulk was a hunted animal. Thor was a god, which up until that point, nobody believed existed. Everybody knew that Iron Man was a heavily armed private bodyguard to one of the richest men in the world – but nobody knew who was in the suit. And, as for the Wasp and Giant-Man, well, the Wasp was a spoiled socialite that no one took very seriously, and Giant-Man wasn't very good with people. In fact, it was only when Captain America –a living legend – showed up, did the Avengers begin to get respectability. And, that's where my story began."

While chronicling how the world would first react to the Earth's Mightiest Heroes, Perez was also doing what he did best: Exploring the little things that often got away from the reader. "I wanted to take this opportunity to divulge the little things that no one noticed. For example, I wanted to show how the servants of Avengers Mansion would not be able to communicate with Ant-Man (another alter-ego of Giant-Man), because he was so small you'd have to use receivers to communicate with him. I also had a scene where Happy Hogan almost catches Tony Stark becoming Iron Man – which would prove that he's not as stupid as people think he is."

"Something else I wanted to give readers was an idea of how loyal Jarvis really was to both his subordinates and his employers," said Perez. "In fact, I had Jarvis quit at the end of the first issue because he was concerned about the safety of the Mansion's employees, with all the sophisticated weaponry it would contain and the constant threat of attack. There was no way Jarvis was going to let other people be in danger. And, it takes Captain America – Jarvis' childhood hero from World War II – personally asking him to stay, while promising that the safety issues for the Mansion will be met, that keeps him on staff. Jarvis could say no to Tony Stark – a man who's worked for Tony's family for years, but he could never say no to his hero, Captain America.

"Jarvis would also find a love interest in the story – one of the other servants – who wants him to fly back to England with her. But like Anthony Hopkins in *The Remains of the Day*, he realises that his work is too important to him; it's who he is. And, he must regretfully decline her invitation – although it breaks his heart to do so."

"At the end of *Avengers Assemble*," Perez added, "reporter Gaynor Green and Lee Kearns (who is revealed to be a villain in the story) get trapped in the Avengers' version of the Danger Room – their Exercise Area – and none of the team is there to come to their aid. Of course, Jarvis finds out that somebody is in the room, so he, Pepper, and Happy attempt to rescue them. Finally, the Avengers do show up and save the day. It is then that the team realizes that the Mansion cannot be opened to the public, and that security has to be increased. They also realize that these two intruders could very well have died; therefore, they agree to have a group of Avengers who are Mansion-bound. Since Cap has no place else to go, he agreed to be part of the group. And, as was established, the new members Hawkeye, Quicksilver, and the Scarlet Witch also lived in Avengers Mansion when they joined the team – and that's one of the reasons they were chosen. The original members knew that when the call was sounded, the world needs full-time Avengers!"

"So, I was going to end the mini-series with the events of *Avengers* #16, when the roster changed. After working so hard at getting the

"SOMETHING ELSE I WANTED TO GIVE READERS WAS AN IDEA OF HOW LOYAL JARVIS REALLY WAS TO BOTH HIS SUBORDINATES AND HIS EMPLOYERS. IN FACT, I HAD JARVIS QUIT AT THE END OF THE FIRST ISSUE BECAUSE HE WAS CONCERNED ABOUT THE SAFETY OF THE MANSION'S EMPLOYEES." –GEORGE PEREZ

respectability and trust of the public, what happens to the Avengers? Everyone except Captain America leaves – only to be replaced by super-humans with criminal records. Of course, as we would eventually learn, the public would be willing to give those new Avengers a chance, because Captain America stayed behind. That's where I would have left it."

But, Perez would never have a chance to tell his story. Although it appeared that everyone was ready to move forward with the project, Perez soon discovered that appearances can be deceiving.

"Angel had to bow out to take over the art chores of Incredible Hulk," Perez explained. "Having lost my penciller, I then asked Ralph, 'Why don't we get this guy by the name of George Perez to draw it?' Because all of the time I wrote the story, I couldn't help imagining what I was going to do with it visually."

Having solved one problem, Perez soon found himself plagued by a larger one. Unbeknownst to him, the House of Ideas would enlist Image Comics' Rob Liefeld and Jim Lee to remake the Earth's Mightiest Heroes during their yearlong, ultra-successful, albeit controversial "Heroes Reborn" event. And,

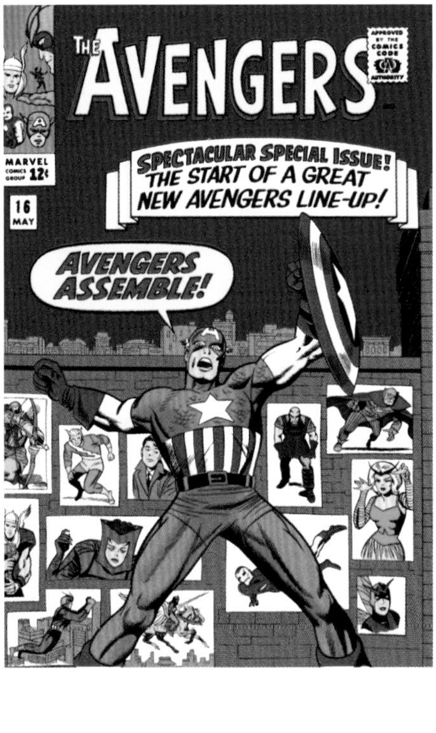
THE AVENGERS
MARVEL COMICS GROUP 12¢
16 MAY
SPECTACULAR SPECIAL ISSUE! THE START OF A GREAT NEW AVENGERS LINE-UP!
AVENGERS ASSEMBLE!

when Marvel finally got the characters back in 1997, new creative teams were brought on (including Perez, who would wind up penciling the top-selling *Avengers* monthly comic) – ultimately leaving Perez with a lost tale.

"I had certain things planned with some of the characters' backgrounds such as Iron Man," Perez added, "that I can't do now since Kurt Busiek wrote his book. And, I would never impose my opinions on other people's stories. But, since he was also the writer of Avengers, and he and I agreed on how to depict specific characters, we were able to incorporate some of those ideas from Avengers Assemble into the series. But unfortunately, *Avengers Assemble* is a dead project, and that's what it must stay."

* * *

Not every Lost Tale I have written about is left wayward in the four-color wind. Some are found by other publishers and through other means. All are extraordinary nonetheless.

Tales such as these:

LEGEND OF THE GREEN FLAME

"People ask me all the time, 'Don't you ever wish you could write Superman or Batman or even Blackhawk,'" award-winning writer Neil Gaiman recalled in 1996. "Well, actually I did. It's just that nobody ever got the opportunity to see it."

Before the movie and television deals, the best-selling novels, and even one of his most successful ventures to date (DC Comics/ Vertigo's acclaimed comic book series, *Sandman*), Gaiman was a freelance writer whose work could be found in the pages of Fleetway's 2000AD., as well as the Original Universe's *Hellblazer*, *Secret Origins* and Swamp Thing. But for a comic book creator who was known for his mythical dreamscapes and unforgettable characters, his work with super-heroes – the traditional four-color mainstay – was few and far between. So, when offered a chance to work on a super-hero project that had the makings of a genuine comic book event, it was an opportunity too good for Gaiman to refuse.

"There was a time in the mid-to-late '80s when *Action Comics*, traditionally a monthly title, went weekly," Gaiman explained. "It became an anthology comic that featured Superman, Green Lantern, the Demon, Catwoman, Blackhawk, Deadman – all these characters rotating in one series. Mark Waid – who has since gone on to fame and glory as a writer – was the editor on the book, and he phoned me up and said, 'We're thinking about doing this giant, 38-page special with all the characters that have been in the current run of the title, and we'd like you to do this last issue of *Action Comics Weekly* before we change it back to a monthly Superman title. Will you write it?' It didn't take me long to say, 'Yes.'"

Having the beginnings of a story in mind, Gaiman looked amongst the extensive list of characters he had to work with in finding the one link that would tie his ideas together. After considering his options, he found his answer – and it was green. Playing up the relationship between Clark (Superman) Kent and Hal Jordan – the intergalactic policeman known as Green Lantern – Gaiman also utilized some of the mythos behind Hal's Golden Age counterpart, Alan Scott. Unlike Hal, the source of Alan Scott's power was supernatural in origin; a theme that's found throughout Gaiman's comic book work. Still, the author is adamant that he had only one thing in mind when plotting out "The Flame is Green."

"The story I basically wanted to tell was about two close friends spending some time together," Gaiman explained, "but with a different spin."

Beginning his "Lost Tale" in 1949, Gaiman reintroduces readers to a very drunk Blackhawk, the renowned World War II flying ace, and

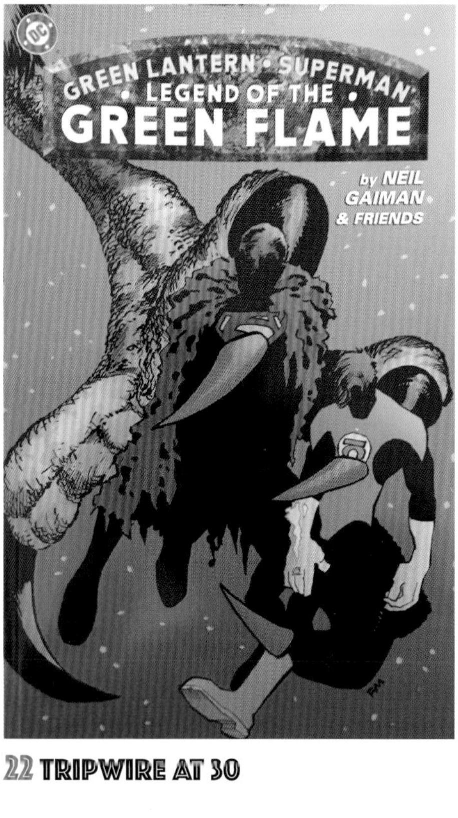
GREEN LANTERN • SUPERMAN
• LEGEND OF THE •
GREEN FLAME
by NEIL GAIMAN & FRIENDS

his associate, Weng Chen – better known to most comics fans as Chop-Chop. According to Gaiman, the two intoxicated war heroes are searching out an abandoned Nazi bunker for a "German secret weapon." But instead, they found what may be the remains of the legendary mystery men, the Justice Society of America – as well as what Weng Chen describes as a "glowing magic lantern." Intrigued by the lamp, the heroes pick it up, give up the search, and head back to the bar.

Gaiman then brings the reader back to the present, where we find Hal Jordan making an unexpected visit to his good friend, Clark Kent. According to the author, Hal has had some rough times of late, so when Clark offers to bring him along on a reporting assignment involving an exhibition at the Metropolis Museum, as well as offer some quality time in the interest of friendship, Hal's all for it.

Later that night, at the exhibition, the two come across Catwoman (who, as Selina Kyle, is staking out the place) as well as the same mysterious artifact that Weng Chen found years earlier. Having discovered the object, Hal turns to Clark and explains how he should return the lamp to its rightful owner. But, before moving the lamp, Hal first attempts to charge his power ring with Clark in attendance – and that's when things go bad.

Gaiman explained that Hal, whose power is science-based, and the magically vulnerable Superman, have unknowingly come across Golden Age Green Lantern Alan Scott's lamp, which as explained earlier, is mystical by nature. And, with Hal trying to recharge his ring using an oath based on cold science, ends up killing Clark and himself.

The story then cuts to a mysterious man in black who Gaiman describes as being held captive (" . . . in an apartment, in all places . . .") by arcane forces. Putting on a his hat and coat, the dark figure summons strange, magical forces, and then vanishes without a trace.

"That's the Phantom Stranger," Gaiman said. "In an earlier mini-series, DC had given him – one of their most mysterious and powerful characters – an apartment. You don't do that."

Bringing the story back, has us catch up with Clark and Hal (now wearing their respective costumes) in the Afterlife, just as they run into one of DC's most bizarre characters – Boston Brand, the Deadman.

"Deadman is a character that always appealed to me," Gaiman admitted. "In fact, I was so fond of the line I was going to use in this story about famous last words, 'Mine were: Hey, from up here it looks like that guy with the hook has a gun,' that I ended up using it when I sat down to write The Books of Magic."

Here, Gaiman also had Superman and Green Lantern mistakenly venture into the outlands of Hell. Meeting up with various nightmare creatures beyond imagining, the two heroes come across one infernal threat after another , until they meet up with a vaguely familiar rhyming demon by the name of Gintear . . . who happens to want them for dinner. But just as they are about ot be devoured, Green Lantern – the bravest man on Earth – pleads to his ring for help. And, in a flash of green, they are gone.

As both Superman and Green Lantern would soon find out, the lamp they had come across in the museum had housed an energy being that was concentrated high magic given form. This "Green Flame" – the true power behind the Golden Age Green Lantern's ring – had essentially brought the heroes back to life, casting them into what Gaiman described as "the very heart of magic itself." Here in a place where both Superman and Green Lantern were most vulnerable, the Green Flame intended to enslave them forever.

Enter the Phantom Stranger.

Having monitored what transpired as only he could, the Stranger arrives just in time to tell Green Lantern that the only chance for escape is to recite his Golden Age counterpart's oath. By saying those magic words, Hal Jordan frees the power ring of the Green Flame's influence, and transports both Superman and himself back to the museum. With the Green Flame once again imprisoned

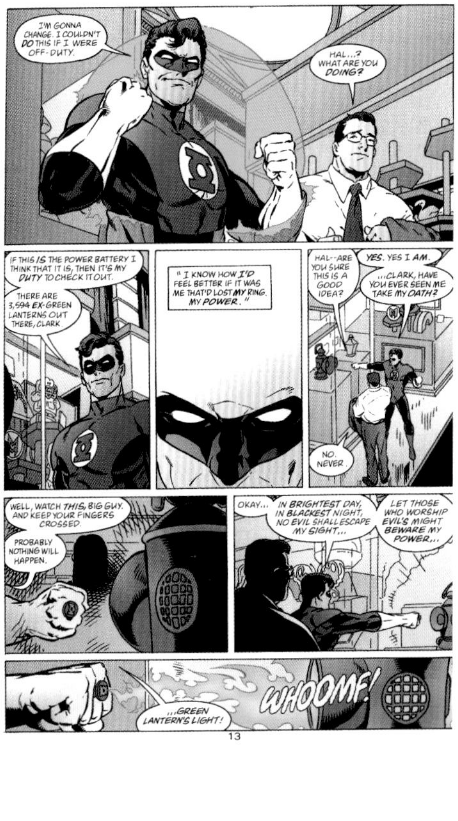
I'M GONNA CHANGE. I COULDN'T DO THIS IF I WERE OFF-DUTY.
HAL...? WHAT ARE YOU DOING?
IF THIS IS THE POWER BATTERY I THINK THAT IT IS, THEN IT'S MY DUTY TO CHECK IT OUT.
THERE ARE 3,594 EX-GREEN LANTERNS OUT THERE, CLARK.
" I KNOW HOW I'D FEEL BETTER IF IT WAS ME THAT'D LOST MY RING. MY POWER. "
HAL--ARE YOU SURE THIS IS A GOOD IDEA?
YES. YES I AM.
...CLARK, HAVE YOU EVER SEEN ME TAKE MY OATH?
NO. NEVER.
WELL, WATCH THIS, BIG GUY. AND KEEP YOUR FINGERS CROSSED.
PROBABLY NOTHING WILL HAPPEN.
OKAY...
IN BRIGHTEST DAY, IN BLACKEST NIGHT, NO EVIL SHALL ESCAPE MY SIGHT...
LET THOSE WHO WORSHIP EVIL'S MIGHT BEWARE MY POWER...
...GREEN LANTERN'S LIGHT!
WHOOMF!
13

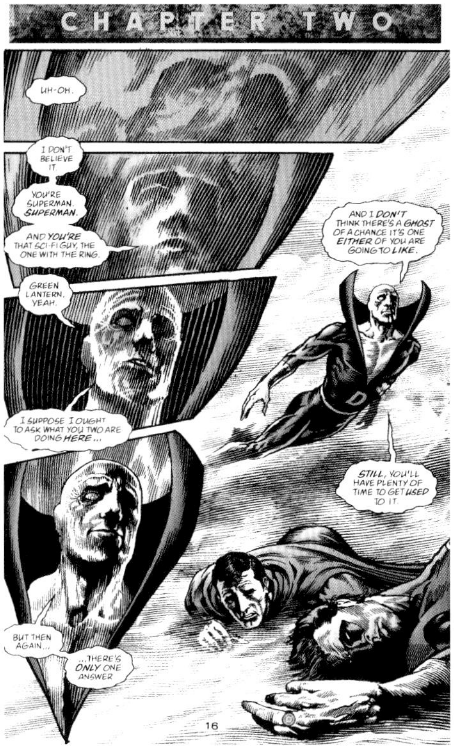
CHAPTER TWO
UH-OH.
I DON'T BELIEVE IT.
YOU'RE SUPERMAN. SUPERMAN.
AND YOU'RE THAT SCI-FI GUY, THE ONE WITH THE RING.
AND I DON'T THINK THERE'S A GHOST OF A CHANCE IT'S ONE EITHER OF YOU ARE GOING TO LIKE.
GREEN LANTERN. YEAH.
I SUPPOSE I OUGHT TO ASK WHAT YOU TWO ARE DOING HERE...
STILL, YOU'LL HAVE PLENTY OF TIME TO GET USED TO IT.
BUT THEN AGAIN...
...THERE'S ONLY ONE ANSWER
16

"DEADMAN IS A CHARACTER THAT ALWAYS APPEALED TO ME...IN FACT, I WAS SO FOND OF THE LINE I WAS GOING TO USE IN THIS STORY ABOUT FAMOUS LAST WORDS, 'MINE WERE: HEY, FROM UP HERE IT LOOKS LIKE THAT GUY WITH THE HOOK HAS A GUN,' THAT I ENDED UP USING IT WHEN I SAT DOWN TO WRITE THE BOOKS OF MAGIC."–NEIL GAIMAN

in the lamp, Gaimen then has Clark and Hal say their goodbyes, with real-life writers (then DC editors) Waid and Brian Augustyn sipping champagne in the background. Gaiman also had some fun by showing Superman flying over a theatre billboard for the popular movie, Fatal Attraction – with only the letters A-C-T-I-O-N left standing.

Having finished the story, Gaiman sent it right off to DC. "I put together a story very much in the continuity DC had that particular week. But, by the time it went off, I had lost Etrigan the Demon – so I had rewritten him as Gintear, which is a bad anagram for Etrigan. I then sent it off again. Unfortunately, this time, somebody decided that too many people knew who the Man of Tomorrow really was, so the Powers that Be made a rule that nobody except Ma and Pa Kent knew Superman's secret identity. Despite working well within John Byrne's revamped Superman continuity, this was a new and sudden rule that had been decided – end of story. I then got a bunch of calls, asking, 'Can you rewrite the story so that Hal Jordan doesn't know that Superman is Clark Kent?' To that, I said, 'You know what? This is a story about two old friends meeting in civvies. One of them has problems, and the other one doesn't. It may not be the greatest story ever written, but at least it has a reason for being there. If I rewrote it so that they bumped into each other in costume during a bank robbery, the story would have no point. Right now, stuff happen, and one of them cheers up a bit in the end. And, that's the last *Action Comics Weekly* as we hand the title back to Superman.'

"After some thought, [DC] finally said, 'How about we pay you off and do a kill fee on it, and get Gerry Conway or Eliot S. Maggin to write it?' I agreed. Then, they asked if they could use my 'Fatal Attraction coming off the marquee gag' at the end of the story, which was fine by me, except nobody told the letterer – which is why he put a word balloon over the ACTION sign, preventing DC from using it in the way I originally intended."

That's not the end of the tale, though. In the year 2000, DC finally released the story as a standalone one-shot, *Green Lantern/ Superman: Legend of the Green Flame*. How that project came to be is another story for another time.

"That was my little outing with super-heroes," Gaiman laughed. "Strange, wasn't it?"

SHERLOCK HOLMES AND THE EMPIRE BUILDERS

"[Joel Meadows and Andy Bennett's *Sherlock Holmes: The Empire Builders*] examines how history could have taken a different turn for the real world using an iconic fictional figure," explained writer Joel Meadows from his London home. Below, we examine the clues he left us readers to discover this brave new world of alternate realities and deadly games. And, of course, the game is afoot!

With that, what is the secret origin of Meadows and Bennett's Sherlock Holmes story? How does it liken to Arthur Conan Doyle's stories of the past? How is it a postmodern epic all its own?

"The genesis of this story goes back to the late '90s," said Meadows. "I have always been a fan of Doyle and Holmes but I also enjoy alternate world stories. The film *Young Sherlock Holmes* by Barry Levinson and produced by Steven Spielberg always stayed with me. So, I started thinking about a story that could tell the tale of an older Holmes, in a world he doesn't understand, stripped of many of his skills. Also, he has to do without the companionship of his right hand man Watson, a situation that leaves him rudderless. It does tie in a little with Doyle's stories but I admit my knowledge of his stories does have a few gaps. It is an ambitious sci-fi epic because it brings real historical figures like the tale's main antagonist Oswald Mosley, a real-life British fascist, and Francis Crick, the scientist who unraveled the DNA helix with his partner James Watson in our actual history. So, by weaving real history with fictional figures like Holmes and Watson hopefully that makes for a compelling setting."

Like in the 2020 print mag, this is another preview – but the stakes have risen. What made Meadows and Bennett decide to offer readers and your growing fan base the excellent action and suspense found in "Prey."

"I really enjoyed writing 'The House That Crime Built' in the (2020) print magazine," said Meadows. "But I wanted to tell a totally different kind of story here. "Prey" is a far more action-motivated story which gives artist Andy Bennett the opportunity to really show off his artistic chops here. It is a chase story but includes enough that it teases the reader and makes them want to read more adventures set in this world."

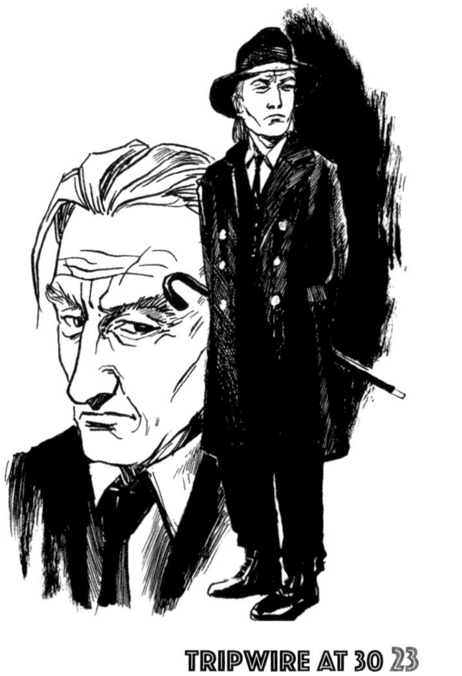

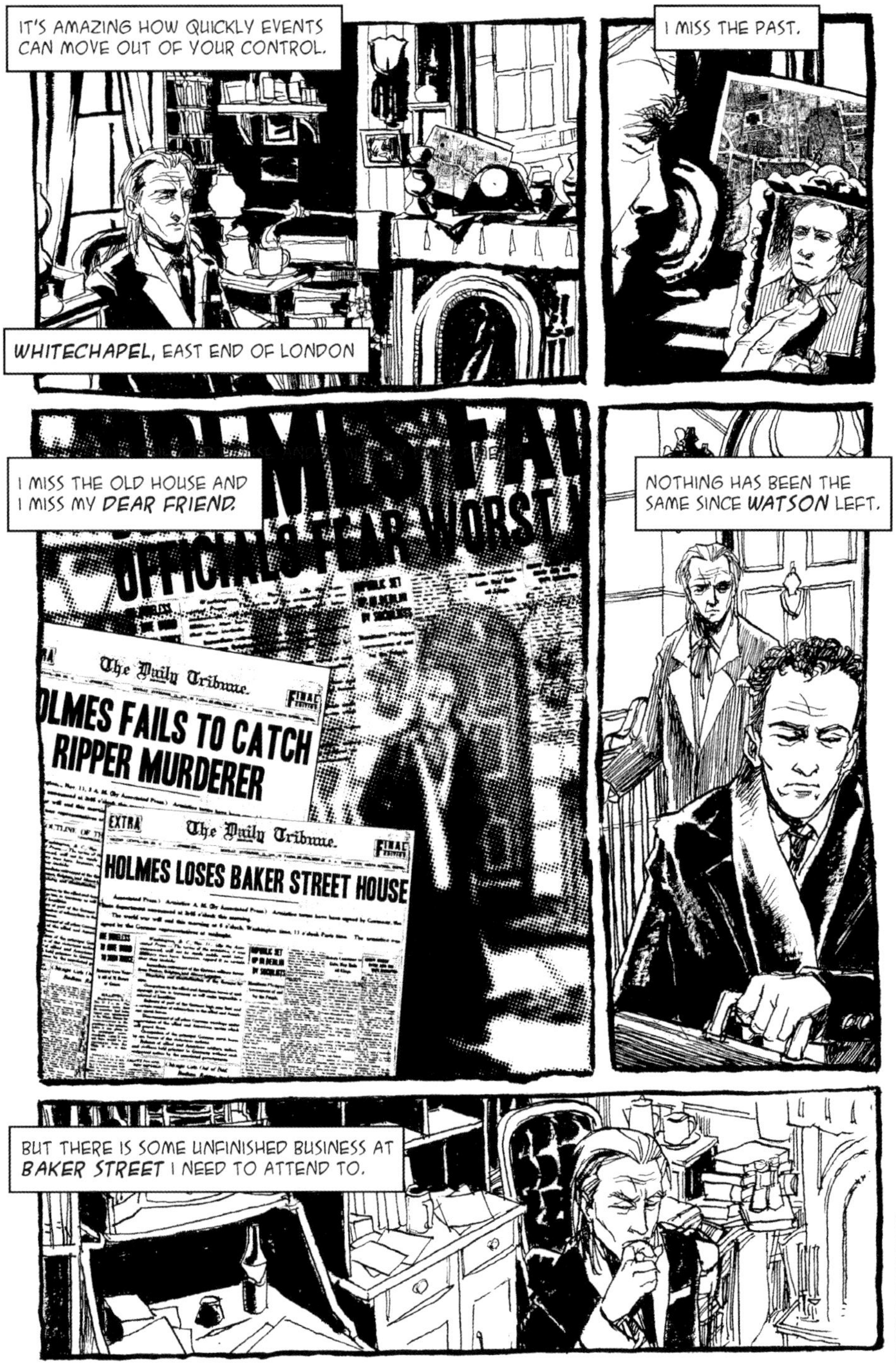
IT'S AMAZING HOW QUICKLY EVENTS CAN MOVE OUT OF YOUR CONTROL.
WHITECHAPEL, EAST END OF LONDON
I MISS THE PAST.
I MISS THE OLD HOUSE AND I MISS MY DEAR FRIEND.
The Daily Tribune
LMES FAILS TO CATCH RIPPER MURDERER
EXTRA
The Daily Tribune
HOLMES LOSES BAKER STREET HOUSE
NOTHING HAS BEEN THE SAME SINCE WATSON LEFT.
BUT THERE IS SOME UNFINISHED BUSINESS AT BAKER STREET I NEED TO ATTEND TO.

There is talk that a number of companies have shown interest in Meadows and Bennett's work. What can Meadows tell us on the aspect of the upcoming series?

"The upcoming series tells the story of how Oswald Mosley comes to power," he said, "how Holmes tries to find his position in this new world and how the pair are brought into conflict through a series of dramatic events. We are introduced to Gurkha Agent Six in 'Prey' and he shall be playing a major role in the full series to come."

When the book makes its debut, is it an ongoing or limited series?

"It will be a limited series of around six issues," Meadows confirmed, "and hopefully it will also be reprinted as a hardcover after it appears as a series of monthly comics."

We have seen two amazing moments into Meadows and Bennett's series – with a third debuting in this very book. Where are they going to take us next?

"People will just have to wait and see where we take Holmes and company," said Meadows. "I have built in a few shocks into the main story which I don't want to spoil for the reader. I really wanted to try and subvert what is such a well-established and familiar fictional character. "

Has writer Meadows plotted out the first arc yet, or is he just as surprised what we've seen as we are?

"I have plotted the first six issue series yet as I thought it was important to know where we are heading with this."

What's the endgame?

"If the first series does well, then I have already considered future stories featuring some of Doyle's other Holmes characters,

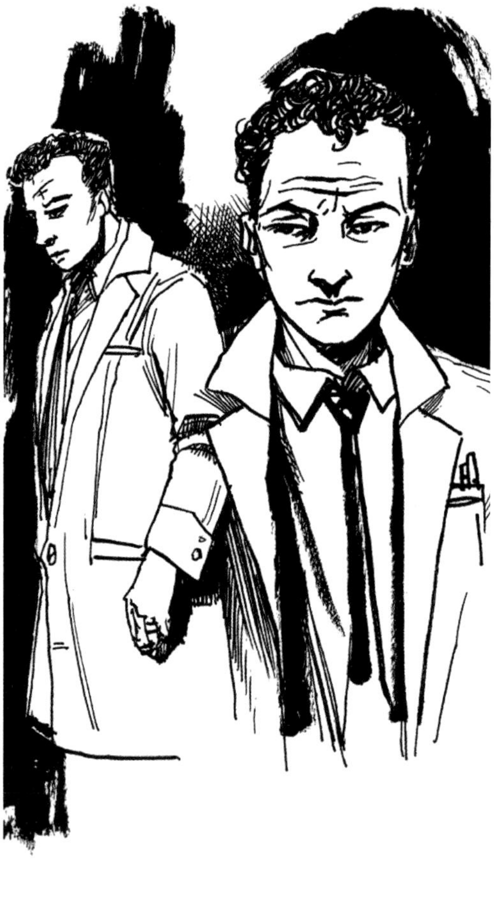

"THE UPCOMING SERIES TELLS THE STORY OF HOW OSWALD MOSLEY COMES TO POWER.HOW HOLMES TRIES TO FIND HIS POSITION IN THIS NEW WORLD AND HOW THE PAIR ARE BROUGHT INTO CONFLICT THROUGH A SERIES OF DRAMATIC EVENTS. WE ARE INTRODUCED TO GURKHA AGENT SIX IN 'PREY' AND HE SHALL BE PLAYING A MAJOR ROLE IN THE FULL SERIES TO COME."–JOEL MEADOWS

"BRADEN CITES GRANT MORRISON'S 'CRITICALLY ACCLAIMED REVAMP OF DC COMICS' ANIMAL MAN; A FOUR-COLOR STORY IMPRESSING UPON ME WHAT IT WOULD BE LIKE IF A FICTIONAL FIGURE CAME TO LIFE,' AS ONE OF THE FORBEARS OF KENT MENACE."– SCOTT BRADEN

including adversary sniper Sebastian Moran who I think would be perfect for a second story arc. But let's just get the first story under our belt first and see where we go from there."

KENT MENACE

The cover of the comic book demands attention, but that's not all it does. The insouciant curls, bold lines, and mysterious reflections in the eyeglasses of Kent Menace invite readers to kindle their imaginations as they engage with what creators Scott Braden and Mike Malbrough call their "all-new weird hero."

The fictional Kent Menace has a back story that's pure pulp – think watery depths, infernal fighting techniques, a pirate king father, and a Tritonblade imbued with the power of time travel, all leading up to an epic battle on which the fate of the world depends.

While Kent Menace faces mythological foes and grapples with making the ultimate sacrifice, here in the real world, Kent's creators have labored long to see their hero brought to life in the pages of their comic book.

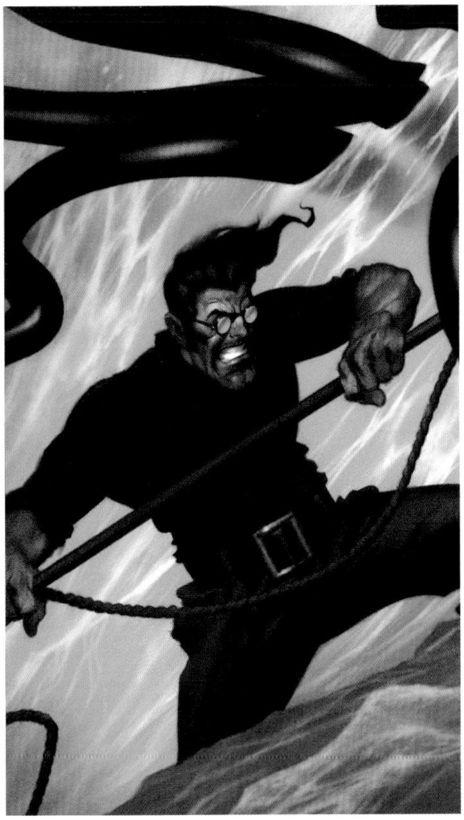

Writer Scott Braden originally conceived the character and backstory in 1999, and it was Braden's collaboration with artist Mike Malbrough that breathed life into the supernatural sailor. Every aspect of the comic is layered with deep, geeky knowledge and reverence for the comic book as a genre.

Kent Menace is a decidedly reflexive, self-referential comic book, and Braden is all too aware of his hero's place in a long line of meta-fiction. Braden cites Grant Morrison's "critically acclaimed revamp of DC Comics' *Animal Man*; a four-color story impressing upon me what it would be like if a fictional figure came to life," as one of the forbears of Kent Menace, a comic book hero who unexpectedly finds himself ripped from the pages of his fictional quests, followed, of course, by nightmarish creatures who threaten the world we puny mortals inhabit.

The creation of a comic book by a writer and an artist is a uniquely collaborative process. Braden didn't deliver a set of instructions to Malbrough; the two fashioned their weird hero together in an endeavor that sparked mutual inspiration and character development. Braden describes one such instance: "For example, in my writer's direction on the bottom panel of the front preview's third page, I only told Mike to draw Kent with other heroes of his making. In turn, he created Boss Monkey – which I named (aren't I clever). Mike is that good – and he makes our comic book world come to vivid life." Braden's description of his collaboration with Malbrough doesn't just describe the creation of Kent Menace, though. In the process, we see mirrored the very act of engaging with the entire genre.

For readers who might not be familiar with the genre, Braden explains why he and Malbrough choose to share their creation in the form of a comic book: "Paraphrasing award-winning scholar Scott McCloud, the comic book is based on a simple idea – placing one picture after another to tell a story. But it's the spaces between the pictures that chronicle the passage of time. It's up to the readers to piece together the story between the panels, and to add all the bits that are literally left off the page and into the imagination. This makes comic book storytelling a very personal

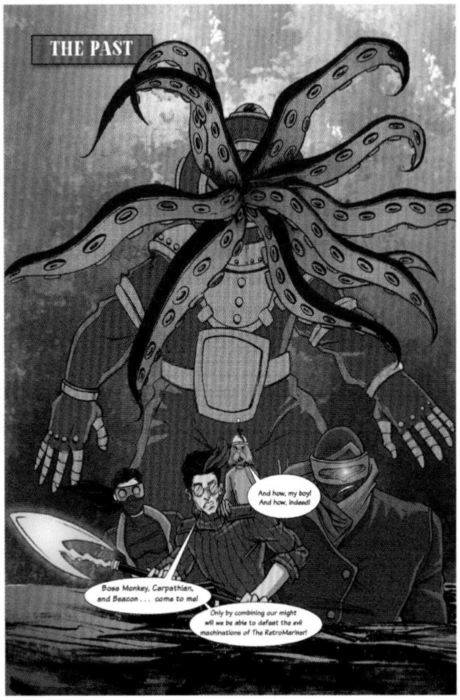
THE PAST
And how, my boy! And how, indeed!
Boss Monkey, Carpathian, and Beacon . . . come to me!
Only by combining our might will we be able to defeat the evil machinations of The RetroMariner!

partnership – an engagement between creators and their readers. Comics are a series of scenes and situations sequentially strung together to tell a story. That's something you just don't get from other modern mediums like movies and television." While comic novices might assume the genre is simplistic, relying on art to create images for readers too lazy to exercise their imaginations, in fact, nothing could be further from the truth.

Kent Menace invites readers to luxuriate in a strange place, suffused with camp, myth, danger, destiny, and necessarily fraught familial ties. While Malbrough's richly textured artwork evokes fantastical,

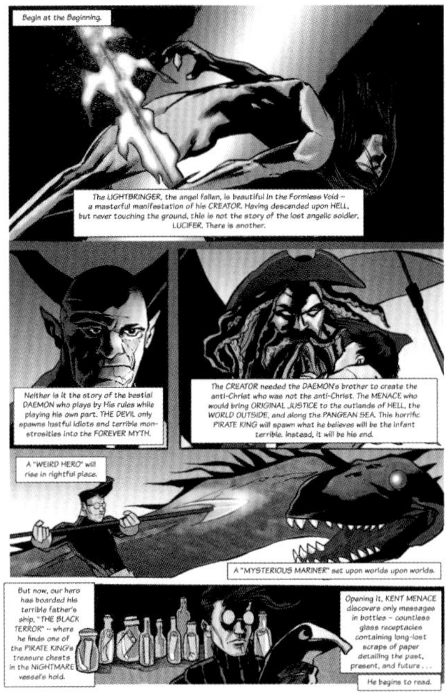
Begin at the Beginning.
The LIGHTBRINGER, the angel fallen, is beautiful in the Formless Void – a masterful manifestation of his CREATOR. Having descended upon HELL, but never touching the ground, this is not the story of the lost angelic soldier, LUCIFER. There is another.
Neither is it the story of the bestial DAEMON who plays by His rules while playing his own part. THE DEVIL only spawns lustful idiots and terrible monstrosities into the FOREVER MYTH.
The CREATOR needed the DAEMON's brother to create the anti-Christ who was not the anti-Christ. The MENACE who would bring ORIGINAL JUSTICE to the outlands of HELL, the WORLD OUTSIDE, and along the PANGEAN SEA. This horrific PIRATE KING will spawn what he believes will be the infant terrible. Instead, it will be his end.
A "WEIRD HERO" will rise in rightful place.
A "MYSTERIOUS MARINER" set upon worlds upon worlds.
But now, our hero has boarded his terrible father's ship, "THE BLACK TERROR" – where he finds one of the PIRATE KING's treasure chests in the NIGHTMARE vessel's hold.
Opening it, KENT MENACE discovers only messages in bottles – countless glass receptacles containing long-lost scraps of paper detailing the past, present, and future . . .
He begins to read.

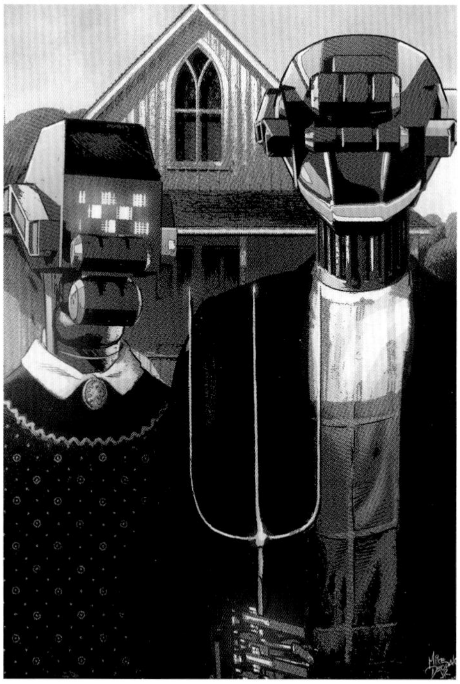

"I LIKE WORKING WITH GRAND METAPHORS. I WANTED TO WRITE A METAPHOR FOR TOXIC MASCULINITY IN A WAY THAT FORCES MEN TO EMPATHISE WITH WHAT IT'S LIKE TO BE ON THE RECEIVING END OF IT."–MARK RUSSELL

otherworldly creatures, there's a deep, wide vein of self-conscious humor that runs through both artwork and writing. The language is, Braden notes, distinctive and appealing to fans of comic books. Braden elaborates: "Comics are as varied as any other medium, but as far as my take on *Kent Menace*, well, I'm all about going over the top. I've read comics since I was five, and I've always been attracted to stories and dialogue that make you think and smile. When I write *Kent Menace*, it's all about having fun and trying to make comics that others would deem fun, too."

As far as the future for *Kent Menace*, Braden and Malbrough have big plans. Scott Braden explained what perils might be in store for the hero himself, and the writer clearly knows where his story is heading. He explains: "as far as our supernatural sailor goes, the End Times bring about final combat and the promise of a new world. With that, Kent must decide whether he has what it takes to put an end to an evil so great that even the Devil himself has joined the fight against it. Does our weird hero have the courage to make the greatest sacrifice of all?"

There's no denying that *Kent Menace* is fun, a melodramatic celebration of life-and-death struggles that invites readers to accompany a strange super-hero on his quest to save the world. But comic is more than just a beautifully rendered romp; it's a celebration of an underappreciated genre that simultaneously engages with serious themes like sacrifice and salvation, while also requiring readers to unleash their imaginations.

NOT ALL ROBOTS

Comics scribe Mark Russell has turned heads and won awards for his myriad works, including *Snagglepuss*, *The Flintstones*, and his "cereal serial" in AHOY's award-nominated *Edgar Allan Poe's Snifter of Terror*. Now, he turns readers' attentions to his engaging "Lost Tale," *Not All Robots*.

What's the secret origin behind Russell's "Lost Tale," which ended up getting illustrated by comix superstar Mike Deodato and published by AWA Studios? What inspired it?

"I like working with grand metaphors," said Russell. "I wanted to write a metaphor for toxic masculinity in a way that forces men to empathize with what it's like to be on the receiving end of it. The impending era of automation seemed like a good place to start. In a world where robots have all the good-paying jobs, control most industries and law-making, it's about what it would be like for men to be reliant on the goodwill of creatures who might, you know, also go crazy and kill them."

When did he first come up with the story? And, how long has he been pitching it to publishers?

"As the title suggests," Russell explained, "I came up with the story idea around the same time the #NotAllMen clapback started to the MeToo movement. To me, it seemed like a real deficit of empathy and an inability to read the room when the guys started protesting their own innocence and sense of victimhood

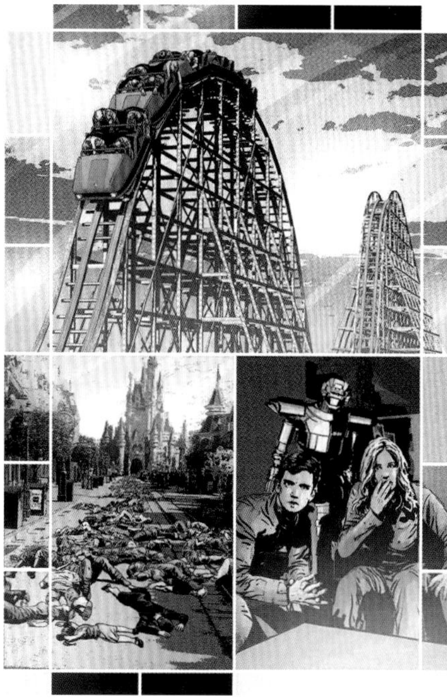

to women who were telling their stories of decades of systematic abuse and harassment. This story was designed to sort of put them in the same boat and also to explore themes of automation and worker displacement, which seems to become more relevant with each passing day."

Russell has submitted this involving story to various publishers. What kind of feedback has he received for his efforts?

"Most publishers I've spoken to have said that they like the story," said the award-winning writer, "but they've had it up to the gills with dystopian sci-fi stories right now."

Above many things, Russell is known by fans for his thought-provoking work. Would *Not All Robots* continue that trend?

"I hope so," Russell said, modestly. "I think the point of science fiction, and perhaps just fiction in general, is to get people to think about themselves while not getting defensive because the story is ostensibly about someone else. That's the effect that I hope this, and most of my work, would have."

Who are the Waltons – and what can Russell tell us about his human protagonists and their place in the story?

"The Waltons are sort of an every-family," Russell explained. "Sort of like the Waltons from the '70s TV series, but in a near-future dystopia instead of a near-past dystopia."

Who are some of the robotic characters that Russell came up with for *Not All Robots*? Are they friend to mankind or foe?

"They are mostly breadwinners and civil servants," said Russell. "Normal 'people.' Because all work has been automated, every family has been assigned a robot to be their source of income and support. These robots think they are the best thing that ever happened to humanity. Whenever one of them goes nuts and kills its family, they just write it off as a small price to pay for all the benefits humans get from their metal overlords."

With robots replacing our labor force on a daily basis, is this dystopian future closer to reality or tailored to be nothing more than fantastic fiction?

"I think it's closer to our current reality than anyone quite realises yet," Russell admitted.

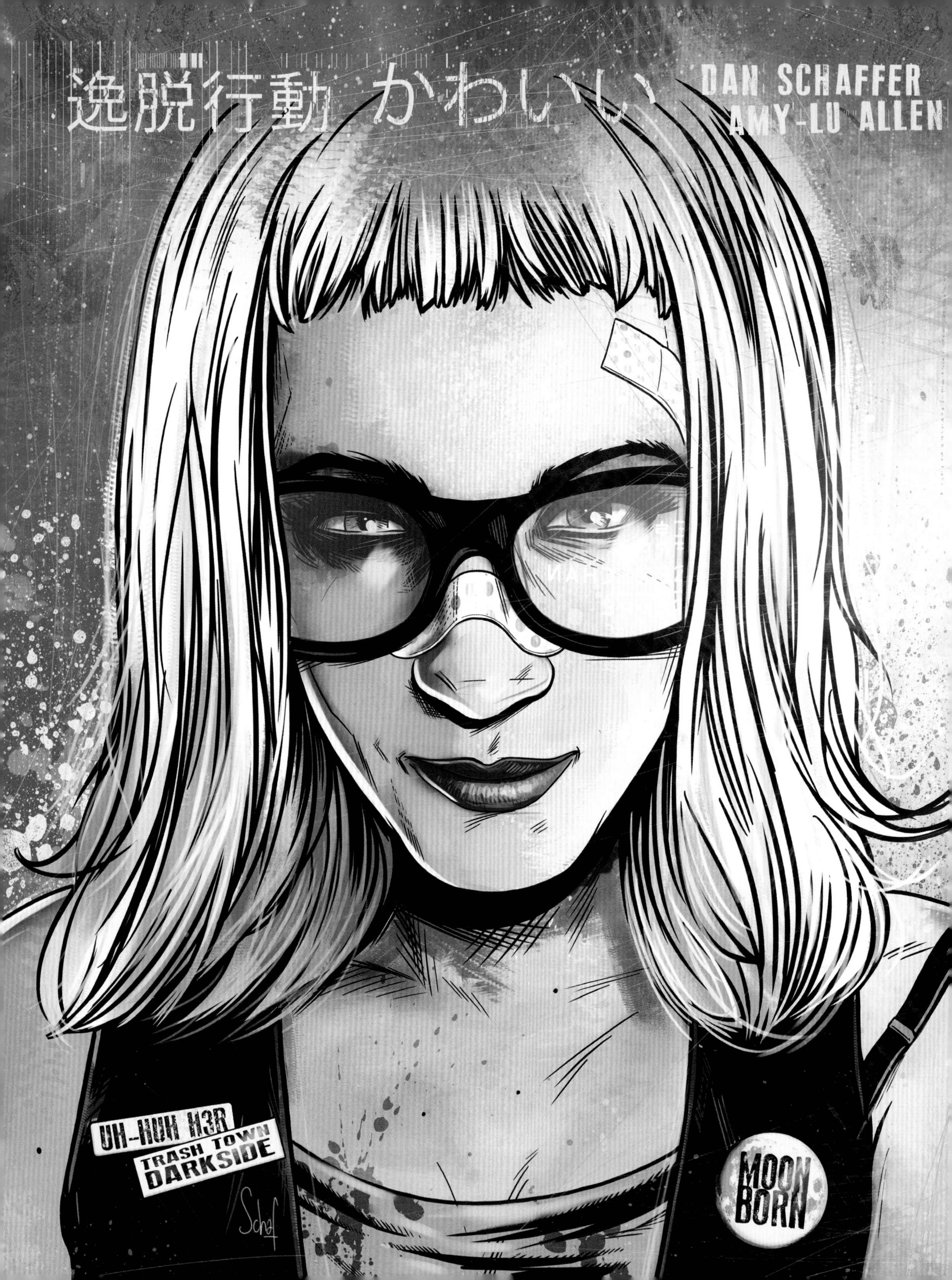
逸脱行動 かわいい
DAN SCHAFFER
AMY-LU ALLEN
UH-HUH H3R
TRASH TOWN
DARKSIDE
Schaf
MOON BORN

30 INDEPENDENT COMIC CREATORS WHO MADE THEIR MARK

Tim Hayes takes a look at 30 independent comic creators including editors who have made their presence known over the past thirty years, 1992-2022...

1 Gilbert and Jaime Hernandez

When Gilbert, Jaime and Mario Hernandez sent their self-published *Love and Rockets* comic to Fantagraphics publisher Gary Groth in 1982, it was the right comic in the right place at the right time, the seed for the indie comics sector that grew in its wake. Four decades on, Gilbert and Jaime have tended their series and its characters in two complementary but very different art styles, not collaborating but still joined at the source for stories about America, family, music, sex, fantasy, reality and wrestling.

LOVE AND ROCKETS
#01
GILBERT & JAIME HERNANDEZ

PEEP SHOW
THE CARTOON DIARY OF JOE MATT

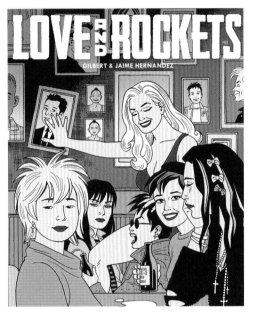

2 Joe Matt

Joe Matt's *Peepshow* painted its main character in a massively unflattering light, that character being Joe Matt. In 14 issues published over as many years, Matt's confessional comic showed the character as a penny-pinching porn-obsessed argumentative pain, with flashbacks to his childhood to show where all this came from. The expressive cartooning helped to make the self-deprecation endearing, but the main influence behind Matt's autobiographical bile is the fertile world of underground comix, as a dedication to Robert Crumb in Matt's later *Spent* made clear.

3 Daniel Clowes

After warming up with *Lloyd Llewelyn* in 1986 Dan Clowes made a splash with *Eightball* in 1989 and never looked back. The *Eightball* anthology started with Like a Velvet Glove Cast in Iron, a *Twin Peaks*-style story of oddball Americana that predated the David Lynch show by six months. Later came *Ghost World*, following Enid Coleslaw (spot the author anagram) through suburbia, and *Art School Confidential*; both of these became films. So did *Wilson*, Clowes's 2010 exploration of a curmudgeonly misanthrope in modern America. *Patience* from 2016 was a lengthy science-fiction romance where the cartoonist's deceptively modest style probed deep into an unfriendly universe.

Eightball
NUMBER 13
FANTAGRAPHICS BOOKS
WHAT?! IT'S MY PUNK LOOK!
BY DANIEL CLOWES
Recommended for mature Readers

4 Adrian Tomine

Drawn & Quarterly began collecting Adrian Tomine's self-published minicomics series *Optic Nerve* in 1995, bringing the artist's atmospheric urban stories to a wider audience. Tomine's expressive faces and heavily spotted blacks showed

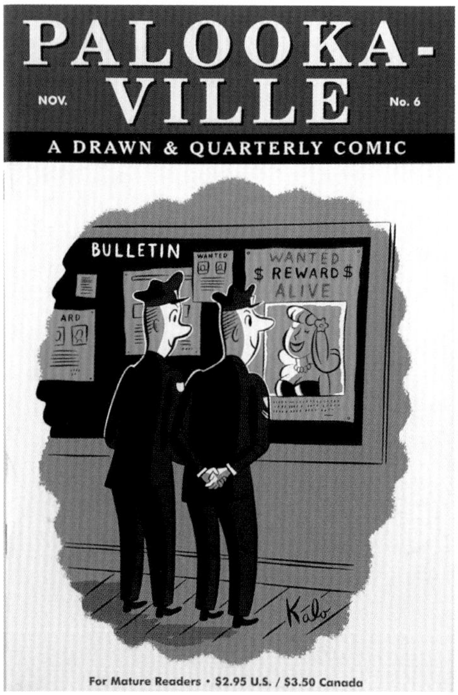
PALOOKA-VILLE
NOV.
No. 6
A DRAWN & QUARTERLY COMIC
BULLETIN
WANTED
$ REWARD $
ALIVE
For Mature Readers • $2.95 U.S. / $3.50 Canada

how the influence of Jaime Hernandez was spreading, but Tomine has experimented with different styles and moods in stories often relating to the artist's Japanese American heritage. *The Loneliness of the Long-Distance Cartoonist* was explicitly autobiographical, processing the universal tribulations of the indie comics artist.

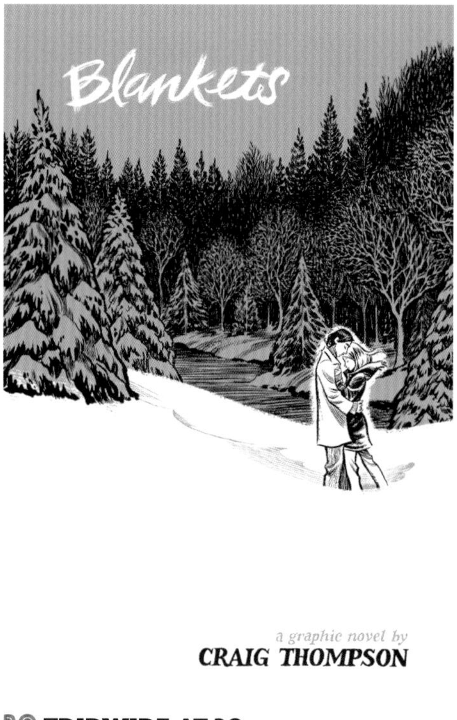
Blankets
a graphic novel by
CRAIG THOMPSON

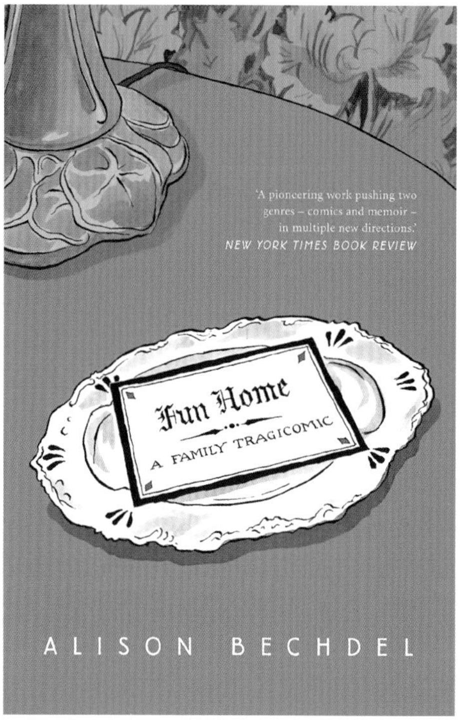
'A pioneering work pushing two genres – comics and memoir – in multiple new directions.'
NEW YORK TIMES BOOK REVIEW
Fun Home
A FAMILY TRAGICOMIC
ALISON BECHDEL

5 Seth

Gregory Gallant, aka Seth, filled the pages of *Palookaville* with small panels and soft lines, plus a feeling for the history of his industry. *It's A Good Life If You Don't Weaken* was about a man fascinated by the long-gone cartoonists of the past, and Clyde Fans was anxious about the damage capitalism does to art. Seth's fixed panel grids jammed onto the page had their own ticking rhythm like a production line, as the story showed commerce driving families apart.

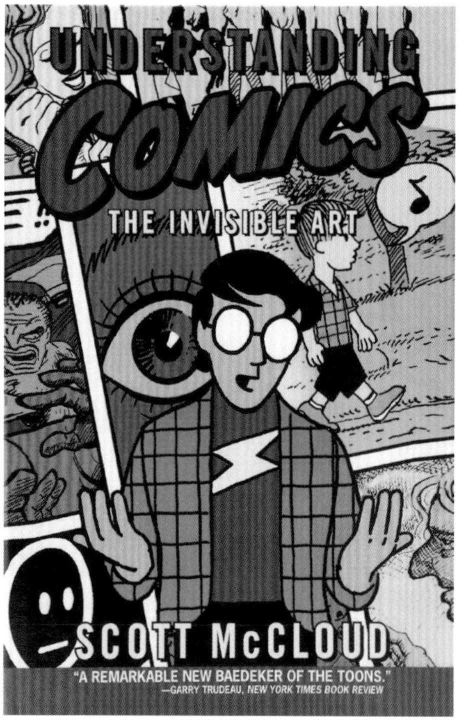
UNDERSTANDING COMICS
THE INVISIBLE ART
SCOTT McCLOUD
"A REMARKABLE NEW BAEDEKER OF THE TOONS."
—GARRY TRUDEAU, NEW YORK TIMES BOOK REVIEW

6 Alison Bechdel

A name known far outside comics, thanks to the Bechdel Test for representation of women in fiction now name-checked regularly in mainstream media. *Dykes To Watch Out For* collected drawings from several publications and magazines, their scratchy ink lines and single panel strips evolving into a regular cast of characters. *Fun Home* was more complex, about the relationship of a lesbian daughter with her father. Most recently for *The Secret to Superhuman Strength* Bechdel's style evolved again, with colour washes and grand landscapes in a story about the modern fixation on self-improvement.

7 Craig Thompson

Good-bye, Chunky Rice, Craig Thompson's first book, put cartoony human and animal characters in front of detailed heavily inked backgrounds. His next, *Blankets*, had more realistic human beings, drawn in curved sexy lines owing a lot to the French artist Blutch. *Habibi* in 2011 followed two suffering children through precisely detailed Orientalist architecture and religious structures. All his books are about making roots and connections, and the occasional flashes of cruelty that get in the way.

8 Scott McCloud

Three decades after Scott McCloud created *Understanding Comics* the book still crops up in every discussion of comics theory, and as a result so does he. It's a worthy volume, and can obscure the other comics that McCloud made previously. *Zot* was a significant 1980s series, an exuberant superhero fantasy with serious cultural undertones. *Destroy!!* satirised superhero violence and, inadvertently, the Image Comics era that wouldn't actually start until six years later. McCloud returned to fictionalised stories with *The Sculptor* in 2015, a big graphic novel about love and death and agitated emotion. But *Understanding Comics* will open all the eventual McCloud obituaries.

9 Raina Telgemeier

Smile, Raina Telgemeier's webcomic of a young girl's dental work and related adolescent anxieties, was picked up for print by publishers Scholastic, and duly reached the kind of audience within that publisher's bookstore reach, and promptly went onto the *New York Times* list of bestselling graphic novels. Her later graphic novels, about friendship, growing up, and digestion, followed the same route with the same results. One of the small number of indie cartoonists known well beyond the direct market for adult indie comics, Telgemeier's free-flowing, funny, accessible cartooning has won fans almost everywhere.

From the #1 New York Times Bestselling Author
Raina Telgemeier
WINNER
Smile
SCHOLASTIC

10 Chester Brown

Chester Brown's *Yummy Fur* first appeared in 1983 and no one reading it was in any doubt about what the young cartoonist wanted to talk about: schizophrenia, onanism, castration, religion and scatology to start with, and then deeper into Brown's free associative absurdity. Some of his comics play formal experiments, like *Underwater* in which a child's lack of language skills garbles some of the dialogue; or *Paying For It* which lays out Brown's views on prostitution with the faces of the women always obscured by word balloons. Sometimes expressive, sometimes sparse, and easy to mock, Brown's books insist that the reader tunes in to Brown's wavelength.

11 Joe Sacco

The label of Comics Journalist is attached so firmly to Joe Sacco that it can hide the other cartoonists who have worked in non-fiction comics, as well as the level of craft that Sacco brings to the job. But the success of *Palestine* and *Safe Area Goražde* brought new focus to the ability of comics to record historical conflict and civilian casualties. *The Great War* went back to the Battle of the Somme and unfolded into a single seven-metre panorama, a formal experiment in the same kind of observation. *Bumf*, Sacco's rude satire of political uselessness, isn't news from a war zone, but was made by someone who had stood in a few of them.

LOUIS RIEL
A COMIC-STRIP BIOGRAPHY
CHESTER BROWN

AUTHOR OF FOOTNOTES IN GAZA AND SAFE AREA GORAŽDE
PAYING THE LAND
JOE SACCO

12 Gary Panter

Jimbo: Adventures In Paradise made a major splash, Gary Panter's rough jagged lines and off-kilter apocalyptic sci-fi story blending LA punk and modernist art styles together in an unlikely but striking fusion. Since then his amiable slacker Jimbo has wondered around *Dante's Purgatory* and *Inferno*, and Panter has dug into Milton's *Paradise Lost* too. 2017's **Crashpad** is Panter at full throttle, a wildly extravagant pondering of the hippie era and its long shadow that lets the artist make his druggy underground comic, after saying he was too young for the genre the first time around.

NOCTURNALS
THE SINISTER PATH
DAN BRERETON

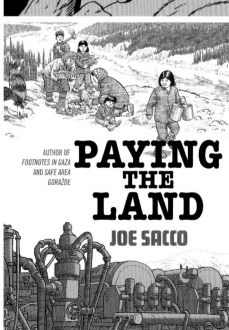

13 Dan Brereton

Alex Ross set a template for painted comics art in the 1990s with lush realism from the Norman Rockwell school. Dan Brereton's painted art goes in another direction entirely, mixing Gene Colan, Wally Wood and Charles Addams in a style that stays emphatically cartoonish and blazingly colourful. A man to call on whenever big destructive creatures come crashing in, Brereton has worked on several mainstream books but his heart belongs to his own *Nocturnals* series, mixing horror comics with pulp fiction. Monsters are for life, not just for Halloween.

14 Paul Grist

Not many UK comics artists spark uproar in The Sun newspaper, but Paul Grist did when he and Grant Morrison created *St Swithin's Day in 1989*. Going solo, Grist self-published *Kane*, the perfect venue for his stylised, angular, humane cartooning and one of the great 1990s cop comics. Image Comics gave a home and high profile to *Kane* and to *Jack Staff*, a multi-generational story of British superheroes that drew on old issues of *Lion* and *Valiant*, but with more jokes. *Mudman* was set in a particularly muddy seaside town of a kind the Somerset-based Grist would know all about, while the strip harked straight back to Stan Lee and Steve Ditko.

15 Shaky Kane

Deadline magazine contained plenty of high voltage 1990s cartooning, but the work by Michael Coulthard aka Shaky Kane had more punch than most. Aggressively harsh lines spun Jack Kirby's blocky energy into a Britain of Tory angst, with the *A-Men* kicking down the doors of anyone having too much fun and Chief Constable James Anderton's face on the Shroud of Turin. More recently Image Comics has given Kane and David Hine room to develop their *Bulletproof Coffin* series, in which a skewed Americana of UFOs and Cold War terror becomes the secret history of US comics.

BRITAIN'S GREATEST HERO!
A PAUL GRIST COMIC!
Jack Staff

16 Woodrow Phoenix

Early work on *Sonic The Comic* and *The Sumo Family* strip in the *Independent* showed off Woodrow Phoenix's energetic characters and lines, but his indie work hasn't been afraid of formal experiment. *The Bride*, about the Bride of Frankenstein character, exists in only one oversized copy, so either you travel to it or it travels to you. *Rumble Strip* used static images of deserted UK roads and eerily pointless traffic signs for an angry complaint about the loss of life on roads and a society in thrall to the motorcar. Phoenix revised it for a US edition retitled *Crash Course*, by which time Covid-19 had emptied the roads for real and given it even more resonance.

IF YOU WANT TO GET AWAY WITH MURDER BUY A CAR
WOODROW PHOENIX
CRASH COURSE

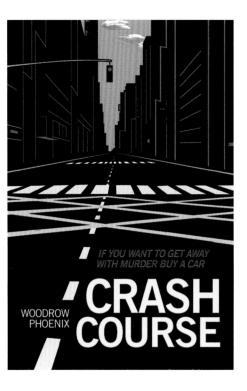

17 Lale Westvind

Lale Westvind's art can be unmistakable from a long way off. It has big bodies and big limbs and big movements rendered in strident risograph colours on pages buzzing with energy. The comics fuse Jack Kirby dynamics with psychedelic sensory overload, or emphasise the psychedelic that's was also part of Kirby's oeuvre. *Grip* from 2018 told a sort-of superhero origin in which a woman's hands are never still, and turned it into a story of empowerment for anyone involved in the physical creation of anything, a comic about labour and purpose.

18 Bryan Talbot

The Adventures of Luther Arkwright began in 1978 and didn't conclude for a decade, but by then the 1980s market for sophisticated comics with subversive attitudes had caught up to it. Bryan Talbot's crowded black and white art and dense ink lines matched the sci-fi intensity of the story, while also embracing roots that went back as far as Hogarth. Talbot's work since always combines political comment with refined comics craft, whether describing the life of Lewis Carroll in *Alice In Sunderland*, or venturing deep into Anglo-French relations via anthropomorphic badgers in the *Grandville* series.

19 Darwyn Cooke

Darwyn Cooke found his niche in comics through work in Bruce Timm's stable of animated DC superheroes, which makes perfect sense considering Cooke's retro art style. But Cooke could turn that style to modernity, violence and brutality without stretching. *The New Frontier* was affectionate about both 1950s comics and 1950s USA, part pastiche but all sincere, while Cooke's adaptations of Richard Stark's *Parker* novels looked at the same country from underneath, all the ingredients of noir rendered in two-colour washes rather than lakes

of black. Cooke's death at 53 robbed comics of a lot.

20 Barry Windsor-Smith

In the 1970s Barry Windsor-Smith's sinuous and sensual art on *Conan The Barbarian* looked like a new level of sophistication in comics, and each time he drew a few issues of *X-Men* or other mainstream series that same craft elevated the stories. *Barry Windsor-Smith: Storyteller* was published by Dark Horse in 1996 but was essentially BWS flexing his muscles, experimenting with format and technique. After years of silence *Monsters* arrived in 2021, a looming thundercloud of a book about cruelty and bereavement that put the Nazis in place as the central evil of the modern world, BWS drawing as if seeing how far into the dark his art could take him.

21 Benjamin Marra

Hugely violent, wildly profane and certain to offend anyone looking to be offended, Benjamin Marra's books are a reaction against po-faced timid cartooning wherever on the political spectrum it comes from. Marra doesn't believe in restraint, and if he wants to draw rappers NWA waging war on the LAPD, or an individual looking a lot like Jesus Christ fighting the Romans with martial arts, or US foreign policy implemented by homicidal psychotics, then that's what will happen. During Covid-19 Marra drew a daily Instagram series that spitballed an endless disjointed series of events into one unending soap opera of micro-aggressions, much as did Covid-19.

22 Ed Brubaker

Prior to his stints scripting superheroes for Marvel, DC and Image for nearly three decades, Ed Brubaker wrote and drew *Lowlife*, an autobiographical comic inspired by creators like the Hernandez brothers which fully engaged with 1990s indie comics' themes about family ties and bad memories. More recently he co-wrote episodes of *Westworld* and Nicolas Winding Refn's acidic noir fantasy *Too Old To Die Young* for TV. As comics have moved to the centre of pop-culture, so the path for indie writers to move into the mainstream of comics and then into adjacent media has become smoother - if they want to take it.

23 Robert Kirkman

Likewise, Robert Kirkman began his career self-publishing superhero comedy strips, spent a few years writing for Marvel and Image, and then started the creator-owned *The Walking Dead* in 2003, first with artist Tony Moore and then Charlie Adlard. The series ran for 16 years and became a TV franchise, putting Kirkman on Hollywood Power Lists and seeing

THE WALKING DEAD
20
100
$3.99
KIRKMAN • ADLARD • RATHBURN

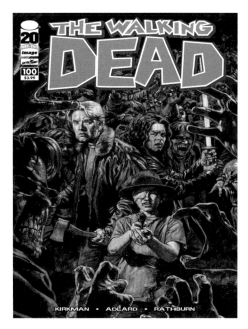

him became an Image Comics partner as well as head of Skybound Entertainment. He has also been involved in a decade of back-and-forth lawsuits over money from the TV show, potentially the biggest ever profits dispute in television history. Which is the territory that indie cartooning can now lead to.

24 Alan Moore

Independent thinker, independent creator, independent thorn in the side of any publisher he feels has let him down although they rarely then change course. Believer in the power of words as the core currency of human imagination, whether in comics, novels or performance art. Inveterate satirist of social ills in ways which haven't changed much in his forty-plus year career, for better or worse. Retired with the conclusion of *The League of Extraordinary Gentlemen* in 2019, but when he changes his mind everyone will be talking about it.

25 Grant Morrison

Hugely inventive writer and originally artist of comics teeming with mind expansion, esoteric knowledge, and frequently laughs. Post-modernist and intellectual, while also deeply cross with revisionist trends and dismantling of old-fashioned Silver Age charm - a writer more happy at DC than Marvel, not coincidentally. Creator of comics that often seem timeless; the ideas in Vertigo comics like *The Filth* and *The Invisibles* have hardly aged at all, since

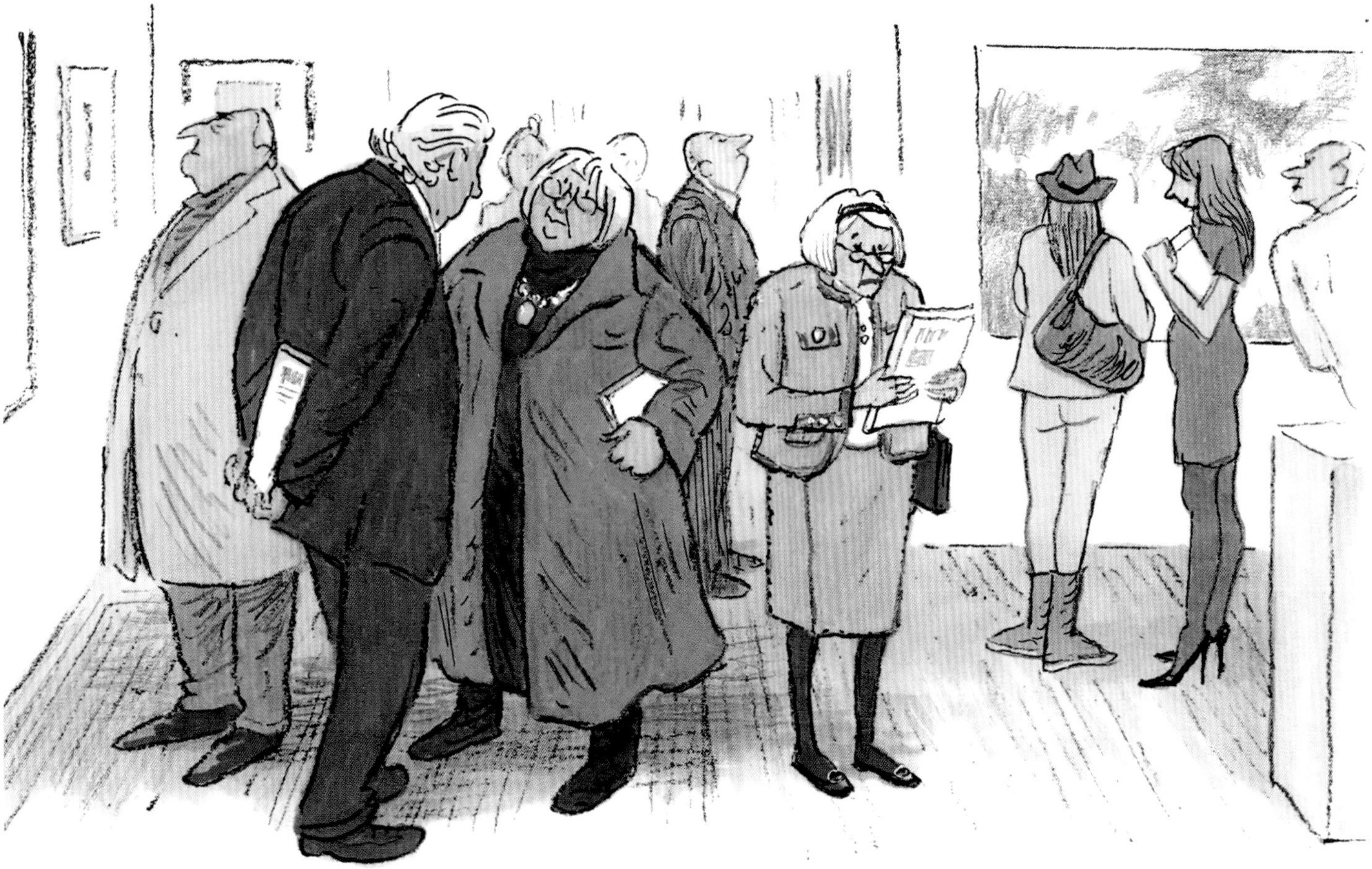

the society Morrison was thinking about is the one we still have. Currently among the creators seeing if Substack is the next big thing for comics publishing. And has written a novel centred on Widow Twankey.

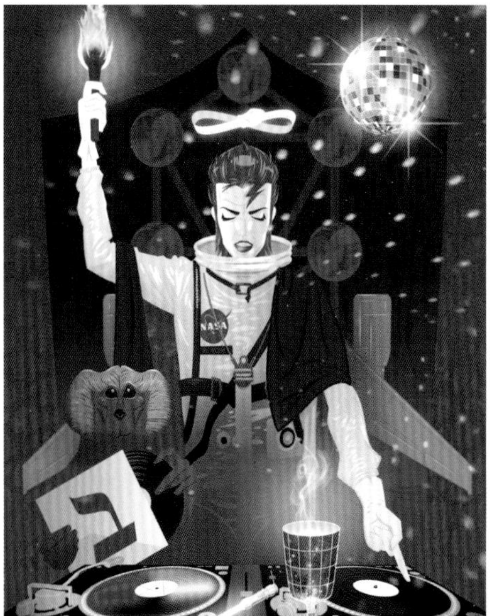

26 Karen Berger

The Vertigo imprint existed for 27 years with Karen Berger as Executive Editor for the first 20, and for those

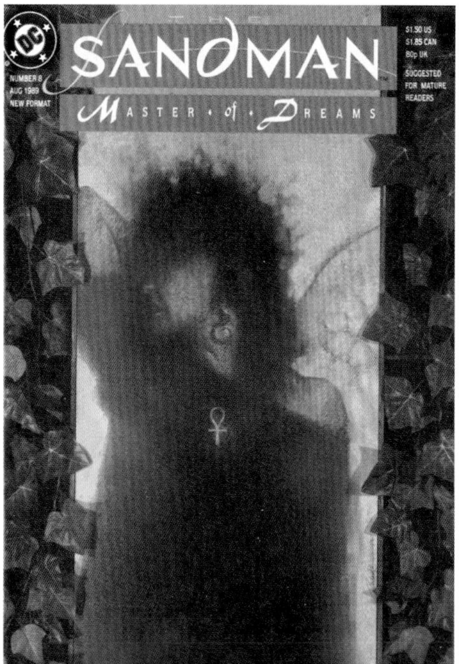
SANDMAN
MASTER · of · DREAMS
NUMBER 8
AUG 1989
NEW FORMAT
$1.50 US
$1.85 CAN
80p UK
SUGGESTED FOR MATURE READERS
GAIMAN · DRINGENBERG · JONES

two decades her influence on the Vertigo stable as a home for creator-owned comics and independent cartoonists was indisputable. Originally a launching pad for the British creators Berger cultivated and enticed into US comics, and with Neil Gaiman's *The Sandman* title as its high-profile motor, Vertigo let the creators of *The Invisibles*, *Enigma*, *Y: The Last Man* and *Preacher*, plus many others, do exactly the work that they wanted to do.

27 Robin and Lorenzo Etherington

Comics by the Etherington brothers appeared in the weekly British children's anthology comic *The DFC* and then in its successor *The Phoenix*, supplying both with a characteristic high-energy drawing style, humorous characters and blazing colours. At the same time they mastered a crowd-funding approach, creating a series of lively and accessible How To books about drawing and writing comics that expanded on free online tutorials and

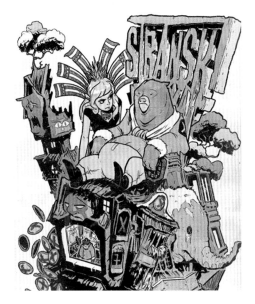

become the most funded artbooks on Kickstarter for three consecutive years. Each volume is funded by, and then reaches, thousands of enthusiastic new creators, making the Etheringtons two of the most high-profile comics educators around.

28 Posy Simmonds

The Guardian's *Posy* strip ran until 1987, bringing Posy Simmonds's delicate cartooning style to a wider broadsheet audience. She continued the association with the newspaper for *Gemma Bovary*, reworking the Flaubert story via English expatriates in France for a strip that was later made into film. The same thing happened with *Tamara Drew*, another story of messy adult relationships and urban vs. rural Britain, that let Simmonds refine her newspaper strip technique with colour for added sophistication. In the *Guardian* work and beyond, Simmonds's cartoons are appreciated by readers of prose literature who might not necessarily seek out comics in other places.

THE ADVENTURES OF
CAPTAIN UNDERPANTS
Action
THRILLS
LAFFS
The FIRST EPIC NOVEL BY
DAV PILKEY
SCHOLASTIC

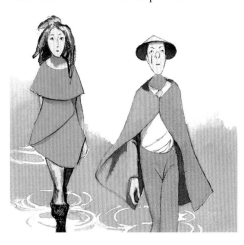

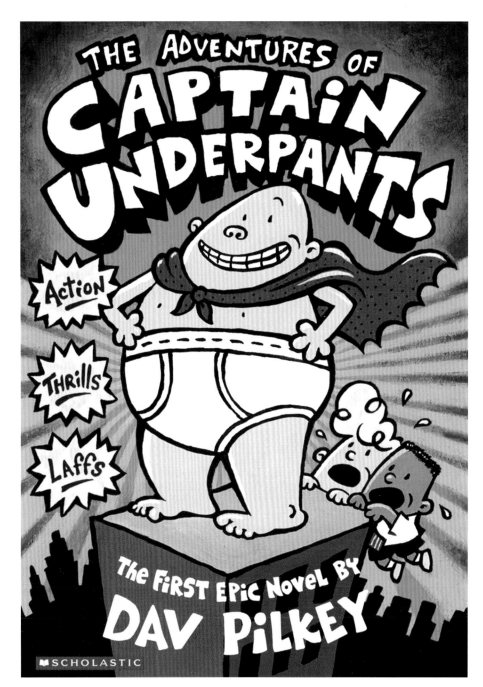

29 Manuele Fior

The soft watercolour art in Manuele Fior's comics suits their dreamy magic-realist mood, stories happening in a not-quite-real world that might be the future or an invented past. And Fior studied architecture, which probably has a lot to do with his constant interest in design and location. *5,000 km Per Second*, winner of Best Album at Angoulême in 2011, was a poignant relatively realistic love story spanning decades, but since then Fior has found ways to incorporate extraterrestrials, mythological characters, telepathy, fine art, and in 2021's Celestia a fantasy version of Venice barricading itself from something bad ravaging the rest of Italy.

30 Dav Pilkey

The numbers do not lie: sales figures of the *Captain Underpants* and *Dog-Man* books for kids have made Dav Pilkey the best-selling comics creator in North America by a comfortable margin. Published by Scholastic, and so tapping into the same bookstore markets as Raina Telegemeir, each book in Pilkey's *Dog Man* series has a print run above five million copies. And there are ten books. As big-time success in comics goes, this is not necessarily the dream of all indie cartoonists, but it fits the description.

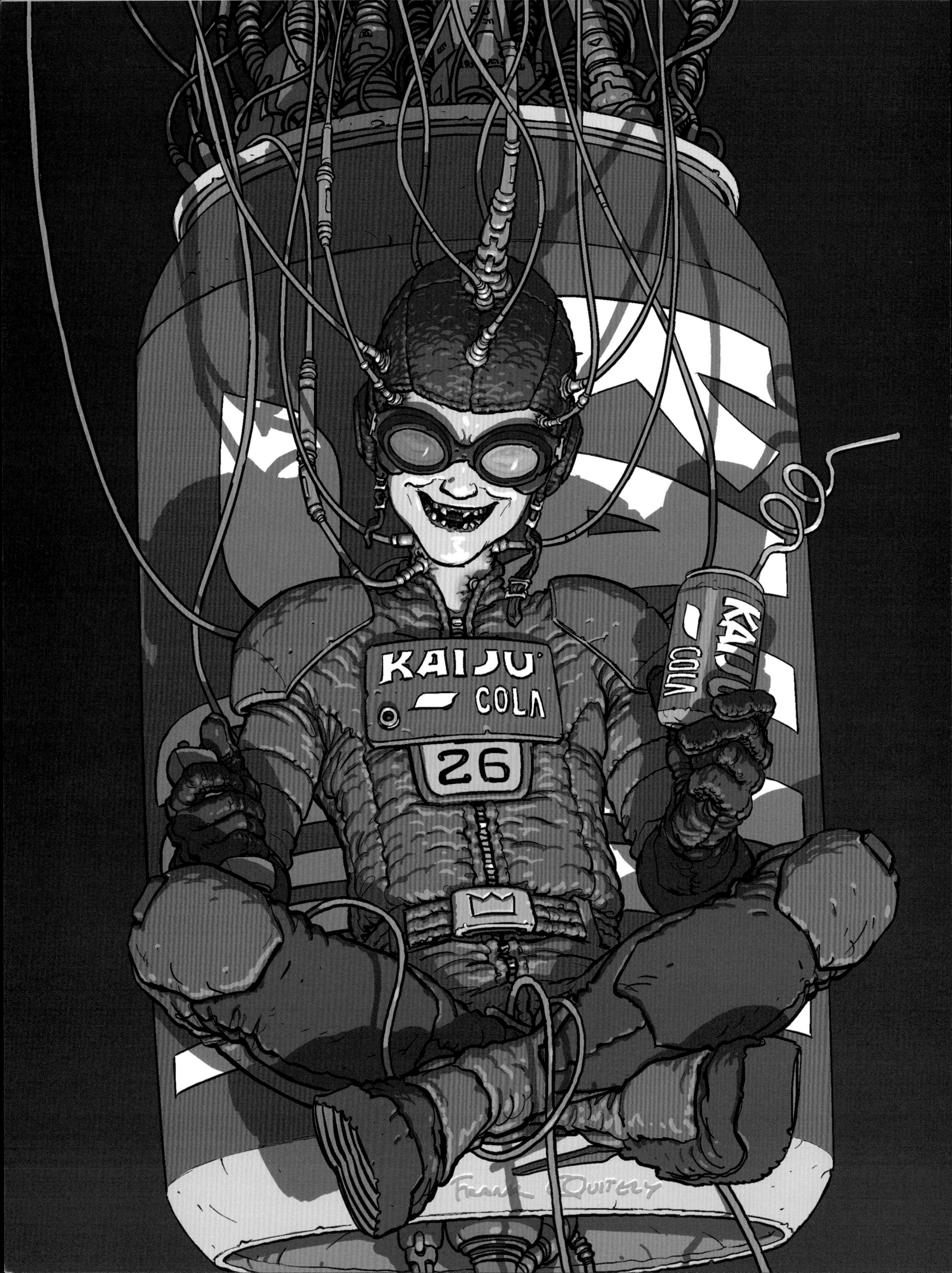
KAIJU
COLA
26
FRANK QUITELY

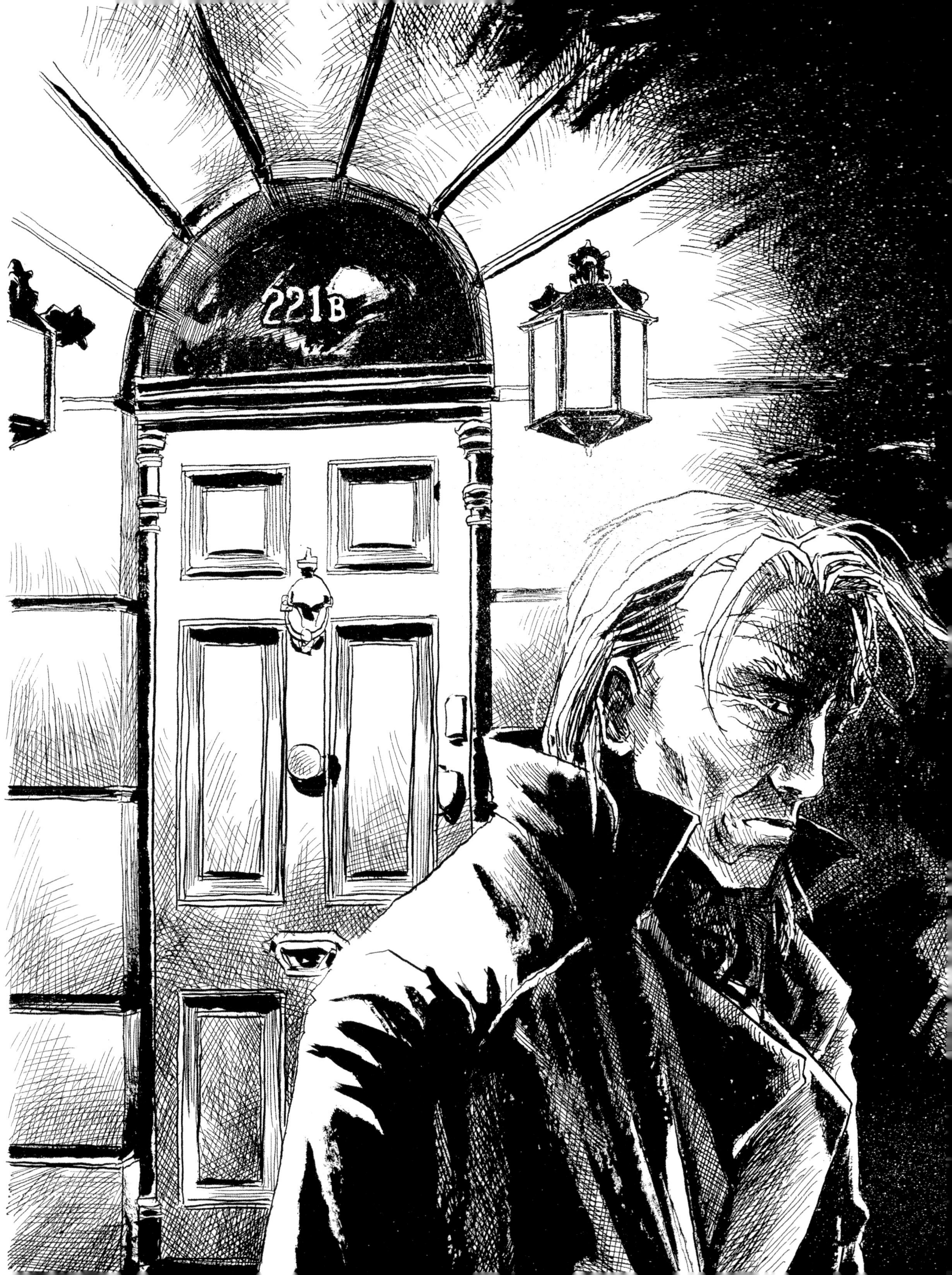
221B

ALWAYS BREAKING NEW GROUND

THE WALKING DEAD
image
ROBERT KIRKMAN
TONY MOORE

BRIAN K. VAUGHAN
FIONA STAPLES
Saga
VOLUME ONE

THE WICKED + THE DIVINE

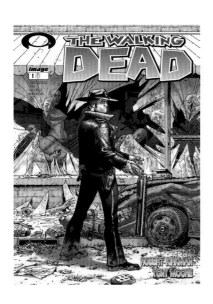

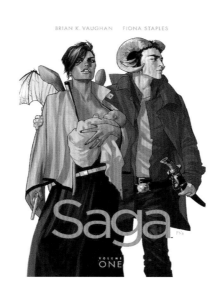

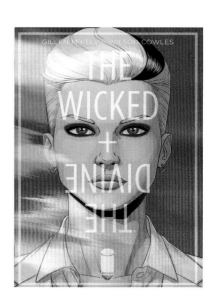

2022 is also the 30th birthday of independent comics powerhouse Image Comics and Scott Braden takes a look at the rollercoaster ride that the company that has brought us the likes of *The Walking Dead*, *Saga*, *The Wicked + The Divine* has enjoyed over the past three decades...

It all began in August of 1990. Comic book upstart Rob Liefeld, with friends and fellow comics professionals Erik Larsen and Jim Valentino, asked then-Malibu Comics publisher Dave Olbrich if he would ever consider publishing projects from them individually or as a trio.

Olbrich's answer made comic book history. And after that landmark decision – as well as the eventual inclusion of superstar artists Jim Lee, Todd McFarlane and Whilce Portacio – Image Comics, and the idea of Image itself, truly became everything all at once.

"The industry said, 'These long standing comic characters are the stars, and you should feel lucky that you are servicing them," said acclaimed writer Kieron Gillen. "Those early Image creators said 'No' and proved they were right. In doing so, they created a place which has creator rights at its absolute core."

At its most popular, Image Comics joined Valiant 1.0 to create its *Deathmate* event, which in turn symbolised both the peak and the decline of comic books in the 1990s. It

ROB LIEFELD
YOUNGBLOOD
image
1 APR $2.50 $3.00 Canada
THE NEXT GENERATION OF HEROES!
1ST EXCITING ISSUE!

SPAWN
image
1 MAY $1.95 $2.35 Canada

mirrored the glamour and near-hysteria of the comics boom, and (as unlikely as it was) did its part to help determine the speciality market's shocking downfall in that same decade.

Although *Deathmate* was announced as a crossover of Image Comics and Valiant, only two of Image's superstar studios participated in the event: Rob Liefeld's Extreme Studios and the one-time Jim Lee/Marc Silvestri partnership, Homage Studios, which was made up of Lee's Wildstorm characters and Silvestri's Top Cow Productions' properties.

"THE INDUSTRY SAID, 'THESE LONG STANDING COMIC CHARACTERS ARE THE STARS, AND YOU SHOULD FEEL LUCKY THAT YOU ARE SERVICING THEM," SAID ACCLAIMED WRITER KIERON GILLEN. "THOSE EARLY IMAGE CREATORS SAID 'NO' AND PROVED THEY WERE RIGHT. IN DOING SO, THEY CREATED A PLACE WHICH HAS CREATOR RIGHTS AT ITS ABSOLUTE CORE." –KIERON GILLEN

Valiant was an up-and-comer, sure, and it was enjoying success by building a new universe around revived Gold Key properties from the 1960s. But having the publisher Image Comics participating in the event – even only in part – carried a lot of cred. Its various studios and their projects were finding themselves on the covers of all the hot comics magazines (like *Wizard*) and setting records – like the first million-selling African-American-produced comic (*Tribe*) and the four-color return of the King of Comics, Jack Kirby (*Phantom Force*), among others.

Needless to say, the excitement behind the project was palpable with fans and the industry as a whole.
To further promote the event, the creators went on a worldwide comic shop tour. According to the silver-foil, $3.95-priced *Deathmate Tourbook* (with embossed cover) made available for purchase by participating shops, the event offered "fans the chance to be part of one of the biggest comics collaborations ever." At the time, that was not a misleading statement.

The Tourbook also declared "*Deathmate* is about the commonality between Image and Valiant and the

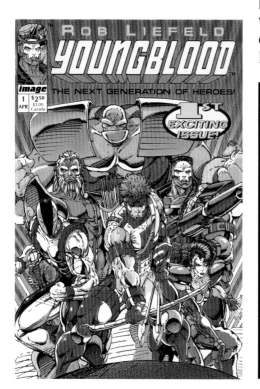

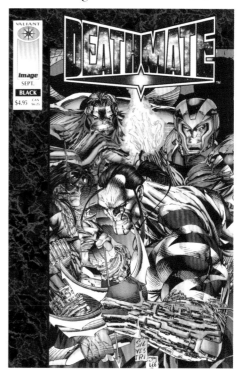

VALIANT
DEATHMATE
image
SEPT.
BLACK
$4.95 CAN $6.25

Shaping the company: Eric Stephenson has been a part of Image for decades now

many similarities both companies share. Both Image and Valiant are based on a natural enthusiasm for the creative process, as well as a love for the comics medium itself."

Direct market retailers and countless comics fans were excited about *Deathmate* from the very beginning. The much-anticipated crossover was a great success, despite its lateness and constant rescheduling. It easily served as one of the high points (creatively and commercially) and low points (retailers were left with a plethora of Deathmate issues once the books shipped late and fans lost interest in the series) of the decade. Still, this four-color meeting between Image and Valiant – as opposed to the Image Boys' own two companywide crossovers *Shattered Image* and *Image United* – excited the industry and shook up fandom for a time, successfully making its mark for readers yet to come. Until it didn't.

It is no secret that Image Comics was originally all about super-heroes. And when the comic book bust came in the mid-90s, fascination with super-characters and their heroics with an adolescent mindset became just that – kid's stuff. Readers wanted more mature books, and, as a result, they wanted their four-color funnies to grow the hell up.

At the same time, Liefeld's Extreme Universe became a thing and left Image – with comics grandmaster Alan Moore symbolically at the helm and, starting with his award-winning and critically acclaimed run on Supreme, transformed the publisher and Liefeld's generic properties into Awesome Entertainment. When that went south, Moore took many of his ideas to Jim Lee, who eventually sold his studio, Wildstorm Productions, and all the varied properties within it, to DC Comics.

With these turn of events, publisher Eric Stephenson quickly realized he needed to shake things up at "The House that The Image Boys Had Built." To start Image Comics' evolution into a 21st century creator-owned powerhouse, he and Valentino brought Robert Kirkman's comic book phenomenon, *The Walking Dead*, and Brian K. Vaughn's comix sensation, *Saga*, to the masses. With that, Image Comics changed forever.

"Since its inception," said Stephenson, "Image has been a home for writers and artists who want the final say over what they create. Image started with seven Marvel artists who wanted to have greater control over their work and could have been limited to that – a home for superstars interested in creating their own characters – but instead, they invited other creators to enjoy the same freedom they had and the longterm benefit can be seen in everything from the global success of *The Walking Dead* to groundbreaking comics and graphic novels like *Saga*, *Monstress*, *The Wicked + The Divine*, *The Department of Truth* and *Reckless*."

MARJORIE LIU
SANA TAKEDA
MONSTRESS
VOLUME FOUR · THE CHOSEN

"My view is that Image Comics evolved into a true home for creator-owned comics," said award-winning creator Jeff Lemire. "By that I mean, we the creators, have total ownership

"SINCE ITS INCEPTION ...IMAGE HAS BEEN A HOME FOR WRITERS AND ARTISTS WHO WANT THE FINAL SAY OVER WHAT THEY CREATE. IMAGE STARTED WITH SEVEN MARVEL ARTISTS WHO WANTED TO HAVE GREATER CONTROL OVER THEIR WORK ...THEY INVITED OTHER CREATORS TO ENJOY THE SAME FREEDOM THEY HAD." –ERIC STEPHENSON

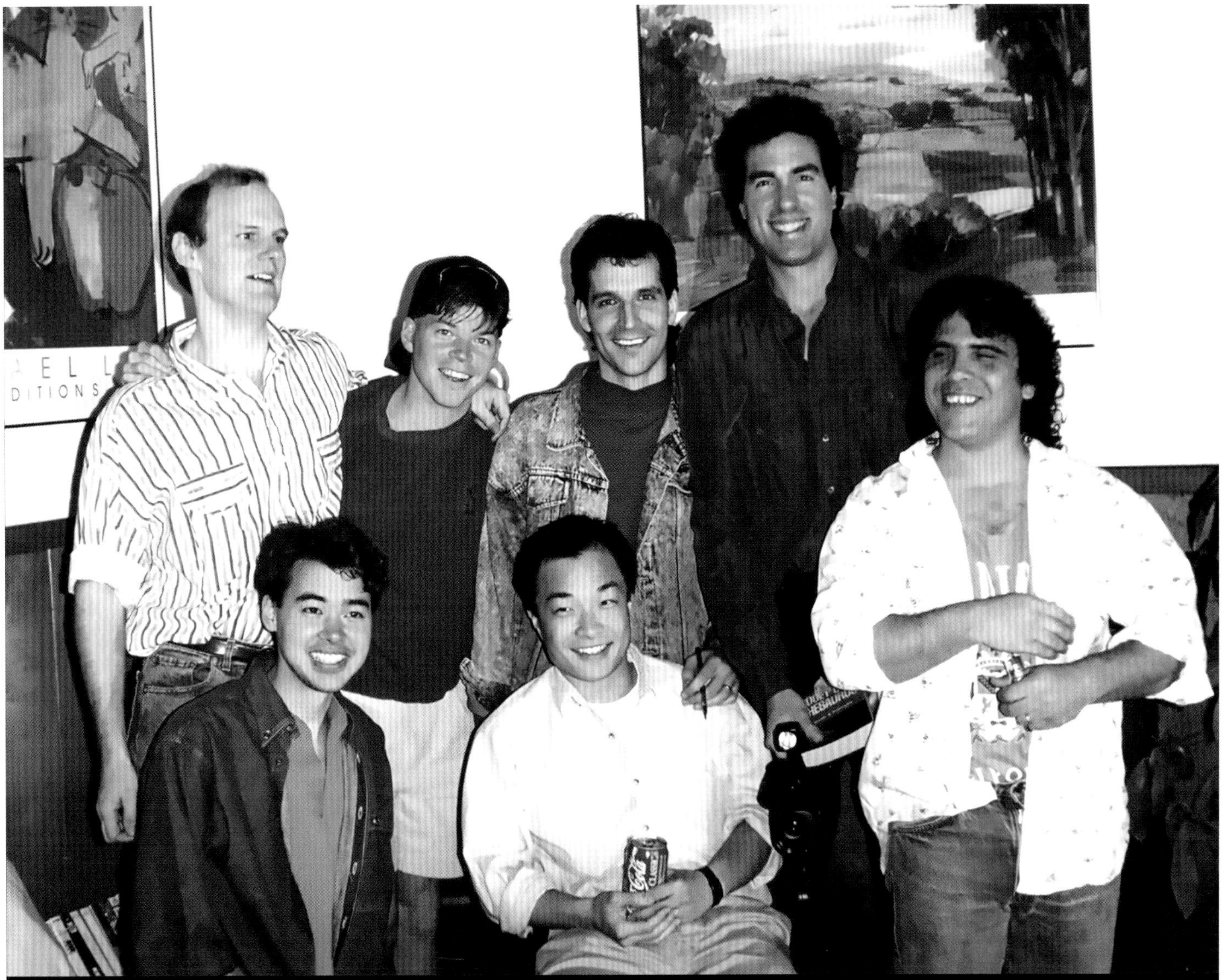
E L L
DITIONS

Making history: The Image founders when the company started back in 1992

and creative freedom, but with the infrastructure of a publisher rather than having to self-publish. The success of Image books allowed creators like myself to build a library of books that I own, or co-own with my collaborators, and that allows me to make a living outside of doing work-for-hire and DC/Marvel."

"As DC became more and more corporate and the truly visionary people there, like Karen Berger, were forced out," added Lemire, "it stopped being a creator-owned friendly environment. Image Comics was the natural spot to take up the mantle. Unlike DC, there is no corporate oversight and Image Comics does not take a percentage of our media rights, etc."

Lemire's collaborator Andrea Sorrentino also sees just how significant Image Comics has been for the world of comics: "I think it's completely safe to say that Image Comics changed the industry. The creators-keeps-the-rights-of-what-they-created approach was revolutionary in the 90s and there are many incredible books that would't be out not only without Image, but even without this new way of thinking on how to create comics.

Knowing you'll completely own (and so, be able to manage all by your choices) the property you're creating is something that really pushed the creators, in past and now, to explore completely different ways of telling comics, of creating them and of publishing them."

Gillen stated, "This is an essay, but you're not paying me for an essay, so let's keep it simple: you do the book at Image, and you have complete control of the rights . . . more and more creators just did the math, and went to Image."

Fellow British comic writer Si Spurrier sees the company's corporate remit at the heart of its continuing success:

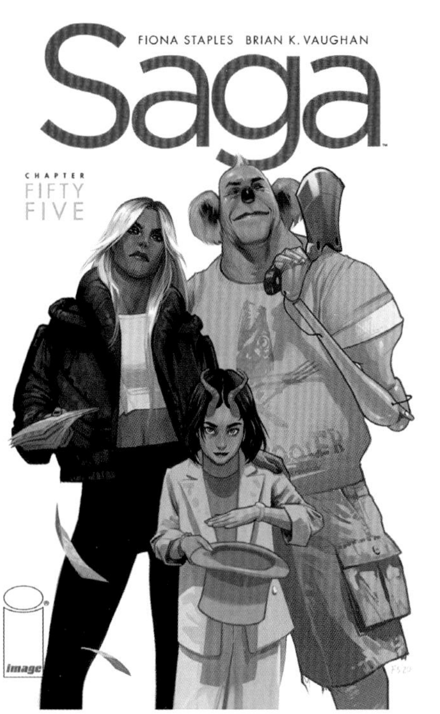
FIONA STAPLES BRIAN K. VAUGHAN
Saga
CHAPTER
FIFTY
FIVE
image

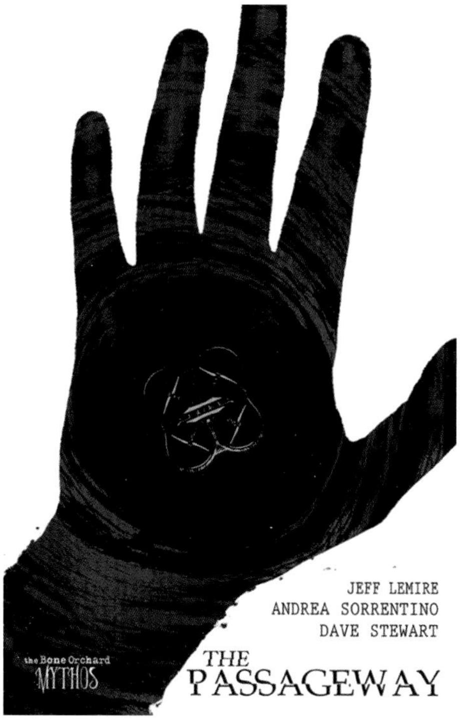
JEFF LEMIRE
ANDREA SORRENTINO
DAVE STEWART
the Bone Orchard
MYTHOS
THE
PASSAGEWAY

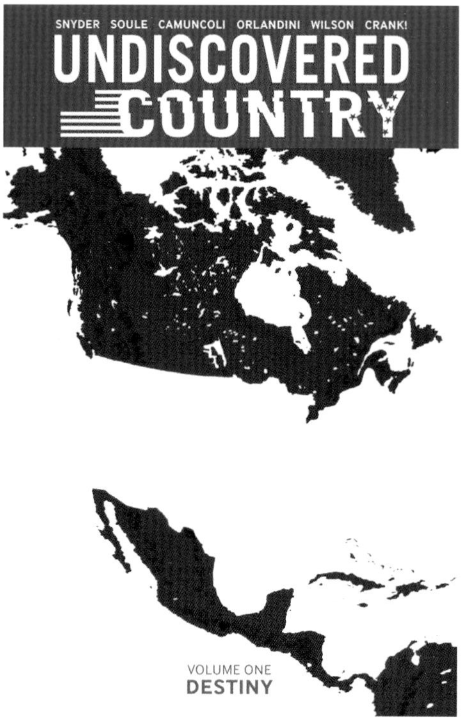
SNYDER SOULE CAMUNCOLI ORLANDINI WILSON CRANK!
UNDISCOVERED
COUNTRY
VOLUME ONE
DESTINY

"To my eye, the cultural and historical significance of Image - by accident or design - derives from precisely the same core mentality as the strategies which have made it such a leader in the field today. Put simply: quality comics derive from creative freedom.

Unpack that a little and what you get is a very sharp rubric. Let the creators make all the decisions, and take all the risks, and the formative pressures which surround a project (primarily: It Better Be Good Or Nobody Makes Any Money) will tend to produce some seriously good shit.

"Whether or not the terms of the current boilerplate deal were in the minds of those first breakaway talents, when they decided they'd be happier and better-off controlling the content rather than producing it on demand, I don't know. But the current deal is quite remarkable. By levying a flat fee rather than taking a cut of each monthly comic, Image tacitly presents itself as providers of a service as opposed to an interested (hence interfering) authority. You might think of Image as a sort of one-stop solution to marketing, printing and distribution. Unlike any other publisher, the readers and the retailers are not Image's customers. We are. The creators. We pay them a set amount to publish our books. In smaller, stranger circles this is the model adopted by what is often sniffily dismissed as "vanity publishing". Hence it's a sign of how brilliantly Image curates its slate -- which books it chooses to publish and those it declines -- that over time the brand has become so trusted by retailers that "New Image #1" connotes a certain level of quality, and guarantees a certain a level of interest.

Sorrentino does see parallels between Image and DC's former independent imprint Vertigo but specific ones, he revealed.

"I think it's a bit easier to draw parallels of the two from a reader's point of view, honestly, because both represent now (in the case of Image) and represented then (in the case of DC Vertigo) a new frontier in bringing something fresh to the table and an environment where creators were and are pushed to create something completely new and to explore new directions in terms of genre, mood, writing and giving readers something exciting and never seen before that the

"IT'S IMPOSSIBLE TO OVERESTIMATE THE IMPACT IMAGE HAS HAD ON BOTH THE INDUSTRY AND THE ART FORM SINCE ITS INCEPTION... IMAGE HAD THE RESOURCES AND THE STAR POWER TO PUT CREATOR'S VOICES AT THE FOREFRONT OF A PUBLISHER WHICH COULD STAND TOE-TO-TOE WITH THE JUGGERNAUTS OF MARVEL AND DC SALES-WISE."

– PHIL HESTER

sole market of the superheroes couldn't always bring (or that they never took so far anyways).

They have also been the showcase of some of the top-notch comics creators ever, so they took so much excellence to the table it's incredible.

At the same time, to be completely honest, I'm not sure if it's fair to compare the two from a creators perspective. I've been in the industry as a pro for less then 15 years now, so I didn't have the chance to work on any Vertigo title. However I've still got the feeling that a part of the property was at that time (or, for some projects at least) still held and coordinated by DC, whereas at Image currently you're the owner, editor and manager of any project you put out (you'll manage the choice of the format, the possible variant artists, the quality of the paper, the international rights and so on) making it for a completely different experience.

DC Vertigo probably changed the way that readers read comics at the time, but I think Image really changed it for what it means for the creators."

"It's impossible to overestimate the impact Image has had on both the industry and the art form since its inception," said comix creator Phil Hester. "I came of age as a professional during the black and white explosion of the mid 80's, so a vibrant indie scene has always been part of my comics landscape. I think that scene would still exist without Image, but Image had the resources and the star power to put creator's voices at the forefront of a publisher which could stand toe-to-toe with the juggernauts of Marvel and DC sales-wise, and also put pressure on them to deal with creators more equitably themselves. Owning your creation outright, with no strings attached, is an unparalleled proposition.

"During Vertigo's heyday, there were any number of publishers offering similar or better deals to creators. I

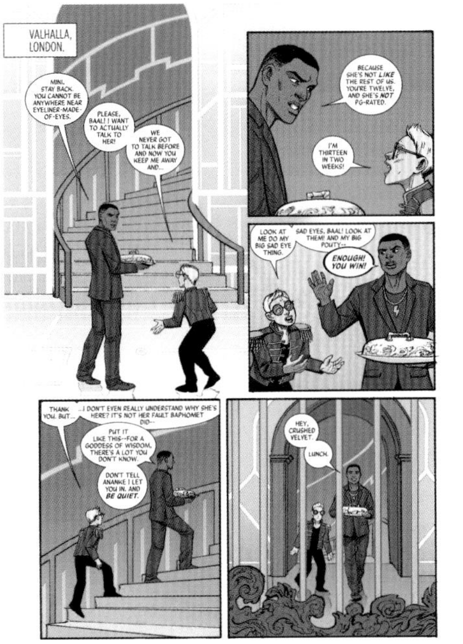
VALHALLA, LONDON.
MINI. STAY BACK. YOU CANNOT BE ANYWHERE NEAR EYELINER-MADE-OF-EYES.
PLEASE, BAAL! I WANT TO ACTUALLY TALK TO HER!
WE NEVER GOT TO TALK BEFORE AND NOW YOU KEEP ME AWAY AND...
BECAUSE SHE'S NOT LIKE THE REST OF US. YOU'RE TWELVE, AND SHE'S NOT PG-RATED.
I'M THIRTEEN IN TWO WEEKS!
LOOK AT ME DO MY BIG SAD EYE THING.
SAD EYES, BAAL! LOOK AT THEM! AND MY BIG POUTY--
ENOUGH! YOU WIN!
THANK YOU. BUT...
...I DON'T EVEN REALLY UNDERSTAND WHY SHE'S HERE? IT'S NOT HER FAULT BAPHOMET DID--
PUT IT LIKE THIS--FOR A GODDESS OF WISDOM, THERE'S A LOT YOU DON'T KNOW.
DON'T TELL ANANKE I LET YOU IN. AND BE QUIET.
HEY, CRUSHED VELVET.
LUNCH.

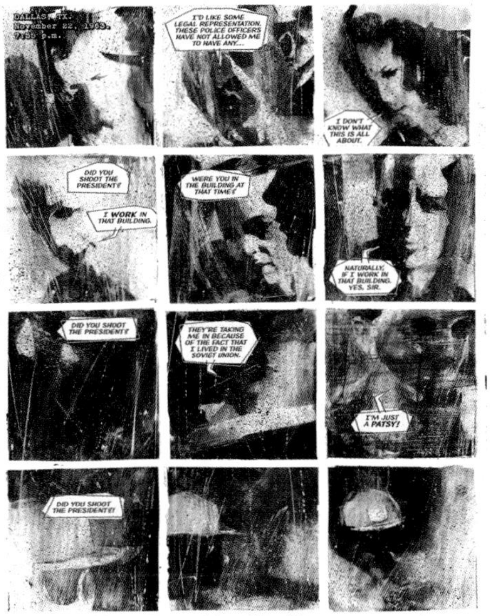
DALLAS, TX.
November 22, 1963.
I'D LIKE SOME LEGAL REPRESENTATION. THESE POLICE OFFICERS HAVE NOT ALLOWED ME TO HAVE ANY...
I DON'T KNOW WHAT THIS IS ALL ABOUT.
DID YOU SHOOT THE PRESIDENT?
I WORK IN THAT BUILDING.
WERE YOU IN THE BUILDING AT THAT TIME?
NATURALLY, IF I WORK IN THAT BUILDING. YES, SIR.
DID YOU SHOOT THE PRESIDENT?
THEY'RE TAKING ME IN BECAUSE OF THE FACT THAT I LIVED IN THE SOVIET UNION.
I'M JUST A PATSY!
DID YOU SHOOT THE PRESIDENT?!

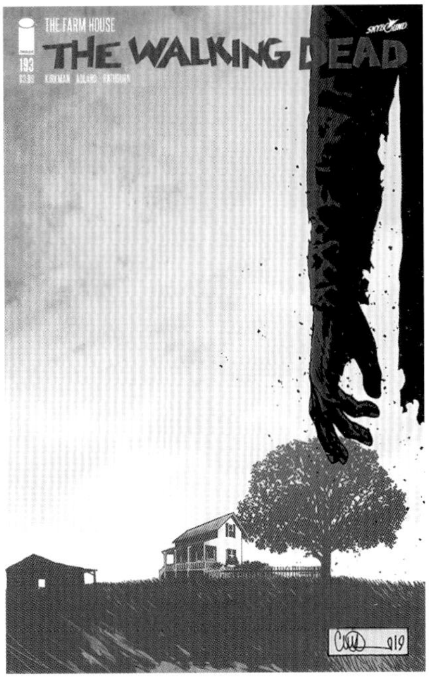
THE FARM HOUSE
THE WALKING DEAD
193

think Dark Horse, Tundra, Kitchen Sink, etc. could have assumed that edgy frontrunner position had things broken one way or another. Editorial at Vertigo was very adept at scouting talent, and could offer some attractive DC franchises to that talent. No matter how seemingly disaffected a creator is, there is a little kid inside of them who carries a torch for Solomon Grundy.

"Also, shops and readers felt some familiarity with the properties, making it easier for them to take chances on new books. Image has been around long enough now, that they have earned that same "established security with daring voices" vibe that Vertigo emanated.

"I feel quite lucky to have plied my trade with both houses."

"I think creativity flourishes when you let writers and artists do the kind of work that excites them as opposed to telling them what you want," said Stephenson. "A pretty common exchange between myself and incoming creators goes along the lines, 'What are you looking for right now?' and then, 'We're looking for whatever you're most excited about.' Or to put it another way, 'independent creatorship' really only works if you stay true to the notion of independence. No one could have asked Brian K. Vaughan and Fiona Staples to come up with a pitch for something like *Saga* – that had to start with them. All the best comics start with writers and artists wanting to scratch some creative itch or figure out how to piece together some creative puzzle that only they can see. Image provides a platform for success, but as I tell creators all the time, we're only as good as they are."

As a part of that, titles like Kirkman's *Invincible*, Gillen's *The Wicked + The Divine*, *Die* and Scott Snyder's *Undiscovered Country*, began to wear the Image "I" while capturing the imaginations of readers worldwide.

They still do.

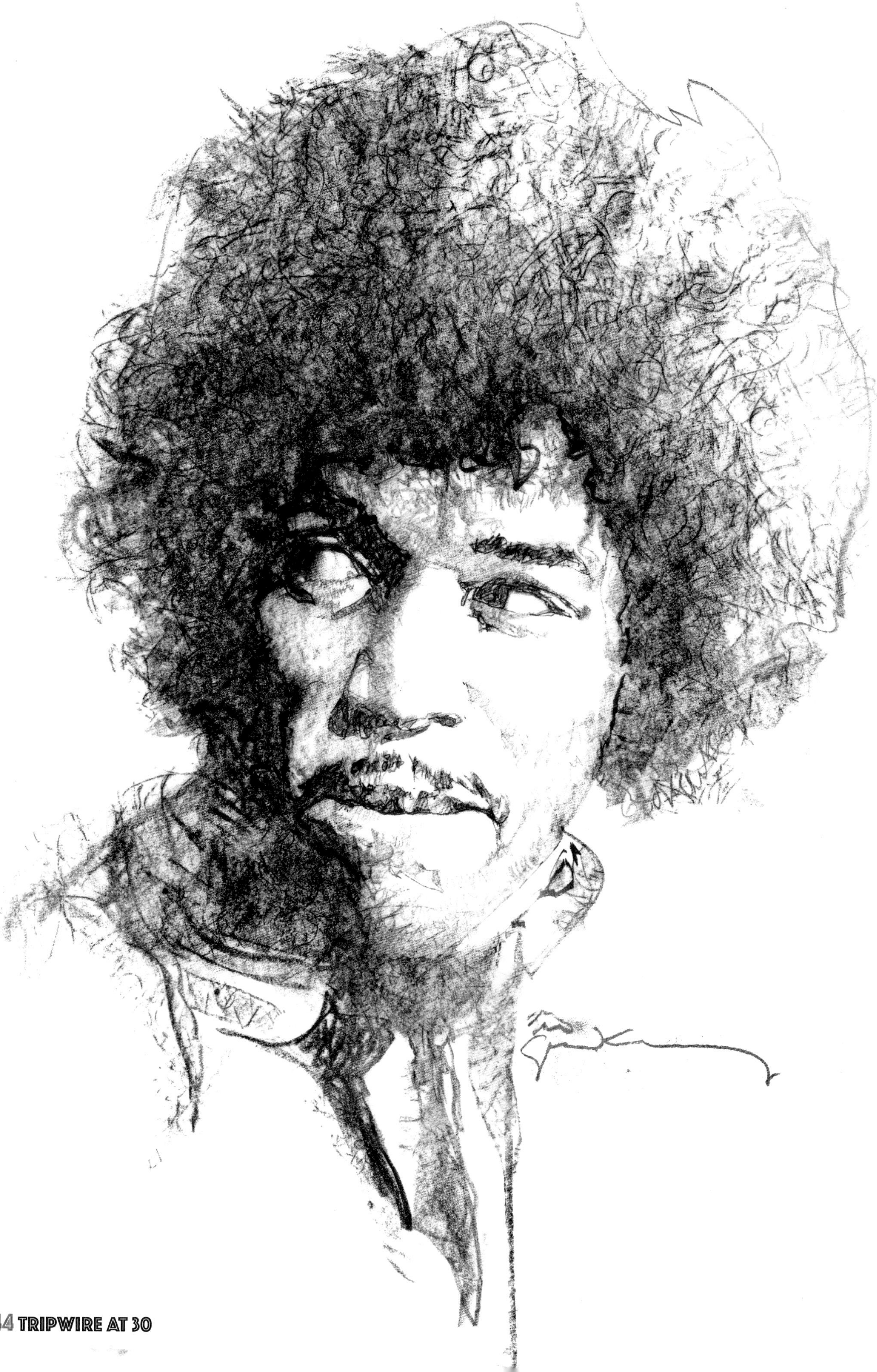

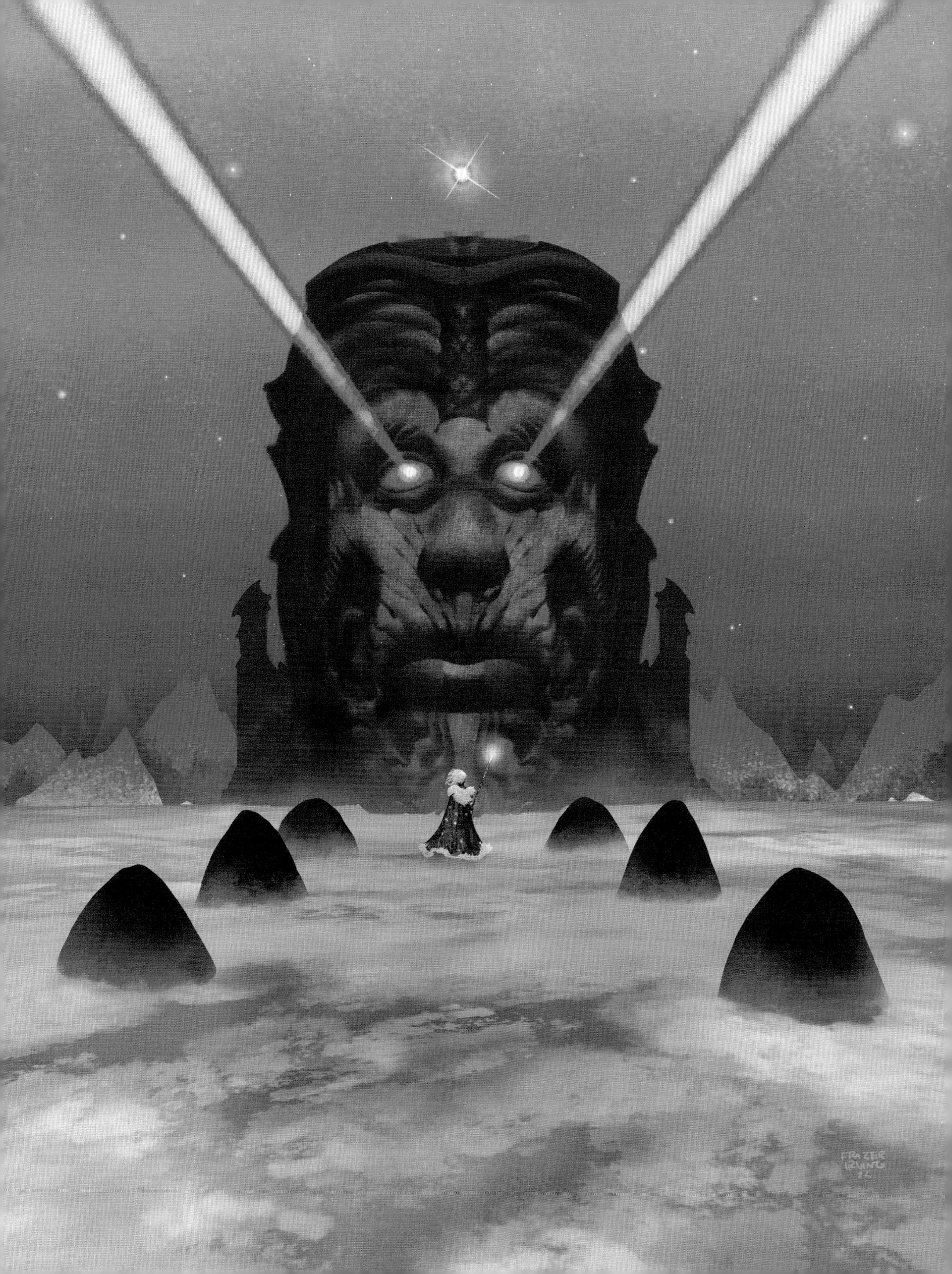
FRAZER
IRVING
12

TOP 30 COMICBOOK MOVIES 1992-2022

THE
GOD
OF
THUNDER
TRUST A FEW
FEAR THE REST
X-MEN
BATMAN BEGINS
JUNE 17

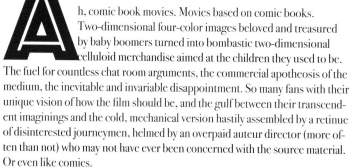

Ah, comic book movies. Movies based on comic books. Two-dimensional four-color images beloved and treasured by baby boomers turned into bombastic two-dimensional celluloid merchandise aimed at the children they used to be. The fuel for countless chat room arguments, the commercial apotheosis of the medium, the inevitable and invariable disappointment. So many fans with their unique vision of how the film should be, and the gulf between their transcendent imaginings and the cold, mechanical version hastily assembled by a retinue of disinterested journeymen, helmed by an overpaid auteur director (more often than not) who may not have ever been concerned with the source material. Or even like comics.

And yet fandom unquestionably would rather they were there. Until as recently as the early noughties there had been very little in the way of high-production event movies featuring our favourite comic characters – diehard fans had until then been starved of such entertainment, being forced to make do with sitting through the two decent Christopher Reeve *Superman* flicks, as well as Tim Burton et al's increasingly shambolic and ludicrous Batman franchise. And where in Midgard was Marvel? Apart from a particularly pedestrian (and no-budget) Spider-Man film the publisher didn't seem to care about the commercial possibilities of a properly made screen transfer. And shoestring, mostly straight to video offerings like *Dr. Strange*, 1990's *Captain America*, *the Punisher* and *Howard The Duck* certainly did the company no favours either, whilst Stan Lee's attempts throughout the eighties and nineties to co-produce a Spider-Man or X-Men film were continually and frustratingly put on hold due to studio bankruptcies, terminated deals (pun intended) and Hollywood's general lack of faith in comic-based properties.

The sea-change in Marvel's cinematic fortunes arrived with the release of 1998's crossover vampire movie *Blade*, starring A-listers Wesley Snipes and Kris Kristofferson. It proved to be a great success which led to a mini-franchise, but more importantly it created the impetus for Marvel to get its act together and produce a quality super-hero film, which turned out to be *X-Men*. The project had languished for the better part of a decade, with a rotating list of high profile industry names linked with it – but once Bryan Singer, fresh from his success with *The Usual Suspects*, had been coaxed on board (after numerous attempts), things finally fell into place. *X-Men*, although not all that inspired a production, at least had some of the hallmarks of Claremont and Byrne's definitive version, which meant profits, and sequels, were a certainty. Clearly there was a demand for big budget versions of other Marvel heroes, and with technology having finally caught up with the concepts outlined in the comic version, Sam Raimi's *Spider-Man* from 2002 raised the bar and proved to be the watershed, the catalyst for a decade's worth of projects to come. The much-maligned medium was finally to be the belle of the cinematic ball, its supporters and enthusiasts validated for their long-term marginalised devotion. Not that it was that monolithic an art form of course – there have been a raft of excellent non-spandex movies, a few of which, such as *Ghost World*, will be spotlighted in the lists below.

And these lists are far from comprehensive – there have been far more comic movies released since 1992 than you would assume the marketplace could stand. Whittling the list down to thirty meant focusing on those movies that represented the best of the crop. All reviews by Tripwire senior editor Andrew Colman...

LOGAN
MARCH 3
5.2.03
AVENGERS
ENDGAME
GHOST WORLD

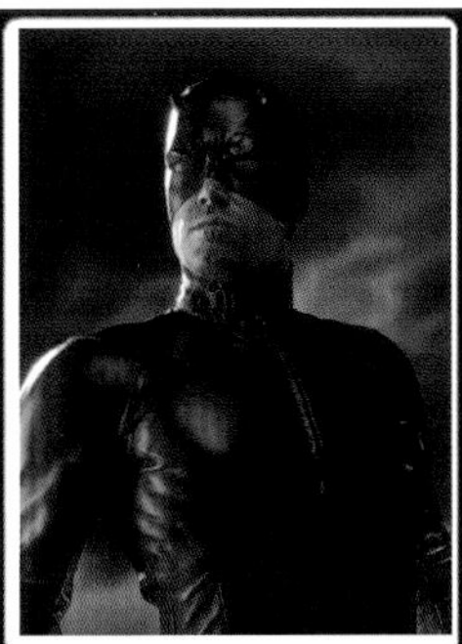

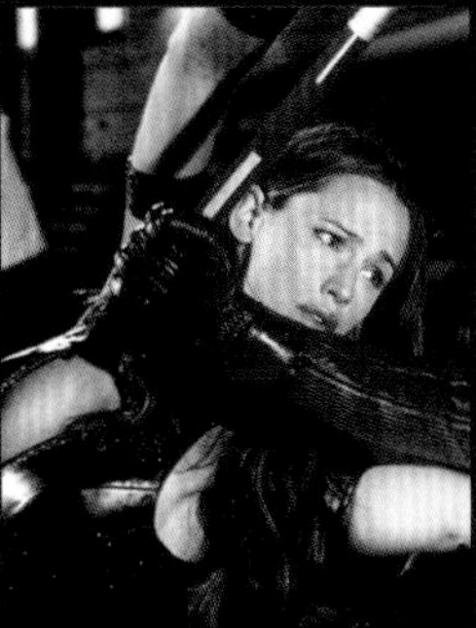

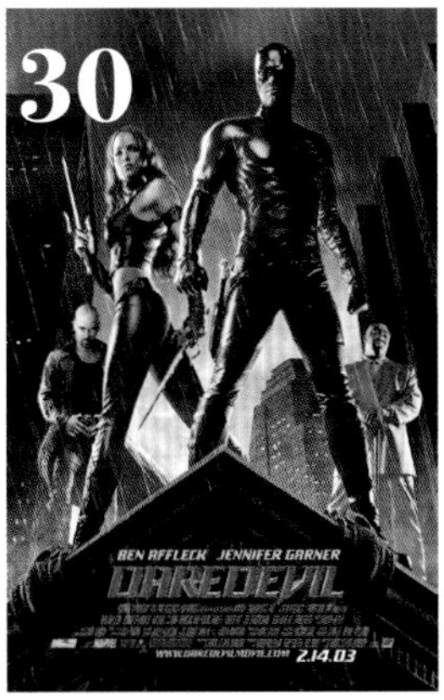

30
BEN AFFLECK JENNIFER GARNER
DAREDEVIL
2.14.03

Daredevil (Mark Steven Johnson, 2003)

A Marvel film out of kilter with all their other releases, *Daredevil* was a studiedly dark and noirish effort, a movie aimed at an older demographic that was also keen to retain its pulpy roots and as a consequence ended up pleasing nobody. Situated in a far more grimy and realistic New York than the one witnessed in *Spider-Man*, the film does at least possess a somewhat decent script and adequate leads, with a suitably imposing turn from the sadly missed Michael Clarke Duncan as the Kingpin. However despite the cast and all the dutiful nods to Frank Miller's celebrated retrofit of the long-running comic series, it promises more than it delivers, particularly with its weak denouement. Some ably handled sequences (Daredevil's origin, Bullseye's viscerally graphic battle scene with Elektra) elevate what is for too much of its length a slick box-ticking exercise. Not deserving of the vilification meted out by fandom, however.

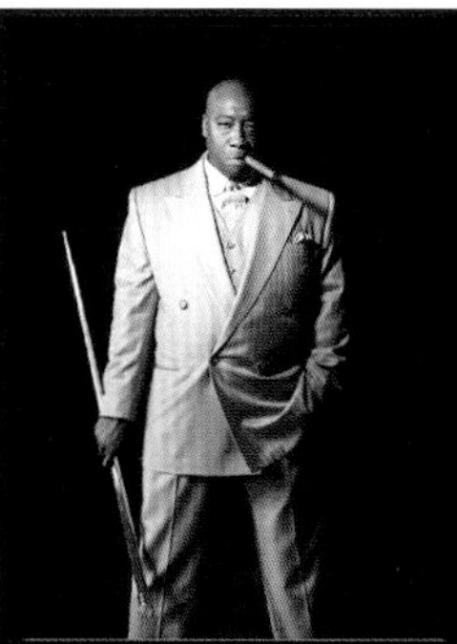

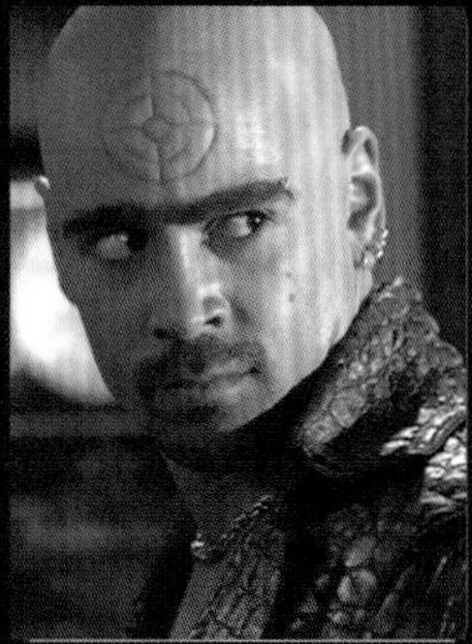

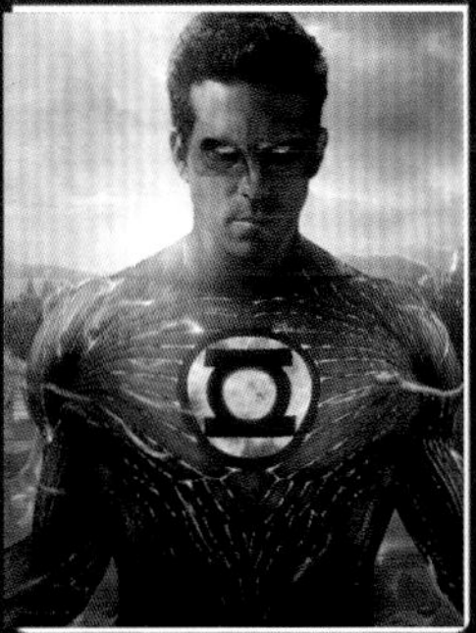

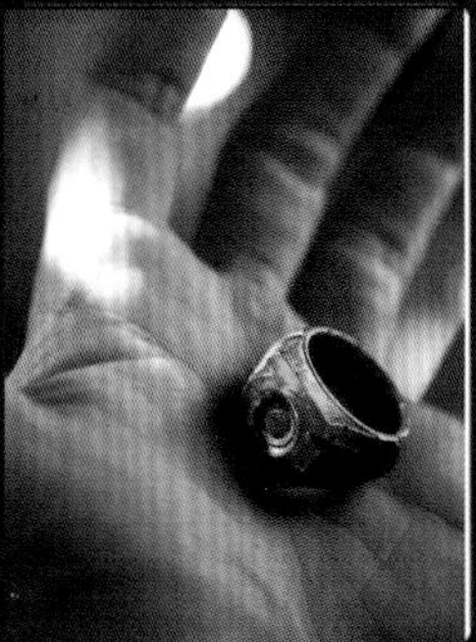

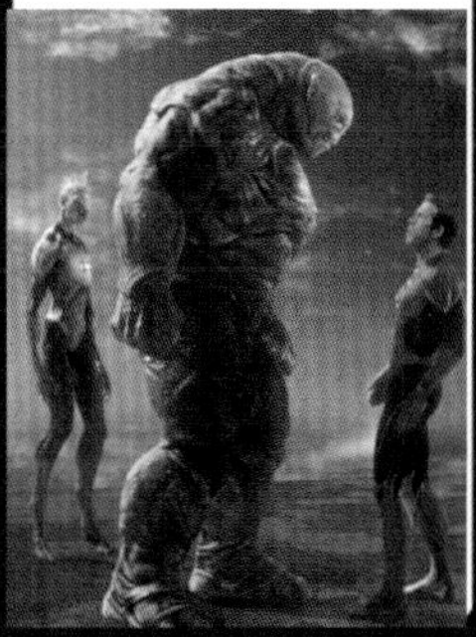

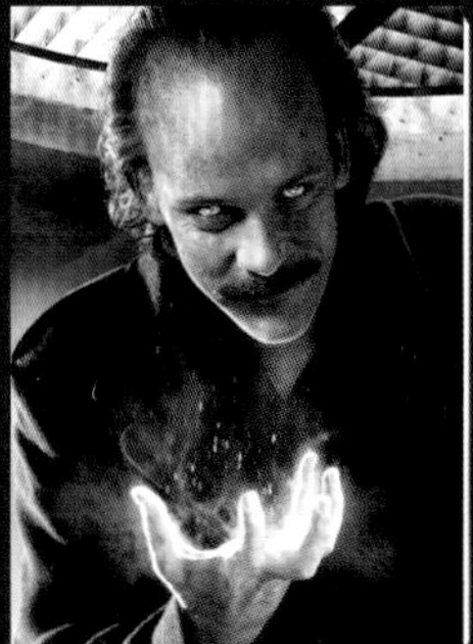

Green Lantern (Martin Campbell, 2011)

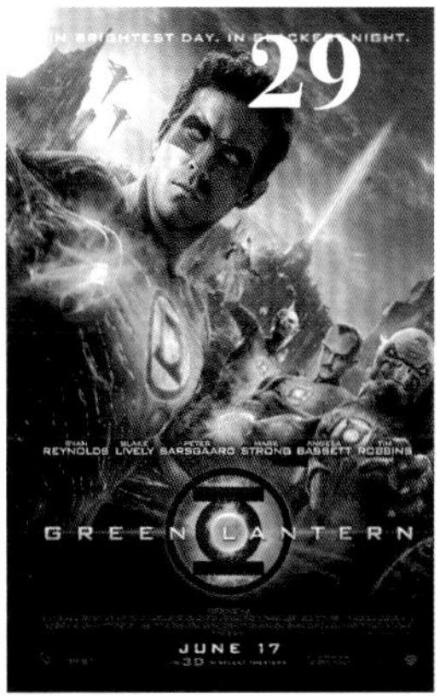

29
GREEN LANTERN
JUNE 17

The first major DC super-hero project not to showcase Batman or Superman, *Green Lantern* was an odd choice for the cinema screen – a cosmic hero from the Eisenhower era, beloved by some corners of old-school fandom but a hitherto unknown for everyone else. Cramming decades of convoluted history, character refits, and high concepts into two hours was always going to be an unwieldy undertaking, which inevitably does lead to the usual shorthand plot developments – Ryan Reynolds's all-too wholesome and diffident Hal Jordan being haphazardly shunted from one phase in his transformation to the next without stopping for breath. Nevertheless the movie, once it hits its stride, does briefly engage when the new Green Lantern heads across space to Oa for a meeting with the Guardians and future foe Sinestro – a sequence that looks excellent. After that, and the obligatory fight with his new rival, there's the half-baked soul-searching, redemptive noises, grandiose finale and routine enemy vanquishing before the closing credits. As offhand as the film is, the potential for a superior sequel is certainly there, but it never got the green light.

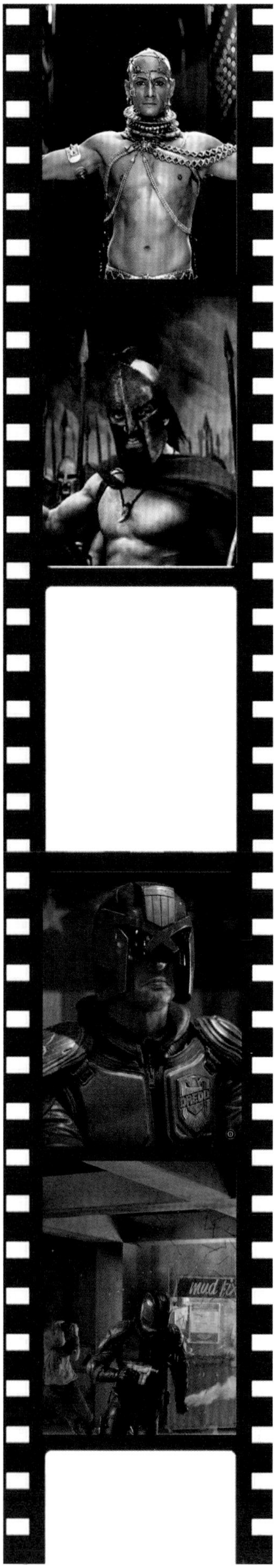

28

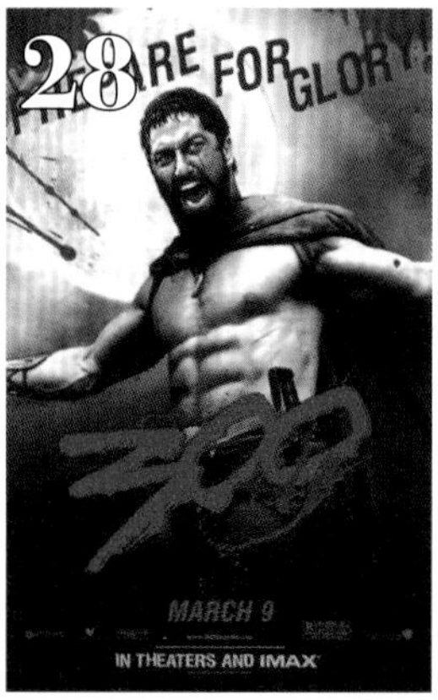
MARCH 9
IN THEATERS AND IMAX

300
(Zack Snyder, 2007)

Snyder's chroma-key swords and sandals epic certainly can lay claim to being as close to the original comic material as any movie, bar *Sin City*. A historical fantasy lifted from the pages of Frank Miller's graphic novel, the movie focuses on the shouty, belligerent King Leonidas (Gerard Butler) leading a paltry band of 300 Greeks against a legendarily insurmountable Persian army. All bare teeth and gruff declamations, Butler's Leonidas is the motor of a fairly simple premise, but there's no question that despite the obviously superficial treatment of this mythical portion of history, the film looks great and has a modest ring of authenticity. A phenomenal success, this visually arresting film is still a curate's egg in its somewhat cynical compulsion to put stylisation and format first. One can lob brickbats regarding its pomposity and self-regard, but the movie still plays, and at the very least was suffused with ambition and the need to validate the source medium. Not a triumph, but by no means a failure either.

27

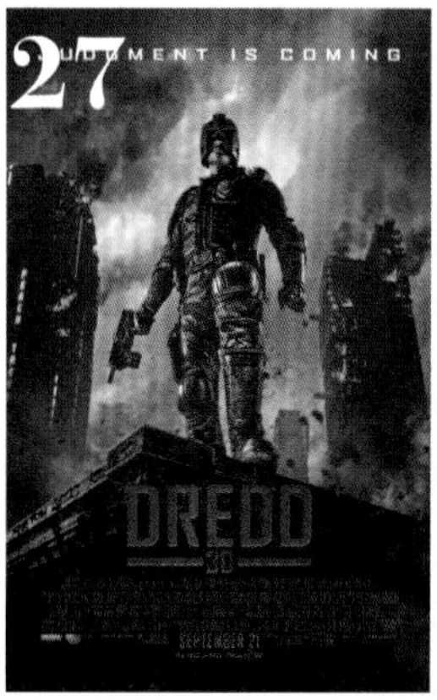
DREDD

Dredd 3D
(Pete Travis, 2012)

Travis's hyperkinetic, stylised revamp of Britain's favourite fascist cop is an engrossingly fun B Movie, a post-urban spaghetti western with lashings of ultraviolence, mazy claustrophobia, and a smidgeon of future-shock context thrown in. Dredd and his newbie partner Anderson are assigned to a tower block in downtown Mega City to shut down a drug pushing ring and find themselves enmeshed in a cat and mouse game with the building's very own Cruella De Ville (and chief nasty) Ma-Ma. As with the source material that it apes, there's little time for character arcs amidst the high-velocity bullets, but the intent and provision here is pure lowbrow crowd-pleasing entertainment, and on that level it succeeds. Old fashioned, reactionary frolics never provided as much guilty pleasure, although you'll prefer to look away when Ma-Ma gets her rather graphic comeuppance at the end. A sleeper hit in the *Robocop* mould then, although a few more ironic one-liners wouldn't've gone amiss.

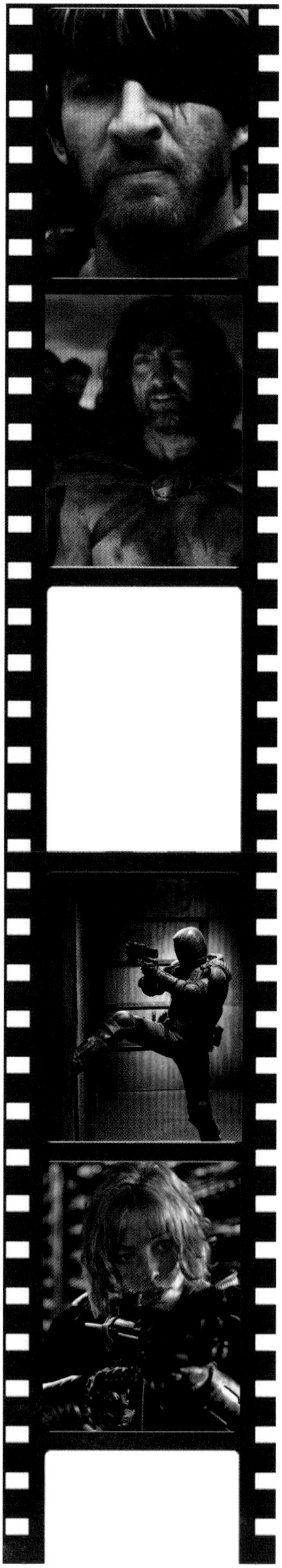

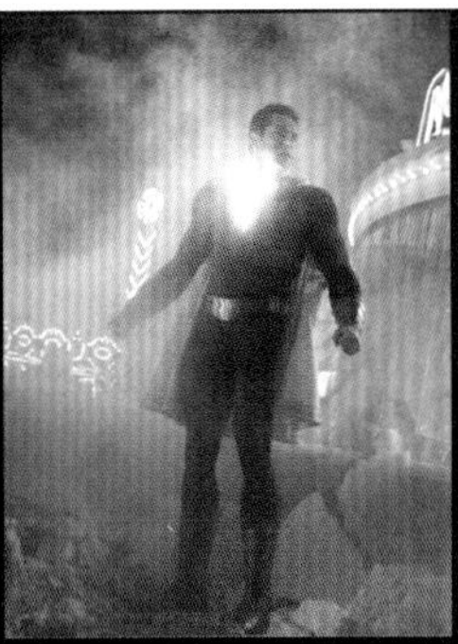
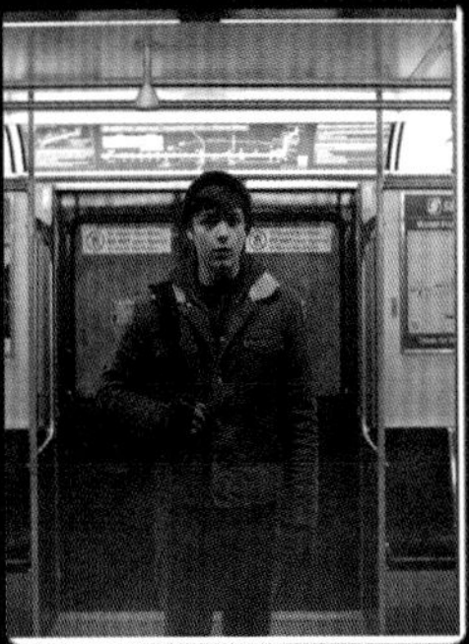
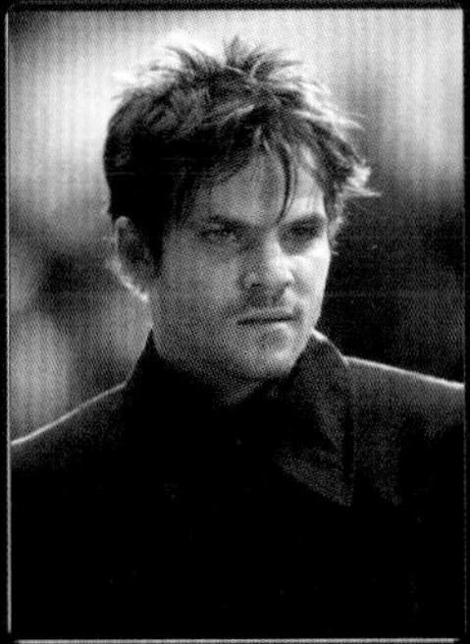
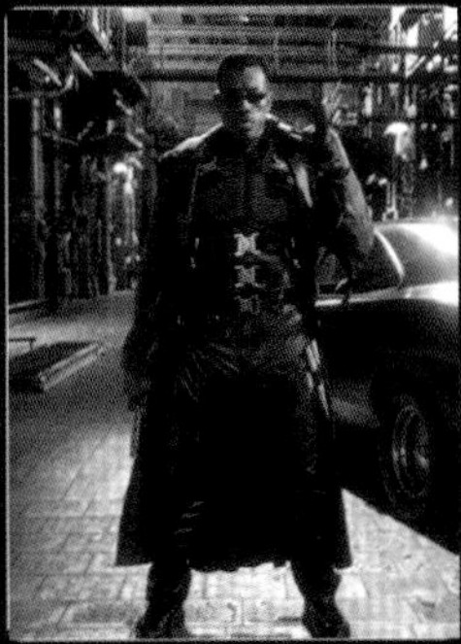

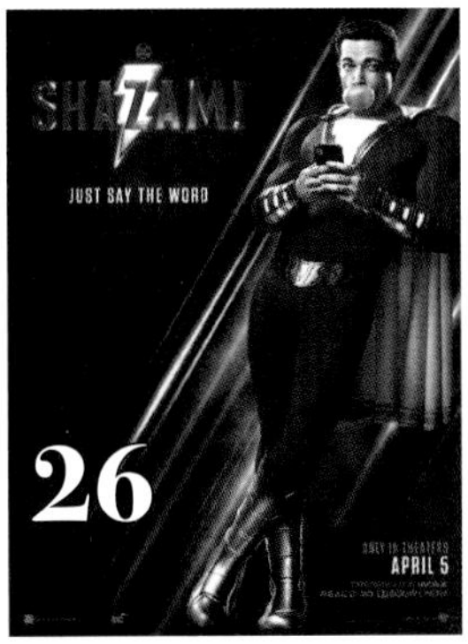
SHAZAM!
JUST SAY THE WORD
26
APRIL 5

Shazam!
(David F. Sandberg, 2019)

The classic CC Beck Captain Marvel, I mean *Shazam!* strips were always lightweight fun, and this movie does manage to capture some of their essence. Billy Batson is an orphaned itinerant who is forced by social services to join a foster family. Befriended by foster brother Freddy Freeman, who is paraplegic, Batson quickly turns saviour at the local high school where the outsider Freeman is regularly bullied despite his issues. On the run from the thugs, he is summoned into another realm by the wizard Shazam, who transforms him into a shiny retro-lummox with a duck-tail haircut, massive abs and immense powers. He's every inch the 1940s version, except more ludicrous. And from there, the hi-jinks ensue. There's enough humour to sustain half of the movie, with the hero Shazam (Zachary Levi) behaving like a gauche, arrested Pollyanna being the entire point. His initial forays into heroism, obviously echoing Tom Hanks's turn in *Big*, are thoroughly entertaining, but never stray into satire or anything deeper than mindless, knockabout farce. At best one could say it's a necessary corrective to all the benighted, doom-laden farragoes generally churned out by DC, and to its eternal credit it eschews any kind of pretence whatsoever. It's never less than charming fluff, with Mark Strong an excellent turn as the villain. There's enough in there to charm even the most curmudgeonly viewer and regardless of the whole thing being Archie on steroids, it's a refreshing change of pace.

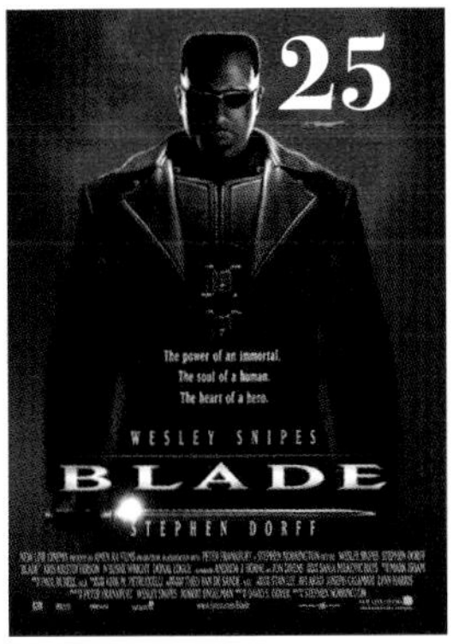
25
The power of an immortal.
The soul of a human.
The heart of a hero.
WESLEY SNIPES
BLADE
STEPHEN DORFF

Blade
(Stephen Norrington, 1998)

"Some motherf---ers always trying to ice skate uphill!" Not the most auspicious endgame line to wrap up this franchise-begetting star vehicle, it has to be said. However Wesley Snipes' biggest box-office success is an assured, reasonably intelligent and quite low-key affair, echoing the source character's early *Tomb Of Dracula* appearances. Detailing the battle between Snipes' vampire hunting "daywalker" and Stephen Dorff's Deacon Frost, a renegade vampire bent on controlling and harvesting humanity, the movie retains an even, moderate pace as it progresses towards its climax. There's a modicum of depth in the characters and their relationships (notably between Blade and his mentor Whistler), and Snipes is excellent in the lead role. Very much an upgrade of a minor yet significant player in the Marvel universe, the film succeeds in splicing two genres together, whilst creating an acceptably benighted milieu. The characterization and script may be dry and throwaway in places but there's no doubt that this was an important project for Marvel, who (like a lot of the industry) may not have expected anything.

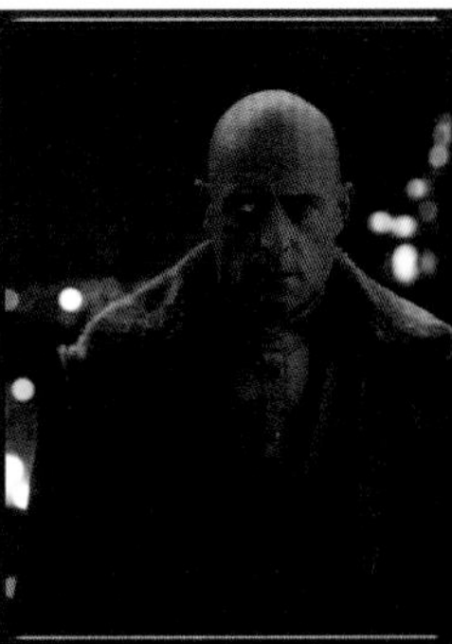
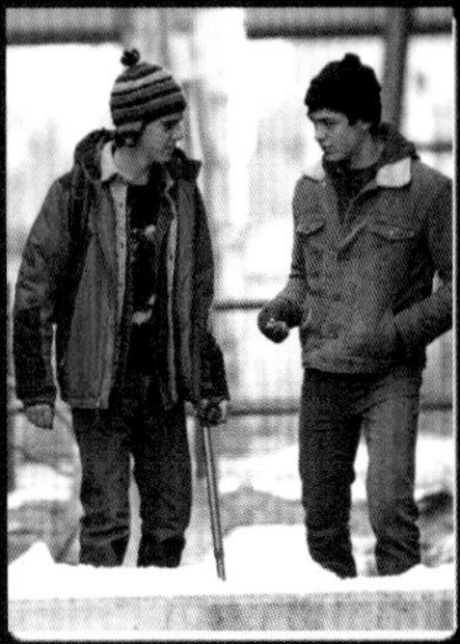
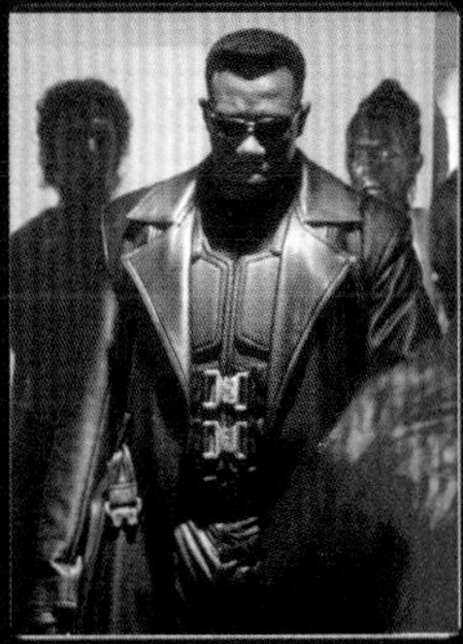
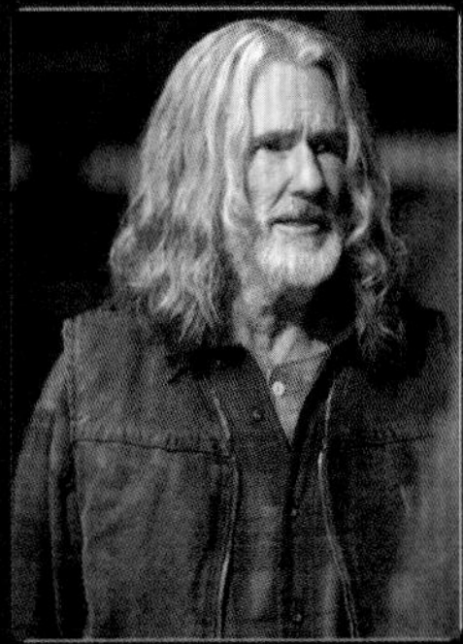

24 Spider-Man (Sam Raimi, 2002)

Obviously not as pivotal a movie as *Star Wars*, *Spider-Man* nevertheless was a hugely significant work in pop culture and the template for many films that came in its wake. Despite its importance, it is still only marginally more than the film that came with the poster – an event product that established genre convention by resorting to cliché, lightweight tropes and unthreatening, wholesome leads. The plot is serviceable and reasonably faithful to the comic, but what stood out for audiences were the special effects and action sequences, with Spider-Man's web-slinging particularly impressive. What was missing however was the sly, knockabout humour that was a touchstone of Lee, Ditko and Romita's classic stories, and pacy direction. Overall, the film's huge success was predicated on not taking chances, maintaining a lightness that bordered on the trite, and providing a framework for sequels, although at least the well-cast Willem Dafoe (as the Green Goblin) managed to chew the scenery whenever he wasn't in that absurd costume. Even though the ownership of Marvel's pantheon of heroes was split amongst several studios, the formula for all successive productions began here.

Captain America: The First Avenger (Joe Johnston, 2011)

The decision by Marvel to ensure that none of its properties received a "grim 'n' gritty" makeover weighed most heavily on this period venture, which is a shame as despite his flag-waving nationalistic undertow, Captain America was always, in the right hands, an underrated, sympathetic character. Not that the film's producers were unaware of his potential – the first half of the movie features an excellent origin sequence and witty historical framing that remarkably doesn't advance the plot or contain ponderous exposition. However once he lands in Italy to begin his mission behind enemy lines everything hurriedly reverts to type, with some well-directed but ultimately run-of-the-mill action set pieces, none of which quite capture the Simon and Kirby spirit. The film's biggest flaw, apart from having an underwhelming supporting cast, is its desire not to offend – the Nazis and their barbarism are barely touched upon, replaced by a cookie-cutter super-villain who is vaguely reminiscent of the Red Skull. It is here, when the story dips into dour genre convention, that the film comes across as a two-hour trailer for the Avengers.

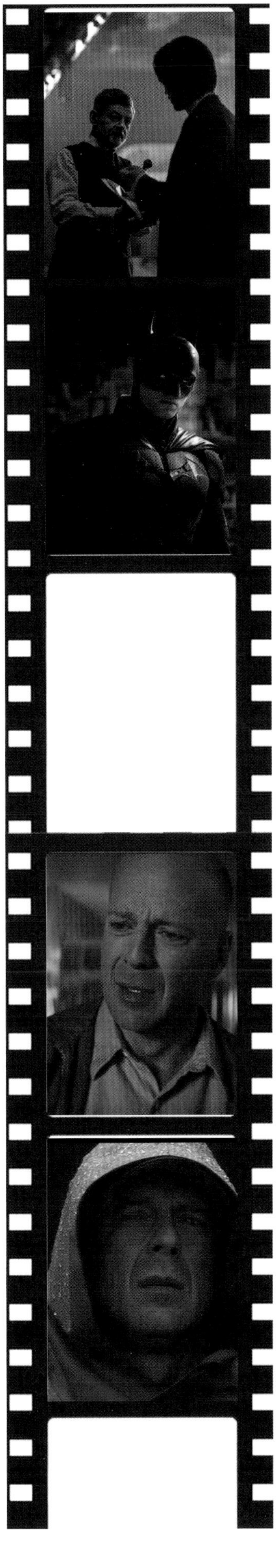

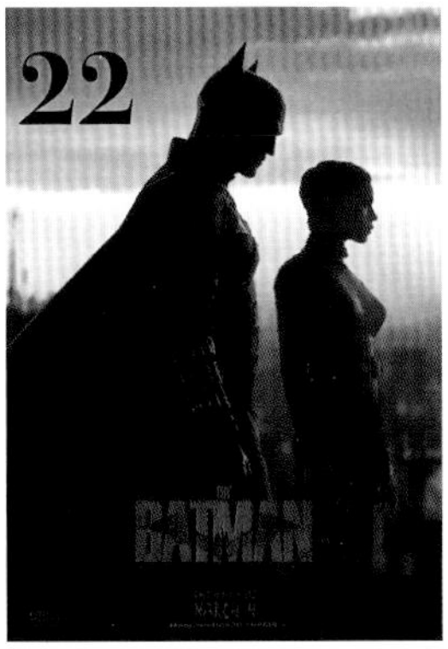

22 The Batman (Matt Reeves, 2022)

Much can be said of Matt Reeves' take on the Dark Knight – that it is an even more revisionist piece than that of obvious influence Christopher Nolan, and that it is painstakingly dark, insistently gritty and far too focused on maintaining a constant tone of noir terror at the expense of characterisation. In other words, it tries too hard, in the way that its predecessor, the recent Joker movie did, offering little in the way of catharsis or indeed engagement. However, it is still a worthwhile addition to the ever-expanding Batman canon, as it does emphasise the detective aspect of the character, something that is often omitted in Bat-movies. Taking its cues from *Batman: Year One* and Englehart and Rogers' celebrated version of the property, The Batman is essentially a slow-burn, episodic affair, as our angst-ridden young protagonist is challenged by a particularly psychotic and misshapen Riddler, who, as is his wont, leaves riddles for him pinned to his victims. As the plot unfolds and the Riddler evades detection, we learn of Bruce Wayne's parents becoming mixed up in organised crime, which connects them to Batman's ally Selina Kyle (Catwoman) and indeed his nemesis. As far as art direction is concerned, it is excellent, one-upping the gothic lite of the Burton movies by some margin, while the general foreboding atmosphere does evoke dread and tension. However, the big reveal is anti-climactic, while the grand guignol denouement seems tacked-on and out of place with the interior feel of the rest of the movie. Paul Dano's Riddler is painfully one note, while Robert Pattinson's Bruce Wayne is the picture of studied, outsider gloom. There's a genuinely good movie lurking in this production, which is somewhat let down by the aforementioned reversion to convention. It's still a worthwhile flick though, which if it had stayed away from prosthetic goonery (the Penguin for example was completely superfluous) would've been an excellent standalone instalment.

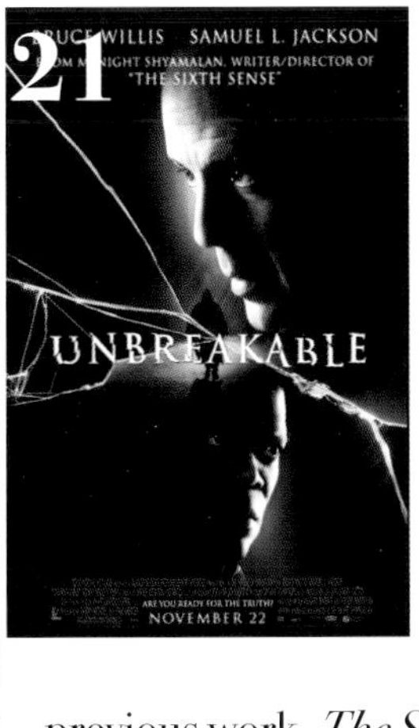
BRUCE WILLIS SAMUEL L. JACKSON
"THE SIXTH SENSE"
UNBREAKABLE
NOVEMBER 22

21 Unbreakable (M. Night Shyamalan, 2000)

Shyamalan's overly low-octane yarn is a clever hybrid of two genres, but wasn't marketed as a comic-book movie, much to the chagrin of its director. Focusing on the everyman David Dunn (Bruce Willis), who, due to the intervention of handicapped comic art gallery owner Elijah Price (Samuel L. Jackson), begins to realize that he has super-powers. The film has similar tropes to the director's previous work, *The Sixth Sense*, with an equally schematic ending. Needless to say, the foreboding atmospherics and Willis's understated performance (one of his best) provide enough tension and suspense for the audience, regardless of the film's measured, stately pace. Despite the rather contrived and unsatisfactory ending, the production is an excellent rejoinder to all the frenetic bombast normally seen in comic movies, with barely any action sequences at all. Shame that the feeble art in Price's gallery was so unrepresentative of the four-color medium, though, but we'll let that go.

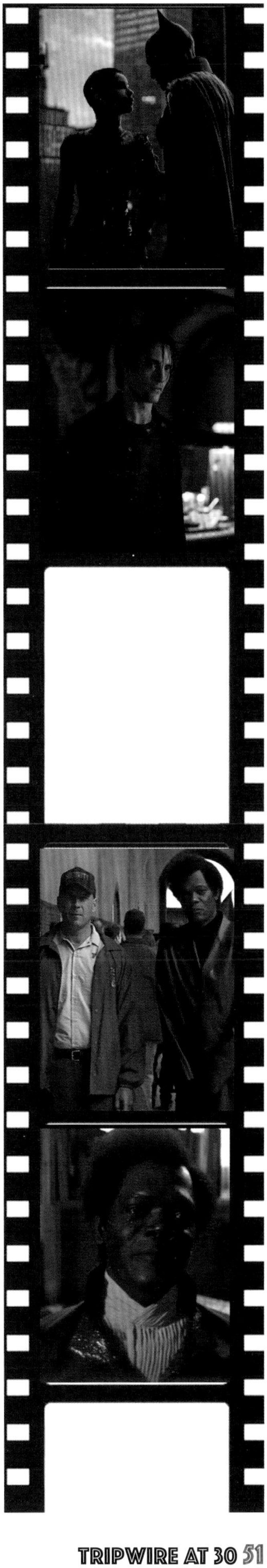

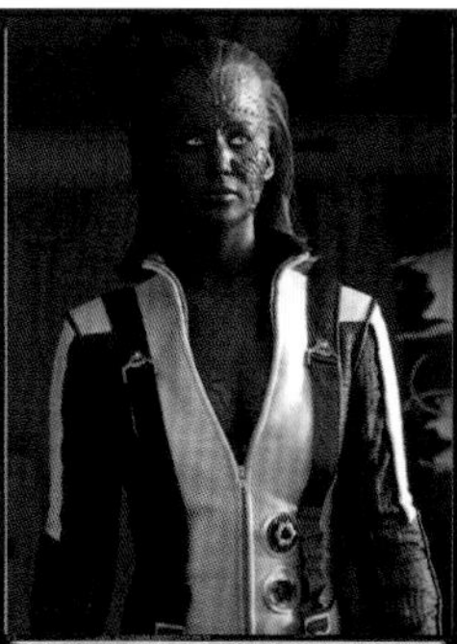

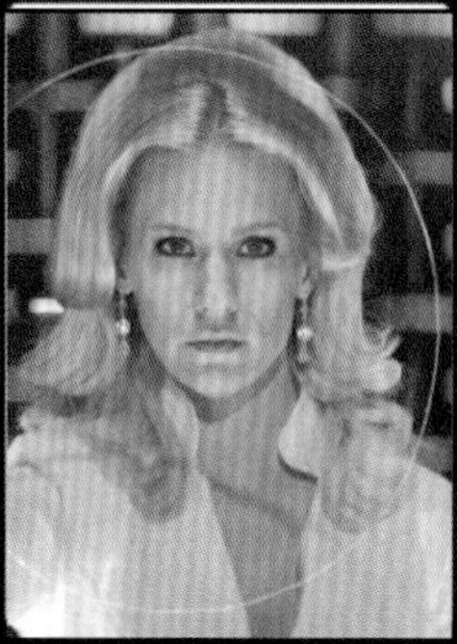

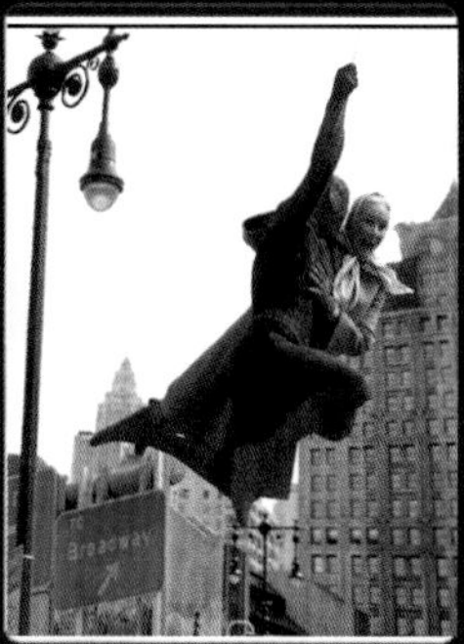

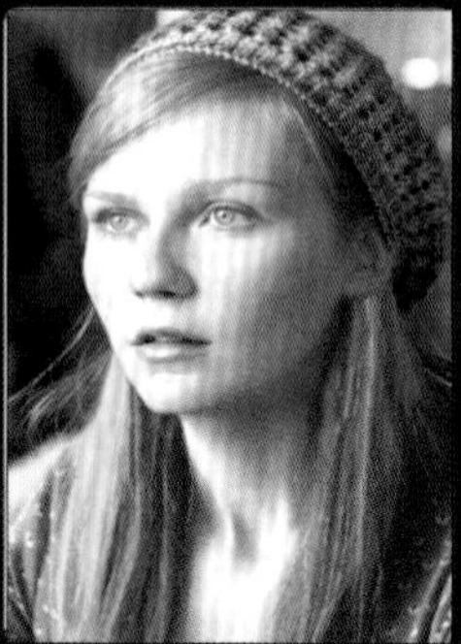

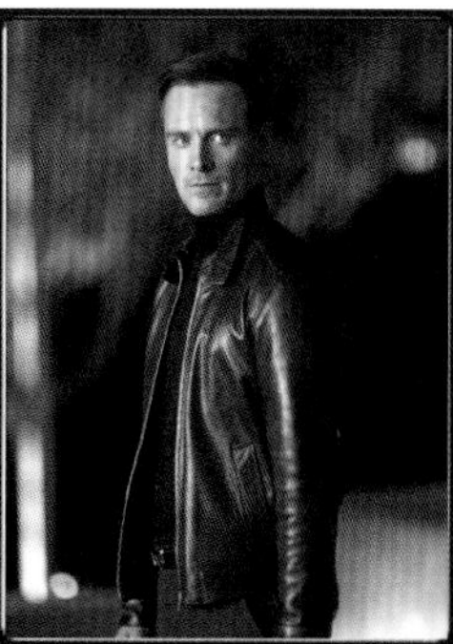

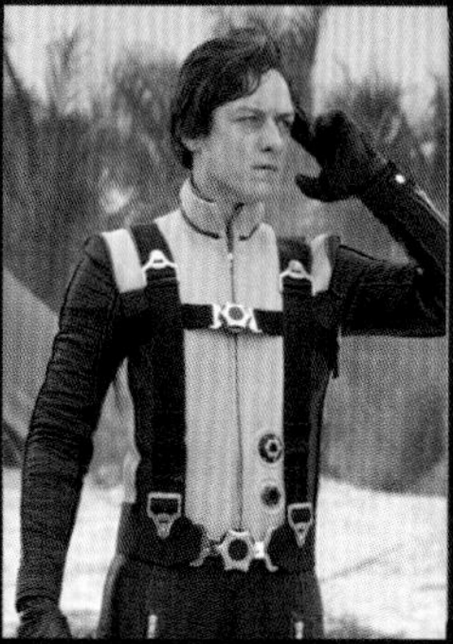

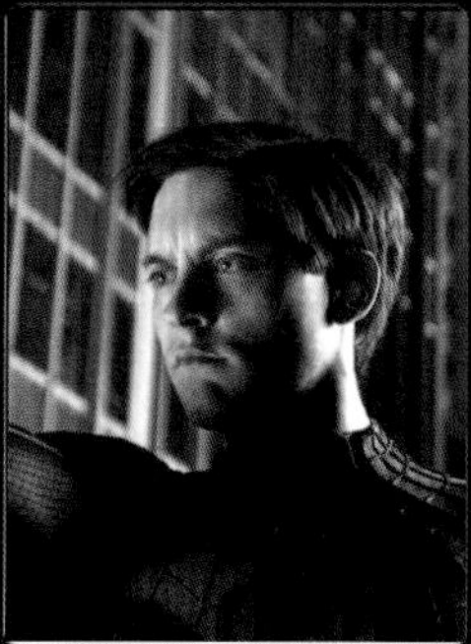

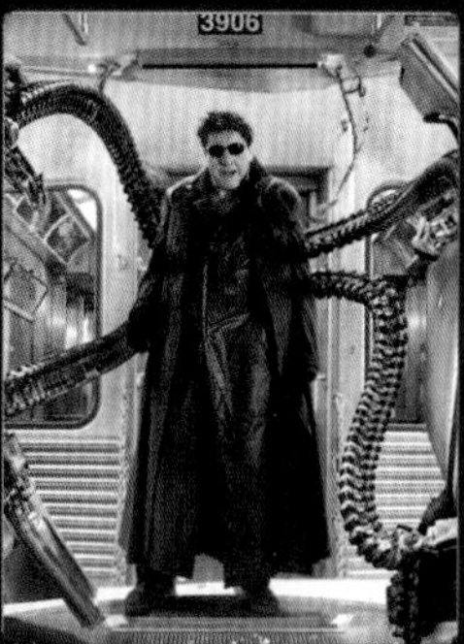

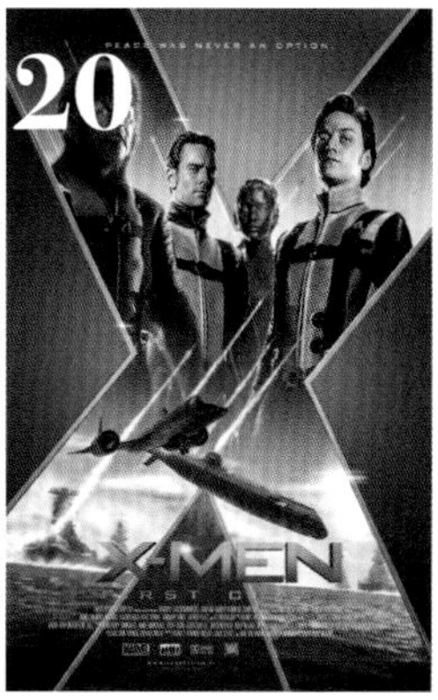
X-MEN

20 X-Men: First Class (Matthew Vaughn, 2011)

Matthew Vaughn's prequel tale relating the origin of the X-Men, Professor Xavier's relationship and initial schism with Magneto, as well as the formation of the Brotherhood of Mutants is a well-crafted and thoughtful slice of entertainment that is thematically strong and cohesive, with excellent performances from the young cast. Focusing on the creation of Xavier and Magneto and their division over their attitude towards non-mutants, this film, primarily set in the early 1960s, is very much in the classic retro comic mould. There are a few contrivances, such as Erik Lensherr's connection to concentration camp guard Schmidt, who becomes Sebastian Shaw, the founder of the renegade Hellfire Club, but the set up (Shaw and his clan of mutants attempt to start World War 3 by pitting the Soviets against the US) works well enough. Where the film succeeds are the committed turns from the two leads, James McAvoy and Michael Fassbender, who never allows his effort to veer towards parody. The nods to the era (there's a certain amount of vintage Bondery involved) are certainly above average, as the theme of what it means to be a mutant is well handled. The film that kept this franchise afloat, for another few instalments.

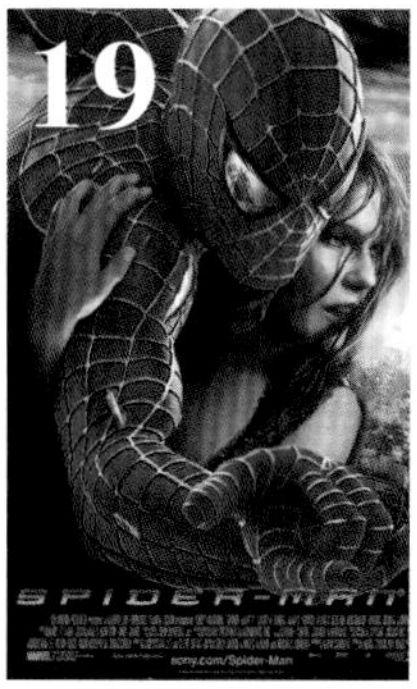
SPIDER-MAN

19 Spider-man 2 (Sam Raimi, 2004)

Marvel's follow-up to 2002's first Spidey movie garnered heaps of praise from the critics due to it being a tighter production than the first outing, along with veteran character actor Alfred Molina's definitive take on Doctor Octopus. And indeed, there's less twee romance in this edition, with Tobey Maguire's hero suffering a breakdown and loss of powers, which (as in the classic Amazing Spider-Man 50) leads him to quit being a superhero. With the subplot (again borrowed from the source material) of Harry (son of the Green Goblin) Osborn's suspicion that his best friend may have had something to do with his father's death, the intrigue and psychology here were certainly ratcheted up further. Peter Parker / Spider-Man is the fall guy here, just as he always had been in the four-color version, having lost Mary Jane to Jonah Jameson's son while finding himself comically incapable of harnessing his powers. However, despite many claiming that the movie had considerably more emotional depth (true to an extent, although there's still plenty of schlocky melodrama), it does recede into formula – yet what carries it of course is Molina's outsize, batty turn as Doc Ock, a glorious portrait of petulant, wigged-out psychosis. Plus, there's an excellent finale, which (yes, it is my barometer) really captures the Lee / Ditko spirit. Lightweight it might be but if ever proof were needed that comic movies were here to stay, this outing was the one.

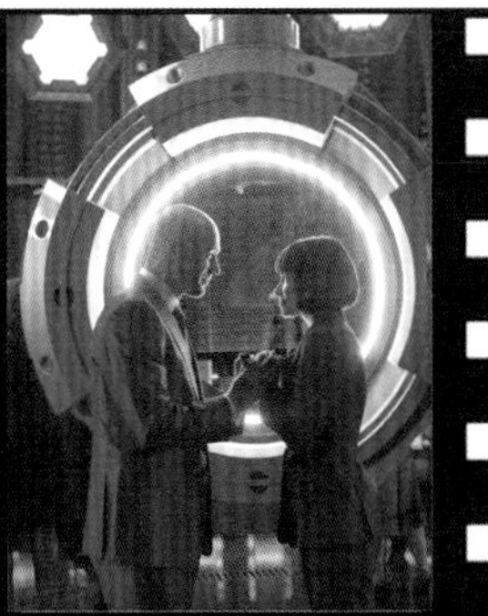

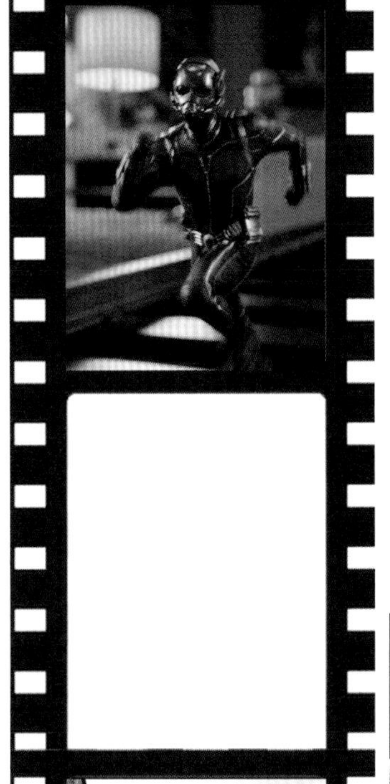

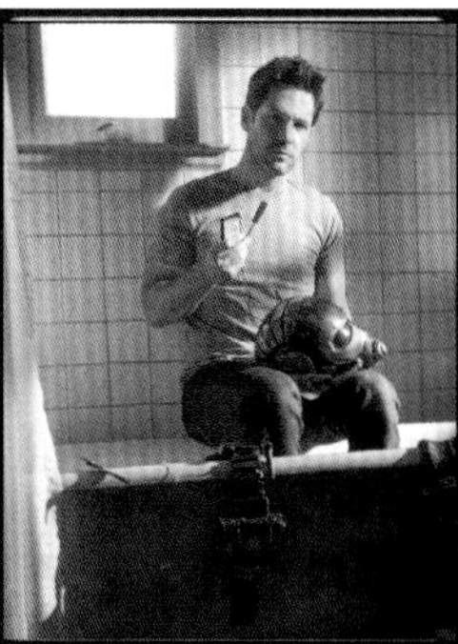

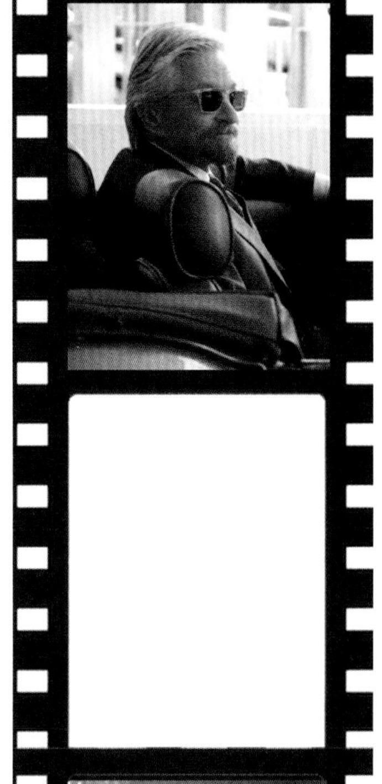

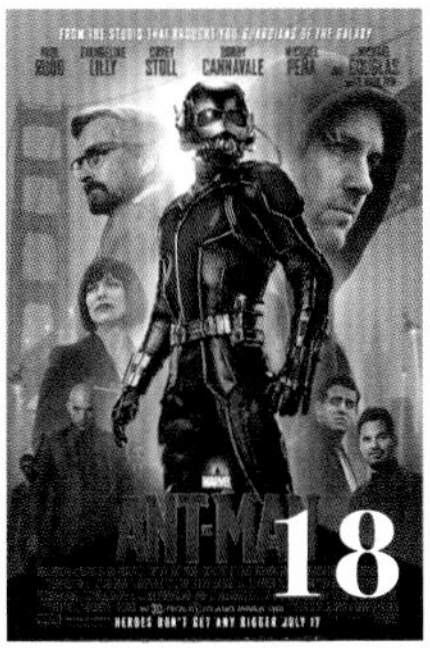

18

Ant-Man (Peyton Reed, 2015)

Ant-Man turned out to be one of the more compulsive big-screen Marvel efforts for quite some time, and proved to be a necessarily upbeat corrective to the rest of the MCU. Michael Douglas played Hank Pym, a doctor who discovers a scientific means of shrinking matter down but is concerned that his discovery will fall into the wrong hands, while Paul Rudd was convict Scott Lang, fresh out of prison, who is picked by Pym to recover his tech so it isn't used to create a mini army of sub-atomic soldiers. Corey Stoll played Darren Cross, who intends to use Pym's Yellowjacket suit for his own nefarious ends. Ant-Man succeeded in conveying the sense of fun and good-time entertainment that are comics' bread and butter with style and wit. One of the first Marvel movies not to take itself too seriously, the 3D it used also worked well here, adding a layer of narrative and a genuinely impressive visual experience. Rudd is excellent casting as convict Lang, Douglas looks very much at ease considering that this is his first spandex movie, Evangeline Lilly is decent enough as Pym's daughter Hope, and the whole package is amusing quality hokum. Ant-Man found the perfect balance between straightforward adventure and ironic humour and showed that Marvel had learnt not to unnecessarily overcook anything to achieve success at the box office. A lightweight but worthwhile instalment.

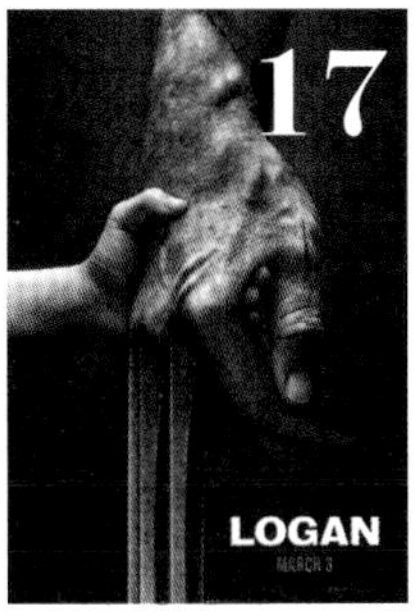
LOGAN

17

Logan (James Mangold, 2017)

The final chapter in the Wolverine trilogy, based as it is on the Mark Millar Old Man Logan story arc is the joker in the pack of (non-comedic) Marvel movies, dispensing as it does with plot armour for the leads, with a negative, hope-free dystopian setting and the lingering sense that whatever Wolvie does, it will have appalling consequences. Innocent people die in this film and there is no moralising to adorn their passing - this is a bleak, relentless, ultraviolent road movie in the *Mad Max* vein, with Patrick Stewart along for the ride to provide gravitas and depth. It's 2029, and there are no mutants to be found, with an aging, deteriorating Logan looking after the 90-year-old Professor Xavier, who is both ill and a serious health hazard to those around him. Stranded in the desert dustbowl, Logan is eventually saddled with both Xavier and Laura, one of many child mutants created by Transigen corporation, led by Richard E Grant's Zander Rice. Transigen's enforcer Donald Pierce, whose mission is to wipe out all the remaining mutant children, gives chase to Logan and his charges who are heading for the north and sanctuary. Apart from the downbeat, doom-laden elements, this is a fairly generic movie with tragedian pretensions, which can't quite develop that sense of aftermath that one experiences with such films. On the plus side, it is uncompromising, its coda redolent of classic revenge westerns (there are excerpts from Shane in it). Both Jackman and Stewart exude resignation and despair, even if we don't get quite enough of Stewart's virtuoso emoting. The critics at the time were falling over themselves to praise this movie, regarding it as a corrective to all the cookie-cutter spandex extravaganzas, but in real terms, the CGI has been replaced by a mountain of viscera, while the plot is as old as Hollywood itself. Nevertheless, this is a decent flick for the ever-reliable Jackman to bow out, and to his credit, he really does put in a shift. You genuinely do care for his fate, along with his mutant friends. A pulpy action fest then, with a familiar premise, but a very good one, and but for Grant and Stewart not being given enough to do, a genuinely touching finale.

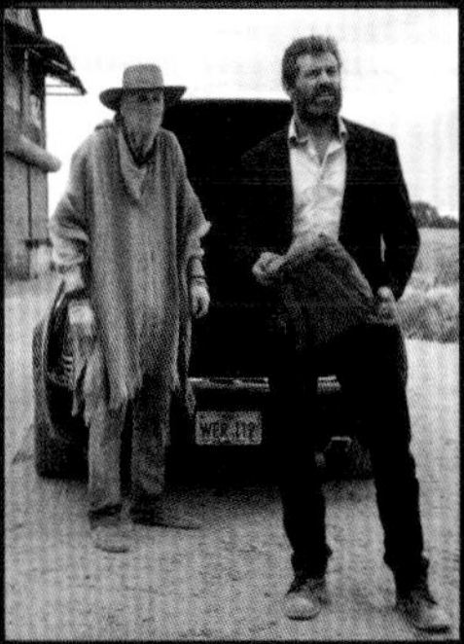

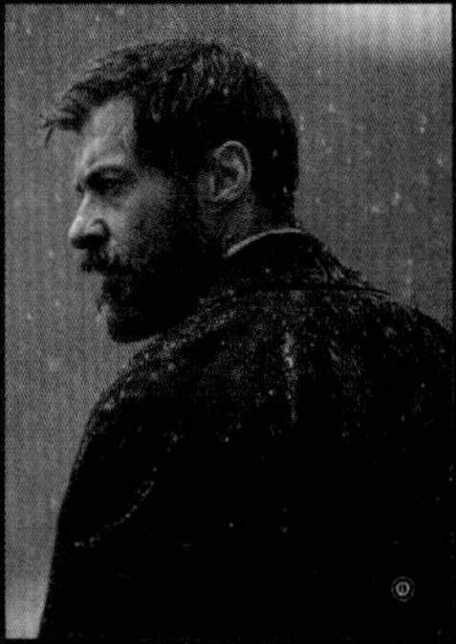

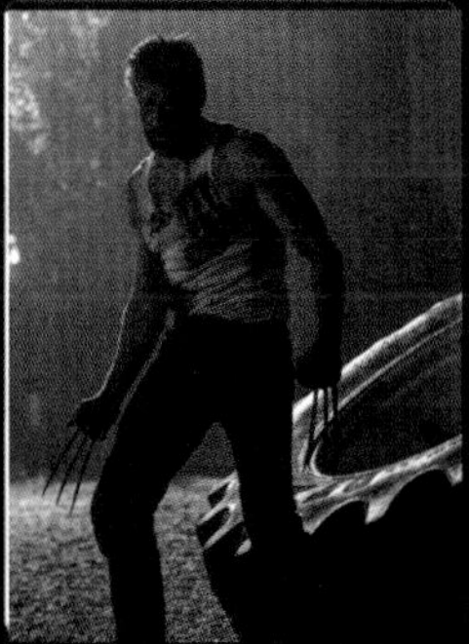

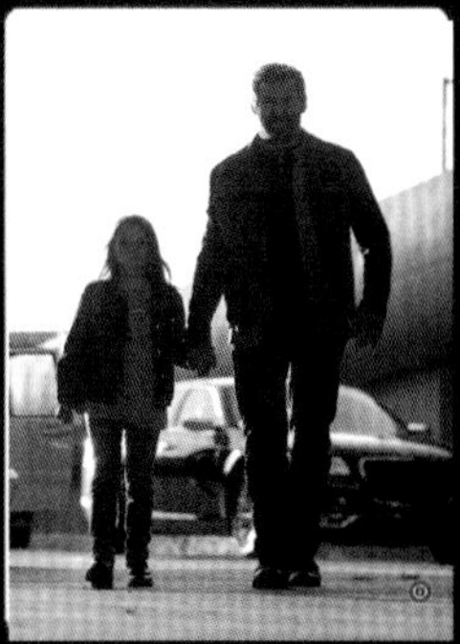

16
AVENGERS
MAY 4

The Avengers (Joss Whedon, 2012)

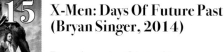

Following on from hits like *Iron Man* and *Captain America*, Marvel's sixth installment of their super-team stable was the ultimate audience pleaser, and an inevitably gigantic success. Such is fandom's slack-jawed approbation for this mega-potboiler, it's somewhat difficult to leave out of our top thirty, and it is indeed here on merit (just) – Whedon does successfully imbue the movie with sufficiently rip-roaring one-liners (well, six of them) and adequate personality conflicts that the enterprise is likeable and entertaining enough. The fanboy in me wanted to delight in finally witnessing all those wondrous Marvel characters chewing the same scenery, and there are certainly some enjoyable moments. But the film does anthologize every cliché in the book, has no thematic depth, doesn't really allow enough of a spotlight on some of the heroes, and can't help but seem like a tag-team bout during the finale, with a rather questionable alien menace providing the destructive hi-jinks for the world's mightiest. Such hyperbolic action segments always worked better through the medium of Buscema or Perez's pencils, so I'll get with the throng and state that Whedon's version made a damn good fist of it, nevertheless.

15
X-MEN
DAYS OF FUTURE PAST
MAY 23

X-Men: Days Of Future Past (Bryan Singer, 2014)

Based on the Chris Claremont and John Byrne classic story arc of the same name, *X-Men Days of Future Past* is a satisfying film transfer that pays the necessary respect to the source material (considering that the original comic story has been hailed as one of the title's best, that is significant). As with the comic, the future-shock elements are all intact – the older Xavier and Magneto, forced into an alliance due to being hunted relentlessly by the government backed Sentinels, opt to send Wolverine back to the early 1970s to alter timelines and prevent the giant anti-mutant robot program from being initiated. Wolverine proceeds to revive the X-Men as a going concern and attempts to stop Magneto from killing President Nixon, the pivotal act that would set everything in motion. Despite not enough time being devoted to certain plotlines and members of the considerable ensemble, the film is a well-paced and balanced work that manages to weave the two timelines together without losing any momentum, while the film plays it straight, evading hokey sentimentality and unnecessary levity. Although the pay off and aftermath is predictable, it is weightier and more palpable thanks to the near-extinction the mutants face. Possibly the best X-Men episode since director Bryan Singer's *X2* some years earlier, the film once again benefits from a heavyweight cast, solid script and tight direction.

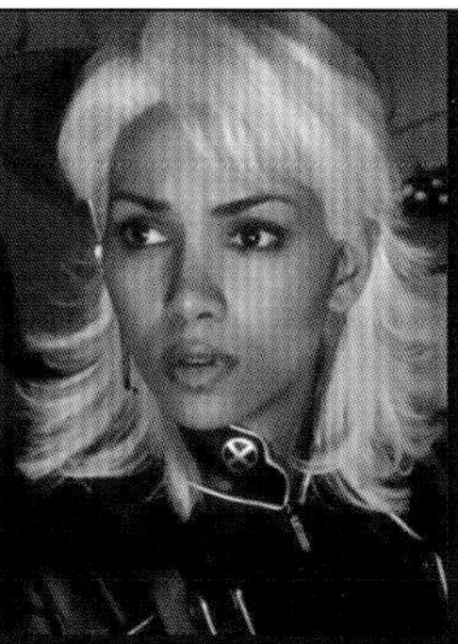

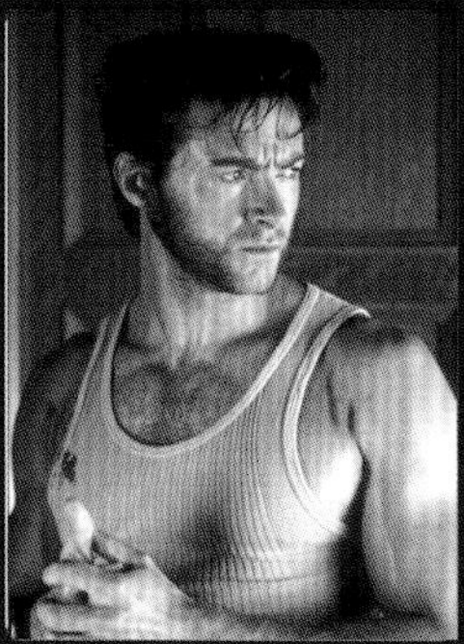

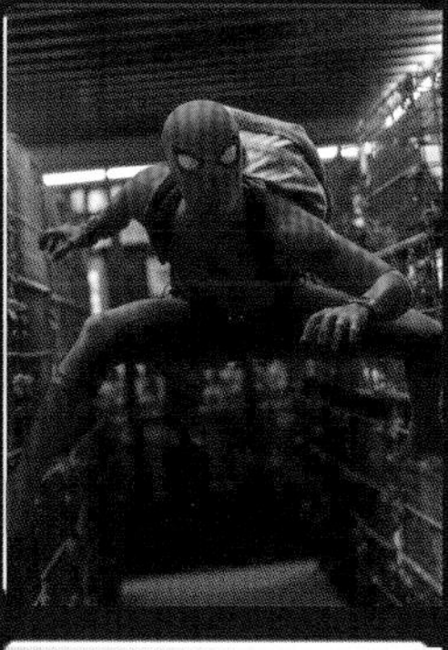

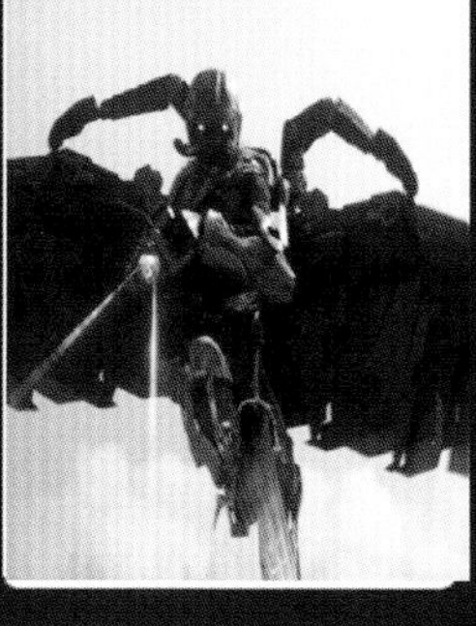

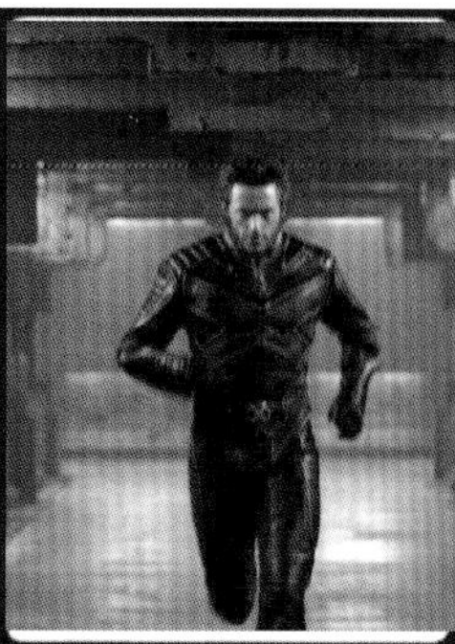

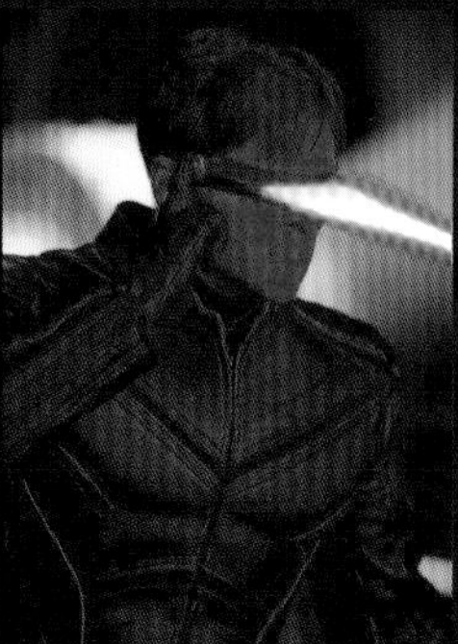

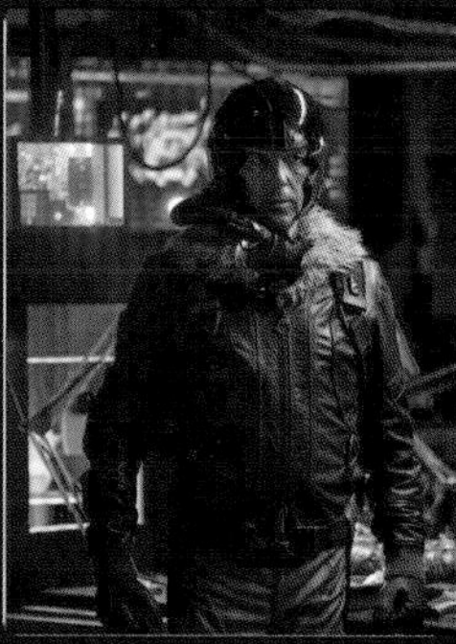

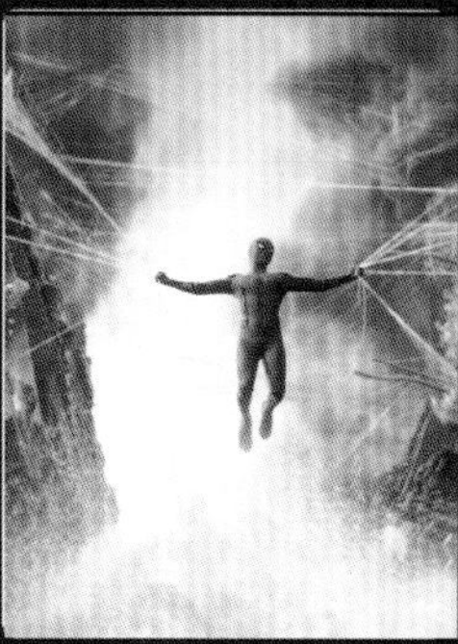

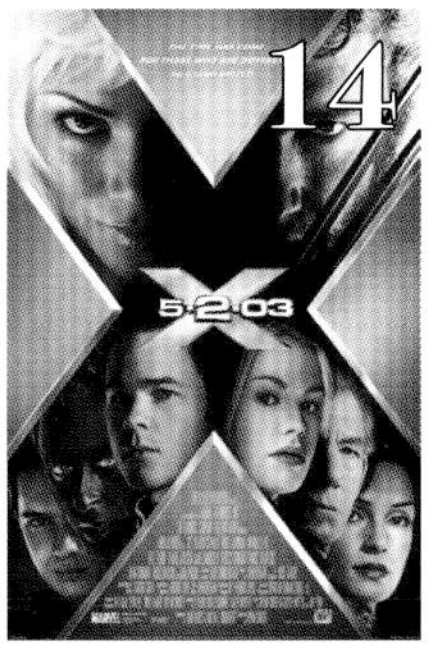
5.2.03

14

X-Men 2 (Bryan Singer, 2003)

Singer's second mutant outing is a classy pulp entertainment that is easily superior to the first – a far darker, better acted piece with sterling performances from Hugh Jackman, Patrick Stewart and Ian McKellen, who are all given some weightier lines to work with on this occasion. Focusing on anti-mutant fanatic William Stryker's (played with some aplomb by Brian Cox) attempt to wipe out the X-Men and their kin, the movie strikes the perfect balance between excellent special effects and the grim hostility faced by the team of outsiders. A film that handles difficult concepts and an ensemble cast quite seamlessly, there's much to enjoy here – the salty interplay between Magneto and Xavier, not to mention the younger X-Men, as well as the enmity between Wolverine and Cyclops. The only film of the three to capture the essence of the original 1970s title, it's an accomplished work that dispenses with mawkish sentiment in favour of realism, and aims for subtlety rather than histrionics. Possibly the best of the Marvel films.

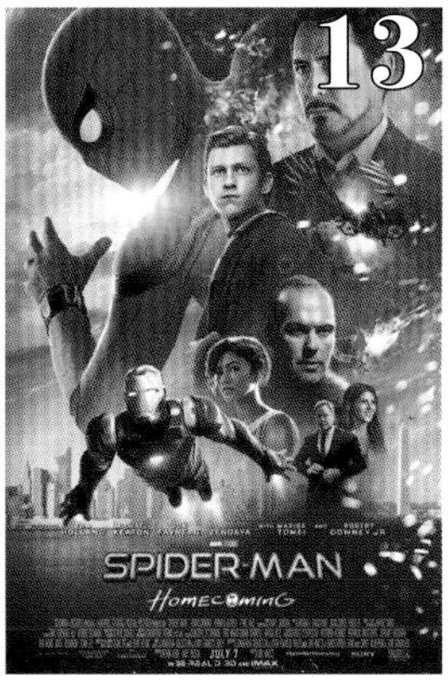
SPIDER-MAN
HOMECOMING

13

Spider-man: Homecoming (Jon Watts, 2017)

Jon Watts, Kevin Feige and Amy Pascal worked the oracle with rebooting old webhead, turning out a film that hit most of the right notes from the off, while effortlessly capturing the spirit of Lee, Ditko and Romita's classic 1960s run. Although very much rooted in the present, the character of Spidey (Tom Holland) on this occasion is now the mawkish, immature high school outsider from his early days, which does play sufficiently well, but what really scores is Michael Keaton's turn as the nemesis of the piece. Keaton was always reliable as the psychotic, wild-eyed villain (he's had one or two such roles before). On this occasion he's playing Batman, I mean Birdman, I mean the Vulture, a man who has appropriated Chitauri technology to build a steampunk winged suit replete with weapons capable of defeating our teenage wall-crawler. The breakneck, offhand pace of the film might've been a little tiresome but for the above average script and occasionally inspired homages, such as the one lifted from *Amazing Spider-Man* 33 (dedicated geeks, I mean aficionados, will spot it). This film is up there as possibly the best of all Marvel projects – there are more amusing one-liners than any previous entry, with the narrative deftly handled, not to mention one or two genuine left-field moments. Shallow it may be but this is entertainment with panache, frequently evading the usual drudge and plodding formula, succeeding in being cinematic while capturing the spirit of comics.

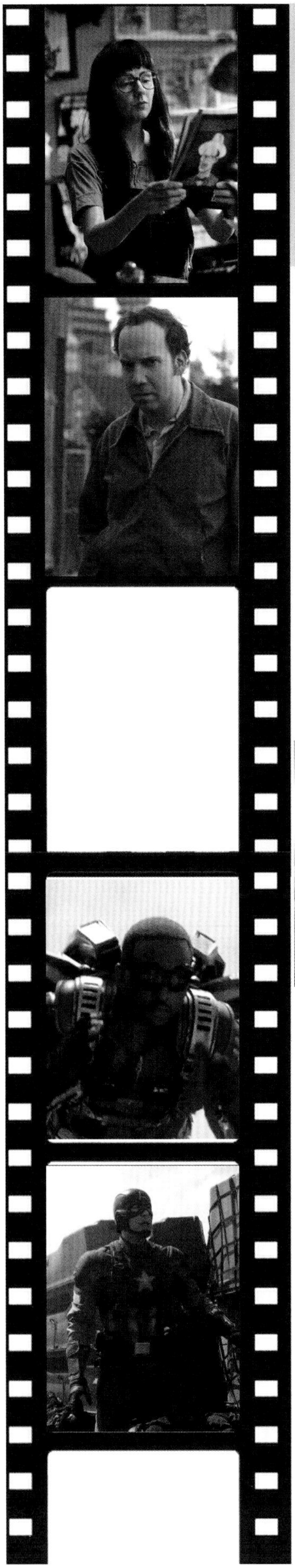

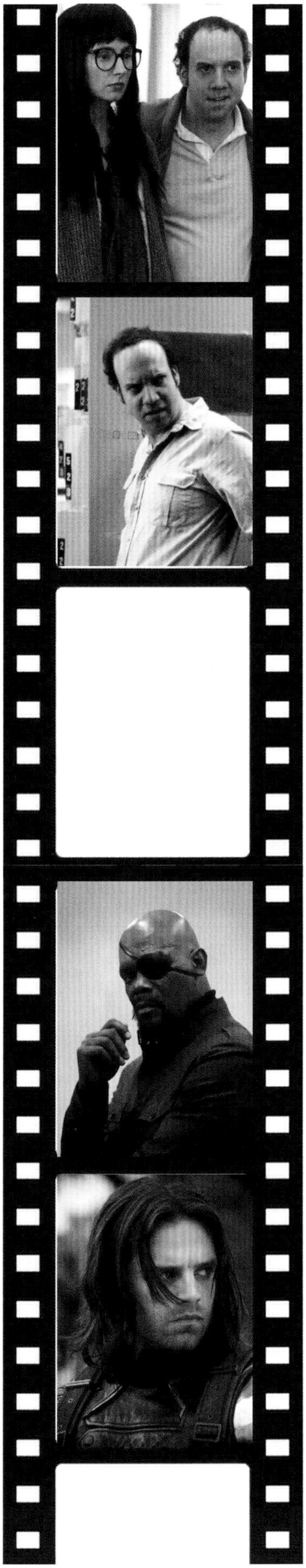

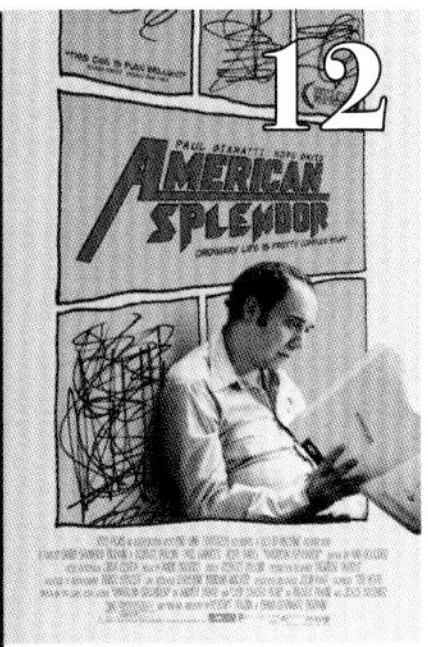
AMERICAN SPLENDOR

12

American Splendor
(Shari Springer Berman and Robert Pulcini, 2003)

The late Harvey Pekar was always the oddest of oddballs on the fringe of pop culture, but his work in his own autobiographical comic rivaled Charles Bukowski's prose in its delineation of inner-city loserdom. Berman and Pulcini's creditable transfer elicits shades of Woody Allen and Albert Brooks in its evocation of Pekar's working class upbringing on the streets of Cleveland. Dealing mainly in the years leading up to and including his appearances on the David Letterman show, the film captures the spirit of the comic by constantly breaking the fourth wall, at one point stopping the actors and letting the real Pekar and his workmates take centre stage. Despite being firmly ensconced on life's bottom rung, whilst befriending characters who are even more socially awkward than he is, the Pekar story is a classic slice of Americana, which like Terry Zwigoff's *Crumb* film does not flinch in its portrayal of these players but ensures that they are humanised. And Paul Giamatti's sympathetic central performance is pitch-perfect.

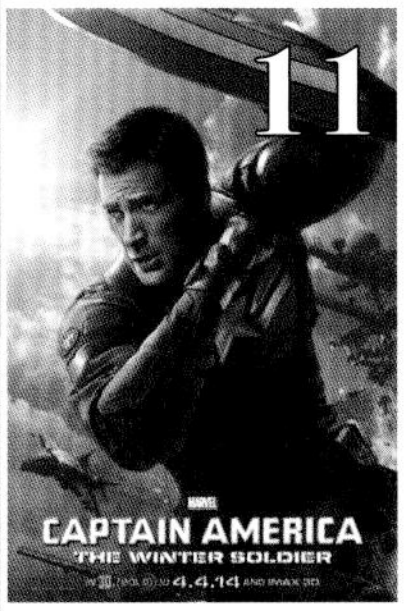
CAPTAIN AMERICA
THE WINTER SOLDIER
4.4.14

11

Captain America: The Winter Soldier (Russo Brothers, 2014)

2014's follow-up to *Captain America: First Avenger* is a compulsive little thriller with Cold War overtones, influenced as it was by films such as *Three Days of the Condor* and *The Manchurian Candidate*. Featuring an extensive cast, the movie (a quasi-Avengers affair) is somewhat of a back to basics work, with Steve Rogers enlisting the Falcon and Black Widow to uncover a hidden conspiracy within the ranks of S.H.IE.L.D., eventually learning that his former partner, Bucky Barnes, has survived World War 2 and been brainwashed into becoming the Winter Soldier. Based on Ed Brubaker's arc from the comic series, the film stood out for critics due to the realistic action sequences and themes of betrayal and paranoia. A polished effort, the film scores due to the decent script and the presence of Samuel L. Jackson, along with Sebastian Stan's portrayal of the title character. It is a little clunky in places, and is somewhat overlong, but the concepts are both interesting and time-honoured, with a great deal of Marvel lore underpinning events. Although the tropes are over-familiar, it still holds its own in this list and does expand on the Captain America mythos. By this point (MCU Phase 2) Marvel was in complete ascendency at the box office, yet this film doesn't rest on its laurels.

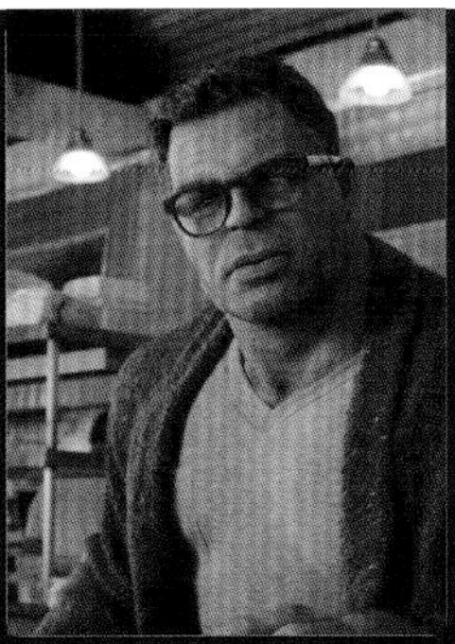

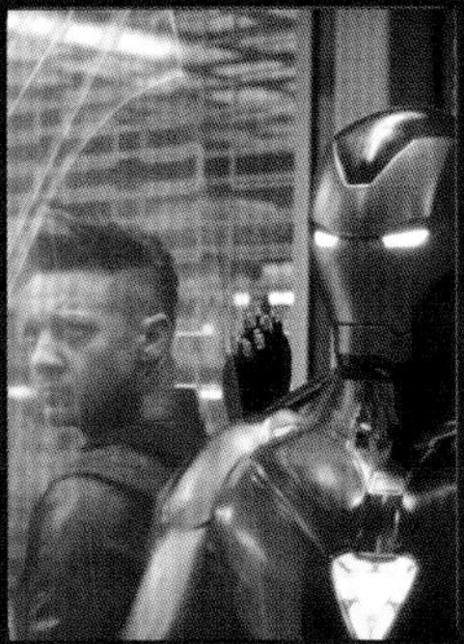

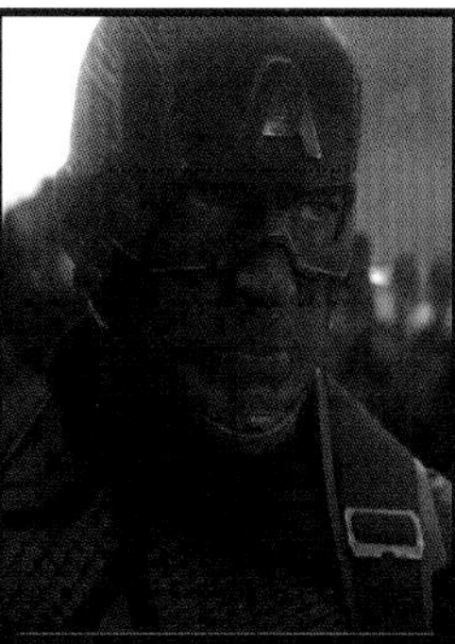

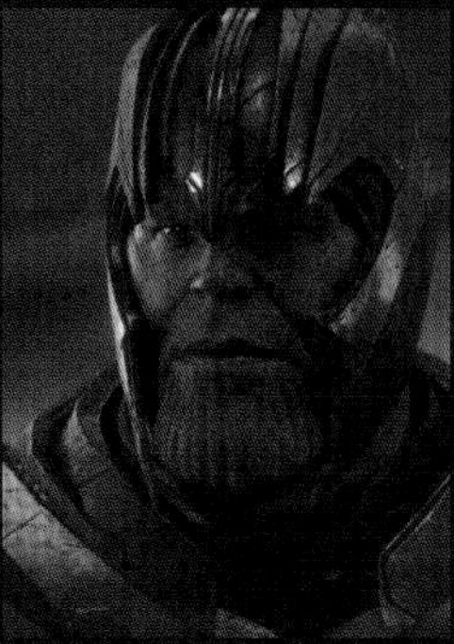

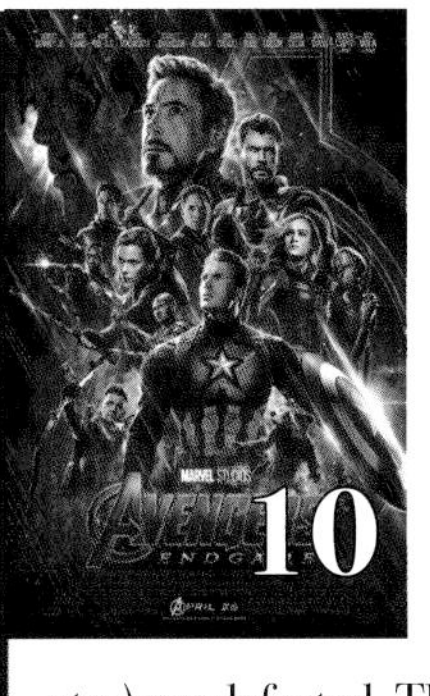

10

Avengers: Endgame (Russo Brothers, 2019)

Continuing as we all know from *Infinity War*, *Avengers: Endgame* features the Big Bad (Thanos, played with lugubrious relish by Josh Brolin) who has killed half the life in the universe. The surviving members, which include polar opposites Captain America (Chris Evans, wholesome, immaculate, but self-aware) and Iron Man (Robert Downey Jr, unkempt, bearded, glib, but the undisputed MCU star) are defeated. There's only one way to reverse this axiomatic mess – time travel (like there was any other way), and thanks to Scott Lang (Paul Rudd)'s deus ex machina presence, it's doable. Groups of surviving Avengers are deployed separately into the near past to retrieve and repair matters, while also getting the chance to revisit key scenes from MCU movies of yore. Where the movie works is that some of the space-time travelling sections work very well – there are some witty and occasional touching moments that are handled with remarkable deftness, as the Marvel heroes either relive their yesterdays or (far too coincidentally) bump into key figures from their lives, or indeed themselves. I can forgive all of this simply because this "heist" section captures the essence of the comic medium. Even if characters aren't allowed the screen time to ruminate on the ramifications of what just occurred to them, it doesn't matter. This isn't high art, and all the plot holes (and there are plenty) mean little compared to what the MCU has evoked here. And the CGI throughout these sequences is pretty impressive. In the end Downey Jr is the lynchpin, and the only character in the project to pontificate eloquently about the Avengers' predicament. But despite his somewhat detached effort, he holds the movie together and makes it a decent follow-up to its predecessor. *Avengers: Endgame* is a worthy, highly watchable entry – a wee bit of a let-down at times, but then I may have expected too much after *Infinity War*. Then again, one cannot ignore how steeped it is in both Marvel history and indeed cinema, and as endcaps to huge, ensemble sagas go, it's a remarkable effort.

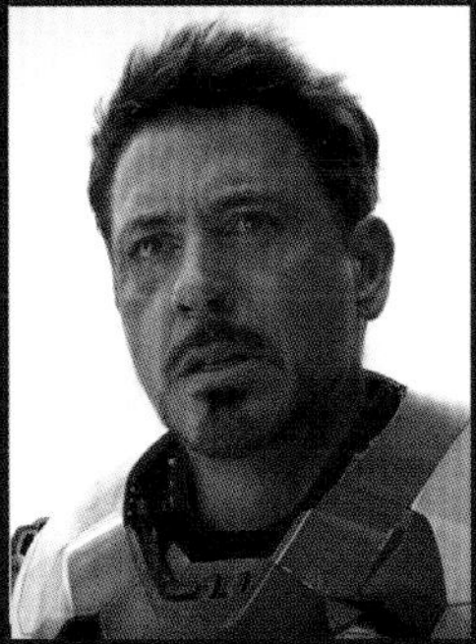

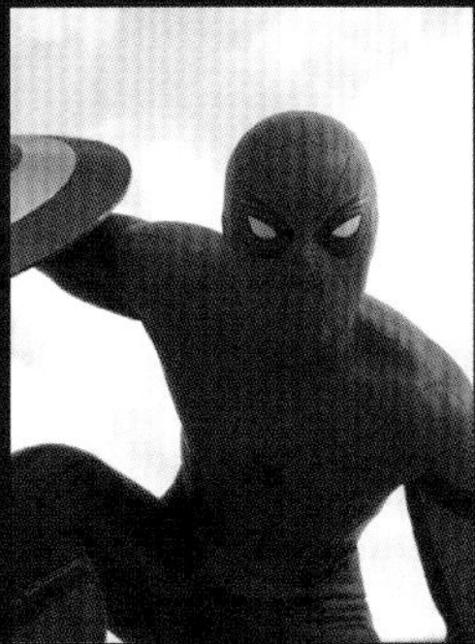

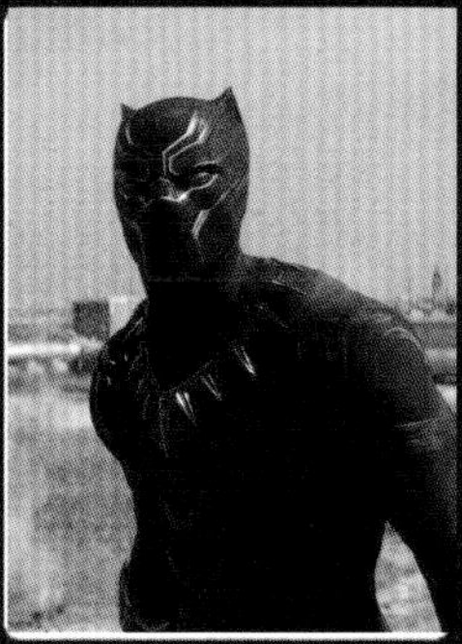

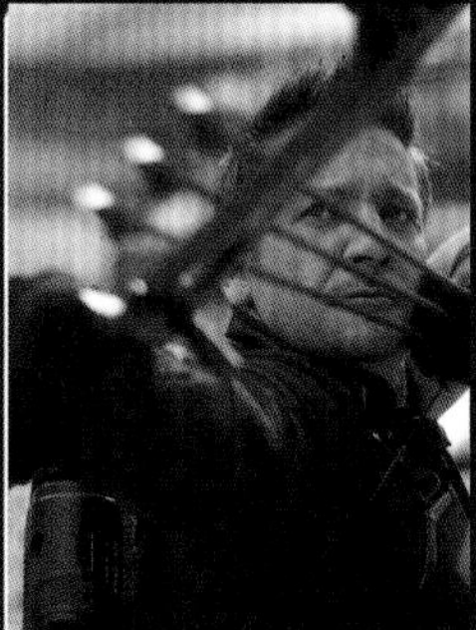

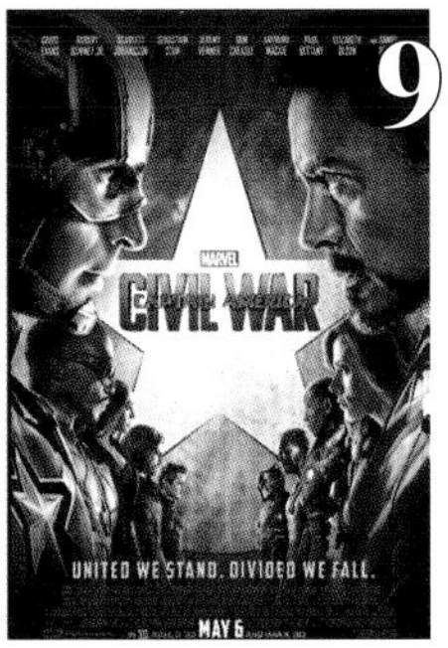
CIVIL WAR
UNITED WE STAND. DIVIDED WE FALL.
MAY 6

9

Captain America: Civil War (Russo Brothers, 2016)

Having super-heroes fight each other, either individually or in teams, was by no means a new concept in comics, and indeed stretches further back than the original Marvel era, but this production managed to take this concept and make it fire on all cylinders. Based on the comic story arc from the mid noughties, this movie is basically *Winter Soldier* and *Age of Ultron* part 2, a sequel to two sequels. Despite being what could have been just another chapter, the film rewards the diehards with a decent script, far better characterisation and a genuine sense of moving matters forward. What could've been a risible set-up (the schism between two factions of Avengers, engineered by Helmut Zemo) featuring the usual clichés and platitudes, turns out to be remarkably assured, with all the characters in the ensemble given time to expand and flourish without allowing the plot to drag. All in all, a slick and confident effort which sustains attention and does, with some reservations, succeed in balancing the required sledgehammer sensibilities with subtle touches and mature storytelling. This instalment was a step forward in Marvel's spandex soap opera, which had threatened to run aground in *Avengers: Age of Ultron*.

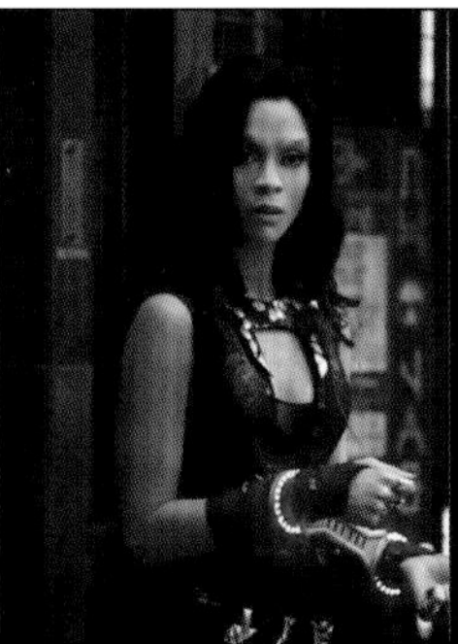

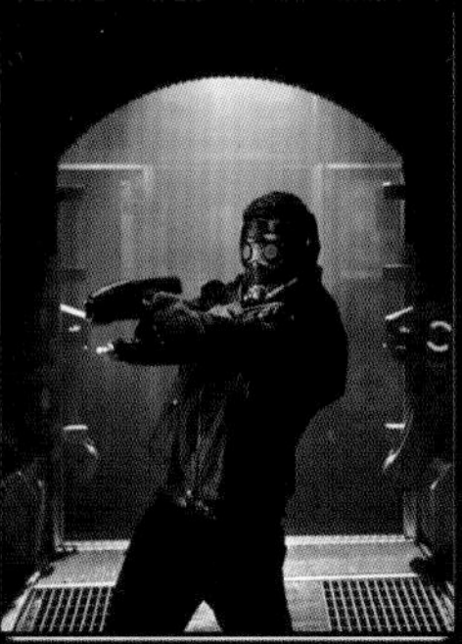

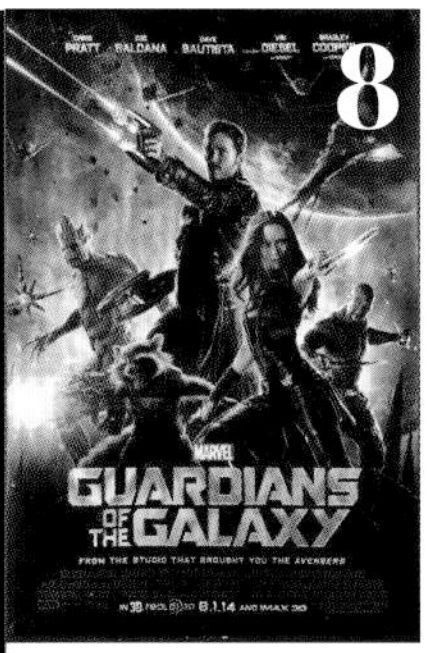
GUARDIANS OF THE GALAXY

8 Guardians Of The Galaxy (James Gunn, 2014)

Guardians of the Galaxy was the surprise hit of 2014, and was Marvel's first attempt at a humorous, irreverent, daringly daft entry in its cinematic universe. No attempt was made to take the canon seriously, nor did it seem too bothered about being liked, even though there were plenty of times when it did grandstand and went for broad if not childlike comedy. Riffing as it did on science-fiction comics and *Star Wars*, the Guardians' universe was remarkably cohesive and always maintained interest. Primarily it was a production that cleverly seemed to eschew cynicism – the cast and crew clearly enjoying the proceedings, but not too much to be self-indulgent. Telling the cosmic tale of human / alien hybrid Peter Quill (Starlord, played by the more than game Chris Pratt) a mercenary who is chased from one corner of the galaxy by the smuggling gang called the Ravagers and Kree renegade Ronan the Accuser, the film focuses on his meeting various other ne'er do wells, such as the animated Rocket Raccoon and talking tree Groot. Lurking in the background is psychotic demigod Thanos, whose adopted daughter Gamora provides Starlord's love interest. Above all what makes this superannuated Saturday morning cartoon work is the characterization, the chemistry between the players and the deftly handled plotting, which to its credit does invoke if not entirely borrow from 1970s Marvel story arcs such as Warlock and Captain Marvel. The threat and drama is kept to a relative minimum, but the movie is amusing and clever enough that you don't mind, such is its lightweight charm. And the soundtrack is rather good too, especially for those of an older persuasion. A popcorn movie in the right sense of the term.

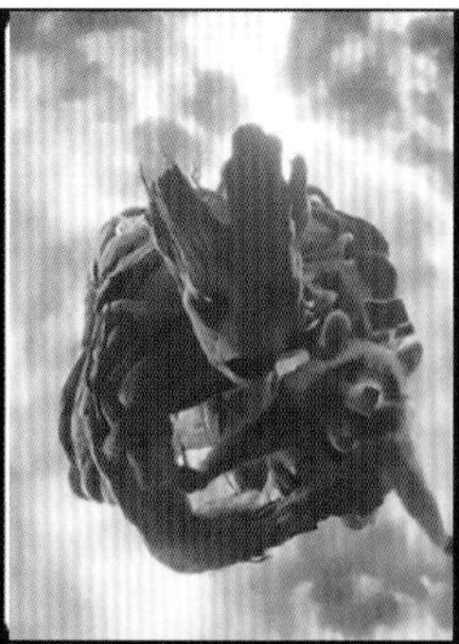

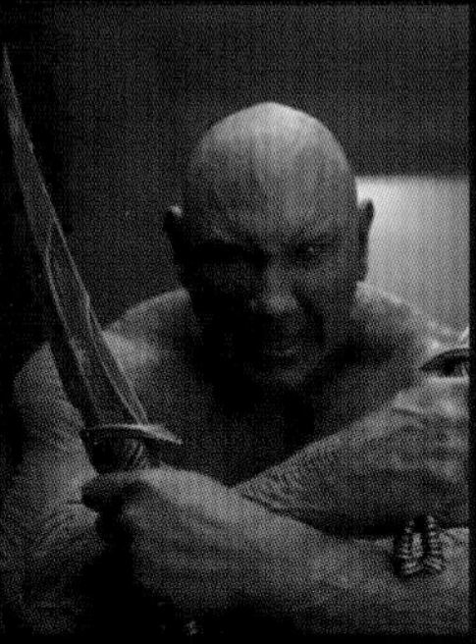

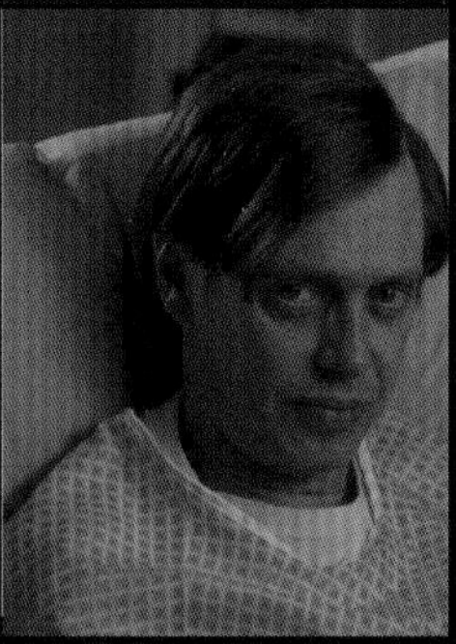

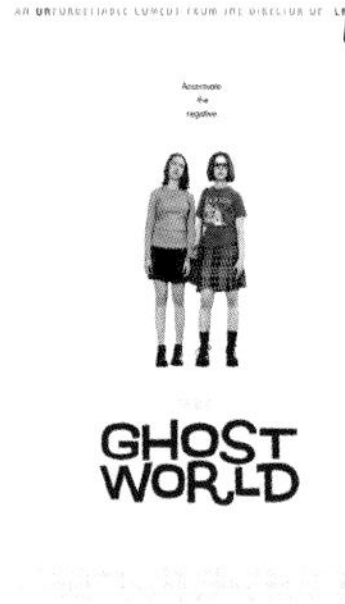
GHOST WORLD

7 Ghost World (Terry Zwigoff, 2001)

Despite the presence of creator Dan Clowes as scriptwriter, *Ghost World* is a considerably different entity compared to his comic-book version. In Clowes's strip, the characters have little room to grow in their solipsistic bedroom pods, whilst in the film, regardless of their at times strident immaturity, the leads do develop and change. Basically a drama about two adolescent girls approaching adulthood in a disconnected, hermetic town, this remarkably involving film details the protagonists' gradual estrangement from their environment and each other, whilst dragging a desultory loner (played with verve by Steve Buscemi) into their orbit. Faithful to the comic's barren tone, the film is an excellent evocation of the pain of introspective youth, its fear of the future and contempt for its surroundings. The two leads, played by Thora Birch and Scarlett Johansson, are perfectly cast, whilst the look of the film, both garish and washed-out, remains consistent throughout. A film that never patronises either the characters or the audience, it's an underrated work that deserves cult status.

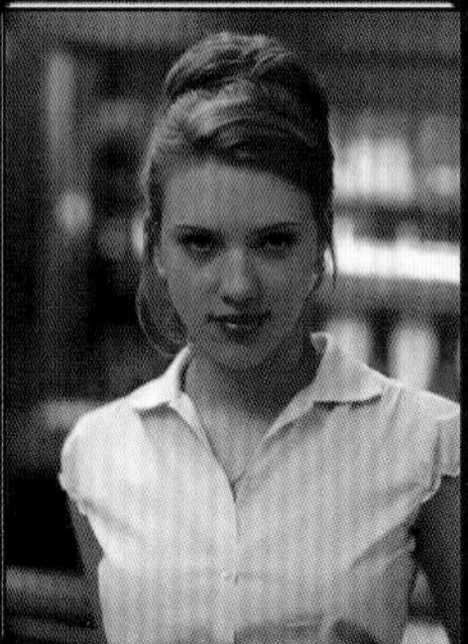

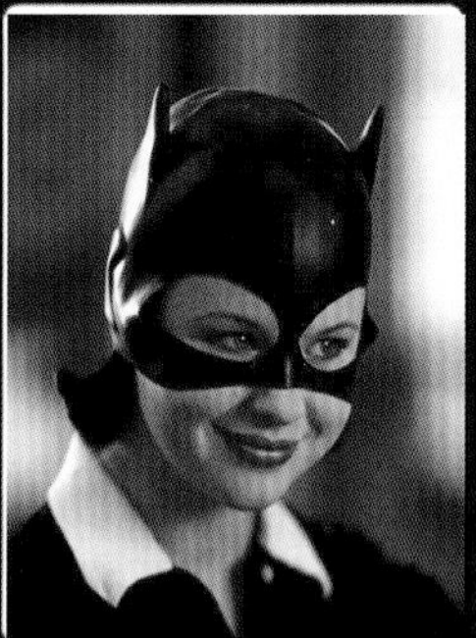

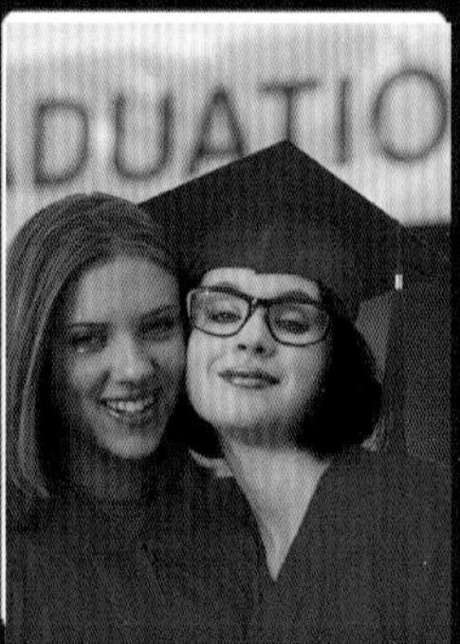

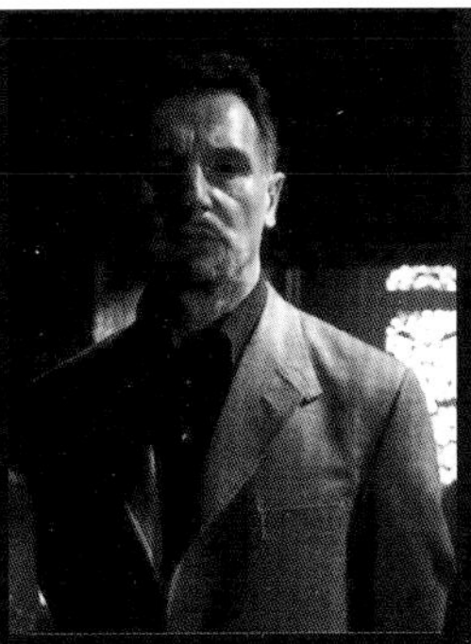

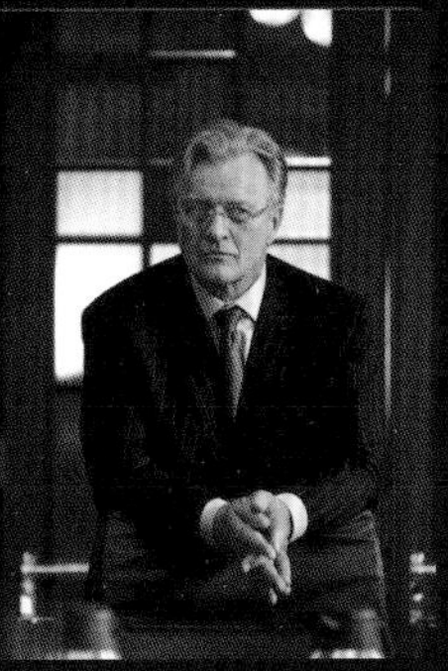

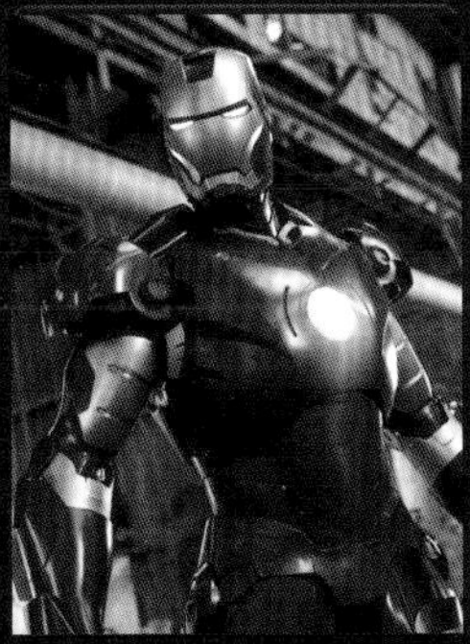

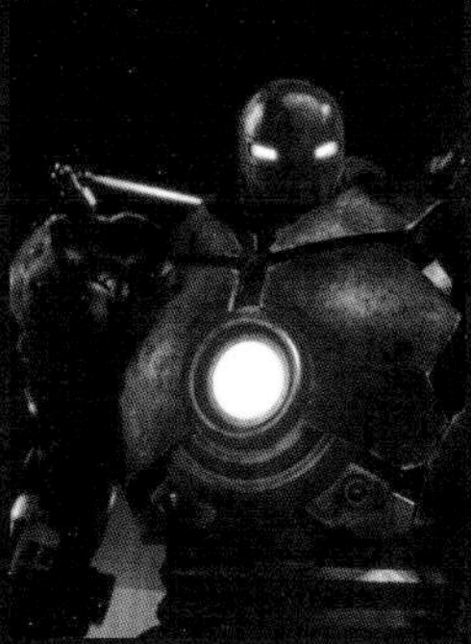

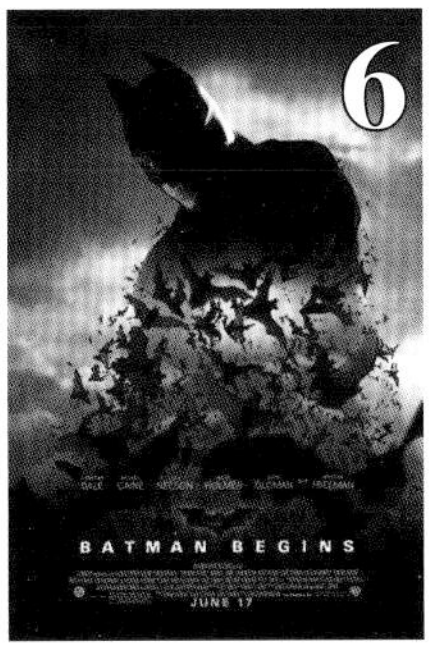
BATMAN BEGINS
JUNE 17

6 Batman Begins (Christopher Nolan, 2005)

Nolan's first attempt at the Dark Knight came with a directive – to restore credibility to DC's only genuinely bankable film property, whilst providing a neat origin adjustment that would create the platform for his trilogy. Very much a pared-down, low-key effort in comparison to Tim Burton's portrayal, the film's more naturalistic dialogue and direction was underpinned by the early 70s version of the comic, along with Frank Miller's classic *Year One*. The plot, which details how the young Bruce Wayne started out as a criminal before being trained by arch-villain Ra's Al Ghul's League Of Shadows, certainly uses the title's backstory effectively, whilst the film's themes of fear, isolation and needing a father figure are all central to the Batman mythos, so it seems that the filmmakers did their homework. Excellent work from Liam Neeson and Cillian Murphy as the enigmatic baddies, as well as Gary Oldman as the future Commissioner Gordon. Without question the interpretation of the character that fandom had been waiting for, and the best was yet to come.

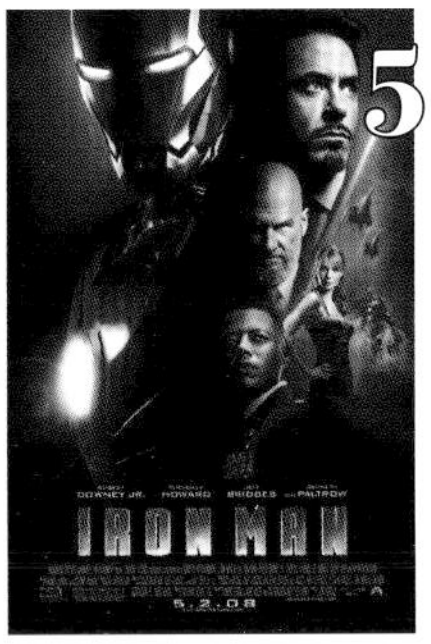
IRON MAN
5.2.08

5 Iron Man (Jon Favreau, 2008)

Perhaps the movie that most accurately replicated the sense of fun and dry humour of the comic-book version, Favreau's effort works due to an intelligent script, and above all the star quality of the film's lead, Robert Downey Jr., who practically reinvents the role as himself. Another step-up for comic-based cinema, the film successfully balances the excellent special effects with developed characterization, which to all intents and purposes, guaranteed success. Nevertheless, the film suffers from the usual pitfalls – the rather jingoistic plot and routine villainry, not to mention the dated nature of some of the supporting cast (despite Favreau's desire to modernize the mise-en-scene) do rankle somewhat, and there's a general offhandedness to the whole affair, as if the filmmakers needed to remind the audience that it's only a comic-book movie, folks. If there is a subtext, it's surreptitiously buried beneath some dazzling action sequences (was there ever a hero more tailor-made for genre cinema?) and RDJ's career-saving performance.

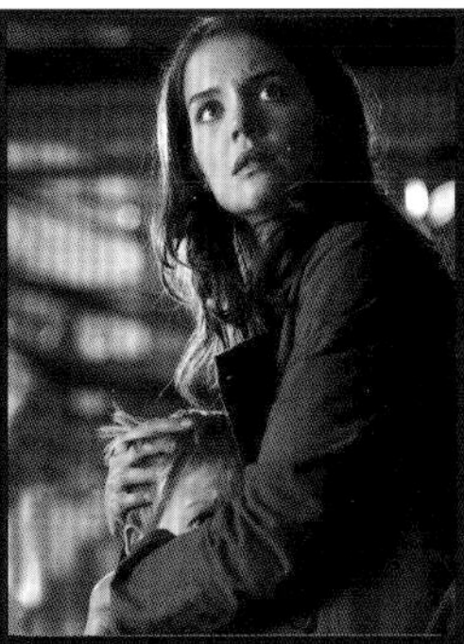

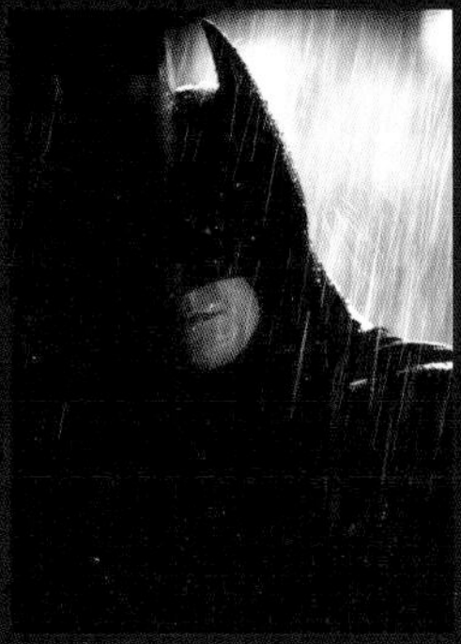

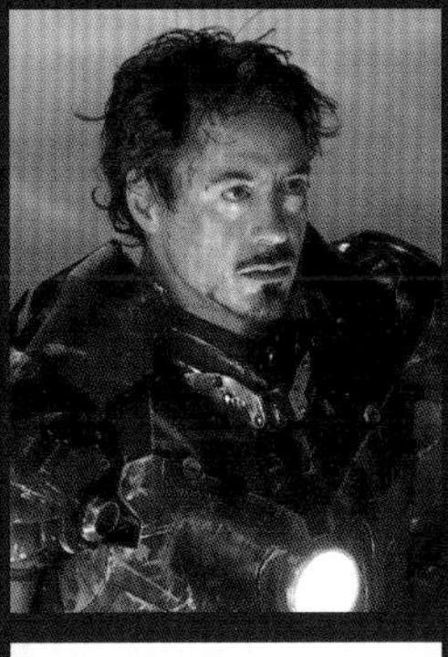

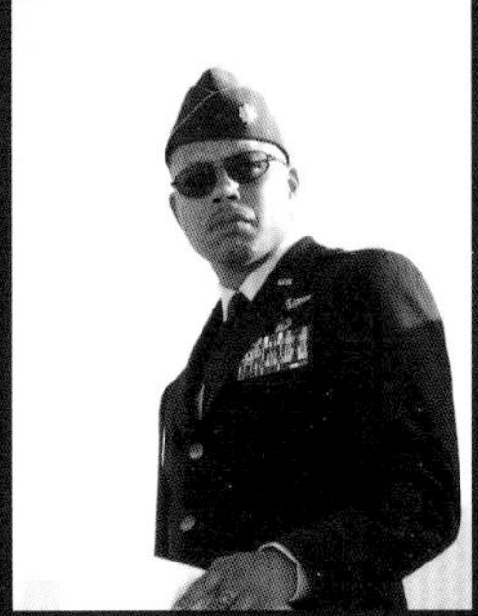

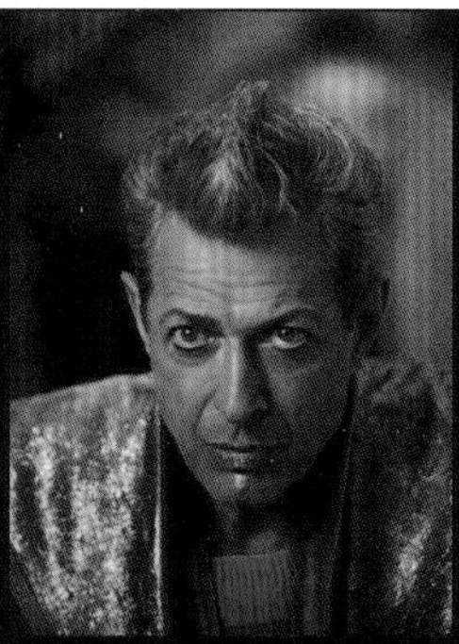

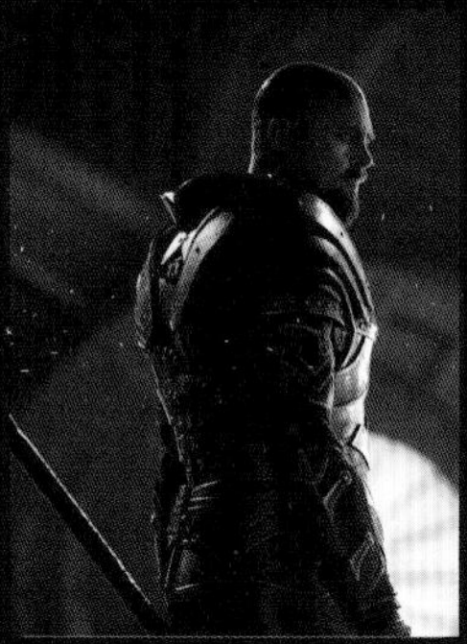

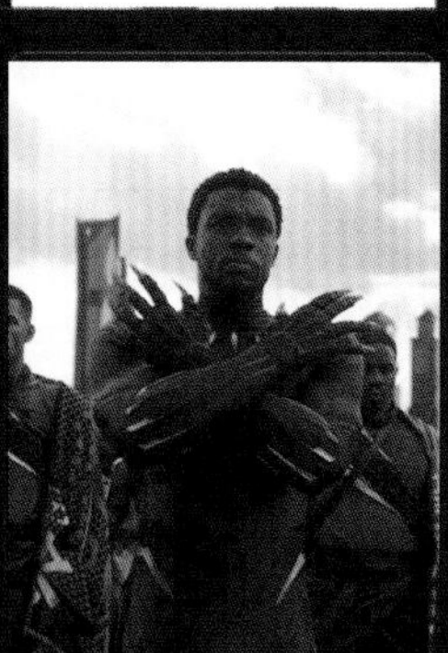

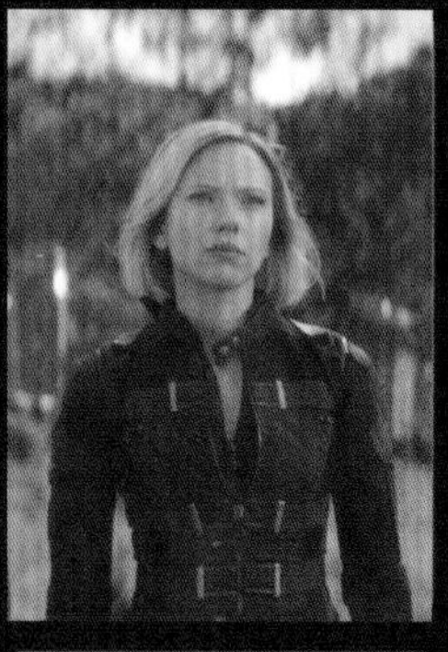

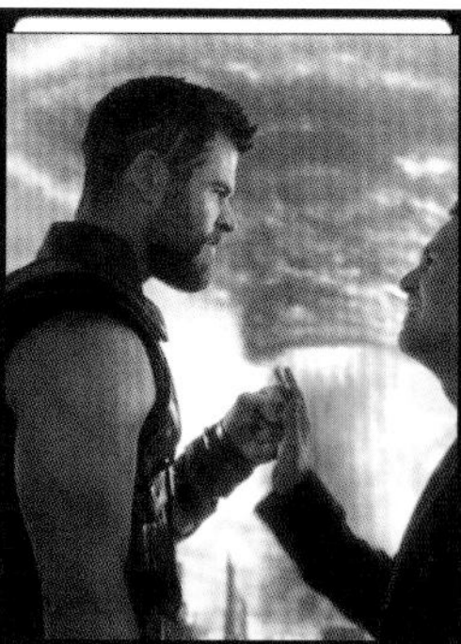

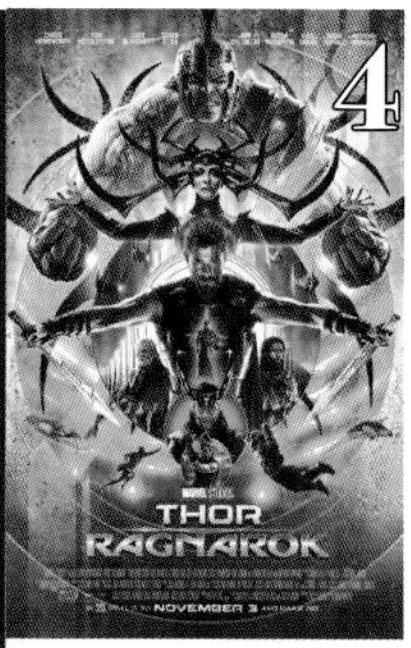
THOR
RAGNAROK
NOVEMBER 3

4

Thor: Ragnarok (Taika Waititi, 2017)

Thor's third outing is a rollicking, enormously funny if somewhat depth-free good time, and rather like *Spider-Man Homecoming* or the first *Guardians* outing, what's on screen captures the spirit of the source material in a far better manner than previously. A lot of this has to be down to lead actor Chris Hemsworth, who deftly excels in balancing the absurdity of it all with the mandatory seriousness involved with the final reel's denouement. Thor returns to Asgard, covertly ruled by his knavish half-brother Loki, in order to locate their father Odin. Odin warns them of the goddess of death Hela who has been released from aeon-length captivity and is hell-bent on exacting revenge. Thor challenges Hela and is savagely defeated, ending up on prison planet Sakaar, where he is captured and enslaved by uber-decadent overlord Grandmaster. It is on this garishly dystopian world that the film's mandate reaches its apex. Adapting plot strands from 2006's *Planet Hulk* tour de force comic series, Thor has to endure endless indignities at the hands of various malefactors, such as Valkyrie and Grandmaster, played with hilariously offhand panache by Jeff Goldblum, shining as he hadn't done for a considerable time. There are some excellent, even grand guignol moments here – it's almost as if, unwittingly, producer Kevin Feige and director Taika Waititi fashioned something ambitious that didn't involve wholesale graphic destruction. There's enough here for the casual viewer and diehard fan to relish, with all the leads seemingly enjoying themselves, especially Hemsworth, who is terrific. A pretence-free affair that raised the bar, leaving us not wanting a whole lot more, but certainly not wanting less. Classy and engrossing pulp entertainment.

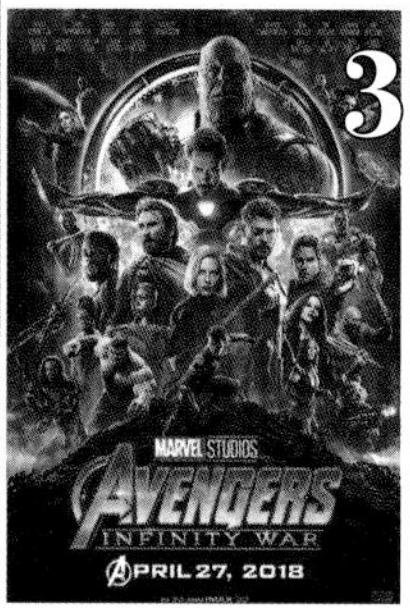
MARVEL STUDIOS
AVENGERS
INFINITY WAR
APRIL 27, 2018

3

Avengers: Infinity War (Russo Bros, 2019)

MCU's Phase 3 provided a breakthrough sense of a studio who, now that the franchise was so embedded in the cinematic landscape, were emboldened enough to take chances. You could claim that the filmmakers were throwing everything at the screen including the kitchen sink, but it would be equally reasonable to say that the foundation work had been done, and now the fun could truly get underway. And it's hard to go wrong when you have Jim Starlin's peerless canon (the entire Thanos saga from the 70s on) to mine. The film dispensed with any kind of framing device, as we immediately laid eyes on the granite form of the film's monster / villain (and virtual protagonist) of Thanos himself, immeasurably powerful against Thor and Loki. Accompanied by some equally gnarled and utterly ruthless henchmen called the Children of Thanos, his goal was to attain all six Infinity Stones in order to have complete dominion of space, time and dimension. Which involved wiping out half the population of the universe in order to save it. It was a moderate departure from the source material, but that was all moot. Such a force of nature would require just about every spandexed good guy in the MCU to defeat him, and that, essentially, is what we get. This film did have something that could be conceivably considered transcendent, which might be a first for a super-hero movie. This is by no means a challenging or world-beating classic, but it was a step by the Marvel Cinematic Universe towards actual, if not demanding, cinema – there's ambition in spades here, needless to say, with the filmmakers attempting to think outside the box, while being frequently entertaining in the process. The last twenty minutes were engrossing rather than the same old tedium, featuring what is a surprisingly beguiling cliff-hanger finale. For a film that often threatens to collapse under the weight of its aspirations and ensemble cast, it's a highly commendable bit of work that goes some way to living up to the hype. For me this is the best Marvel movie, bar none.

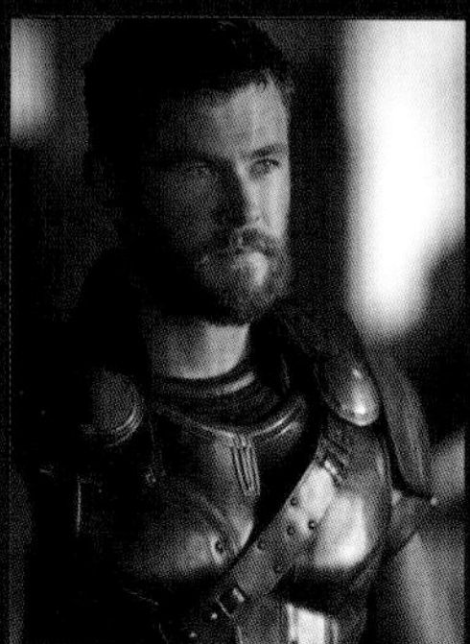

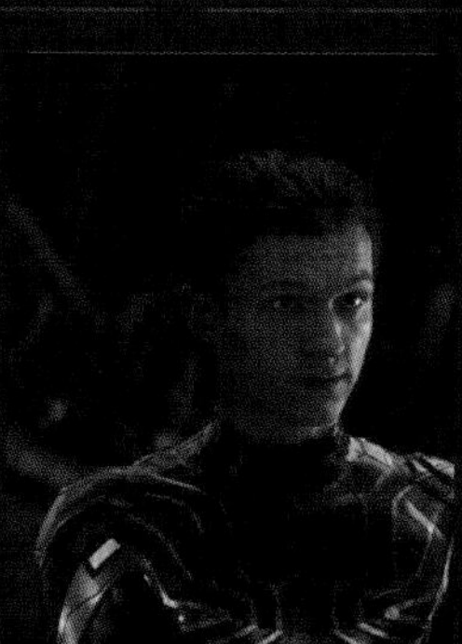

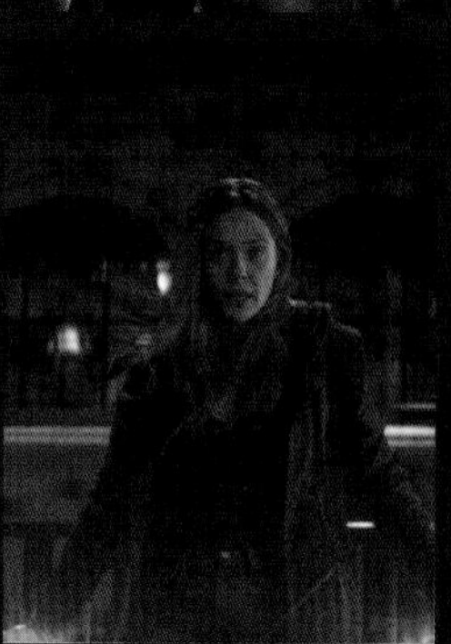

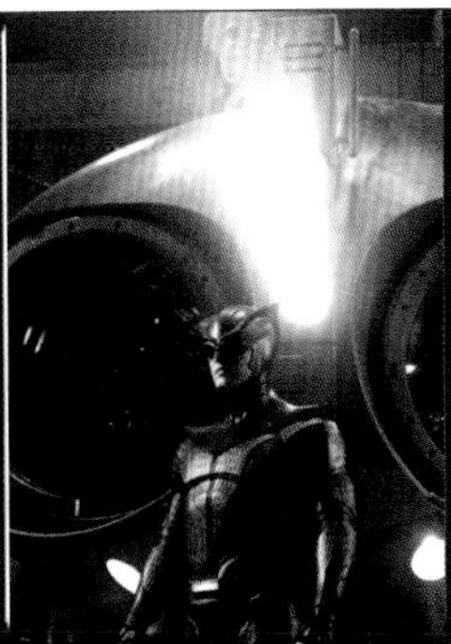

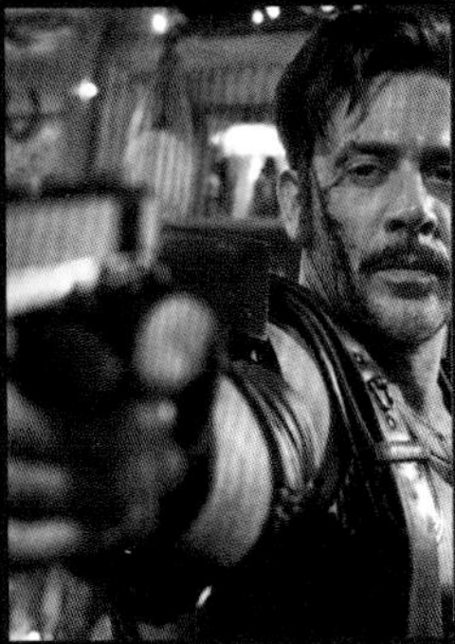

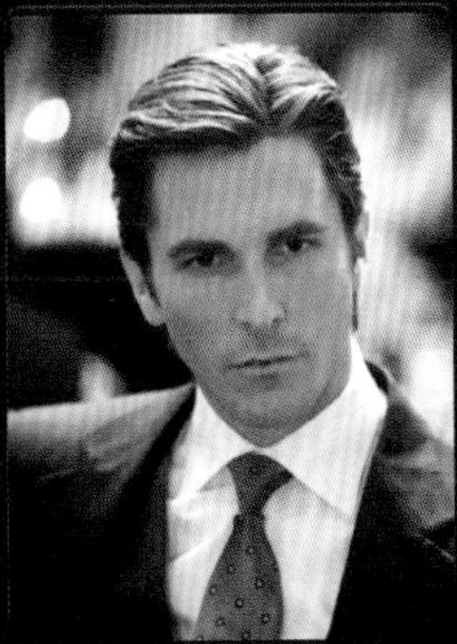

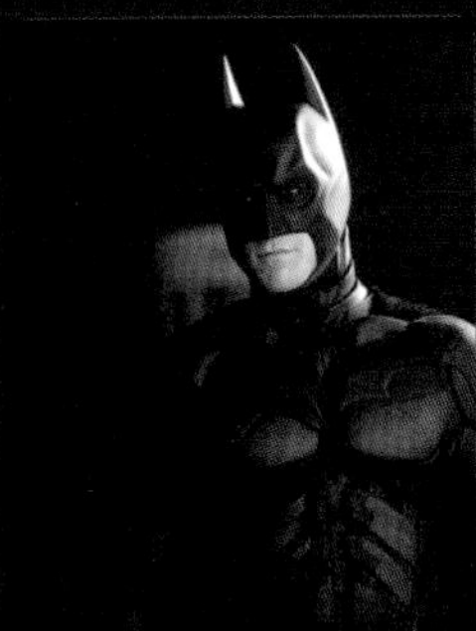

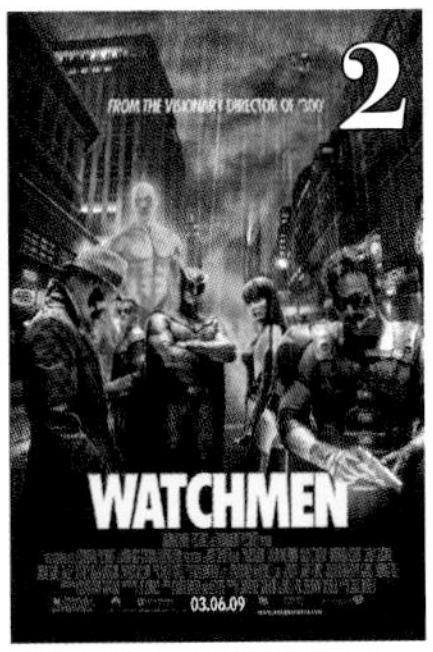
FROM THE VISIONARY DIRECTOR OF "300"
WATCHMEN
03.06.09

2

Watchmen (Zack Snyder, 2009)

Dismissively considered the "unfilmable film" during its extended period in development doldrums, Snyder's *Watchmen* movie arrived on cinema screens to general bemusement and indifference – after all, who would be interested in a subversive appraisal of the medium featuring unfamiliar, skewed characters with no star actors? Meanwhile devotees of the graphic novel would no doubt see it as flat, superficial and reductive. On second viewing however it becomes clear that the original misgivings regarding the project were back to front – the adaptation could not fail with such painstaking storyboards in place, and indeed it doesn't. There are the clunky montage scenes, backed by some rather too obvious song choices, and the ending lacks the intensity of the book, but the movie plays, and plays surprisingly well. What's most impressive is how the film doesn't succumb to portentousness, and manages to entertain, whilst its production values do justice to the source – in short, it retains that vital comic spirit. The tagline states that Snyder is the visionary here, but make no mistake, this is Moore and Gibbons' vision. Which in the end is all we could ask for.

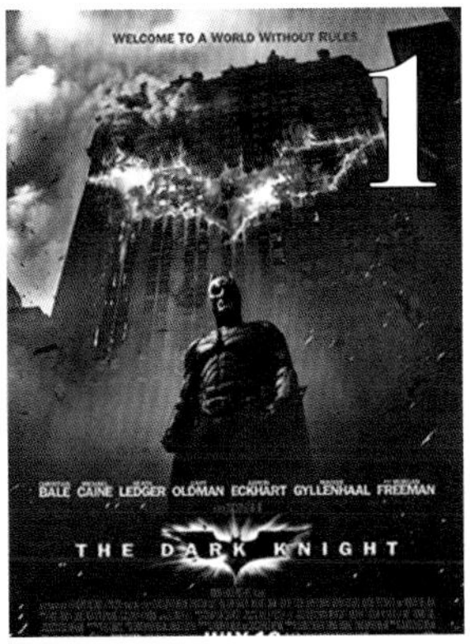
WELCOME TO A WORLD WITHOUT RULES
BALE CAINE LEDGER OLDMAN ECKHART GYLLENHAAL FREEMAN
THE DARK KNIGHT

1

The Dark Knight (Christopher Nolan, 2008)

Nolan's baroque tour de force remains the only example of a comic-based film that asks questions of its audience – a subversive, cutting-edge work that maintains thematic cohesion and is dizzyingly entertaining with it. Central to the film of course is Heath Ledger's Joker, who once on screen confounds and baits audience expectation with demonic, ruthless alacrity – a genuine mercurial psychopath compared to Nicholson's subdued clown. Nolan's remit as director is to willfully ignore and play havoc with convention, and to keep the viewer as in the dark and off-balance as the players – the ferry scene for instance being a point where one simply doesn't know what's coming next – quite a feat in modern cinema. Not that the cast don't play their part – Bale's Batman is a commanding presence, whilst Eckhart's performance as the doomed Harvey Dent is moving and thoroughly believable. Evoking the brutal urban gothic of graphic novel masterworks like *The Long Halloween* and *The Killing Joke*, one could argue that the movie is a dark, psychological thriller with a gadget-laden costumed hero in tow – a "serious and mature" revisionist piece that transcends rather than elevates. And you'd be half-right – it's actually what comic books are capable of. Hats off to Mr. Nolan.

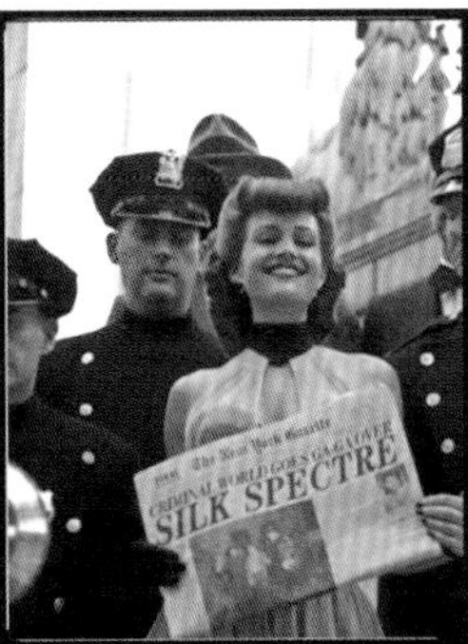
SILK SPECTRE

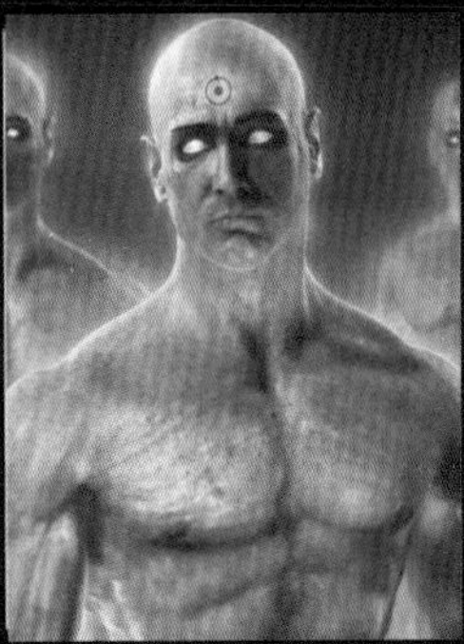

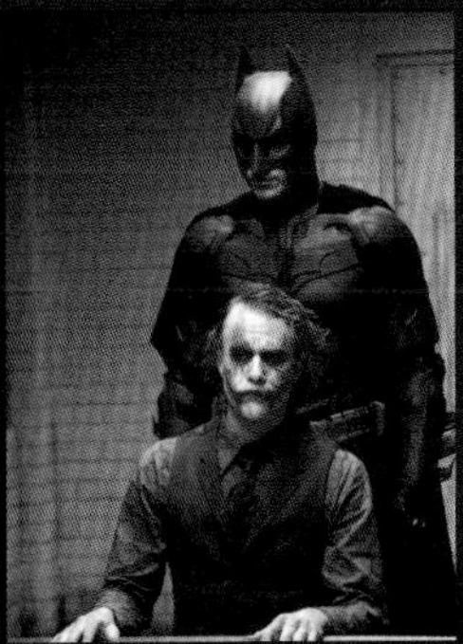

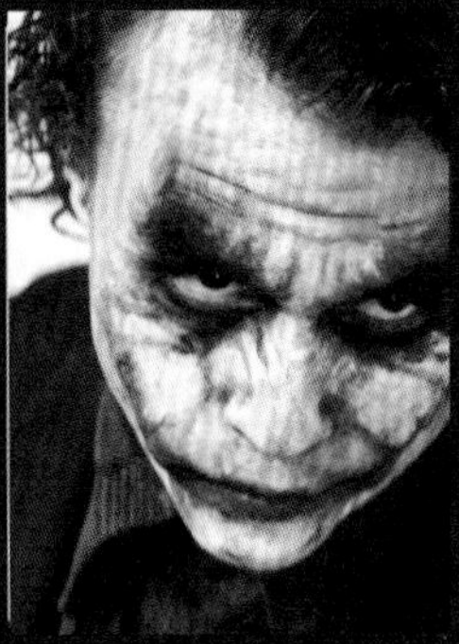

30 YEARS OF TRIPWIRE IN COVERS

Tripwire has covered a lot of different subjects in its 30 years of history and here's 30 of its covers over the decades...

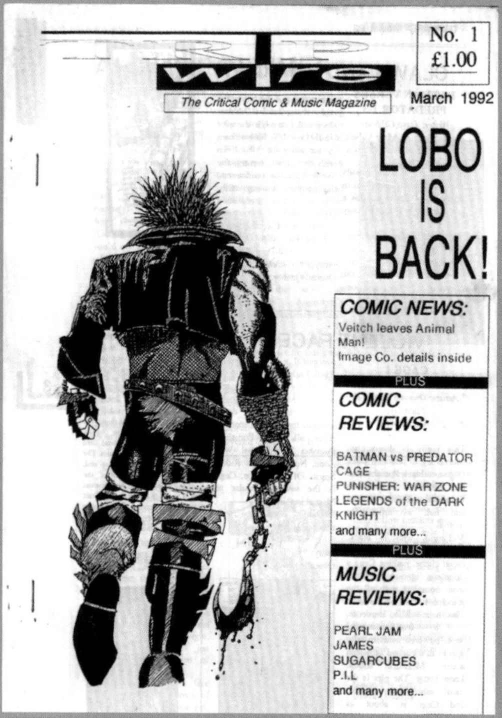
TRIP wire
No. 1
£1.00
The Critical Comic & Music Magazine
March 1992
LOBO IS BACK!
COMIC NEWS:
Veitch leaves Animal Man!
Image Co. details inside
PLUS
COMIC REVIEWS:
BATMAN vs PREDATOR
CAGE
PUNISHER: WAR ZONE
LEGENDS of the DARK KNIGHT
and many more...
PLUS
MUSIC REVIEWS:
PEARL JAM
JAMES
SUGARCUBES
P.I.L
and many more...

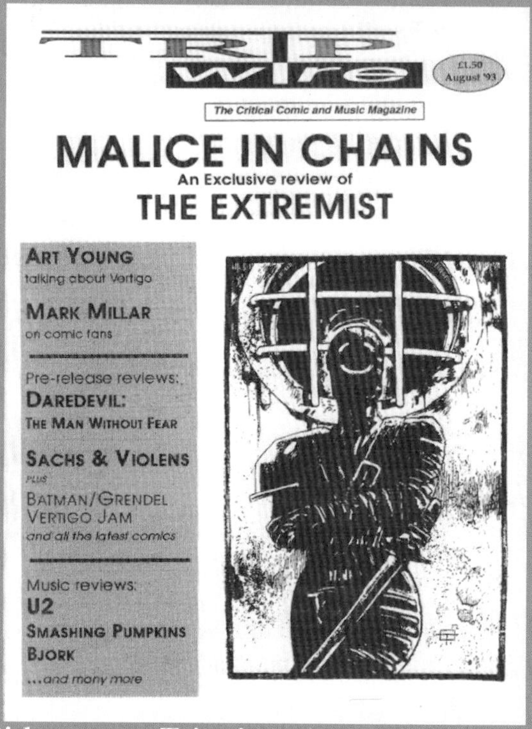
TRIP wire
£1.50
August '93
The Critical Comic and Music Magazine
MALICE IN CHAINS
An Exclusive review of
THE EXTREMIST
ART YOUNG
talking about Vertigo
MARK MILLAR
on comic fans
Pre-release reviews:
DAREDEVIL:
THE MAN WITHOUT FEAR
SACHS & VIOLENS
PLUS
BATMAN/GRENDEL
VERTIGO JAM
and all the latest comics
Music reviews:
U2
SMASHING PUMPKINS
BJORK
...and many more

From left to right: Tripwire volume 1 #1 March 1992 Lobo Simon Bisley cover • Tripwire volume 1 #4 August 1993 Ted McKeever Extremist cover • Tripwire volume 1 #8 Dec 1994 Duncan Fegredo Face cover • Tripwire volume 1 #9 May1995 Frank Quitely Blackheart cover

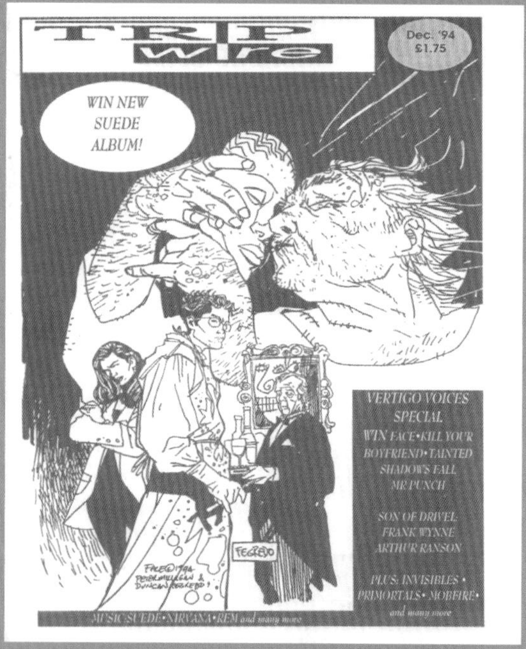
TRIP wire
Dec. '94
£1.75
WIN NEW SUEDE ALBUM!
VERTIGO VOICES SPECIAL
WIN FACE•KILL YOUR BOYFRIEND•TAINTED
SHADOWS FALL
MR PUNCH
SON OF DRIVEL
FRANK WYNNE
ARTHUR RANSON
PLUS: INVISIBLES •
PRIMORTALS• MOBFIRE•
and many more
MUSIC:SUEDE•NIRVANA•REM and many more

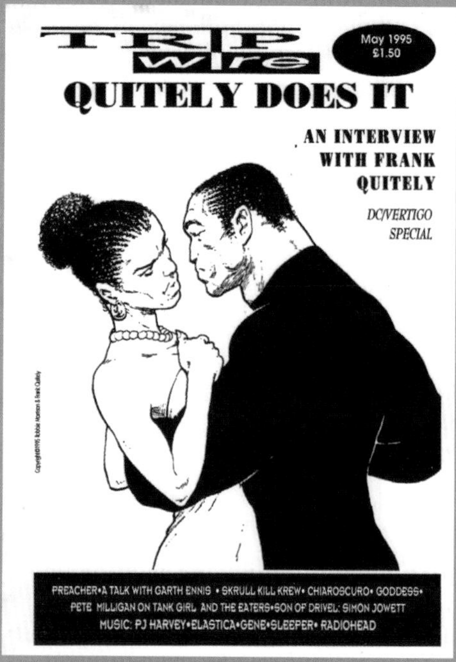
TRIP wire
May 1995
£1.50
QUITELY DOES IT
AN INTERVIEW WITH FRANK QUITELY
DC/VERTIGO SPECIAL
PREACHER•A TALK WITH GARTH ENNIS • SKRULL KILL KREW• CHIAROSCURO• GODDESS•
PETE MILLIGAN ON TANK GIRL AND THE EATERS•SON OF DRIVEL: SIMON JOWETT
MUSIC: PJ HARVEY•ELASTICA•GENE•SLEEPER• RADIOHEAD

TRIP wire
No.12 Spring 1996 £1.50 UK $2.50 US $3.50 CAN
KINGDOM COME

TRIPWIRE
COMICS AND MUSIC
SUMMER '96 No. 13
£1.50 UK $2.50 US $3.50 CAN
HELLBOY
WIN KINGDOM COME
PLUS MUSIC
THE CURE
MANIC STREE PREACHERS
and many more
BATMAN GRENDEL II

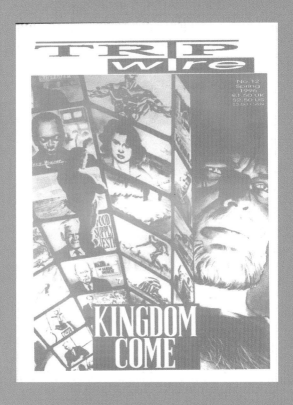

From left to right: Tripwire volume 1#12 Spring 1996 Kingdom Come Alex Ross cover • Tripwire volume 1 #13 Summer 1996 Frank Quitely Flex Mentallo cover • Tripwire volume 1 #14 mid-summer 1996 Miker Mignola Hellboy cover • Tripwire volume 1 #16 sprimg 1997 Frank Quitely 2020 Visions cover

TRIPWIRE
COMICS AND MUSIC
£1.50 UK $2.50 US $3.50 CAN
MID SUMMER '96 No. 14
HELL AND BACK
MIGNOLA SPELLS OUT HELLBOY'S FUTURE
ASTRO CITY
TEEN TITANS
MUSIC
PRINCE, ELECTRONIC, 808 STATE, PLACEBO

SPRING '97 No 16
TRIPWIRE
COMICS AND MUSIC
£2.50 UK $3.95 US $4.95 CAN
JAMIE DELANO
GRANT MORRISON
MIKE MIGNOLA
JAMES ROBINSON
STEVEN SEAGLE
FRANK QUITELY

TRIPWIRE
COMICS AND MUSIC
TAKING THE REINS
CHRIS BACHALO ON THE X-MEN

TRIPWIRE
LIVING IN AMERICA
ALEX ROSS ON UNCLE SAM

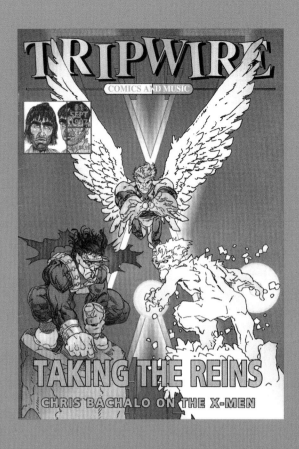

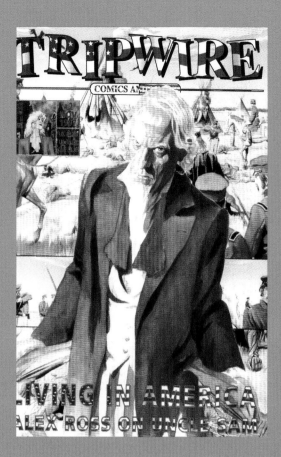

From left to right: Tripwire volume 2#1 sept 1997 X-Men Chris Bachalo cover • Tripwire volume 2 #2 nov 1997 Uncle Sam Alex Ross cover • Tripwire volume 2 #3 dec 1997 Chase Batman JH Williams III cover • Tripwire volume 2 #8 dec 1998 Bryan Talbot Heart Of Empire cover

comics and music
dec/ jan '97-'98 £2.50 uk $3.95 us
Tripwire
LITTLE SISTER
williams and johnson on DC's chase
YEAR OF THE BAT
long halloween
new year's evil
heroes return
bowie: starman?
black grape symposium john lennon spice girls soundgarden

Tripwire
comics and music
ON HER MAJESTY'S
BRITANNIC REQUEST
REM: for buck's sake!

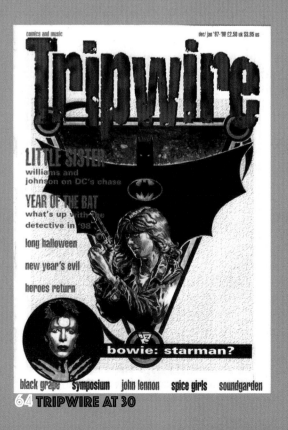

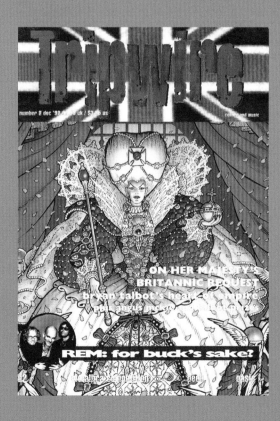

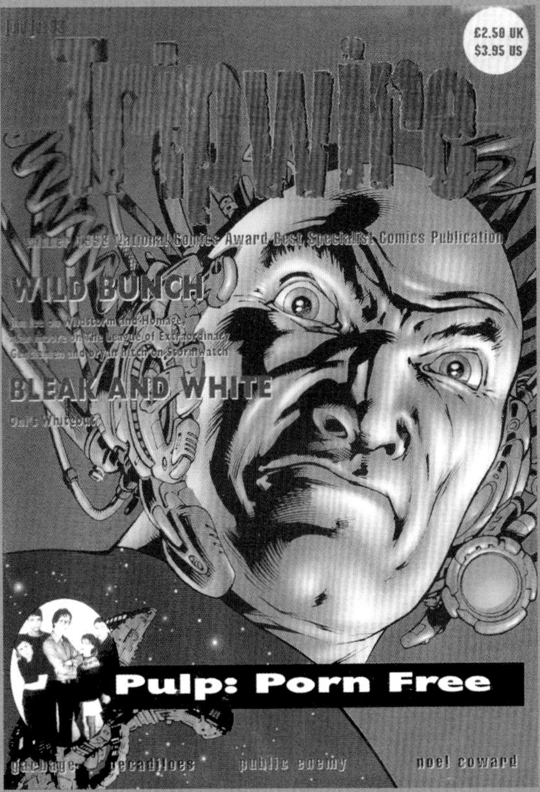
£2.50 UK
$3.95 US
Tripwire
WILD BUNCH
BLEAK AND WHITE
Pulp: Porn Free
public enemy
noel coward

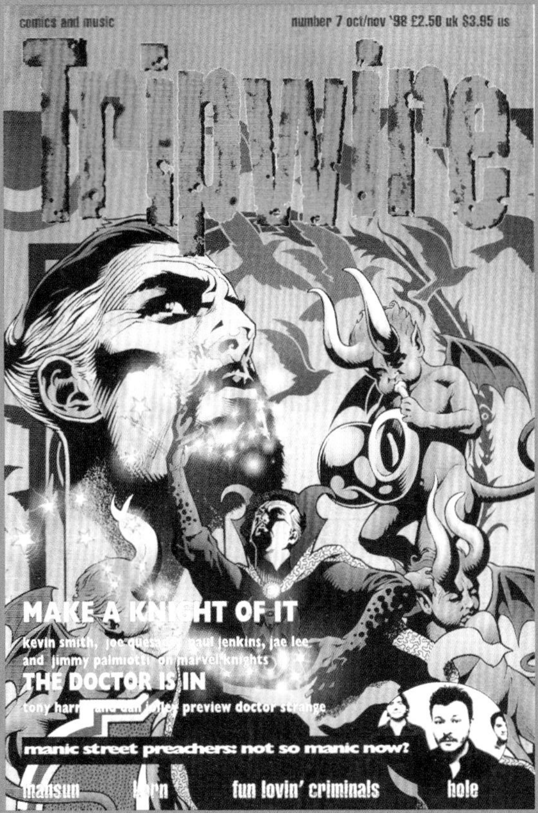
comics and music
number 7 oct/nov '98 £2.50 uk $3.95 us
Tripwire
MAKE A KNIGHT OF IT
THE DOCTOR IS IN
manic street preachers: not so manic now?
fun lovin' criminals
hole

From left to right: Tripwire volume 2#5 June 1998 The Authority Jim Lee cover • Tripwire volume 2 #7 oct 1998 Tony Harris Doctor Strange cover • Tripwire volume 2 #9 feb 1999 Mike Mignola Hellboy cover • Tripwire volume 2 #10 apr1999 JH Williams III Promethea cover

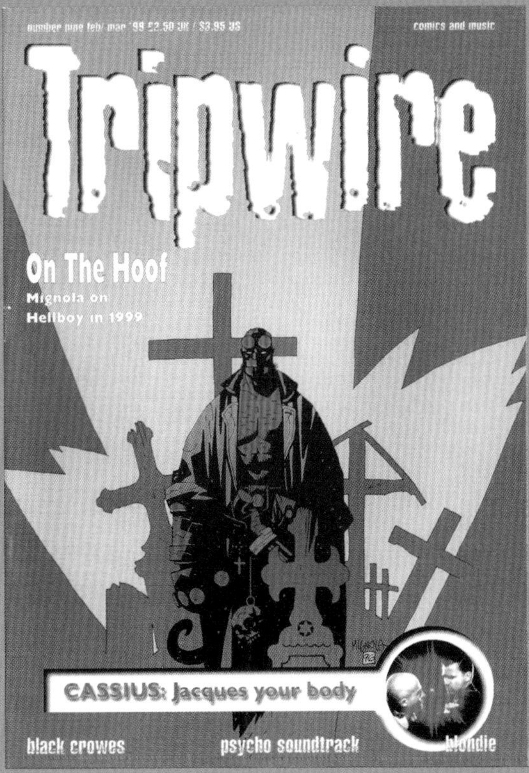
comics and music
Tripwire
On The Hoof
Mignola on
Hellboy in 1999
CASSIUS: Jacques your body
black crowes
psycho soundtrack
blondie

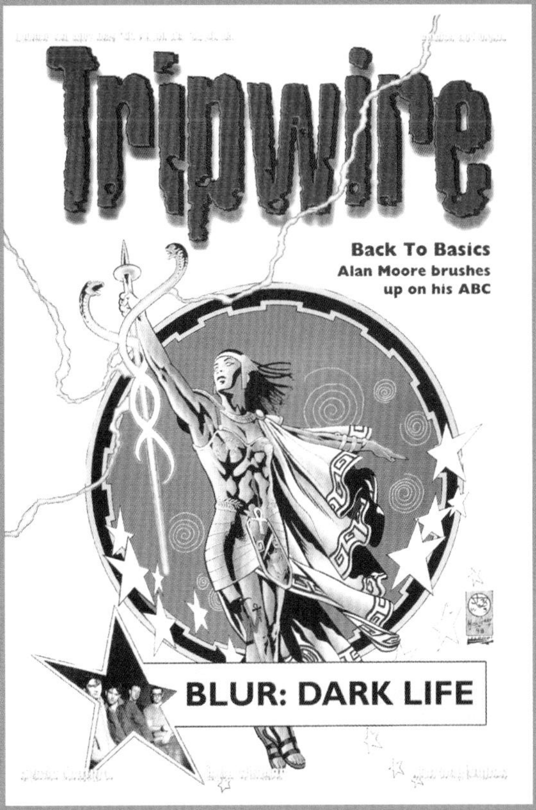
Tripwire
Back To Basics
Alan Moore brushes
up on his ABC
BLUR: DARK LIFE

MUSIC
comics
Tripwire
MAY JUNE
1
INTRODUCING: THE ASTONISHING
X-MEN
Suede:
Gary Glitterati
Catatonia:
No Sleep Til Llandudno
TRIPWIRE MONTHLY
Vol 3#1 May June 99
99p UK $1.75 US

Tripwire
Preaching To The Converted
Steve Dillon and Axel Alonso
on the end of Preacher
PLUS Peter Hogan on
Sandman Presents
witness
austin powers ost
rem live

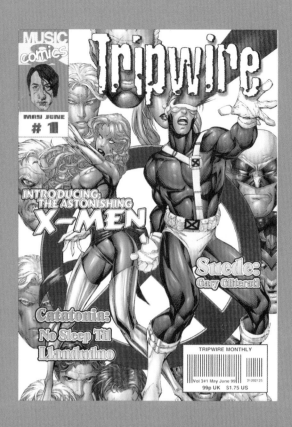

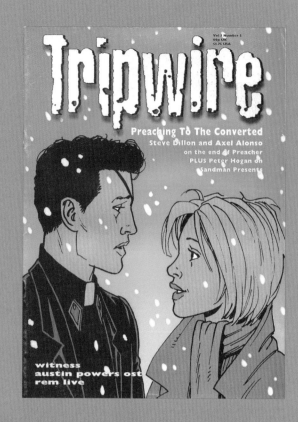

From left to right: Tripwire volume 3#1 May/Jun 2000 Astonishing X-Men cover • Tripwire volume 3#3 Jun/Jul 2000 Steve Dillon Preacher cover • Tripwire volume 3 #4 Aug 2000 David Mack Daredevil cover • Tripwire volume 4 #1 Oct 2000 JH Williams III Promethea cover

Tripwire
comics and music
volume 3 number 4
$2.25 US
99p UK
DANCING WITH THE DEVIL
David Mack on his Daredevil
plus
Paul Jenkins looking back at the Inhumans
Jim Shooter on Unity 2000
Astro Turf: Supergrass

£2.50 UK $3.95 US
U.S. EDITION VOL 4 No. 1
TRIPWIRE
BE ASTOUNDED
BY THE LATEST MUSICAL ENDEAVOURS
BYWATER & JOWETT
BISHOP & DIGGLE
PRESENTS THE FASTEST BLADE OF THE STEPPES
ALAN MOORE WITNESS THE
AMAZING FEATS OF NORTHAMPTON'S GIANT

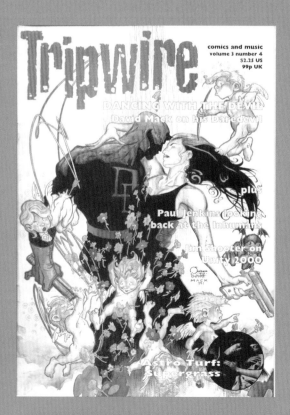

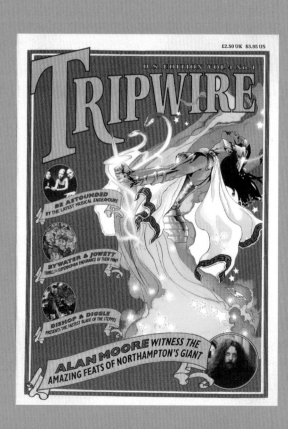

£2.50 UK $3.95 US
VOL 4. No. 2
TRIPWIRE
BRIAN BENDIS
The MAN
WHO WROTE
TOO MUCH
A Baffling
Detective Mystery
THE DUTCH DANDY GANG

THE MIGHTY WORLD OF
£2.50 UK $3.95 US
VOL 4. No. 3
TRIPWIRE
PAUL JENKINS
BLUR
DARK VICTORY

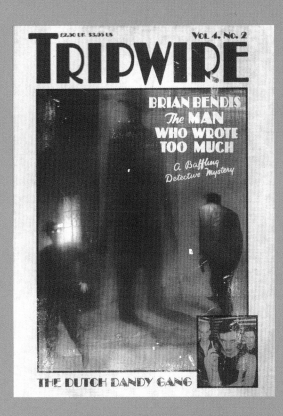

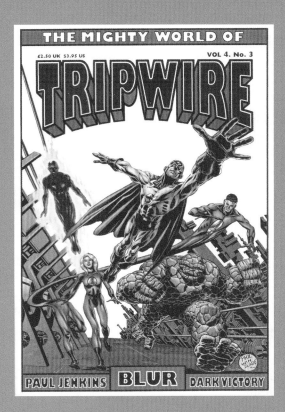

From left to right: Tripwire volume 4#2 Nov 2000 Alex Maleev Sam & Twitch cover • Tripwire volume 4 #3 Dec 2000 Phil Winslade The Sentry cover • Tripwire volume 4#4 Feb 2001 Matt Wagner Grendel cover • Tripwire volume 4 #5 April 2001 Mike Mignola Hellboy cover

£2.50 $3.95 us
Vol. 4 No. 4
Tripwire
The Devil May Care
Matt Wagner on Grendel and more

£2.50 $3.95US. VOL.4. NO.5.
TRIPWIRE
THE WORM TURNS
Mike Mignola
on
Hellboy Conqueror Worm
WILL EISNER
HOWARD CHAYKIN
and
ED HILLYER

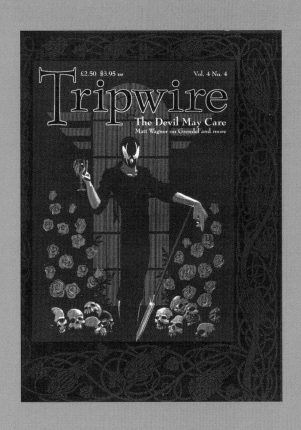

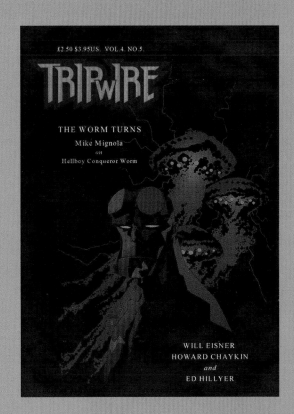

dec/ jan 02
volume four number nine
£2.50 UK/ $3.95 US
tripwire
comics and related culture
SPEAKING FRANKLY
FRANK MILLER on DARK KNIGHT STRIKES AGAIN,
the state of the industry and much more

mar/apr 02
volume four number ten
£2.50 UK/ $3.95 US
tripwire
comics and related culture
STORMY WEATHER
the retooled Wildstorm with editor Scott Dunbier and creators Ed Brubaker, Joe Casey, Sean Phillips, Ashley Wood and Colin Wilson...

Tripwire volume 4#9 Dec 2000/ Jan 2001 Frank Miller Dark Knight Strikes Again cover • Tripwire volume 4#10 March 2001 Sean Phillips Point Blank cover • Tripwire volume 4#11 Jun/ Jul 2002 Alan Moore photo cover • Tripwire volume 5#1 April 2003 Daredevil TV show cover

jun/jul 02
volume four number eleven
£2.50 UK/ $3.95 US
tripwire
the magazine of illustrated erudition
speaks about
THE LEAGUE OF EXTRAORDINARY GENTLEMEN VOLUME TWO, the future of America's Best Comics and much more...

april 2003
£3.50 UK / $5.95 US
TRIPWIRE
COMICS·FILM·TV·ANIMATION·GAMES
THIS ISSUE
Star Trek
CSI
Phil Hale
Hellboy
Judge Dredd
Hellblazer
GOING FOR THE BULLSEYE
Enter The World Of Marvel's Daredevil
NEW

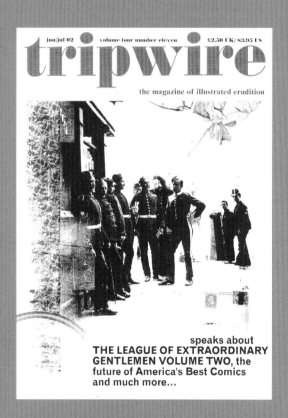

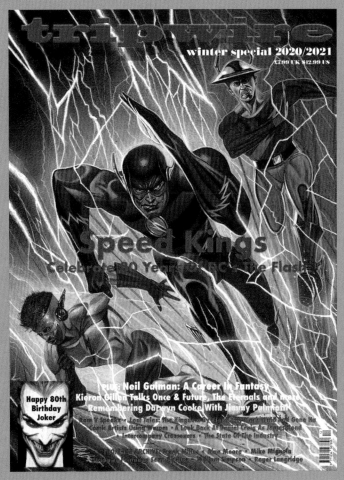

tripwire
winter special 2020/2021
£7.99 UK $12.99 US
Speed Kings
PLUS: Neil Gaiman: A Career In Fantasy
Kieron Gillen Talks Once & Future, The Eternals and More
Remembering Darwyn Cooke With Jimmy Palmiotti
Happy 80th Birthday Joker

tripwire
the genre magazine
£8.99 UK/ $13.99
A HELL OF A RIDE:
DARK HORSE COMICS AT 35
Happy Birthday To Portland's independent powerhouse
B.P.R.D.
PLUS: HAPPY 40TH BIRTHDAY INDY
Drew Struzan Talks Indiana Jones
FANTASTIC FOUR AT 60
Marvel's First Family Hits A Milestone
SHARPER IMAGE
Liam Sharp On A Career In Comics

Tripwire winter special 2020/2021 David Michael Beck Flash 80th anniversary cover • Tripwire winter special 2021 Mike Mignola Dark Horse 35th anniversary cover

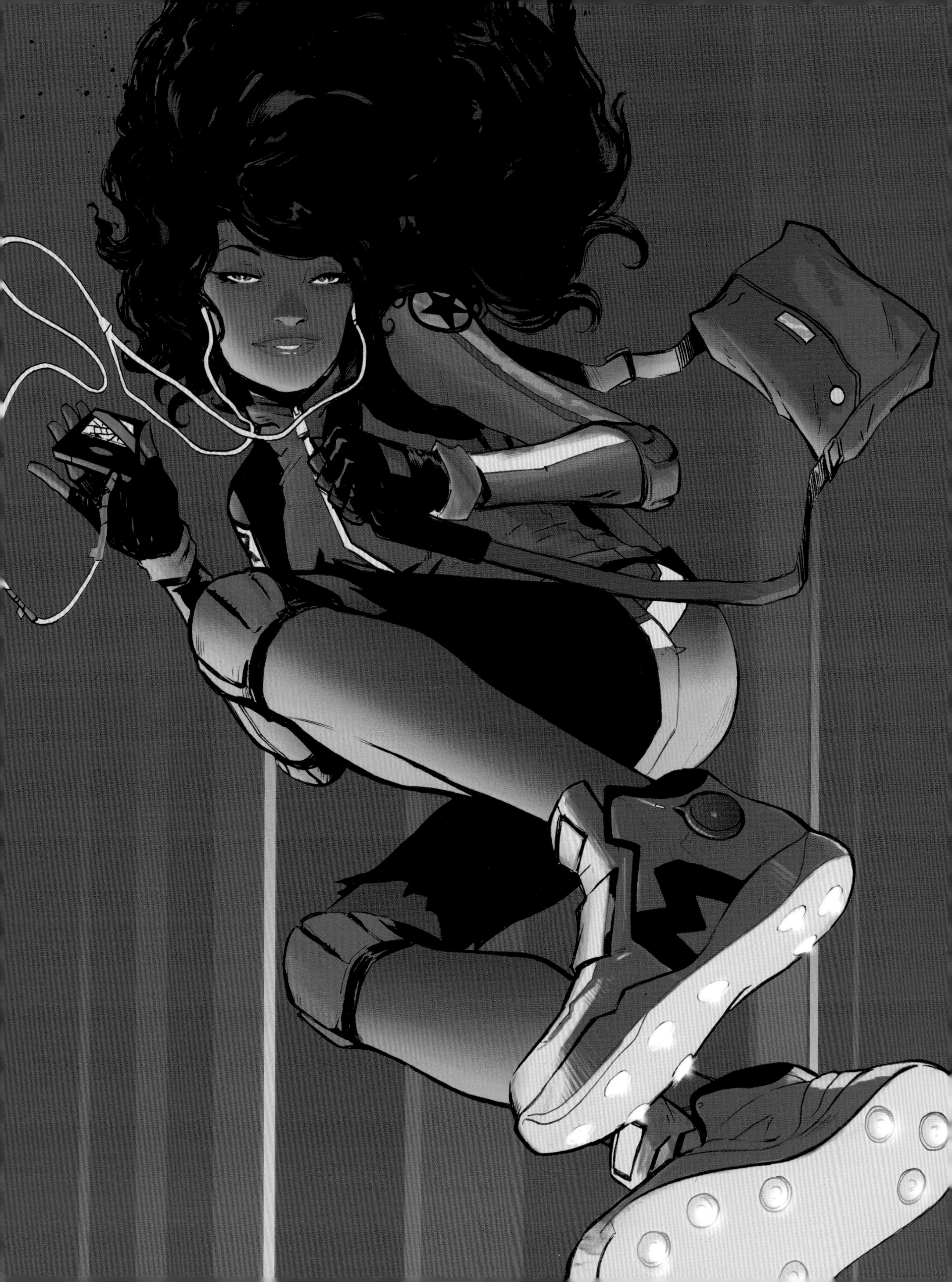

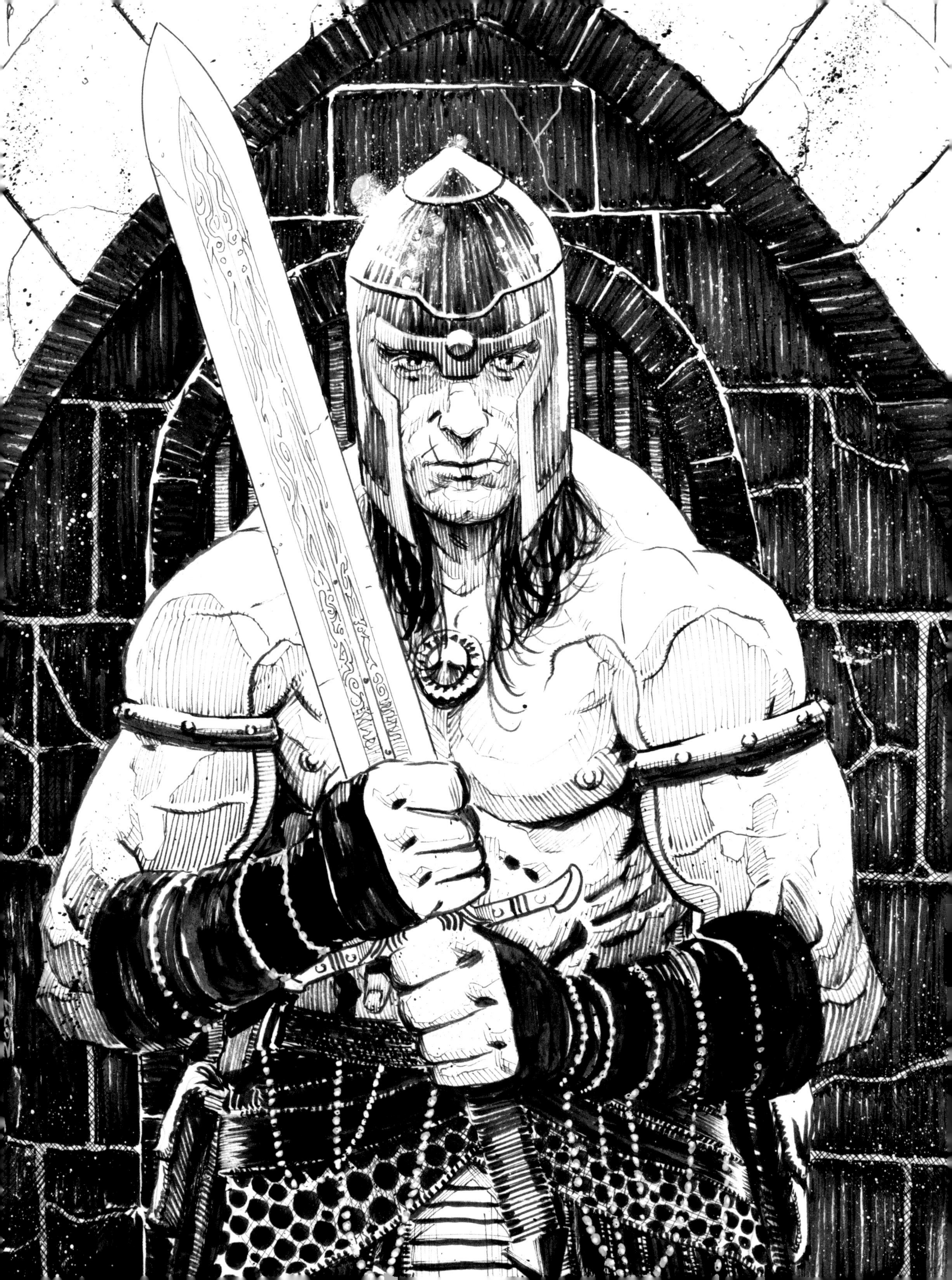

30 YEARS OF TRIPWIRE INTERVIEWS

Here's a selection of quotes taken from 30 years of Tripwire interviews both in print and online with every mover and shaker in comics and related industries

"I've always been a big fan of old-fashioned pulpy, horror fiction. It just got to the point where I needed a character to base these stories around." – Mike Mignola on why he created Hellboy, TRIPWIRE Volume 1 #14, Mid-summer 1996

"I consciously designed this character to be an old-fashioned good guy and so yes it's ironic that he's from hell" – Mike Mignola on why he created Hellboy, TRIPWIRE Volume 1 #14, Mid-summer 1996

"I want to do comics because they're the one place where I can put my ideas on paper."– Mignola on why he continues to work in comics, TRIPWIRE Volume 4#5 May 2001

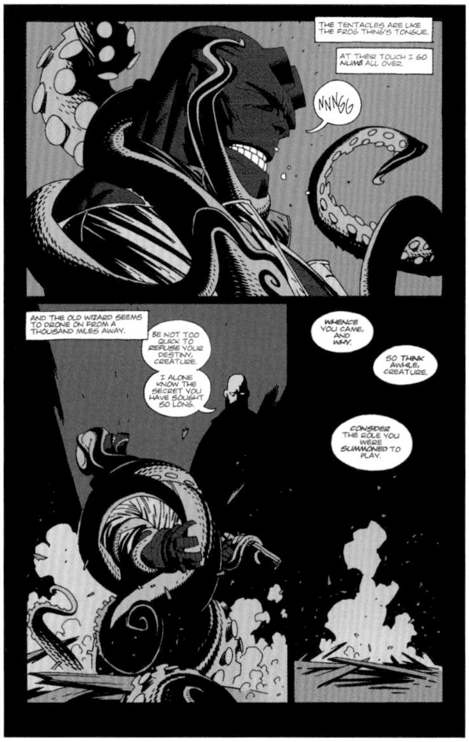
THE TENTACLES ARE LIKE THE FROG THING'S TONGUE.
AT THEIR TOUCH I GO NUMB ALL OVER.
NNNGG
AND THE OLD WIZARD SEEMS TO DRONE ON FROM A THOUSAND MILES AWAY.
BE NOT TOO QUICK TO REFUSE YOUR DESTINY, CREATURE.
I ALONE KNOW THE SECRET YOU HAVE SOUGHT SO LONG.
WHENCE YOU CAME, AND WHY.
SO THINK AWHILE, CREATURE.
CONSIDER THE ROLE YOU WERE SUMMONED TO PLAY.

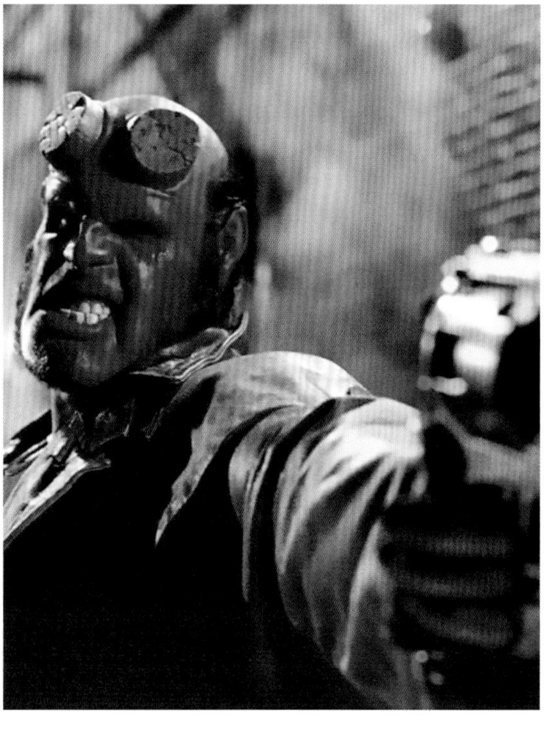

"It feels like I have won the lottery. I was content to have no involvement but Del Toro wanted it to be Mike Mignola's *Hellboy*. So they wanted me. Del Toro's *Blade 2* was a warm-up for Hellboy. This film is being done because of *Blade 2*, that film gave Del Toro the greenlight, and if it didn't greenlight then *Hellboy* would never have been made" – Mike Mignola on Hellboy the movie from TRIPWIRE Volume 5#1, April 2003

"I think Guillermo and I, we worked very closely on the first one. I've worked very closely with him on the second one also. I've been in preproduction for two solid months with him. But my role is a little different. In the first one, it was figuring out how to translate Hellboy into a film. Now that problem has been solved and I'm still there to do some really rough early design stuff but I am real busy trying to run everything else and ever since I saw *Pan's Labyrinth*, I thought 'You don't need me.' I don't want to get in the way. Not that I had any doubts about Guillermo doing the first film but certainly after Pan's Labyrinth, I'm just going 'You do what you do.' I had nothing to do with Pan's Labyrinth. I want you to make THAT movie again', so all I've been doing is whispering in Guillermo's ear for the last couple of months. 'remember Hellboy is your first post- Pan's Labyrinth film? You set the bar pretty high' so

I'm just thrilled..." – Mignola on Hellboy 2, TRIPWIRE Annual 2007

"With this series, I've looked back at the various mythologies that have provided models for such characters as the Flash to Hawkman and onwards but beyond that, I've also considered characters and archetypes created during the Victorian adventure- fiction of the 1900s." – Alan Moore on League of Extraordinary Gentlemen, TRIPWIRE Volume 2#5, May/June 1998

"The Victorian period saw the beginnings of a variety of archetypes that have since become commonplace in the comic book medium. For example, I remember Stan Lee and Jack Kirby acknowledging that the Hulk was originally modeled after Robert Louis Stevenson's Dr Jekyll and Mr Hyde, while the Invisible Girl, as well as all invisible characters, were rooted in HG Wells' *Invisible Man*, a book first published in 1897." –Alan Moore on League of Extraordinary Gentlemen, TRIPWIRE Volume 2#5,May/June 1998

"When I was writing it, I became obsessive and decided that if there were any walk-on characters, they would all be from somewhere in the fiction of the nineteenth century. We mention Anna Kypo, also known as Nana, the murders in the Rue Morgue and we've even got some characters from *the Pearl*, the pornographic magazine. It is a big toyshop because we can basically deal with any characters in literature."– Moore on

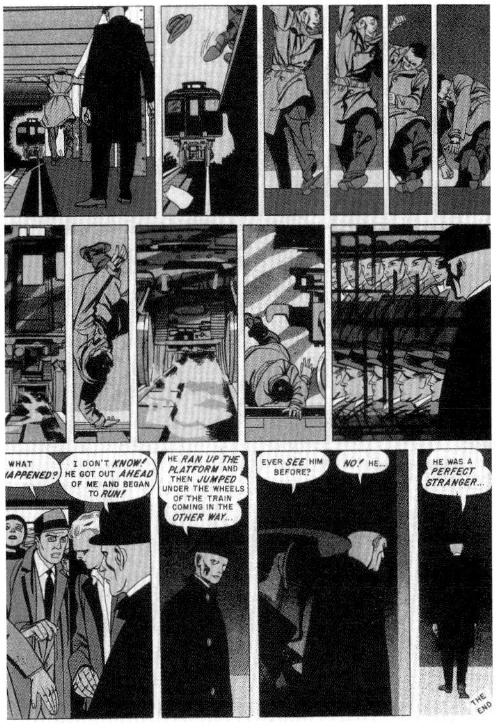
WHAT HAPPENED?
I DON'T KNOW! HE GOT OUT AHEAD OF ME AND BEGAN TO RUN!
HE RAN UP THE PLATFORM AND THEN JUMPED UNDER THE WHEELS OF THE TRAIN COMING IN THE OTHER WAY...
EVER SEE HIM BEFORE?
NO! HE...
HE WAS A PERFECT STRANGER...
THE END

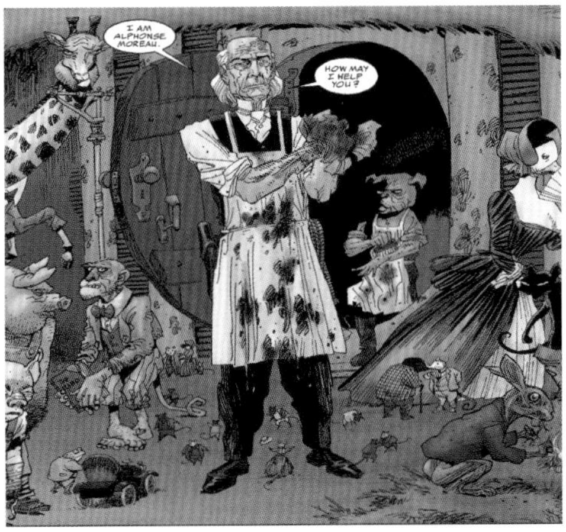
I AM ALPHONSE MOREAU
HOW MAY I HELP YOU?

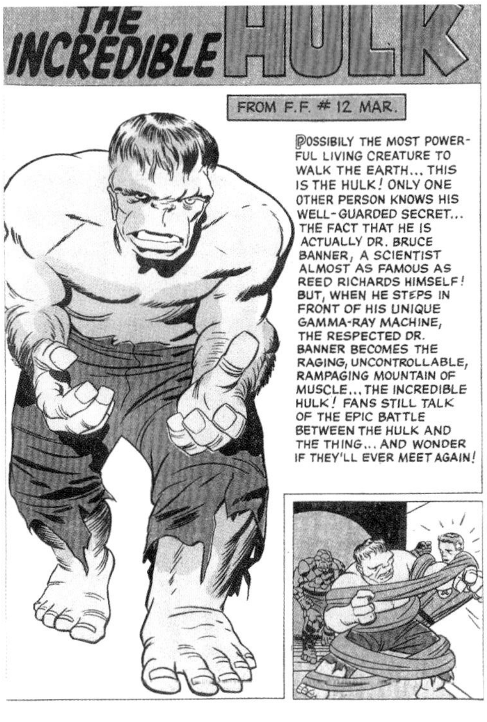
THE INCREDIBLE HULK
FROM F.F. # 12 MAR.
POSSIBILY THE MOST POWERFUL LIVING CREATURE TO WALK THE EARTH... THIS IS THE HULK! ONLY ONE OTHER PERSON KNOWS HIS WELL-GUARDED SECRET... THE FACT THAT HE IS ACTUALLY DR. BRUCE BANNER, A SCIENTIST ALMOST AS FAMOUS AS REED RICHARDS HIMSELF! BUT, WHEN HE STEPS IN FRONT OF HIS UNIQUE GAMMA-RAY MACHINE, THE RESPECTED DR. BANNER BECOMES THE RAGING, UNCONTROLLABLE, RAMPAGING MOUNTAIN OF MUSCLE... THE INCREDIBLE HULK! FANS STILL TALK OF THE EPIC BATTLE BETWEEN THE HULK AND THE THING... AND WONDER IF THEY'LL EVER MEET AGAIN!

explaining the cameos in the first *League of Extraordinary Gentlemen* series, TRIPWIRE Special A, November 1998

"Comics these days are too divided up. There used to be an incredible range of stories, everything from *Little Nemo* to Bernie Krigstein's *Master Race*. It was a rich field. It seems to me that we don't really have entry level comics. It's definitely true to say that we don't have that many adult comics for people over thirty either, apart from some Fantagraphics and Drawn & Quarterly material." A League of His Own? – Alan Moore bemoaning the limited choices for readers at the time, TRIPWIRE Special A, November 1998

"I suppose that people could accuse me of wallowing in those elements under the guise of postmodernism and they'd probably be right. I don't think that you get an unpleasant atmosphere after reading the stories. It's more British attitudes that are being pilloried rather than the targets of those attitudes. What makes it funny is this idea of a supremacist Britain that ruled the entire world." – Moore talking about some of the more contentious content in *League of Extraordinary Gentlemen*, Special A, November 1998

"I was down in Wales minding the chickens during the time that the whole thing blew up. Jim Lee is a gentleman. He came over here, rather than do it over the phone or get an underling to do it, with Scott Dunbier to talk to me. ...He did have trepidations because I think that they had both been worried about my response. When I got out of the cab at the station and he saw that I had my stick with me, he told me that I half expected me to beat him like a red haired stepchild."– Moore talking about the sale of Wildstorm to DC, TRIPWIRE Special A, November 1998

"All you've got to do with these ideas is strip away some of the scar tissue that people have allowed to accumulate. Ideas don't get old, it's only us that get jaded."–Alan Moore on his approach to *League of Extraordinary Gentlemen*, TRIPWIRE Special A, November 1998

"Everybody goes on about superheroes as if they're characters. They're not. They're a name and a chest emblem.

"I think that, as the characters grow, the story really starts to work well, they start to tell you things about themselves. I know it sounds a bit pretentious and a bit arty but the writer becomes a vessel for the characters" – PETER MILLIGAN, Spiked Milligan, Volume 1 #2, Sept

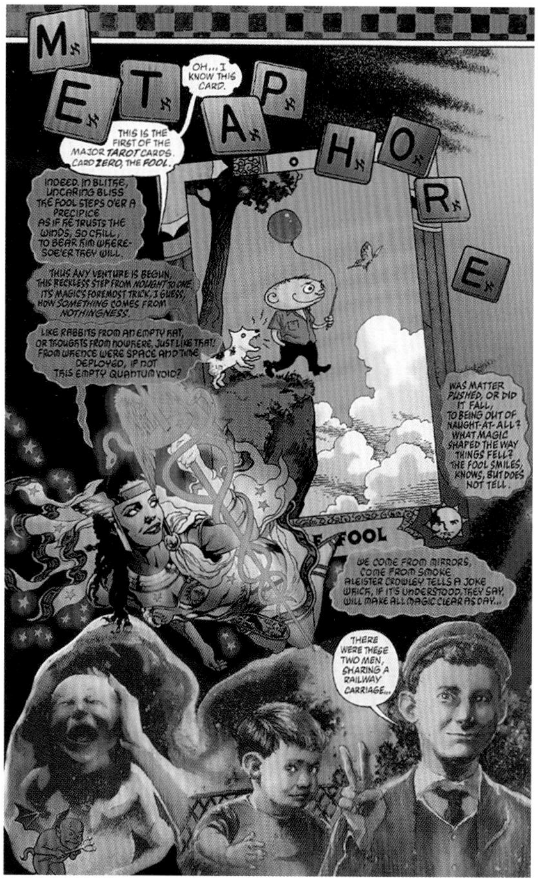
METAPHORE
OH... I KNOW THIS CARD.
THIS IS THE FIRST OF THE MAJOR TAROT CARDS. CARD ZERO, THE FOOL.
INDEED. IN BLITHE, UNCARING BLISS THE FOOL STEPS O'ER A PRECIPICE AS IF HE TRUSTS THE WINDS, SO CHILL, TO BEAR HIM WHERE-SOE'ER THEY WILL.
THUS ANY VENTURE IS BEGUN, THIS RECKLESS STEP FROM NOUGHT TO ONE. IT'S MAGIC'S FOREMOST TRICK, I GUESS, HOW SOMETHING COMES FROM NOTHINGNESS.
LIKE RABBITS FROM AN EMPTY HAT, OR THOUGHTS FROM NOWHERE, JUST LIKE THAT! FROM WHENCE WERE SPACE AND TIME DEPLOYED, IF NOT THIS EMPTY QUANTUM VOID?
WAS MATTER PUSHED, OR DID IT FALL, TO BEING OUT OF NAUGHT-AT-ALL? WHAT MAGIC SHAPED THE WAY THINGS FELL? THE FOOL SMILES, KNOWS, BUT DOES NOT TELL.
FOOL
WE COME FROM MIRRORS, COME FROM SMOKE ALEISTER CROWLEY TELLS A JOKE WHICH, IF IT'S UNDERSTOOD, THEY SAY, WILL MAKE ALL MAGIC CLEAR AS DAY...
THERE WERE THESE TWO MEN, SHARING A RAILWAY CARRIAGE...

Someone like Batman, he's an icon and back when you started reading the early DC, you'd have three stories in one issue of Detective and none of them would acknowledge that the others even happened." – Moore on creating America's Best Comics, TRIPWIRE Volume 2#10

"They know what my position is with this – I don't want any money from it, I want the money to go to Dave Gibbons and I want my name taken off of it. If they do that I will not make a squeak about the film. If they go for some other novelty option like they did with *V For Vendetta* then I'm in for another year of excoriating them in every interview I do until they remove my name from it."– Moore on *Watchmen* the film, TRIPWIRE Annual 2007

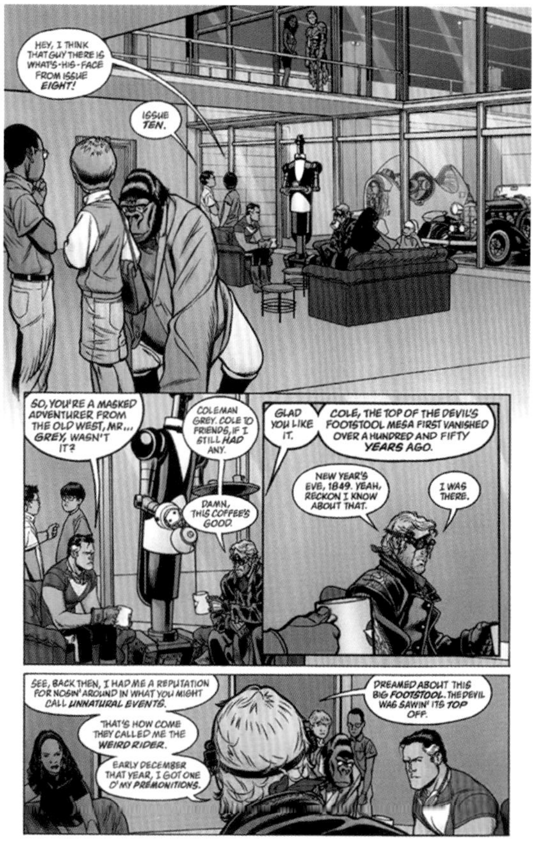
HEY, I THINK THAT GUY THERE IS WHAT'S-HIS-FACE FROM ISSUE EIGHT!
ISSUE TEN.
SO, YOU'RE A MASKED ADVENTURER FROM THE OLD WEST, MR... GREY, WASN'T IT?
COLEMAN GREY. COLE TO FRIENDS, IF I STILL HAD ANY.
DAMN, THIS COFFEE'S GOOD.
GLAD YOU LIKE IT.
COLE, THE TOP OF THE DEVIL'S FOOTSTOOL MESA FIRST VANISHED OVER A HUNDRED AND FIFTY YEARS AGO.
NEW YEAR'S EVE, 1849. YEAH, RECKON I KNOW ABOUT THAT.
I WAS THERE.
SEE, BACK THEN, I HAD ME A REPUTATION FOR NOSIN' AROUND IN WHAT YOU MIGHT CALL UNNATURAL EVENTS.
THAT'S HOW COME THEY CALLED ME THE WEIRD RIDER.
EARLY DECEMBER THAT YEAR, I GOT ONE O' MY PREMONITIONS.
DREAMED ABOUT THIS BIG FOOTSTOOL. THE DEVIL WAS SAWIN' ITS TOP OFF.

"I'd prefer to be a starving artist somewhere, to be honest. Just a bit of food to eat, enough room and space to throw paint on huge canvasses, have exhibitions adn talk to pretentious arseholes, you know? 'Cause there's something that really fascinates me about the whole art world." – SIMON BISLEY, The Bisley/ Morrison Tapes Part One, Volume 1 #6, Feb 1994

"But the thing is that basically you do these books, no matter if these guys recognise you or you're on the Late Show and the book's gonna sell 2,000 copies at most if it's lucky. Most modern literature is selling something like 2,000 copies when it comes out. I mean, even the lowest-selling comic that I've done has never sold less than 35,000. The sales are so much higher in comics and you're reaching more people."–Grant Morrison, The Bisley Morrison Tapes Volume 1#6 Feb 1994

"It wouldn't surprise me if someone comes up with an idea which then enters the field and begins to resonate, causing other people to have the same idea, in the same way that experimental rats learming a maze in California influence the morphic field of all rats in China to learn the same maze."– GRANT MORRISON, The Invisible Man Part One Volume 1 #7, Sept 1994 (Maggie Knight)

"You have to teach yourself to at least be able to imagine what it would be like to be the servant of a Lovecraftian ultra-terrestrial cult or a fifteen-year-old boy with no money and no future. Bad writers write every character as themselves and every narrative voice the same, which is the writer's own."– GRANT MORRISON, Volume 1 #7, Sept 1994, (Maggie Knight)

"We worked quite closely together while we were setting this up. Working from vague suggestions from me, Steve [Dillon] became entirely responsible for the look of the characters. The only time I stuck my oar in was on the Saint of Killers. Steve wanted him to look like Lee Marvin but I wanted a more Clint Eastwood look. In the end, he became an amalgamation. He's got Lee Marvin's haggard looks but he's got Clint's killer eyes." – GARTH ENNIS on Preacher, "Now Hear The Word of The Lord Volume 1#9, Apr 1995(Tim Pilcher)

DC
VERTIGO
THE INVISIBLES
SEP 94
$2.95 US
GRANT MORRISON
STEVE YEOWELL

HELLO?
HELLO? IS THERE SOMEONE DOWN THERE?
YEAH. UNDER HERE. I CAN'T MOVE!
OH. WELL, HOLD ON. I'LL GET SOMEONE.
DON'T GET SOMEONE. GET ME OUT OF HERE.
HANG ON. I'M COMING DOWN.
I CAN SEE THE PROBLEM. THERE'S A REFRIGERATOR ON YOUR LEGS.
CAN YOU MOVE IT?
I DON'T KNOW. CAN YOU STILL BREATHE?
YEAH. SORT OF.
DUMB PLACE TO GO EXPLORING.
WHO ASKED YOUR OPINION?
OH. GEE. I DIDN'T REALIZE I WASN'T WANTED. WELL, NICE MEETING YOU.
HAVE FUN UNDER THERE.
14

"I see art as a journey, it's always progressing in some direction or another. It's something I'm very conscious of and I'm always aware that I'm changing it. I look at other artists to see what they're doing."– CHRIS BACHALO, Death Becomes Him, Volume 1 #11, Winter 1995

"I'm just a fan of art in general. Anything from sculpture to Renaissance art, Leonardo and Michelangelo, Botticelli, Titian, Van Eyck and I really enjoy the French Impressionists."–CHRIS BACHALO, Death Becomes Him, Volume 1 #11, Winter 1995

"The first battle was with myself. I didn't bother in school. I wrote short stories and and I was good at drawing and I was in a dream world. Not unlike Simone in [*Girl*]. It never occurred to me to actually work...The problem with the working class background is that it can be

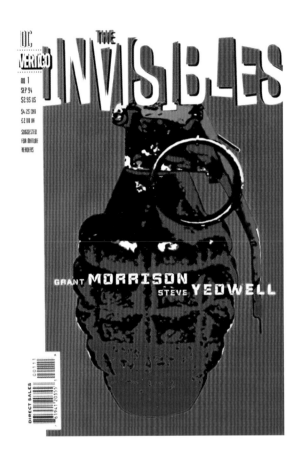

quite closed."–PETER MILLIGAN on *Girl*, The Changing Man, Volume 1 #13, Summer 1996

"Coming from someone who is so socially well adjusted it is quite strange, isn't it? I guess because heir madness is a mirror to the society that makes them so. But perhaps because they are on the outside of society that they sometimes allow us a view." –PETER MILLIGAN on his obsession with outcasts, The Changing Man, Volume 1 #13, Summer 1996

"I think there's a British sensibility to my writing that still holds true even though I'm in America. I think that the roots to my artistic intentions or whatever that I went into comics with when I lived in England, are still present in *Starman* and in the work I do. I think people of my generation, all of us are a little bit the children of Alan Moore."– JAMES ROBINSON, An Englishman in Opal City (Christopher Woodward), Volume 1 #16, Spring 1997

"I've only been to Miami once. It seemed to fit just right for this noir story. The strange thing is that Miami seems to be the wrong place

WHAT'S THE MATTER? YOU SHY OF GIRLS?
YOU GOT EL ESCULTOR VICTIMS BEEN THROUGH THAT CLUB...? BARRIO GIRLS WHO SHOULDN'T BE ABLE TO AFFORD THE COVER...?
YOU NEED TO KNOW WHO FINANCED THEM... AND MAYBE MY LITTLE HAITIAN, TOO?
SO. SWALLOW, HOMBRE. ASK ME?
GET OUT! YOU'RE STINKING UP MY CAR.
GIMME A BREAK. THIS BEACH IS FOR LOS ANIMALES...
SO. YOU STILL GOT ONE SHOE TO BEAT THEM OFF.
YOU'RE SUCH A BITCH, HECTOR.
BUT THEN, AIN'T WE ALL?
BEST GET YOUR SHIT TOGETHER HERE, ATLANTA...
23

for a noir story because it's all neon and pastel colours with tropical heat. But it works quite well. Miami for me is the cheap end of American culture, which gives it a perverse attraction."– JAMIE DELANO on *2020 Visions*, Grave New World, Volume 1 #16, Spring 1997

"Sometimes I get frustrated with comics just because, like any medium, it has its limitations and sometimes I want to do things that you can't necessarily do in a comic book. I'm underway with a novel. I've written about three or four chapters. When I find a bit of time and when I'm in the right mood, I do another chapter. I've been thinking about TV or drama but I was put off by *Neverwhere*."– JAMIE DELANO, Grave New World, Volume 1 #16, Spring 1997

"The problem is I've been so heavily engaged in cutting new ground that the taste for going back over old territory no longer stays with me. While I've been doing Spirit covers [for Kitchen Sink's reprint series], I've never really wanted to continue doing it." – WILL EISNER, Spirit in the Sky (Steve Darnall), Summer Special 1997

"I really think now I needed the distance on

it to do it correctly. I'd have to say I was able to get back to Mage with that sort of distance whereas I think if I had done it then it would have resembled Grendel more than I would have liked."–MATT WAGNER on *Mage: The Hero Defined*, Magic Circle, Summer Special 1997

"It's the story that everybody tells a zillion times. The key to making it truly mythic is to personalise it like Mike [Mignola] has done with Hellboy, like I'm trying to do here with Mage. When it becomes an internal quest, it becomes mythic."–MATT WAGNER on *Mage: The Hero Defined*, Magic Circle, Summer Special 1997

"The feel is traditional Western but there are anachronistic elements, modern elements that I'm looking at through the lens of that genre. I think that genre fiction done right can tell any kind of story."–JEFF MARIOTTE on *Desperadoes*, A Change Of Image, Volume 2 #1, Sept 1997

"The main reason why we work together so often is that he is very much the cinematographer to my director."–JEPH LOEB on working with Tim Sale, Bat To Basics, Volume 2 #3, Dec 1997 - Jan 1998

"Since *The Godfather* made the family system work so well, particularly in the case of characters like Tessio and Clemenza, we decided to utilise it."–JEPH LOEB on

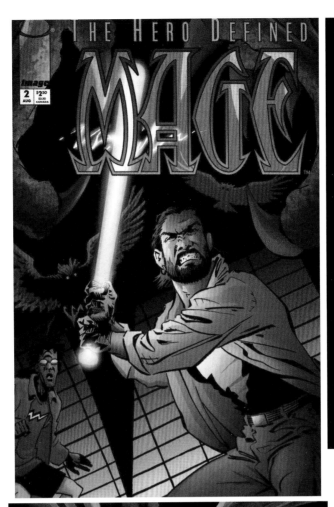

"It's the story that everybody tells a zillion times. The key to making it truly mythic is to personalise it like Mike [Mignola] has done with Hellboy, like I'm trying to do here with Mage. When it becomes an internal quest, it becomes mythic" – MATT WAGNER on Mage: The Hero Defined, Magic Circle, Summer Special 1997

parallels between *The Godfather* and *Batman: The Long Halloween*, Bat To Basics, Volume 2 #3, Dec 1997 - Jan 1998

"The characters that we fancied creating new stuff with were always the characters that we considered second tier and they just haven't had their moment in the sun. These characters require a lot of motivation and creative juices from the writers and artists to keep it fresh and interesting." –JOE QUESADA on setting up the Marvel Knights line, Knights To Remember, Volume 2 #7, Oct-Nov 1998

"I've told this one in a completely different way [to Luther Arkwright]. The first book was very self-consciously experimental and I wasn't interested in doing the same thing again. The story's a lot more linear and accessible. I tried to write a classic adventure story, which is actually a great deal of fun."–BRYAN TALBOT on *Heart of Empire*, Historical Differences, Volume 2 #7, Oct-Nov 1998

"Again with the cynic bullshit. I think people misname an honest, no bullshit approach to life as cynicism. As I have said before, I'm not a cynic – I'm a romantic realist. I may have mellowed a bit in the last few years, but only on the inside. What is misperceived as cynicism is actually a healthy scepticism."– HOWARD CHAYKIN on that 'cynic' question, Cold Warriors, Volume 4#5, May 2001

"[Milton Caniff] was a tremendously strong influence, as was George Herrimann. Caniff, Herrimann and Segar [the creator of *Popeye*–ed]. These were the men I was studying most assiduously because I felt that they made the greatest underlying contribution to the work I did."–WILL EISNER on who influenced him, Speak Easy, Volume 4#5, May 2001

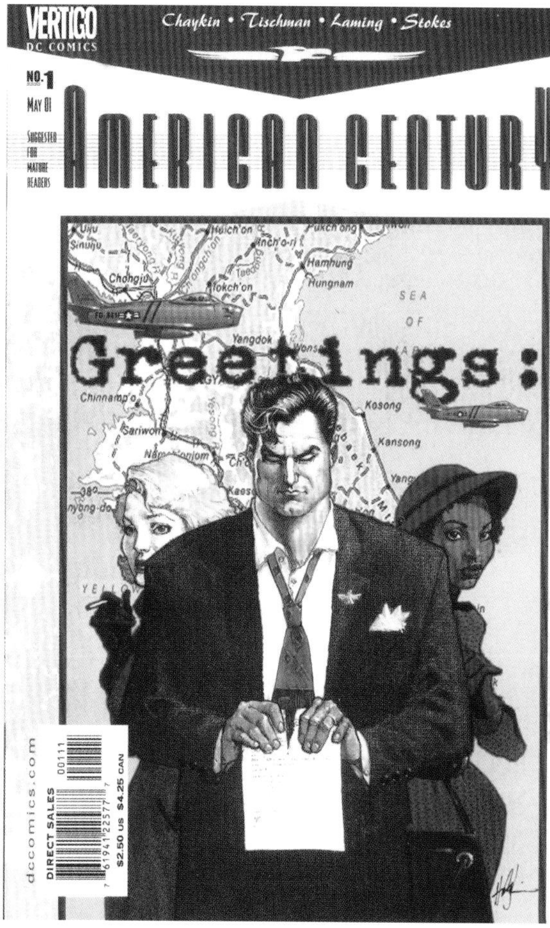
VERTIGO
DC COMICS
Chaykin • Tischman • Laming • Stokes
NO.1
MAY 01
SUGGESTED FOR MATURE READERS
AMERICAN CENTURY
Greetings:

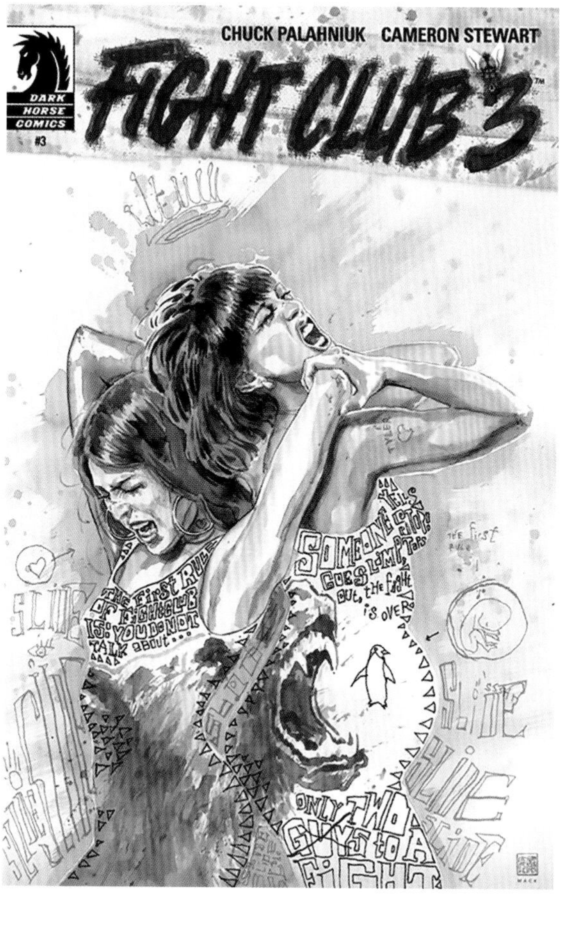
CHUCK PALAHNIUK CAMERON STEWART
DARK HORSE COMICS
#3
FIGHT CLUB 3

"Both the novel and the film have established their audiences. They'd both be tough acts to follow, that's why the third interpretation had to be as a comic. I've since fallen in love with the ordeal of writing a comic script, and the license it allows me. I can depict things that would be forbidden in film – the army of dying kids from FC2 – and depict things that would seem too unreal and phony if presented in just prose. It's that ability to portray a Little Nemo in Dreamland fantasy that prompted me to do Fight Club 3. Picasso said something like Art is the lie that tells the truth better than the truth. I wanted to use comics to depict an Art Bell, Ground Zero, late night-radio type of story using the established Fight Club characters. Our fantasies tell a greater truth about us." - CHUCK PALAHNIUK on *Fight Club 3*, Return To The Fight Club, tripwiremagazine.co.uk, December 2018

"The thing about movie posters is that it's very different from other products. They only have one weekend to sell the idea to come and see what we've done. There's other things like the trailers that keep people interested. But what the poster is supposed to be for initially is to excite people about the possibilities of the movie. So a poster has to tell people something about the spirit of what the director and the story had in mind. So I think a good poster is one that does that: inspires, excites and gives people a sense of the product. But for me personally because when I was doing it, I always had in mind the commercial uses of it" – DREW STRUZAN, Movie Masterclass, TRIPWIRE 54, Summer 2010

"I had a good classic education, drawing and painting. I learnt to paint and draw in all different kinds of styles historically and modern. Then I got into the industry and that's why I didn't have my own style. I could paint like anybody and when I was young, they would say 'We need a Rockwell and he's not around any more' so I did a Rockwell. If they said: 'We need something that looks Art Nouveau' so I read up on the style which took me to Mucha. When I was working in the record industry, a book came out on JC Leyendecker and he'd been kind of forgotten over the years but when the book came out he became very popular again. So everybody wanted a Leyendecker for their artwork. So that's where my influences came from. So I paint in many styles and techniques but it was the industry that required certain ways of painting; they wanted naturalism." – DREW STRUZAN, Movie MasterclassTRIPWIRE 54, Summer 2010

"It's good I had this much time away from superheroes. Off doing *Sin City* and *300* and *Martha Washington* with Dave Gibbons and all that crazy stuff with Geof Darrow, I got to travel wide and far. So, to turn around and take another gander at Superman and Batman and Wonder Woman and the rest, well, I can only say I have fresh eyes. Fresh as a little kid's."- Frank Miller on returning

TIM ROBBINS
MORGAN FREEMAN
THE SHAWSHANK REDEMPTION
10TH ANNIVERSARY
CASTLE ROCK ENTERTAINMENT

I'M DONE TALKING.
GET OUT OF MY CAVE.

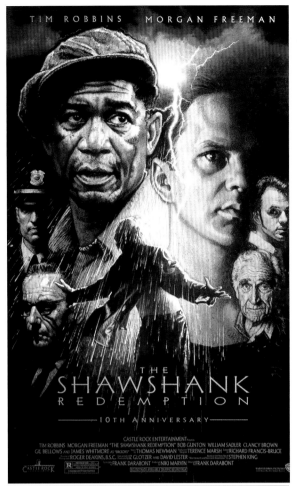

to superheroes for *Dark Knight Strikes Again*, TRIPWIRE Volume 4#9, December 2001

"Batman's one of the few gods in the superhero pantheon. Most of the rest –Spider-Man, The Flash, etc., – fit the classical definition of heroes, not gods. They haven't the same stature. Zeus may have fathered them, but they have human mothers. They haven't the stature of gods. But Batman has that stature. And he's the only superhero god with no overtly superhuman power. He's the dark, passionate, volcanic god, Nietzsche's Dionysus– in conflict with Apollo, the god of reason and order, aka Superman. That's one side of Batman. Then there's the Year One Batman, the young, rough-and-tumble crimefighter who exists among us, who is one of us, a man who might've been normal but for his parents' murder. A guy driven by that calamity to hunt down criminals. A vigilante, but a human one. A guy who makes mistakes, who is kind of disturbing to be around, not the kind of guy you'd want to have a pint with, necessarily. But he manages to do the right thing and save the right people when the chips are down. Those are just two of my versions of Batman, and I'm just one among many others who have a take or two on Batman. A great character." Frank Miller on the different approaches to

Batman, TRIPWIRE Volume 4#9, December 2001

"My inspirations are vastly different and innumerable, some of whom are the illustrators from the 20th century, like Mc Ginnis, Cornwell and the others. I find valuable inspiration in even the minute details of brushwork or patterns and the hard to perceive balance and grace of an overall composition such as in Mucha's work, borrow these little things I love, learn from them and re-invent them in my own way." – Jeremy Mann on his influences, A Life Lived In Art, tripwiremagazine.co.uk, April 2016

"Artists need to grow and change and artists need to create the things which resound to them the most in the changing times of their lives. Having gone from suburbia to the big city at the time when I was studying art, the excitement of those new surroundings infused themselves into the paintings I was creating. An artist can paint anything they desire in their own style, or voice, and find it not only liberating, but exciting through the struggle to that realisation. And, secondly, an artist should paint mostly the things they love (in terms of: inspired by, interested in, and infused with a passion for). The last few years, having moved from the city to a house in suburbs again, living in a more solitary state, my desires have turned inward

"Cityscapes have qualities I love to paint for reasons other than figures and will forever be a large part of me, but these days the balance has shifted to these beautiful creatures of melancholy a shift which I am aware of in self-reflection which lets me know I'm on the right bumpy path." – JEREMY MANN, Inside The Mind Of A Fine Art Original

to the worlds of emotional connection, dreams, stories, and all the mish-muck our torrid little dramas play during our time on stage. Cityscapes have qualities I love to paint for reasons other than figures and will forever be a large part of me, but these days the balance has shifted to these beautiful creatures of melancholy, a shift which I am aware of in self-reflection which lets me know I'm on the right bumpy path." – Jeremy Mann on how artists should change and evolve, Inside The Mind Of A Fine Art Original, tripwiremagazine.co.uk, Jan 2018

"Gil Kane was my first serious art crush. I loved his work from the moment I became aware of it, back in 1960, on the Silver Age revival of *Green Lantern*. I never did any actual hands-on work for Gil –trust me when I say it–to call my work inept is to credit it with far more value than it merited. I ran errands for Gil, and listened to and absorbed the monologue that ran from the beginning to the end of a work day. Gil was a deeply opinionated man, but unlike opinionated people these days, he was also profoundly well informed. The year I spent working for him so utterly informs my way of thinking – about the creative process of comics, as well as just about everything else in my life and experience. The only way I can imagine repaying this debt is to pass it on to others in kind.

Gil was a difficult man, with complex, not to mention slippery ethics, but I loved him dearly, warts and all, and miss him an awful lot." - Howard Chaykin on his relationship with his mentor Gil Kane, Changing The Rules Of The Game, tripwiremagazine.co.uk, 2016

"In the first place, while I believed otherwise at the time, *[American] Flagg!* is not a mainstream comic book. Rather, it was my first serious attempt to synergise graphic ideas, narrative themes and visual syntax into a cohesive whole.
Even if it had reached the mass market, I don't believe it would have met with any great or profound love, simply because it pissed all over many of the very tropes that comic fans hold dear. The book featured an untrustworthy, vaguely dishonest sidewinder of a hero – a liberal mugged by reality, in Ed Koch's famous phrase.

Flagg! is packed with a slew of unlikeable supporting characters operating in a vulgar and unsettling place, with an equally difficult world view. Skeptical rather than cynical, the book is easy to read as nihilistic, when in fact it's mostly a screed about the Reagan administration.

And that's only the content. Visually, graphically, textually, narratively, the book isn't easy to read – and doesn't congratulate its reader for being there, the way 'the hero with a wound' traditional comic book formula does so well.

On the other hand, an entire generation of artists and writers grew up on it. And despite the current trend of nice driving out the good, in which talent has

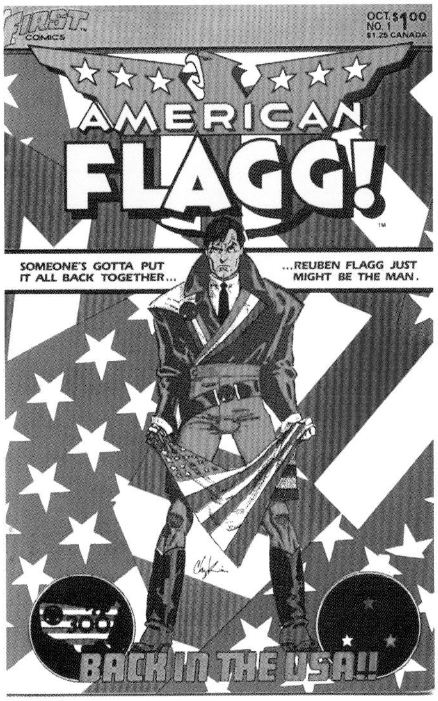
FIRST COMICS
OCT. $1.00 NO. 1 $1.25 CANADA
AMERICAN FLAGG!
SOMEONE'S GOTTA PUT IT ALL BACK TOGETHER...
...REUBEN FLAGG JUST MIGHT BE THE MAN.
BACK IN THE USA!!

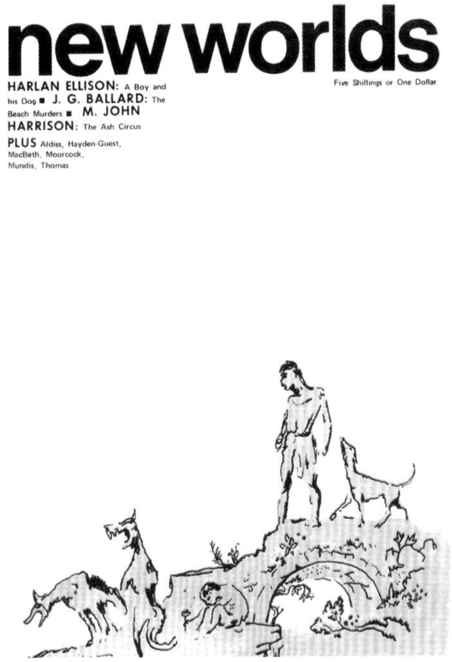
new worlds
Five Shillings or One Dollar
HARLAN ELLISON: A Boy and his Dog ■ J. G. BALLARD: The Beach Murders ■ M. JOHN HARRISON: The Ash Circus
PLUS Aldiss, Hayden-Guest, MacBeth, Moorcock, Mundis, Thomas

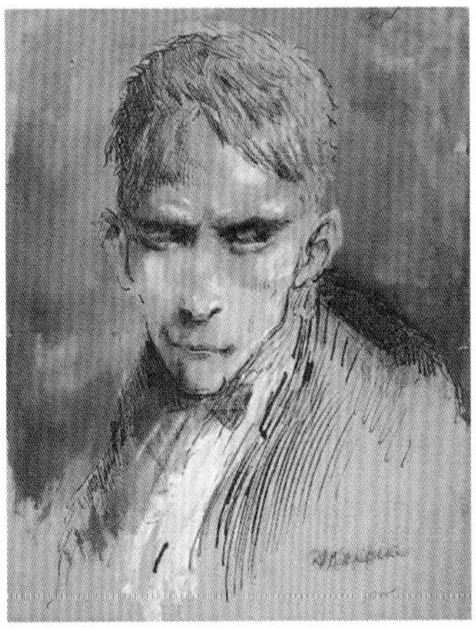

to apologise and pander to an audience that operates under the mistaken impression that it has the right not to have its feelings hurt, *Flagg!* opened the door to an entirely new vocabulary for telling stories in comics.

Mark Chiarello has described me as one of the architects of the modern comic book, by which I assume he's basically referring to the two dozen issues of *American Flagg!* that I both wrote and drew.

I humbly accept that with good grace."-Howard Chaykin on his series *American Flagg!*, Changing The Rules Of The Game, tripwiremagazine.co.uk, 2016

"What Ballard, Bayley and I had talked about was a magazine that wasn't strictly an SF magazine but which borrowed the best techniques from SF to try to produce a new kind of contemporary fiction which would replace, for us at least, the moribund social fiction which was dominant in the early 60s. We weren't interested in improving SF as much as we wanted to find forms and methods which would allow us to write about the real world around us. The first editorial we ran had a title something like 'a new fiction for the space age' and argued that so far only William Burroughs was getting close. We wanted to find ways of condensing narrative, or packing the maximum number of narratives into a piece. We were as much involved with the contemporary arts – i.e. the pop art of Paolozzi, Hamilton and others – modern music as exemplified by Messiaen and so on –as we were with SF. We wanted to see what we could do with all this stuff. SF as such was just the engine which dropped off the rocket once it was spaceborn." - Michael Moorcock on creating *New Worlds*, The Fantasy Grand Master Speaks, Tripwire Annual 2008

"Like Burroughs, he was more an inspiration than an influence. His work continues to inspire because of the powerful originality of its language, its superb visual imagination – it is, as I've said before, sui generis. It is a fantasy with no supernatural elements, entirely the creation of an individual mind. This is partly why it isn't imitated in the way Tolkien is imitated. It is original in the way that Blake was original." – Michael Moorcock on Mervyn Peake, The Fantasy Grand Master Speaks, Tripwire Annual 2008

"I have a ton of them. Honestly. Times together laughing come to mind and so many of them. I have stories for sure, but they are not for everyone. So many. So many drinks. So many nights out. So many embarrassing situations. Each time I think of one, I laugh and know there is no way I can explain it adequately. The time we had dinner with some DC people and he made them buy him the biggest lobster and steak the restaurant had because he felt he was getting shafted out of money, so he wanted to make them pay for it." –Jimmy Palmiotti on Darwyn Cooke, Casting A Huge Shadow, Tripwire Winter Special 2020-2021

"We create for the ALL-AGES

Parker
Darwyn

THE PHOENIX PRESENTS
VON DOOGAN
and the CURSE of the GOLDEN MONKEY
By LORENZO!
PACKED with PUZZLES!
A SUPER-PUZZLE ADVENTURE COMIC!

"If you could say one thing about all my work including Wicked + Divine, Die and Once & Future is how the stories that we tell ourselves as people delude and confuse us. " – KIERON GILLEN on what themes run through his work, English Beat, Tripwire Winter Special 2020-2021

market. Kids' comics suggest something simplistic (and plenty of titles take the easiest path) but truthfully I never wrote a story for Titan or *the DFC* or *the Phoenix* or *the Dandy* that I didn't create with a potential adult reader in mind. Almost any subject matter can work in the all ages market and there's no reason why a comic that appeals to a 7-year-old can't also be appealing to a 70-year-old. When we started out, our early frames of reference were Asterix and Futurama. We liked the idea of visually appealing worlds that could be built into engaging spaces for grand stories."–Robin Etherington on who they create their work for, Brothers In Art, Tripwire Winter Special 2020-2021

"If you could say one thing about all my work including *Wicked + Divine*, *Die* and *Once & Future* is how the stories that we tell ourselves as people delude and confuse us. That's Arthur. You mentioned the Victorians but you didn't mention the French. You've also got very Germanic elements, with people taking the myth of Arthur and running

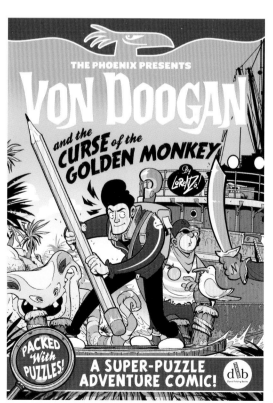

with it. Lancelot for example was added to the legend when the French people needed someone to empathise with." - Kieron Gillen on what themes run through much of his work, English Beat, Tripwire Winter Special 2020-2021

"Great concept; great writing; great actors; and great directors. The film industry never rides on one talent or one idea. The mixing of many talents makes this industry work. I don't think you can underestimate the influence of Harrison Ford and the mix of Steven Spielberg and George Lucas. We live through Indy's adventures. That's the magic of movies and the gift of talent." –Drew Struzan on *Indiana Jones*, Happy 40th Birthday Indiana Jones, Tripwire Winter Special 2021

"It did. It's back in now for some reason, I don't know why. Certain elements of craft are coming back in as well. I'm sure it's cyclical, people are going to tire of it at some point because they'll be glutted. On a personal level, when I met those portrait painters and saw what they were considering when they painted, what their priorities were, how their approach worked. It was so different from illustration. I had to learn how to paint over again. That was the most shocking thing and I had to be willing to do lousy paintings for a while, even now, until it became habitual; because you can't be micro-managing every second of working with the brush." - Phil Hale on switching from illustration to fine art, Broad Strokes, Tripwire Annual 2009

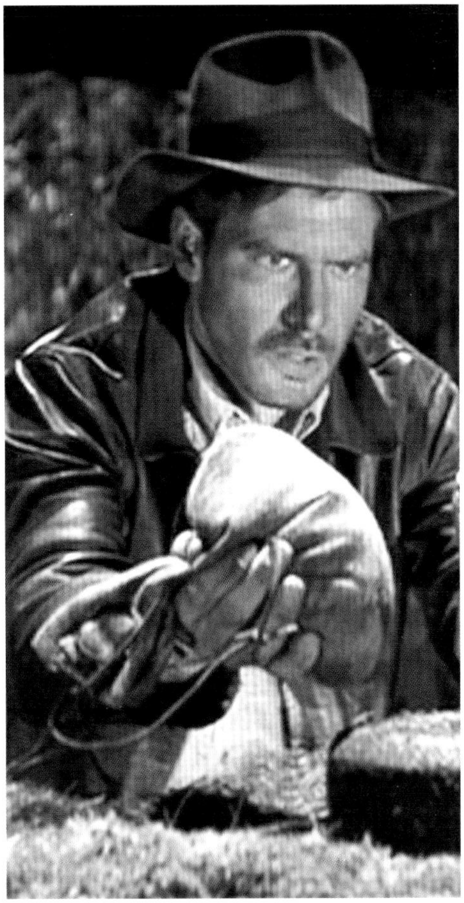

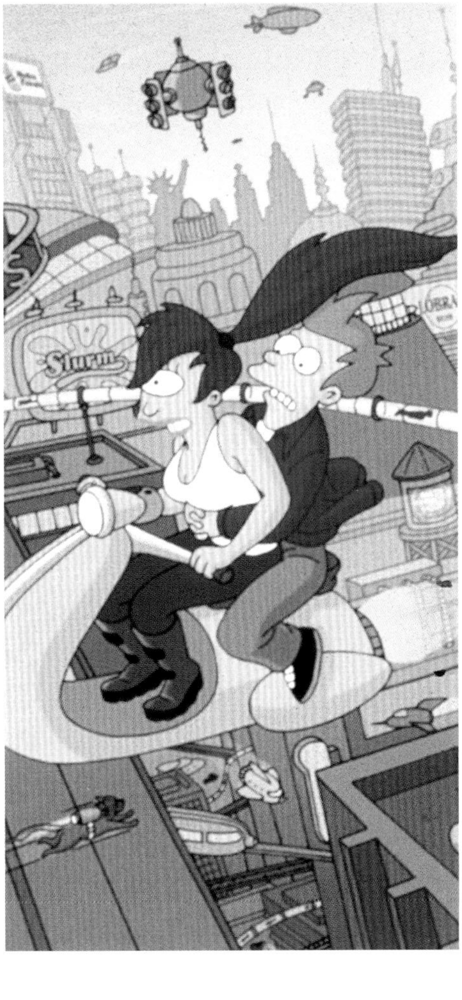

" I don't think you can underestimate the influence of Harrison Ford and the mix of Steven Spielberg and George Lucas. We live through Indy's adventures." - DREW STRUZAN on why Indiana Jones is still popular, Happy 40th Birthday, Tripwire Winter Special 2021

"In the first incarnation of *Futurama*, we were off the Twentieth Century Fox lot and now I have the opportunity to walk back and forth between the shows and do very sitcom-style entrances when I walk into the room. But David [X Cohen] does the hard thing of editing and directing the voice actors. He also supervises the writing. And you'll agree, David, that we have an incredible team."– Matt Groening on the division of labour for *Futurama* in its second iteration, Future Shocks, Tripwire#55 July 2010

"I was in the Army for about three years. I volunteered. I had Signal Corps training. I was supposed to go overseas and repair communications wires... But just as I was about to ship over, they found out that I had worked in comic books and they needed a writer in the training film department. So I got yanked out and sent to Astoria, New York, where the Army had their training film department." – Stan Lee on what he did during the Second World War, It's A Marvelous Life, Tripwire Annual 2009

THE CREATORS WE HAVE LOST 1992-2022

Tripwire's editor-in-chief Joel Meadows takes a look at the creators the industry has lost over the past thirty years

The last thirty years have seen a lot of major comic creators pass away, many some of the most important figures in our industry.

The first creator to pass in 1994 was legend **Jack Kirby (right),** a man who with the aid of Stan Lee, co-created the Marvel Universe. Without him, there would be no Thor, no Avengers, no Captain America and no Marvel Cinematic Universe.

Next in 1998, two significant figures passed away. The first was editor and writer **Archie Goodwin (bottom right)**, who had a CV that included working as an editor at Marvel and DC and writing *Batman* and the acclaimed *Manhunter* at DC. He was one of the most respected people in the comics industry and his loss was a huge one.

The other figure to pass away in 1998 was a more controversial one: Batman co-creator **Bob Kane (middle right)**. It took years for fellow creators Bill Finger and Jerry Robinson to receive their proper credit as the co-creators of DC's Dark Knight Detective and in Robinson's case, his most iconic villain, The Joker.

In 2000, we lost **Gil Kane (top right)** , a veteran artist with an

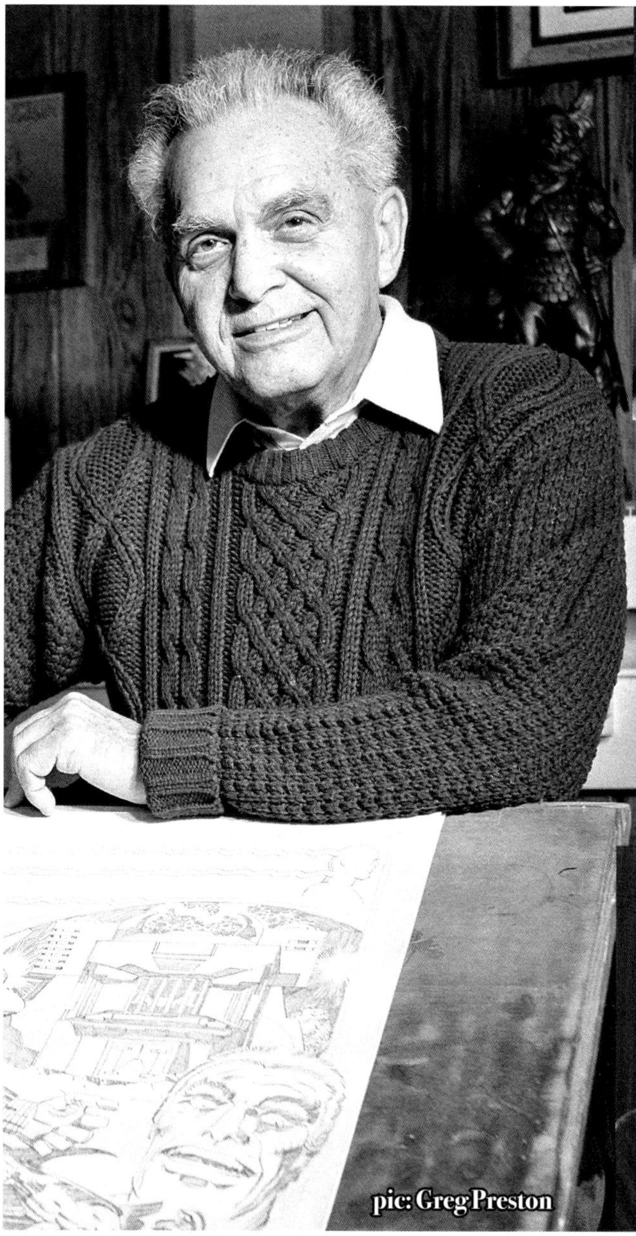

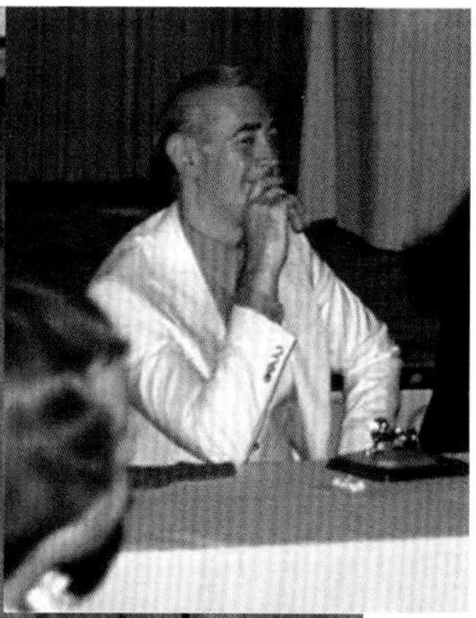

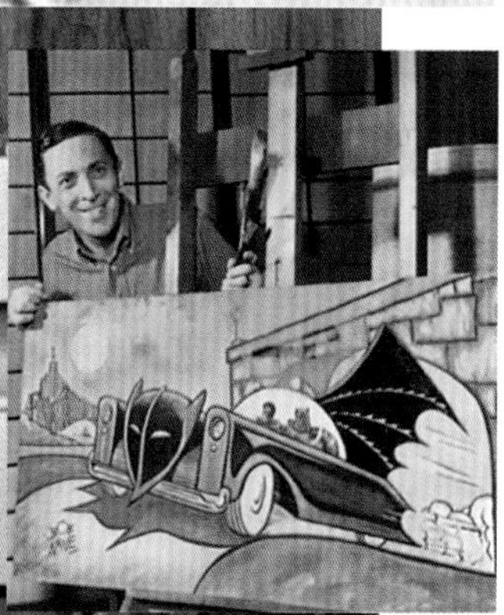

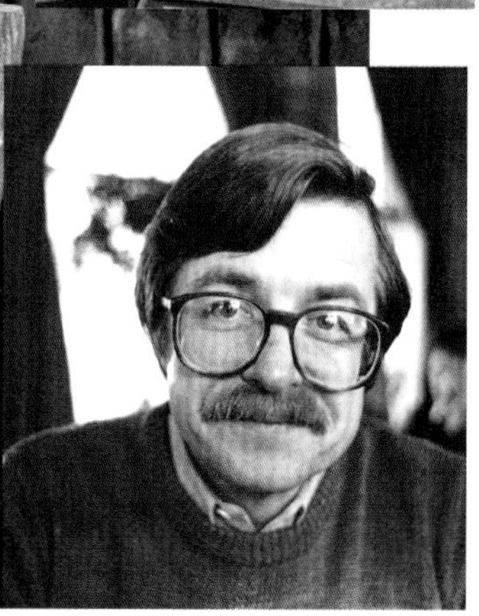

pic: Greg Preston

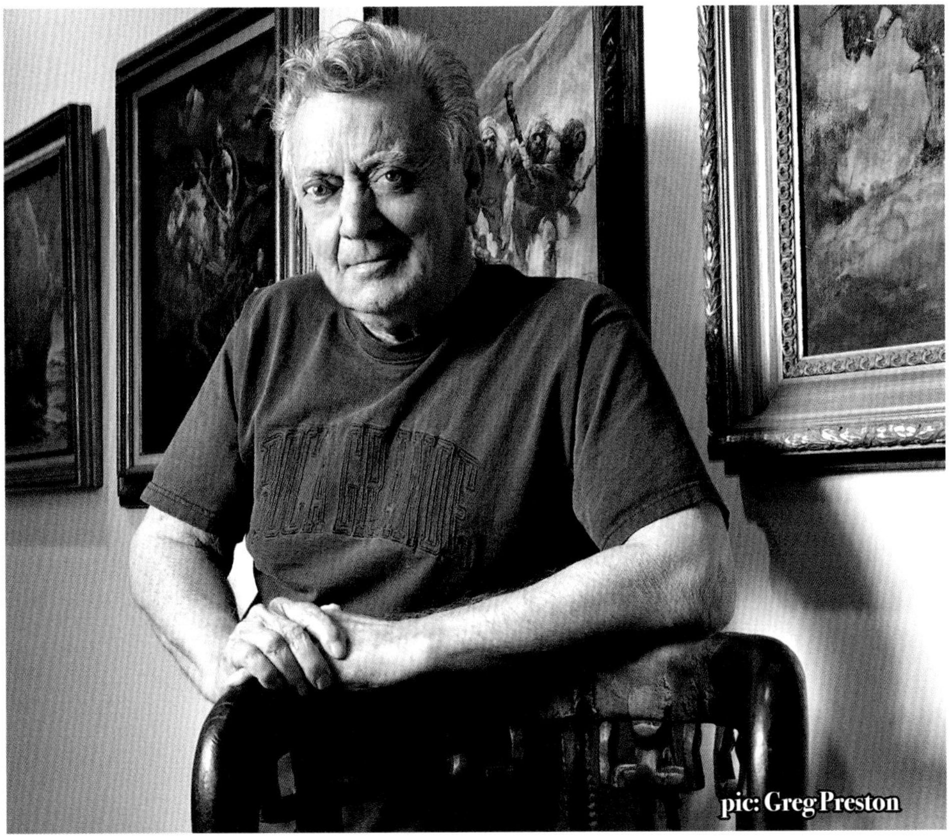
pic: Greg Preston

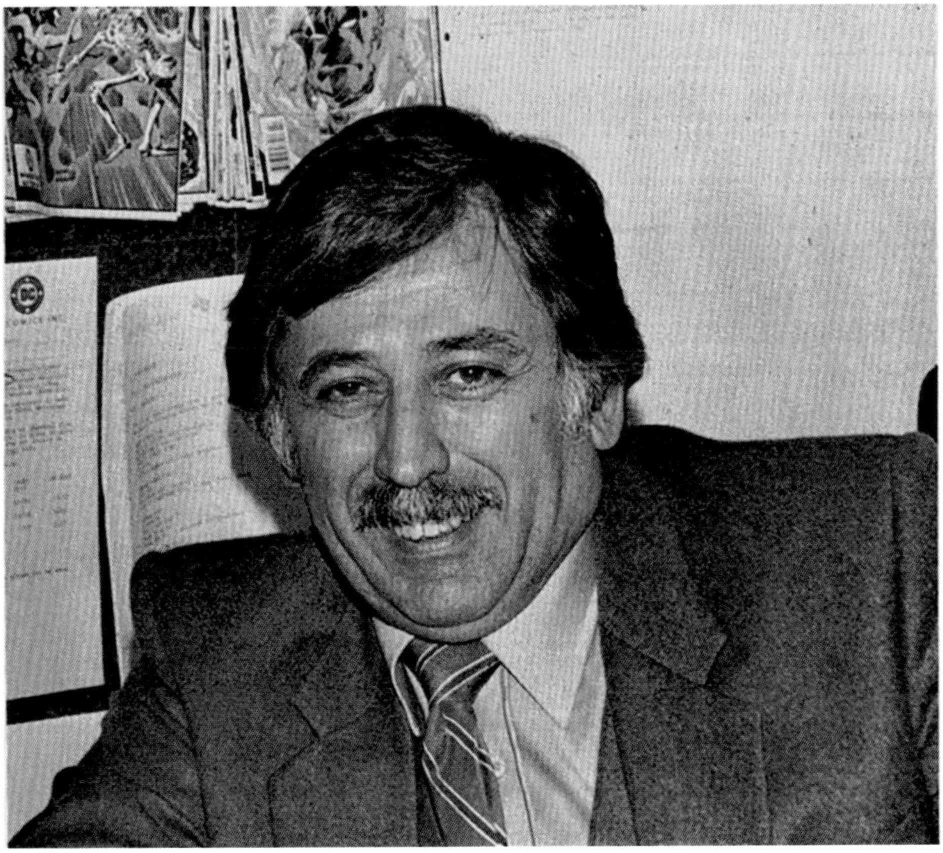

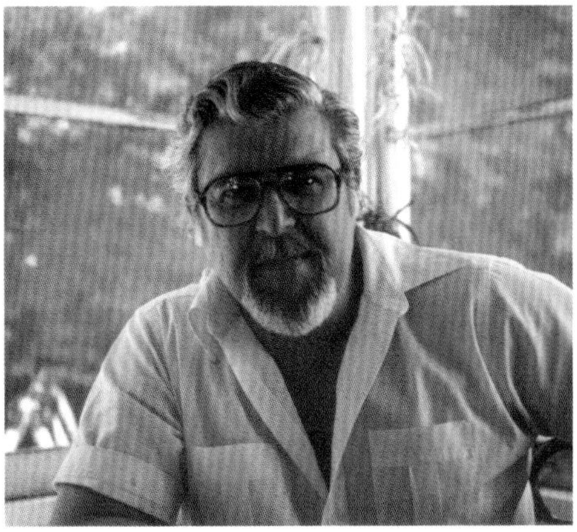

instantly distinct style whose work had graced the pages of some of Marvel and DC's most well-known books like *Captain Marvel*, *John Carter*, *Green Lantern* and *Superman*.

2002 saw the loss of **Robert Kanigher**, a DC stalwart writer and editor at DC for decades who was best known for his work on their war books, predominantly with his artistic partner Joe Kubert. Kanigher worked on characters like *Sgt Rock* and *Enemy Ace*, making their war line the best-regarded in the industry for many years.

The same year saw comics lose one of its greatest Silver Age figures, artist **John Buscema (top right)**, whose powerful line art at Marvel on books like *Silver Surfer*, *The Avengers* and *Conan* garnered him an international following. He also drew *The Punisher* at the House Of Ideas.

In 2005, an early champion of creators' rights, **Will Eisner**, left us. Eisner had a career that spanned seven decades, described as the godfather of the graphic novel. His body of work included the groundbreaking Spirit in the 1940s and later on on with work like *A Contract With God*, *A Life Force* and *Dropsie Avenue*. San Diego Comic-Con's annual awards are named after him.

In 2008, Top Cow artist **Michael Turner** lost his life at the very young age of 36, a creator who made a splash with series like *Witchblade*, *The Darkness* and *Fathom*.

The same year, Golden Age cover genius **Craig Fleissel**, who was responsible for some of the most elegant covers on the pre-Batman *Detective Comics*, passed away.

Frank Frazetta (top left), the master of science fiction and fantasy art whose work crowned *Conan* and Edgar Rice Burroughs book covers but whose

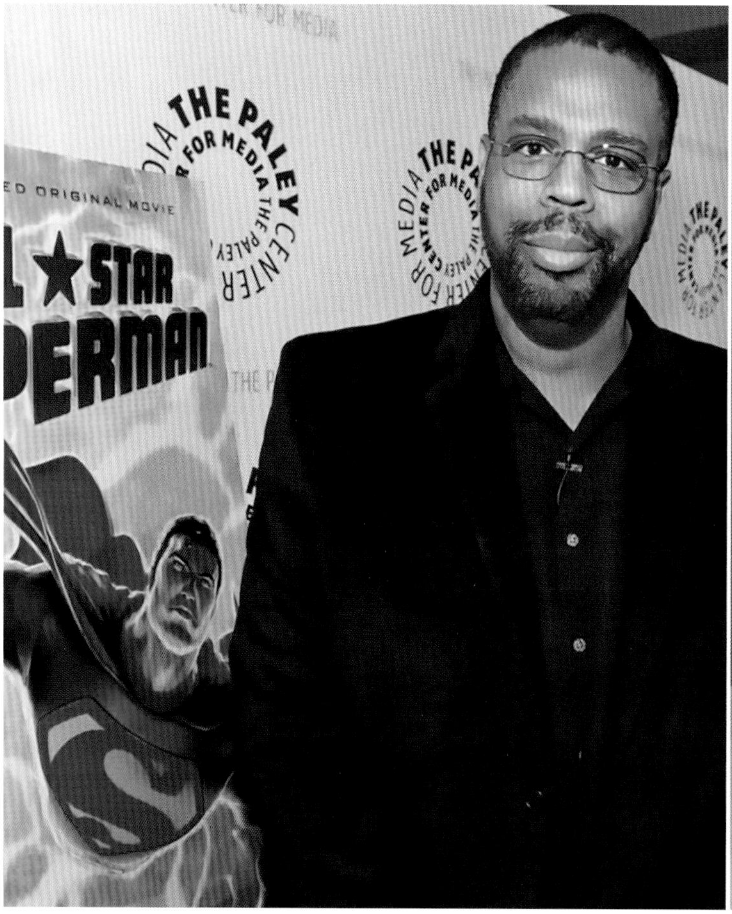
THE PALEY CENTER FOR MEDIA
ALL ★ STAR SUPERMAN

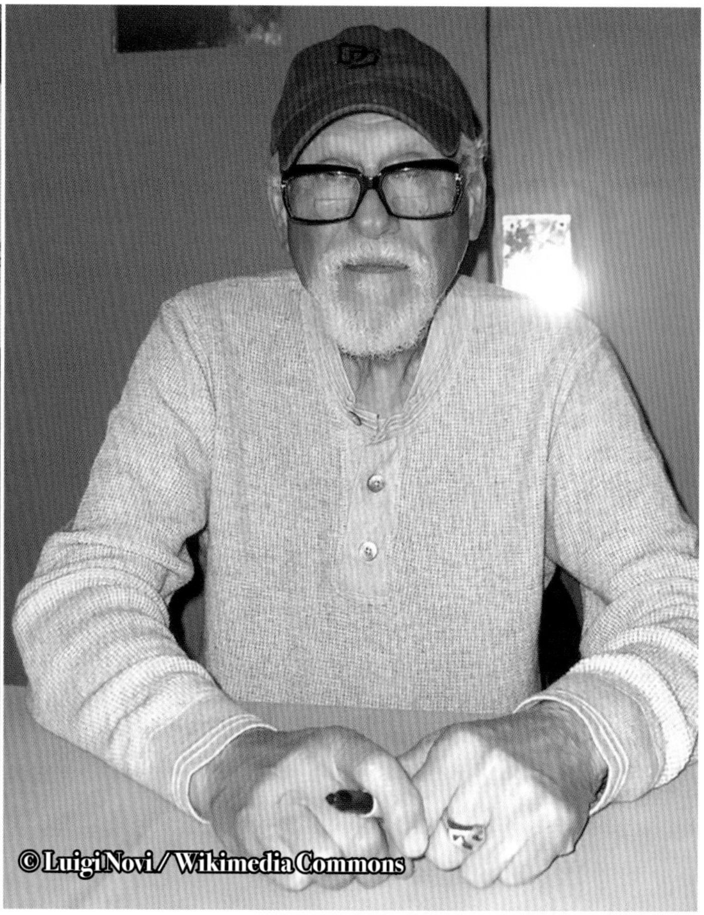

© LuigiNovi / Wikimedia Commons

comic art career included iconic covers for Gaines' EC in the 1950s, passed away in 2010.

In the same year, the industry also lost fellow EC veteran **Al Williamson**, who also moved on to draw newspaper strips like *Star Wars* and *Secret Agent X*.

Dick Giordano (previous page, bottom left) was DC's executive editor during the 1980s but he was also a very talented inker working with Neal Adams on many of his best-loved Batman stories. Giordano also died in 2010.

Jeffery Catherine Jones, who died in 2011, was part of 1970s The Studio with Berni Wrightson, Barry Windsor-Smith and Michael Kaluta, bringing fine art sensibilities to bear with their work. Jones painted many covers for DC's horror and fantasy line as well as working for *Heavy Metal* and *Epic Illustrated* in the 1980s.

The same year saw the industry lose master of comics horror **Gene Colan (top right)**, whose CV included Marvel's seminal *Tomb Of Dracula* plus *Daredevil* at Marvel and a stint drawing *Batman* at DC. His moody linework won him fans around the world.

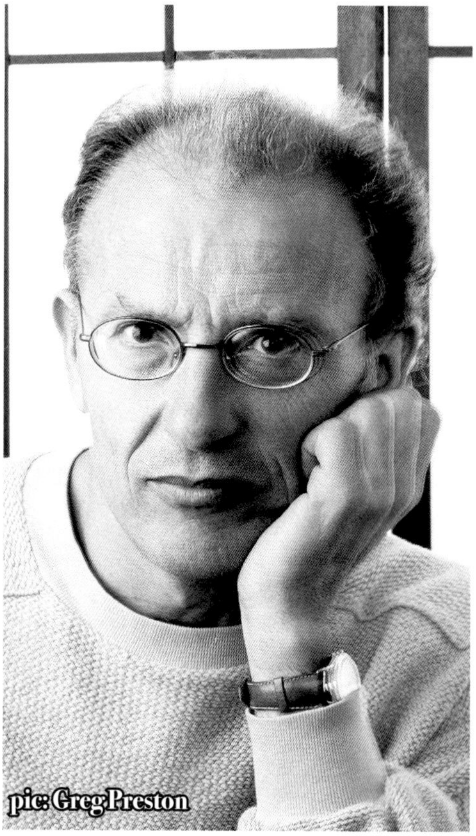

pic: Greg Preston

In 2011, **Jerry Robinson**, the artist whose greatest claim to fame was as the creator of Batman's most infamous adversary The Joker, left us. He also coined the name 'Robin'.

Also in 2011, Jack Kirby's regular collaborator and friend **Joe Simon**, who was also a writer and editor as well as an artist and inker, passed away. Simon co-created *Captain America* with Kirby in the 1940s.

In the same year, African-American writer and editor **Dwayne McDuffie (top left)**, who co-founded Milestone, home of books like *Static*, *Icon* and *Shadow Cabinet*, died at a very young age in surgery but he cast a huge shadow that continues to this day.

Moebius (bottom middle) was a French artist whose impact passed far beyond the French comics industry, casting a huge shadow over US comics. Outside of France, he is probably best-known for *Blueberry*, *Arzach* and *The*

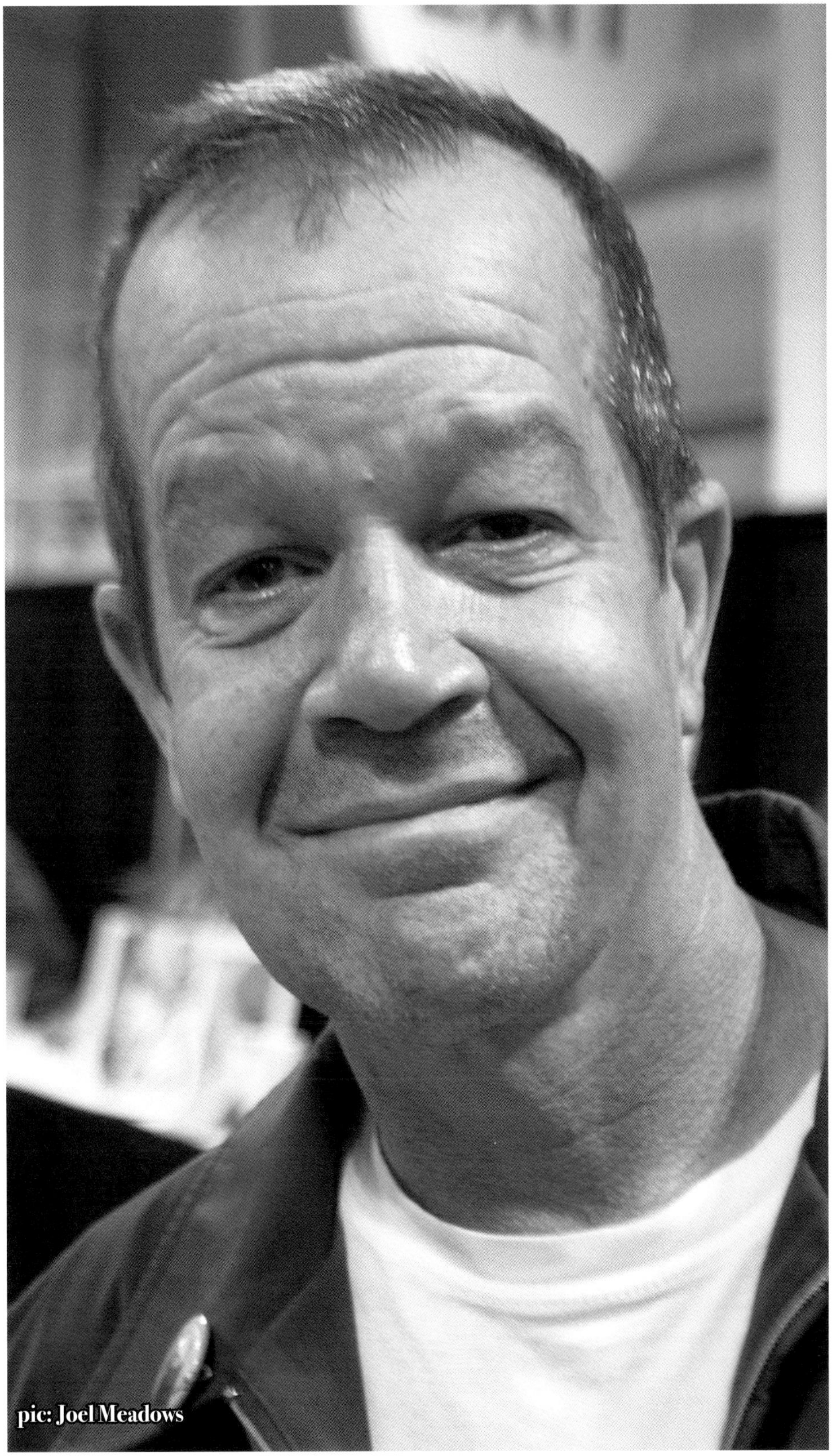

pic: Joel Meadows

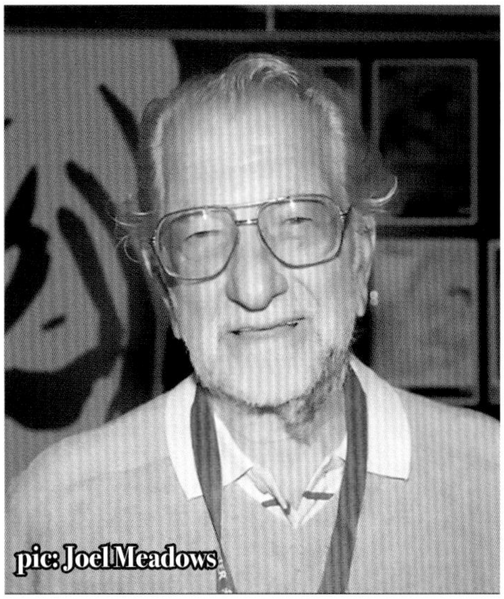

pic: Joel Meadows

Incal. His passing in 2012 was a major blow to the industry.

The same year we lost **Joe Kubert (top right)**, whose career spanned eight decades as an editor, a writer, an artist and also the man who founded the school that still bears his name. His work on DC's war books like *Sgt Rock* and *Enemy Ace* with writer Robert Kanigher set a high watermark for the genre in comics which has never been matched since.

Steve Dillon, one of the greatest British comic artists whose work in publications like *2000AD* and Warrior but also at DC with titles like *Hellblazer* and *Preacher*, died in 2016 leaving a huge legacy as one of the finest storytellers in modern comics.

2016 also saw the industry lose one of *MAD Magazine*'s Usual Gang Of Idiots **Jack Davis**. Davis was well-known for his spoofs of classic films like *Raiders Of The Lost Ark*, *Gone With The Wind* and *MASH*.

The same year saw the loss of **Darwyn Cooke (left)**. Cooke started as an animator and it was this unique approach that got hin noticed first with his *Batman: Ego* oneshot. Cooke went on to write and draw *DC: The New Frontier* as well as issues of DC's *Jonah Hex* and *All-Star Western*. His final run of work was adapting Donald Westlake's *Parker* books into graphic novels at IDW.

In 2017, modern horror artistic master **Berni Wrightson**, who was part of The Studio with Jones, Windsor-Smith and Kaluta, left us. His body of work included the modern gothic of DC's *Swamp Thing* but also adapting Mary Shelley's *Frankenstein* and creating scores of memorable covers for DC's horror books.

In the same year, Wrightson's collaborator **Len Wein** left us. Wein was a writer and editor for both Marvel and DC, on books like *New Teen*

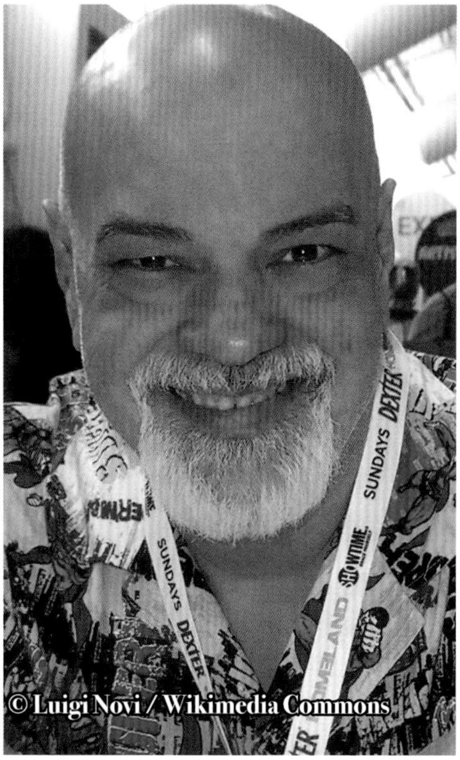
© Luigi Novi / Wikimedia Commons

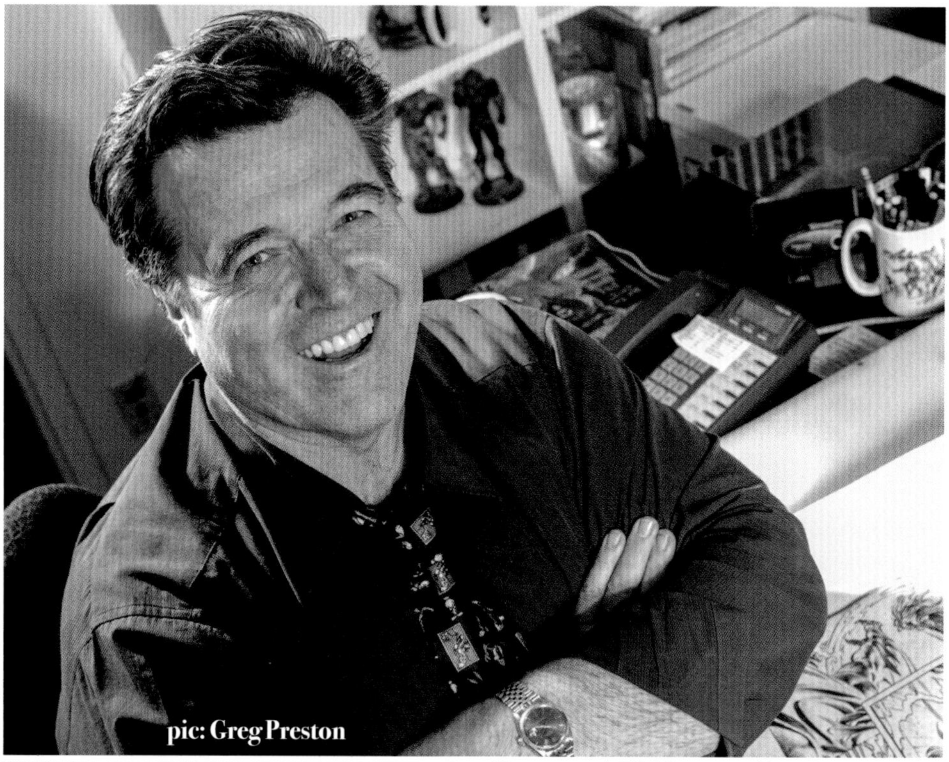
pic: Greg Preston

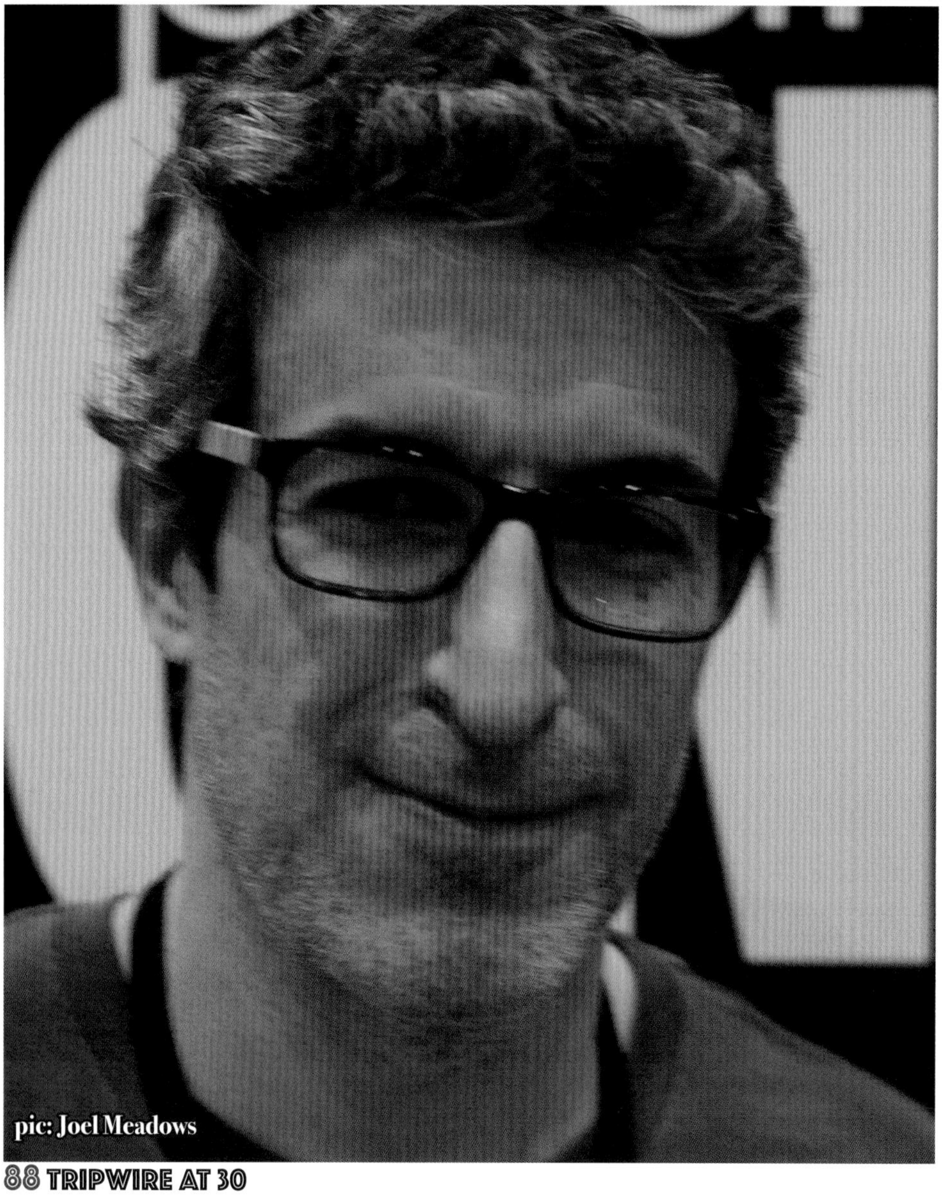
pic: Joel Meadows

Titans and *X-Men* equally talented at both disciplines.

Harlan Ellison, who left us in 2018, was better known as a science fiction writer and TV writer on shows like *Star Trek* and *The Outer Limits* but he also wrote comics for publishers like Dark Horse and DC. He was one of the most important genre writers of the latter half of the 20th century.

The same year, **Stan Lee** left us. Lee was co-creator of Marvel's Silver Age characters like The Avengers, Thor, Spider-man, The Hulk and Fantastic Four. He was Marvel's editor-in-chief throughout the 1960s and, when Marvel began making movies in the early 2000s, he would appear as an onscreen cameo.

Lee's collaborator **Steve Ditko** also left us the same year. Ditko co-created Spider-man with Lee at Marvel. He began his career at Charlton with *The Question* and moved on to Atlas.

Also in 2018, **Norm Breyfogle**, an artist who made his name drawing *Batman* with writers Alan Grant and John Wagner at DC, passed away. His kinetic linework made him one of the most popular portrayers of the Dark pic: Joel Meadows

Knight Detective. He also worked for Marvel a little later in his career.

The same year, **Russ Heath** passed away. Beginning his career at Timely, it was his long run at DC on their war comics that really made his name as an artist. He created some of the finest war comic covers.

In 2020, the industry lost **Mort Drucker**, who like Davis specialised in film and TV satires at *MAD Magazine*. He also created album covers for Anthrax and magazine covers for world-renowned publications like *Time Magazine*.

In the same year, *Asterix* co-creator **Albert Uderzo** passed away. The French comic artist had a career that spanned many decades.

In 2021, **John Paul Leon (bottom left, previous page)** lost his battle with cancer. An artist who began his career at Milestone publishing with book *Static*, he showed off his versatility working on series like *Batman* and *Wintermen* for DC and *The Further Adventures of Cyclops and Phoenix* at Marvel.

2022 has been a fairly unkind year so far with the industry losing some heavyweight figures:

Brian Augustyn (below) was a writer who also worked as an editor at DC. He is best-known for writing Flash spin-off *Impulse* and Elseworlds Batman stories *Gotham By Gaslight* and its follow-up *Master Of The Future*.

pic: Thomas Healy

Neal Adams (top right,previous page) was a legendary artist whose career began in the 1970s where he made his name with groundbreaking work on books like Batman, Green Lantern and Strange Adventures at DC and Avengers and X-Men at Marvel. He brought an illustrative sensibility to his work.

Tim Sale (above right) was a comic artist who began his career in the 1980s who went on to build up a fan following thanks to his work on the acclaimed *Batman: The Long Halloween* at DC and his series of miniseries at Marvel like *Spider-man: Blue* and *Hulk: Grey*, all with collaborator Jeph Loeb.

George Perez was the artist who shaped superheroes in the 1980s thanks to his work first on Marvel's *Avengers* and later on DC's top-selling *New Teen Titans* with writer Marv Wolfman. In the 1990s he was the artist on Marvel's hit *Infinity Gauntlet*.

Alan Grant (inset, top right) was a British writer and editor who worked at *2000AD* for many years. He wrote Judge Dredd with his regular collaborator John Wagner and he also co-wrote *Batman* for many years with Wagner and later on his own with artist Norm Breyfogle.He was one of the most important figures in modern British comic publishing.

These are all figures who shaped the industry so we felt we had to comemmorate them and this list is by no means complete.

30 YEARS OF THE WORST HEADLINE PUNS

Over 30 years, TRIPWIRE has been responsible for some pretty cringeworthy headline puns. So we have sat down and picked out the one hundred worst offenders in chronological order from print and online…

Spiked Milligan
(interview with Peter Milligan, Volume 1#2, Sep '92)

Malice in Chains
(cover strap for review of The Extremist#1, Volume 1#4, August '93)

Automatic For the Steeple
(review of Jesus & Mary Chain's The Sound of Speed, Volume 1#4, August '93)

They're Only In It For The Mummy
(review of Scarab#1, Volume 1#5, November '93)

Bog Standard
(review of Swamp Thing#140, Volume 1#6 February '94)

Heart of The Motter
(review of Heart of The Matter OGN, Volume 1#7, September 1994)

Cooper Scooper
(review of Alice Cooper: The Last Temptation, Volume 1#7, September 1994)

That's Not The Way To Do It
(Review of Mr Punch, Volume 1#8, Dec '94)

Tekno For An Answer
(Review of Neil Gaiman's Mr Hero The Newmatic Man#1 and Leonard Nimoy's Primortals#1, Volume 1#8, Dec '94)

Quitely Does It
(Frank Quitely interview on Blackheart and Missionary Man, Volume 1#9, May '95)

Peter Cooked
(Peter Milligan interview, Volume 1#9, May '95)

Ellis' Ire Land
(review of Ruins#1 and Doctor Strange#80, Volume 1#10, Summer '95)

Sunday Mourning
(review of Death The Time of Your Life#1, Volume 1#11, Winter '95)

Better The Devil You Know
(review of Hellboy Wake The Devil#1-2, Volume 1#13, Summer '96)

On The Wayne
(Review of Batman 530-531, Batman Shadow of The Bat 50-51, Batman Black and White#1, Volume 1#13, Summer '96)

Robin us Blind
(review of Nightwing #1, Volume 1 #14, Mid-summer '96)

Situationist Vacant?
(review of The Invisibles Volume 2 #1, Volume 1#15, Winter '96)

Down The Tube
(Review of BBC's Neverwhere, Volume 1#15, Winter '96)

Never Mind The Pollacks
(review of Timebreakers #1-2, Volume 1#15, Winter '96)

Raising Hell
(Mike Mignola Hellboy interview, Volume 1#16, Spring '97)

House of Old Dears
(Review of Cable -1, Daredevil -1, Uncanny X-Men -1, X-Men -1, Deadpool -1, Silver Surfer -1, Summer Special '97)

Crock Circus
(review of Kiss: Psycho Circus#1, Volume 2#1, Sept '97)

The Gene Genie
(interview with Chris Bachalo on X-Men, Volume 2#1, Sept '97)

The Shite Album
(review of Be Here Now by Oasis, Volume 2#1, Sept '97)

HEADLINE ACTS
Sapphire and Steal
(interview with Vince Danks and Roger Gibson on Ariel Press, Volume 2#2, Nov '97)

Stars and Strife
(Uncle Sam feature, Volume 2#2, Nov '97)

Hammered Horror

(review of Man Thing#1-2 and Werewolf by Night#1, Volume 2#3, Dec '97-Jan'98)
Emotional Bagge
(review of Hate#25-29, Volume 2#4, Mar-Apr '98)
We'll Always Have Harris
(Tony Harris interview on Starman, Volume 2#4, Mar-Apr '98)
Porn Free
(review of Pulp's This Is Hardcore, Volume 2#5, Jun-Jul '98)
Byrne's Victims?
(review of Sensational Spider-man 32-33, Amazing Spider-man 440-441, Peter Parker Spider-man 96-97 and Spectacular Spider-man 262, Volume 2#7 Oct-Nov '98)
Knights To Remember
(feature on launch of Marvel Knights with Joe Quesada, Jimmy Palmiotti and key creators, Volume 2#7 Oct-Nov '98)
Hells Belles
(review of Batman/ Hellboy/ Starman #1-2, Special A, Nov '98)
Historical Differences
(feature on Heart of Empire with Bryan Talbot, Volume 2#8, Dec '98)
The Unforgiveably Dire
(Review of U2's The Best of 1980-1990, Volume 2#8, Dec '98)
On The Hoof
(Feature on Hellboy and plans for 1999 with Mike Mignola, Volume 2#9, Feb-Mar '99)
James Robinson's Justice
(review of All-Star Comics#1, Adventure Comics#1, All-American Comics#1, Smash Comics#1, Sensation Comics#1, Star Spangled Comics#1, Thrilling Comics#1 and All-Star Comics#2, TRIPWIRE Volume 2#10, Apr-May '99)
The Anderson Tapes
(interview with Brett Anderson of Suede, Volume 2#10, Apr-May '99)
Jedi, Steady, Go
(cover strap for Star Wars Episode One coverage, Volume 3#3, Jul-Aug '99)
Better Latex Than Never
(Interview with Nick Dudman on Star Wars Episode One, Volume 3#3, Jul-Aug '99)
Dancing With The Devil
(interview with David Mack on Daredevil, Volume 3#4, Sep-Oct '99)
Cutting Hedge
(Review of Swamp Thing#1, Spring Special '00)
Knights To Forget
(review of The Punisher #1-6, Marvel Boy #1-2, Volume 4#1, Jul '00)
Alphabet Soupçon
(feature on Alan Moore on ABC and League of Extraordinary
Gentlemen, Volume 4#1, Jul '00)
Born To Be Mild
(Review of Neil Young's Silver And Gold, Volume 4#1, Jul '00)
The Man Who Wrote Too Much
(Interview with Brian Bendis, Volume 4#2, Nov 2000)
Nice Knight For It
(Interview with Marvel's Joe Quesada, Volume 4#3, Dec 2000)
Sale of The Sentry
(Review of The Sentry#1-5, Volume 4#3, Dec 2000)
Chaykin All Over
(Review of American Century#1, Volume 4#4, Feb 2001)
Classless of '77?
(Review of 2000AD Progs 1223-1226, Volume 4#4, Mar 2001)
A Design for Strife
(Review of Manic Street Preachers Know Your Enemy, Volume 4#5, May 2001)
Getting Shafted?
(Review of Green Arrow #1-4, Volume 4#6, Jul 2001)
Elektra Assassinated
(Review of Elektra#1, Volume 4#7, Oct 2001)
Life of Brian
(interview with Brian Bendis on Daredevil, Volume 4#7, Oct 2001)
Bat To Basics
(interview with Greg Rucka on Batman, Volume 4#8 Nov 2001)
Speaking Frankly
(interview with Frank Miller on Dark Knight Strikes Again, Volume 4#9 Dec 2001-Jan 2002)
Skill and Crossbones
(feature on Obergeist: The Empty Locket, Volume 4#10, Apr 2002)
Biblical Proportions
(interview with Kyle Baker on King David, Volume 4#10, Apr 2002)
Ahead of The Game
(interview with Mike Mignola on Amazing Screw On Head, Volume 4#11, June 2002)

Quatermain and The Pit
(review of League of Extraordinary Gentlemen Volume 2#1-2, Volume 4#12, Aug 2002)
State of Independents
(feature on independent publishers, Volume 4#12, Aug 2002)
Cooking The Books
(interview with Darwyn Cooke on DC The New Frontier, Volume 5 #1, Apr 2003)
Dredding The Future
(Interview with John Wagner on Judge Dredd, Volume 5 #1, Apr 2003)
A Man of Wealth and Taste
(Interview with Mike Carey on Hellblazer and his career, Volume 5 #1, Apr 2003)
The Man Without Peer...
(feature on Daredevil movie, Volume 5 #1, Apr 2003)
No.1 With A Bullet
(feature on Bulletproof Monk, Volume 5 #2, Jun 2003)
Doing The Write Thing
(interview with J.Michael Straczynski on his career, Volume 5 #2, Jun 2003)
Seeing Red
(interview with Cully Hamner on Red, Volume 5 #3, July 2003)
Hero Worship
(feature on Heroes TV series, Annual 2007)
The Devil's In The Details
(feature on Hellboy in comics and on the big and small screen, Annual 2007)
Bongo Players
(feature on Matt Groening, Bill Morrison and Ian Boothby on Simpsons comics and Simpsons on TV, Annual 2007)
Baked Alaska
(feature on 30 Days of Night the movie, Annual 2007)
The Empire Strikes Back
(feature on British genre TV resurgence, Annual 2008)
Back To The Futurama
(feature on Futurama, Annual 2008)
Behind The Screens
(features on Pinewood Studios, ILM and storyboard artist Martin Asbury, Annual 2008)
It's No Joke
(feature on Watchmen the movie, Superhero Special 2009)
Millar's Crossing
(feature on Kick-Ass the the movie, Superhero Special 2009)
Gutter Presence
(interview with Rich Johnston, Superhero Special 2009)
The Mark of Kane
(feature on Solomon Kane, Annual 2009)
Gripping Yarns
(interview with John Fleskes of Flesk Publications, Annual 2009)
King of The Stone Age
(interview with Joe Kubert on Tor, Annual 2009)
Crime Does Pay
(interview with Ian Rankin on Hellblazer, Annual 2009)
Treading The Boards
(interview with storyboard artist Trevor Goring, Annual 2009)
Teenage Kicks
(feature on James Bond in comics and Young James Bond, Annual 2009)
New Worlds Order
(interview with Michael Moorcock on his career, #54, 2010)
Cut To The Quick
(feature on Madam Samurai, #54, 2010)
Changeling of The Guard
(interview with J.Michael Straczynski on Superman and Wonder Woman, #54, 2010)
Creating a Stark Reality
(feature on Double Negative's work on Iron Man 2, #54, 2010)
Hard Boiled
(interview with Jason Aaron, #55, 2011)
London Made Him
(interview with Christopher Fowler on his career, #55, 2011)
Royal Blood
(interview with Michael Moorcock on Elric, #55, 2011)
Turning The Other Cheek
(interview with Walt Simonson on The Judas Coin, ,#55, 2011)
MAD Man
(interview with Sergio Aragones, #55, 2011)
Taking The Law Into Their Own Hands
(feature on the history of 2000AD, Digital 0.01, April '11)
Bringing The Hammer Down
(feature on Thor the movie, Digital 0.01, April '11)

Barbarous Behaviour
(feature on Slaine The Horned God, Digital 0.02, July '11)
Getting In The Saddle
(feature on Blueberry, Digital 0.02, July '11)
First Class Entertainment
(feature on X-Men First Class the movie, Digital 0.02, July '11)
Sense of Dredd
(feature on Dredd 3D movie, Digital Dredd Special, Nov '12)
He Is The Law
(interview with Karl Urban on Dredd 3D movie, Digital Dredd Special, Nov '12)
Deadpool On Arrival
(Review Of Deadpool, tripwiremagazine.co.uk, Februarty 2016)
That's A Strike
(Ten Days Of The Coen Bros: Day Six: The Big Lebowski review, March 2016)
Absence Of Malice?
(Ten Days Of The Coen Bros: Day Six: Part Three: The Man Who Wasn't There review, March 2016)
Back In The Ring
(Chuck Palahniuk Fight Club 2 interview, tripwiremagazine.co.uk, June 2016)
On The Wayne
(Eight Days Of Christoper Nolan: Day Eight: The Dark Knight Rises review, tripwiremagazine.co.uk, July 2017)
Lost In Space
(Eight Days Of Christoper Nolan: Day Eight: Interstellar review, tripwiremagazine.co.uk, July 2017)
Pan's People
(Eight Days Of Guillermo del Toro: Day Five: Pan's Labyrinth review, tripwiremagazine.co.uk, February 2018)
A Mann For All Seasons
(Jeremy Mann interview, tripwiremagazine.co.uk, March 2018)
Boxing Clever
(David Mack Fight Club 3 interview, tripwiremagazine.co.uk, January 2019)
English Beat
(Kieron Gillen interview, Tripwire Winter Print Special Winter 2020/2021)
Brothers in Art
(Etherington Brothers interview, Tripwire Winter Print Special Winter 2020/2021)
Selfmade Attitude
(SelfMade Hero interview, Tripwire Winter Print Special Winter 2020/2021)
Harnessing Technology
(Wacom tablet interviews, Tripwire Winter Print Special Winter 2020/2021)
Thinking Differently
(Ram V interview, Tripwire Winter Print Special Winter 2020/2021)
Crossing Universes
(Intercompany crossovers, Tripwire Winter Print Special Winter 2020/2021)
Casting A Huge Shadow
(Darwyn Cooke interview with Jimmy Palmiotti, Tripwire Winter Print Special Winter 2020/2021)
Speed Kings
(80 years of The Flash feature, Tripwire Winter Print Special Winter 2020/2021)
Dream Career
(Neil Gaiman feature, Tripwire Winter Print Special Winter 2020/2021)
Kicking Off The Marvel Age
Speaking Frankly
(Frank Miller interview, tripwiremagazine.co.uk, Oct 2021)
(Fantastic Four At 60, Tripwire print special winter 2021)
Claws And Effect
(40th anniversary, An American Werewolf In London, Tripwire print special winter 2021)
Artfully Done
(Alistair Little interview, Tripwire print special winter 2021)
Classics Illustrated
(Folio Society feature, Tripwire print special winter 2021)
It's Not The Years, It's The Mileage
(Indiana Jones Raiders Of The Lost Ark 40th Anniversary, Tripwire print special winter 2021)
Portraits With Character
(photo feature, Tripwire print special winter 2021)
Looking Sharp
(Liam Sharp interview, Tripwire print special winter 2021)
Pulling The Strings
(Guillermo del Toro Pinocchio Teaser, tripwiremagazine.co.uk, January 2022)
Making Us An Offer We Mostly Can't Refuse
(review of The Godfather Trilogy 4K, tripwiremagazine.co.uk, April 2022)
Extinction Agenda
(review of Jurassic World: Dominion, tripwiremagazine.co.uk, June 2022)
The Gene Genie
(Better Call Saul interview, tripwiremagazine.co.uk, July 2022)

HEAVY METAL 45

Scott Braden takes a look at 45 years of cultural comics phenomenon *Heavy Metal*, who brought European sensibilities to the US for the first time...

Forty-five years after its groundbreaking launch on newsstands, *Heavy Metal Magazine* has proven itself as much more than just a magazine. It was—and still is—a cultural phenomenon. It is a staple in the art and comics community and known as the premiere storyteller of cutting-edge illustrated science fiction, fantasy, and horror.

Originally published in the United States by National Lampoon, *Heavy Metal Magazine* is a direct descendant of its internationally renowned French parent publication, *Métal Hurlant*. After a European trip in 1975, National Lampoon contributor Tony Hendra expressed interest in European comics and the National Lampoon team began to seek out European comic material. In 1976, National Lampoon Editor Sean Kelly singled out *Métal Hurlant* and brought the French comics and art publication to the attention of publishing partner Matty Simmons and National Lampoon President Leonard Mogel. It was perfect timing as Mogel was departing for Germany and France to jump-start the French edition of *National Lampoon*.

Métal Hurlant debuted in early 1975 from Les Humanoïdes Associés, an association that Philippe Druillet, Jean-Pierre Dionnet, Jean Giraud

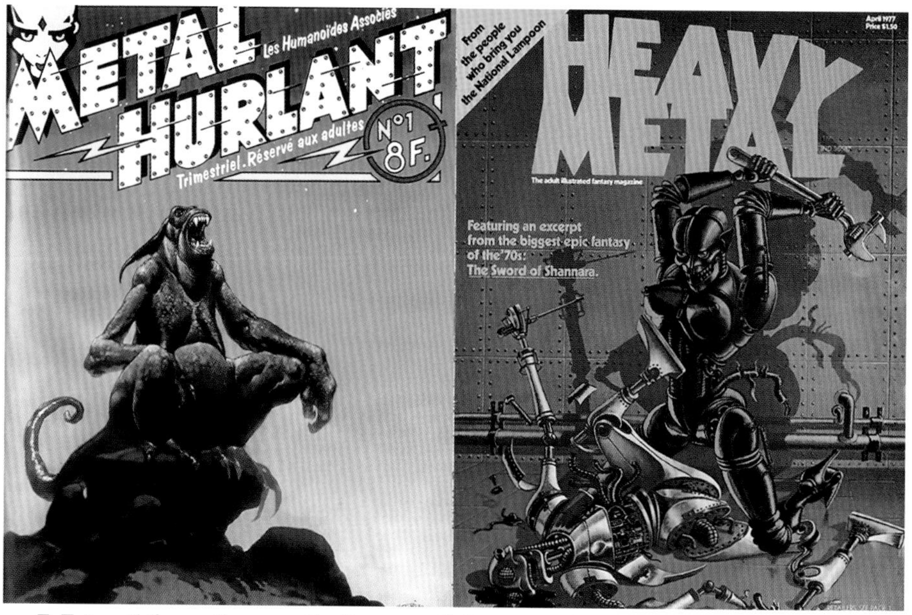
MÉTAL HURLANT
Les Humanoïdes Associés
Trimestriel. Réservé aux adultes
N°1 8F.
From the people who bring you the National Lampoon
HEAVY METAL
April 1977 Price $1.50
Featuring an excerpt from the biggest epic fantasy of the '70s: The Sword of Shannara.

Métal hurlant debuted in early 1975 from Les Humanoïdes Associés, an association that Philippe Druillet, Jean-Pierre Dionnet, Jean Giraud (Mœbius), and financial director Bernard Farkas formed in 1974.

(Mœbius), and financial director Bernard Farkas formed in 1974. Upon Mogel's return from Paris in 1976, he reported that the French publishers had agreed to an English language version, and suggested the title *Heavy Metal* to be used for the first issue debuting in 1977. The English translation of Métal Hurlant is "Screaming Metal" or "Howling Metal", but the National Lampoon team thought that Heavy Metal made more sense due to the "heavy" deep philosophical content and the connection to the popular musical genre.

Heavy Metal Magazine debuted in the States as a glossy, full-color monthly magazine published by HM Communications, Inc. The cover of the initial April 1977 issue declared itself to be "From the people who bring you the *National Lampoon*", and the issue primarily featured reprints from *Métal Hurlant*, as well as material from National Lampoon, a colourised portion of Vaughn Bodē's *Sunpot*, and an excerpt from Terry Brooks' *The Sword of Shannara*.

Heavy Metal Magazine was the first publisher to bring European legends like Mœbius, Enki Bilal, Philippe Druillet, Milo Manara and Pepe Moreno to the U.S. while showcasing non-mainstream American superstars like Richard Corben, Vaughn Bodē, Bernie Wrightson and Frank Frazetta.

July 1977
$1.50
HEAVY METAL
The adult illustrated fantasy magazine
Featuring:
Eleven pages of Moebius's "Harzak"
The conclusion of Vaughn Bodé's "Sunpot"
Love, Death, ESP, and Intergalactic Super Spies
LES HUMANOIDES ASSOCIES

Since Heavy Metal was a magazine, it was able to evade the restrictive Comics Code Authority that confined the subjects of American comic books in the past

Published monthly, *Heavy Metal Magazine* has featured serialised and standalone comic stories, artist galleries, short stories in prose, and interviews. Since *Heavy Metal* was a magazine, it was able to evade the restrictive Comics Code Authority that confined the subjects of American comic books in the past. That allowed *Heavy Metal* to print explicit content that couldn't be found elsewhere in comics, breaking down boundaries and allowing creators complete freedom to explore not just sexuality and violence but also deep-reaching philosophical sci-fi concepts. The magazine has become an icon in not just the adult realm, but the entire art and storytelling community, as a bastion of counterculture and home for thrilling, subversive, no-holds-barred content.

Kevin Eastman, co-creator of the *Teenage Mutant Ninja Turtles*, took over publication of the magazine in May 1992 and continued to run the company until 2014, when it was sold. In 2019, CEO Matthew Medney, Chief Creative Overlord and Publisher David Erwin, Associate Publisher & Chief Sales Officer Kris Longo, and Executive Editor Joseph Illidge took over and have taken *Heavy Metal Magazine* and the company to new heights, adding a podcast network, a growing slate of comics and prose novels, a series of NFTs and Web3 worldbuilding, and starting Heavy Metal Studios with President Tommy Coriale to build a slate of television and film projects in partnership with

ADULTES
6
trimestriel
METAL HURLANT
8f50
canada $2
LE MAJOR GRUBER de MŒBIUS
Bilal.Tardi.Corben.Masse...

HEAVY METAL
February 1982
$2.00
WPS 36587
The adult illustrated fantasy magazine
GREG HILDEBRANDT

In 2019, CEO Matthew Medney, Chief Creative Overlord and Publisher David Erwin, Associate Publisher & Chief Sales Officer Kris Longo, and Executive Editor Joseph Illidge took over and have taken Heavy Metal Magazine and the company to new heights

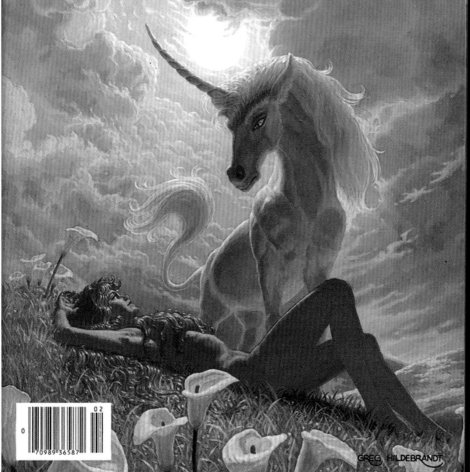

top-tier management firm Range Media Partners as a co-producer.

"As real life becomes stranger than fiction and technological advancement accelerates at blinding speed, Heavy Metal will continue to push the envelope of genre fiction and celebrate legendary artists like Juan Gimenez and Ken Kelly while opening the doors to tomorrow's visionary creators. Reaching for the stars is our duty," said Joseph Illidge, Executive Editor.

In addition to the magazine, the company is known for the 1981 Canadian-American, fantasy-tinged, animated anthology film for adults, *Heavy Metal*, directed by Gerald Potterton and produced by Hollywood giant Ivan Reitman and *Heavy Metal Magazine*'s own Mogel. Among the many voice actors who lent their talents to this film include comedy troupe Second City's John Candy, Joe Flaherty, and Eugene Levy, as well as Harold Ramis, Richard Romanus, August Schellenberg, and John Vernon, among others. The screenplay was written by Daniel Goldberg and Len Blum. The soundtrack, with songs from popular rock artists, including Black Sabbath, Blue Öyster Cult, Don Felder, and more, is also beloved by fans.

The *Heavy Metal* film is an anthology of various science fiction and fantasy stories tied together by a single theme of an evil force that is "the sum of all evils". It was adapted from stories from *Heavy Metal Magazine* and featured shorts inspired by the likes of such legends as Bernie Wrightson and Richard Corben, among others. The film also introduced the world to Taarna, *Heavy Metal*'s iconic warrior heroine. Like the magazine, the film was geared towards adults due to its graphic cutting-edge content, told

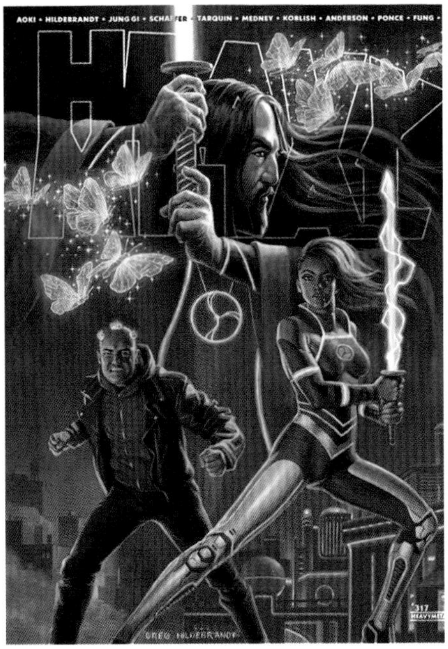
AOKI • HILDEBRANDT • JUNG GI • SCHAFFER • TARQUIN • MEDNEY • KOBLISH • ANDERSON • PONCE • FUNG
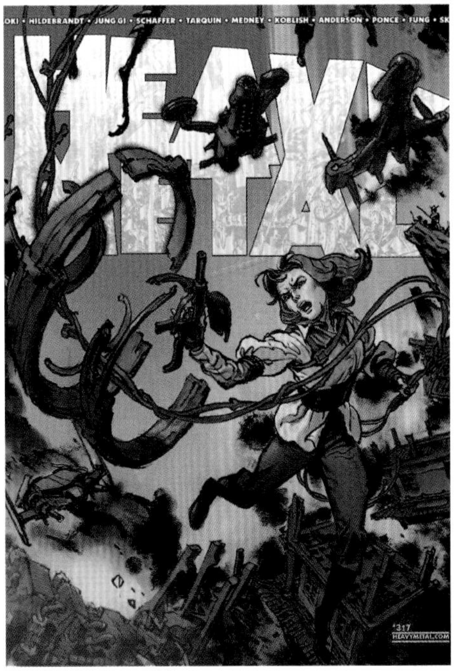
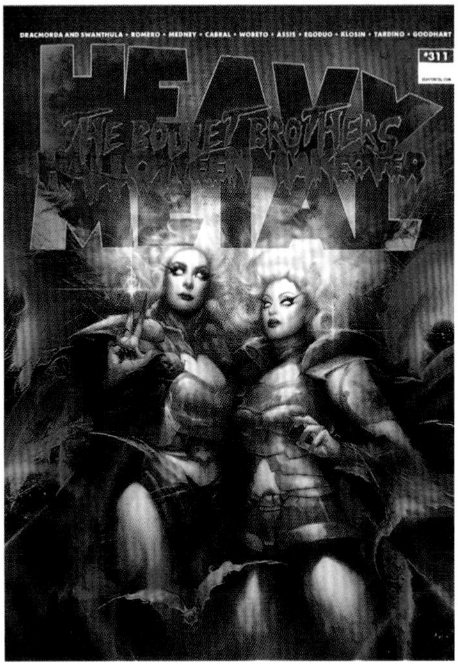
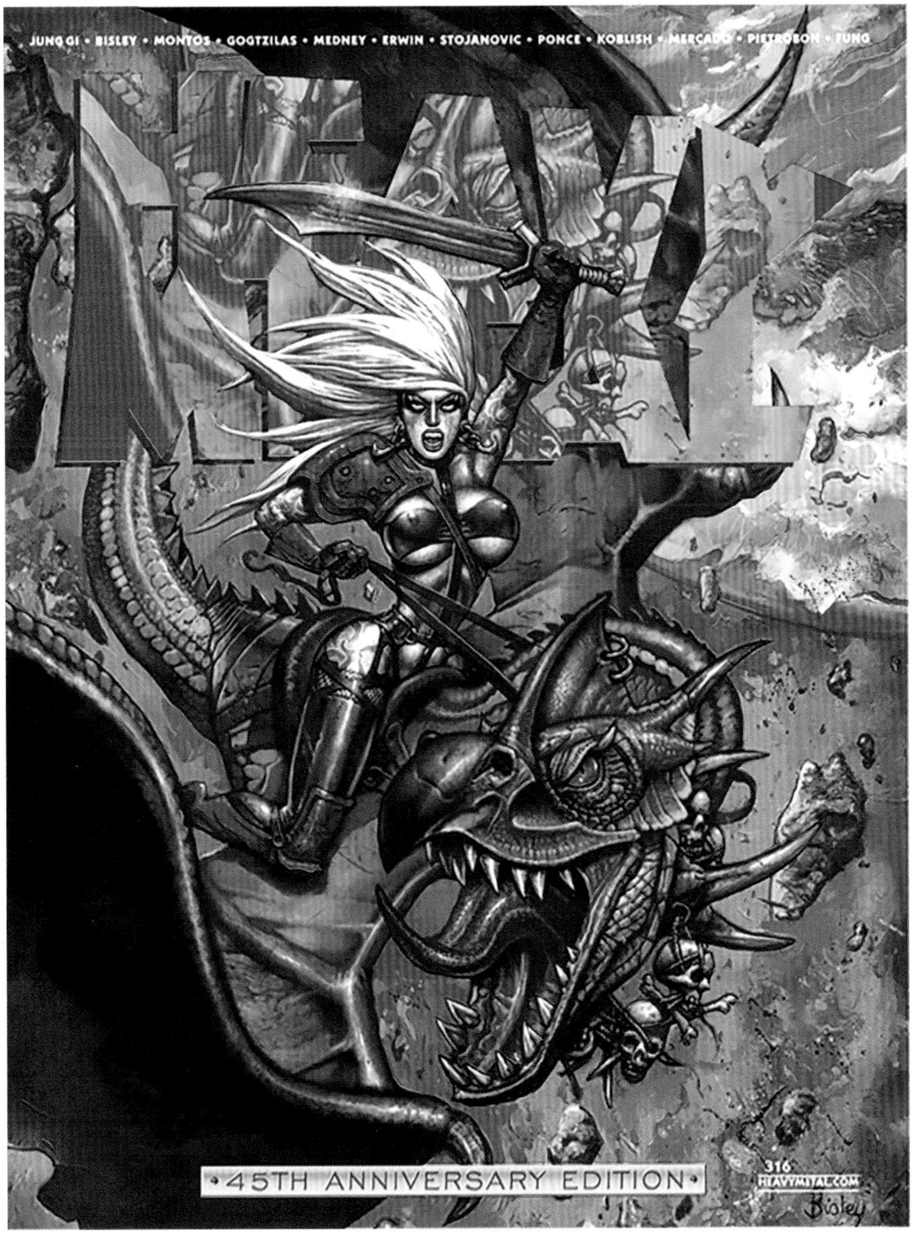
JUNG GI • BISLEY • MONTOS • GOGTZILAS • MEDNEY • ERWIN • STOJANOVIC • PONCE • KOBLISH • MERCADO • PIETROBON • FUNG
• 45TH ANNIVERSARY EDITION •
316
HEAVYMETAL.COM

through the lens of imaginative genre fiction with a focus on stunning mind-bending art. Its production was boosted by having several animation houses working simultaneously on different segments. Since its release, the film has become a cult classic in pop culture.

The trend-setting magazine has inspired some of the most famous blockbusters in film history, including *Blade Runner* ("Do Androids Dream of Electric Sheep?" was printed in the magazine) and *The Fifth Element*, and the company published the official *Alien* graphic novel in 1979 (Alien artist H.R. Giger was a contributor to both *Métal Hurlant* and *Heavy Metal Magazine*). Award-winning filmmakers like Guillermo del Toro and Zack Snyder

Heavy Metal is known for its vast and rich history in art and storytelling, and the company continues to not only live up that legacy but is bringing it even further into the future.

February 2022
$13.99
HEAVY
The adult illustrated fantasy magazine
GREG HILDEBRANDT

HEAVY METAL

"Managing a 45-year-old legacy can be a daunting business, but we view this as quite simply our time to remind the world how pop culture has caught up to *Heavy Metal*." – Kris Longo, associate publisher, Heavy Metal

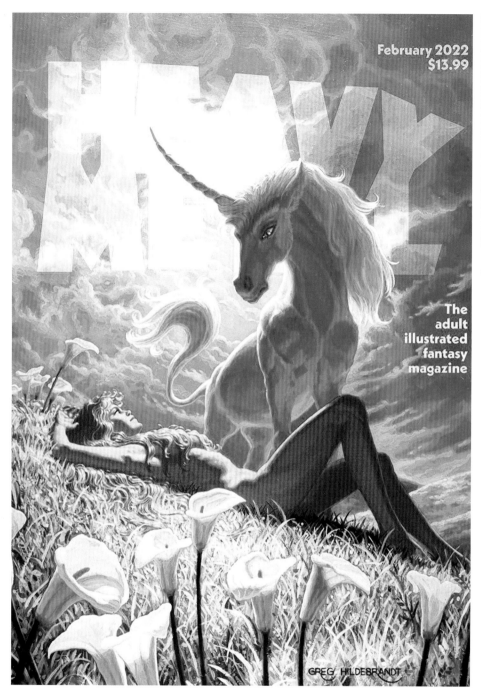

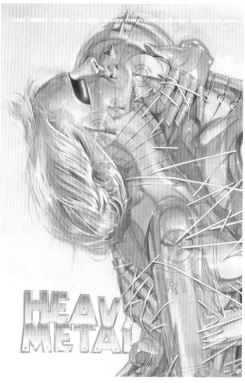

have cited the influence of Heavy Metal on their work, and Netflix's popular animation anthology *Love, Death, & Robots* is a modern reinterpretation of the magazine.

"Directly and indirectly, our legacy has shaped the current landscape of popular culture. If the embryo of the idea or character did not literally appear on the pages of *Heavy Metal*, those pages inspired so many of today's writers, directors and showrunners to create challenging and compelling sci-fi, fantasy and horror content.

Managing a 45-year-old legacy can be a daunting business, but we view this as quite simply our time to remind the world how pop culture has caught up to Heavy Metal," said Associate Publisher & Chief Sales Officer Kris Longo.

Heavy Metal is known for its vast and rich history in art and storytelling, and the company continues to not only live up that legacy but is bringing it even further into the future. Exciting new content from the company includes projects like Christopher Priest's *Entropy* comic series, screen adaptations of Blake Northcott's *Arena Mode* novel and Dan Fogler's *Moon Lake* graphic novels, recent collaborations with artists and creators like Hajime Sorayama, Kim Jung Gi, Greg Hildebrandt, Steve Aoki, Seth Green, and the Boulet Brothers, and monthly magazine issues filled to the brim with stunning illustrations and thrilling tales. As President Tommy Coriale told *Variety* in a recent interview, "Our message to our fans and to Hollywood is one and the same – buckle the f–k up, *Heavy Metal* has arrived."

COMIC BOOK TRENDS IN THE TIME OF TRIPWIRE 1992 - 2022

Scott Braden offers us a selection of the trends in comic books during the lifespan so far of Tripwire Magazine: 1992-2022: from the death of some major fictional figures in the the industry to gender swaps and more…

To say the trend of the "Dark Age" of Comics started in a vacuum with the coming of the 1980s four-color masterpieces would be foolish – and we here at *Tripwire: The Genre Magazine* are anything but fools. Of course, there was Marvel Comics' *X-Men* #137, where Chris Claremont and John Byrne killed the nigh omniscient Phoenix; as well as Frank Miller's *The Dark Knight Returns* and Alan Moore & Dave Gibbons *Watchmen* for DC Comics. But, before that, there were the EC Comics stories of the 1950s. Decades later, the drug addiction of Speedy (DC Comics' sidekick to its "Emerald Archer"), the death of Gwen Stacy (the fair-haired first love of Marvel Comics' "Web-Slinger"), and the coming of the House of Ideas' high-calibre anti-hero, The Punisher – all in the 1970s.

The trend of "Darker Tales" did not miss the Tripwire Era either. With the coming of the premier international genre magazine came the death (and rebirth) of Superman, and the death of The Caped Crusader's second Robin (Jason Todd). There was the not-so far-fetched transformation of Katar Hol's home planet of Thanagar (Hawkworld) into a totalitarian police state; the breaking (and healing) of Batman's back; and not to be left out, the period where Wolverine lost his nigh-invulnerable adamantium metal lining of his bones and claws.

Then, about three decades earlier in the 1960s, within the pages of DC Comics' *Lois Lane* #106 (scripted by legendary war comics scribe Robert Kanigher and featuring art by Werner Roth & Vince Colletta); fans witnessed the transformation of white-bread Lois Lane into an African-American woman for an undercover assignment. Not to be outdone in the 1990s, Frank Castle – The Punisher – became black for a New York minute via his best-selling Marvel Comics title, and the House of Ideas' young super-team of the New Warriors found themselves in a parallel, utilitarian, African-dominated America (courtesy of The Sphynx) where Caucasians were on the lower tier of class society and the likes of Reed Richards – one of the Marvel Universe's most brilliant men in any reality – aspired to be nothing more than a janitor in the top-selling dystopian storyline, "Forever Yesterday."

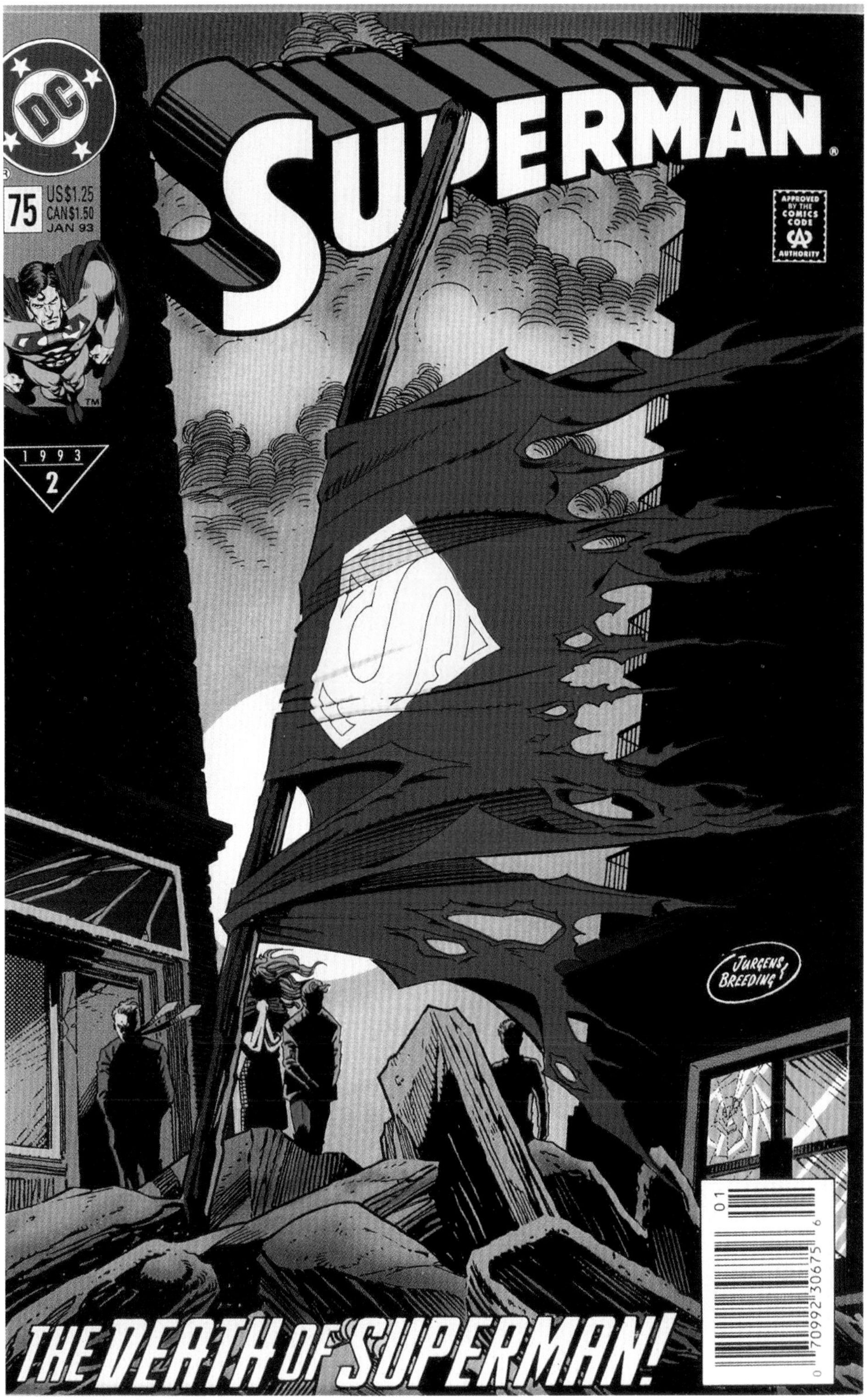
SUPERMAN
75
US$1.25
CAN$1.50
JAN 93
1993
2
APPROVED BY THE COMICS CODE AUTHORITY
JURGENS/ BREEDING
THE DEATH OF SUPERMAN!

Another popular trend during the time of Tripwire was the painted comic. Multiple award-winning painter and storyteller Alex Ross was at the forefront of this movement with his works *Marvels* (with Kurt Busiek), as well as *Kingdom Come* (with Mark Waid) for the Distinguished Competition.

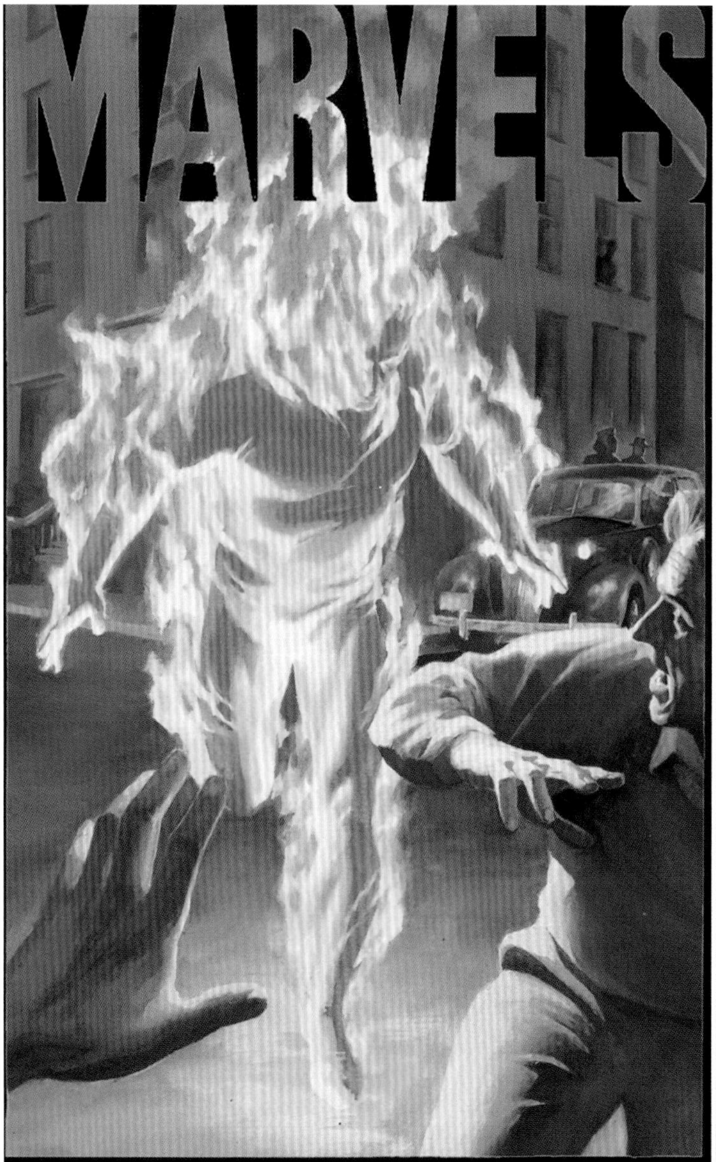
MARVELS

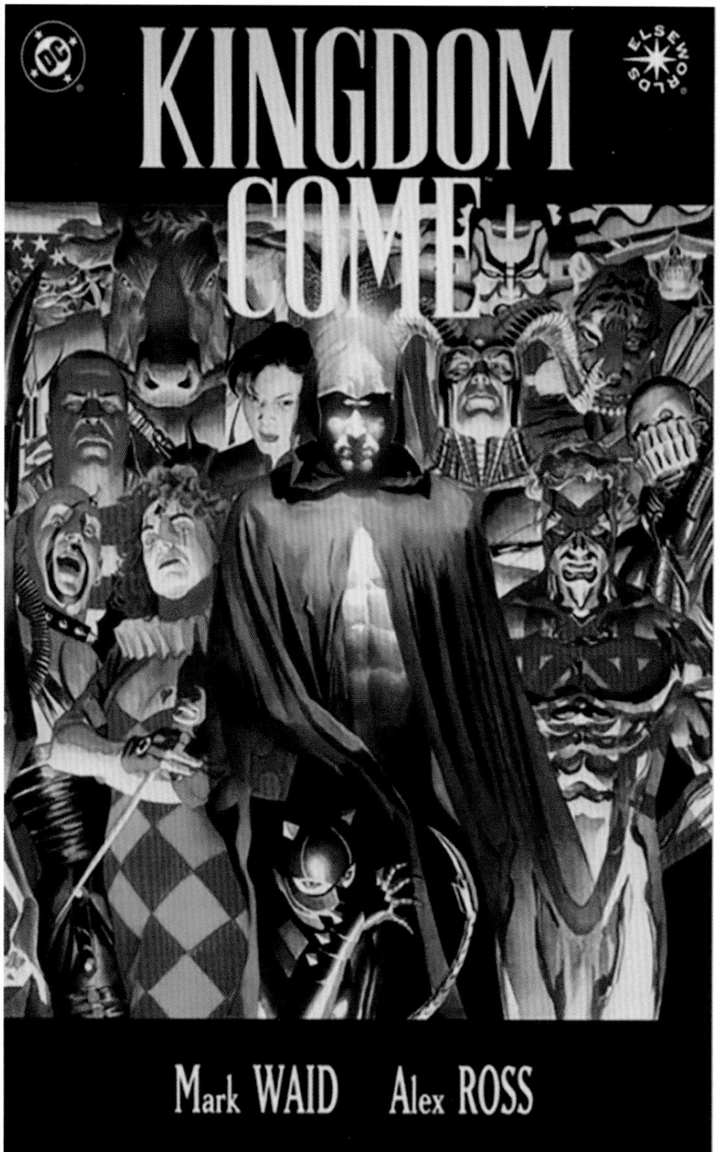
DC
KINGDOM COME
ELSEWORLDS
Mark WAID Alex ROSS

ANOTHER POPULAR TREND DURING THE TIME OF TRIPWIRE WAS THE PAINTED COMIC. MULTIPLE AWARD-WINNING PAINTER AND STORYTELLER ALEX ROSS WAS AT THE FOREFRONT OF THIS MOVEMENT WITH HIS WORKS MARVELS WITH KURT BUSIEK), AS WELL AS KINGDOM COME (WITH MARK WAID) FOR THE DISTINGUISHED COMPETITION. THESE WORKS WERE FOLLOWED BY THE HOUSE OF IDEAS' VARIED TALES OF THE MARVELS IMPRINT RELEASES, INCLUDIN CODE OF HONOR RUINS AND OTHERS.

These works were followed by the House of Ideas' varied "Tales of the Marvels" imprint releases, including Code of Honor, Ruins, and others. On the independent front, there was Dan Brereton's *Nocturnals*, and the spectacular painting he did on Howard Chaykin's *Thrillkillers* for DC.

Although originally popular in the 1960s through the '80s as well, the trend of new characters taking over long-held super-hero roles during the time of Tripwire also saw a growing movement. For example, Dennis O'Neil and Joe Quesada's creation Azrael became a dark Batman, John Ridley's Future Batman took over the role of Bruce Wayne, and one-time sidekick The Falcon earned his wings and became Captain America. Then, there was Spidey's clone, Ben Reilly, who became Spider-Man; the "Four Supermen" (Steel, Superboy, The Eradicator, and The Cyborg) took over the Man of Steel during his absence; and Hal Jordan became The Spectre as a fallout of the DC company crossover, *Zero Hour*.

Then, beginning in the 2000s, there was the trend of making established characters gay – like the Golden Age Green Lantern. Never mind that living legend Roy Thomas had him happily married off to the Golden Age Harlequin and the father of Infinity Inc. members Jade and Obsidian. Nope, just a little retcon and he's homosexual.

Not that there aren't strong gay characters in comics from

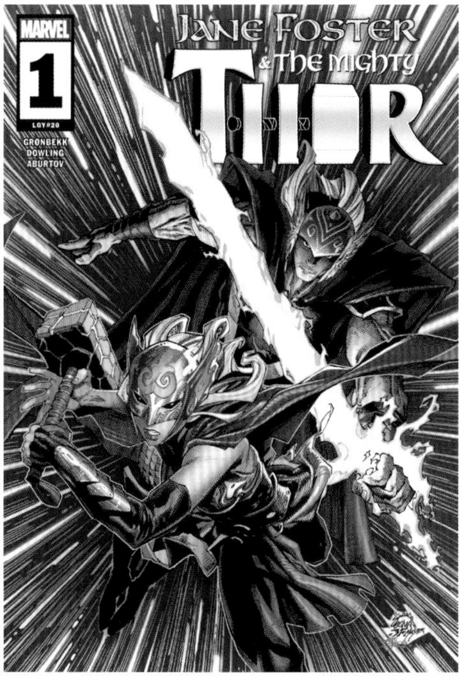
MARVEL
1
JANE FOSTER & THE MIGHTY THOR
GRONBEKK
DOWLING
ABURTOV

their inception. Look at Apollo, Batwoman, Midnighter and Northstar – fan-favourite heroes all. Still, that doesn't stop the Big Two from taking established characters like Tim Drake (the third Robin) and the Son of Superman Jon Kent and making them LGBT. Pandering? Maybe. Strong characters? A must!

Then, there is Marvel's relatively recent obsession with gender-swapping their classic heroes. Here's the current list: Thor (Jane Foster), Iron Man (Riri Williams as Ironheart), Captain Carter, and Spider-Man (Tom DeFalco's Spider-Girl and Spider-Gwen), Gwenpool, Silk, and of course, the House of Ideas' second and fourth Captain Marvels (Monica Rambeau and former Ms. Marvel/Binary herself, Carol Danvers). DC Comics got into the act, too, in the early 2000s with the 52 addition of the female Question.

Ladies first, I guess.

With all these transformative trends above, it is almost no wonder that comic book fans long for the old days and old ways of four-color fun. Ladies and gentlemen, boys and girls, let us present the concept of "The Homage Comic."

As a companion to the winning team's acclaimed *Marvels*, Kurt Busiek and Alex Ross joined artist-extraordinaire Brent Anderson to explore archetypes and concepts of comics past with their multiple award-winning *Astro City*. Whether at Image, Jim Lee's Homage Comics, DC Comics' Vertigo or back round at Image, it is one series that is a must-read.

Simultaneously, comix grandmaster Alan Moore paid homage while mapping out the history of comicdom in his extensive revamping of Rob Liefeld's *Supreme*. This examination of comics past continued in with the pages of Awesome Entertainment's sole company crossover, *Judgment Day*.

When Liefeld's Awesome

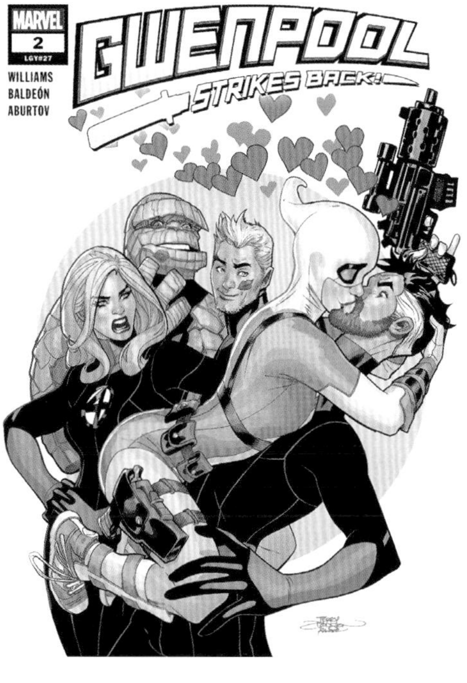
MARVEL
2
GWENPOOL
STRIKES BACK!
WILLIAMS
BALDEÓN
ABURTOV

Entertainment closed shop, Moore examined pulp and science-fiction-based genres at the Jim Lee-helmed America's Best Comics, including the sole creator-owned super-hero (or rather, science-hero) comic book property he has with former *2000 AD* artist Kevin O'Neill, *The League of Extraordinary Gentlemen*.

Divining the same comic book hoodoo that Moore did, John Byrne examined the very beginnings of DC Comics "Man of Tomorrow" and "Darknight Detective" – and the

AS A COMPANION TO THE WINNING TEAM'S ACCLAIMED MARVELS, KURT BUSIEK AND ALEX ROSS JOINED ARTIST-EXTRAORDINAIRE BRENT ANDERSON TO EXPLORE ARCHETYPES AND CONCEPTS OF COMICS PAST WITH THEIR MULTIPLE AWARD-WINNING ASTRO CITY IT IS ONE SERIES THAT IS A MUST-READ.

possible futures that would come from the two costumed champion's origins in real time, with first the Captain America/Batman crossover, and then within the pages of three *Superman & Batman: Generations* projects.

Last but not least, Moore disciple Warren Ellis got into the act first within the pages of *Stormwatch*, where he created iconic characters that mirrored all of comics archetypes. He then examined popular culture on a broader scale within the pages of his and artist John Cassaday's compelling *Planetary*.

These trends remain with us to this day. But, worry not: New ones are just over the horizon for us to see. And see we shall.

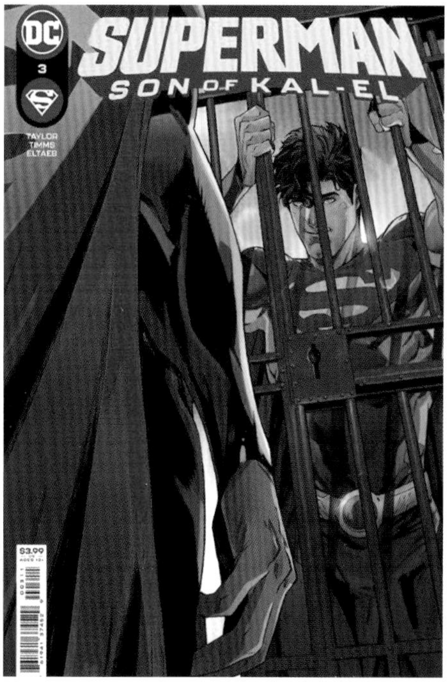
DC
SUPERMAN
SON OF KAL-EL
3
TAYLOR
TIMMS
ELTAEB

30 YEARS OF CAPTURING CREATIVES

Over the next thirteen pages, here's photos taken by Tripwire editor-in-chief Joel Meadows over the past thirty years of figures in the worlds of comics, film and TV...

Liam Sharp, Fitzrovia, London, July 2022 • Alan Moore, signing, Gosh Comics, London, July 2008 • Andy Serkis, New York Comic Con, New York, Oct 2014 • Guillermo del Toro, Covent Garden, London, June 2009 • Helen Mullane, Thought Bubble convention, Yorkshire, Nov 2021 • Louise Simonson, Lucca, Italy, Oct 2018 • Walter Simonson, Suffern, New York, Oct 2017 • Posy Simmonds, Kings Cross, London 2017 • Grant Morrison, New York Comic Con, Oct 2010 • Dave McKean, Kent, Oct 2010 • Mike Perkins, Thought Bubble convention, Yorkshire, Nov 2021 • Christopher Fowler, King's Cross, London, May 2016 • Michael Moorcock, St James, London, June 2011

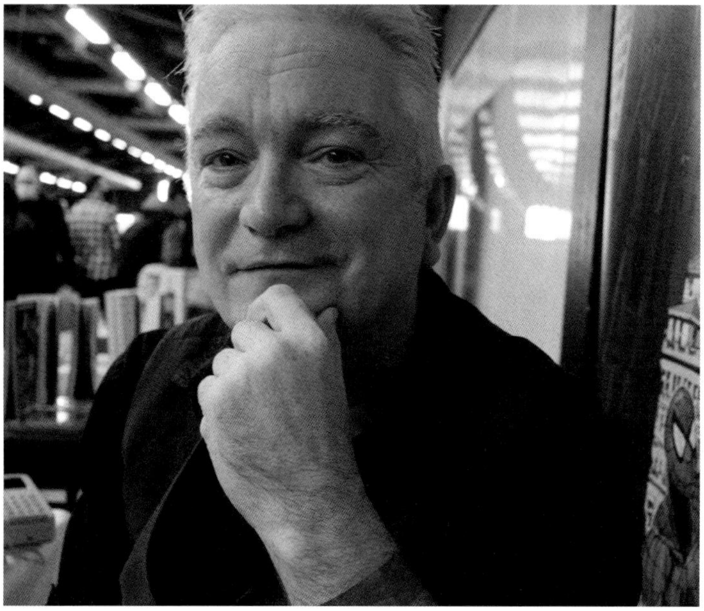

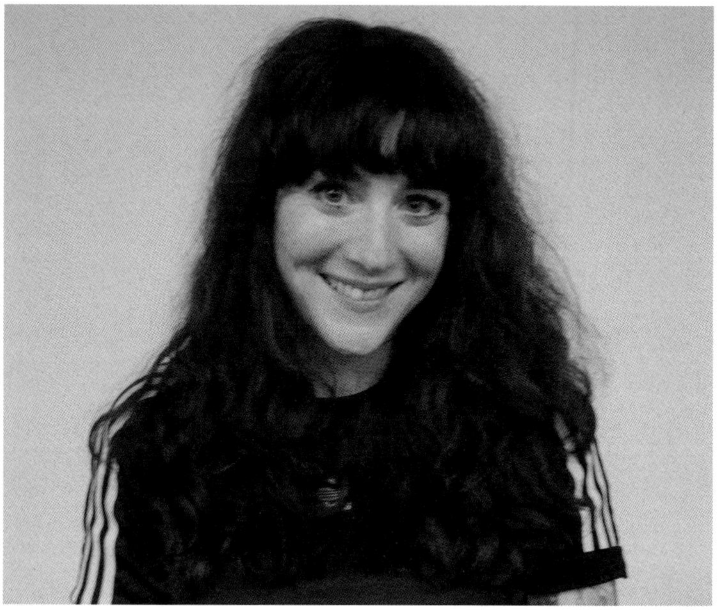

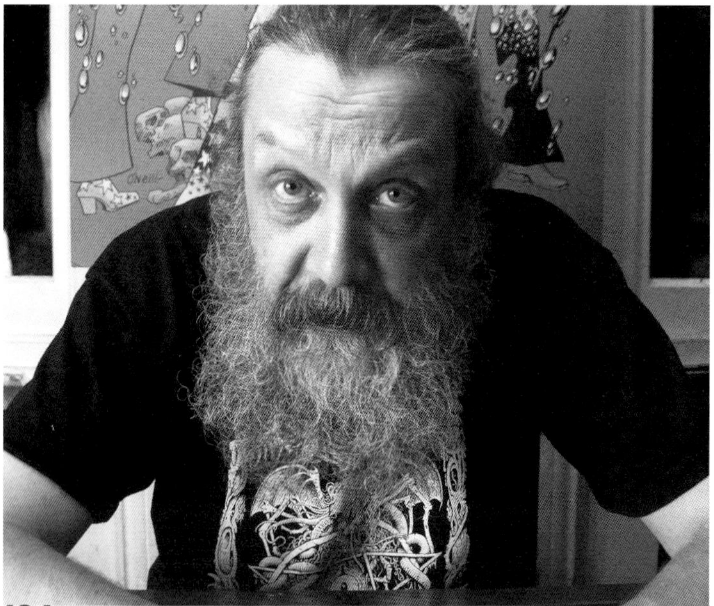

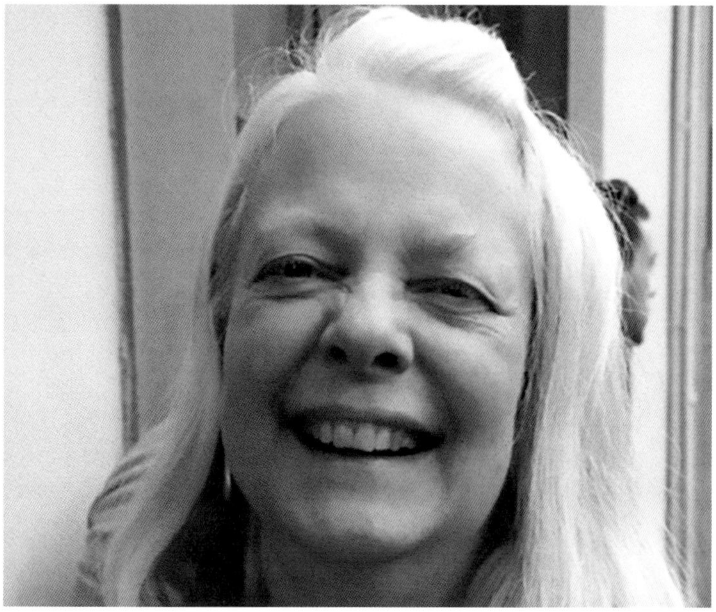

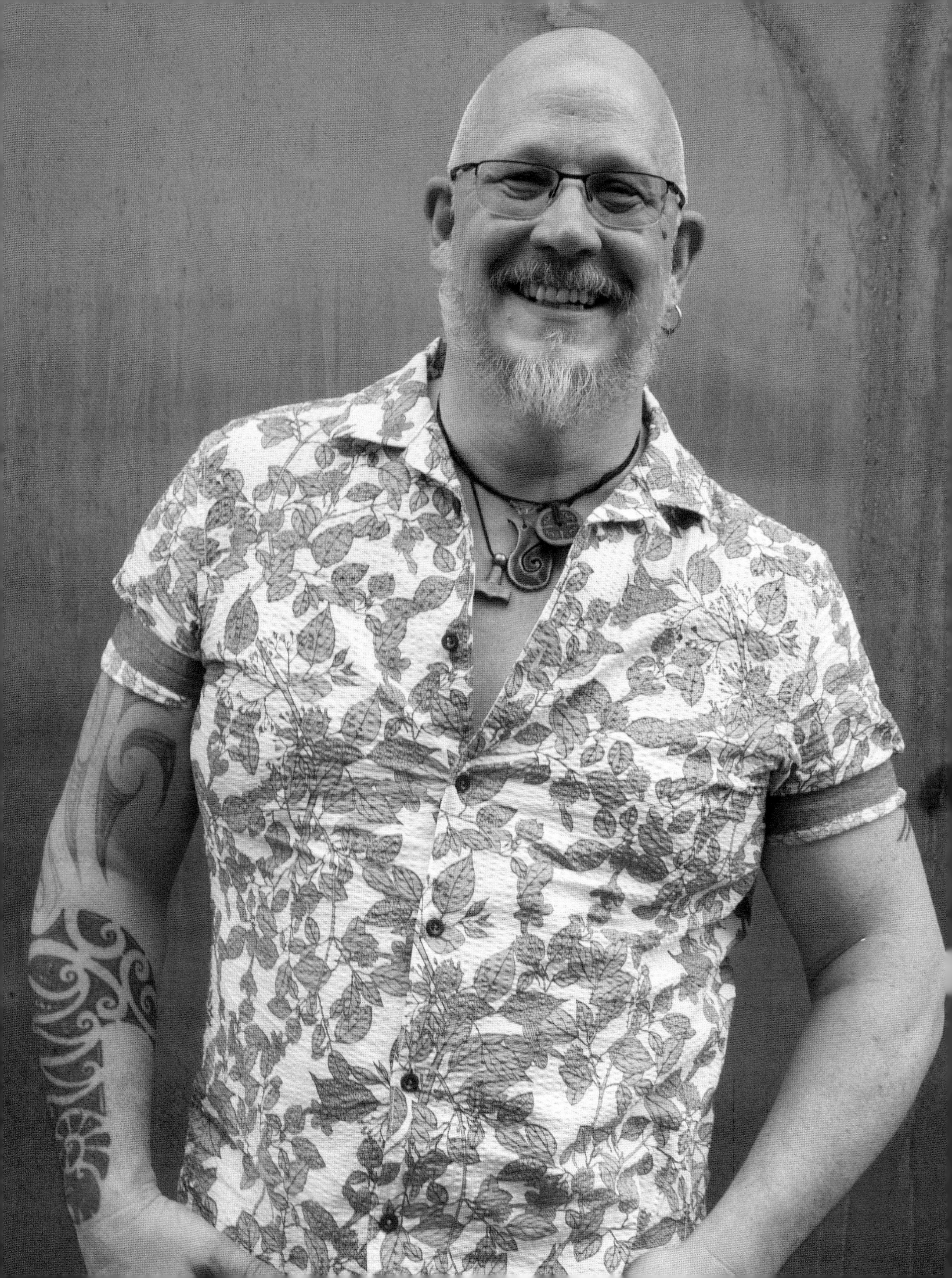

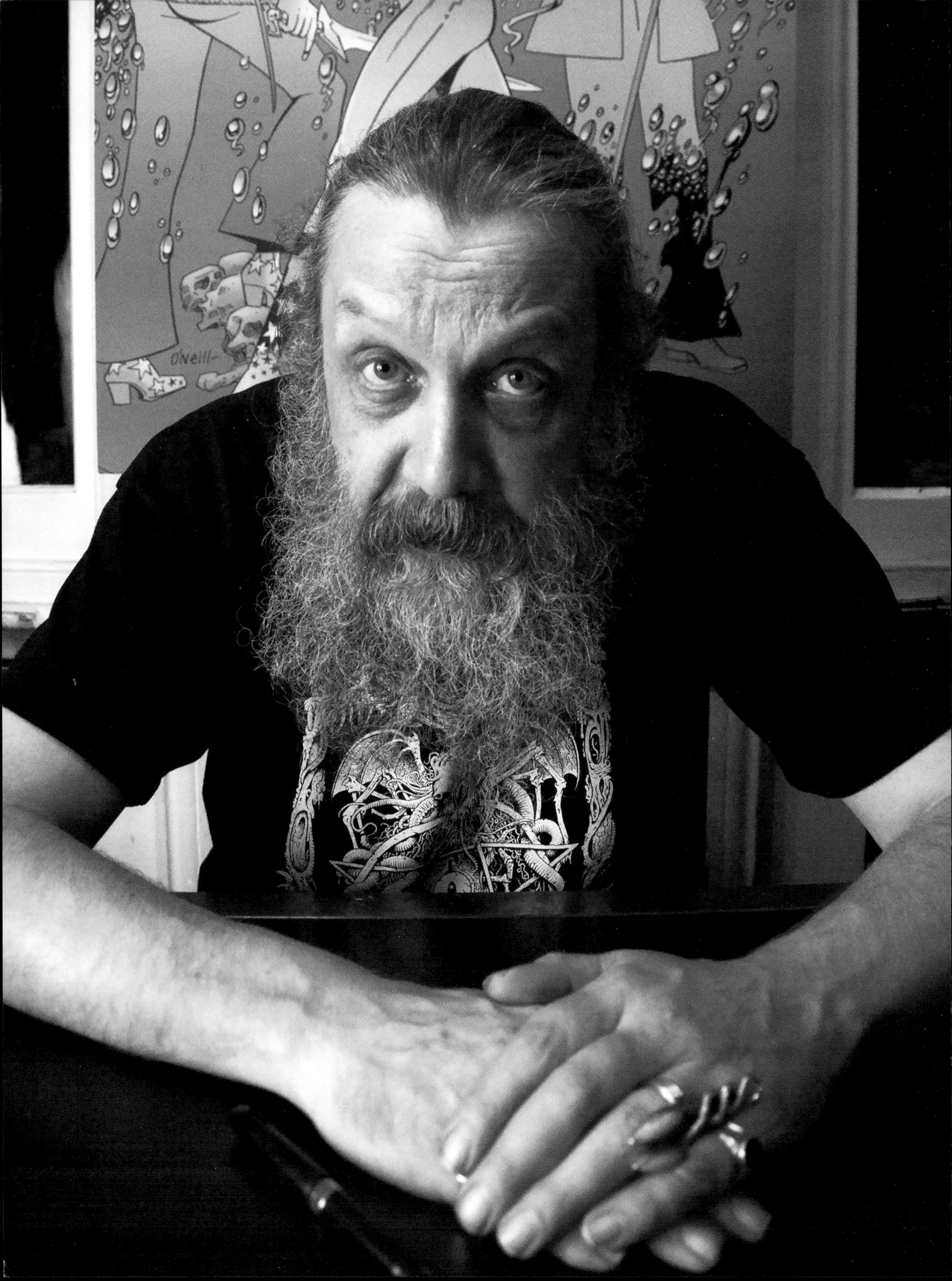
O'Neill

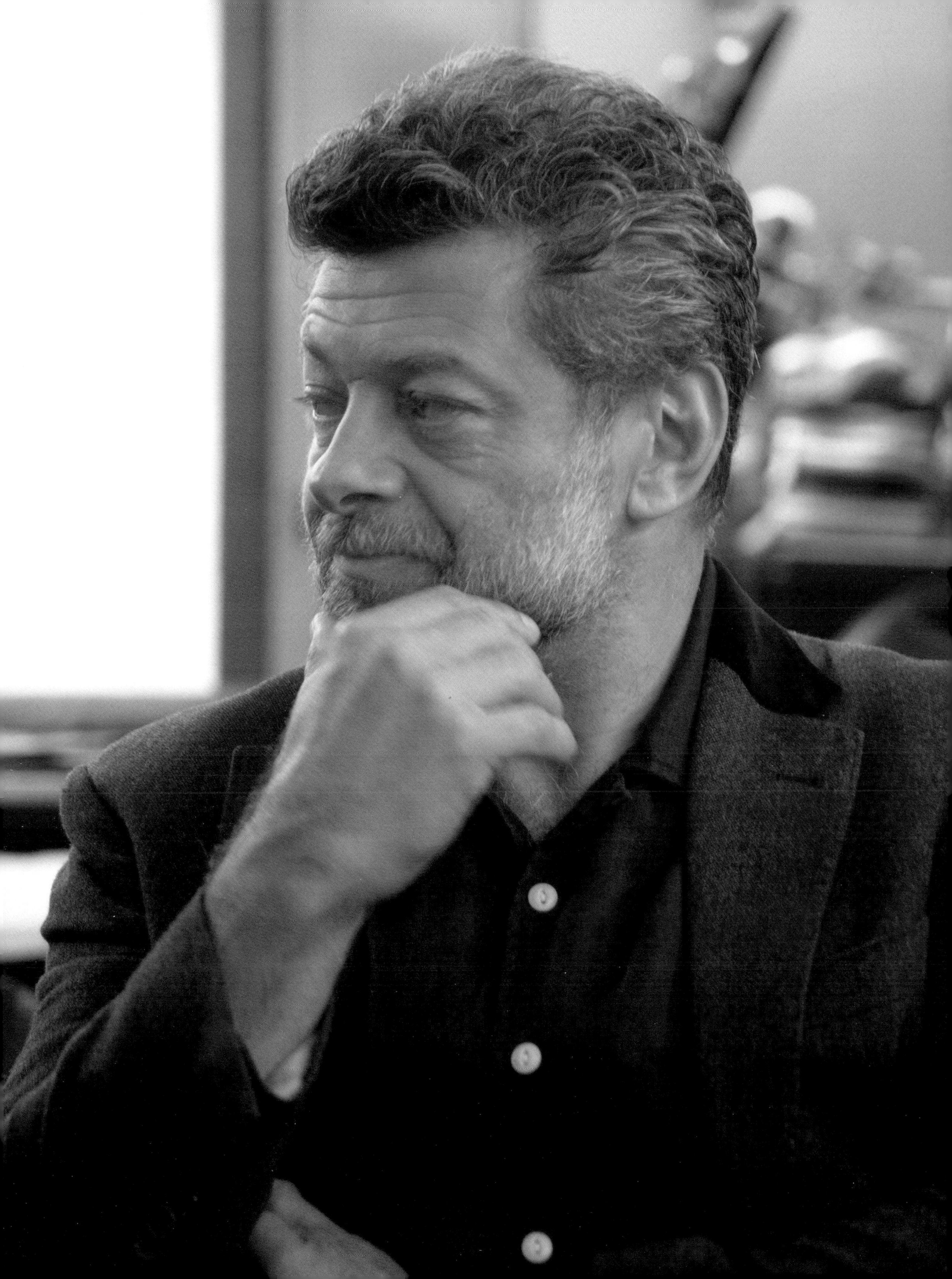

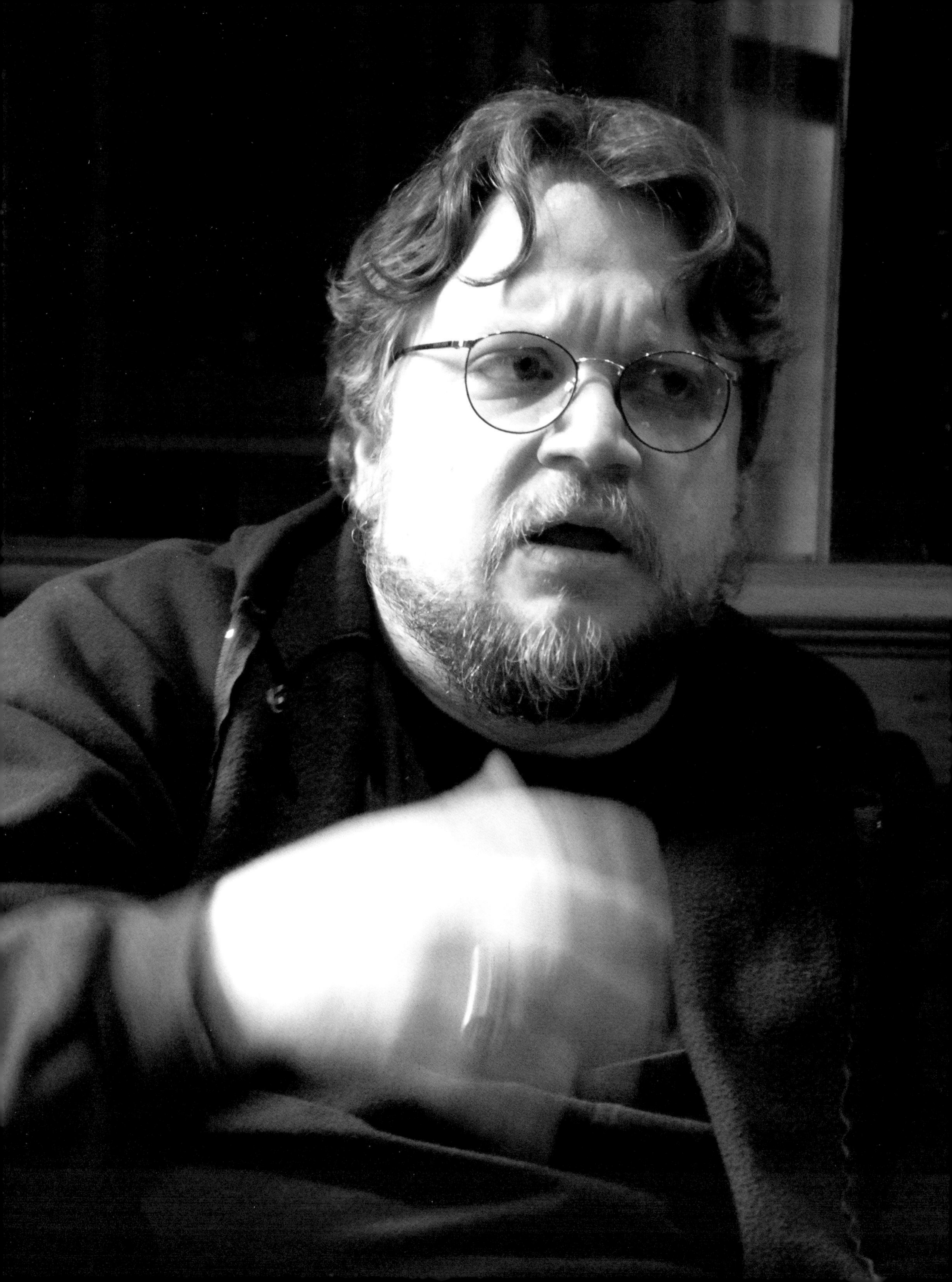

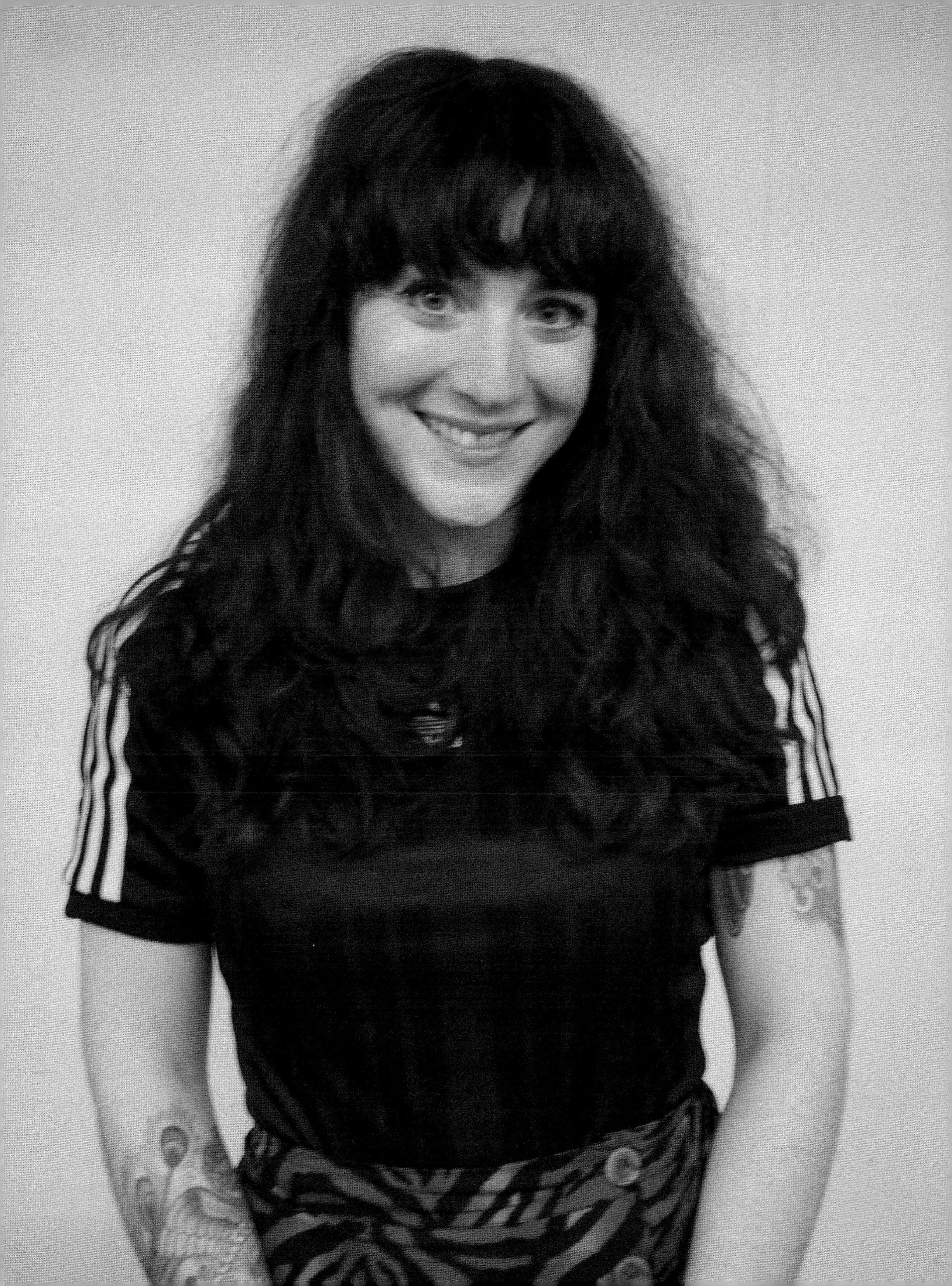

LUCCA

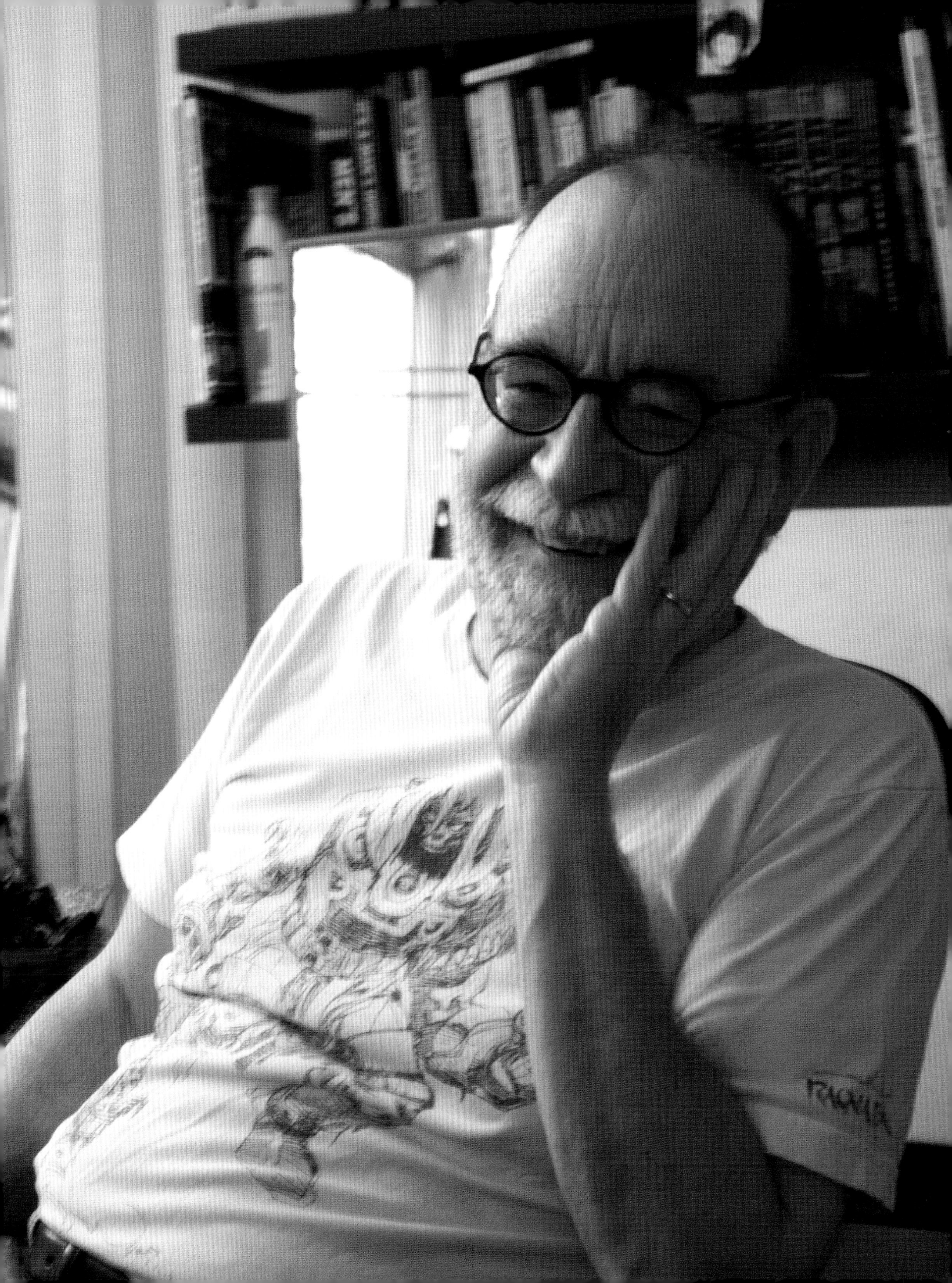

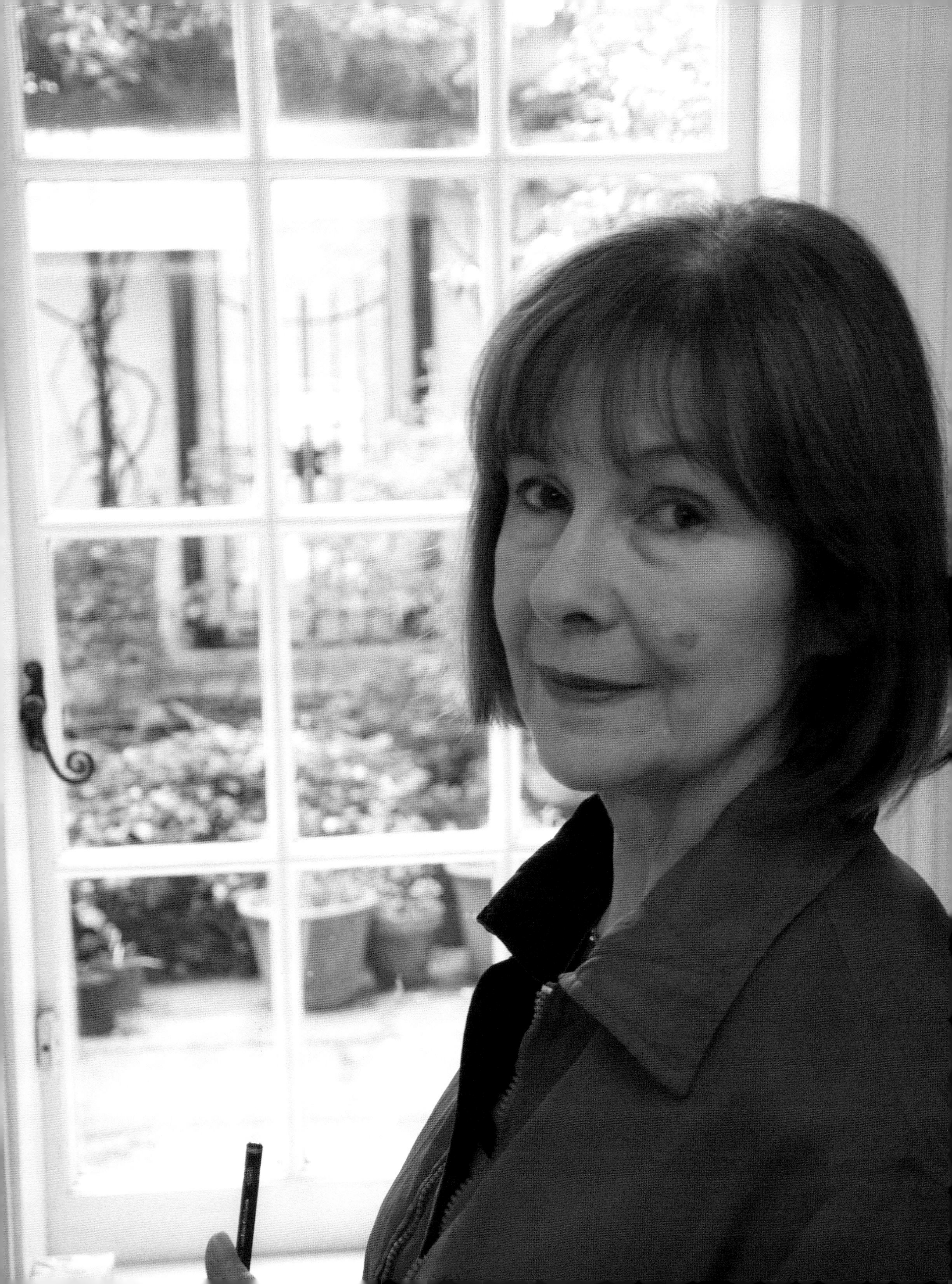

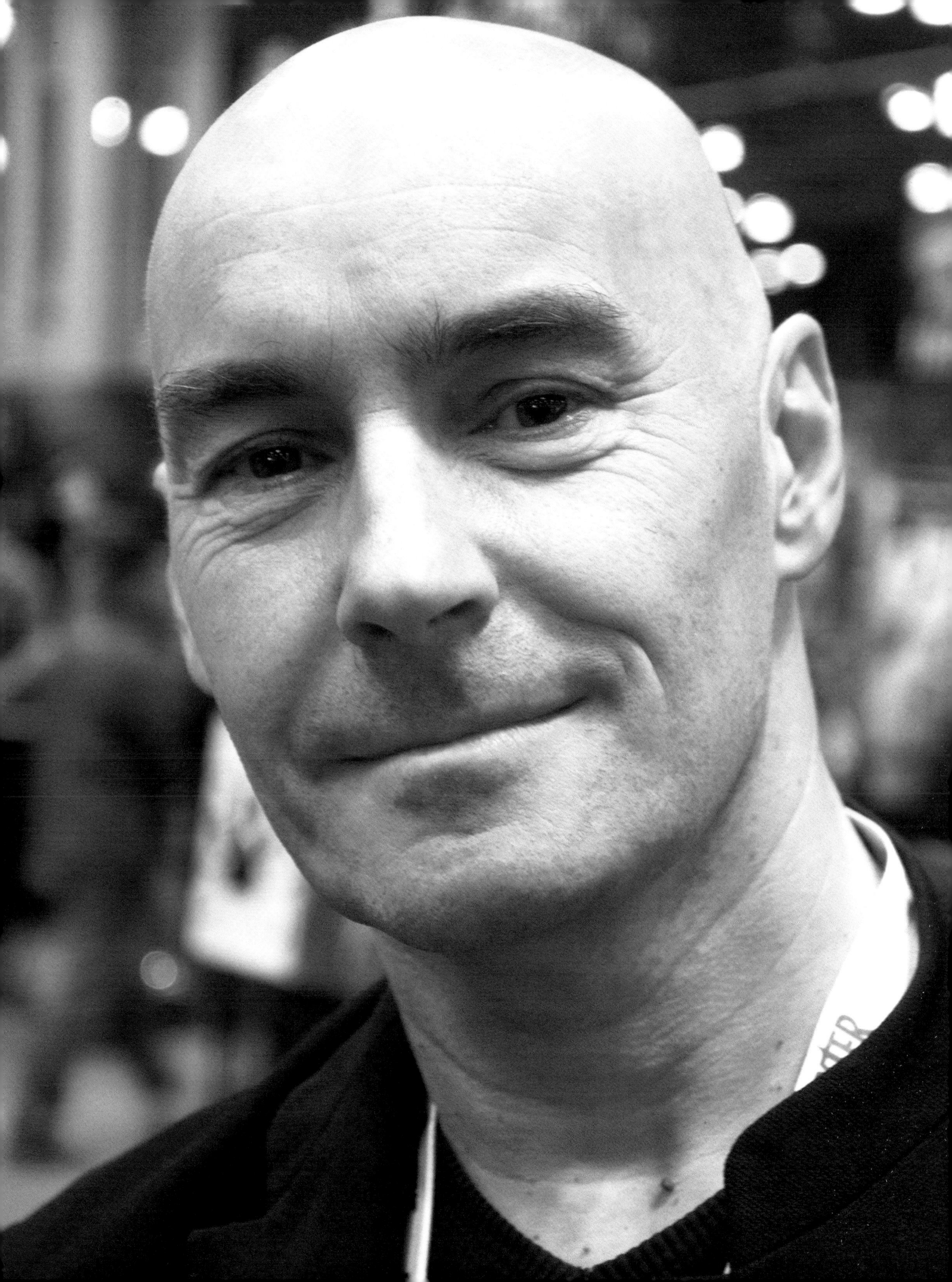

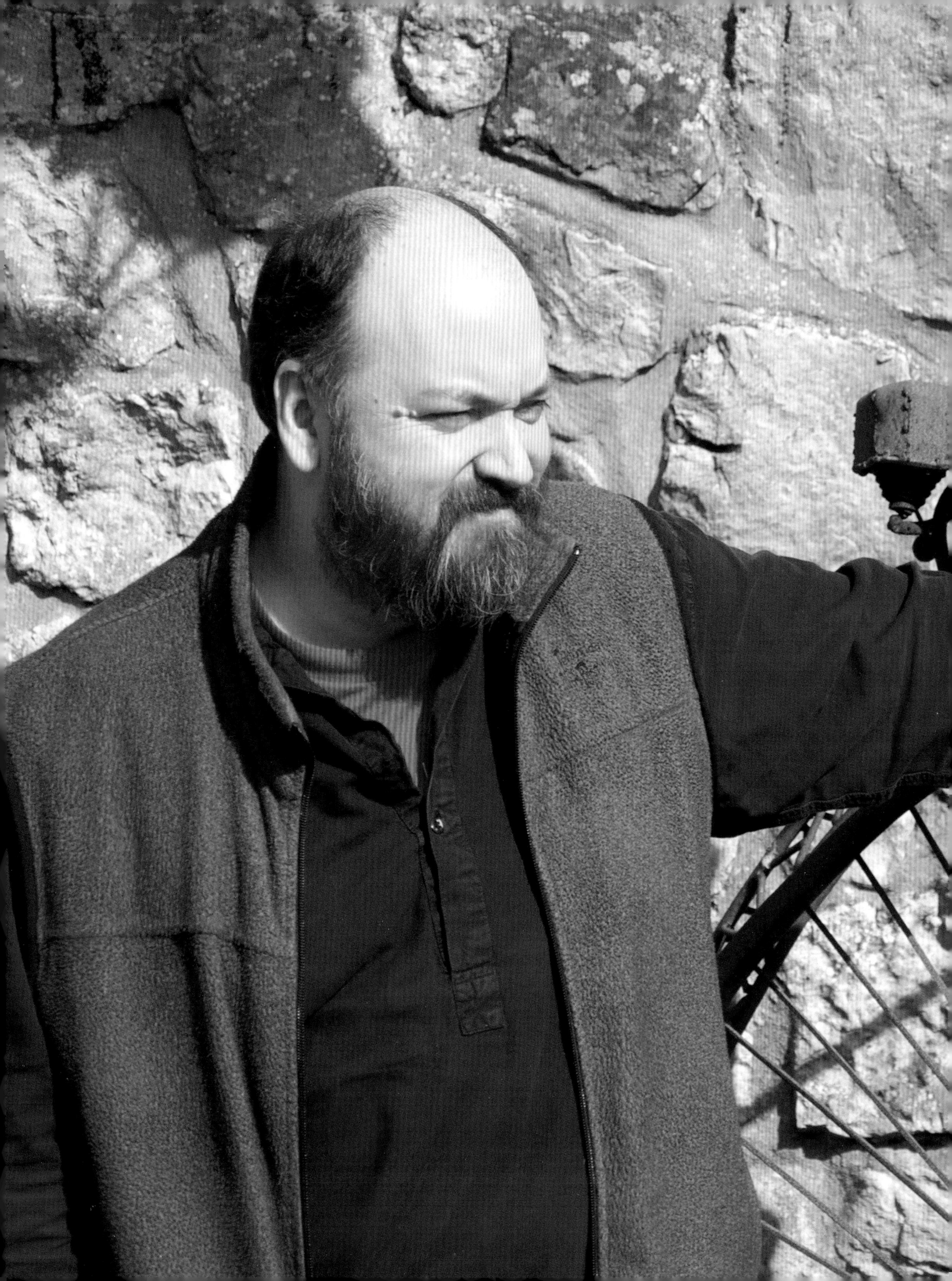

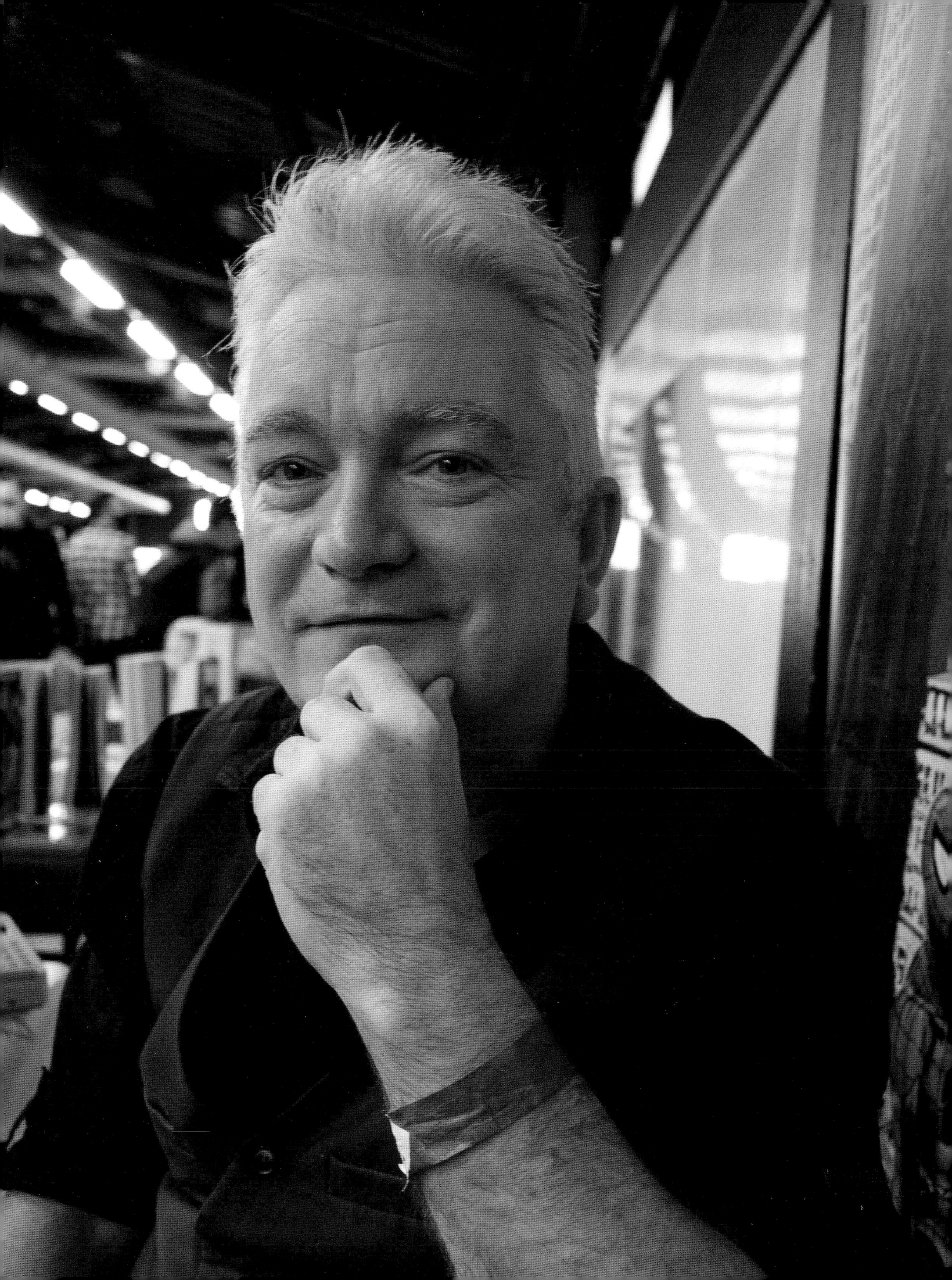

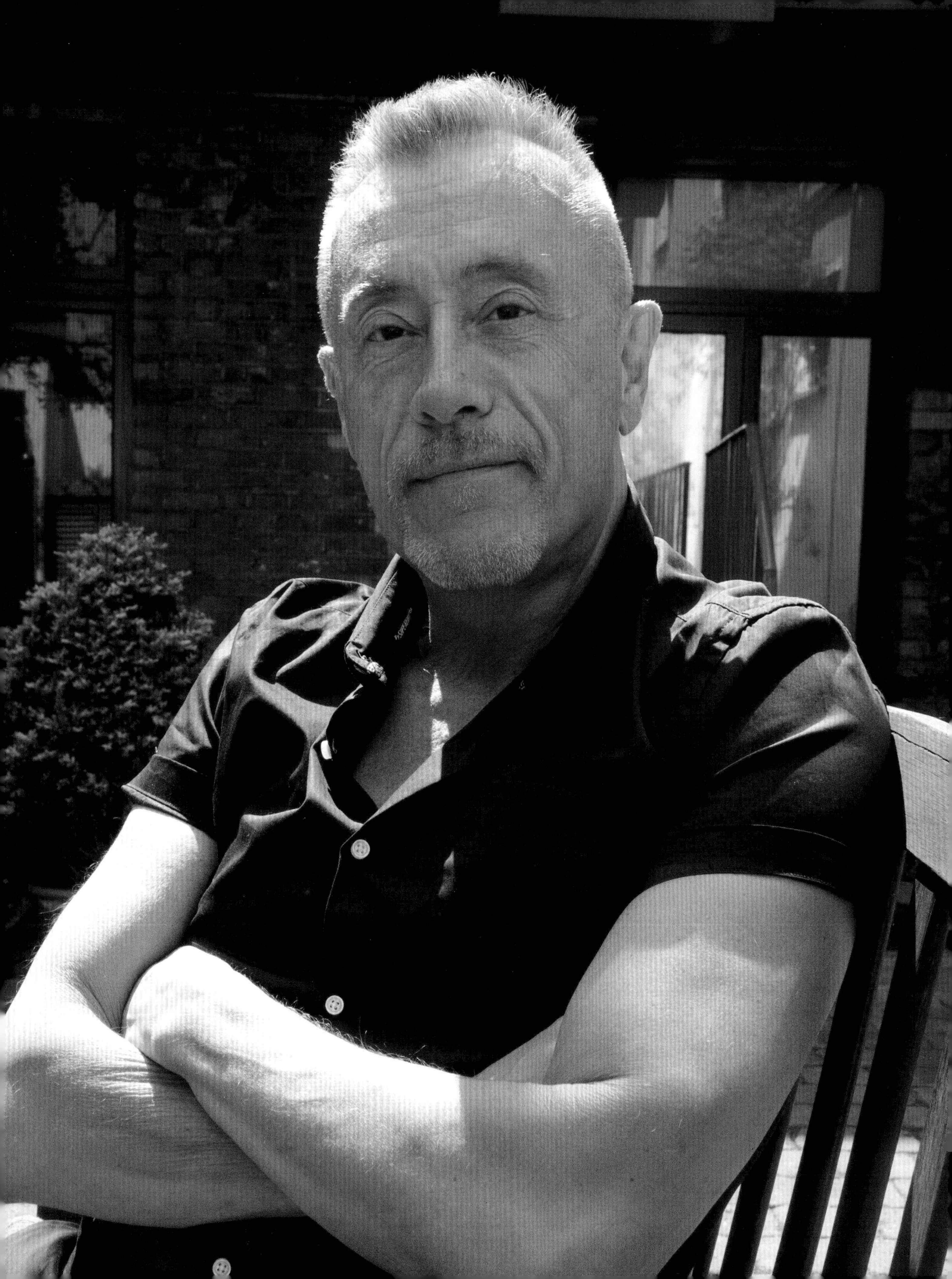

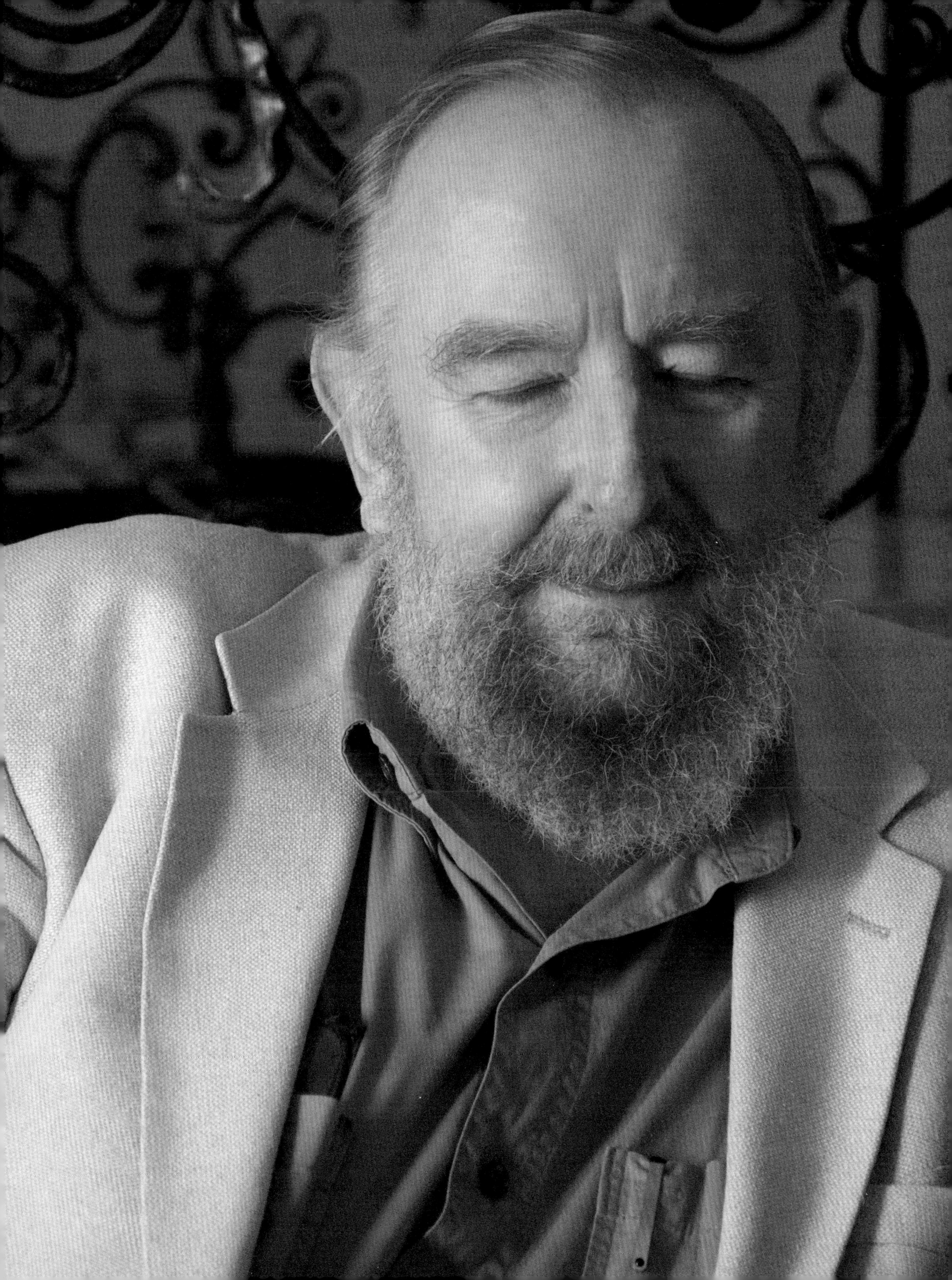

UNLIMITED EDITIONS

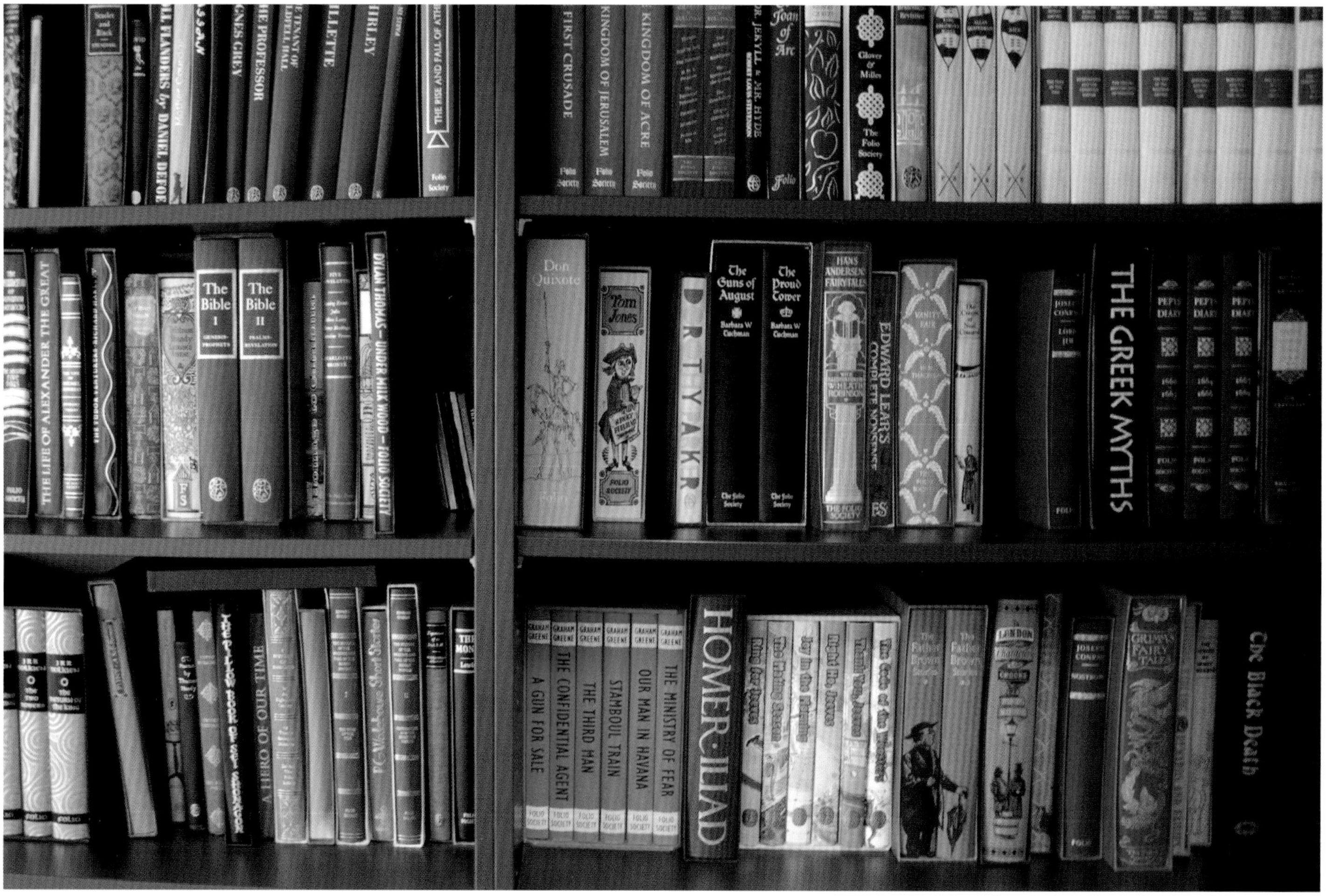
FIRST CRUSADE
KINGDOM OF JERUSALEM
KINGDOM OF ACRE
THE PROFESSOR
THE LIFE OF ALEXANDER THE GREAT
The Bible I
The Bible II
DYLAN THOMAS – UNDER MILK WOOD – FOLIO SOCIETY
Don Quixote
Tom Jones
The Guns of August
The Proud Tower
Barbara W Tuchman
THE GREEK MYTHS
A GUN FOR SALE
THE CONFIDENTIAL AGENT
THE THIRD MAN
STAMBOUL TRAIN
OUR MAN IN HAVANA
THE MINISTRY OF FEAR
HOMER · ILIAD
A HERO OF OUR TIME
The Black Death

FOLIO SOCIETY AT 75

The boutique limited edition publishing house The Folio Society celebrates its 75th birthday this year and Tripwire's editor-in-chief Joel Meadows went to their offices in London near Tower Bridge to talk about the history, genesis and evolution of the company with its publisher Tom Walker

This year isn't just our anniversary but it also marks the 75th anniversary of London boutique publisher The Folio Society.

Tripwire hasn't just been about comics, film and TV but also art and illustration so a look back at the Folio Society with its publisher Tom Walker fits perfectly in this anniversary book.

I went down to The Folio Society's offices in London near Tower Bridge to meet Walker.

The offices are located in a fairly gentrified part of London, a place for tourists and visitors. But the offices are a little off the beaten track there.

The offices feature a library of almost every Folio Society edition published since its inception in 1947 with the rest in a huge warehouse elsewhere.

Wandering along its shelves, you are struck by the range of books Folio has put out over the past seven decades.

Tom Walker meets me and we head to grab lunch nearby.

He fills me in on the genesis of the company back in 1947:

"It was started by someone called Charles Ede and the impetus came out of the post War depression and lack of materials at the time. There's a brilliant essay by John Banville, in our edition of Fleming's *Casino Royale* a while ago talking about the luxury of Bond and how that was so attractive to people after post-War austerity and there was the same motivation here. Charles Ede wanted to make books which were going to last, which were well produced and which were classic in nature. Illustration was there right from the start as was high production values. So the first Folio edition was *Tolstoy's Tales* in 1947 and there were a handful of books produced in 1947, 1948 and 1949, some of which we still have in print. That's not continuous prints which would be

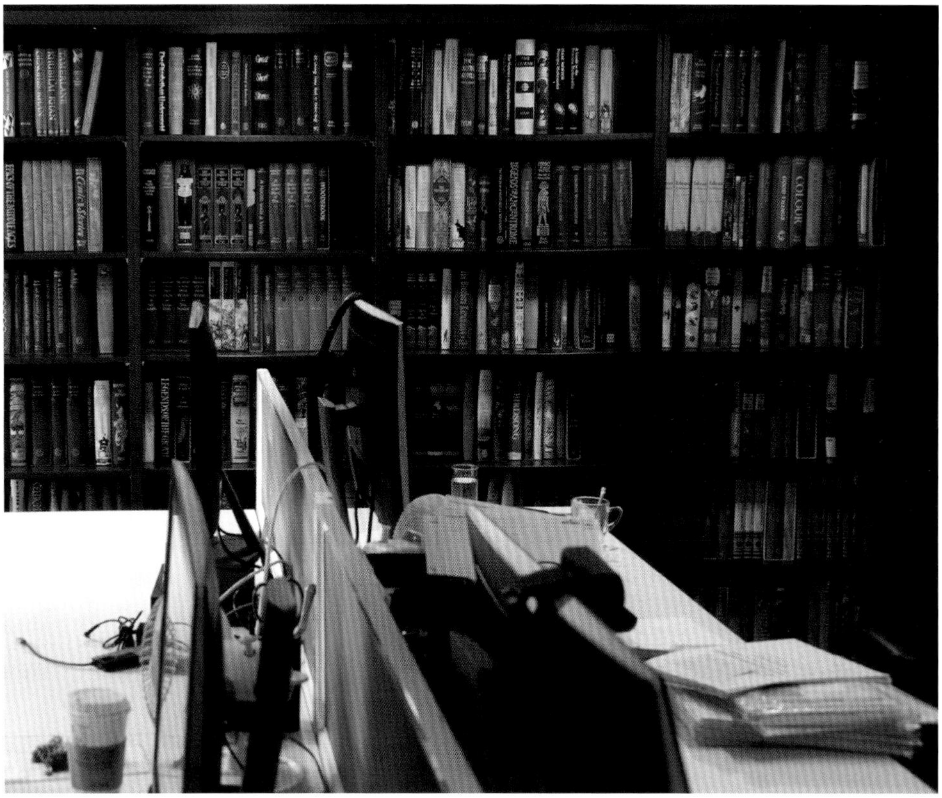

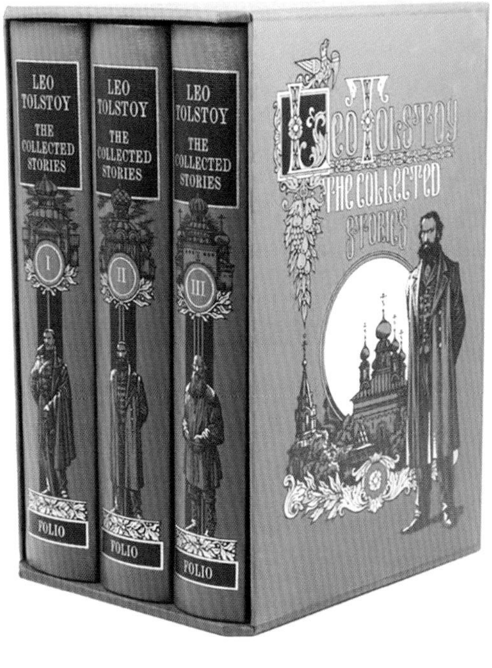
LEO TOLSTOY
THE COLLECTED STORIES
I
II
III
FOLIO
LEO TOLSTOY
THE COLLECTED STORIES

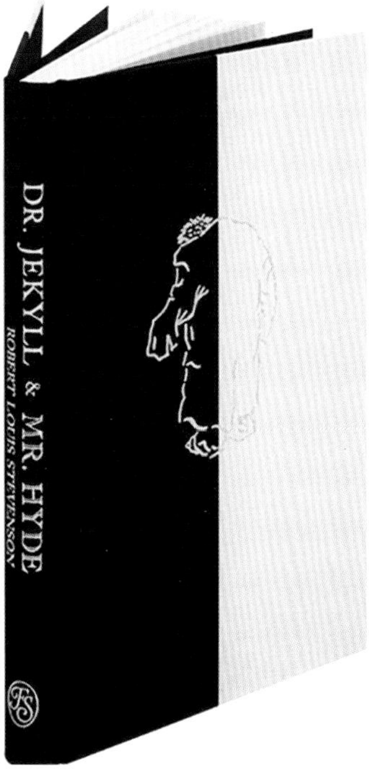
DR. JEKYLL & MR. HYDE
ROBERT LOUIS STEVENSON

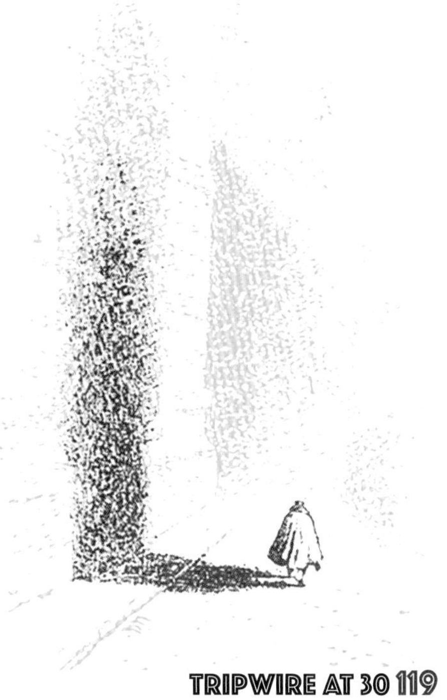

even more impressive but with *Jekyll and Hyde*, we commissioned Mervyn Peake to illustrate that back in 1948 and that has been brought back into print. Then in the 1950s and 1960s it gradually grew. The thread of very high production values has always been there as has community.

In the 1970s and 1980s, it built more internationally so the type of books that we were doing were still very canonical and classics. Then in the 1990s and 2000s, it became a book club and membership model and people would come in and buy into the idea of the Folio Society. That changed around five or six years ago when we opened it up to a wider readership so anyone could come in."

He takes a break from his lunch and continues.

For Walker, it is one particular aspect which really appeals to him: "Now what I love about Folio is it still has the community aspect as we have the online community and the engagement level like we had in the 1980s and 1990s. But it has become a more inclusive organisation and the type of books that we are doing are much broader now. I still see Folio as a classic book publisher but that's in a much wider variety of genres now with fantasy, sci-fi, children's as much as the Victorian novel. The threads are still there and production values are still absolutely crucial to what we do as well as illustration, design and community as they have been so from the start."

The Folio Society has found that being forced to adapt has been something positive for the company, Walker reveals.

"I think the advantage that we've found in the last few years has been we've had to change. For me the big exciting change have been in the way that we think about book design rather than thinking about series consistency like back in the 1990s when every

"'NOW WHAT I LOVE ABOUT FOLIO IS IT STILL HAS THE COMMUNITY ASPECT AS WE HAVE THE ONLINE COMMUNITY AND THE ENGAGEMENT LEVEL LIKE WE HAD IN THE 1980S AND 1990S. BUT IT HAS BECOME A MORE INCLUSIVE ORGANISATION AND THE TYPE OF BOOKS THAT WE ARE DOING ARE MUCH BROADER NOW'"

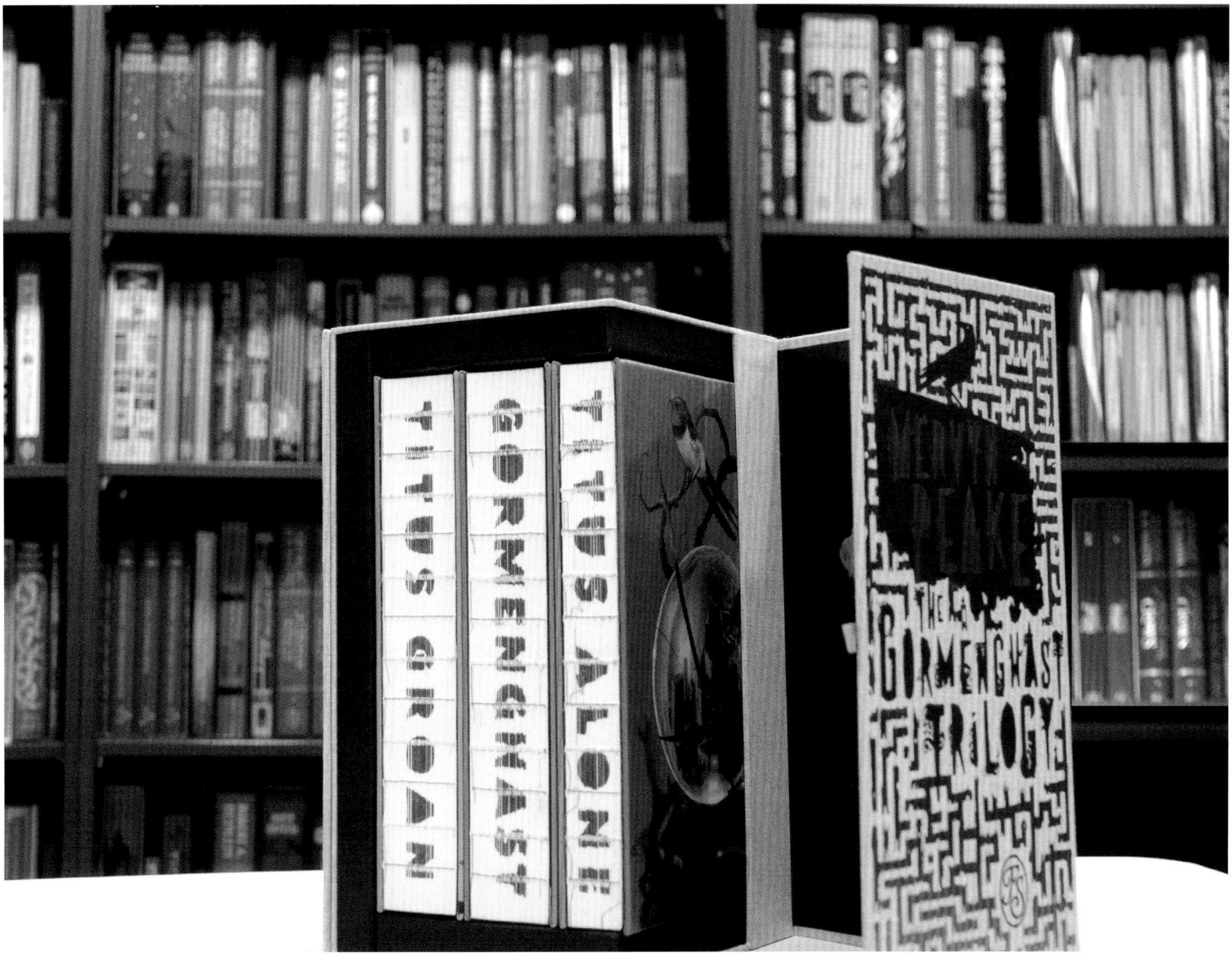
TITUS GROAN
GORMENGHAST
TITUS ALONE
PEAKE
THE GORMENGHAST TRILOGY

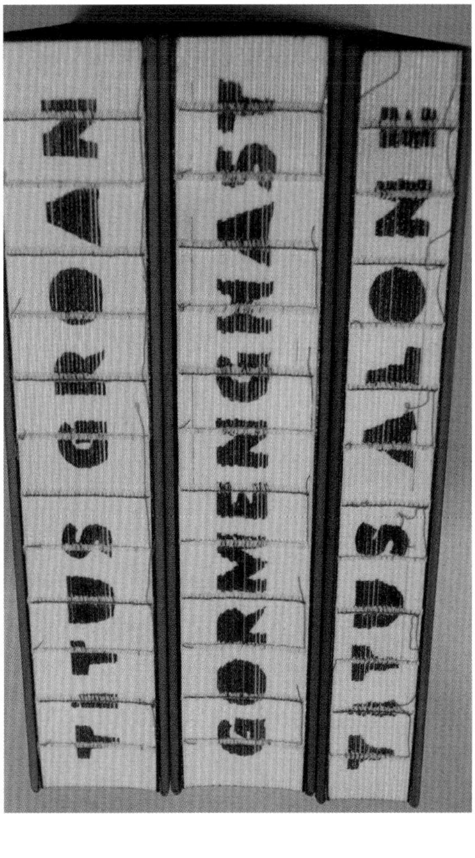
TITUS GROAN
GORMENGHAST
TITUS ALONE

"SO LIKE *GORMENGHAST* WHICH YOU WERE JUST LOOKING AT JUST NOW WHICH PEAKE ILLUSTRATED ORIGINALLY - HOW DO YOU MODERNISE THAT WHILE STILL KEEPING IT CLASSIC, HOW DO YOU INTRODUCE A NEW GENERATION OF READERS TO IT AND HOW DO YOU CREATE THE BEST POSSIBLE EDITION?" – TOM WALKER

Austen would look the same and every Hardy would look the same. There was a beauty to that but now we treat every book individually. When I put a book in the programme, it's treated from scratch and we think: 'How would we make the best possible edition of this?'

So like *Gormeghast* which you were just looking at just now which Peake illustrated originally - how do you modernise that while still keeping it classic, how do you introduce a new generation of readers to it and how do you create the best possible edition? Folio has changed very dramatically and not just in the way that it sounds. We now sell 95 per cent online and we sell to an international audience.

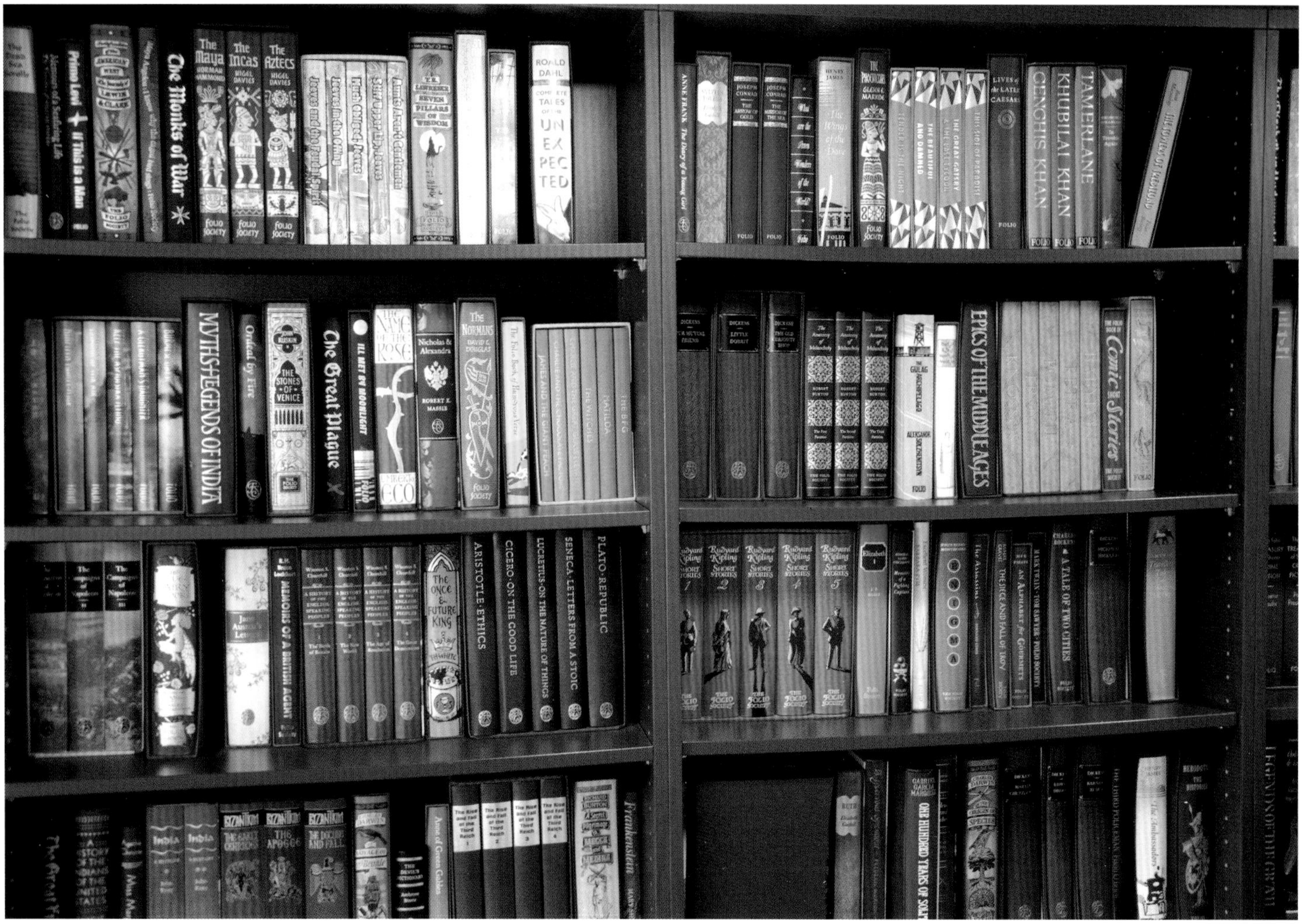

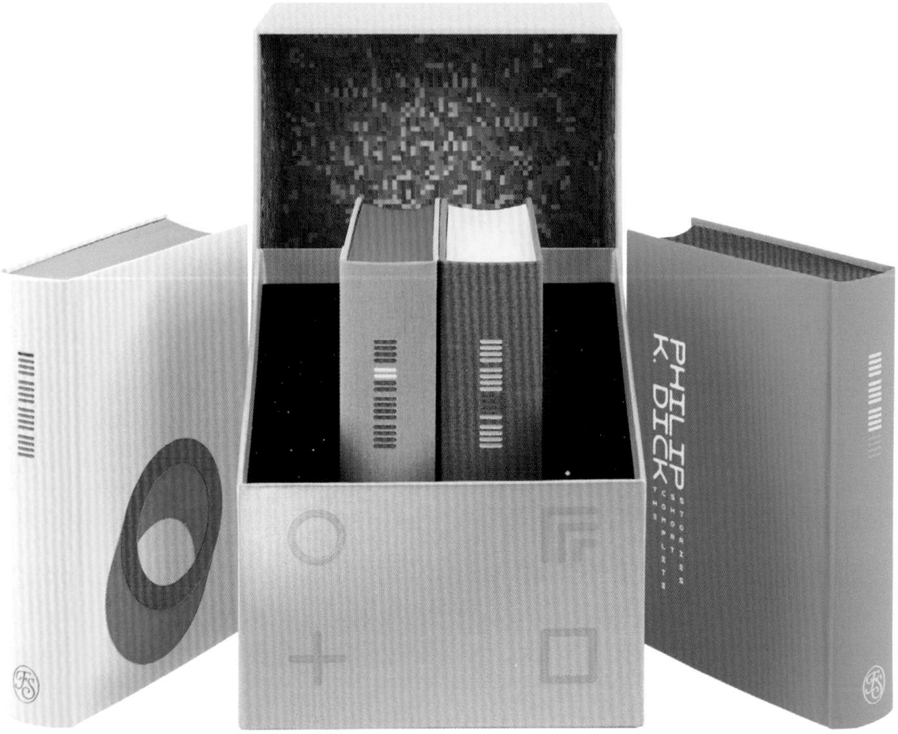

What we do is niche but book illustration is a niche thing so in order to find that audience you have to go internationally. There's a deep well of obsessive enthusiasts who if you are authentic and you mean it and get it right. If you're actually a fan of the books in the same way that people who are buying it are, you can find people online who will love what you do. We have changed with the times in a lot of different ways but the consistent approach is that design and illustration community."

The Folio Society has really specialised in lavish limited editions in recent years and this has really borne fruit as Walker admits.

"You can find particularly with the limited editions, these days if you miss out on the email you quite often miss out entirely. We printed 1000 copies of *Lord Of The Rings* and we

sold them out in 36 hours."

Unlike many other book publishers, Folio doesn't have a partner company in the US to distribute its titles:

"Folio sells all over the world and we distribute from our warehouse just outside of London. We operate solely from London and we don't have an office anywhere else. We distribute internationally from our warehouse. We mostly print in Italy and the UK and a little bit in Germany. It does sound like a slightly ridiculous system but it does work," he admits.

When asked to choose the one title that the company is most proud of, Walker does pick a slightly unconventional choice:

"I could give you a multitude of titles. But if I had to pick one, even

though it's a bit of a cheat, it would be the *Philip K Dick Collected Short Stories*. It's a cheat because it's a series of stories but I think Philip K Dick is on that intersection of the literary and the sci-fi similar to Ballard or someone like Bradbury. I fee like they are similar in tone. But he's got that pulp Americana and that grounded element to his storytelling but he's also a lot broader than that. So the

Philip K Dick estate came to us for that project and it's the only place where you can find those stories all published in one edition. We commissioned 24 different illustrators so it felt like one edition really reaching out into the world, both fantasy and sci fi and regular literary illustration. The design for the book was also really really top notch. There's a new selected short stories which came out of that,

"**FOLIO** SELLS ALL OVER THE WORLD AND WE DISTRIBUTE FROM OUR WAREHOUSE JUST OUTSIDE OF LONDON. WE OPERATE SOLELY FROM LONDON AND WE DON'T HAVE AN OFFICE ANYWHERE ELSE. WE DISTRIBUTE INTERNATIONALLY FROM OUR WAREHOUSE. WE MOSTLY PRINT IN ITALY AND THE UK AND A LITTLE BIT IN GERMANY. IT DOES SOUND LIKE A SLIGHTLY RIDICULOUS SYSTEM BUT IT DOES WORK" – TOM WALKER

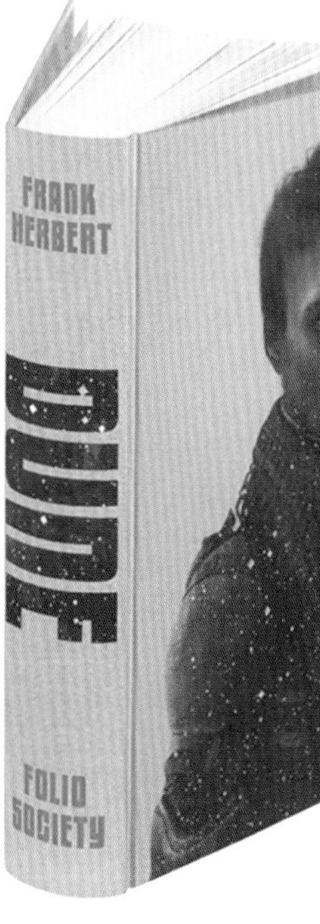
FRANK HERBERT
DUNE
FOLIO SOCIETY

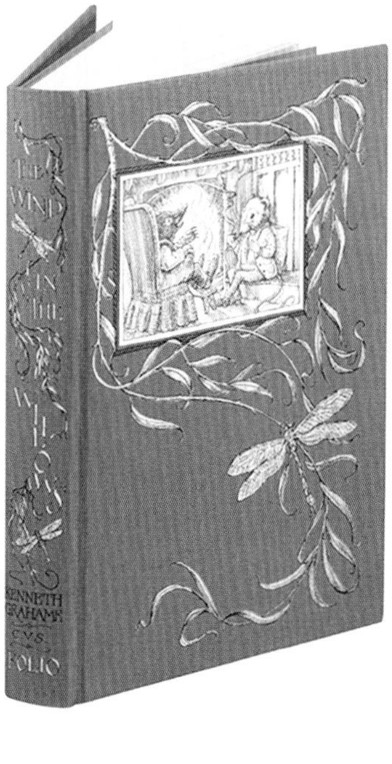
KENNETH GRAHAME
FOLIO

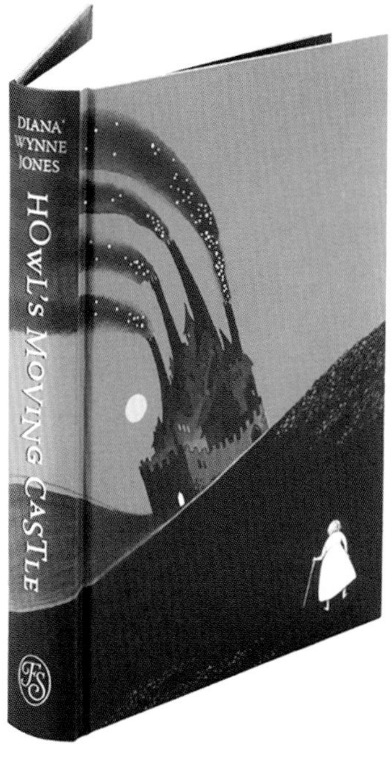
DIANA WYNNE JONES
HOWL'S MOVING CASTLE

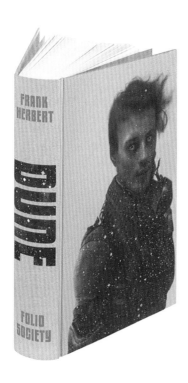

a slimmed-down version with all 24 illustrators. I do have lots of different favourites but that would probably be the big one that I choose. Also it's part of this new trend of limited editions which has attracted a new audience and they're selling out in very short order."

The Folio Society does have a range of titles that do well for them but Walker picks out a few that have really exceeded their expectations when he is asked about their most successful books so far.

"It depends how you look at it whether it's units or revenue. If you look at revenue obviously that will change over time with inflation. I would say that the books that comes to mind are probably four. You've got *Dune* which came out in 2015 and that was really a game changer because it introduced relatively contemporary science fiction into the Folio orbit and that changed the business on its own. There's *The Lord Of The Rings* limited edition which as I mentioned was one of the fastest selling in terms of everything that we've ever had. *Wind In the Willows* has been a real perennial favourite for twenty or thirty years. It continues to sell extraordinarily well. *Howl's Moving Castle* which I was not expecting but

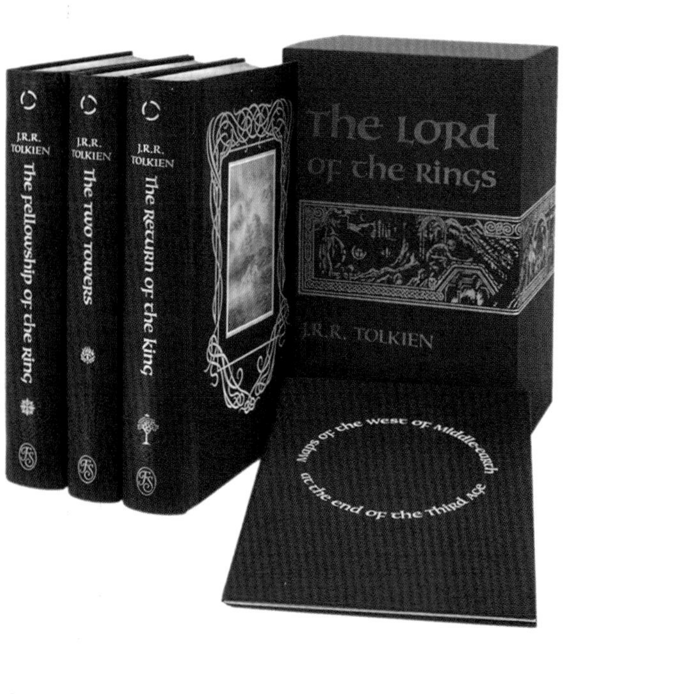
J.R.R. TOLKIEN
The Fellowship of the Ring
J.R.R. TOLKIEN
The Two Towers
J.R.R. TOLKIEN
The Return of the King
The Lord of the Rings
J.R.R. TOLKIEN
Maps of the West of Middle-earth at the end of the Third Age

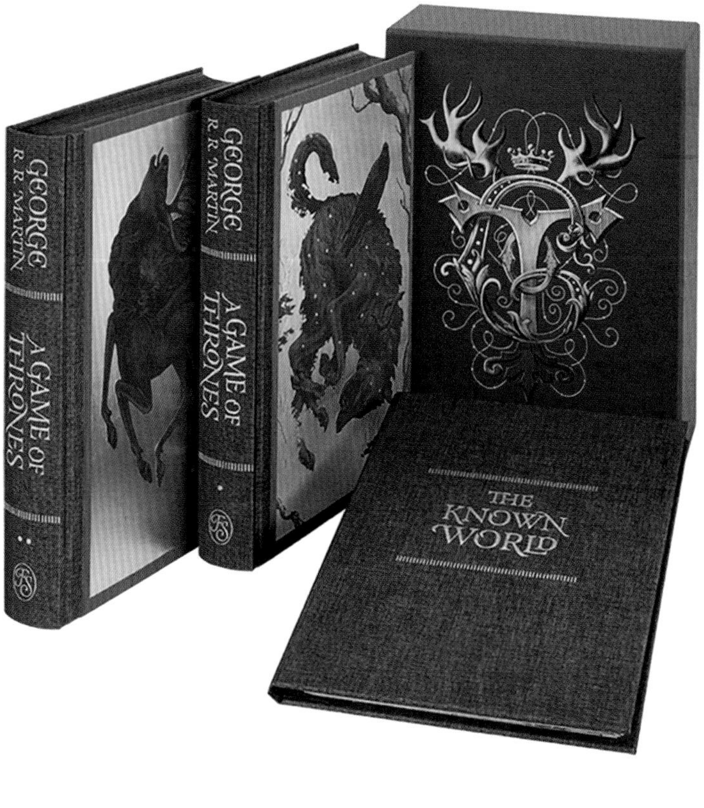
GEORGE R. R. MARTIN
A GAME OF THRONES
GEORGE R. R. MARTIN
A GAME OF THRONES
THE KNOWN WORLD

MARVEL
HULK
HULK
Selected by ROY THOMAS
THE INCREDIBLE HULK
IS HE MAN OR MONSTER OR... IS HE BOTH

"THE FUNDAMENTAL THING IS HAVING SOMEONE HERE WHO LOVES IT AND HAS A VISION FOR WHAT IT COULD BE. AND THERE'S SOMEONE OUT THERE WHO WOULD LOVE TO ILLUSTRATE IT AND DESIGN IT AND THERE IS SOMEONE WHO COULD WRITE A NEW INTRODUCTION WHICH WOULD PUSH IT." -TOM WALKER

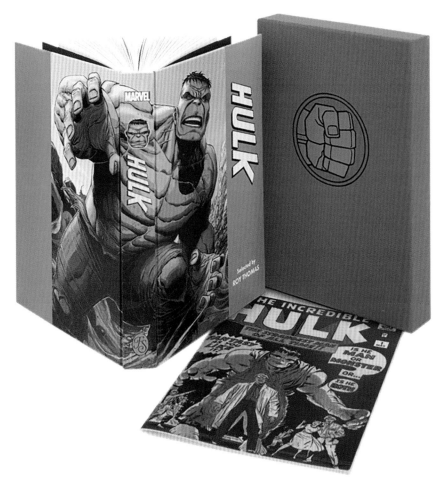

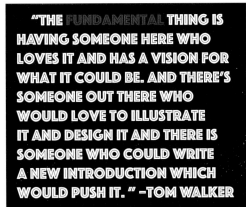

certainly found its audience very very quickly and people absolutely adore that. It did very well indeed. The other one is *Game Of Thrones*. I can't not mention that as that was another game changer in terms of the fact that you've got the science fiction audience and the fantasy audience parallel but different.*Game of Thrones* found us a whole new market."

In terms of the criteria for producing a Folio Society edition, there is something at the core which helps the title to really click with its audience, Walker points out as we wrap up our lunch.

Fear and Loathing in LAS VEGAS

"There are lots of things but the thing that I have found fundamentally over the years is someone in Folio has got to love it otherwise it does not work. In the past I have made decisions which are purely commercial which I think 'That's going to be a winner.' But it doesn't quite fit with what what my idea of what a Folio book is and they never work. You need to have someone in the business who absolutely obsesses over it. So someone has got to want to make it the best possible edition that it can be. That's a fundamental thing.There are lots of other different considerations like does it work as an illustrated book because some books don't and does it have an audience we can find? There are some audiences that we don't know how to find where they are.There isn't enough of an intersection with our own audience. The fundamental thing is having someone here who loves it and has a vision for what it could be. And there's someone out there who would love to illustrate it and design it and there is someone who could write a new introduction which would push it."

There are also more practical considerations as well, he points out.

" Also the question is whether we can get the rights to the work as well."

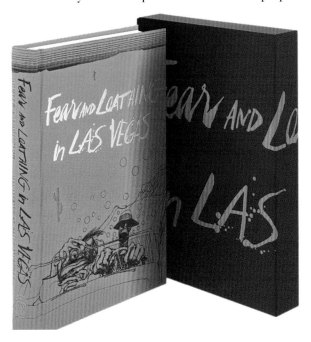

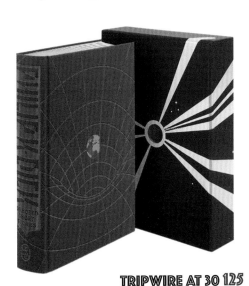

With the Folio Society evolving in recent years, their demands and specifications have also grown more complicated too: "Our specifications as a publisher have got a lot more complex in recent years. Folio went through a phase of stripping down so we would publish illustrated editions in clothbound editions. Now if you take something like the Christmas list, you are printing on page edges or a book which is in art silk. We're using so many different materials and it's got an awful lot harder and I would say now that material availability and supply chain issues have become such a big thing. Paper in a way is relatively straightforward although very very expensive. The cost of our materials has gone up forty or fifty per cent. Paper is less of an issue as it's the other materials that are proving more tricky to source. Printers are demanding a six month lead time rather than a two month lead time. It's definitely harder than it's ever been. Supply chain issues are far greater than they ever were. Three years ago you would be looking at one or two of the links in the chain but now you have to look at all the links in the chain like the foil coming by ship from Taiwan. On the upside of this, there is a lot of innovation in the print industry at the moment and that is being driven partly by publishers like Folio demanding different ways of doing things. I think there is a growing market for design led books and that even pre pandemic was led by a printing industry that was being more innovative than it used to be. Even in the UK now, there's real investment in high quality innovative thinking."

The company just became employee-owned, which is another very unusual move for a book company.

Walker's passion for quality books is infectious and, 75 years after it was first started, the Folio Society continues to create books like no other publisher. Its future is definitely in very good hands.

30 OF THE MOST BEAUTIFUL FOLIO EDITIONS

The Gormenghast Trilogy
Mervyn Peake
Illustrated by Dave McKean

Fear and Loathing in Las Vegas
Hunter S. Thompson
Illustrated by Ralph Steadman

A Perfect Spy
John le Carré
Illustrated by Sam Green

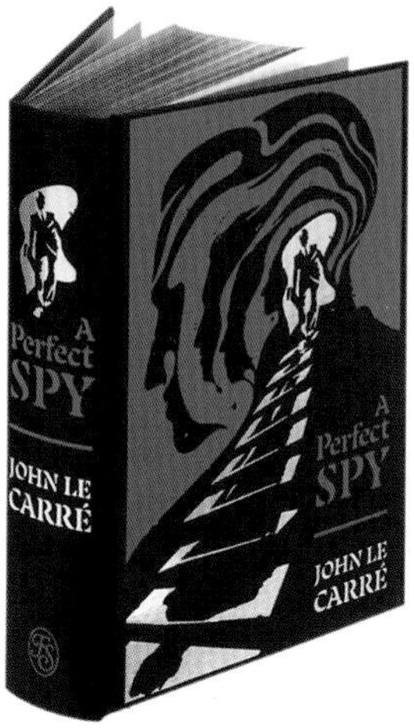
A Perfect SPY
JOHN LE CARRÉ
A Perfect SPY
JOHN LE CARRÉ

Anna Karenina
Leo Tolstoy
Illustrated by Angela Barrett

A Feast for Crows
George R. R. Martin
Illustrated by Jonathan Burton

The Roald Dahl Collection (Set 1)
Roald Dahl
Illustrated by Quentin Blake

Dracula
Bram Stoker
Illustrated by Angela Barrett

The Man With the Golden Gun
Ian Fleming
Illustrated by Fay Dalton

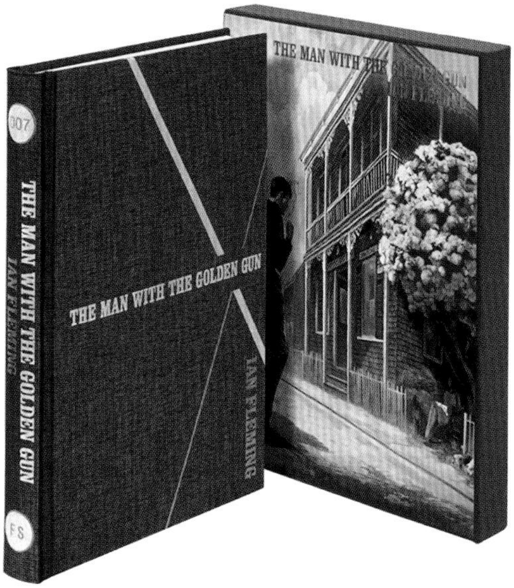
007
THE MAN WITH THE GOLDEN GUN
IAN FLEMING
FS
THE MAN WITH THE GOLDEN GUN
IAN FLEMING

The Great Gatsby
F. Scott Fitzgerald
Illustrated by Sam Wolfe Connelly

Dune
Frank Herbert
Illustrated by Sam Weber

The Book of the New Sun
Gene Wolfe
Illustrated by Sam Weber

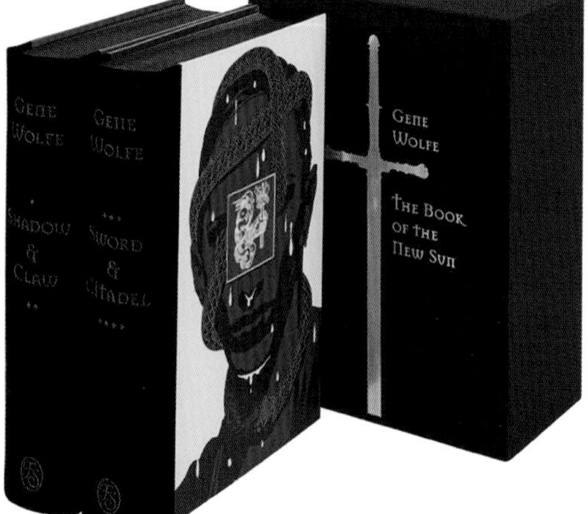
GENE WOLFE
GENE WOLFE
GENE WOLFE
THE BOOK OF THE NEW SUN

Do Androids Dream of Electric Sheep? & A Scanner Darkly
Philip K. Dick
Illustrated by Andrew Archer and Chris Skinner

Stranger in a Strange Land
Robert A. Heinlein
Illustrated by Donato Giancola

Planet of the Apes
Pierre Boulle
Illustrated by David de las Heras

Something Wicked This Way Comes
Ray Bradbury
Illustrated by Tim McDonagh

I Am Legend
Richard Matheson
Illustrated by Dave McKean

His Dark Materials
Philip Pullman
Illustrated by Peter Bailey

A Game of Thrones
George R. R. Martin
Illustrated by Jonathan Burton

American Gods
Neil Gaiman
Illustrated by Dave McKean

The Lord Of The Rings
J. R. R. Tolkien
Illustrated by Eric Fraser and Ingahild Grathmer

The Handmaid's Tale
Margaret Atwood
Illustrated by Anna and Elena Balbusso

RICHARD MATHESON

THE AMAZING ADVENTURES OF KAVALIER & CLAY
MICHAEL CHABON

PHILIP K. DICK
THE MAN IN THE HIGH CASTLE
FOLIO SOCIETY

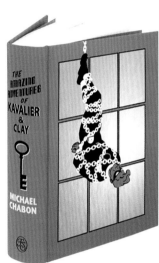

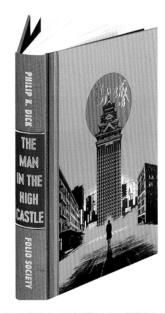

The Illustrated Man
Ray Bradbury
Illustrated by Marc Burckhardt

The Tale of Peter Rabbit
(Limited Edition)
Beatrix Potter

Doctor Zhivago
Boris Pasternak
Illustrated by Leonid Pasternak

The Murder of Roger Ackroyd
Agatha Christie
Illustrated by Andrew Davidson

The Selected Adventures and Memoirs of Sherlock Holmes
Arthur Conan Doyle
Illustrated by Max Löffler

The Amazing Adventures of Kavalier & Clay
Michael Chabon
Illustrated by Chris Samnee

The Lord of the Rings (Limited Edition)
J. R. R. Tolkien
Illustrated by Alan Lee

A Clockwork Orange
Anthony Burgess
Illustrated by Ben Jones
£39.95

I, Robot
Isaac Asimov
Illustrated by Alex Wells

The Man in the High Castle
Philip K. Dick
Illustrated by Shan Jiang

THE RISE AND FALL OF DC'S VERTIGO

Scott Braden takes a look at the genesis, evolution and eventual demise of DC's renowned imprint which launched characters like Preacher, The Sandman, Swamp Thing and more and creators like Grant Morrison, Garth Ennis, Neil Gaiman, Dave McKean, Frank Quitely and many others in its long and turbulent history…

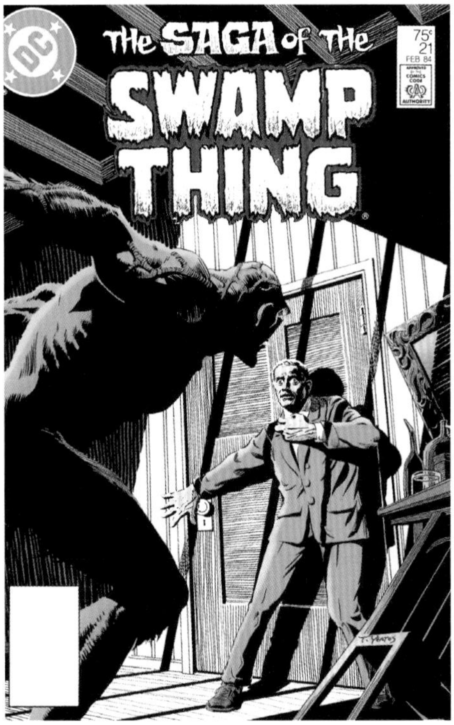
The SAGA of The
SWAMP THING
75¢
21
FEB 84

As an 80s indie rock band once stated, "Alan Moore knew the score."

His work on *The Saga of the Swamp Thing* and other mainstream DC Comics titles struck a resounding chord with readers. In fact, his and the work of fellow English writers Jamie Delano, Neil Gaiman and Peter Milligan, as well as Scottish scribe Grant Morrison, introduced comics fans to a more sophisticated sort of sequential storytelling. And fans of the four-color medium couldn't get enough.

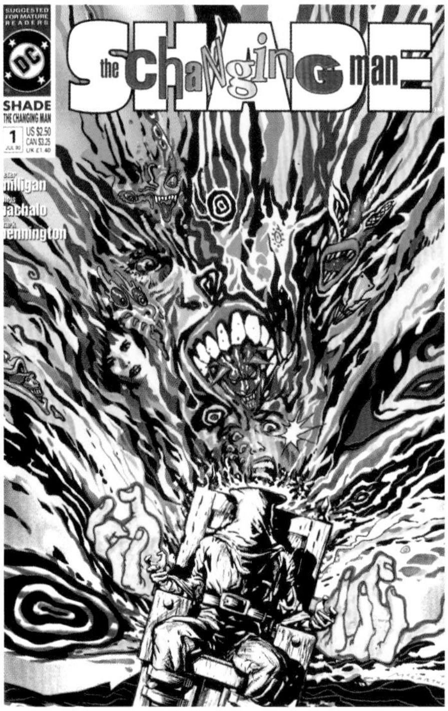
SUGGESTED FOR MATURE READERS
SHADE the Changing man
SHADE THE CHANGING MAN
1
milligan
bachalo
pennington

"I THINK IT ALL GOES BACK TO KAREN [BERGER]...SHE WAS NOT A TYPICAL DC EDITOR, BECAUSE SHE DIDN'T GROW UP LOVING COMICS AND WASN'T THERE TO DO HER OWN VERSIONS OF THE JUSTICE LEAGUERS WHO'D ENTHRALLED HER IN THE PLAYPEN (BECAUSE THEY HADN'T)." - TOM PEYER

Enter Vertigo: The legendary DC Comics imprint suggested for mature readers.

The Vertigo imprint began publishing titles and related product in 1993. Spearheaded by imprint editor Karen Berger, all DC titles bearing the Vertigo logo catered to not only more mature readers, but more sophisticated writers and artists as well. Berger saw this in part from her experience as an assistant editor for EC Comics alum Joe Orlando. By working with the comic book legend, she was able to build up her expertise working on the "sophisticated suspense" books (a company euphemism for "horror" titles) that were later published under the Vertigo banner.

"I think it all goes back to Karen," said former Vertigo editor and current AHOY Comics editor-in-chief Tom Peyer. "She was not a typical DC editor, because she didn't grow up loving comics and wasn't there to do her own versions of the Justice Leaguers who'd enthralled her in the playpen (because they hadn't). So the design, art, and story concepts of Vertigo weren't influenced that much by mainstream comic books. Now nearly all comics are aimed at adults, and the grinning, punch-throwing visuals of comics' first 60 years are no longer dominant. You can see hints of Vertigo everywhere you look."

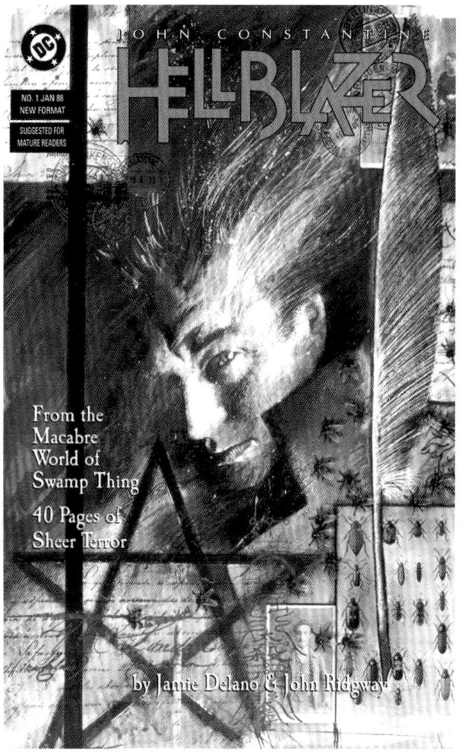
JOHN CONSTANTINE
HELLBLAZER
NO. 1 JAN 88
NEW FORMAT
SUGGESTED FOR MATURE READERS
From the Macabre World of Swamp Thing
40 Pages of Sheer Terror
by Jamie Delano & John Ridgway

"Let's see: Vertigo was a big deal, obviously, and we all knew it at the time," AHOY's Stuart Moore said, who was a founding editor for the line. "I'd been working with Karen at DC for about three years when Vertigo launched, and even before that, she'd been laying the foundation for

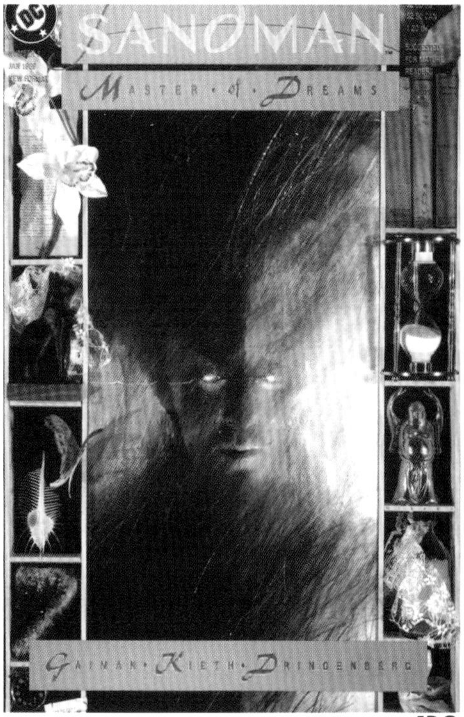
SANDMAN
Master of Dreams
GAIMAN · KIETH · DRINGENBERG

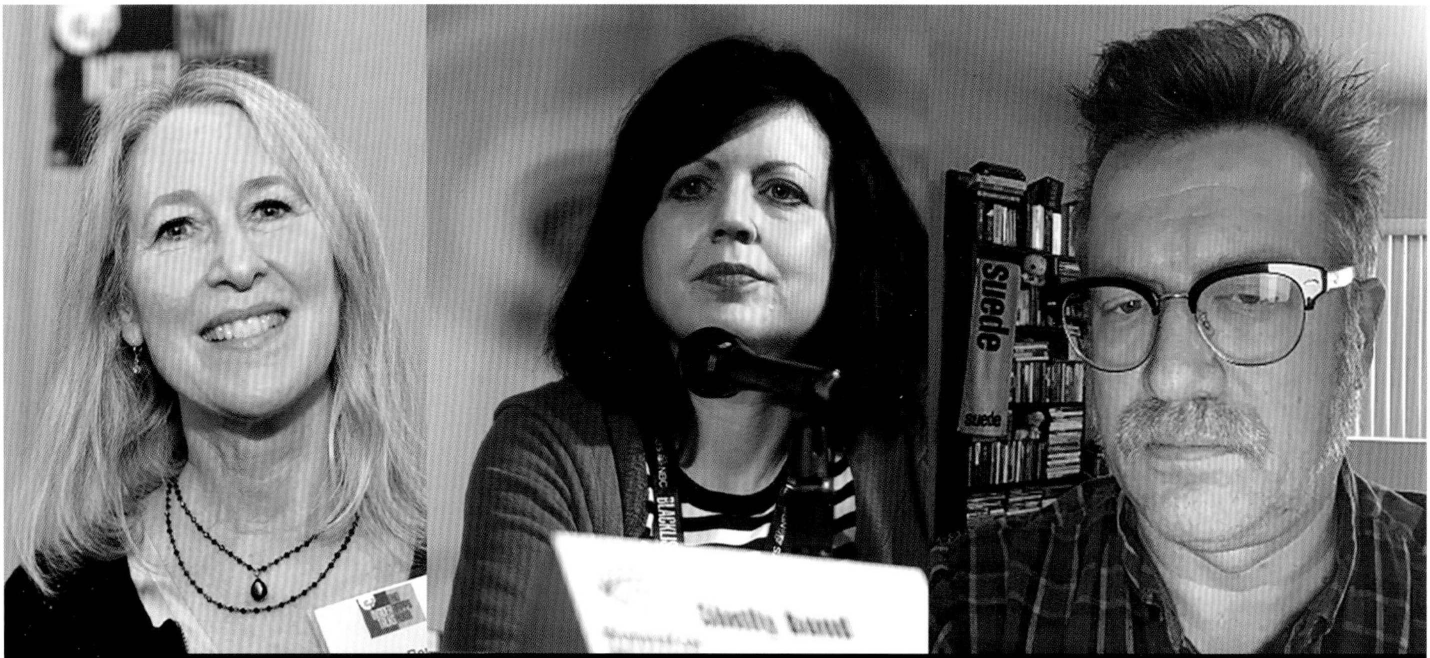
suede
suede

Vertigo heads through the years: (from left) Karen Berger (pic: Kendal Whitehouse), Shelly Bond (pic: Gage Skidmore) and Jamie S Rich

the imprint with a pretty stunning roster of talent. It was a time when a lot of things came together; I looked at it as a synthesis of 'mainstream' comics with the vibrant indie comics movement of the '80s, which was beginning to crest and fade as DC and Marvel crowded the market with titles, and as indie dollars shifted over to the rising Image Comics stars. The third element, of course, was what we called 'The British Invasion.' The U.K. had a great comics industry, but the number of titles was small enough that it couldn't really support the number of talented writers and artists coming up. Vertigo provided a place for them, and a lot of them moved over or sideways to superhero comics from there."

"Thanks to Karen Berger and the editors she assembled around her between the late 1980s and early 2000s," said Delano, "I was lucky enough to find myself in a creative environment receptive to the kind of stories I was inclined towards writing. There being few to zero publishers with a similar ethos at the time, and personally having little interest in adding to the 'superhero' canon, I doubt I would have been able to persist in 'mainstream' comics for as long as I did without Vertigo and its precursor

"THANKS TO KAREN BERGER AND THE EDITORS SHE ASSEMBLED AROUND HER BETWEEN THE LATE 1980S AND EARLY 2000S," SAID DELANO, "I WAS LUCKY ENOUGH TO FIND MYSELF IN A CREATIVE ENVIRONMENT RECEPTIVE TO THE KIND OF STORIES I WAS INCLINED TOWARDS WRITING" - JAMIE DELANO

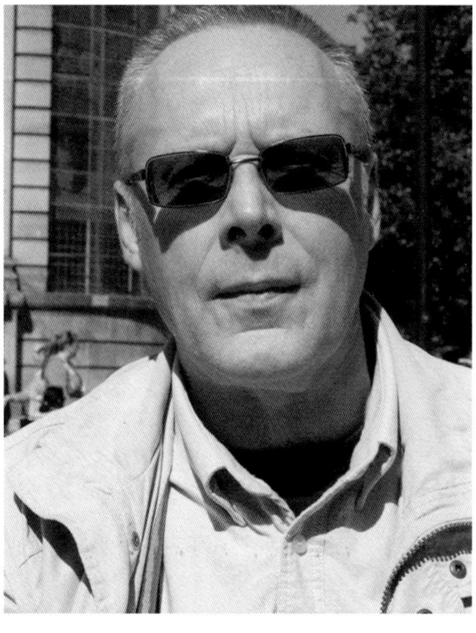

regime. Some may assess this as a good thing; others may shrug with disinterest. I just count my blessings. Vertigo trusted its creators to deliver storytelling and content innovation with minimal (but occasionally astute) editorial interference; a strategy – I would suggest – rewarded by the enduring quality of its output."

After decades at the helm, Berger found herself forced out by the Powers that Be at DC Comics in the early 2000s, replaced by Shelly Bond. She, in turn, was then replaced by Jamie Rich who was replaced by Mark Doyle. And then, with Doyle and the entire comic book line gone with him, that was that.

Looking back at their output, the Vertigo writers, thanks to their sensibilities, brought something new and fresh to American comics. Berger was quick to realize this and enlisted talent from the weekly British comic anthology, 2000 AD, as well as during trips to the United Kingdom, specifically UKCAC – a famed comic convention in London that ran from 1984 to 1997.

Several of DC's existing releases

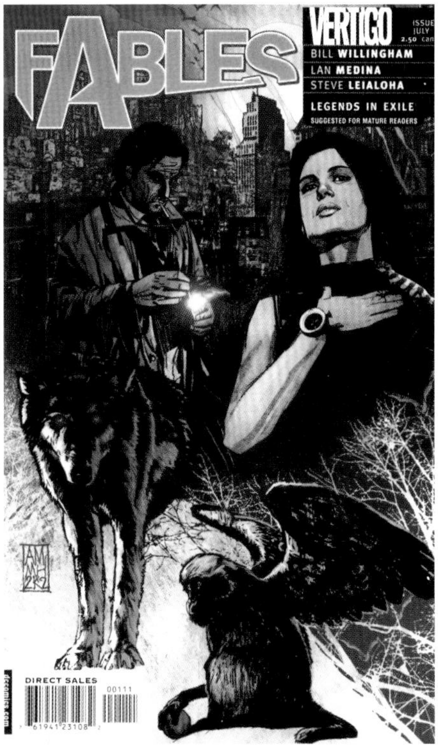
FABLES
VERTIGO
BILL WILLINGHAM
LAN MEDINA
STEVE LEIALOHA
LEGENDS IN EXILE
SUGGESTED FOR MATURE READERS
DIRECT SALES

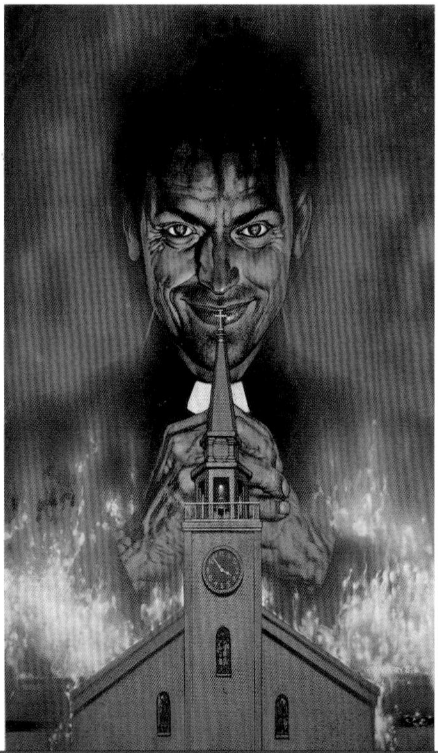

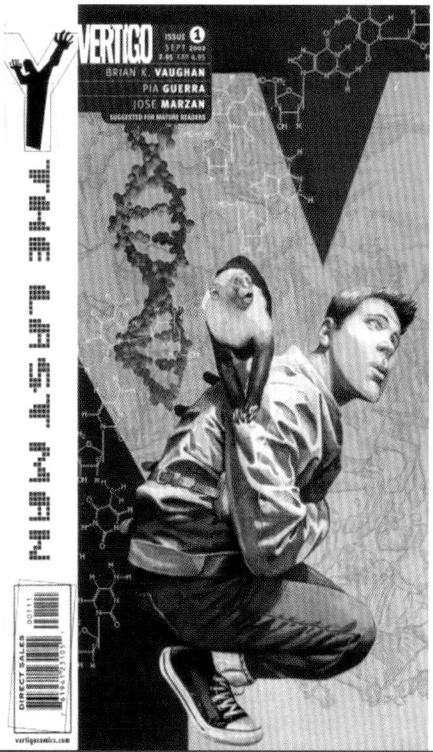
VERTIGO
ISSUE 1
SEPT 2002
BRIAN K. VAUGHAN
PIA GUERRA
JOSE MARZAN
SUGGESTED FOR MATURE READERS
Y THE LAST MAN
DIRECT SALES
vertigocomics.com

LOOKING BACK AT THEIR OUTPUT, THE VERTIGO WRITERS, THANKS TO THEIR SENSIBILITIES, BROUGHT SOMETHING NEW AND FRESH TO AMERICAN COMICS. BERGER WAS QUICK TO REALIZE THIS AND ENLISTED TALENT FROM THE WEEKLY BRITISH COMIC ANTHOLOGY, 2000 AD, AS WELL AS DURING TRIPS TO THE UNITED KINGDOM, SPECIFICALLY UKCAC – A FAMED COMIC CONVENTION IN LONDON THAT RAN FROM 1984 TO 1997.

such as *The Sandman*, *Hellblazer*, *Animal Man*, *Doom Patrol*, *Shade, the Changing Man* and *Swamp Thing* immigrated to the Vertigo camp, while new titles and limited series were likewise added to the growing Vertigo line. Collected versions of many Pre-Vertigo titles bore the Vertigo stamp even though they were originally published under the standard DC Comics banner.

Each issue of a Vertigo title typically contained adult-orientated material including nudity and profanity. Thematically, the stories tended to revolve around supernatural or crime-noir based storytelling themes, and had little in common with the brighter, more

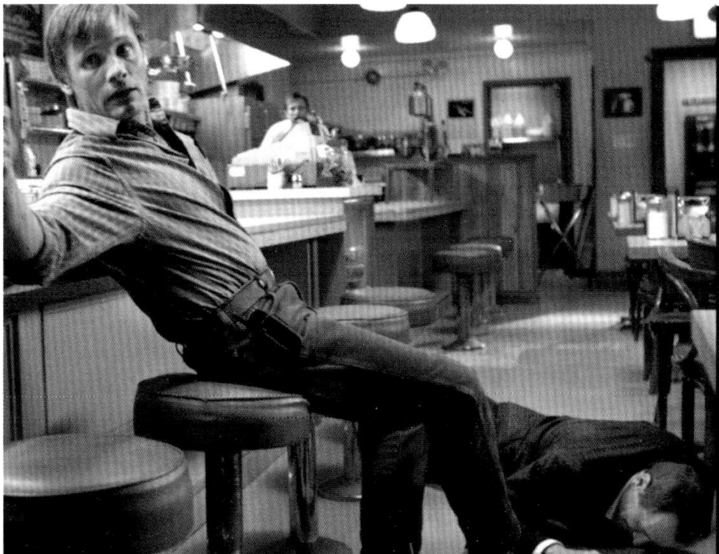

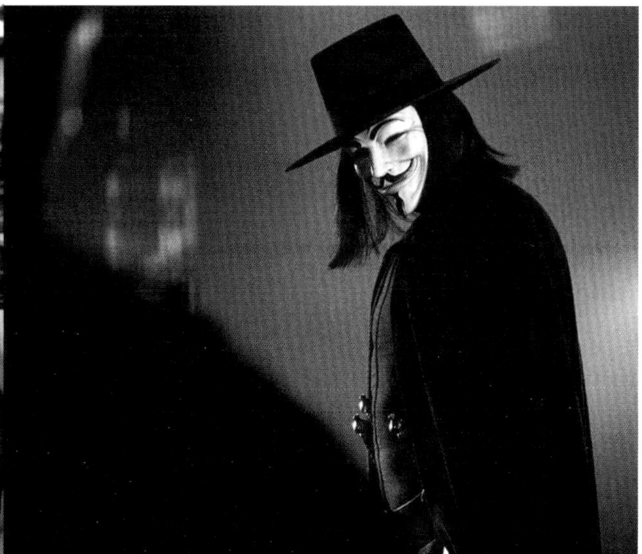

Spreading its wings: A History Of Violence (above left) and V For Vendetta (above right), two films based on comics from DC's Vertigo stable

animated super-hero venues of the mainstream DC Universe.

Besides the now-legendary EC Comics and its luminary creators like Orlando, Wally Wood, Harvey Kurtzman etc. who changed comics forever back in the 1950s, Vertigo's progenitors also included Warren Magazines with its *Creepy* and *Eerie* anthology horror titles released in the '70s. And, of course, another forerunner for Berger's star-studded imprint was Marvel's Epic Comics and Magazine line from the 1980s. Led by comic book editor-extraordinaire Archie Goodwin – who also worked for Warren in his younger years – it offered international audiences comic material unlike any other U.S. company at the time.

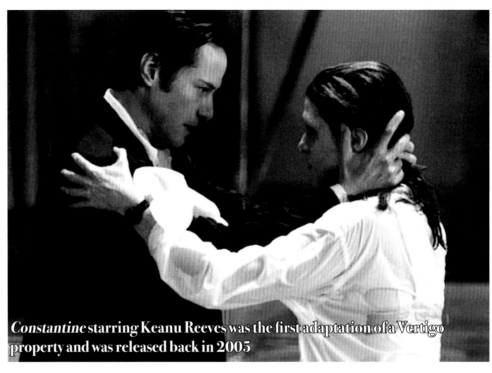

Constantine **starring Keanu Reeves was the first adaptation of a Vertigo property and was released back in 2005**

While many Vertigo titles take place within the proper continuity of the greater DC Universe, there are many more which exist in their own singular continuity, separate not only from the DCU, but from other Vertigo titles as well. For example, Garth Ennis' award-winning series, *Preacher*, does not share continuity with any other DC or Vertigo title with the exception of its own spin-off titles and neither did crime comic *100 Bullets*, co-created by Brian Azzarello and Eduardo Risso.

As stated previously, many titles published by DC before Vertigo was founded were reprinted under the Vertigo name, such as *V for Vendetta*. To follow that up, the line saw its first movie in 2005, named *Constantine*, based on the comic book series *Hellblazer* – the postmodern occultist chancer and creation of Moore and artist Rick Veitch. Later that year, A History of Violence was released in cinemas, and in 2006, the Moore-written *V for Vendetta* appeared on the silver screen.

In 2009, Vertigo launched Jeff Lemire's quirky sci-series *Sweet Tooth*, which ran for four years.

In 2011, with the introduction of Pandora, both Vertigo and Wildstorm were treated as separate universes before merging with the mainstream DCU, in contrast to having crossovers as before. And in 2020, amidst a

VERTIGO
NOW A MAJOR MOTION PICTURE!
V FOR VENDETTA
ALAN MOORE
DAVID LLOYD
WITH STEVE WHITAKER AND SIOBHAN DODDS

THIS ALWAYS HAPPENS...
NO IT DOESN'T. ANYWAY, WHY CAN'T WE PLAY MY TAPE?
'CAUSE IT DISTURBS ME, YOU LISTENIN' TO THAT STUFF. WHAT'S WRONG WITH THE KING? CAN'T GO WRONG WITH THE KING.
YES, YEH FUCKIN' CAN. LOOK, I'VE GOT THIS ONE HERE--
KLIK
LONDON IS FLOODING, IIIIII LIVE BY THE RIVAAAHH--
AN' YOU LIGHT MY MORNIN' SKYYYY, BURNIN' LUHUVV...
KNEW A CRACK DEALER BY THE NAME OF PETAH, HAD TO BUCK 'IM DOWN WIT' MY NINE MILLIMETAH...

DC
VERTIGO
HELLBLAZER
GARTH ENNIS
STEVE DILLON

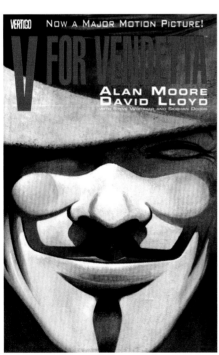

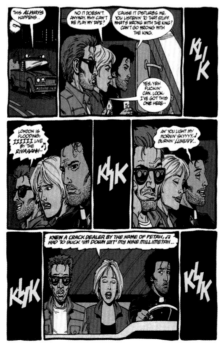

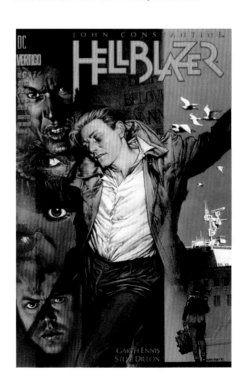

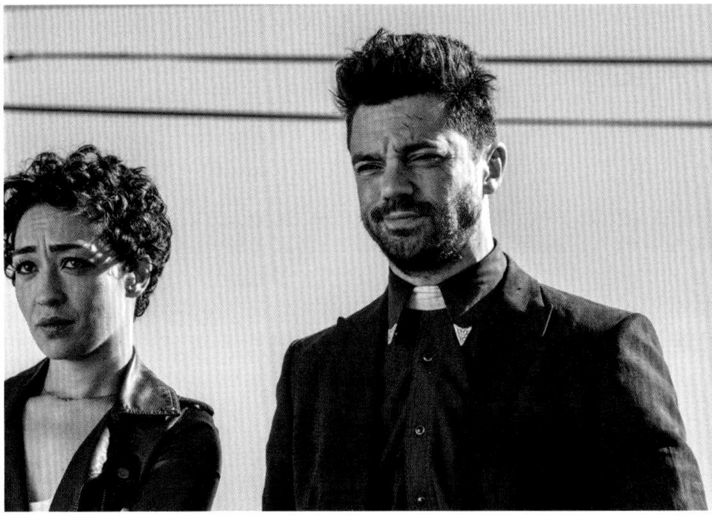

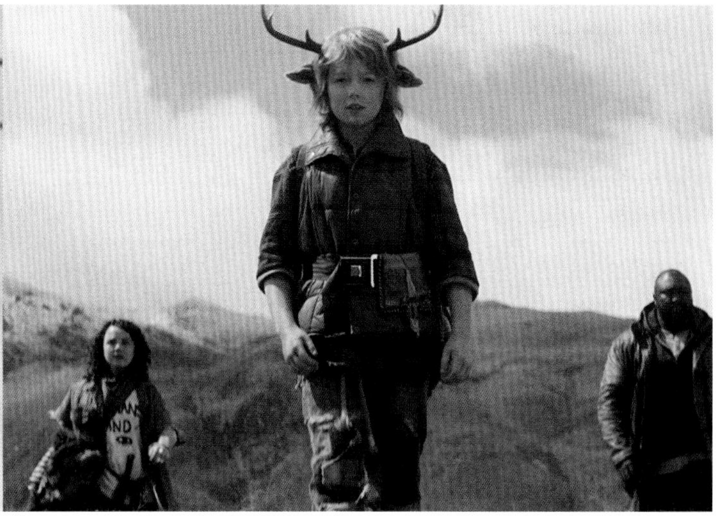

Preacher **starring Dominic Cooper and Ruth Negga (above left) was adapted by HBO for four seasons while *Sweet Tooth* (top right) came to Netflix in 2021, *Doom Patrol* (below left) is still running on HBO while The Sandman (below right) started on Netflix in August 2022**

worldwide pandemic that symbolically mirrored the comic book line's omega moment, Vertigo was discontinued.

THE IMPACT OF THE IMPRINT CONTINUED TO BE FELT WITH HBO'S ADAPTATION OF ENNIS AND DILLON'S PREACHER AND NETFLIX BRINGING LEMIRE'S SWEET TOOTH TO THE SMALL SCREEN IN 2021.

In the years during Vertigo's decline and fall, as well as following it, comic book upstarts AHOY Comics, BOOM!, Dark Horse Comics, and Image Comics began to steal the once-great line's thunder, finally ending up filling the void left by the demise of the publishing giant. These innovative publishers offered keen readers critically acclaimed and commercially successful releases like *The Wrong Earth* and *High Heaven* (AHOY Comics); *We Only Find Them When They Are Dead*, *Something is Killing the Children*, and *Once and Future* (BOOM!), Hellboy and *Zombie World*, as well as the Berger Books imprint (Dark Horse Comics); and *The Walking Dead*, *Saga*, and *Undiscovered Country* (Image Comics); among others.

Today, these publishers continue where Vertigo left off, building on its legacy but forever being shaded by the legendary comic book line's long shadow. Of course, fans who experienced the fruit of Vertigo's richness on comic shop stands from the early '90s – and into the 21st century – would expect nothing less.

Turn over to see 30 creators who came to the fore thanks to the imprint

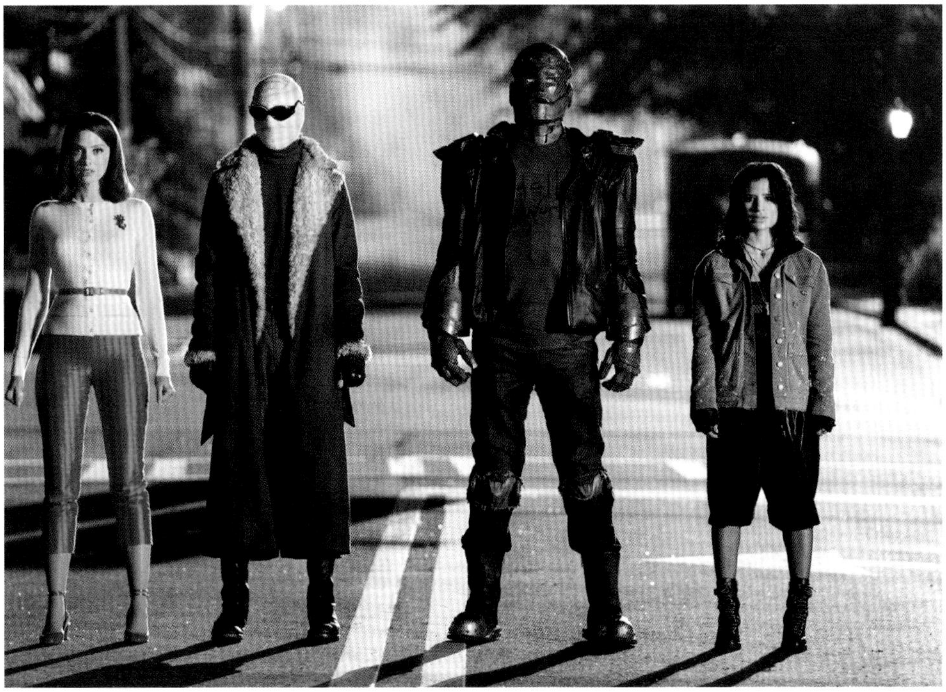

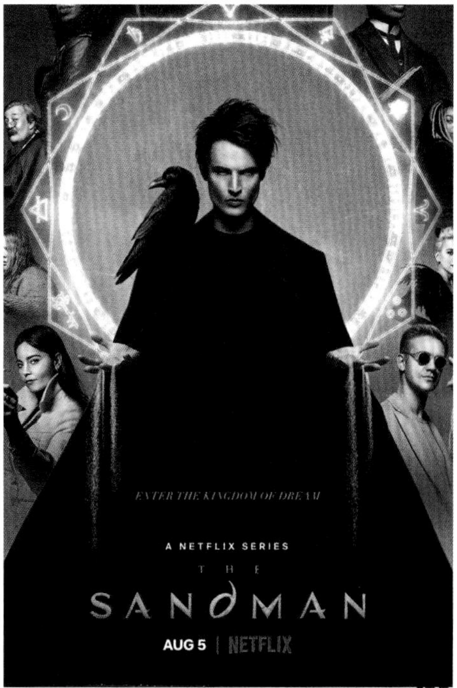
A NETFLIX SERIES
THE
SANDMAN
AUG 5 | NETFLIX

30 CREATORS BROUGHT TO PROMINENCE THANKS TO VERTIGO

Here's 30 creators whose careers were given a boost through DC's imprint ...

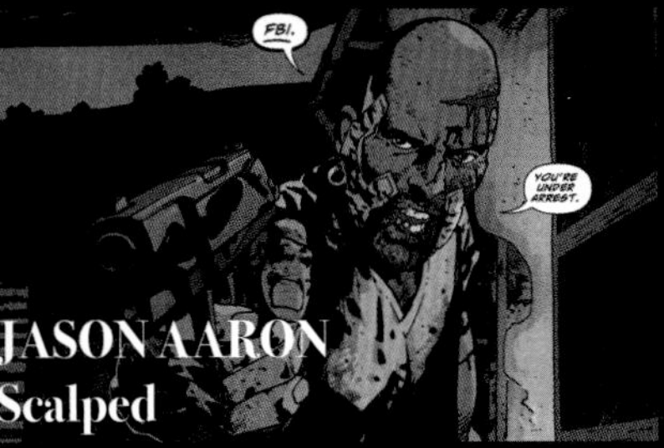
FBI.
YOU'RE UNDER ARREST.
JASON AARON
Scalped

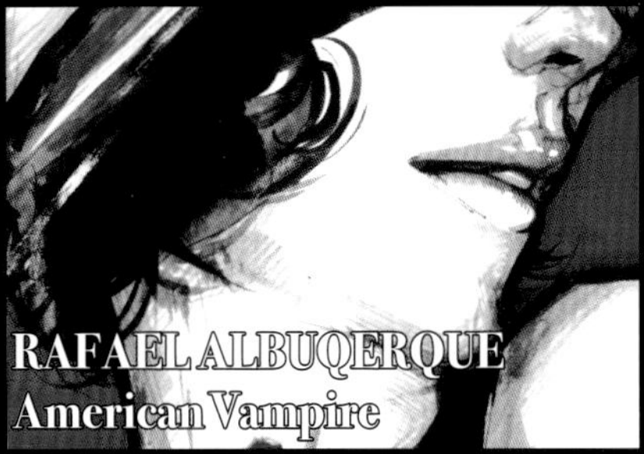
RAFAEL ALBUQUERQUE
American Vampire

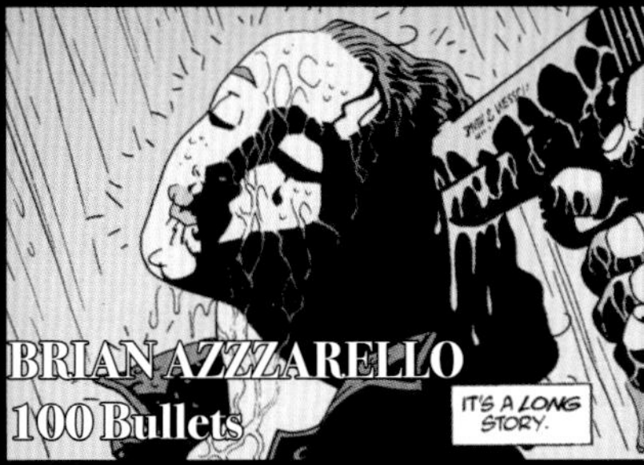
IT'S A LONG STORY.
BRIAN AZZZARELLO
100 Bullets

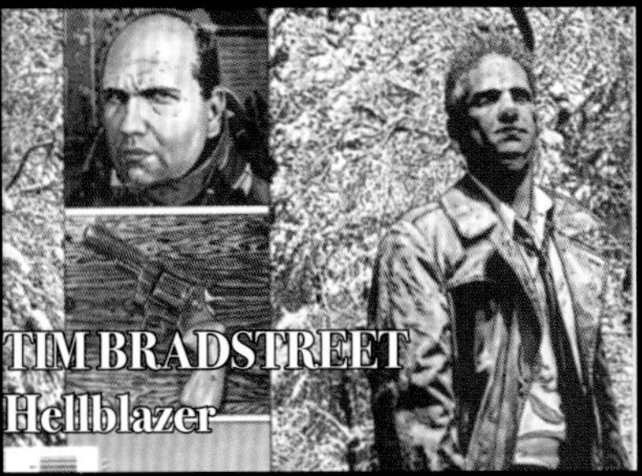
TIM BRADSTREET
Hellblazer

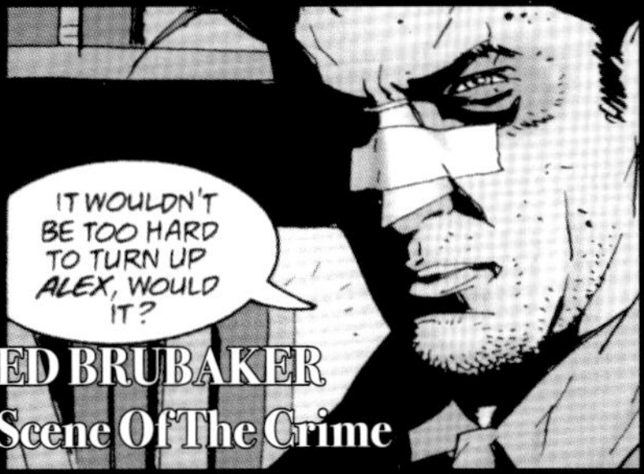
IT WOULDN'T BE TOO HARD TO TURN UP ALEX, WOULD IT?
ED BRUBAKER
Scene Of The Crime

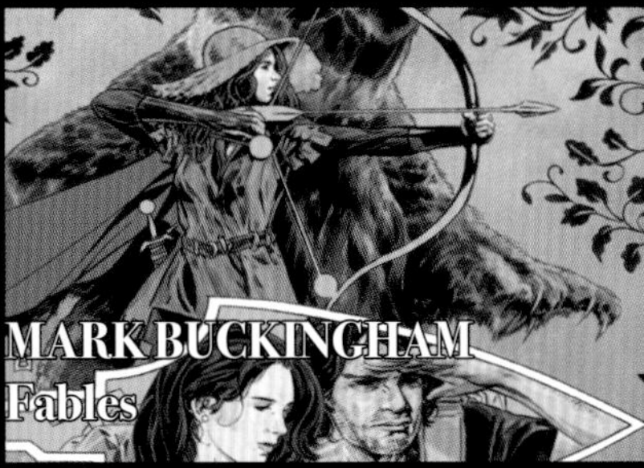
MARK BUCKINGHAM
Fables

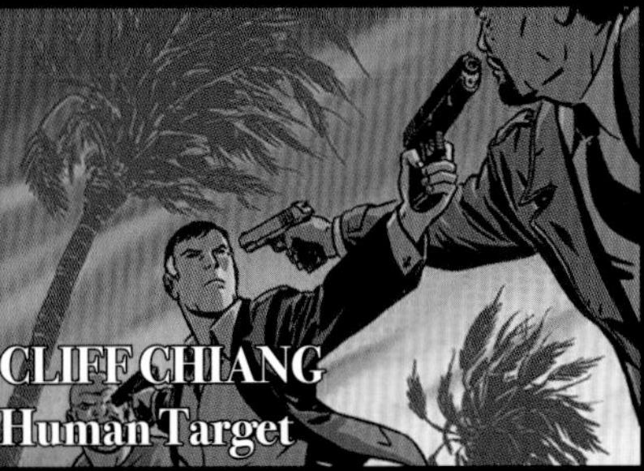
CLIFF CHIANG
Human Target

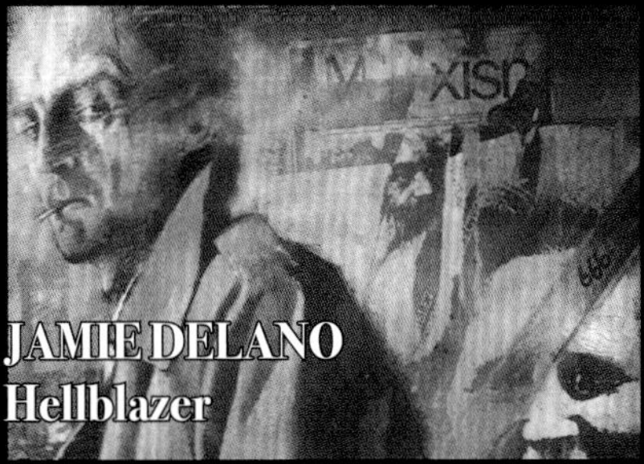
JAMIE DELANO
Hellblazer

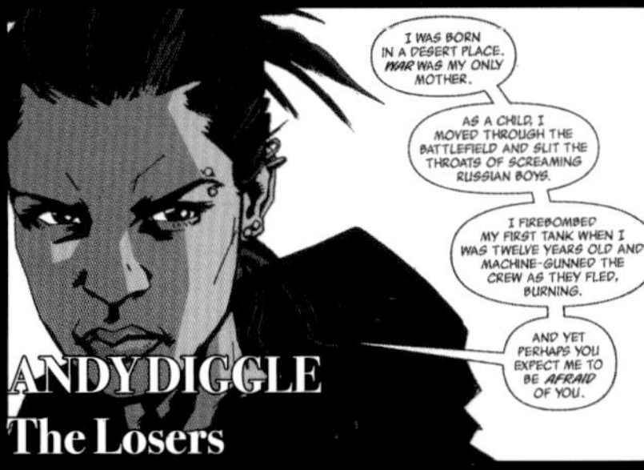
I WAS BORN IN A DESERT PLACE. WAR WAS MY ONLY MOTHER.
AS A CHILD, I MOVED THROUGH THE BATTLEFIELD AND SLIT THE THROATS OF SCREAMING RUSSIAN BOYS.
I FIREBOMBED MY FIRST TANK WHEN I WAS TWELVE YEARS OLD AND MACHINE-GUNNED THE CREW AS THEY FLED, BURNING.
AND YET PERHAPS YOU EXPECT ME TO BE AFRAID OF YOU.
ANDY DIGGLE
The Losers

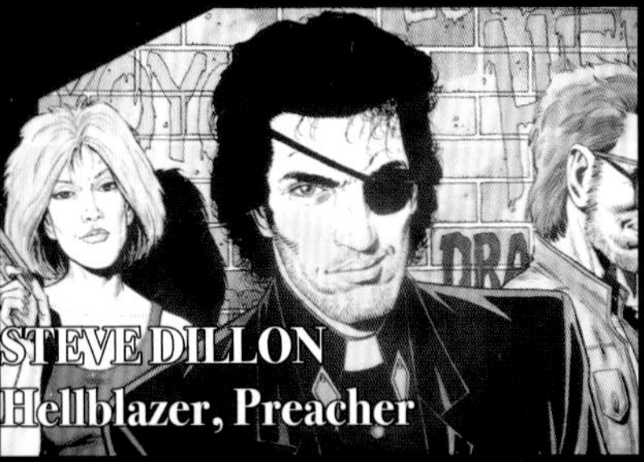
STEVE DILLON
Hellblazer, Preacher

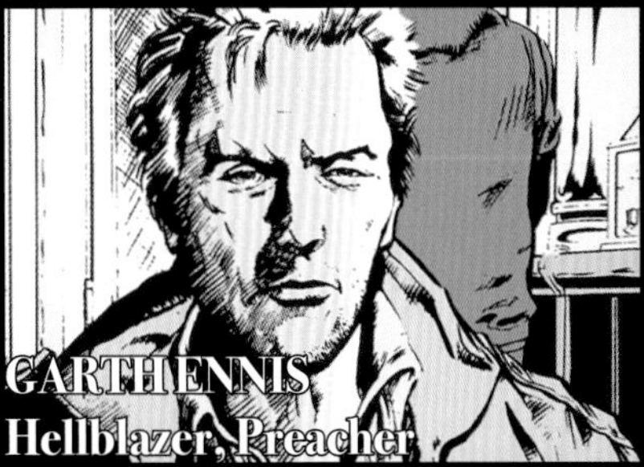
GARTH ENNIS
Hellblazer, Preacher

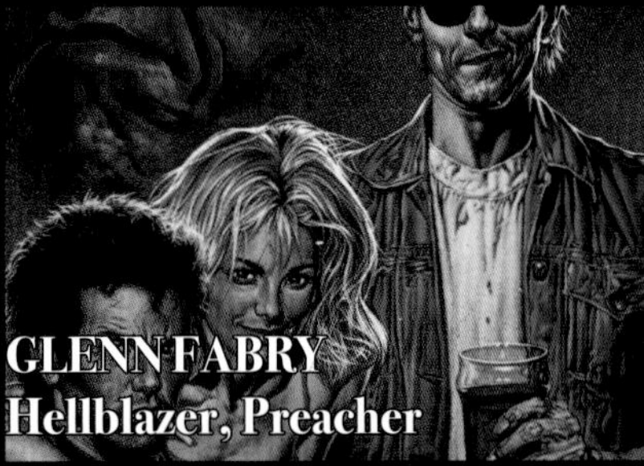
GLENN FABRY
Hellblazer, Preacher

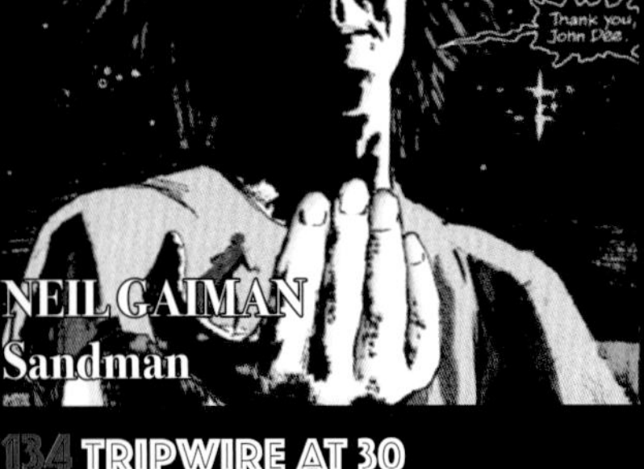
Thank you, John Dee.
NEIL GAIMAN
Sandman

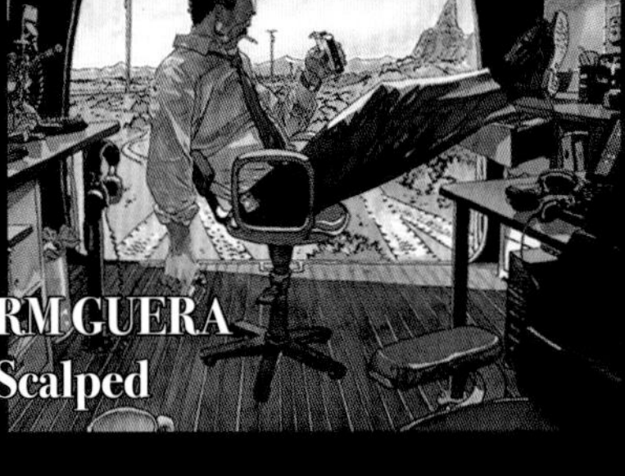
RM GUERA
Scalped

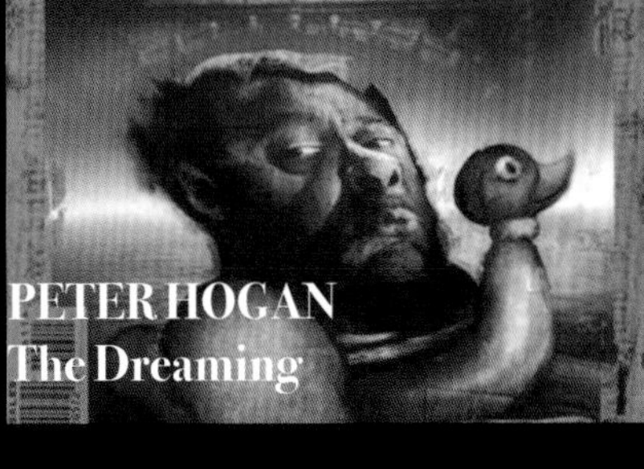
PETER HOGAN
The Dreaming

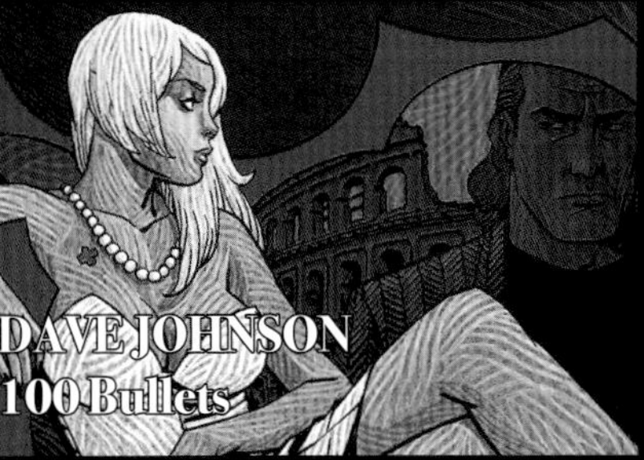
DAVE JOHNSON
100 Bullets

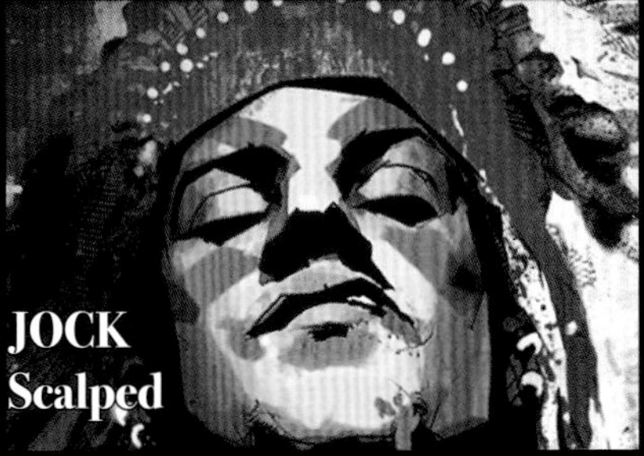
JOCK
Scalped

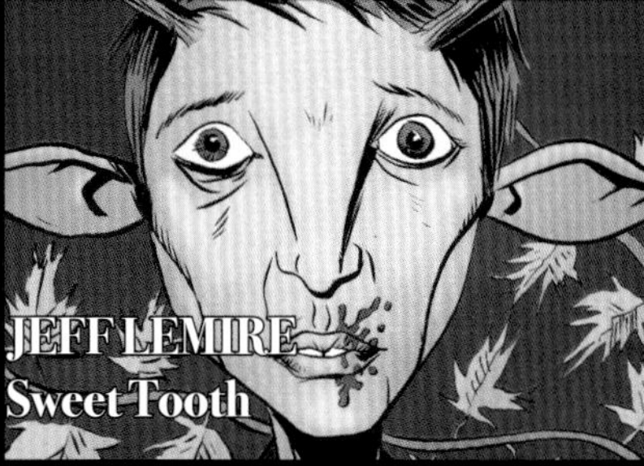
JEFF LEMIRE
Sweet Tooth

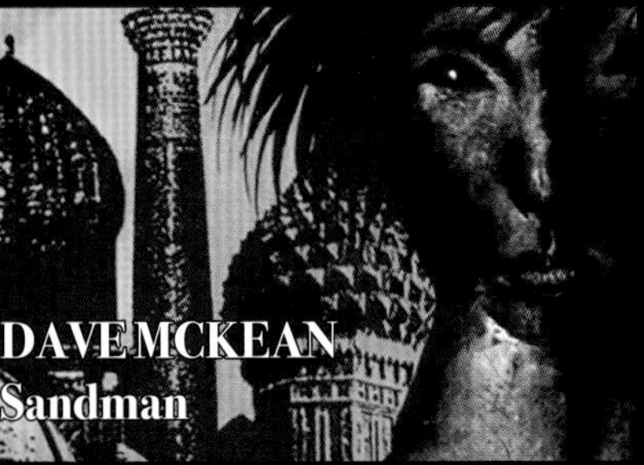
DAVE MCKEAN
Sandman

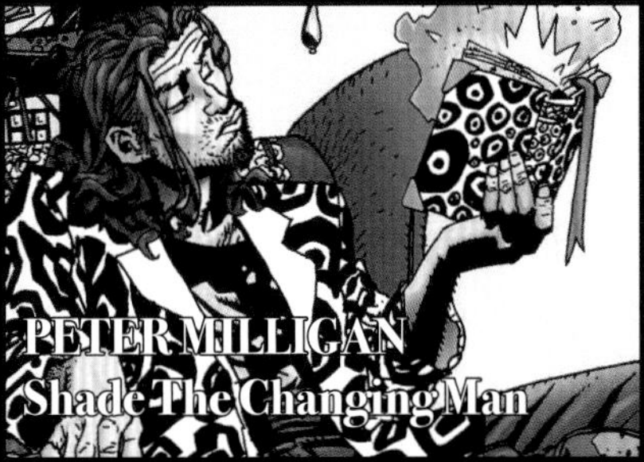
PETER MILLIGAN
Shade The Changing Man

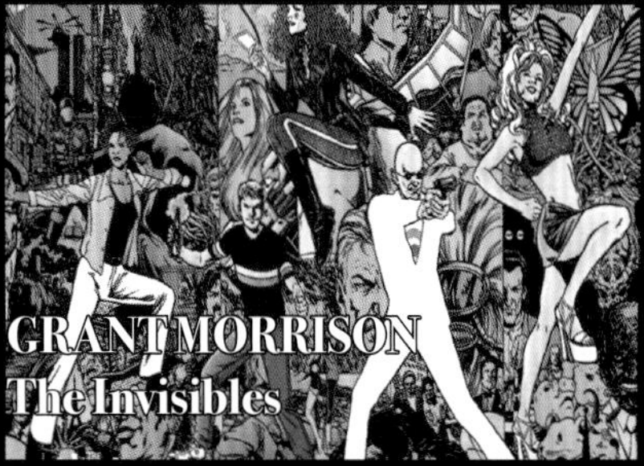
GRANT MORRISON
The Invisibles

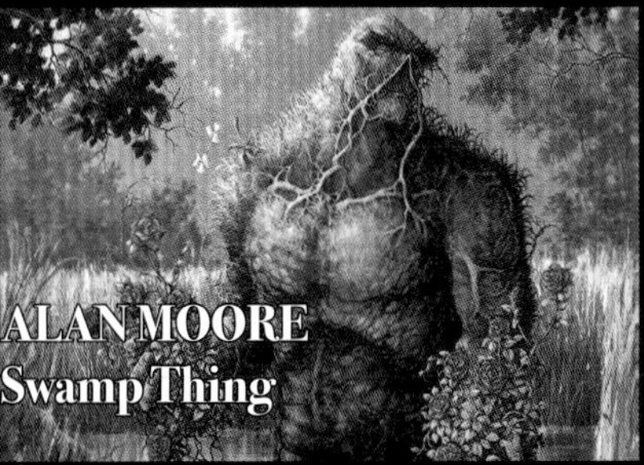
ALAN MOORE
Swamp Thing

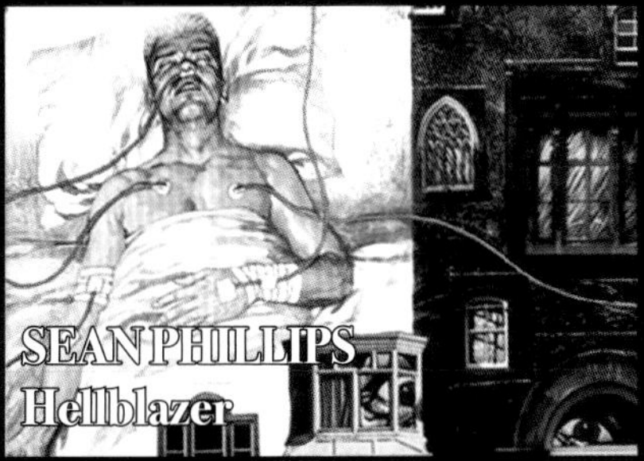
SEAN PHILLIPS
Hellblazer

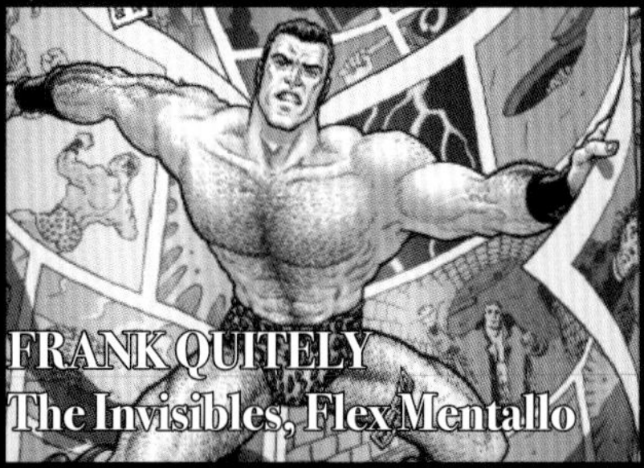
FRANK QUITELY
The Invisibles, Flex Mentallo

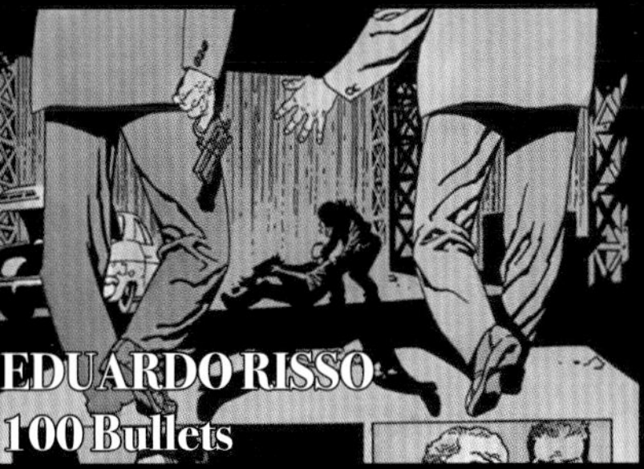
EDUARDO RISSO
100 Bullets

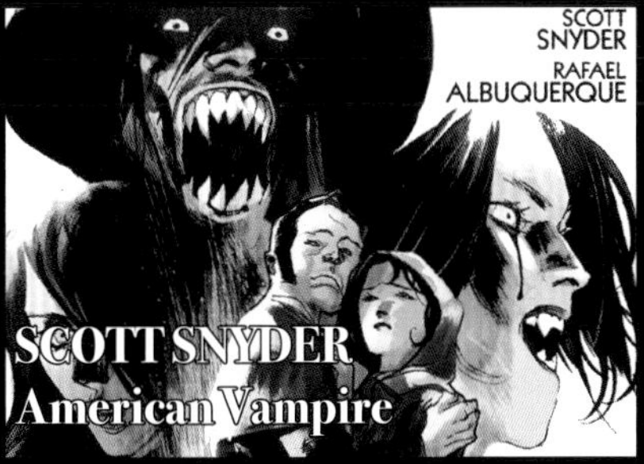
SCOTT
SNYDER
RAFAEL
ALBUQUERQUE
SCOTT SNYDER
American Vampire

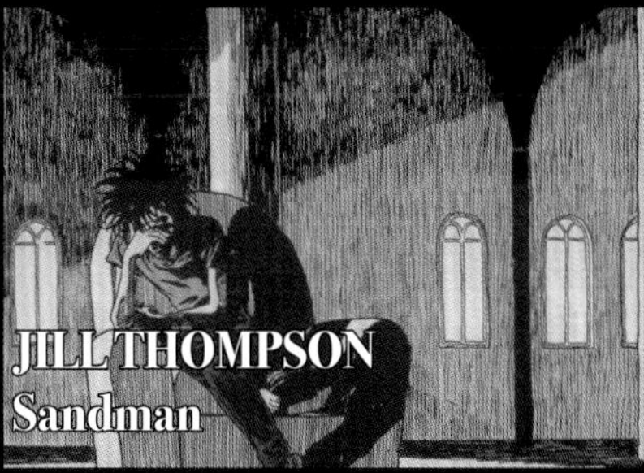
JILL THOMPSON
Sandman

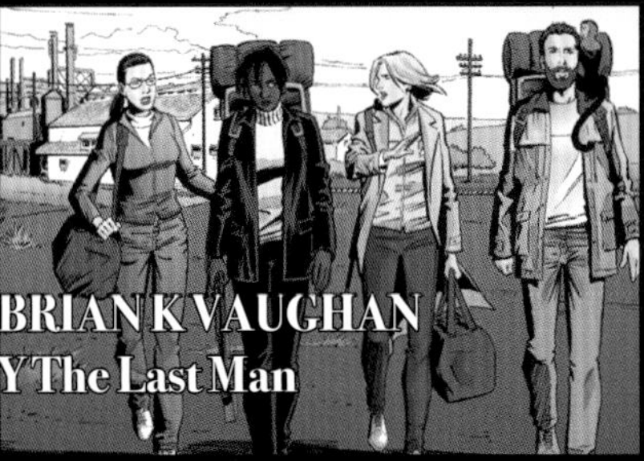
BRIAN K VAUGHAN
Y The Last Man

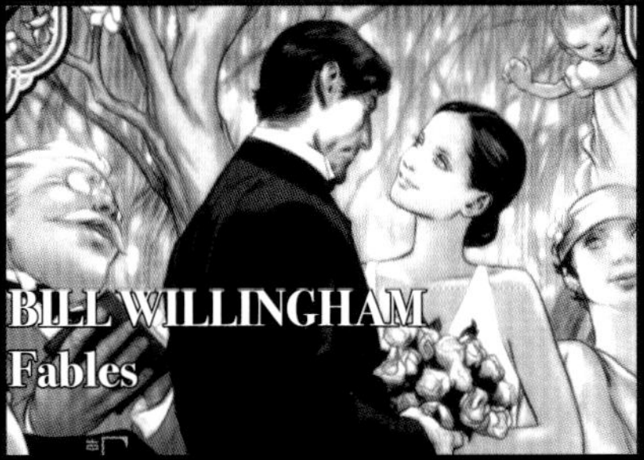
BILL WILLINGHAM
Fables

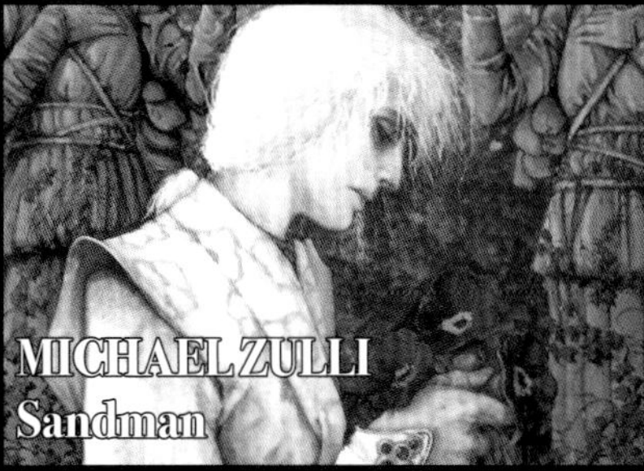
MICHAEL ZULLI
Sandman

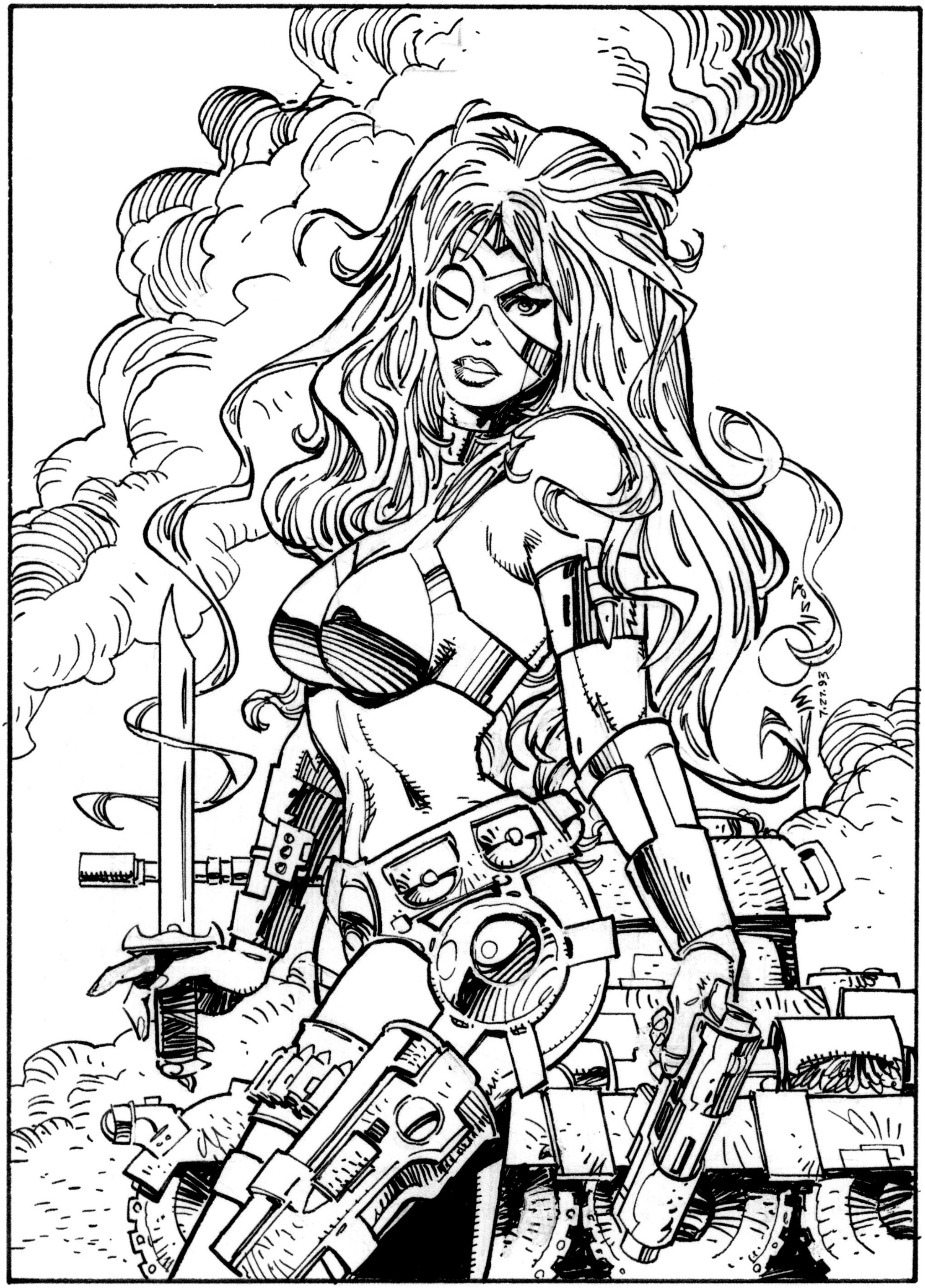

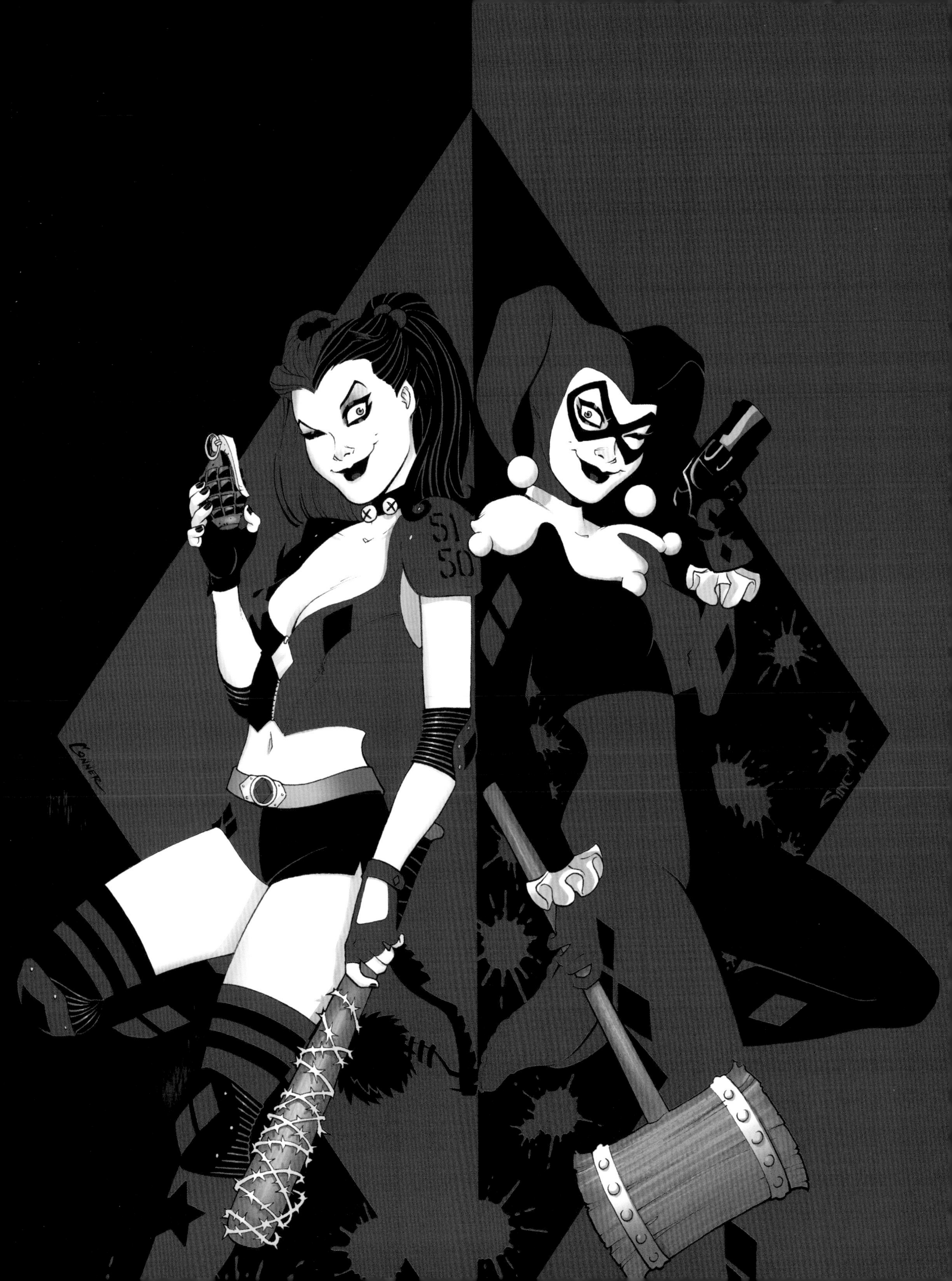
51
50
CONNER

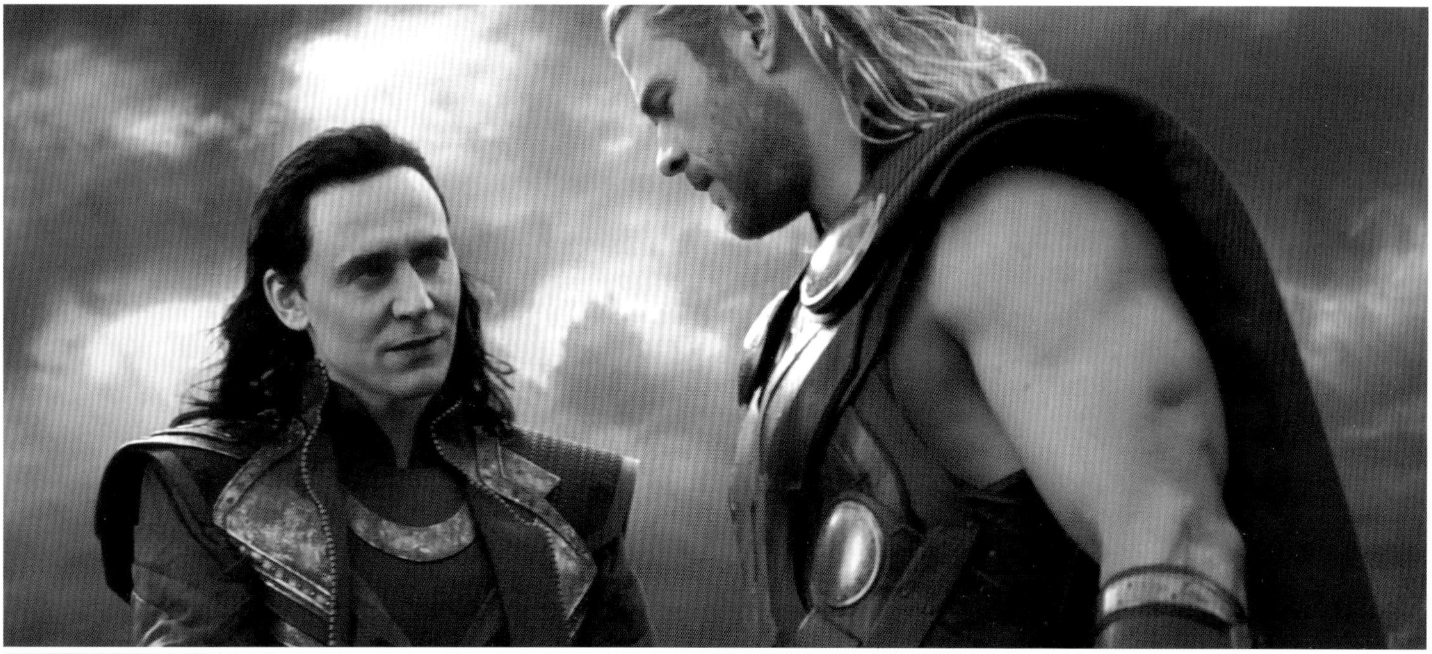

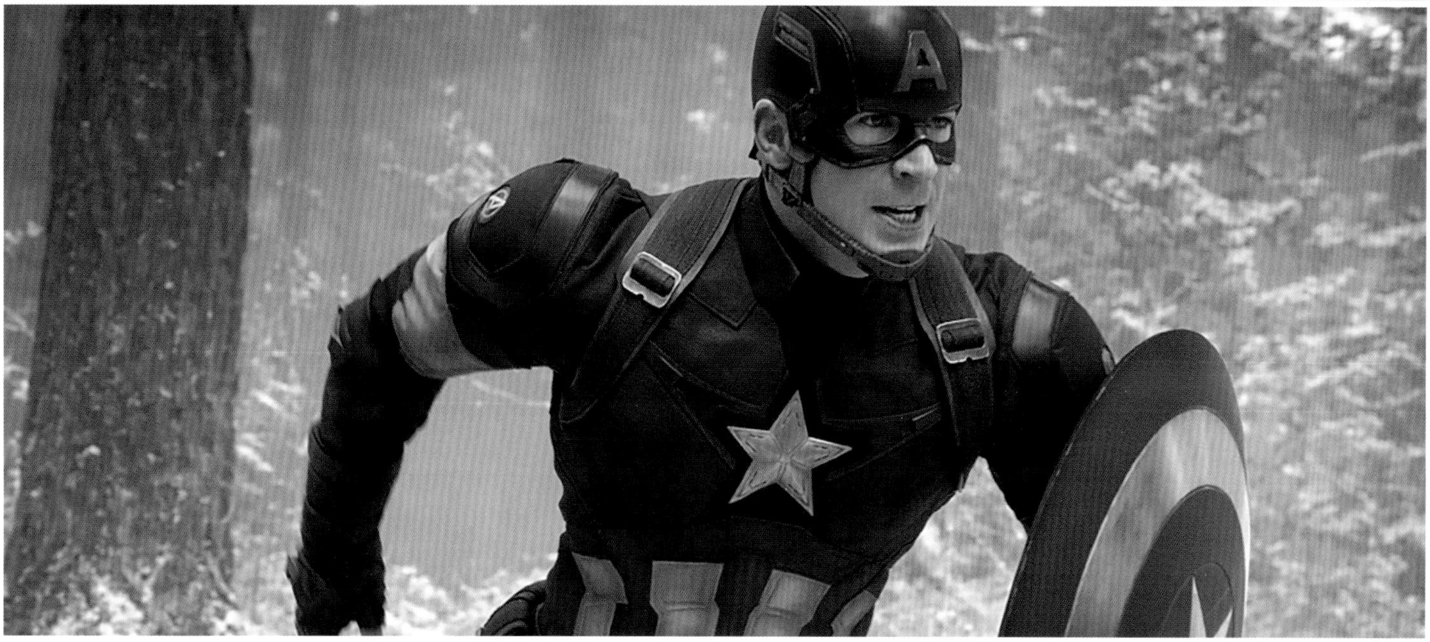

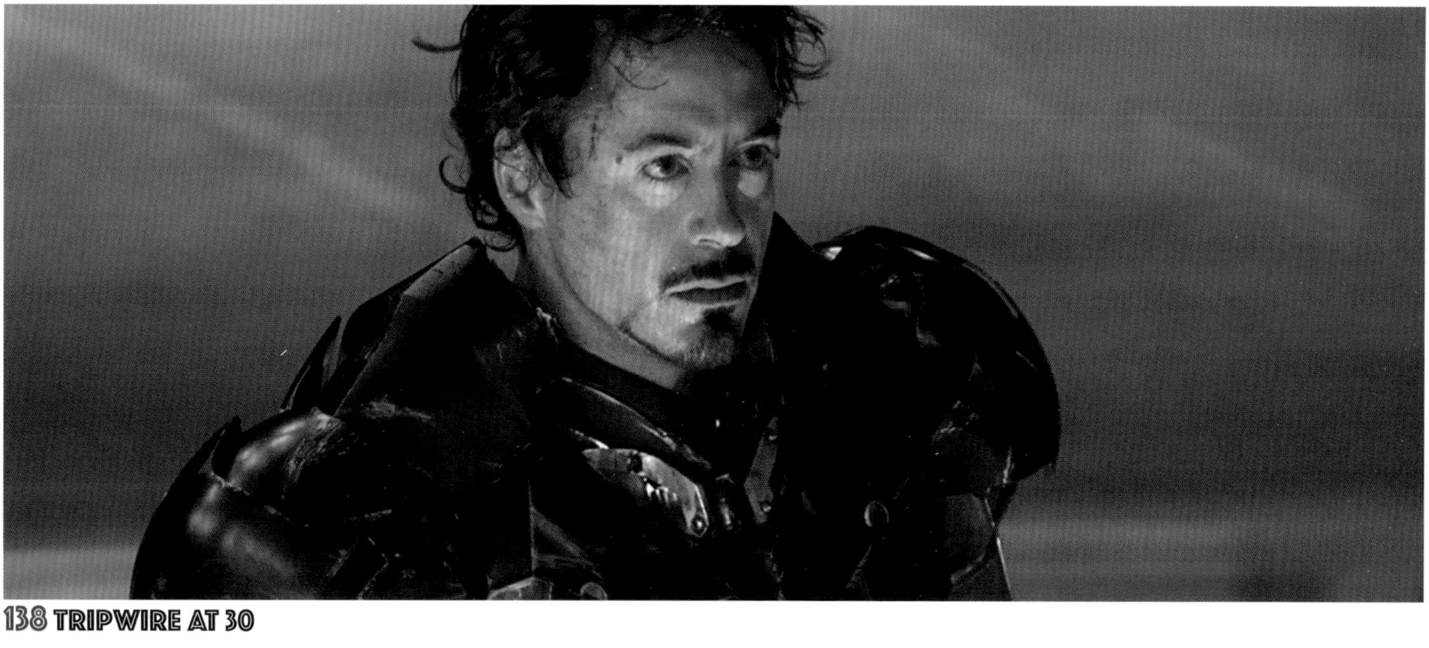

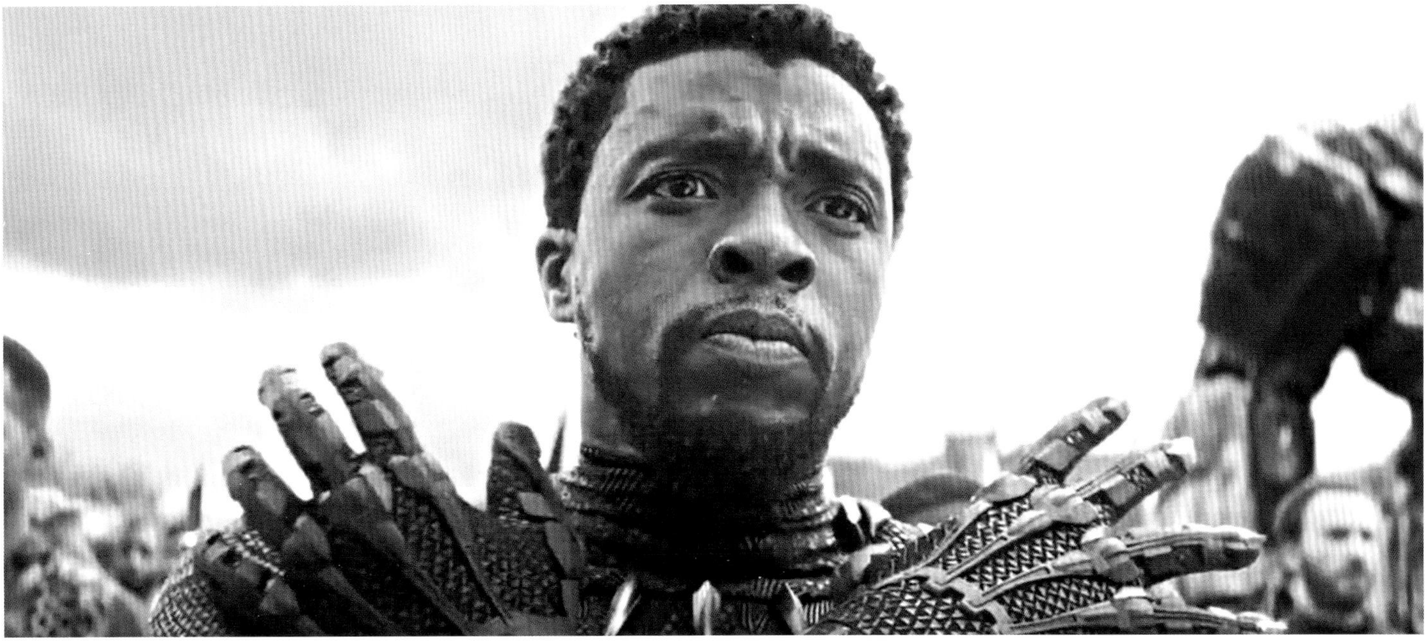

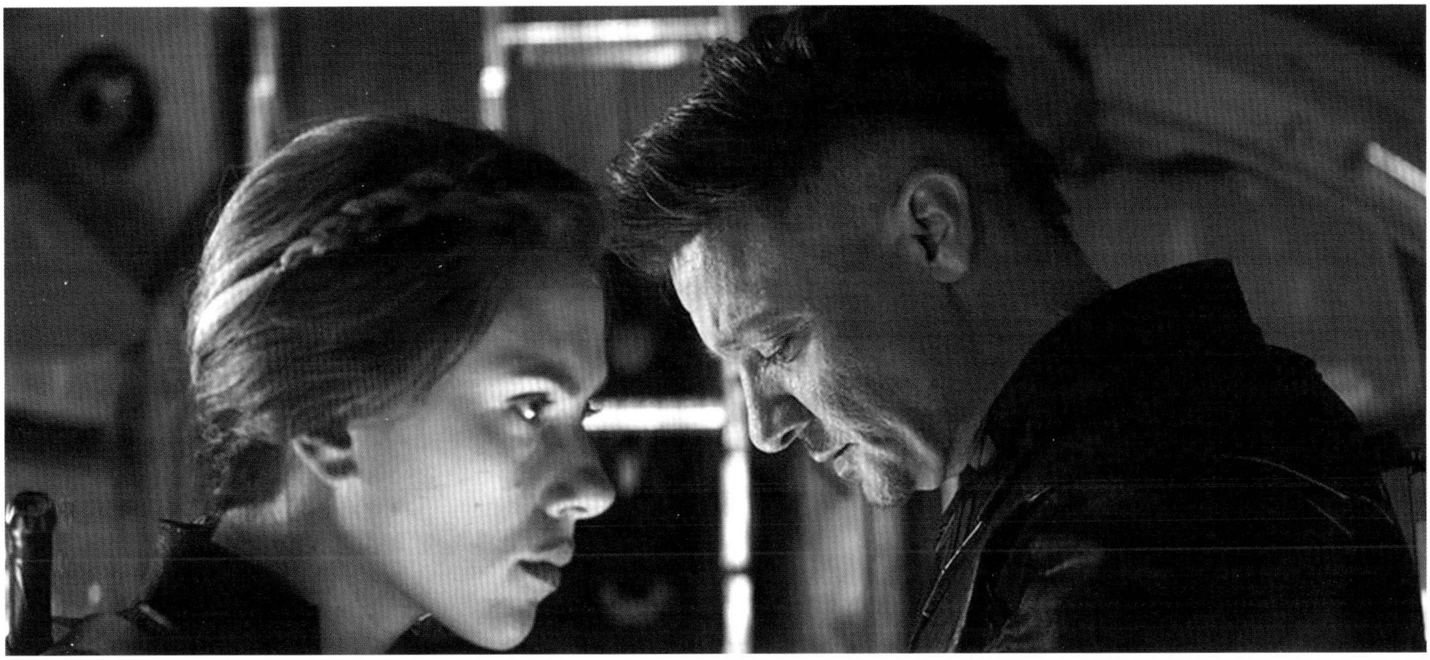

THE MARVEL AGE OF MOVIES

Since 2008, Marvel Studios has moved from a rank outsider to the dominant cultural force on the big screen. Tripwire's editor-in-chief Joel Meadows takes a look at the rise of the biggest movie studio on the planet...

In 1992, Marvel was a successful comic company but film success had eluded them. DC had two popular Batman films directed by Tim Burton but the House of Ideas couldn't compete. It took until 1998 and Wesley Snipes' *Blade* to show that they could beat their long-term rival on the big screen.

Blade led to Sam Raimi's *Spider-man* starring Tobey Maguire as the teenage webspinner, making an impressive $825m at the box office when it was released back in 2002. Marvel had arrived at the cinema.

It was the hiring of one Kevin Feige as associate producer on Bryan Singer's *X-Men* movie made by Fox in 2000 which was to prove to be one of the company's canniest (or uncanniest) moves.

X-Men 2 and *X-Men The Last Stand* both did decently at the box office, grossing $407m and $460m respectively, but they never quite managed to match the success of *Spider-man*, which spawned two sequels. The last one came out back in 2007 but it was seen as a failure even though it grossed a fairly amazing $894m worldwide. It had taken them over a decade but Marvel had worked out what it took to compete with their distinguished competition.

2008 was a watershed year for Marvel movies: it saw the release of *Iron Man*, directed by Jon Favreau and starring Robert Downey Jr. Downey Jr was an actor whose career needed severe rehabilitation after taking a nose dive in the 1990s but he proved to be a very popular choice.

At the time, the actor was a risky choice as Feige recalled in an interview with CinemaBlend back in 2021: "I was lucky enough to be involved in early *Spider-Man* films and *X-Men* films. But we wanted to do an *Iron Man* movie. And I do think, still, the biggest risk – which seems outrageous to say

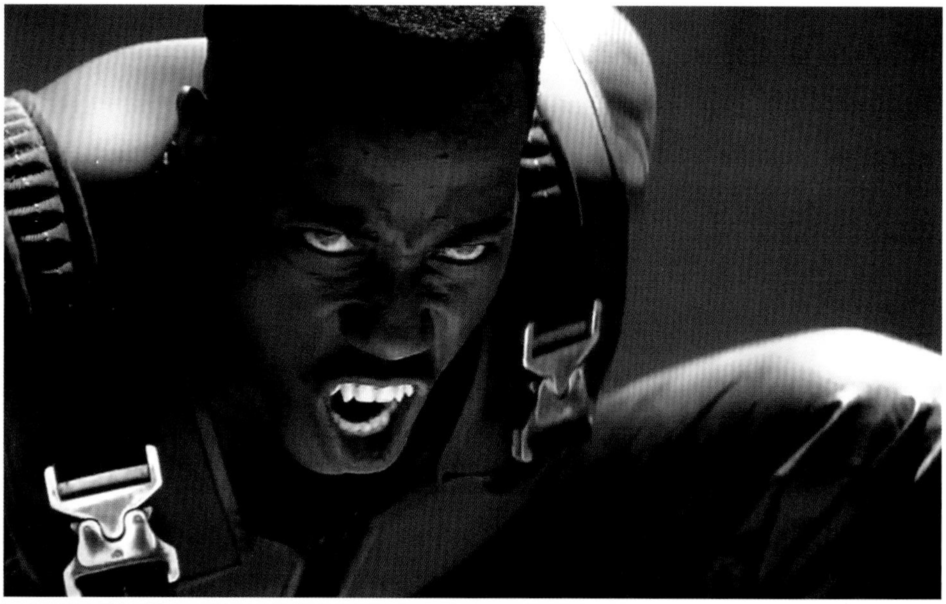

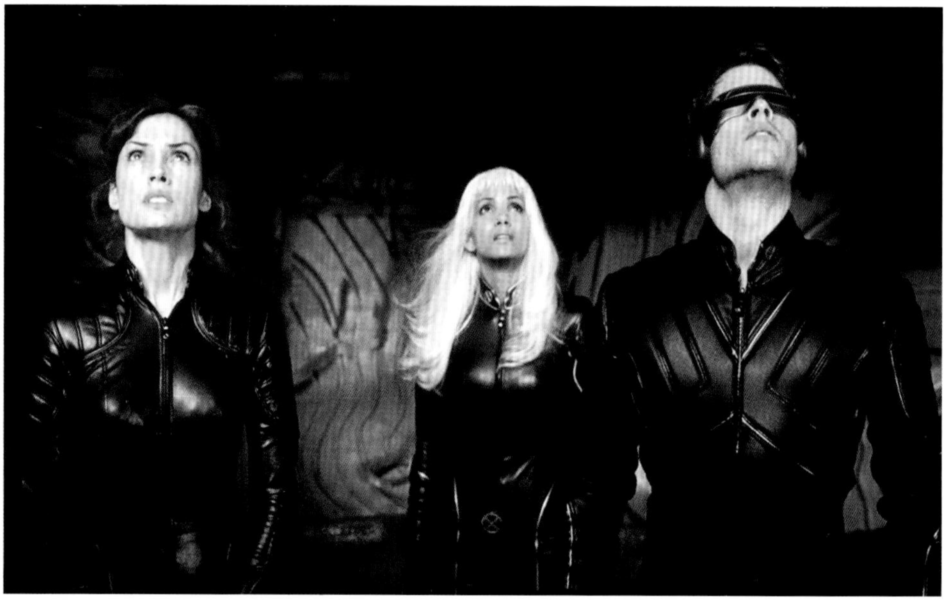

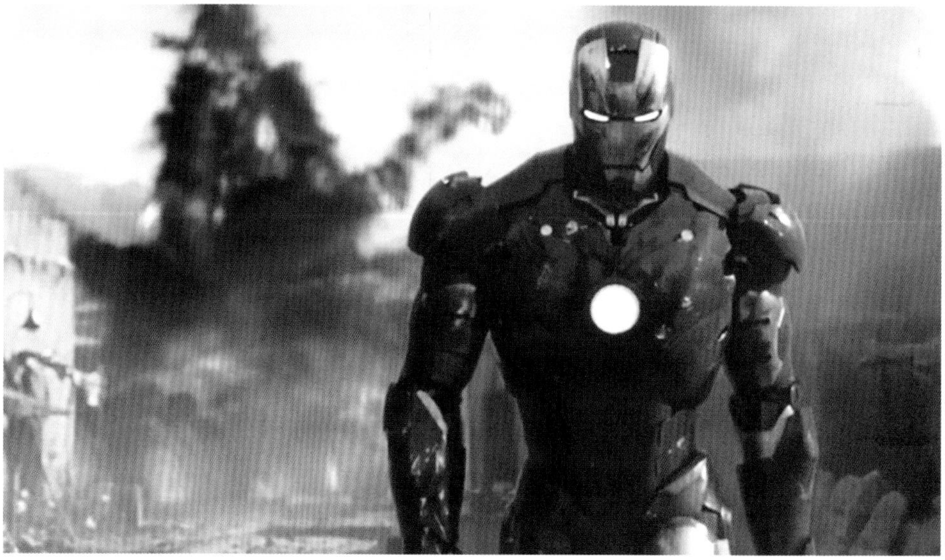

Laying the ground work: Without Blade (1998, top) and X2 (2003, middle) for Iron Man (bottom, 2008) would not have happened

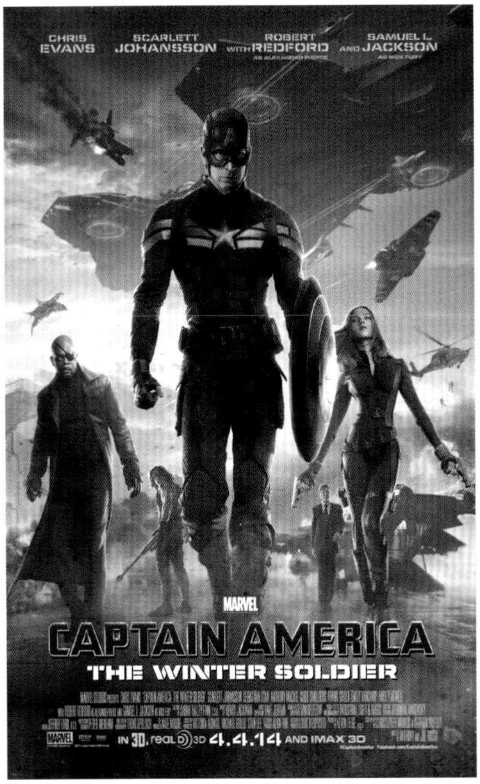
CHRIS EVANS
SCARLETT JOHANSSON
WITH ROBERT REDFORD
AND SAMUEL L. JACKSON
MARVEL
CAPTAIN AMERICA
THE WINTER SOLDIER
IN 3D, realD 3D 4.4.14 AND IMAX 3D

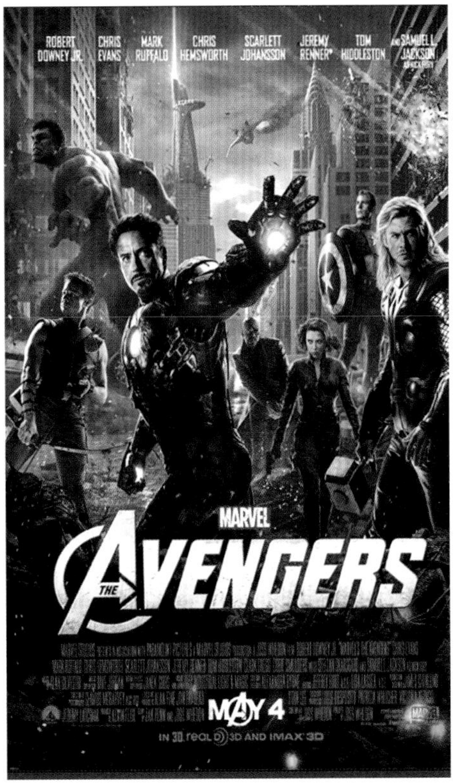
ROBERT DOWNEY JR.
CHRIS EVANS
MARK RUFFALO
CHRIS HEMSWORTH
SCARLETT JOHANSSON
JEREMY RENNER
TOM HIDDLESTON
AND SAMUEL L. JACKSON
MARVEL
THE AVENGERS
MAY 4
IN 3D, realD 3D AND IMAX 3D

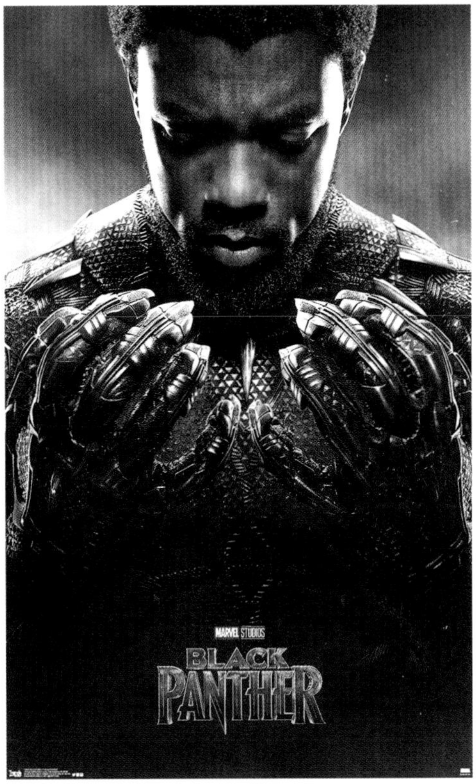
MARVEL STUDIOS
BLACK PANTHER

"I WAS LUCKY ENOUGH TO BE INVOLVED IN EARLY SPIDER-MAN FILMS AND X-MEN FILMS. BUT WE WANTED TO DO AN IRON MAN MOVIE. AND I DO THINK, STILL, THE BIGGEST RISK – WHICH SEEMS OUTRAGEOUS TO SAY NOW – WAS CASTING ROBERT DOWNEY JR. IT WAS BOTH THE BIGGEST RISK AND THE MOST IMPORTANT THING IN THE FOUNDING OF THE MARVEL CINEMATIC UNIVERSE."– KEVIN FEIGE

now – was casting Robert Downey Jr. It was both the biggest risk and the most important thing in the founding of the Marvel Cinematic Universe. Without Robert, we wouldn't be sitting here today. I really believe that."

Iron Man made a fairly decent $585.8m at the box office and it kicked off the Marvel Cinematic Universe.

In 2009, Marvel was bought by Disney, which gave them a huge amount of clout internationally and began the House of Mouse's acquisitive streak which continued for many years.

Iron Man led to *The Incredible Hulk* the same year, which starred Edward Horton as the titular monster. It had a disappointing box office, only grossing $265m. It led to Hulk being recast by Mark Ruffalo later on. But despite this performance, Marvel continued and 2010 saw *Iron Man 2*, with Downey Jr returning as the millionaire superhero Tony Stark. *Iron Man 2* made more than its predecessor, grossing $624m internationally.

The year after, *Thor* debuted with the first appearance of the fellow Avenger played by Chris Hemsworth. It did decently enough taking in $450m at the box office. But Marvel hadn't quite reached the stratospheric heights that they hit later on with their cinematic efforts.

In the same year, we also saw the debut of Chris Evans as US patriotic hero Captain America in *Captain America: The First Avenger*. Just like *Thor*, it did decently enough but still a little bit lowkey taking in $370m.

It took the release of *The Avengers*, titled *The Avengers Assemble* in the UK, to really take things to the next level. Teaming up all of Marvel's big screen heroes in one place, the film passed the $1bn mark which was a huge milestone for them at the time.

The magic continued as *Iron Man 3*, which saw Downey Jr return again to the flying suit, grossed $1.2bn which proved that the Avengers' popularity wasn't just a fluke.

However *Thor: The Dark World*, the second outing for Hemsworth flying solo as the Norse god, only managed to take in $645m. But it is a lot higher than its progenitor

LOKI
MARVEL STUDIOS
LOKI
Disney+
Original Series Now Streaming

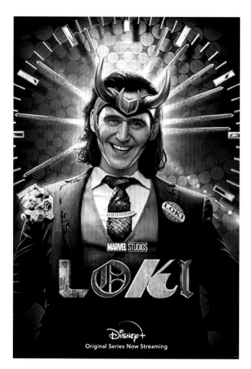

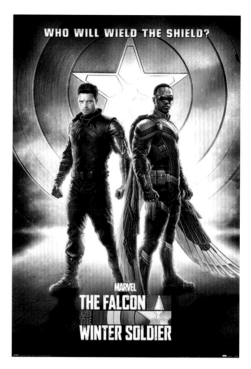

and it proved that the success of The Avengers increased audience interest in Marvel's properties.

The second Captain America film, *The Winter Solder*, was released in 2014 and it took $715m, again a lot more than the first one.

By 2014, Marvel, free from other studios to distribute them, were a major player in the world cinema market, just six years after the release of *Iron Man*.

From 2014 to 2019, Marvel ramped up their releases with films like *Black Panther*, *Avengers: Infinity War* and *Avengers: Endgame* easily passing the $1bn mark and breaking box office records on a regular basis.

The pandemic in 2020 caused Marvel to have a major rethink. But they were very canny as they switched from cinema to the small screen, turning to Disney Plus to move things forward. In 2021, Marvel produced *WandaVision*, *The Falcon and The Winter Soldier* and *Loki*, waiting for the world to return to normality.

In the same year, Marvel released *Black Widow*, which made $380m, which is a respectable figure as the first Marvel movie to come out after the pandemic. Also in 2021, Marvel with

MARVEL STUDIOS TRANSFORMED THE FILM LANDSCAPE BACK IN 2008 AND THEY HAVE BEEN DOING IT EVER SINCE.

Sony released *Spider-man No Way Home*, which took in an incredible $1.9bn at the box office. In 2022, Marvel's *Doctor Strange In The Multiverse Of Madness* came just short of $1bn, hitting $954m, which again is pretty impressive.

Marvel managed to weather the year and a bit of the pandemic, with its latest offering, *Thor: Love And Thunder* at $600m as of this writing. Later this year, Marvel releases *Wakanda Forever*, which would have been Black Panther 2 if we hadn't lost its star Chadwick Boseman so tragically early. It will be interesting to see if the film studio can keep the momentum going with the announcement of a tranche of new films at San Diego Comic-Con in July 2022.

Director Taika Waititi who has directed two Marvel movies (*Thor: Ragnarok* and *Thor: Love And Thunder*) sees working in the Marvel

MARVEL STUDIOS
WandaVision
Disney+
Original Series Streaming Jan. 15

WHO WILL WIELD THE SHIELD?
MARVEL
THE FALCON
AND THE
WINTER SOLDIER

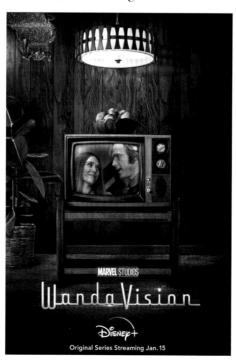

Movie Universe as one he enjoys, he said in an interview for ABC TV in 2022:

" "It's obviously beautiful. It's a great experience. It's really the only major studio experience I've had on this scale. And, you know they're family. I trust them very much and they trust me and it just seems to work."

Despite the box office success of the Marvel movies, one thing that has escaped them is awards. But Feige does understand why this is the case as he revealed in an interview also on cinemablend: "I think we are always at a deficit because of the Marvel logo and because of a genre bias that certainly exists. I just loved that for a shining moment there with *Black Panther* that was put aside and the work was recognised for the achievement that it was."

2022 has also seen a number of new Marvel TV series launch: *Ms. Marvel*, *Moon Knight* and *She-Hulk: Attorney-At-Law*.

One thing is for certain: Marvel Studios transformed the film landscape back in 2008 and they have been doing it ever since, adapting to the changes that the film industry and the world has thrown at them.

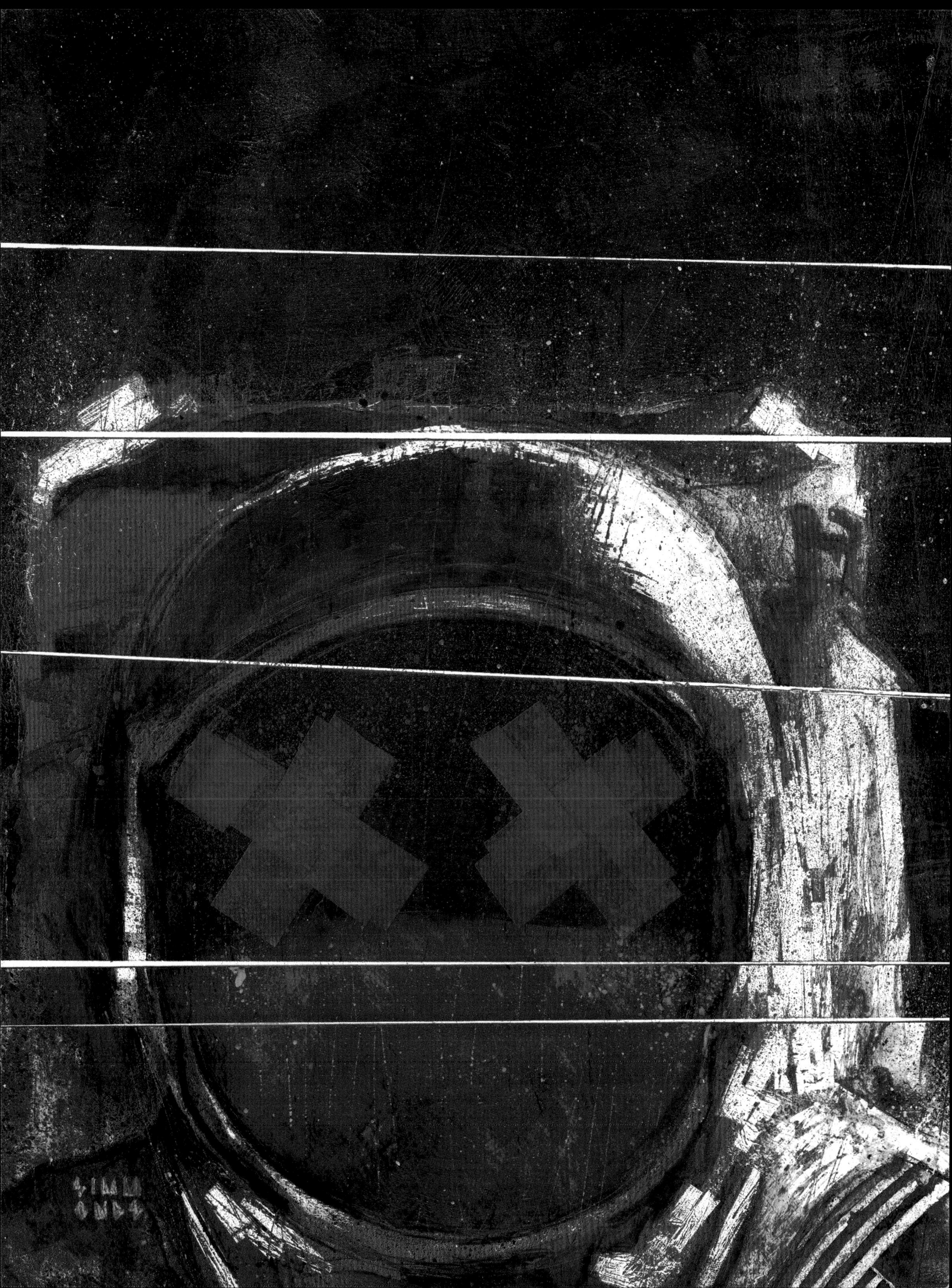
SIMM
ONDS

30 YEARS OF COMIC-RELATED TV SHOWS

Tripwire's contributing writer Robert Cave takes a look at 30 years of comic-related TV series...

When the first iteration of *Tripwire* hit comic shops three decades ago, the whole world of broadcast media was a different place. In the US, MTV was just over a decade old, and multi-channel pay TV packages were the hot new thing, while in UK most viewers still only had access to the standard four terrestrial channels. Modern streaming services providing on-demand access to almost unlimited quantities of film and TV was the stuff of a madman's dream.

Back in that old world, popular comic book series were not the subject of fevered bidding wars between rival media companies. Consequently comics-based adaptations, in either live-action or animated form, were a far rarer occurrence and TV itself was widely regarded as a less prestigious, lower budget artform and cinema's poor relation. How times have changed! Today, traditional broadcasters have sought to update their offerings as they attempt to compete with streaming platforms that

provide an all-you-can-eat buffet of film and TV. All of them have invested heavily in commissioning all manner of scripted episodic drama series and have increasingly come to view comics as a valuable source material from which "content" can be mined. There's now so much TV being produced that it's virtually impossible to keep up with it all, so with that in mind I present here my subjective list of (over) thirty significant shows from the past thirty years. Truly, there has never been a better time to be a fan of comics-related TV.

Batman The Animated Series (1992-95)

The brainchild of Bruce Timm, Paul Dini and Mitch Brian, B*atman: The Animated Series* first hit Fox Kids in September 1992, reinvigorating and unifying the Batman mythos for a new generation. Critically acclaimed by fans to this day, it served as a launching point not just for Timm and Dini's fan-favourite Harley Quinn character, but also for over a decade's worth of shared DC Animated Universe continuity.

X-Men Animated Series (1992-1995)

The X-Men's most successful TV series to date debuted in October 1992, also on Fox Kids, and lasted for 5 seasons. During its run it revisited the highlights of Marvel's mutant continuity up to that point, remixing it for a wider TV audience and, it was hoped, a new generation, something that it wildly succeeded at, as evidenced by the existence of the *X-Men '92* comics, which are directly inspired by the cartoon.

The Maxx (1995)

Sam Kieth's distinctive and singular comic took the conventions of superheroes and subverted them to the point that its hero was just a powerless, homeless bit player in the wider psychological traumas of the women who care for him. Mixing liberal doses of Jungian theory, feminist thought, and a visual aesthetic that owed equal amounts to Vaughn Bode and Dr. Seuss, Kieth's vision was adapted into a short-lived animation that ran on MTV in 1995, bringing a very idiosyncratic story to the channel's equally sizable audience.

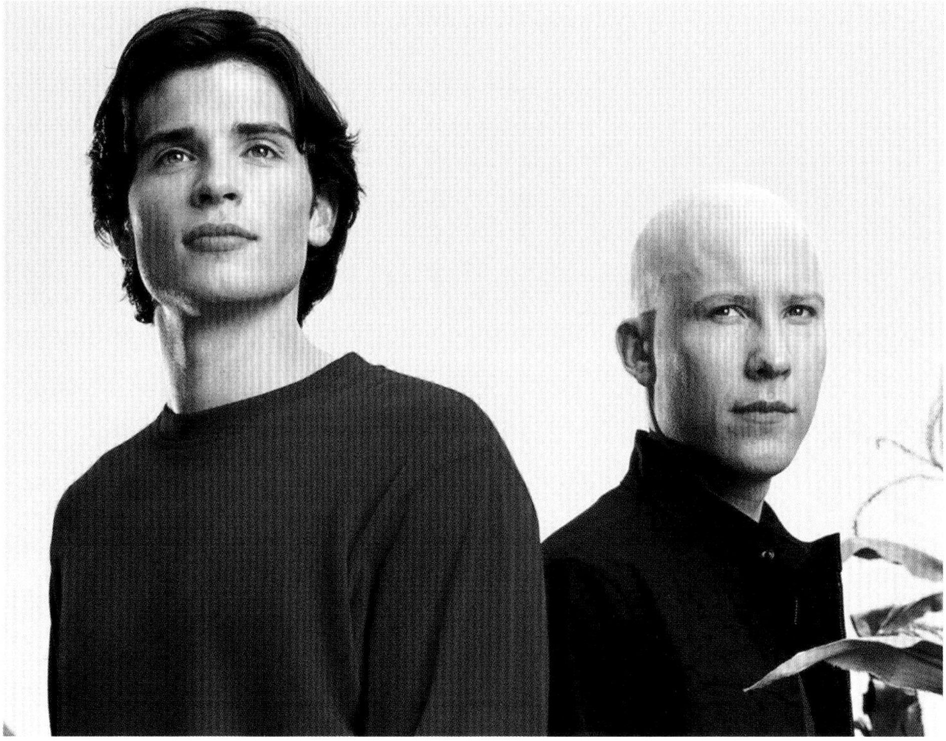

Lois & Clark: The New Adventures of Superman (1993-1997)
The history of live-action TV adaptations of Superman goes back to 1950s, but ABC's 1990s TV incarnation sought to broaden the character's appeal for more casual primetime family audiences by giving him equal (second?) billing to his love-interest, the journalist and career gal Lois Lane. The show's engaging scripts and playful performances by Teri Hatcher and Dean Cain in the lead roles focused the show on the couple's romance while the outlandish fights, foes and threats kept comic fans happy.

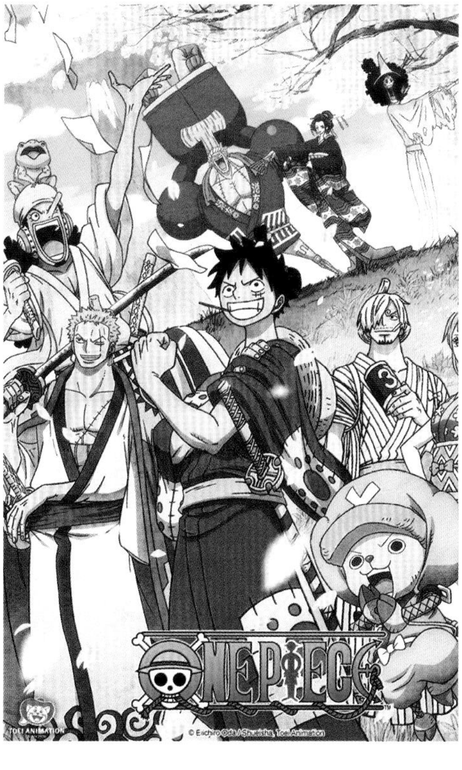
ONE PIECE

Sabrina The Teenage Witch (1996-2003)
Yes, the recent Netflix version might be cooler and more relevant to modern audiences, but Melissa Joan Hart's 90s sitcom gave Archie comics its first live-action TV success, with ratings averaging over ten million viewers during its initial Friday-night run on ABC. Those figures dropped precipitously when the show moved to the WB network in late 2000, but that didn't prevent the show stacking up an impressive seven season run. In contrast, the character's recent horror-inflected adventures on Netflix were brought to an untimely end by the complications of filming during Covid after just two seasons.

One Piece (1999-)
Based on the still ongoing massive manga mega-hit by Eiichiro Oda, *One Piece* follows the adventures of Monkey D. Luffy, a wannabe Pirate King whose body is given the properties of rubber after he inadvertently eats a Devil Fruit. In addition to numerous TV specials and theatrically released movies, the manga has spawned an equally successful anime adaptation on the Fuji TV network that is now in its 20th season and still going strong. It seems Luffy and his crew, The Straw Hat Pirates, are not going to run out of adventures any time soon.

Smallville (2001-2011)
A mere four years after adult Superman had settled down and got married in *The New Adventures of Superman*, the WB network took the character back to his teenage roots in Smallville. Set before his move to Metropolis and both his journalistic or superheroic careers, *Smallville* initially eschewed the fights and tights in favour of the teen drama of a young Clark Kent and friends, who include a young Lex Luthor. The show soon developed a dedicated fanbase, clocking up a formidable 218 episodes over its ten-season run.

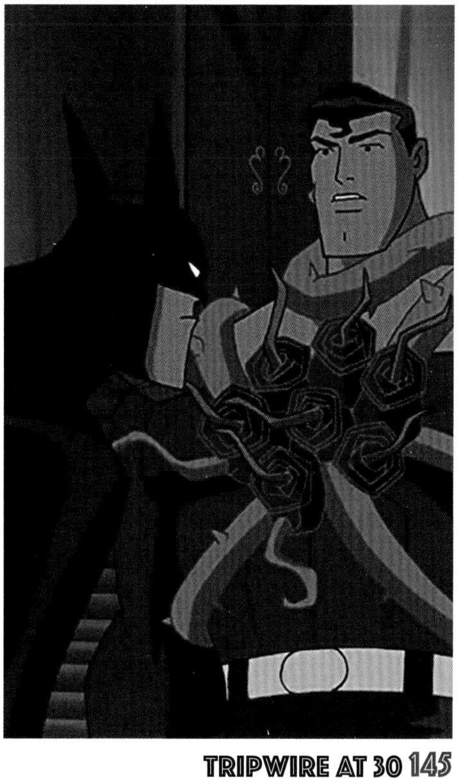

Justice League Unlimited (2004-2006)

The eighth and last series in the popular DC Animated Universe, which started with *Batman The Animated Series*, *Justice League Unlimited* proved to be both a popular and resilient series that was originally commissioned by the Cartoon Network. The show expanded the League's roster of heroes and helped further cement John Stewart's place as the pre-eminent Earth-based Green Lantern for a generation of fans. However, over time, rival unrelated DC TV and movie spin-offs impacted on the shows ability to include various characters and the series ended its run on Toonami after three series.

The Walking Dead (2010-2022)

Bettering *Smallville's* season count, but still some way off of *One Piece's*, *The Walking Dead* is an eleven-season colossus of comics to live-action TV adaptations. US cable TV channel AMC took a very cautious gamble commissioning a mere six-episode first season of Robert Kirkman, Tony Moore and Charlie Adlard's iconic post-apocalyptic zombie-infested survival horror epic, but the show proved popular enough to demand not just many additional seasons, but also various webisodes and at least four spin-off series, as well as *The Talking Dead*, a chat/discussion show in which celebrity fans and guests chew over the events of the latest Walking episodes.

Arrow (2011-2020)

The CW, a joint venture between CBS and the WarnerMedia empire, struck ratings gold with Greg Berlanti, Marc Guggenheim, and Andrew Kreisberg's TV adaptation of DC's **Green Arrow** comics series. Despite being one of DC's less widely-known characters, at least among non-comic readers, Arrow's show runners succeeded in organically growing both their own audience and their own interlinked TV universe, dubbed the Arrowverse by fans, as a direct counterpoint to Marvel's cinematic universe. This extended live-action TV universe even outlasted the show that spawned it.

Agents of S.H.I.E.L.D. (2013-2020)

Following in the wake of the first *Avengers* movie, which loudly and decisively brought Marvel Studios various film franchises into a single shared continuity, Disney's ABC network took the opportunity to bring that cinematic universe to the small screen with Marvel's *Agents of S.H.I.E.L.D.* Despite Gregg Clark reprising his movie role as a resurrected Agent Coulson, and various thematic and narrative links to the films, S.H.I.E.L.D. felt as if it was being kept at a slight distance from the rest of the MCU and should probably be viewed as something of a dry run for the more tightly interconnected Marvel Studios TV series that later debuted on the Disney+ streaming service.

Teen Titans Go! (2013-)

In a time of live-action superhero dominance, series developers Michael Jelenic and Aaron Horvath proved that there was also plenty of appetite for shorter kid-friendly comedy-centred animation about rambunctious teen superheroes getting into various unsupervised adventures. Then they demonstrated that the same approach could also sustain an equally successful (short) animated feature with *Teen Titans Go! To the Movies* in 2018.

The Flash (2014-2023)

Grant Gustin made his debut as the Wally West version of The Flash in two stories in *Arrow*'s second and third seasons before going on to headline his own series, the first spin-off from what would become known as the Arrowverse. Throughout its run, the show has adroitly juggled the scarlet speedster's convoluted backstory with lighter tales, such as the musical team-up episode, Duet, co-starring Melissa Benoist's Supergirl. With a ninth, and final, season planned for 2023, *The Flash* is also set to be the last main Arrowverse show standing. It will be interesting to see what kind of ending the showrunners have for this bold experiment in shared universe TV storytelling.

Gotham (2014-2019)

Apparently, the idea for a Batman prequel series was first floated at Warner's TV division in the early 2000s, but this pitch was cast aside in favour of the Superman prequel series, *Smallville*. Fortunately for its fans, Bruno Heller and Danny Cannon succeeded in bringing their take on the on the concept at Fox. With David Mazouz playing a younger, pre-Batman Bruce Wayne edging painfully slowly towards the Batmask, much of the show's focus instead shifted onto Ben McKenzie as James Gordon and

a rotating cast of proto-Batvillains. Ultimately lasting five seasons, *Gotham* was eventually succeeded by a further prequel series that focused on the even earlier adventures of Bruce Wayne's butler, Alfred Pennyworth.

Supergirl (2015-2021)

The first season of *Supergirl* was filmed in bright, sunny LA and broadcast on CBS, one of the three largest networks in the US, before moving to the less mainstream channel The CW and shifting production to Vancouver. The channel switch facilitated the show's assimilation into The CW's Arrowverse, and served as a springboard for The CW's version of Superman, played by Tyler Hoechlin. Hoechlin would later go on to headline his own series, *Superman and Lois*, which was revealed to take place separately from wider Arrowverse's continuity in its second season finale.

Daredevil/ Jessica Jones (2015-2019)

While ABC brought the MCU to traditional TV broadcasting with *Agents of S.H.I.E.L.D.*, Netflix introduced the Marvel brand of superheroics to streaming with its own shared universe of less-prominent "ground-level" characters. These shows were produced to be part of the wider MCU, but their continuity was deliberately kept at arms-length from Marvel's non-Netflix output. Regardless, the shows, particularly *Daredevil* and *Jessica Jones*, met with widespread acclaim from fans and critics alike. Although the Netflix/Marvel deal came to an end after just 4 years, it is significant that Marvel Studios opted to stick with Charlie Cox, the actor Netflix cast as Daredevil, for their upcoming *Daredevil: Born Again* miniseries, rather than re-casting.

Legion (2017-2019)

Produced for FX before the 2019 Fox-Disney merger completed, showrunner Noah Hawley's *Legion* is arguably one of the most impressively imaginative and daring live-action comic book adaptations ever created. A feat all-the-more surprising because the show is centred on a comparatively minor figure from the *X-Men* comics, David Haller, the schizophrenic son of the team's founder Professor X. The show actively revels in the fundamental unreliability of its narrative and employs everything from animation to interpretive dance routines and musical numbers to convey the various conflicts at play in David's shifting perception of reality. Dan Stevens is nothing short of excellent in the title role and is supported by the equally impressive talents of Aubrey Plaza, Jean Smart and Jemaine Clement.

Doom Patrol (2019-)

Originally commissioned as part of the short-lived DC Universe subscription video-on-demand (SVOD) service,

Doom Patrol is an adaptation of the comic about a team of traumatised and deeply damaged misfit superheroes. The key influence here is Grant Morrison's iconic absurdist and frequently surreal late-80s/early 90s run on the title. It is to showrunner Jeremy Carver's immense credit that he and his writing team so successfully capture both the humanity and the strangeness of Morrison's work as they craft their own jazz-like improvisations around the themes he established.

Lucifer (2016-2021)

Loosely based on the fallen angel from Neil Gaiman, Sam Keith and Mike Dringenberg's acclaimed *Sandman* comic (and his subsequent solo comic adventures), the Fox TV adaptation of *Lucifer* transformed the title character actor, played by Tom Ellis, into some supernatural Sherlock Holmes figure, serving as a consultant to the Los Angeles Police Department. But perhaps the most significant thing about the show was how it was saved from cancellation after three series and resurrected for a further three-series run on Netflix, a feat that captured the shifting TV landscape as streaming services begin to challenge the dominance of traditional broadcast networks. Interestingly,

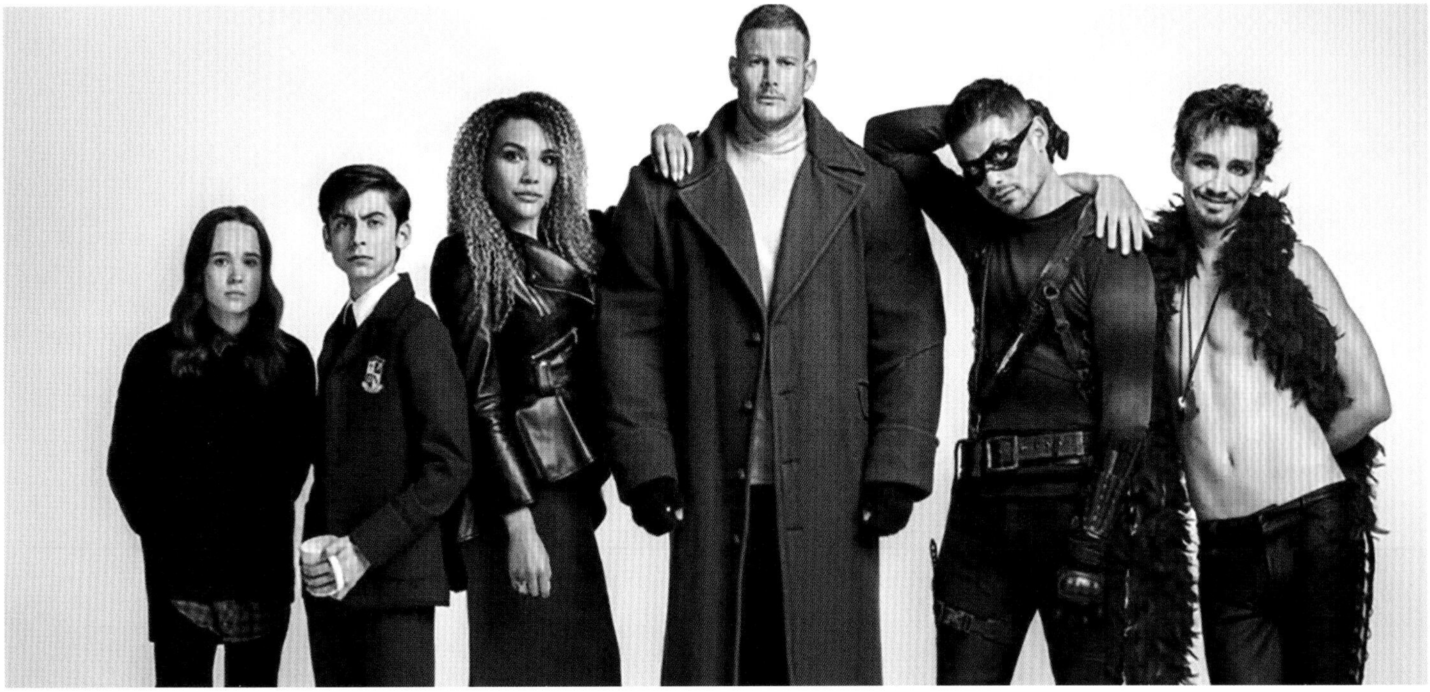

Netflix went on to successfully produce their own version of another former Fox commission, Joe Hill and Gabriel Rodriguez's *Locke & Key*, which Fox developed as a pilot back in 2011.

Preacher (2016-2019)
AMC's TV adaptation of Garth Ennis and Steve Dillon's anarchic, and frequently scatological, theologically themed western sees conflicted preacher Jesse Custer endowed with the power to literally compel others to do whatever he tells them to do. Custer then embarks on a journey that takes him from a crisis of faith to an ultimate confrontation with God. The series had a long and arduous path to its live-action TV adaptation, including extended periods in movie development hell, as well as a spell as a project for HBO. Ultimately, it took Sam Catlin, Evan Goldberg, and actor/comedian Seth Rogen to finally bring the controversial and playfully obscene comic to the small screen for a successful four-season run.

Umbrella Academy (2019-)
Based on Gerard Way and Gabrial Bá's award-winning Dark Horse comics series, *Umbrella Academy* follows the complex adventures of a group of superhumans conceived under mysterious circumstances and born on the same day in 1989. Forged into a team by their adopted father, the Umbrellas fight to avert an apparently imminent apocalypse in their own time, as well as a further apocalypse in the past caused by the failure of the assassination of JFK. Fittingly for a show that deftly dances over all manner of unusual and unexpected events, when cast member Elliot Page contacted series creator Steve Blackman to share the news of his gender transition, that transition was written in to the already completed scripts for the show's third season.

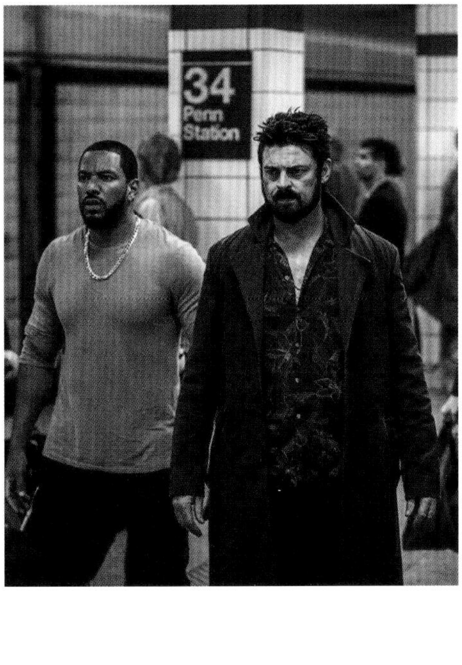
34
Penn
Station

The Boys (2019-)
Originally envisaged as a movie adaptation, the live-action version of Garth Ennis and Darick Robertson's scabrous superhero satire about a bunch of vigilantes aiming to take down various murderous, self-important and self-obsessed "superheroes", spent years in development hell before being redeveloped in 2016 as a TV series by Eric Kripke. Like a live-action rendering of cartoon violence, the show's splatter-stick humour revels in its own outlandish excesses, and found a natural home at Amazon Prime, whose streaming platform is much less restrictive than traditional US networks or cable channels. Indeed, it is exceedingly difficult to imagine any of them would have gone near a TV adaptation of *The Boys*. With a further animated series, *Diabolical*, in 2022, and an additional series in the works, it looks likely that *The Boys* franchise has a promising future for a while to come.

Harley Quinn: The Animated Series (2019-)

After making her debut in *Batman: The Animated Series*, Harley Quinn finally graduated to getting her own adult-orientated show in 2019 on the DC Universe subscription Video-on-Demand service. Although primarily an irreverent and frequently mildly sweary comedy, the key draw for fans is probably Harley's burgeoning romantic relationship with fellow Bat-villainess Poison Ivy, which finally reaches fruition at the end of the show's second season with the pair officially becoming a couple.

Watchmen (2019)

Where Zack Snyder's 2009 movie sought to adapt Alan Moore and Dave Gibbons legendary 12-issue miniseries, Damon Lindelof's HBO series styled itself more as a televisual sequel to Moore and Gibbons' series. Set some 34 years after the events of the comic, The TV show features various new characters and highlights the events of the 1921 Tulsa Race Massacre, which saw racist mobs attack and kill residents and destroy buildings and property in an affluent black neighbourhood in Greenwood, Oklahoma. These events have largely been supressed from public memory. Despite receiving numerous awards and critical acclaim, Lindelof declined

to return to *Watchmen* for a second series, leaving HBO to subsequently reclassify the show as a limited series.

Crisis on Infinite Earths (2019)

While not technically a TV series, The CW's final massive crossover event really warrants its own entry for the sheer audacity of its scope. Not content with merely crossing over the main shows that comprise The CW's Arrowverse, the event's planners also brought in stars from variety of other TV series based on DC comics character, both past and present. Actors ranging from Burt Ward (Robin in the popular 1960s *Batman* TV series) to the cast of *Doom Patrol* and *Lucifer* and even the writer of the original *Crisis on Infinite Earths*, Marv Wolfman, all appearing.

WandaVision (2021)

The Disney+ series *WandaVision* marked Marvel Studios' first foray to producing its own TV series set in the Marvel Cinematic Universe after subsuming the old Marvel Television division previously based at the ABC network, another Disney-owned operation. Focusing on Elizabeth Olsen's Scarlet Witch, the show explores her character's bereavement and trauma in the aftermath of the events of Avengers: Endgame. In addition to its slow-build emotional punch, *WandaVision* delivers a wonderful sense of closure while also setting up numerous ongoing plot threads for the future, including a possible sequel series.

Loki (2021)

Marvel Studio's third miniseries for Disney + was a wonderfully inventive six-parter that focused on Tom Hiddleston's unpredictable, chaotic Loki character and the Time Variance Authority, a bureaucratic organisation policing the continuity of the Marvel Universe. While joyously playful and fun, the series was also brilliant at exploring potential new directions for the MCU, as well as establishing a potent new supervillain to replace Thanos, the overarching threat lurking in the background of the first 20-odd MCU films.

Ms. Marvel (2022)

In contrast to Marvel Studios' earlier Disney+ series, which largely focused on already established characters from the MCU, *Ms. Marvel* saw the TV debut of Pakistani-American Kamala Khan (Iman Vellani), a teen hero who is set to make the opposite journey from the small to big screen. However, what may be more significant for Marvel movie fans is that while the show keeps the character's cultural origin largely consistent with her comics version, the origins and nature of her powers have changed considerably, seemingly to bring them more into line with the energy powers of Carol Danvers (Brie Larson) and Monica Rambeau (Teyonah Parris), whom she is set to star alongside in the MCU feature *Marvels* in 2023.

Papergirls (2022-)

Based on Brian K Vaughn and Cliff Chiang's Image comics series, *Papergirls* made its debut on Amazon Prime in 2022. Both the comic and TV series tell the tale of four almost-teenage paper delivery girls working in suburban Ohio in 1988 who stumble into a time travel war that takes them far away from their temporal comfort zone. While the 80s setting and profusion of walkie-talkie bicycle action have led to comparisons to *Stranger Things*, the

Papergirls comic series actually predates the Netflix show, and its focus on the emotional fallout as our young heroines confront futures they never imagined for themselves gives the series an emotional heft all its own.

Sandman (2022-)

The much-anticipated screen adaptation of Neil Gaiman's iconic comic series has finally arrived. Fans have spent literally decades casting their own choices of actors to fill each role in the comic. Fortunately for us all, Gaiman was in no rush to see someone else produce their version of the series that helped make his name as a writer. Instead, he busied himself with numerous other projects, biding his time and gaining new skills as these projects spawned their own films and TV adaptations. Eventually, as his authorial stature grew, Gaiman was able to maximise his influence across the production of his tale's eventual transition to TV. The result is a gorgeous series that inhabits a dream spot, simultaneously cleaving close to the source text's narrative, and the wide variety of visual styles provided by Gaiman's many artistic collaborators, while also adapting itself for a modern audience.

30 GRAPHIC NOVELS YOU SHOULD READ

Here are 30 graphic novels in no particular order that we feel people should read from the fields of US, UK, European and Japanese comics...

LONE WOLF AND CUB
VOLUME 1
THE ASSASSIN'S ROAD
By KAZUO KOIKE & GOSEKI KOJIMA

30

Lone Wolf And Cub: The Assassin's Road
Writer: Kazuo Koike
Artist: Goseki Kojima
Dark Horse Comics

Lone Wolf And Cub started publication in its native Japan back in 1970, created by writer Koike and artist Kojima. Over its existence, it built up a huge following, winning fans in US comics like Frank Miller, who of course went on to make a splash with comics like *Dark Knight Returns* and *Daredevil*. *Lone Wolf And Cub* first saw an English translation through First Comics back in 1987, spearheaded by Miller.

First Comics then published the entire saga from 2000 onwards. *Lone Wolf And Cub* is a Japanese cultural phenomena, spawning six films and a television series.

GARA GARA
GARA GARA
IS THAT YOUR CHILD, SIR?
HE IS.
HOH...

The Assassin's Road introduces us to Ogami Itto, a disgraced samurai who wanders 17th century Japan with his son, Daigoro. He has become a sword for hire, with his almost supernatural skills as an assassin and his ability to be at least two steps ahead of anyone else who is foolish enough to stand in his path.

The nine tales contained in this volume showcase Koike and Kojima's unsurpassed panache as comic creators. Kojima's kinetic art lends excitement and a savage beauty to Koike's fast-moving scripts. Running in black and white gives it a extra impact. Economy is the order of the day here with the pair packing so much into short 20 to 30 page stories. Koike brings 17th century Japan into sharp focus here, offering us a fascinating glimpse into the Edo era that the story is set in. Each story is an inventive look at Japan's history. *Lone Wolf And Cub* is as close as you can get to having Kurosawa on paper too, following in the tradition of that director's samurai stories like *Yojimbo* and *Seven Samurai*. It is an epic, widescreen tale with this first volume making readers hungry for more adventures.

Its shadow can still be seen in modern popular culture with the first season of Disney Plus' *The Mandalorian* owing a bit to Koike and Kojima's seminal work.

The entire saga which spans 7000 pages is one of the most impressive ever committed to comics in any language and *The Assassin's Road* is a wonderful entrypoint into Koike and Kojima's exceptional series. **JOEL MEADOWS**

SHKK
CHOK
AH!
SHK KCHNNG

29

Parker: The Martini Edition Vol.1
Parker: The Martini Edition: Vol.2 Last Call
Writer/ Artist: Darwyn Cooke with contributions by writer Ed Brubaker and artist Sean Phillips
IDW Publishing

PARKER
The Martini Edition
Last Call

the martini edition

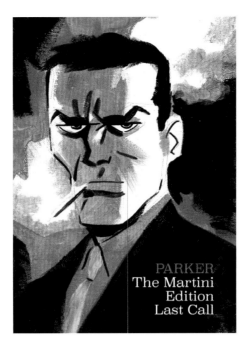

Darwyn Cooke's career in comics only lasted for less than twenty years but his legacy continues to be massive. After years working in superhero comics for DC and Marvel, the last seven years of his career and sadly his life were taken up with adapting Donald Westlake's *Parker* novels for comics. These two oversized slipcase hardcovers reprint Cooke's adaptations of Westlake's books but also include a lot of extra material as well.

The Martini Edition Vol.1 came out in December 2011, while the writer-artist was still with us. Clocking in at a very impressive 335 pages or so, we get oversized reprints of his adaptations of *The Hunter*, *The Man With The Getaway Face* and *The Outfit* as well as an interview that the late comics journalist Tom Spurgeon conducted with Cooke too which also features contributions from fellow modern comics noir writer and friend of Cooke's Ed Brubaker.

There is a cinematic graphic simplicity to Cooke's art that plays to the strengths of the comic form while also managing to subvert it as well. The oversized format here really adds to the drama of his work as does the duotone colour scheme for each story as well. There is a timeless starkness to Cooke's lines which really lends each tale impact for the reader. Cooke also knows when to tell a scene without extraneous dialogue too and these are some of the most impressive pieces here. The Hunter which introduces us to protagonist Parker is a classic slice of hard-boiled noir with him battling against criminal endeavour *The Outfit*. *The Man With The Getaway Face* offers us a Parker short about a heist he signs up for while *The Outfit* is a tale which sees Parker once again up against the criminal organisation that wants him dead. *The Seventh*, the final tale, is even shorter than *The Man With The Getaway Face* but Cooke manages to pack a great deal into this 10 pager. The book wraps up with a portfolio of single page images created by Cooke which were inspired by the *Parker* films featuring the likes of Jack Palance, Lee Marvin and even Michael Caine.

The Martini Edition Vol.1 is a gloriously lavish reproduction of Darwyn Cooke's Parker adaptations, offering them in a format that really gives the stories room to breath.

Vol.2 gives us what acts as a tribute to Cooke who sadly died back in 2016, representing his adaptations of *The Score* and *Slayground* plus a new short story by Ed Brubaker and Sean Phillips featuring Westlake's character Grofield and a roundtable between editor Scott Dunbier and Cooke's friends Ed Brubaker and Bruce Time. *The Score*, about a heist that Parker is involved in that goes very pear-shaped, is another beautiful noir tale with Cooke's use of duotone really creating impact for the reader while *Slayground*, about our protagonist trapped in ironically titled theme park Fun Island, really experiments with the comic format. The Brubaker and Phillips short is a very sweet visual eulogy to Cooke, with Phillips adapting his art a little to mirror Cooke. The roundtable offers readers a little bit of insight into Cooke's personality from his friends. The book closes with full page colour images from a series of planned fully illustrated Parker novels which unfortunately Cooke never got to complete.

Both of these books act as a celebration of Cooke, a creator who brought so much to comics in his short time in the industry. He cut his teeth as a comic artist drawing superheroes but with Parker, it really felt like his natural milieu as a creator. Inhabiting the world of duplicitous dames and the films of Steve McQueen and Robert Mitchum, Darwyn Cooke was the perfect creator to bring Westlake's creation to life. Cooke loved comics and he loved the detective form as well, two things that are more than evident here throughout. It is very hard to really do justice to his work here in a short review but fans of comics and detective fiction should consider picking both of these volumes up. Cooke was a true original, versatile and with a unique warmth and passion to his work. Cooke's *Parker* has a boldness to it which belies the sheer force of will and effort underneath. We should raise a glass to this man who brought so much to the medium and editor Scott Dunbier has done a great job assembling both of these volumes.

JOEL MEADOWS

28

Manhunter
Writer: Archie Goodwin
Artist: Walter Simonson
DC Comics

When this strip ran as a backup in 1973 in *Detective Comics*, the story goes, DC's flagship title was in trouble. By the end of its seventh chapter, the issue-length Gotterdammerung, Goodwin and Simonson had steadied the ship. *Manhunter* is an exercise in economy.

Editor Archie Goodwin brought artist Walter Simonson, who was reasonably green at this time, to illustrate this sparse tale of intrigue. *Manhunter* took the DC character of the same name by Joe Simon and Jack Kirby and refashioned him into a modern day adventurer complete with skills like no other hero.

In eight- page installments, Goodwin and Simonson managed to pack more story into these segments than some creators do in a long run. Taking cues from Peter O'Donnell's *Modesty Blaise* comic strip series, *Manhunter* doesn't waste a panel in telling its story of Paul Kirk, a man manipulated by the sinister Council, who searches for closure and retribution.

Another thing to note here is the inclusion of Eastern weaponry, popular on the big screen with Bruce Lee at the time, but this is a number of years before Frank Miller popularised this in the pages of *Daredevil.* So Goodwin and Simonson were ahead of the curve.

Simonson has always been known as the consummate storyteller but *Manhunter* was the series that first brought him to people's attention. His sinewy artwork and elegant panel composition brings something which is cinematic but still very much playing to the strengths of the four-color page.

The fnal part of the original *Manhunter* tale, *Gotterdamerung*, sees Goodwin and Simonson team Paul Kirk with Batman in a 22 page story which offers a truly dramatic crescendo for the tale that has been unfolding, giving them room to breath while not sacrificing the tight storytelling that the reader has become accustomed to up to this point.

The volume ends with *Manhunter The Final Chapter*, a silent story that was published after Goodwin passed away and it is the perfect endcap to Paul Kirk's journey. Archie Goodwin was an exceptional writer and Simonson, even though his work was a little bit primitive here, brings considerable energy to every panel.

Manhunter is a masterclass in comic storytelling and this hardcover book, beautifully reproducing this series, should be on every superhero comic aficionado's bookshelf.

JOEL MEADOWS

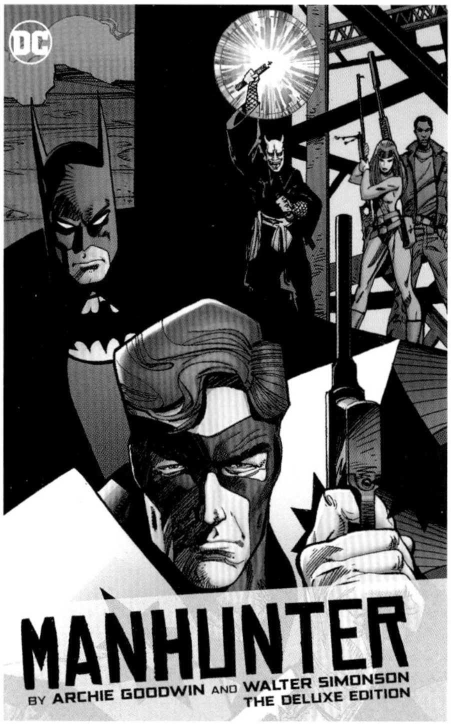
DC
MANHUNTER
BY ARCHIE GOODWIN AND WALTER SIMONSON
THE DELUXE EDITION

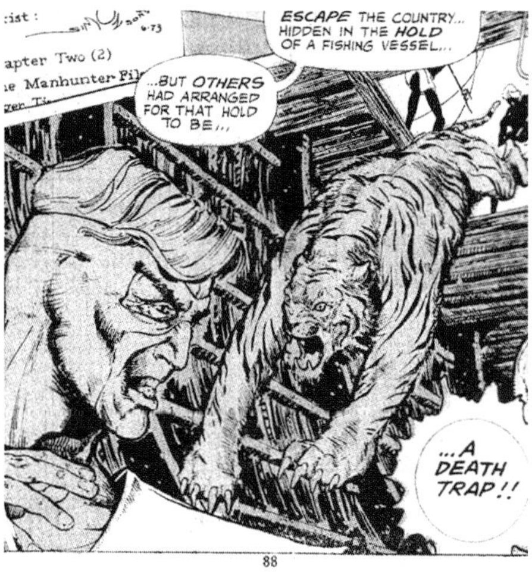
ESCAPE THE COUNTRY... HIDDEN IN THE HOLD OF A FISHING VESSEL...
...BUT OTHERS HAD ARRANGED FOR THAT HOLD TO BE...
...A DEATH TRAP!!
88

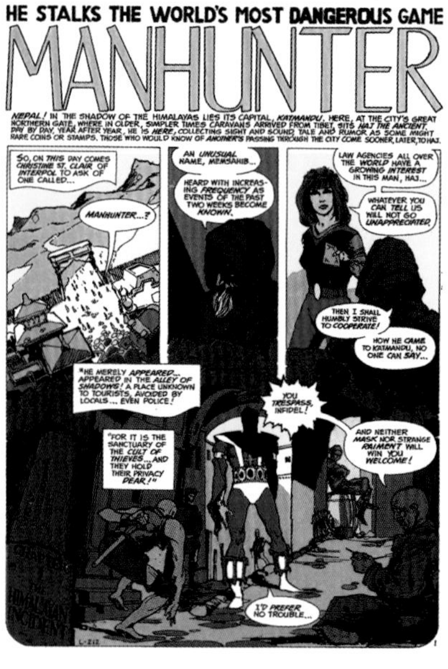
HE STALKS THE WORLD'S MOST DANGEROUS GAME
MANHUNTER
NEPAL! IN THE SHADOW OF THE HIMALAYAS LIES ITS CAPITAL, KATMANDU. HERE, AT THE CITY'S GREAT NORTHERN GATE, WHERE IN OLDER, SIMPLER TIMES CARAVANS ARRIVED FROM TIBET, SITS HAJ THE ANCIENT. DAY BY DAY, YEAR AFTER YEAR, HE IS HERE, COLLECTING SIGHT AND SOUND, TALE AND RUMOR AS SOME MIGHT RARE COINS OR STAMPS. THOSE WHO WOULD KNOW OF ANOTHER'S PASSING THROUGH THE CITY COME SOONER, LATER, TO HAJ.
SO, ON THIS DAY COMES CHRISTINE ST. CLAIR OF INTERPOL TO ASK OF ONE CALLED...
MANHUNTER...?
AN UNUSUAL NAME, MEMSAHIB...
HEARD WITH INCREASING FREQUENCY AS EVENTS OF THE PAST TWO WEEKS BECOME KNOWN.
LAW AGENCIES ALL OVER THE WORLD HAVE A GROWING INTEREST IN THIS MAN, HAJ...
WHATEVER YOU CAN TELL US WILL NOT GO UNAPPRECIATED.
THEN I SHALL HUMBLY STRIVE TO COOPERATE!
HOW HE CAME TO KATMANDU, NO ONE CAN SAY...
"HE MERELY APPEARED... APPEARED IN THE ALLEY OF SHADOWS! A PLACE UNKNOWN TO TOURISTS, AVOIDED BY LOCALS... EVEN POLICE!
"FOR IT IS THE SANCTUARY OF THE CULT OF THIEVES... AND THEY HOLD THEIR PRIVACY DEAR!"
YOU TRESPASS, INFIDEL!
AND NEITHER MASK NOR STRANGE RAIMENT WILL WIN YOU WELCOME!
I'D PREFER NO TROUBLE...

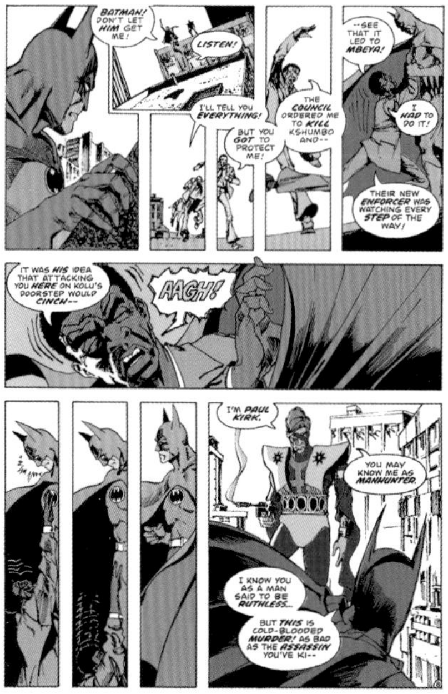
BATMAN! DON'T LET HIM GET ME!
LISTEN!
I'LL TELL YOU EVERYTHING!
BUT YOU GOT TO PROTECT ME!
THE COUNCIL ORDERED ME TO KILL KSHUMBO AND--
--SEE THAT IT LED TO MBEYA!
I HAD TO DO IT!
THEIR NEW ENFORCER WAS WATCHING EVERY STEP OF THE WAY!
IT WAS HIS IDEA THAT ATTACKING YOU HERE ON KOLU'S DOORSTEP WOULD CINCH--
AAGH!
I'M PAUL KIRK.
YOU MAY KNOW ME AS MANHUNTER.
I KNOW YOU AS A MAN SAID TO BE RUTHLESS...
BUT THIS IS COLD-BLOODED MURDER! AS BAD AS THE ASSASSIN YOU'VE KI--

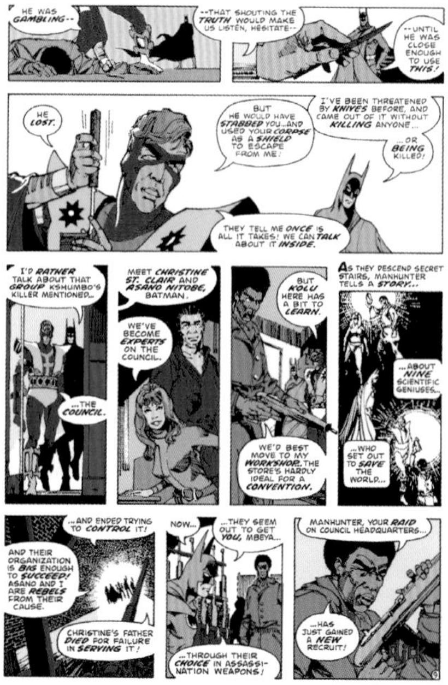
HE WAS GAMBLING--
--THAT SHOUTING THE TRUTH WOULD MAKE US LISTEN, HESITATE--
--UNTIL HE WAS CLOSE ENOUGH TO USE THIS!
HE LOST.
BUT HE WOULD HAVE STABBED YOU...AND USED YOUR CORPSE AS A SHIELD TO ESCAPE FROM ME!
I'VE BEEN THREATENED BY KNIVES BEFORE, AND CAME OUT OF IT WITHOUT KILLING ANYONE...
...OR BEING KILLED!
THEY TELL ME ONCE IS ALL IT TAKES! WE CAN TALK ABOUT IT INSIDE.
I'D RATHER TALK ABOUT THAT GROUP KSHUMBO'S KILLER MENTIONED...
...THE COUNCIL.
MEET CHRISTINE ST. CLAIR AND ASANO NITOBE, BATMAN.
WE'VE BECOME EXPERTS ON THE COUNCIL.
BUT KOLU HERE HAS A BIT TO LEARN.
WE'D BEST MOVE TO MY WORKSHOP... THE STORE'S HARDLY IDEAL FOR A CONVENTION.
AS THEY DESCEND SECRET STAIRS, MANHUNTER TELLS A STORY...
...ABOUT NINE SCIENTIFIC GENIUSES...
...WHO SET OUT TO SAVE THE WORLD...
...AND ENDED TRYING TO CONTROL IT!
AND THEIR ORGANIZATION IS BIG ENOUGH TO SUCCEED! ASANO AND I ARE REBELS FROM THEIR CAUSE.
CHRISTINE'S FATHER DIED FOR FAILURE IN SERVING IT!
NOW...
...THEY SEEM OUT TO GET YOU, MBEYA...
...THROUGH THEIR CHOICE IN ASSASSINATION WEAPONS!
MANHUNTER, YOUR RAID ON COUNCIL HEADQUARTERS...
...HAS JUST GAINED A NEW RECRUIT!

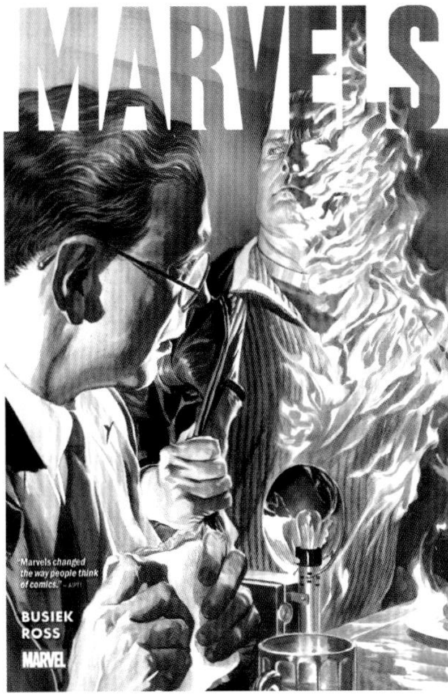
MARVELS
"Marvels changed the way people think of comics."
BUSIEK
ROSS
MARVEL

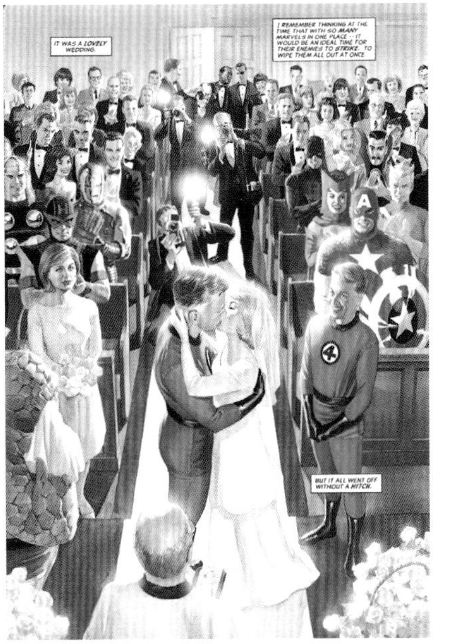
IT WAS A LOVELY WEDDING.
I REMEMBER THINKING AT THE TIME THAT WITH SO MANY MARVELS IN ONE PLACE -- IT WOULD BE AN IDEAL TIME FOR THEIR ENEMIES TO STRIKE. TO WIPE THEM ALL OUT AT ONCE.
BUT IT ALL WENT OFF WITHOUT A HITCH.

27

Marvels
Writer: Kurt Busiek
Artist: Alex Ross
Marvel Comics

"It's scary. It's exciting. It's thrilling. All of it at once."

Have you ever wondered what it would be like if superheroes were real? You're mowing the lawn and suddenly the Human Torch comes streaking across the sky. Going for a jog and you suddenly see Spider-Man hanging from the side of skyscraper. You're sat at your desk in your office, and there is the almighty shadow of Galactus making everything go that much darker. 1994's *Marvels*, written by Kurt Busiek and illustrated by Alex Ross, takes this conceit and runs with it, examining the history of the Marvel universe through the perspective of Phil Sheldon, a photojournalist whose entire life becomes intertwined with that of those costumed gods that walk amongst the population.

The story begins in 1939 when young reporter Sheldon attends a presentation of a new android created by Phineas T. Horton. This creation catches fire on exposure to air creating a Human Torch, and a whole new world of fantastic beings, that seem to enthral and appal ordinary humans in equal measure, begins. Soon more meta-humans, such as Namor, appear on the scene and the world as it has been known changes forever. And all the time Sheldon is there to document these wonderful – and terrible – happenings. In the 60s he sees the Fantastic Four and the Avengers emerge to the awe of humanity. But – with the X-Men and mutantkind emerging – this awe turns to hatred and fear, partly magnified by the very newspapers he works for.

Even when Galactus is stopped from devouring the Earth by Reed Richards and his cohort, humanity begins to turn on our heroes much to the chagrin of Sheldon. But in the 80s, his faith is shaken when – in the midst of defending the honour of Spider-Man – he becomes friends with a young girl called Gwen Stacey whose story is destined to end in tragedy...

On a simplistic level, *Marvels* is just a paean to Marvel Comics, a chance to revisit classic moments and battles throughout its history. But it's reframing of numerous iconic moments in Marvel history, while certainly celebratory, is also an attempt to examine the role of ordinary humans within the Marvel universe. Comic book battles are usually there for visceral entertainment. But here, as Namor rampages through the streets, we have frightened residents being evacuated into hiding places by the US army. There's a tangible sense of fear and the human cost of living in a world in which gods seems to walk amongst us.

Indeed, much of the book deals with just how humankind reacts with both joy and jealousy at the new normal they face. There's relief that these super powered beings seem to be capable of dealing with any threat. But there's also a sense of impotence, of ordinary humans feeling that they've been left behind by evolution. It gives rise to hatred and fear, with the persecution directed at mutants directly paralleling the racial tension in the United States during the 60s and 70s (rather appropriate given Stan Lee's stated reason for why he and Jack Kirby created the X-Men). The book also gives some interesting insight into J Jonah Jameson and why he consistently seems to hate Spider-Man and his costumed brethren.

Throughout all this, we experience everything through the character of Phil Sheldon. The conceit of using an ordinary person to comment on the extraordinary – something Alex Ross would go on to use numerous times in such stories as *Kingdom Come*, *Uncle Sam* and *Earth X* – is well used here. Sheldon is a sympathetic and complex character, acting as both reader avatar and the moral conscience of humanity. His awe and fear at his constant interaction with superheroes is tempered by the everyday realities of life. As we follow him getting older, we're also reminded of what is traditionally verboten in the world of comic books: the passing of time. As he gets older and wiser, his opinions and ideas change, his view of life alters. It makes for a marked counterpoint for – 'event' style reboots notwithstanding – the general stasis in which comics usually take place.

Aside from the emotional and human script from Busiek, another reason for Marvel's success is, unsurprisingly, Alex Ross' now infamous photorealistic art. The comic book aesthetic of primary colours and eye popping visuals from the likes of Ditko and Kirby are given a realistic makeover. While the colour scheme is undoubtedly more muted than the original stories, everything is no less grandiose than it was before. Indeed, it inspires a certain amount of awe – and maybe even trepidation – when we see familiar scenes rendered with a sheen of realism. Often the action is framed from a POV where the superheroes battle above us – the gods fight in the heavens whilst we look fearfully upon them.

While *Marvels* is – in and of itself – a superlative piece of work that every fan should have on their shelf, you'd not do wrong to get your hands on the recently published 25th Anniversary edition of the book which is an absolutely amazing piece of work. With everything related to the work (such as the prologue, a later published epilogue and a myriad of alternative covers) it does the work of Busiek and Ross justice. There's Busiek's complete script, intros and interviews from Busiek and Ross (both new and reprinted from previous collections) which provide comprehensive information on the metamorphosis of the project and – best of all – a complete commentary on the entire thing. Pointing out many of the references to Marvel history it's a wonderful accompaniment to the story. Also, in their commitment to realism (or their obsessiveness), Busiek and Ross made sure all the newspapers in the story were fully written and realised. This edition now allows you to read them in all their glory.

With real life locations – New York instead of Metropolis – and characters who seemed slightly more in tune with real-life events (especially in the 60s and 70s), the Marvel Universe always had their foot closer to the real world than their counterparts at DC. *Marvels* emphasises this reality while also creating a complex and fascinating – treatise on the heroes and humans that makes up their universe.

LAURENCE BOYCE

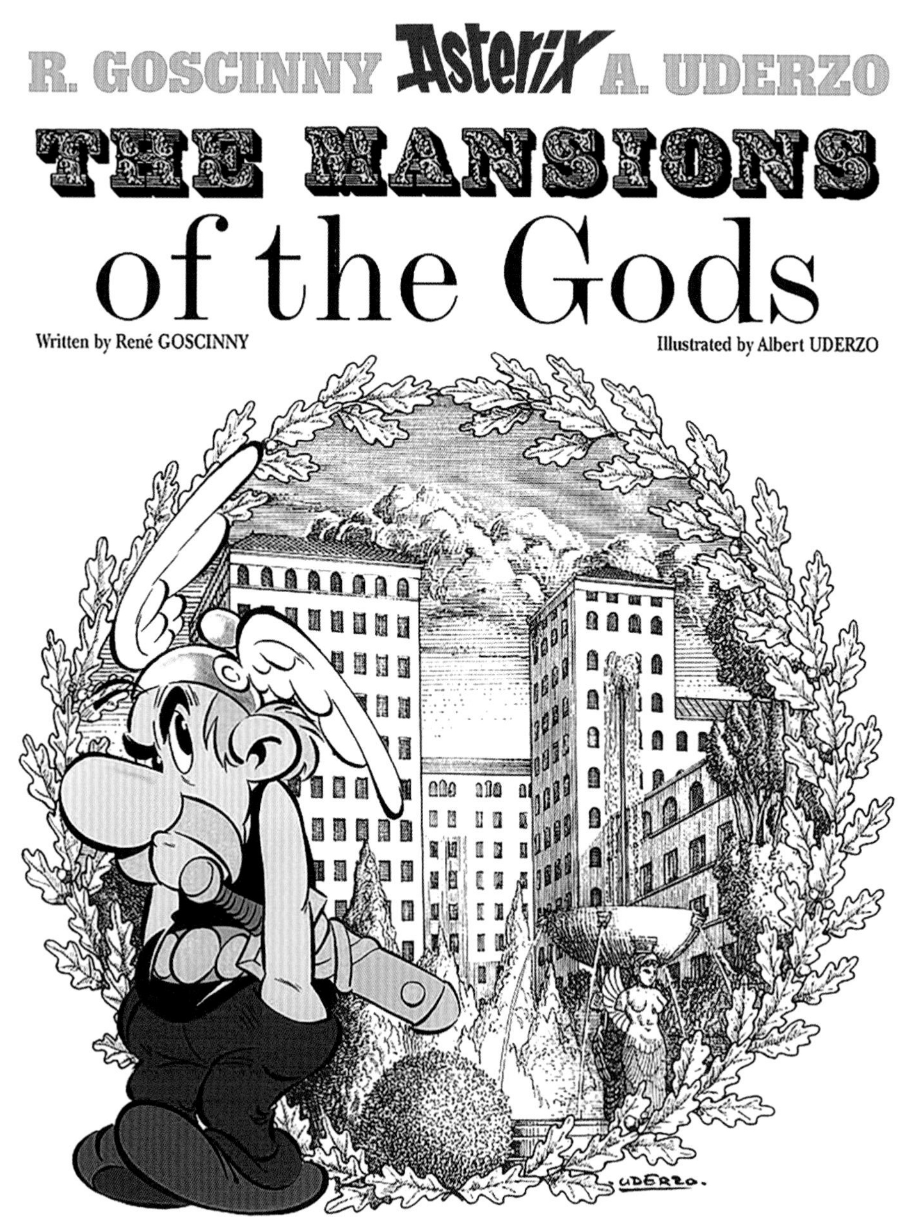
R. GOSCINNY Asterix A. UDERZO
THE MANSIONS
of the Gods
Written by René GOSCINNY
Illustrated by Albert UDERZO
UDERZO.

26

Asterix: The Mansions Of The Gods
Writer: Rene Goscinny
Artist: Albert Uderzo
Publisher: Hodder

France's greatest comic book export reached its zenith in 1969, with *Asterix in Spain*, and continued with a run of peerless albums that ended in 1975's *Asterix and the Great Crossing*. Picking a favourite entry out of the ten adventures that were published in those six years is nigh-on impossible – an equal would be *Asterix and the Roman Agent*, with *Asterix in Switzerland*, *Soothsayer* and *Laurel Wreath* very close contenders. In the end, *Mansions of the Gods* just shades it for me, as in this particular instance, the Gaulish ensemble are unwittingly battling for the very soul of the village against Julius Caesar's most assiduous plan to defeat them – by co-opting them and forcing them to integrate through bringing the city of Rome and its trappings to their doorstep.

In its early period, Goscinny and Uderzo's series mainly relied on light yet affectionate stereotypes (except with the Goths) and knockabout, slapstick humour. The pun-heavy dialogue was less sophisticated, and the supporting cast of villagers had yet to develop. Of course, there were some terrific episodes from that era, especially *Asterix the Gladiator*, *Asterix and Cleopatra*, *Asterix and the Big Fight* and of course *Asterix in Britain*, the latter a brilliantly plotted work which parodied all aspects of typical Brits, yet was never hostile (it was probably as genial a Gallic portrayal of us as there had been up until then). However the Paris riots of 1968 proved to be pivotal – a moment in history that forced many French comic artists and writers to reconsider their cultural position and subsequently to add a political or at least contemporary component to their oeuvre. Goscinny and Uderzo were certainly no exception to this sea change.

The story is somewhat more involved than usual – Julius Caesar hatches a cunning plan to undermine and disperse the rebellious Gauls by gentrifying the forest area next to their village. Caesar enlists an architect who is billeted at one of the garrisoned camps near the villagers to bring Roman civilisation to their area under the banner of "The Mansions of the Gods". The nonplussed Gauls, baffled by the architect's behaviour, initially play cat and mouse with this new interloper – they regrow all the trees uprooted by his slave workers, thereby destroying his morale. Eventually however Asterix and Obelix relent in order for the slaves, bolstered by Getafix's magic potion, to be freed on completion of the first block of flats. This inevitably backfires on the villagers as the newly-arrived Roman expats visit the village, colonising it with their couture, values and of course wealth. Before long, the villagers are fighting bitterly amongst themselves for trade, and all unity and common interest evaporates.

As always it is Asterix, using his intelligence rather than his fists, who, with Obelix's help, rescues the village from disintegration by frightening one of the Mansions residents into leaving before replacing him with Cacofonix and his unbearable racket. In the end, what could've been the last gasp for the village turns once again into triumph. Goscinny and Uderzo added further weight with a wonderful coda at the end – when asked by Asterix whether they would always manage to stop the course of events as they had just done, druid Getafix responds that that would be impossible, despite having time on their side. The book closes with the beguiling words – "a victory over the Romans and over the inexorable passage of time". A rare existential moment for the strip, and one which stays with you.

Asterix and the Laurel Wreath and *Switzerland* satirised Roman decadence, pampered mores and hierarchies and did so with immense aplomb (one could not imagine such adult content in their earlier Asterix efforts!), while *Roman Agent* and *Soothsayer* were equally masterful in a similar manner to Mansions, on both these occasions the warfare being one of gaslighting and misinformation. Yet thematically *Mansions of the Gods* is the pinnacle, with Goscinny and Uderzo sending up marketing, advertising and the clash between the Luddite villagers and their unwitting nemeses – the idealised brochure for the housing project being a particularly witty effort.

Also by this point the characterization was first rate, with bitter enemies Fulliautomatix and Unhygienix, not to mention Vitalstatistix and the rest of the villagers, all present, correct and fully-formed. Obelix is no longer the childlike sidekick prone to acts of sulking while Uderzo's art by this stage had reached virtuoso level, and a match for any Gallic artist, including Moebius and Druillet. His storytelling (a lot was crammed into those 44 pages) is also a model of brevity and focus. As European comic books go, this is about as good as it gets, and every bit as brilliant as when I first read it over forty years ago.

ANDREW COLMAN

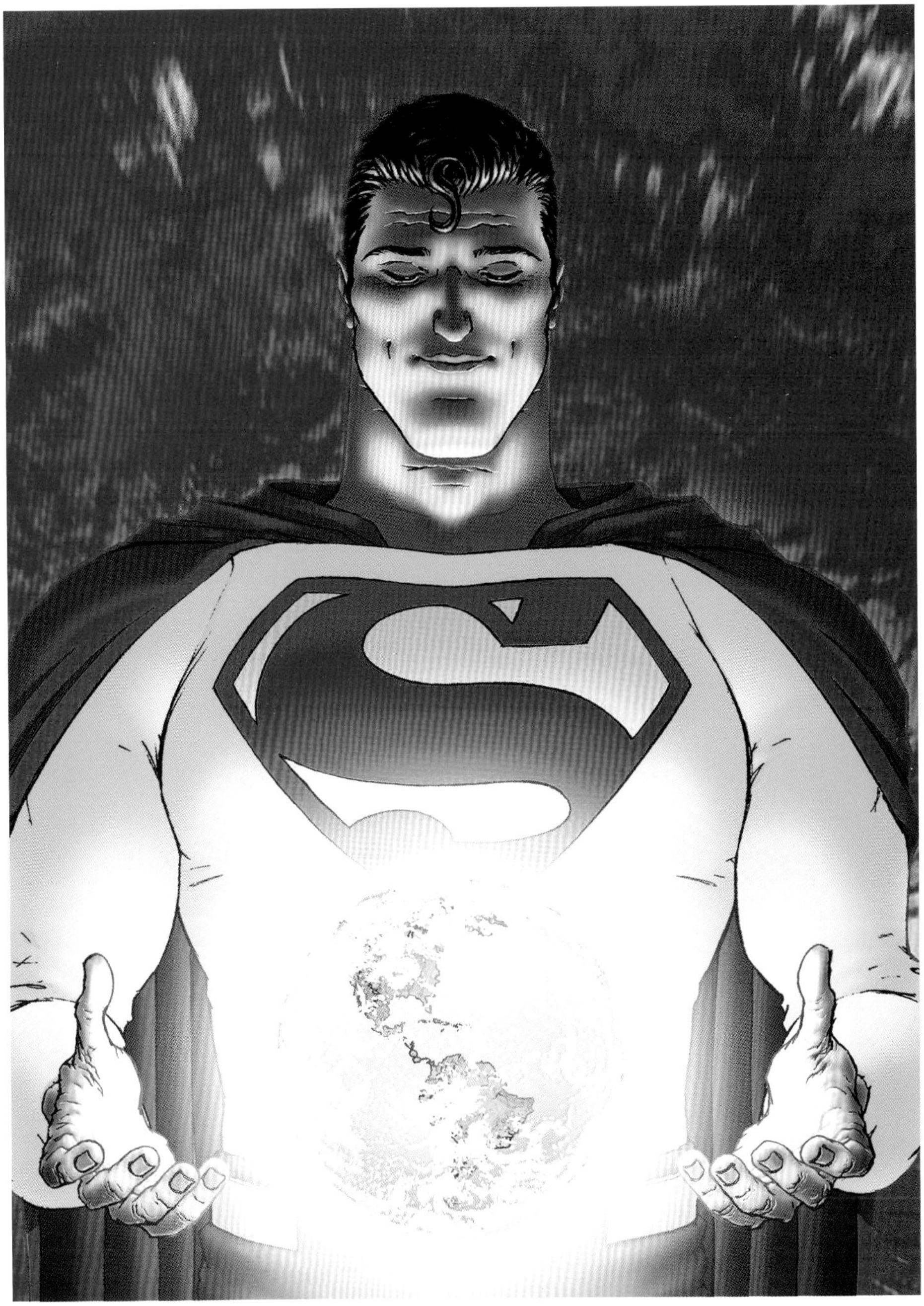

25

Absolute All-Star Superman
Writer: Grant Morrison
Artists: Frank Quitely and Jamie Grant
Colours: Jamie Grant
Publisher: DC

All-Star Superman was part of the short-lived All-Star line that DC published in the first decade of this century. *All-Star Batman and Robin* was a title written by Frank Miller and drawn by Jim Lee which didn't quite connect with readers. But *All-Star Superman*, which ran for 12 issues was a modern triumph. Writer Grant Morrison at his best is able to pull out the essence of iconic mainstream comic characters and here with his regular artistic collaborator Frank Quitely, finished by Jamie Grant, is perhaps the ultimate Superman story. The Superman here is the embodiment of benevolent power, at the end of his superheroic journey and Quitely depicts him throughout as a physically heroic alien figure.

Even though *All-Star Superman* only ran for 12 issues, Morrison and Quitely pack in everything a classic Man Of Steel needs. We have Lex Luthor, of course, plus Bizarro as you've never seen him before plus other Superman staples like The Parasite making an appearance. It all builds to an emotional crescendo which manages to be both sad and hopeful at the same time.

All-Star Superman works because it is quirky, idiosyncratic but also a very warm and emotional tale. Morrison's relationship between Superman/Clark Kent and Lois tips its hat to the Christopher Reeve and Margot Kidder movie dynamic, with real trust and love at its heart. Quitelty brings so much too to the world of Superman, imbuing every scene with passion and fire. Inker Jamie Grant who finishes Quitely's pencils here brings something new to the Scottish artist's work and the colouring here is also magnificent.

Reading the introduction here from famous art director Chip Kidd really helps to put everything into context too. Morrison and Quitely's Superman is classic yet contemporary, conventional while being subversive at the same time and Absolute All-Star Superman is an elegant and exquisite representation of this iconic run, with some intriguing behind the scenes sketch work in its back matter. Despite its relatively short existence, sometimes a series comes along that just works on every level and *All-Star Superman* set the bar very high for Superman stories. Still one of Morrison and Quitely's finest pieces of work.

JOEL MEADOWS

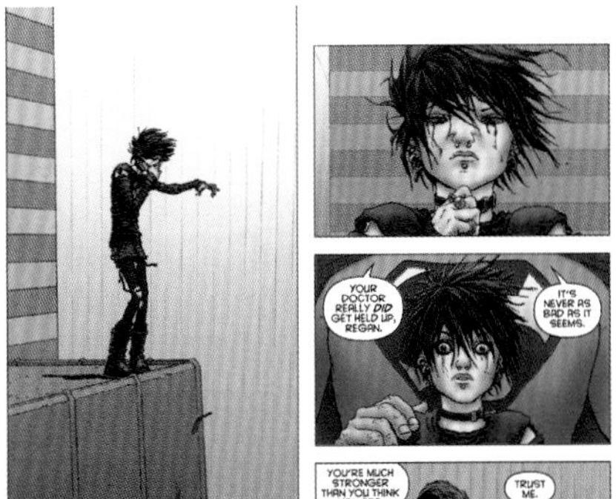
YOUR DOCTOR REALLY *DID* GET HELD UP, REGAN.
IT'S NEVER AS BAD AS IT SEEMS.
YOU'RE MUCH STRONGER THAN YOU THINK YOU ARE.
TRUST ME.

24

Batman: Year One
Writer: Frank Miller
Artist: David Mazzucchelli
Colourist: Richmond Lewis
DC

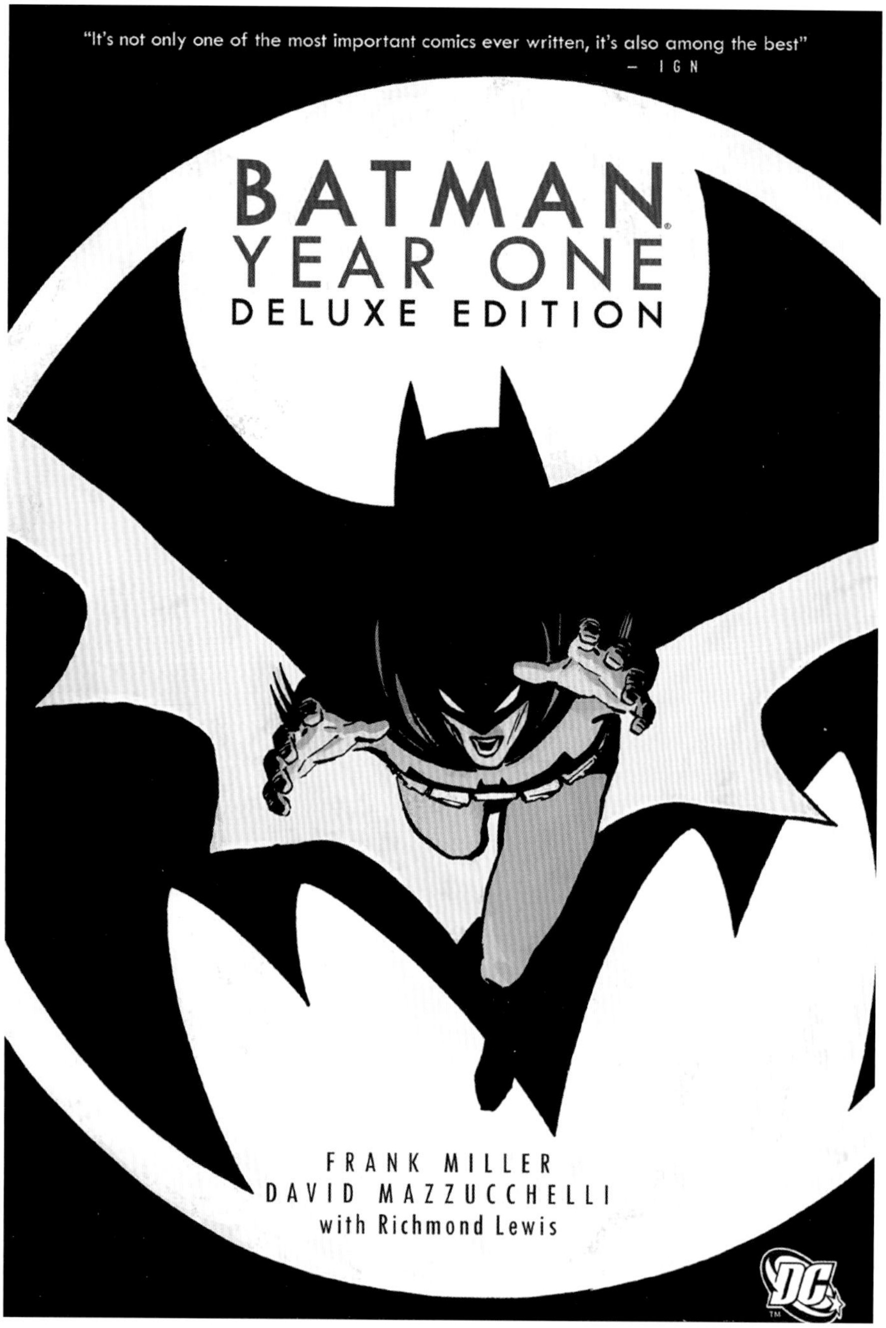
"It's not only one of the most important comics ever written, it's also among the best"
– IGN
BATMAN
YEAR ONE
DELUXE EDITION
FRANK MILLER
DAVID MAZZUCCHELLI
with Richmond Lewis
DC

In the 1980s, Frank Miller owned mainstream superhero comics. His career began in 1979 when he took over as writer-artist on Marvel's *Daredevil* title and created his own niche during four years on that book, later with artist Klaus Janson. He then went on to create *Ronin*, a dystopian sci-fi adventure he wrote and drew for DC in 1983. Of course he is probably still best known for writer and pencilling *Batman The Dark Knight Returns* in 1986-1987. He returned to the Dark Knight Detective with this four issue story that ran in *Batman* from 404 to 407, with him retelling Batman's origin collaborating again with his Daredevil: Born Again partner, David Mazzucchelli.

Batman: Year One does tell a story that most people who are fans of Batman are familiar with but Miller with Mazzucchelli introduce new elements to the mythos, offering a kinetic, noirish take on Bruce Wayne becoming Batman. It is its seeming simplicity that marks it out as one of the finest Batman stories of the modern era. Miller understands economy of language and creates characters just through a few lines which seem at first glance to be just throwaway but they are so much more. The world that Miller throws policeman James Gordon into is a demi-monde of bent coppers, bizarre prostitutes and the concept that he is one of the only straight policemen in the city is one that works really well here. *Year One* is sweeping and cinematic in its writing and plot. Miller draws on things like Friedkin's *The French Connection* and even Scorsese's *Taxi Driver* to bring his unique vision of Gotham to life.

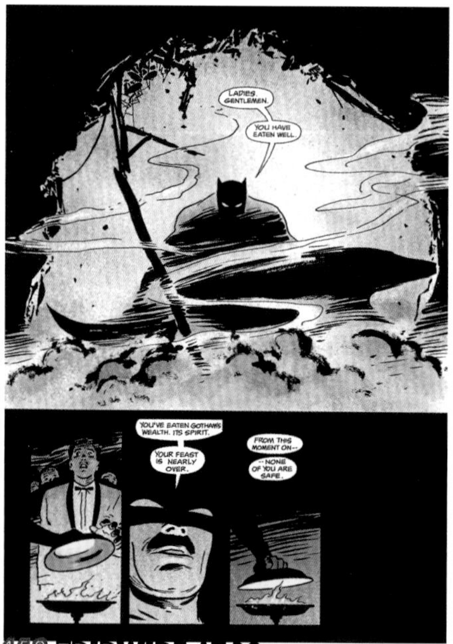
LADIES. GENTLEMEN.
YOU HAVE EATEN WELL.
YOU'VE EATEN GOTHAM'S WEALTH. ITS SPIRIT.
YOUR FEAST IS NEARLY OVER.
FROM THIS MOMENT ON--
--NONE OF YOU ARE SAFE.

And it's not just Miller here who lends so much to the overall richness of the story. Mazzucchelli is magnificent with his elegant lines and amazing storytelling and composition adding to Miller's new take on Batman's genesis. There are so many pages here that demand more than a cursory glance, forcing the reader to look deeply at his lines. His Batman is a German expressionist set of marks on the page, fluid and always moving. As he displayed on *Daredevil: Born Again*, Mazzucchelli is the master of simplicity with every stroke there for a reason. You can't imagine anyone else, even Miller himself, illustrating this story.

The colouring by Richmond Lewis is also a major player here too with her work lending so much to Mazzucchelli's lines. The palette she picks is perfect, using a range of subtle colours. Lewis is the artist's wife which may explain why they work so effortlessly together.

I was blown away by it when I first read when it initially came out back in 1987 and *Batman: Year One* is still an important, exquisite modern superhero tale created by two people who work so well in concert with each other. If people haven't read it, it's the perfect Batman graphic novel to immerse yourself in while you are stuck inside. Miller was rarely better and it cemented Mazzucchelli's reputation as one of the finest practitioners of modern comic illustrators.

JOEL MEADOWS

GREG RUCKA
STEVE LIEBER
WHITEOUT
COMPENDIUM

23

Whiteout Compendium
Writer: Greg Rucka
Artist: Steve Lieber
Oni

Whiteout and *Whiteout: Melt* are two detective tales featuring US Marshal Carrie Stetko who is stuck in Antarctica. When *Whiteout* came out back in 1998, Oni was just a fledgling company and writer Rucka had written a few very well-received detective novels. Even though it was Rucka's first comic script, you really wouldn't know it. He uses the Antarctic setting brilliantly and his dialogue is razor sharp. Lieber is the perfect artistic partner here too with his wonderfully expressive faces and simple yet effective action sequences. The fact that *Whiteout* is in stark black and white really makes it impactful for the reader. Stetko has great chemistry with British secret service agent Lily Sharpe here and Rucka really gives his protagonists unique voices. A clever, inventive murder story which takes place in such an unusual setting, Whiteout was a very strong and assured comics debut.

Its follow-up, *Whiteout Melt*, wasn't quite as good as its predecessor partly because of the absence of Sharpe. Here we see Stetko team up with Russian GRU agent Aleks Kuchin to get to the bottom of some stolen nuclear weapons and Russian special forces who are bent on taking them back to Russia. There is still decent rapport between her and Kuchin but the reader misses the back and forth between Stetko and Sharpe a little. Lieber is still on top form artistically, bringing the inhospitable world of the Antarctic to life with style and élan once again. Melt is still a very decent detective story showing off Rucka's economy as a writer.

Rucka and Lieber have planned a third adventure with Stetko called *Thaw* but it hasn't happened as yet.

Whiteout and *Whiteout: Melt* are two very well-delineated slices of comics crime fiction. The first tale does read a little better than the second but *Melt* is still a very good piece of work. Rucka is one of the best comic writers to debut in the last twenty years or so and Lieber is a classically talented artist who manages to feel vintage yet contemporary at the same time.

JOEL MEADOWS

DAMN BITCH!

22

Akira
Writer/ Artist: Katsushiro Otomo
Dark Horse

AKIRA
1
KATSUHIRO OTOMO
アキラ

The next choice is the seminal manga title *Akira*. Some series transcend the genre they are created for and this manga sci-fi classic is definitely one of those titles. Katsushiro Otomo's post-apocalyptic science fiction epics is set in neo Tokyo, 38 years after World War Three and deals with a teenage bike gang. The gang contains two friends, Kaneda and Tetsuo, who find themselves part of a Japanese government conspiracy that involves the former site of the Olympics in Tokyo and mysterious figures who possess strange psycho-kinetic powers. At the heart of this is Akira, who could hold the key to everything.

Originally published in Japanese way back in 1982 and 1983 in Young Magazine, and then translated into English and published by Marvel's Epic imprint in the 1980s.

Just like *Lone Wolf and Cub*, which featured earlier on in this list, Akira has broken out of simply being a Japanese comic series and has achieved iconic status around the world. In 1988 it was adapted as an anime film, which was very well received and it got a worldwide release four years later in 1992.

Akira is a wonderfully executed science fiction epic with Otomo's vision of Neo Tokyo offering something bold and original for the reader. He is just as much at ease in the talking head scenes as he is in the frenetic bike chases. There is a visceral quality to Otomo's lines too which take certain scenes flying off the pages as well. The interplay between Kaneda and his former friend Tetsuo is well-handled too while Kay is a female character who develops as the story progresses.

Akira feels like an ambitious science fiction movie which explains why it made the jump to anime. In terms of creating the look of Neo Tokyo, Otomo has paid as much attention to detail as a production designer would for a film. His concepts are magnificent and the city is as much a character in the story as Kaneda, Kay and Tetsuo. There has been talk of it getting adapted again as a live action Hollywood production but each time, they have discussed shifting the story to the US. This would be a huge mistake as *Akira* works because of its Japanese setting and if you took its Japanese culture out of the equation, it would just feel like another generic sci-fi movie with some cool kit. There is an off-kilter feel here that American science fiction finds it hard to replicate.

Almost forty years old, *Akira* still has the power to smack the reader in the face and it more than deserves its place here. **JOEL MEADOWS**

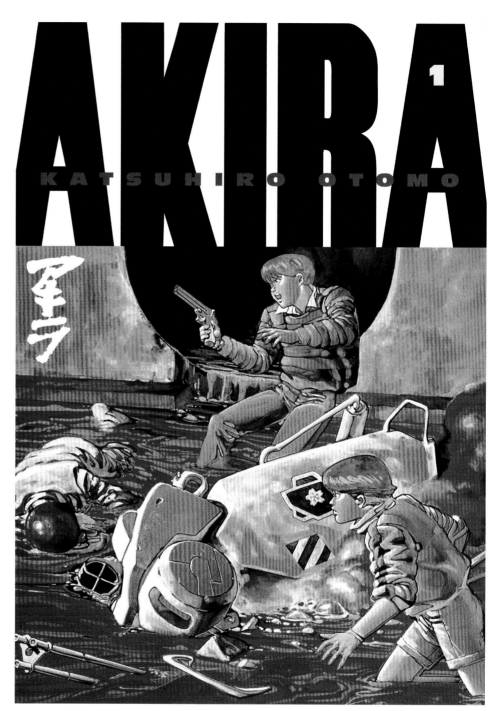

21

Sensible Footwear – A Girl's Guide
Writer/ Artist: Kate Charlesworth
Myriad Editions

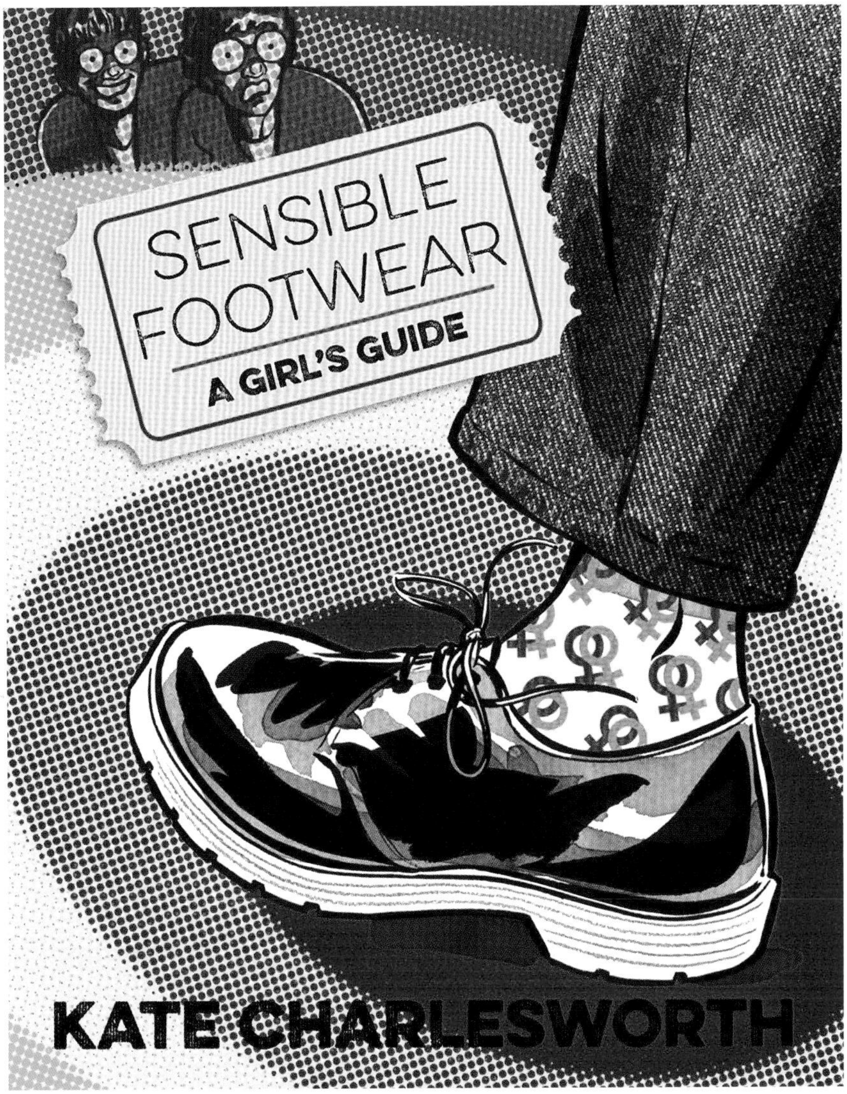
SENSIBLE FOOTWEAR
A GIRL'S GUIDE
KATE CHARLESWORTH

Charlesworth is a veteran of the UK cartooning scene, from her Twice Nightly strip in the Manchester Evening News in the early 70s to work with *the Guardian*, *New Scientist*, *The Pink Paper* and more, in addition to longer form works like the quite superb *Sally Heathcote, Suffragette* (with Mary and Bryan Talbot), and of course her much-beloved character Auntie Studs (some of which she was reposting daily during Lockdown on her Twitter). *Sensible Footwear* has been a labour of love, years in the making; I would hear bits and pieces about it and I was eager to read it. It was well worth the wait.

The book is partly Kate's story, from her birth in 1950s Barnsley through to growing up, feeling different, trying to figure out what she wanted, who she was (this in a time when sexuality – especially anything deviating from the Sacred Norm – was simply not discussed), to that great life experience of moving out of the home, going off to college and the freedom to explore yourself more, meeting new people, new ideas, through to the women's movements of the 70s and beyond, the LGBT groups springing up, especially in the wake of Stonewall, fighting for fairness and equality that anyone should have. And just as Sally Heathcote pointed out that the Suffragette movement was never "just" about getting the vote for women, but about fighting for a whole raft of social problems to be solved, from poverty to health to education, *Sensible Footwear* shows that those women's movements and the gay rights movements were not just fighting for rights for themselves, but for those rights to be enjoyed by everyone (consider, for instance how the authorities would use the vague wording of the Obscene Publications Act to try and shut down gay publications or bookshops, but then also use the same act against any other groups they didn't care for, from the infamous *Oz* trial to Knockabout Comics' Tony Bennett fighting them and HM Customs to reprint classic underground comix).

Woven through Kate's story is a walk through the Queer history of British culture, from the days when homosexuality wasn't merely frowned on but actually illegal, but still appearing with wonderful cheek in mainstream popular culture through radio shows like *Round the Horne* to looking for role models and idols wherever they could be found in that more repressed era of society (Diana Rigg and Honor Blackman in *The Avengers*, powerful women who took no nonsense, the wonderful Dusty Springfield, of course). As it does, the book reminds the reader that no matter your orientation, that gay culture has been a part of the general British pop culture for decades, even when some weren't overly aware of it.

The artwork makes great use of colour and shading to suggest different times and subjects, switching to a more collage-style approach between eras, mashing up elements from different decades to give a flavour of the time. For those of us of a certain age this also leads to a number of highly enjoyable "Oh, I remember that or him or her", be it the burning injustice of the vile, openly homophobic Section 28 imposed by the government, the devastation of the AIDS era (and the brutal, horrible way many in authority and the media used the diseases as a way not to offer help to sufferers but to stigmatise them further), or Edinburgh' first Pride March. Gay, straight, trans, bi, pan or asexual, lots of these moments were important milestones in the way our shared society and culture has developed, and *Sensible Footwear* reminds us of that communal aspect of our culture. The book is also wonderfully, delightfully warm, often smile-inducing, laced with humour, leaving you with a similarly pleasurable feeling to having spent time drinking and chatting with an old friend.

JOE GORDON

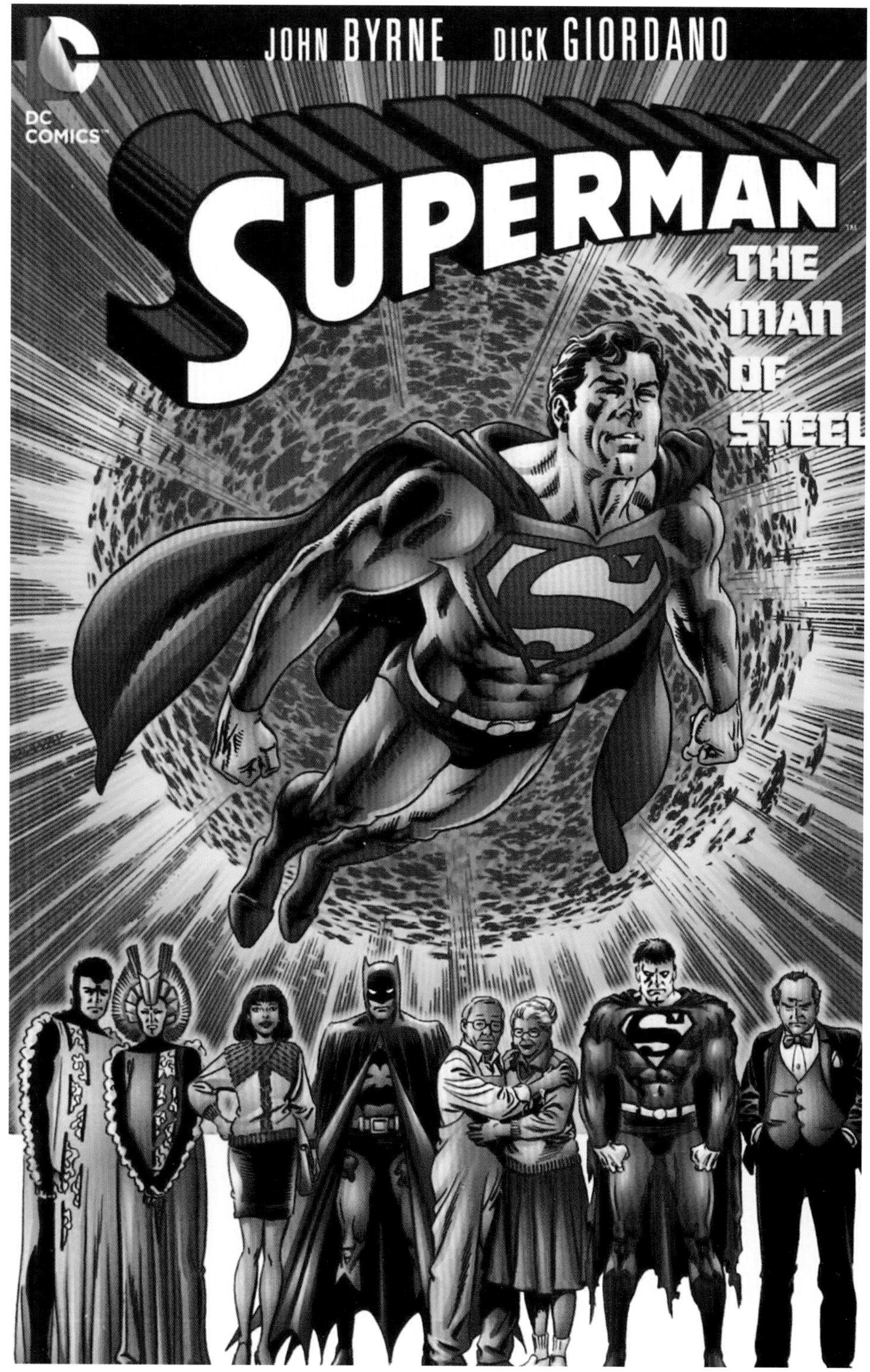
JOHN BYRNE DICK GIORDANO
DC COMICS
SUPERMAN
THE MAN OF STEEL

20

Superman: The Man Of Steel
Writer: John Byrne
Artists: John Byrne with Dick Giordano
Letterer: John Costanza
Colours: Tom Ziuko
DC

John Byrne's retelling of Superman's origin, *Superman: Man Of Steel*, was an instant hit for DC. When this came out back in 1986, Byrne was best known as a stalwart of DC's competitor Marvel and so it came as a bolt out of the blue when he turned his attention to DC's most iconic superhero.

Superman had suffered for decades in bland, unengaging stories and so something had to be done to bring him out of his slump. DC poached Byrne from Marvel and from the start here, where we see Byrne's take on the Man of Steel's Kryptonian origins, he doesn't waste any time setting the scene for the character's genesis.

Familiar characters like Lois Lane, Lex Luthor, Bizarro and Ma and Pa Kent are reintroduced by Byrne. They are the familiar figures but he has given each of them a little tweak just to bring them up to date. Much like Morrison and Quitely's *All-Star Superman* twenty years or so later, Byrne takes the essence of all of these archetypes and brings something fresh to them. Cameos from Batman are very well-handled too and Byrne tells his tale in just six chapters with no flab and no padding.

Visually Byrne's Superman is the embodiment of hope and positivity, taking his cue from Christopher Reeve in the iconic films but also giving him his own more personal approach. The introduction by Byrne, who was born in England but moved to Canada when he was fairly little, puts his Superman in a very interesting context. Here is this creator born in England and raised in Canada who is taking on the ultimate American hero, so he's an outsider tackling another outsider figure. Ray Bradbury's introduction is also fascinating. He gets to the nub of just why it is that throughout our modern era, Superman is there. He reflects the mores of the period he is created in and *Man Of Steel* is definitely a very 1980s approach to the character. Inker Dick Giordano gives Byrne a very polished sheen to his pencils and letterer Costanza and colourist Tom Ziuko lend the whole thing a very classy feel.

Superman: Man Of Steel is a wonderful heartfelt tribute to the character with Byrne injecting new life into Superman. Set just after DC's *Crisis On Infinite Earths*, *Man Of Steel* offers a new perspective on DC's most familiar creation. **JOEL MEADOWS**

19

Preacher Deluxe Edition Book One
Writer: Garth Ennis
Artist: Steve Dillon
Colourist: Matt Hollingsworth, Pamela Rambo
Vertigo/ DC

Garth Ennis
Steve Dillon
PREACHER
Book One
"Just about the best thing to come along since comics started finding their way into books."
— The Washington Post
VERTIGO

Ennis and Dillon's post-*Hellblazer* tour de force from the 1990s starts as it means to go on, in a hellbound landscape brimming with venal, salty, misshapen players, apocalyptic tropes and the blackest of black (if not gross-out) humour – one of Ennis's key calling cards of course. Jesse Custer's preacher ends up being imbued, mid-sermon natch, with the soul of Genesis, the offspring of an angel and a demon, which possesses enough power to challenge God himself. And that is just for openers. Custer's benighted world, even when he is abroad from his Texan dark lands in New York with vampiric chum and comic relief Cassidy and girlfriend Tulip, is ugly, mean-spirited and perpetually on the verge of bursting into flames.

It takes a while to get going, the story's rock 'n' roll, cooler-than-thou attitude at times wearing, while every lead or secondary character is hiding an expansive backstory or grim secret. For such a feted and celebrated work (the television spin-off ran for four series) one would expect it to carry a reasonable bite upon rereading it, which needless to say it does – but with so much plot to get through, it takes a while to coalesce into the gripping, compulsive gem we all remember. The first few chapters introduce us to the Adephi, Seraphim and of course, the Saint of Killers – all interesting ideations that have yet to gel in this volume – indeed, Custer's relationship with God is merely the MacGuffin for the meat of the matter. And once things come to a head in New York, everything kicks into gear.

And they go up considerably more when Jesse and Tulip get reacquainted with his "family", which is as good a story arc as Ennis and Dillon ever conceived – a cinematic journey through the most brutal recesses of Southern Gothic, which, rather like the rest of this book, certainly doesn't pull any punches. *Preacher* Volume 1, which reprints the first twelve issues of the title, is a rollicking, picaresque, irreverent ride through the seedy underbelly of America that pushed the envelope further than Ennis and Dillon's previous, equally-lauded efforts. The particularly graphic imagery, Fellini-esque hijinks and spaghetti-western milieu mean it lacks the weight of *Hellblazer*, even if Jesse Custer does come across like an Americanised John Constantine.

Garth Ennis must have had a movie version in mind when he began the series, and with Steve Dillon's excellent filmic pencils (very few artists could tell a story as well as the much-missed maestro) it's easy to see what an obvious choice it was to make the transfer. Yes, it is a title that at times betrays its age, and is wilfully cynical, but there is heart in there eventually, and it's a cracking, unputdownable read that is still very much preferable to the AMC iteration. One of the best titles of the 90s. **ANDREW COLMAN**

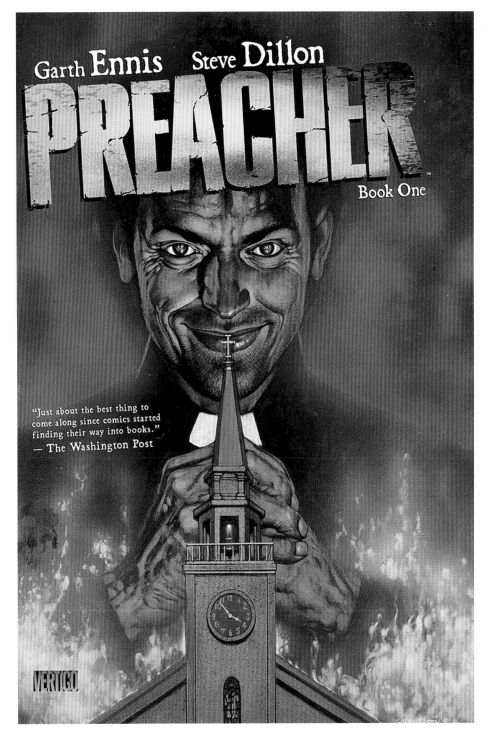

MARK WAID

ALEX ROSS

KINGDOM COME

18

Kingdom Come
Writers: Mark Waid and Alex Ross
Artist: Alex Ross
Letters: Todd Klein
Black Label DC

While it perhaps seems a bit reductive to say that *Watchmen* is nothing more than a reflection of Alan Moore being a 'bit grumpy', it's fair to say that the seismic effect of said comic book was both positive and negative. While it remains one of the most striking examples of what the medium could actually do when in the hands of someone who understood it, it – and other works such as *The Dark Knight Returns* – left many pale imitators in its wake: comics that thought that equated intelligence with constant darkness and depressing storylines. The 90s saw many other comics rebel against this notion: often with an 'X' in the title they became orgies of OTT colour and violence, the brainless

entertainment ying to the yang of contemplative brooding.

Against this backdrop, and the general comic book crash of the 90s, came *Kingdom Come*. An earnest attempt to 'reclaim' the heroes of the Silver Age and rally at some of the excesses of the comic book industry at the time, the 'Elseworlds' branded event sees traditional superheroes come up against a new generation whose amoral ways become an affront to the values built by those previously.

The Joker dies as the hands of superhero Magog: an execution served after the Clown Prince of Crime heads to trial for the mass murder of numerous Daily Planet employees, amongst them Lois Lane. With overwhelming public support for Magog's actions, the Justice League and Superman have disappeared from view: their values seemingly out of touch with the rest of society. But the new generation of heroes engage in indiscriminate violence, the line between hero and villain almost unrecognisable. After a battle instigated by Magog goes awry, millions are killed and Superman returns with the Justice League intent on restoring order and teaching the true meaning of truth and justice. But the generational battle becomes more complex with Bruce Wayne in the background and Lex Luthor making his own plans with a brainwashed Captain Marvel.

While things get ever more critical and complicated – with Superman considering a prison for the malcontents who don't hold to his ideas – The Spectre appears to Norman McCay, an unassuming minister, who tells him he must bear witness to the forthcoming superhuman apocalypse.

Those who are fans of Alex Ross, who co-wrote this with Mark Waid, will recognise

many of the tropes that would typify much of his previous and subsequent work. The ordinary protagonist who becomes an observer of superhero actions. A tale that deconstructs traditional superhero tropes, heavy on continuity and celebration of the past. A piece that deals with issues of morality and fragility amongst the godlike beings who inhabit the worlds of comic books. All these ideas are present throughout in a piece that revels in the epic, the grandiose. Yet, despite these epic set-pieces, this is also a piece that allows the characters to muse and reflect, with large swathes dedicated to examining the nature of good and evil, of right and wrong. In the hands of lesser writers these moments may seem didactic and dull. But here there pacing is excellent – save a denouement which seems a little too glib for its own good – with the more contemplative moments allowing much needed respite from the more OTT moments.

While *Kingdom Come* is in many ways a riposte to the fast and loose morality of many of the comic book superheroes of the era, it doesn't indulge in beatifying the golden and silver age of superheroes. Superman's prison is a quasi-fascistic measure whose morality is thorny as those he seeks to control. But, while the story is set to end in destruction and death, there is a much consistent sense of hope here. That for all their problems, for all their struggles our heroes are just that: heroes. Even amongst the darkest times they will fight for what is right and realise the error of their own ways. The world may be dark but their light will ultimately shine through.

The characterisations here are great, a series of grizzled and aged heroes all dealing with their own issues. Superman is haunted by the death of Lois – and a society that has seemingly rejected his values. Wonder Woman is similarly hardened and disgraced in own home country. An exoskeleton wearing Bruce Wayne is as Machiavellian as ever. But they are still recognisable heroes, with a strong sense of right and wrong. Their faith may have been shaken – and it will take an ordinary human to remind them of the right path. Also intriguing is the centring of Captain Marvel whose very existence – halfway between ordinary human and god – becomes a key plot point.

Ross' realistic gouache artwork is superb here. With characters believably aged – Bruce Wayne is all silver hair and crevassed face – Ross still emphasises their heroic statues. The likes of Superman all feel like they've carved out of granite, and they cast a continually imposing presence. And, as with works such as *Marvels*, his realistic style reminds us of the human and grounds the world of gods to a human dimension.

Kingdom Come has become an important milestone in DC history, with many elements being woven into contemporary DC lore as well as other mediums (such as the recent TV adaption of Crisis on Infinite Earths). It still has a tremendous power to this day, not only as a constantly enthralling piece of work, but also as an example of an industry coming to terms with its past, present and future.
LAURENCE BOYCE

17

Jonah Hex: Counting Corpses
Writers: Justin Gray, Jimmy Palmiotti
Artists: Paul Gulacy, Darwyn Cooke, Dick Giordano, Jordi Bernet and Billy Tucci
Letters: Rob Leigh
Colours: Rob Schwager, Paul Mounts and Dave Stewart
DC

Back in the 2000s, Jimmy Palmiotti and his writing partner Justin Grey brought DC's iconic former Confederate soldier turned bounty hunter back to the DC line first in his own book, *Jonah Hex*, which ran from 2005 to 2011 and then was replaced with *All-Star Western*, which ran for another three years. This collection reprints six tales taken from the *Jonah Hex* title, illustrated by some very impressive artists indeed.

The first tale, The Hyde House Massacre, is drawn by DC and Marvel legend Paul Gulacy. What is most extraordinary is that 14 out of the story's 22 pages are silent, devoid of any dialogue. Gulacy has always been a very atmospheric and haunting artist and this Hex one off shows that he has lost none of his impact. Hex has been hired to rescue a woman and her father and manages to strike a lucrative bargain with the woman by the tale's end.

The second story, The Great Silence, sees Palmiotti and Grey team up with one of their finest collaborators, the late great Darwyn Cooke. Here we see Hex team up with Tallulah Black, his fellow bounty hunter and occasional lover and we get to see a slightly more human side to Hex. Cooke was spectacular at capturing action as well as emotion and this story is some of the finest modern Western comic work. Cooke was all about simplicity and conveying so much in just a few lines.

The third story, Divining Rod, is by Neal Adams' former inker and DC's executive editor Dick Giordano. He was better known as an inker rather than a full artist but he was a more than serviceable penciller and so it's rather cool to have him included here as this was one of his last professional jobs in

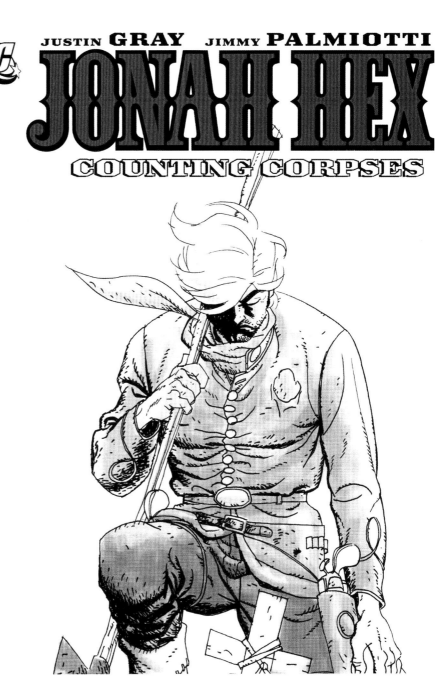

JUSTIN GRAY   JIMMY PALMIOTTI
JONAH HEX
COUNTING CORPSES

comics. He was a very fine storyteller so it's great to see him strut his stuff.

The fourth story, Too Mean To Die, by Spanish comics great Jordi Bernet, sees Hex hiding out in a swamp from men bent on killing him and a little like Cooke, Bernet is the master of the line, eliciting so much with just a few simple strokes. His European approach is refreshing here and he reteams with Palmiotti and Grey in the final tale here, Shooting Stars.

Between these two stories is You'll Never Dance Again, a story of betrayal and vengeance that sees Hex enlist dance hall girl Lana, whose motives are less than pure here, to help him acquire the bounty on a pair of robbers.

Artist Billy Tucci captures the action well although he sometimes lacks the subtlety and nuance of the other illustrators in this volume.

Bernet's final tale, Shooting Stars, is a classic Hex tale of bizarre alliances and wrongfooting your opponent.

Palmiotti and Grey brought something fresh and new to Jonah Hex, lending it a Leoneesque spaghetti western feel and these are six wonderful self-contained stories of DC's most interesting and iconic Western creation. It is a shame that the company doesn't have space for a Hex book as part of its line currently but you can't keep a good bounty hunter down for long.
JOEL MEADOWS

16

Absolute Batman: The Long Halloween
Writer: Jeph Loeb
Artist: Tim Sale
Colours: Gregory Wright
Letters: Richard Starkings and Comicraft
DC

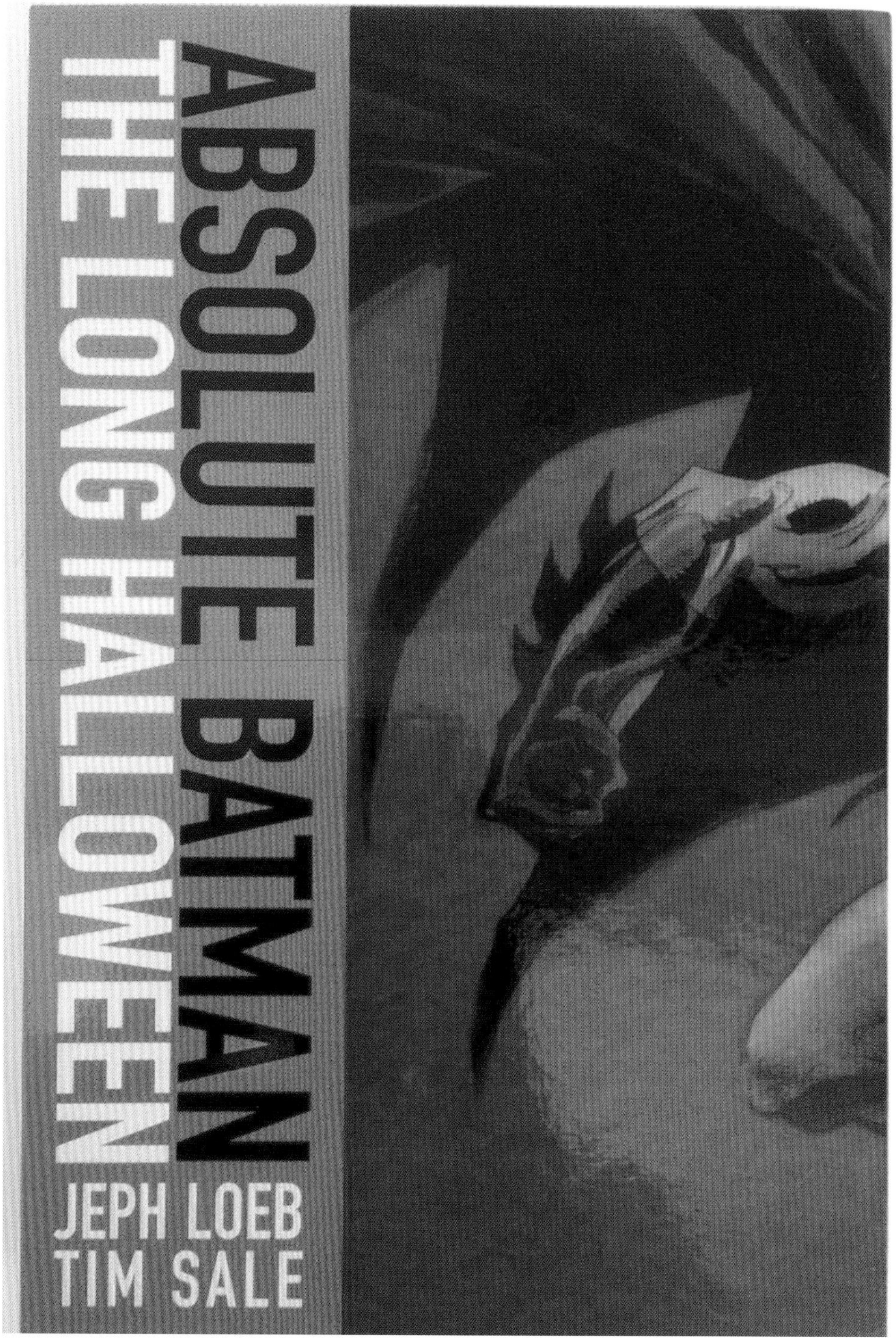
ABSOLUTE BATMAN
THE LONG HALLOWEEN
JEPH LOEB
TIM SALE

Set earlier on in Batman's career but after *Batman: Year One*, Jeph Loeb and Tim Sale have constructed a Dark Knight epic which was easily the equal of Frank Miller's work on the character.

Gotham is a city at war with two rival gangster families, the Falcones and the Maronis, vying for ultimate power in the criminal demi monde. On the side of law and order is Captain Jim Gordon and district attorney Harvey Dent. They make a pact with Batman to bring down the criminal fraternities that are ripping Gotham apart. But there is another spanner in the works, a serial killer everyone has named the Holiday killer who takes great pleasure in dispatching some of the more unsavoury figures in the city.

So Dent, Gordon and Batman are forced to unravel a murder mystery at the heart of Gotham. Batman villains like The Joker, Poison Ivy, Calendar Man, Catwoman and The Scarecrow are also part of the rich tapestry that Loeb weaves here.

Batman: The Long Halloween is arguably the most ambitious Batman story ever created. It owes a great deal to films like *The Godfather*, *The Godfather Part II* and even *Goodfellas* as the internecine struggle between the warring gangs is just as important to it as the more outlandish elements. Loeb gives Gordon and Dent their unique voices here and he also imbues characters like The Joker and Catwoman, who continues to play both sides, with their own foibles and idiosyncracies.

Visually it is also a wonderfully cinematic tale too with Sale with the aid of colourist Gregory Wright using a subtle colour palette and dramatic camera angles to ramp up the filmic qualities here. Murders take place in black and white and single and double page spreads are utilised here to set a very deliberate pace or to make a very intentional dramatic point. Sale also plays with light and shadows to set tone and shift mood to suit the story.

Sale takes from the European tradition of comic art while still remaining very American. The oversized format of the Absolute format gives his art an extra impact, allowing his work to really breathe.

Miller and Mazzucchelli's *Batman: Year One* was a shot of fresh air when it came out but *Batman: The Long Halloween* was the next step for the Dark Knight Detective. It is a brilliantly realised inventive whodunit with a cast of compelling players and art which never lets up, building on and ratcheting up the tension. Loeb and Sale worked together on a lot of different series but *Batman: the Long Halloween* is them at their zenith as a creative team. What makes this extra poignant is the early passing away of Tim Sale in summer 2022 so this now stands as a tribute to the artist and what he could achieve creatively.

JOEL MEADOWS

SAVAGE TOWN

Philip BARRETT
Declan SHALVEY
Jordie BELLAIRE
Clayton COWLES

15

Savage Town
Writer: Declan Shalvey
Artist: Philip Barrett
Letters: Clayton Cowles
Colourist: Jordie Bellaire
Image

Declan Shalvey and Philip Barrett's graphic novel about gang warfare set in Limerick city is a brutal tale that has a keen authentic voice – despite its brevity, the cadences, slang, and attention to detail have an immediacy that completely immerses the reader. Regardless of the bleak, hard-boiled and for the most part dowdy setting, all the characters are unmistakably real, the drab streets a compulsive backdrop for the protagonist's journey of bitter survivalism.

Lead character Jimmy Savage is the anti-hero of the book, an outsider forced to adapt quickly in a town that has no sentiment and even less empathy. A traveller caught between two warring families, the Hogans and the Dawsons, his story inhabits a territory that is reminiscent of Ennis and Dillon's canon, with elements of Shane Meadows at his bleakest, and (as the author himself has mentioned) Roddy Doyle. As the focal point of the tale, Savage proves to be barely more sympathetic than the two factions he is caught between, but there is a palpable depth to him – the relationship with his own family, and especially his martinet of a mother, all provide the humanity.

There is much to savour in this outing – Barrett's delineation of the back streets, sink estates and pubs is unassuming but deceptively detailed. The rest of the supporting cast are considerably fleshed out, the oppressive street noir a relentless player in itself, with each panel exuding a foreboding menace. What also impresses are the more implied elements – the fact that Blackie, as the sole African-Caribbean character, is treated with more respect than Jimmy (and indeed nearly everyone else) is a strange anomaly that speaks volumes about the community's mind set. And then there are the unwritten codes of honour – when Jimmy realizes that Frankie, his childhood friend and mentor, has betrayed him, they both casually accept the violent shadow play that must be enforced. The violence itself is naturalistic and gruesome, committed by its perpetrators with both alacrity and resignation – a far cry from its portrayal in mainstream comics, and deeply nihilistic.

As author Declan Shalvey has pointed out, the book has been a pet project that required time that wasn't available, due to constant other series he was working on as an artist taking precedence. With Philip Barrett on board – a talent deserving of wider recognition – he was able to complete the book with panache. His remit – to write a graphic novel in a city that has (to the best of my knowledge) been overlooked and marginalised, is a departure, but it is partly for that reason that everything fell into place.

If Shalvey and Barrett have proven one thing, it's that they are excellent storytellers, with barely a panel wasted. And the oath-edged asides, snide little aggressions and local vernacular that pepper the narrative keep you locked in. Good stuff.

ANDREW COLMAN

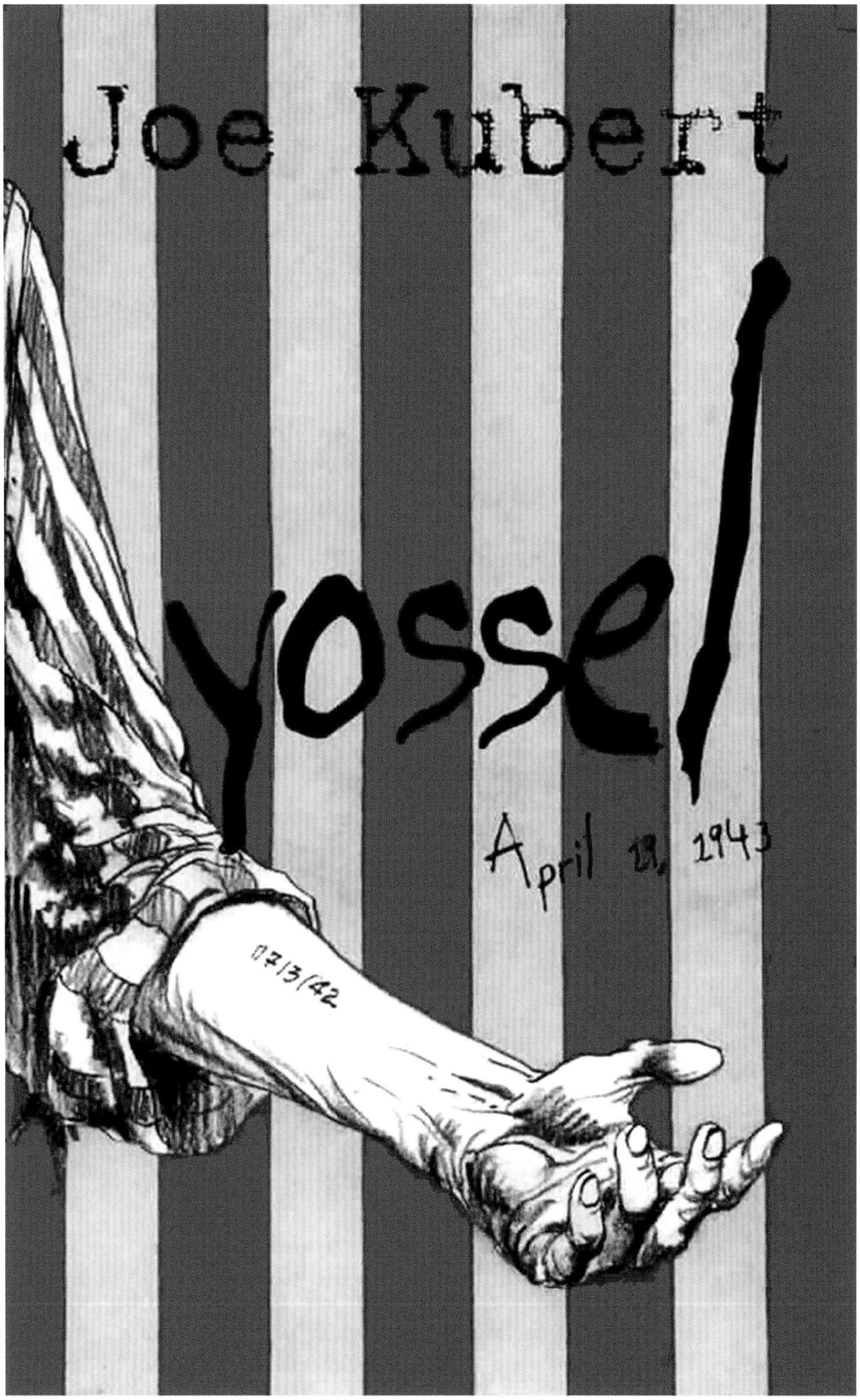
Joe Kubert
yossel
April 19, 1943
07/3/42

14

Yossel
Writer/ Artist: Joe Kubert
Letterer: Pete Carlsson
DC

Towards the end of his career, Kubert moved towards more hard-hitting material and away from his superheroes and adventure tales. *Yossel* is a 120 page original graphic novel about a young boy, the eponymous Yossel, who finds himself in the Warsaw Ghetto after losing his parents in the death camps. He has survived simply because of his ability to draw, something that the Nazis find eerily charming and so Kubert offers us this haunting tale of a boy who is witness to some of the most horrendous acts in modern history. In fact, he shows that art can sometimes be a conduit for survival and escape even in the most hopeless situations. In his introduction, he mentions that being a comic artist has always been something that he has been lucky to have as a major facet of his life.

Kubert explains his visual approach here in his introduction. *Yossel* is created purely in pencils rather than pen and inks and this offers a greater immediacy for the reader.

The creator varies the viewpoint a little here with the town's rebbe recounting his time in the death camp as a Sondercommando, one of the Jews who worked with the Nazis, and how he escaped from there.

Yossel possesses a harrowing simplicity in its imagery and, despite the fact that Kubert escaped with his family to America when he was little, so this isn't an autobiographical tale, there is such empathy here evoked by Kubert that the reader can't help but be drawn into his compelling narrative. Also the visual research here depicting places like the death camp feel like Kubert definitely did his homework and there is a sense of desperation and hopelessness all the way through here although there are positive notes too in the bleakness.

This also has a quote from master graphic novelist Will Eisner (*Contract With God, The Spirit*) on its cover and this work is easily the equal of any of Eisner's books too.

Joe Kubert was a writer, an editor and a fantastic artist. Here with *Yossel* he showcases his versatility as a creator, illustrating that his work was always about nuance, emotion and subtlety. His previous work in the superhero and war fields always showed he was a cut above many of his contemporaries but here he takes things to another level. *Yossel* is obviously a very hard read but it's one of the most ambitious works of the career of a true comics genius and it should be far better known than it actually is. Haunting and heartfelt, it points to the power of comics.

JOEL MEADOWS

13

London's Dark
Writer: James Robinson
Artist: Paul Johnson
Letterer: Woodrow 'Trevs' Phoenix
Titan Books

In the 1980s, *Escape Magazine* was a comic strip magazine edited by Paul Gravett and Peter Stanbury and it published two original graphic novels. One was *Violent Cases* by Neil Gaiman and Dave McKean and the other was this one.

London's Dark, published back in 1989, was the debut of writer James Robinson and Paul Johnson was an artist who went on to work for publishers like Vertigo and Fleetway. Its story is a simple one: it tells the tale of Jack Brookes, an air raid warden in London in 1940 who has been asked to investigate a young fortune-teller who appears to have upset one of his neighbours by informing her that her son, who she thought had died in the bombings had in fact been murdered. Jack falls for the fortune-teller but finds himself in mortal danger from a gang of brutal murderers.

It's only 48 pages long but Robinson, with the assistance of artist, Johnson weave a tale of revenge and intrigue that holds the reader's attention tight. Johnson left comics a long time ago which is a shame because he is an experimental storyteller who brings London during the war to life with real style and he works well with Robinson. He is able to jump between photographic and a more traditional comic line as an artist with ease too. Also the fact that this is in black and white gives it extra impact for the reader. The cover, which is in colour, sets out the book's intentions very succinctly as well. Letterer Trevs (Woodrow) Phoenix rounds out the team well too.

Robinson went on to write DC's *Starman* series and you can see an embryonic version of some of his unique touches as a writer here. He has a very good ear for dialogue and the interplay between Brookes and fortune-teller Sophie Heath are very

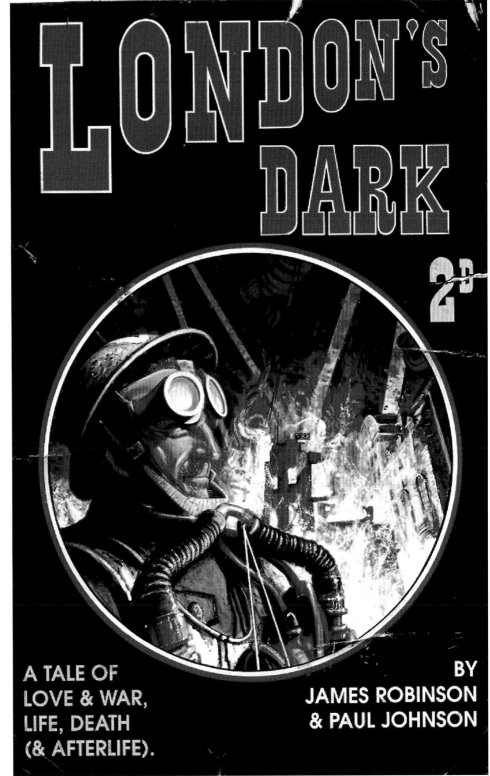

A TALE OF LOVE & WAR, LIFE, DEATH (& AFTERLIFE).

BY JAMES ROBINSON & PAUL JOHNSON

well-handled. There is a two page text section which explains Heath's unique abilities 18 pages into the story which is a little bit jarring but it doesn't disrupt the tale, giving Robinson the opportunity to show off his prose skills. It also offers an extra insight into her as a character. *London's Dark* effectively tips its hat too to the films of Ealing and the 1940s and 1950s British cinema, to the work of filmmakers like David

Lean, the Boulting Brothers and Powell and Pressburger and authors like Graham Greene.

Its short page count means that it tells its story and then leaves. At no point does it feel like Robinson has resorted to any padding.

London's Dark is a very British noirish period graphic novel which effortlessly captures the feel of its time period. **JOEL MEADOWS**

12

The Judas Coin
Writer/ Artist: Walter Simonson
Letters: John Workman
Colourist: Lovern Kindzierski
DC

The Judas Coin was published in 2012 and was an anthology one-shot graphic novel that follows the 30 pieces of silver that Judas Iscariot was paid to betray Jesus through time and through the DC universe.

The book opens with a four page intro putting everything into context and then we have the first story, a tale of DC's Golden Gladiator set in 73 AD in the Roman empire, Blood Peace. Simonson employs a different style for each of his tales here and this has a *Look and Learn* adventure feel to it without sacrificing that Simonson feeling. In and out in just 13 pages, it's a wonderful intro to the book showcasing a Roman agent who gives his all for Rome.

We move onto The Viking Prince tale, Black Blade, Silver Heart, which shifts the action to over 900 years to 1000 AD. Taking another classic little-known DC character, the Viking Prince, whose stories were mostly drawn by Joe Kubert, Simonson gives us a 15 page Viking adventure again with a more open style which plays with the page construction. Two stories down and Simonson hasn't disappointed yet.

WALTER SIMONSON
THE JUDAS COIN
DC COMICS

INRI
THERE WAS ONCE A MAN WHO BETRAYED A FRIEND FOR THIRTY PIECES OF SILVER.
HE BETRAYED HIM WITH A KISS.
THE FRIEND WAS CRUCIFIED.

The third tale features Captain Fear, set on the Spanish Main in 1720, Mutiny. Simonson has previous experience with this character as Fear was one of his first professional jobs for DC. A classic pirate story, where again the artist toys with his style, with some wonderful sound effects courtesy of letterer John Workman, again Simonson does what he had to do in a mere 17 pages. The story of the coins play their part here too in a tale of betrayal and revenge.

Then we jump to 1881 and a fun short starring DC's classic Western character Bat Last. Shorter than the rest, Simonson does something very intriguing with his panel borders here and because of its short page count, only 8 pages long, it never outstays its welcome. The writer realises the power of brevity and he displays his understanding of the medium with rare skill here.

The penultimate story, Heads Or Tails, sees the book head to modern Gotham and here Simonson literally turns things on their heads. Each double page spread is a horizontal story page, broken up into a series of horizontal panels. Simonson has made no secret of his love for newspaper strips like *Modesty Blaise* and the *James Bond* strips and this Batman tale which has Two-Face get his hands on the Judas Coin is like a clever tribute to the newspaper strips that the creator admires so greatly.

It all ends with Manhunter 2070, probably the most obscure DC character here who appeared in DC's *Showcase* book in the early 1970s, in a sci-fi tale he called An Epilog-2087. Simonson introduces a touch of manga and anime in his art here and it's definitely the most experimental we have ever seen him before although the Two-Face story comes close to that. We also get a short sketch gallery at the end to offer readers a little glimpse into his approach to the book.

So Simonson has taken us on a rollercoaster ride through the DC universe in just 96 pages. I can't think of another comic creator who would want to push the envelope and try a format like *The Judas Coin* with their work. Here he shows off his versatility and variety as an illustrator. Many decades into his career, the book shows a creator who is still keen to experiment and push his work and one who is still at the peak of his prowess. Colourist Kindzierski is the perfect match for Simonson's lines and letterer Workman is exceptional as ever.

The Judas Coin is a standalone anthology graphic novel which offers glimpses into various facets of DC's publishing history over the decades created by a true comics original voice.

JOEL MEADOWS

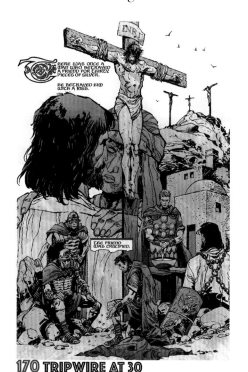

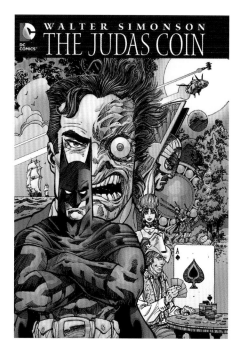

11

The Tale Of One Bad Rat
Writer/ Artist: Bryan Talbot
Titan/ Dark Horse

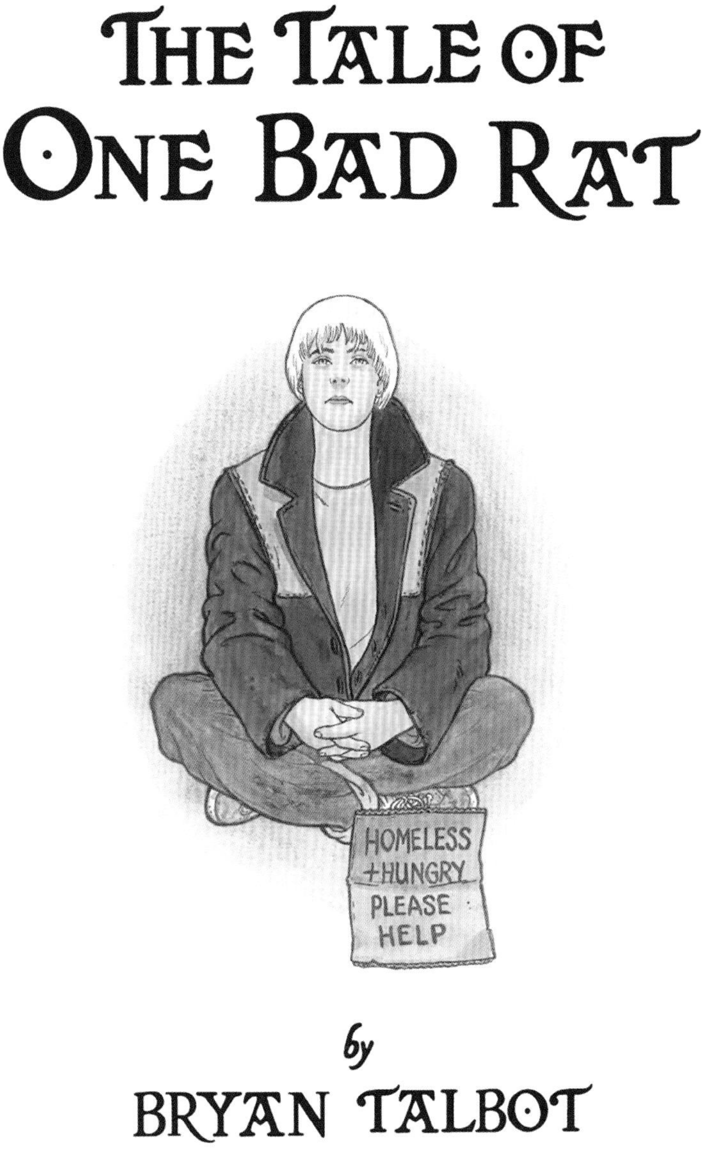
THE TALE OF ONE BAD RAT
HOMELESS +HUNGRY PLEASE HELP
by
BRYAN TALBOT

The very hard-hitting *A Tale Of One Bad Rat* is by veteran British comics creator Bryan Talbot. Comics is a great vehicle for telling serious stories and Talbot is one of comics' finest ambassadors. This graphic novel weaves the story of teenager Helen Potter, a runaway who has been forced to leave home after she is abused by her father. Helen is obsessed with children's author Beatrix Potter, as Helen was the writer's real first name, and creates an imaginary friend in the shape of the one bad rat as a way of coping with her awful life, her abuse suffered and her circumstances. She is a very sympathetic figure and Talbot really brings her to life here with real nuance and subtlety.

It is on the surface a very simple story but Talbot brings empathy, imagination and emotion to bear here, offering healing for Helen through a serious of events. Visually it is very powerful indeed with Talbot's graphic lines communicating very directly with the reader. He has stripped back his artistic style a little here to make it feel a little bit like the illustrations in Potter's children's books. The colouring is very effective too, using a flat palette to compliment Talbot's art. He has always been a very good storyteller and he keeps the pace up here, offering a tale of credible redemption for Helen while using settings like London and the Lake District, where Potter lived for some time in real life, to wonderful effect. There is drama and conflict here and all the way through you are rooting for her to make her life and her situation better partly through her obsession with her true-life namesake.

The best comic creators are able to utilise the four colour format to do something important with their work that makes a real difference. It certainly isn't an easy subject to tackle but Talbot created something here with passion and sympathy that is the equal of the best TV dramas on the subject. It feels like he really did his homework here too and that is another reason why this book packs such a punch for the reader.

Comics should make you think and stop in your tracks sometimes and *A Tale Of One Bad* Rat, one of Talbot's most personal stories, is a work of deep profound emotion with much to say to the reader.

JOEL MEADOWS

10

Judge Dredd – America
Writer: John Wagner
Artist: Colin MacNeil
Rebellion

"Rights? Sure. I'm all for rights. But not at the expense of order. That's why I like to see that Statue of Judgement standing there, towering over Liberty. Kind of a symbol.

Justice has a price. The price is freedom."

I've had a strong desire to revisit *Judge Dredd: America* recently. Having just read the *Judges Omnibus Volume 2* by Mike Carroll, Maura McHugh and Joseph Elliott-Coleman, a prose series which explores the early days of the Judge system and how it replaced the traditional policing in what used to be America, before the Atom Wars and Mega City One, I've been pondering some of the issues the stories raised, Trying to replace a broken, corrupt judicial system with one which is truly impartial, where the colour of your skin or your wealth will not matter, only the crime, leading to instant justice. But at the cost of freedom, liberty and, ultimately democracy. The three tales in Judges reminded me of Wagner and MacNeil's *America*, one of my all-time favourite Dredd stories, and I had to revisit it.

America begins with a beautiful but very sad looking woman, preparing for a stage show, staring into the dressing room mirror in a nightclub, as the dialogue recounts a doomed love for a woman, America, and how through tragic events she was lost, betrayed. The story is being told by Bennett Beeny, an entertainer, a man who has known America Jara – Ami – since she was born in a neighbouring apartment when he was a toddler. They grew up together, the best of friends, but as they got older and she went off to college, they drifted apart. He was deeply in love with her, but knew she cared for him, but not romantically. Their previously tightly-bound lives move apart with age, and besides, Ami has something else, a fire within her, a fire that burns for the restoration of liberty and the overthrow of the totalitarian Judge system.

Ami joins the Dems protest group – the citizens demanding the return of democratic control of their city, but when peaceful mass protest is met by dirty tricks and heavy-handed violence, she and others abandon peaceful means and form Total War, a terrorist group who will use violence and murder to achieve their aims. It's at this point Ami and Bennett's lives cross paths again, accidentally, when he recognises her posing as a "slabwalker" (a street sex worker) in a set-up to ambush and kill Judges, with Bennett shot in the cross-fire. As he painfully recovers Ami covertly visits the now wealthy and successful Bennett, and tells him of what was done to her on that peaceful march that drove her to resort to violence, and also to ask for his financial help. He begs her to stop, to stay with him, but he knows she won't.

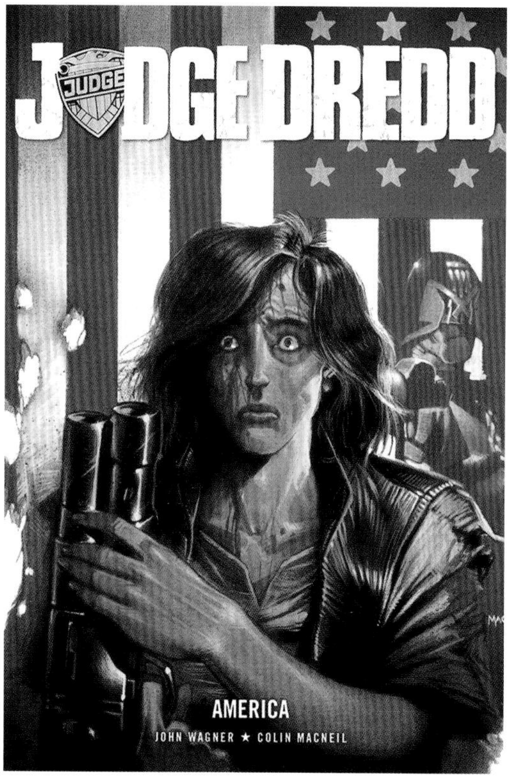
JUDGE DREDD
JUDGE
AMERICA
JOHN WAGNER ★ COLIN MACNEIL

She's committed to the cause, and that cause is planning something big, something violent, with his money to fund it, an idea he can't stomach.

There are so many fascinating, compelling elements to *America*. Wagner, the Dreddfather, delivers a script that weaves in the Big Issues – morality, freedom, justice, human rights – but also the personal, human-level problems – friendship, love, trust and betrayal. Those Big Issues resonate as much today as they did back in the early 90s, perhaps even more – we only have to think about the Draconian laws brought into Western democratic nations following the horror of 9-11, intrusive measures, curbs on freedoms and rights, but "for our safety", of how many will sacrifice some freedoms for safety, or at least the feeling of safety, and how others are happy to use that to garner more power to themselves.

There's the question of violence, from the state, from the individual – Total War are so sure of their cause they will kill for it, not just their enemies, but if innocents are in the way, they are unfortunate collateral. But the Judges are just as stubborn and violent in turn, and there's an argument that their fascist, violent state has effectively created a violent monster in return. It's a question our own troubled world has pondered – why would someone be prepared not just to kill, but to murder innocents for their cause? What drives someone to terrorism? A sense of desperation, of no other avenues being available, mixed with a burning anger for bloody revenge. Not that this story condones their methods here, nor the Judges, and that's where much of the power of this story comes from, that mixed morality where none can truly hold the moral high ground, but at the same time when we see monsters, we also see the wretched circumstances that made them into monsters.

But while those major moral musings are important, for me it is the personal touches that really ground America. The childhood friendship between Ami and Bennett is beautiful, and Wagner perfectly captures that moment so many of us will remember, of friends from our youngest days, the people we thought inseparable from us, who grew and moved off as we all got older, the pangs of longing for a deep, desperate love that may never be returned, but which remains there, pure, unfulfilled. The moments when Ami is back in Bennett's life, the thing he has dreamed of all his life, but is she using him, his love, just to get the money she needs for The Cause? Almost certainly, and yet she clearly loves Bennett too, she sees a life she could have had with him, content, wealthy, safe, loved, but the price would be to ignore the wrong she sees in the world, and she cannot turn her back on that.

MacNeil's painted artwork is stunning, some of the finest to grace the pages of Dredd over the decades. We see a Judge towering over Ami and Bennett when they are children – there was never a time Judges weren't there, a threatening presence in their lives – the armoured lawman standing over the small children, Bennett scared, Ami defiant, determined to protect her friend. Elsewhere MacNeil uses that child's perspective, depicting the Judges from a low perspective, so the reader is looking up at them, standing powerfully above, fascistic power incarnate. Moodily lit and deftly using colour, MacNeil is as effective as showing bloody violence – from the Judges, from the terrorists – as he is the tender moments, the childhood flashbacks, and some iconic scenes (a bloody America with the flag of that now vanished Republic facing hordes of heavily armed Judges before the Statue of Liberty). Both he and Wagner craft a central character, a woman who is immensely strong, powerful, driven to stand for her principles regardless of cost, and yet also clearly marked by that cost, but knowing no other way to live with herself but to carry on.

It's a powerful tale, dramatically, morally, emotionally – we have conspiracy, we have action, we have a fight between opposing ways of living, but we also have romance, and betrayal and happiness and regret, and an ending that will break your heart. It's a story not afraid to depict one of the comics' biggest characters as a brutal, freedom-repressing fascist, another lens to view the complex world of Dredd through, and one which makes you think, makes you feel, and comes all wrapped up in that glorious, painted artwork.

JOE GORDON

9

These Savage Shores
Writer: Ram V
Artist: Sumit Kumar
Colourist: Vittorio Astone
Letters: Aditya Bidikar
Vault Comics

Horror romance These Savage Shores is by Ram V and artist Sumit Kumar. Ram V is a writer who has been in the ascendancy over the last three years and he is currently the regular writer on DC's Detective Comics as well as writing Swamp Thing for them too. Vault is a company which has become one of the best purveyors of modern horror comics too. These Savage Shores is an elegant and very sophisticated tale of the East India Company, who are bent on doing new deals with the rulers along the silk route. But they haven't counted on Bishan, a mythic figure and his lover Kori, who find themselves in the middle of the war between the British and the Indians. The story also throws a particularly nasty vampire figure into the mix, who acts as a catalyst for events and you have a very exciting and pacy horror romance tale with a dash of history and adventure.

Ram V has constructed this tale with style and nuance. It feels like a very canny hybrid of Kipling, Stoker's Dracula and the Arabian Nights with a very contemporary feel at its centre too. He tackles the intrigue between the British and the Mysore inhabitants with a deft hand. Bishan, the timeless figure who may or may not be a monster, is a genuinely intriguing figure. He may well be a monstrous character and he sometimes behaves like one but then he seems to achieve redemption through his love for Kori. Kori is a creation that Ram V brings to life with aplomb, a woman who finds herself at the heart of an obsessive love affair, one which is doomed to end in tragedy. She feels like a classic literary archetype.

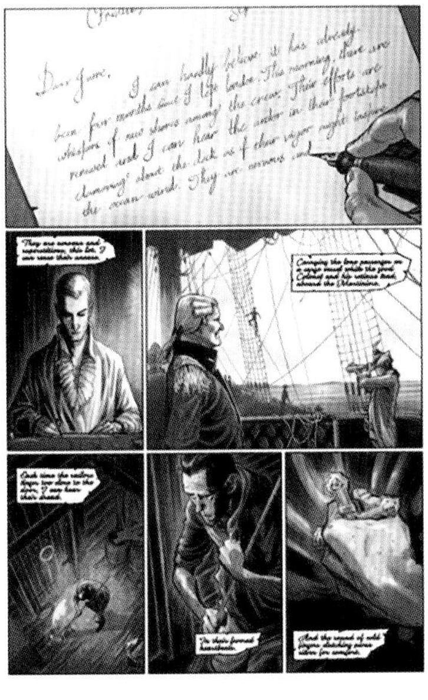

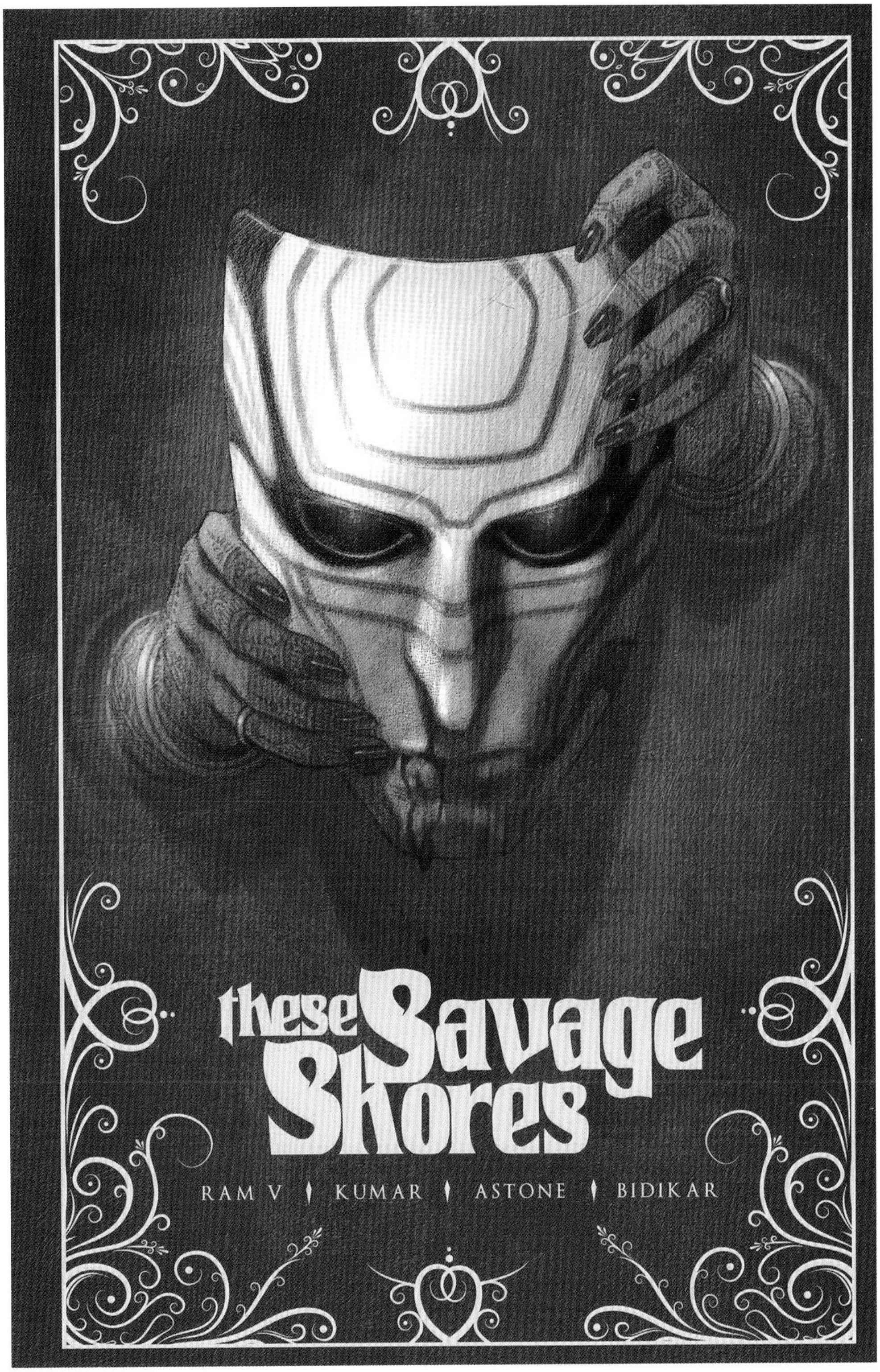
these Savage Shores
RAM V | KUMAR | ASTONE | BIDIKAR

Artist Kumar is fantastic, creating sweeping Indian vistas and equally at home drawing people as he is with the environments they inhabit. Colourist Vittorio Astone manages to bring his lines to life with the deep richness of his tones, really giving this an extra layer and letterer Aditya Bidikar rounds out the package.

Tales of vampires and timeless creatures have been around for centuries but Ram V and Kumar with the sizeable assistance of Astone and Bidikar have synthesised all of these familiar elements to create something which feels fresh yet which includes all of the elements that are present in classic adventure stories to connect with the reader.

Ram V already has an individual voice as a writer that means he will be around a long time, and Kumar is the ideal artist to bring his vision here to life. These Savage Shores is visceral, smart and strangely modern despite its period setting. Even though it has only been around for six years, Vault has already shown that it can offer exceptional comics and graphic novels and *These Savage Shores* is a statement of intent that can't be ignored.

JOEL MEADOWS

FRANK MILLER ★ DAVE GIBBONS

GIVE ME LIBERTY

★ AN AMERICAN DREAM ★

8

Give Me Liberty
Writer: Frank Miller
Artist: Dave Gibbons
Colourist: Robin Smith
Dark Horse Comics

Give Me Liberty is a sci-fi series originally published back in 1990 by Dark Horse. The Martha Washington of the title is an African-American girl who grows up in the poor Chicago

neighbourhood of Cabrini Green. Through various situations she first finds herself arrested and then as an officer in Pax, the Peace Corps of the story. But this is our world with a step taken to the side and so it is a world led by US president Rexall, a slice of speculative fiction that's only a short distance away from our own.

Miller's collaboration with Gibbons on the art is an effective one and Gibbons brings Miller's fractured version of the US, a country literally at war with itself led first by a scary demagogue president and then a flawed but basically good man, to life on the page with real aplomb and confidence. His art has always had a very European feel and he takes it to a whole other level here although it still possesses those uniquely British idiosyncrasies that Gibbons has always used to his advantage.

Miller has carved out a post-apocalyptic US that is corrupt, riven with deep-seated rivalries and created a protagonist in Washington who is flawed, human and someone the reader roots for throughout this four part story. His satirical approach is a similar one to *Dark Knight Returns*, mocking a society that has cracked and splintered.

As a sci-fi epic, it also owes something to Otomo's *Akira* and there are even echoes of Kubrick and Burgess' bold dystopian vision *Clockwork Orange* here too a little. *Give Me Liberty* also shows how technology can be twisted and abused to maintain power for those in charge. It has a few of those classic Miller moments that lift his work above his contemporaries like some classic lines of dialogue chosen and deployed at precisely the right time.

Robin Smith's colours are the perfect foil for Gibbons' lines as well, providing tone and mood throughout.

Give Me Liberty is an extremely ambitious collaboration between two of comics' finest creators at the top of their career and there is real chemistry between Miller and Gibbons. They returned to Washington a number of times afterwards but this first tale is their strongest.

JOEL MEADOWS

7

Trinity
Writer/ Artist: Matt Wagner
Colourist: Dave Stewart
Letterer: Sean Konot
DC

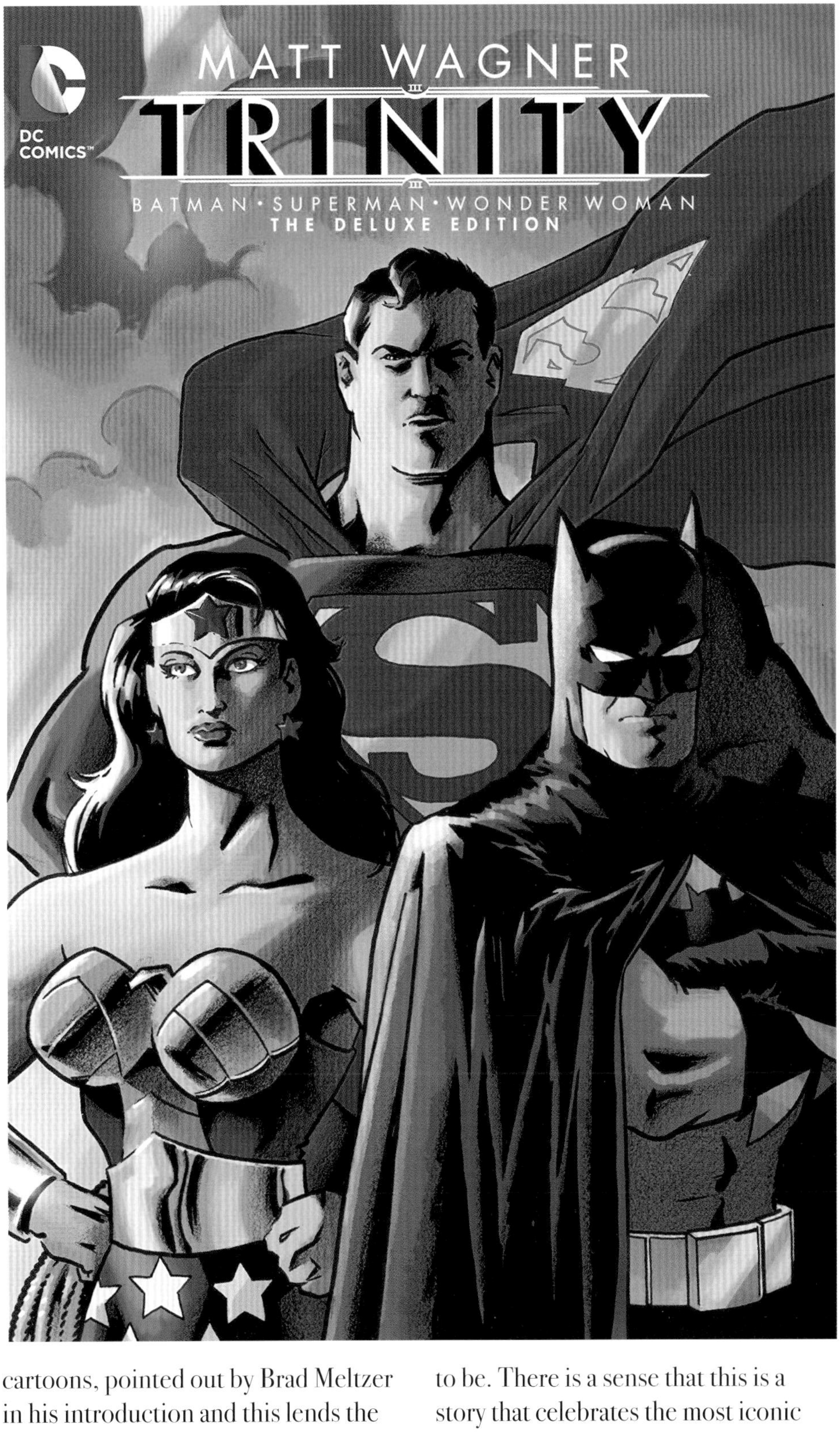
DC COMICS
MATT WAGNER
TRINITY
BATMAN • SUPERMAN • WONDER WOMAN
THE DELUXE EDITION

Trinity was originally published back in 2003 as individual issues and collected a year later. It is a fairly simple tale of how Batman, Superman and Wonder Woman first teamed up in the DC Universe to take on Batman's greatest adversary Ra's Al Ghul who has freed Bizarro and plans to take over Wonder Woman's home island of Themiscyra.

Visually, Wagner with the assistance of master colourist Dave Stewart invests each of DC's three most iconic creations with a different feel and using a slightly different visual language. Batman skulks in the shadows, Superman takes to the skies like a Greek god and Wonder Woman heroically soars. Wagner's Ra's Al Ghul is elegant yet sinister, a real counterpoint to the way we are used to seeing him depicted by Neal Adams.

His cartoony art here really lifts the action to life off the page with some masterful storytelling and he is a very versatile creator. He is as comfortable and proficient weaving fist fights between Wonder Woman and Ra's Al Ghul's minions as he is showing the more human side of characters like Clark Kent. He also utilises the coluring and the tones to make specific points about character. In the first issue, the scene where Clark Kent sits with Bruce Wayne in Wayne's limousine, Wayne is shrouded in shadow while Kent is bathed in sunlight. Gotham here is a city that lives much of its existence in darkness while Metropolis is somewhere which is located in the light. Wagner also tips his hat to things like the Fleischer cartoons, pointed out by Brad Meltzer in his introduction and this lends the story a pace and an energy that it may have lacked otherwise.

Trinity is the perfect introduction to the chemistry between Superman, Batman and Wonder Woman and it is its self-contained nature as a story that displays what an exceptional writer and artist Matt Wagner is and he continues to be. There is a sense that this is a story that celebrates the most iconic aspects of its three principle characters and as with all of the best creators, he makes it look effortless. DC hasn't always treated these three characters properly over the years but Matt Wagner's *Trinity* gets to their heart and offers a tale of adventure which is heartfelt and warm. **JOEL MEADOWS**

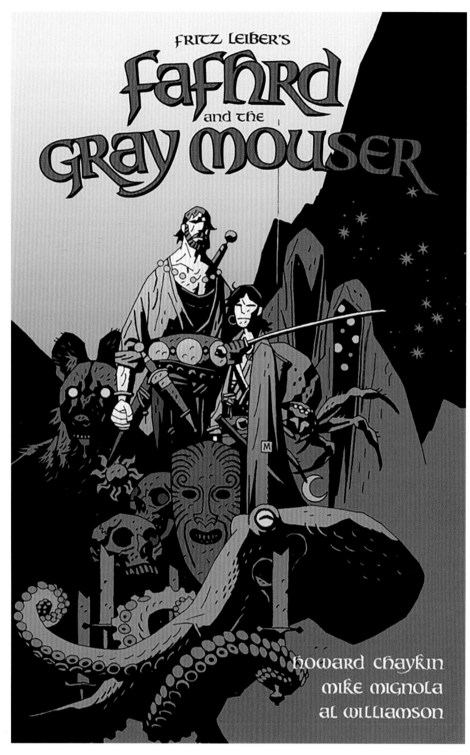

FRITZ LEIBER'S
Fafhrd
and the
GRAY MOUSER
howard chaykin
mike mignola
al williamson

6

Fritz Leiber's Fafhrd And The Gray Mouser
Writer: Howard Chaykin
Artists: Mike Mignola & Al Williamson
Colourist: Sherilyn Van Valkenrburgh
Letterer: Michael Heisler

Dark Horse Comics
This is Dark Horse's trade paperback of Chaykin and Mignola's adaptation of Fritz Leiber's classic fantasy novels featuring mismatched pair Fafhrd and The Gray Mouser. Originally published as four issues through Marvel's defunct Epic Comics imprint back in 1990, it was reprinted as a collection by Dark Horse in 2007.

Writer Chaykin has a connection to Leiber's creations going back in the 1970s as he was the artist on DC's *Sword and Sorcery* shortlived book, drawing the late great Denny O'Neil's scripts. Here he is the scripter teamed up with future superstar Mike Mignola who is inked by industry legend Al Williamson.

The pair are ginger-haired Fafhrd and dark-haired Gray Mouser, two thieves and ne-er-do-wells who find themselves on a serious of outlandlish adventures in and around the fictional city of Lankhmar. Chaykin perfectly brings Leiber's bawdy fantasy tone to life here in its dialogue and the interplay between the pair while Mignola's slightly rougher style than he came to use later on means that it all moves along at a breakneck speed. Colourist Van Valkenbergh's subtle tones are also the perfect foil here.

Fafjrd and Mouser are no high-born warriors like Howard's Conan or Moorcock's Elric and so they are forced to use their wits to get themselves out of their predicaments. Battling a series of supernatural threats, the pair show off their prowess as fighters and also as tricksters and thieves. Leiber's creations predate figures like Moorcock's Elric but you can see just how they have influenced more modern fantasy geniuses like the aforementioned Moorcock. Leiber was a contemporary of Conan creator Robert E Howard but these are a lot more tongue in cheek than Howard.

Mignola talks in the afterword about how getting to draw this series was a dream job for the artist as he had been a fan of Leiber and Moorcock for many years.

For fans of bawdy, quirky fantasy, *Fritz Leiber's Fafhrd And The Gray Mouser* is a rowdy, sharp adventure collection, capturing the spirit of the source material perfectly.

JOEL MEADOWS

5

Why I Hate Saturn
Writer/ Artist: Kyle Baker
Vertigo/DC Comics

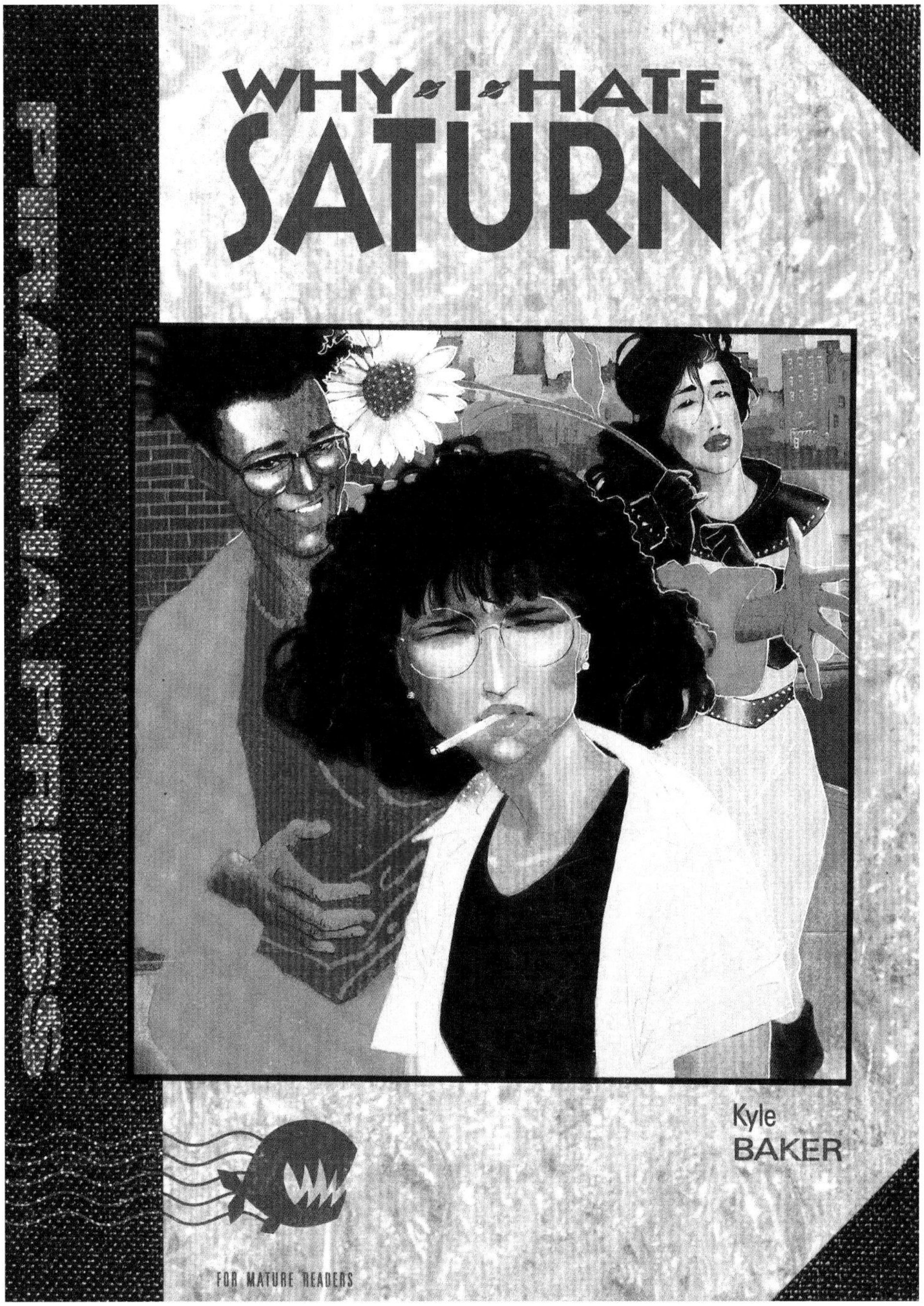
WHY I HATE SATURN
PIRANHA PRESS
Kyle BAKER
FOR MATURE READERS

Kyle Baker is a comics creator with a uniquely idiosyncratic approach to everything he works on. *Why I Hate Saturn* is a brilliantly sharp and witty standalone graphic novel originally published by DC's defunct Piranha Press imprint back in 1990.

It tells the story of magazine columnist Anne Merkel and her bizarre sister Laura and their existence through a series of interconnected vignettes over 200 pages.

Why I Hate Saturn is presented not in the traditional comic format with word balloons and captions but every panel is accompanied by a caption which includes dialogue. Drawn in a grayscale monotone throughout, Baker's broad artistic strokes create a truly illustrative experience displaying his assured grasp of figures and settings. Baker has won a number of Eisner awards for his work but his body of work has been so diverse over the years (drawing *The Shadow* for DC, drawing *Captain America* for Marvel, working in animation, adapting Lewis Carroll's *Alice In Wonderland*) that he is a hard creator to pin down in just one genre.

Why I Hate Saturn is the sort of book that if it was published about fifteen years later, it would have been adapted into an HBO TV series. Baker has imbued central protagonist Anne and her bizarre sister Laura with real human warmth and emotion. The book is well-paced and entertaining throughout as well, with razor-sharp dialogue and a genuinely engaging group of supporting characters. In some ways, this book almost feels like a modern version of Will Eisner as it is so seeped in the culture of New York but through a 1990s indie movie prism. Baker manages to mock the cultural obsessions of the time with precision and panache.

It does seem like this book and his other original graphic novels like *Cowboy Wally Show* and *King David* have been largely forgotten by the modern comic-reading audience but Baker is the master of the quirky modern graphic novel form, able to distill his ideas so expertly into a single standalone story with verve and intelligence. This book went into four printings at DC which is fairly impressive. It is worth tracking down Baker's other OGNs as well as he has an approach like no other in the current field.

Why I Hate Saturn is an erudite and genuinely memorable illustrated tale by one of the most versatile giants of modern comics.

JOEL MEADOWS

4

Fearful Symmetry: Kraven's Last Hunt
Writer: JM DeMatteis
Artists: Mike Zeck and John Beatty
Colourists: Mike Zeck and Ian Tetrault
Letters: Rick Parker
Marvel

MARVEL
the AMAZING SPIDER-MAN
HERE LIES SPIDER-MAN
KRAVEN'S LAST HUNT
DEMATTEIS • ZECK

This is a modern Marvel classic. The 1980s saw a lot of different writers and artists subvert and reinvent the superhero genre. *Fearful Symmetry: Kraven's Last Hunt* takes one of Spider-man's most flamboyant foes, Sergei Kravinoff aka Kraven The Hunter, and place him in a darkly gothic tale. Kraven intends to bring down Spider-man by taking his place and sapping him of his power. He also manipulates the hero through one of his other adversaries, Vermin.

Kraven's Last Hunt is a very powerful and visceral Spider-man tale. Writer DeMatteis takes all of the classic Spidey elements like his relationship with Mary Jane and his obsession to be New York's saviour and ramps everything up to a new frenzied level. Zeck and Beatty offer a vintage Spider-man tale with a more modern twist visually. This is during Spider-man's black costume period and that fits in better with this rather grim story than his bright and breezy red suit would have done. Kraven is a suitably intense counterpoint for Spidey too, a villain who has this rather skewed sense of his own honour who believes that Spider-man is a totemic figure rather than just a man in a suit, with the spider representing an archetype which led to the destruction of his own life. He entombs Parker in a graveyard, which shows the extreme lengths he is prepared to go to in the name of his demented mission. It's fairly deep for a Spider-man comic and DeMatteis has always been a writer who has been able to tackle big issues in the pages of a four-colour adventure. He even manages to weave in a quote from William Blake's The Tyger poem, which the title *Fearful Symmetry* is taken from too.

You can draw comparisons here with *Daredevil: Born Again* although Kraven is a less vindictive figure than The Kingpin thanks to his misguided moral code. Also, *Fearful Symmetry* is at its core an urban horror story.

The story ends on a redemptive note but it is quite a draining ride for the reader. Spider-man has been responsible for a number of memorable comic stories but *Kraven's Last Hunt* is certainly the finest Spidey tale in the more modern era. DeMatteis has always been one of the best mainstream superhero writers and this tale proves his versatility.

Over thirty years old now, it has lost none of its punch and Zeck and Beatty are the perfect team to take DeMatteis' powerful vision and bring it to life on the page. **JOEL MEADOWS**

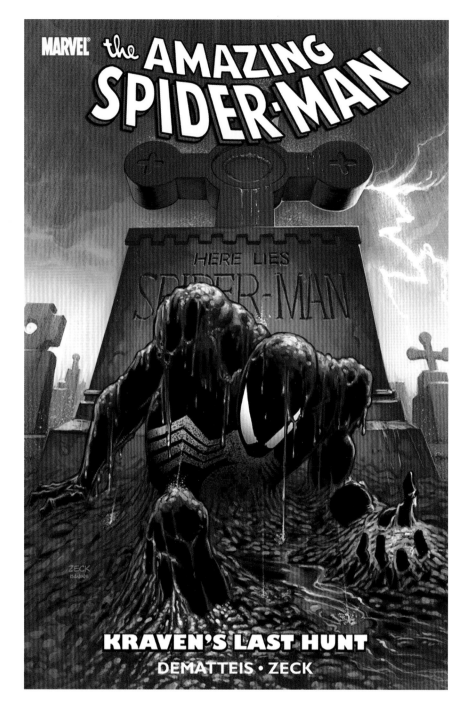

3

Fun Home
Writer/ artist: Alison Bechdel
Houghton Mifflin

While she might now be most famous for the Bechdel-Wallace test, a heuristic exploring gender representation in cinema, the book that really brought Alison Bechdel widespread attention and literary success is her autobiographic novel *Fun Home*.

First released in 2006 by mainstream book publisher Houghton Mifflin, *Fun Home* is a memoir told in a comic strip format that follows twin narrative threads; the author's lyrical exploration of her own sexual identity and her yearning desire to reconcile that identity with that of her dead father. Despite never having read any of Bechdel's work before *Fun Home*'s release, I was nevertheless very aware of her already significant body of work. Bechdel honed her cartoonist's craft while building up a fiercely loyal audience with her *Dykes to Watch Out For* strips. These were serialised in various gay and lesbian periodicals before publication in collected editions that had become a mainstay of the queer comix canon. It seemed clear to me that her first concerted foray into longform narrative comics would mark a significant evolution for her as a creative cartoonist, and that this was an evolution that I, as a someone interested in all aspects of comics as a medium, wanted to witness first-hand and at the earliest possible opportunity.

I was not disappointed. I bought my copy of the hardcover upon its release, rather than waiting for the cheaper paperback, and devoured it over the next few days. I'm not sure what I had expected going in. I had read a synopsis that indicated that the book's title referred to the funeral home that was as the intergenerational family business but was surprised that this aspect of their household life seemed so peripheral to both the book's narrative thrust and to the Bechdel family's finances. I suppose it is not unusual for people need to hold down multiple different jobs to make ends meet, and while I get that the title's allusion to fun houses and deceptive appearances in general, my sense that the name doesn't fit with the contents of the book still niggles at the back of my head each time I reread it.

As I say, the book's true focus is on Bechdel and her father, who was run over and killed by a delivery truck when she was 19, and her attempts to explore both their separate identities and shared relationship.

As an English graduate, the book's constant literary references certainly

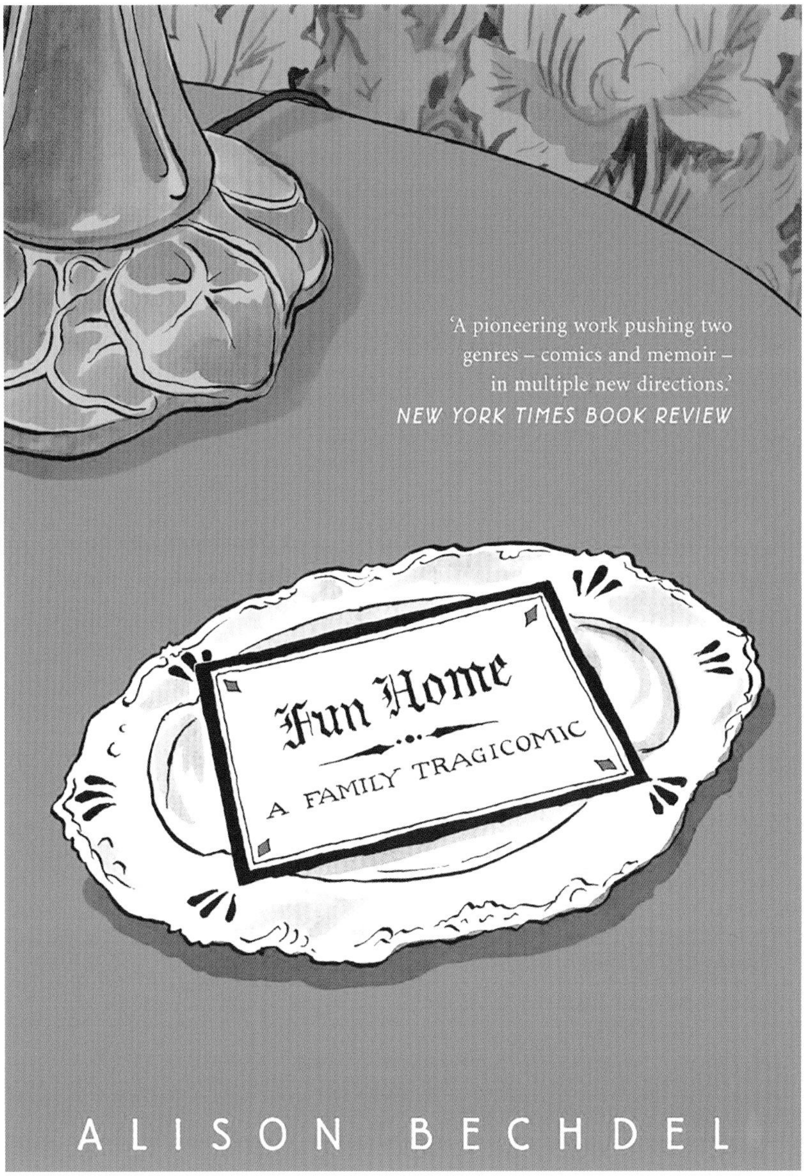
'A pioneering work pushing two genres – comics and memoir – in multiple new directions.'
NEW YORK TIMES BOOK REVIEW
Fun Home
A FAMILY TRAGICOMIC
ALISON BECHDEL

appealed to me, but they are not mere affectations on the part of the author. Rather, they betray Bechdel's anxiety and uncertainty, her reliance on interpretation and external sources to bolster and support her own subjectivity remembrances. Bechdel's almost pathological need for supporting evidence and artifacts is further echoed by her art, frequently recreating the photographic references from which she is constructing her narrative. Equally, the various texts quoted are illustrated in precise typographic detail right down to and including any typos that existed in the source material. The only place that Bechdel's painstakingly faithful recreation of these texts becomes slightly alienating is where Bechdel recreates her parents' handwritten letters. Cursive text is often beautiful, and it certainly conveys character while also adding visual variety, but I must confess that I occasionally struggled to make out these sections and frequently found myself wishing that the author had simply quoted these epistles as herself in her own in-strip voice with its more legible standard comics lettering.

Isolated legibility issues aside, *Fun Home* remains an incredibly engaging read. One that conjures up the visceral experience of growing up with in a dysfunctional family in a small rural American town where societal expectations are expected to trump any aspirations that run counter to small-town convention.

Post publication, Fun Home became an instant hit with readers and critics alike, claiming a spot on the coveted *New York Times* Best Seller list as well as spawning a successful Tony-winning musical adaptation. But perhaps *Fun Home*'s most sincere recommendation comes not from its proponents but from its detractors, who have campaigned on various spurious grounds to get the book banned, withdrawn or otherwise made unavailable to the reading public. If there are folks who want to stop you getting hold of a book, that's got be a great sign that a book well worth reading. **ROBERT CAVE**

2

Nick Fury Agent Of S.H.I.E.L.D
Writers: Stan Lee, Roy Thomas
Artist: Jim Steranko
Marvel

Nick Fury's strip in *Strange Tales* had already been going for some fifteen issues before writer Stan Lee and artist Jack Kirby decided to move on from the title. With Colonel (formerly Sergeant) Fury and his own counter-intelligence agency S.H.I.E.L.D. very much a product of their time, Kirby's concepts had already drawn upon spy novels and movies, with outlandish yet innovative ideas, such as the LMDs (Life Model Decoys). When John Buscema, who had just returned to Marvel in 1966, was handed the artistic reins in *Strange Tales* 150, he was more than a little irked that he had to slavishly follow Kirby's layouts. The decision was then made to hire an untried newcomer to take over pencilling the strip that occupied one half of the title (the other half being the Doctor Strange run) – a certain Jim Steranko.

Like many artists who arrived at Marvel in the mid to late 1960s, Steranko began as a Kirby clone, producing work that was a somewhat primitive take on the King's efforts. However within ten issues of the strip Steranko, who had remarkably been given the scripting duties by Lee as well, had not just made Nick Fury his own, but had surpassed Kirby's vision, channelling the veteran artist (many Kirby tropes were retained throughout) while maturing rapidly as a storyteller. From issue 160 to 168, after which Fury got his own iconic book, Steranko threw everything he had at the series, seamlessly splicing op art, Dali-esque surrealism and cinematic sweep with the super

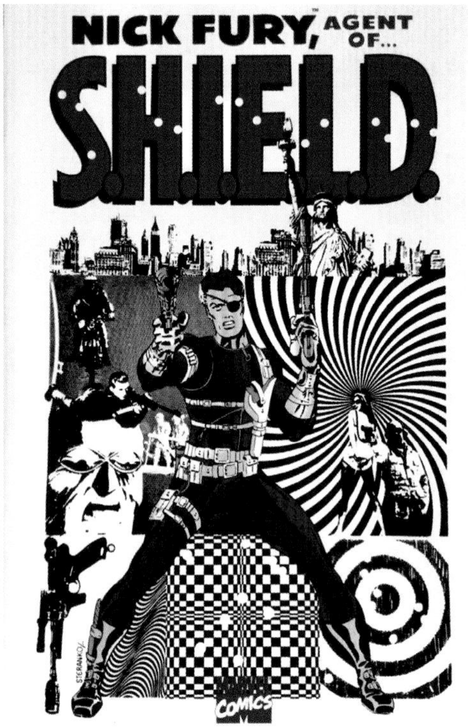
NICK FURY, AGENT OF...
S.H.I.E.L.D.
STERANKO
COMICS

heroics, effectively turning the strip into a psychedelic, widescreen spectacle. Steranko, who was arguably the first branded "superstar" artist at Marvel (despite Kirby's pre-eminence) had soaked up his mentors' work within a year, transcending it while remaining faithful to its spirit. Out of nowhere he inhabited the soul of the medium.

Of course, there is the familiar 1960s daftness in the series – Fury himself having barely changed from his wartime iteration, chewing stogies and using more or less the same expressions and cadences as the Fantastic Four's Ben Grimm, even while battling the supreme Hydra, the Yellow Claw or A.I.M. What is fascinating looking at this book from a pop cultural perspective is how it matched the development of big budget espionage thrillers such as Bond, drawing directly from them (one scene has Fury falling through the floor and into the clutches of a "monster celaphopod", straight out of the pages of *Dr. No*) and in turn influencing them. Steranko may not have created Fu Manchu analogue the Yellow Claw, or Hydra, a S.P.E.C.T.R.E. copy, but he made the antagonists, like everything else, his own, putting Fury in a skin-tight combat suit replete with gizmos and gadgets that regularly come to his rescue with seconds to spare, while battling giant, baroque robots like the Dreadnought or the Yellow Claw in armour. And then there was the glitz, glamour and of course plenty of women in tight costumes, especially love interest Countess Valentina De Fontaine (she had to be called something like that!), swiping from the Avengers television show, rock poster and album iconography, and photomontages.

Steranko was a magpie steeped in comic history who drew from every conceivable source to produce the ultimate 60s escapist fantasy – dated certainly, and as distant from reality as one could get, but these are positives in what is the most envelope-pushing, bravura and filmic Silver Age series of all. Worth checking out even if you're not all that familiar with comics.

ANDREW COLMAN

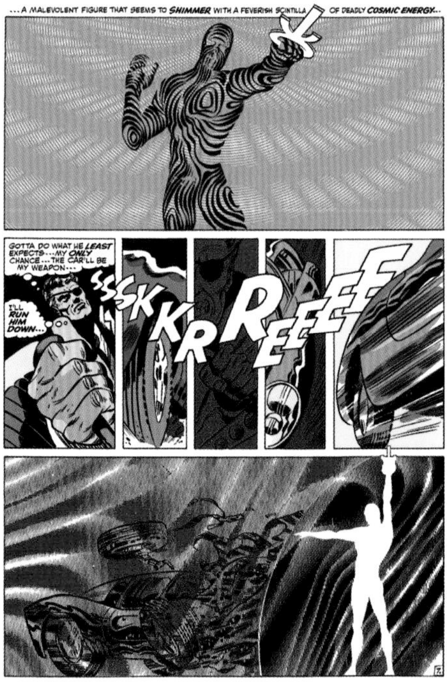
...A MALEVOLENT FIGURE THAT SEEMS TO SHIMMER WITH A FEVERISH SCINTILLA OF DEADLY COSMIC ENERGY...
GOTTA DO WHAT HE LEAST EXPECTS...MY ONLY CHANCE...THE CAR'LL BE MY WEAPON...
I'LL RUN HIM DOWN...
SSSKKRRREEEEF

1

Gemma Bovery
Writer/ artist: Posy Simmonds
Jonathan Cape

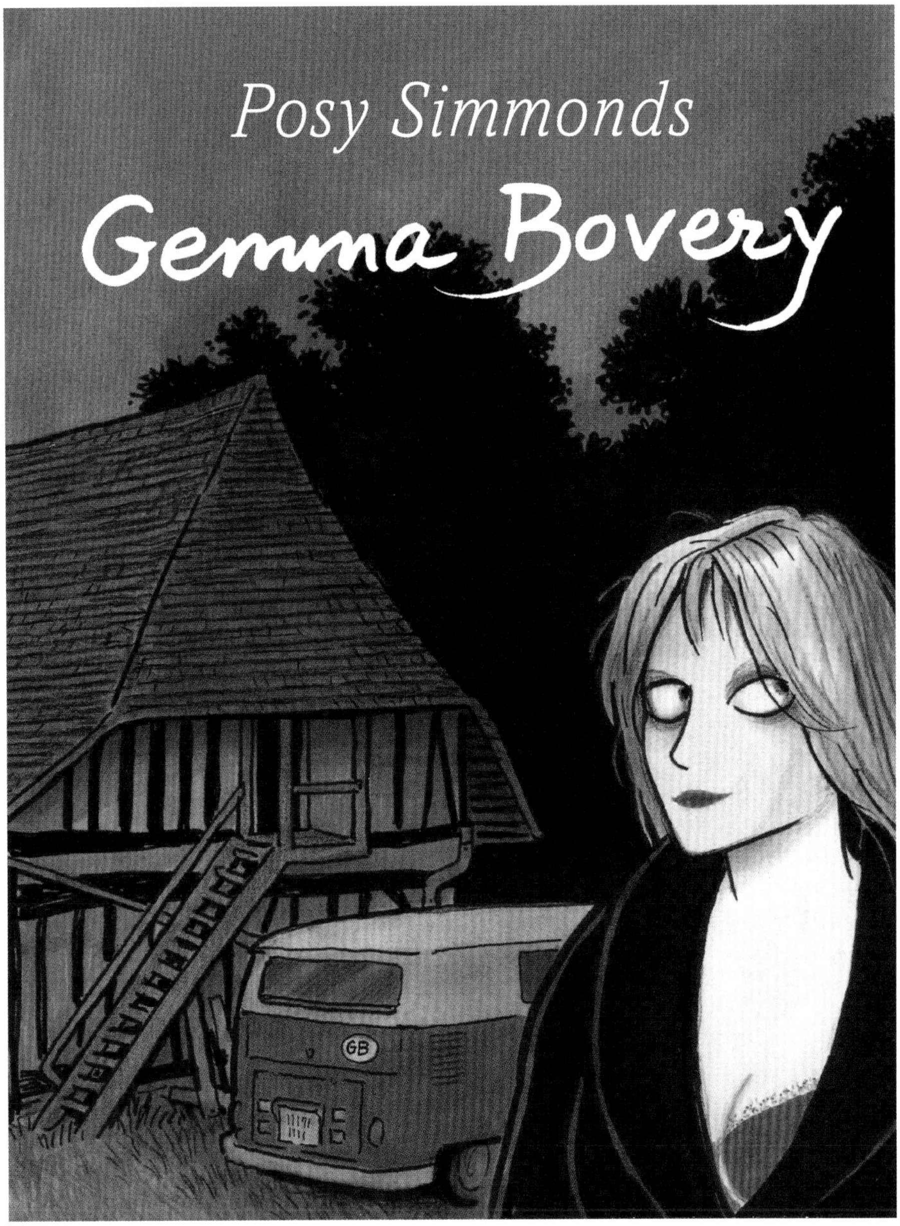
Posy Simmonds
Gemma Bovery
GB

The doyenne of British cartoonists and illustrators, Posy Simmonds MBE is one of the UK's greatest, most successful living comic creators. Her works' diverse audience spans from the very young to the mildly decrepit and she found a natural home for her work in the Guardian newspaper, where she penned a decade-long strip featuring the everyday middle class, middle-aged misadventures of Mrs Wendy Weber and her friends and family. A further decade on, Simmonds returned to *the Guardian* with *Gemma Bovery*, a sophisticated and intricately plotted longform comic that was her most ambitious work up to that date. Its title and narrative heavily references, and playfully parallels, Gustave Flaubert's 19th century novel of provincial manners, *Madam Bovary*.

Partially composed during its serialised run and published a page at a time, the narrative hangs together incredibly well, bolstered in part by Simmond's willingness to employ a wide variety of narrative devices and multiple narrators, juxtaposing the comic strip elements with more standalone illustrations and separate larger blocks of text from Gemma's diaries. In addition to this playfulness, Simmonds also has great fun toying with her audience's expectations, raised by her volume's various literary allusions. How does Simmonds' titular Gemma relate to Flaubert's Emma Bovary, whose disastrous love affairs and spending habits ultimately lead to her downfall? From the book's very opening we know that Gemma is dead, and the rest of the story is leaden with an inescapable sense of impending doom. However, Simmonds tale is not simply some rote retelling of classic literature but a new story in-its-own-right, one that swaps the unrealistic romantic expectations and taste for luxury of Flaubert's heroine with a gentle satire on the morals and manners of the expatriate English middle class attempting to live their dreams and escape the confines of English social convention in Northern France.

As a reader, I have long been more faithful and consistent in buying comics in various shapes and forms and somewhat less habitual in my newspaper purchasing. Consequently, I missed great chunks of the story in its initial serialised run. However, I was keen to read the narrative as a whole and so sought out the somewhat unusually shaped paperback collection as soon as it was released in 1999. Its tall yet slightly shallower form marks it out from every other book on my shelf, but its formalistic and narrative inconformity are a significant part of the book's charm. While American comics have influenced and to some extent come to set expectations about the form and content of comic books and graphic novels across the English-speaking world, Simmonds work comes out of a very different cultural milieu, drawing on a very different set of traditions influences and cultural preoccupations that are both and self-consciously literary and equally self-consciously English. Her book is awash with hide-bound English class obsessions that are all-the-more apparent when contrasted with the lives and obsessions of the book's French characters.

Simmonds' illustration style is also incredibly expressive, mixing grey washes and graphite textures over the simple inked pencils of her earlier output, giving the whole book its own distinctive look. The silvery greys that shade into darker tones echo the moral ambiguity of both the title character and its narrator, the French baker Joubert, who's interest in Gemma is at least semi-prurient. And then there is Gemma herself, a young and beautiful woman very much in the mould of Princess Diana; they both share the same heavy-lidded eyes and methods of coping with their respective unhappy marriages.

In 2014 the book spawned a successful film adaptation of the same name starring Gemma Arterton in the title role. In the *gulp* almost quarter century since its initial publication, *Gemma Bovery* remains a defiantly unusual book – one that gloriously captures a now-vanished pre-Brexit world in which France was still viewed as a desirable and accessible place for Brits to live. Well worth perusing.
ROBERT CAVE

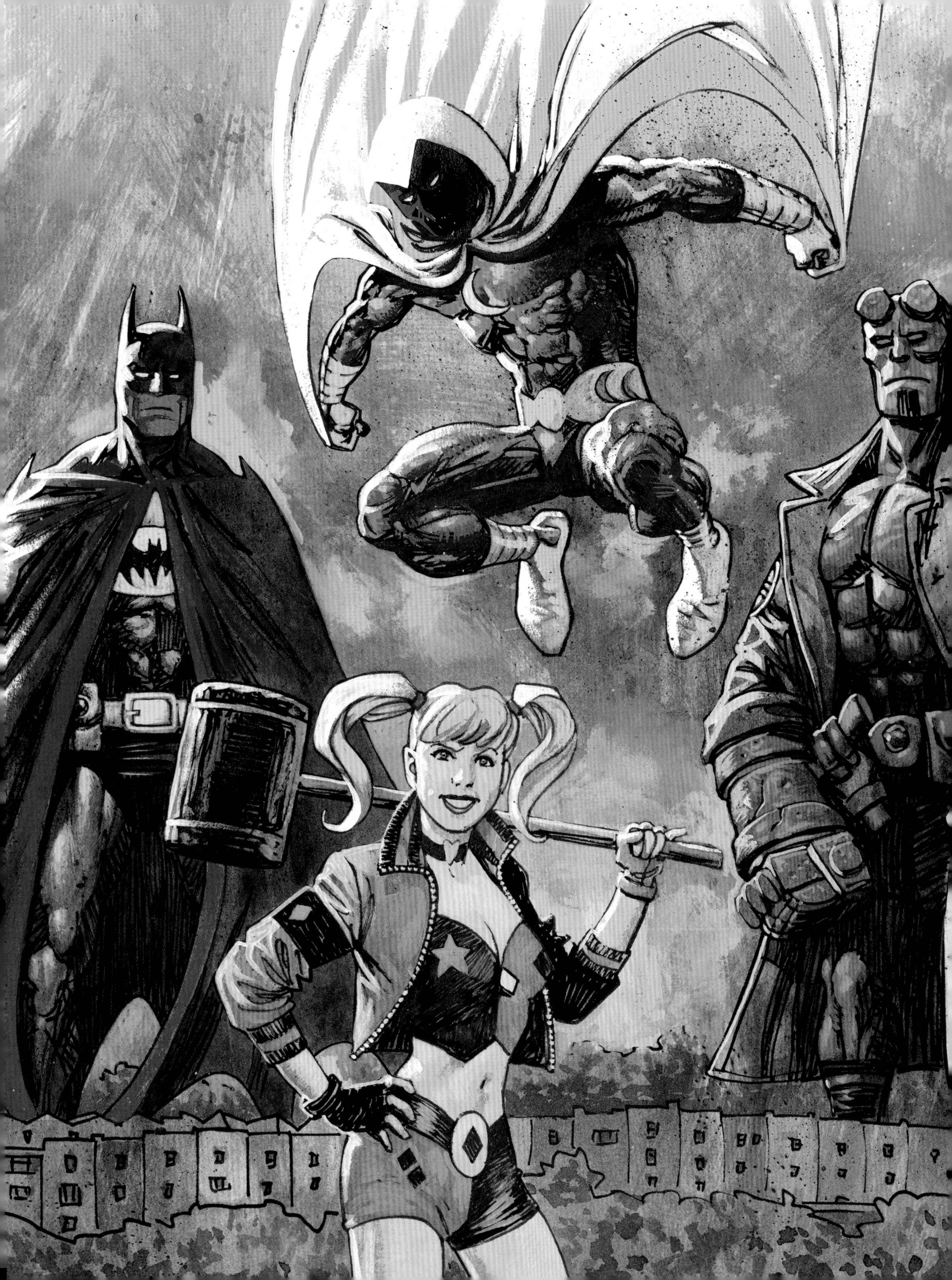

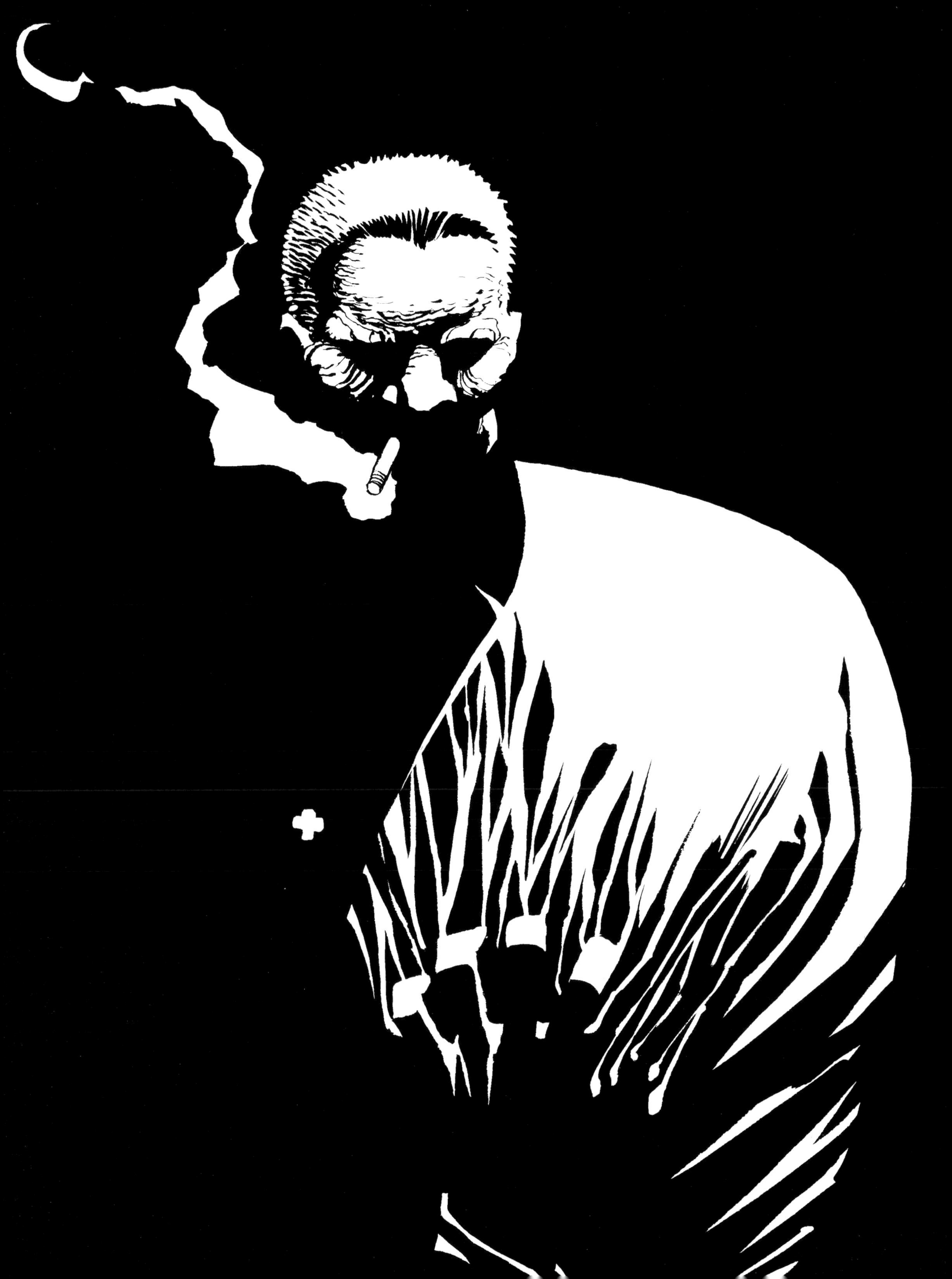

20 YEARS IN THE MAKING...

Tripwire editor-in-chief and editor of this book Joel Meadows introduces the Sherlock Holmes And The Empire Builders comic strip, with three short comic stories printed here including the debut of The Secret Files Of Oswald Mosley...

SHERLOCK HOLMES
THE EMPIRE BUILDERS

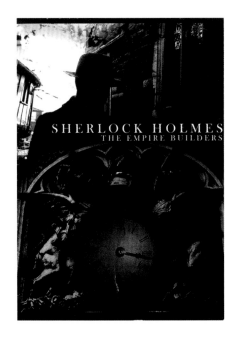

[Scott Braden] asked me if I had any comic series that might be appropriate for his Lost Tales series and I thought of Sherlock Holmes and The Empire Builders. After chatting to him I decided that it was time to have another go at getting this series out there.

The three *Sherlock Holmes and The Empire Builders* strips are over twenty years in the making. This strip began life with another artist the very beginning of this century. I had always enjoyed Sherlock Holmes and I was also a fan of alternate history tales by the likes of Michael Moorcock and Bryan Talbot.

I can't remember how I was first introduced to Andy Bennett or by who but we clicked instantly. We put together a proposal which included fake travel posters, fake newspaper articles from the world of the *Empire Builders* and a short introducing the series. We sent it round to a number of publishers but sadly despite our efforts, no one took the bait. So I stuck it in a drawer and forgot about it.

Fast-forward to 2018 and my friend Scott Braden had returned to write for us and contribute to *Tripwire*. He asked me if I had any comic series that might be appropriate for his Lost Tales series and I thought of *Sherlock*

WHITECHAPEL 3978 , PLEASE.
THERE MUST BE SOME WAY THAT I CAN MAKE THINGS RIGHT.

SHERLOCK HOLMES
AND THE EMPIRE BUILDERS
UNCOMMON GOOD
WRITTEN BY: JOEL MEADOWS
DRAWN BY: ANDY BENNETT
LETTERED BY: DAN O'CONNELL
WITH THANKS TO
THE WORKS OF ARTHUR CONAN DOYLE
THERE'S SOMETHING I NEED YOU TO DO.
WATSON'S SON IS BEING COMMITTED TODAY.
I WANT YOU TO PERSONALLY OVERSEE HIS INCARCERATION.
WHAT IF ANYONE TRIES ANYTHING? I'D FEEL A LOT HAPPIER IF I COULD TAKE ONE OF SIX'S MEN.
THAT'S OUT OF THE QUESTION, I'M AFRAID. WITH EUSTON'S SECONDMENT TO INDIA AND THE SECURITY SERVICES IN NEED OF FRESH BLOOD AFTER THE WHOLE HOLMES DEBACLE, SIX CAN'T REALLY SPARE ANY MEN.
YOU UNDERSTAND THE IMPORTANCE OF THIS TASK, DON'T YOU?
OF COURSE, SIR.
WHERE IS WATSON BEING TAKEN TO?
HE'S BEING TRANSPORTED TO THE COLONEY HATCH ASYLUM. IT'S ISOLATED AND THE SECURITY THERE IS THE BEST IN THE SOUTH OF ENGLAND. ANYWAY, WE DON'T HAVE TO WORRY ABOUT THE REBELS TRYING ANYTHING AFTER THE THRASHING WE GAVE THEM IN THE TEMPLE.

I HATE THIS FILTHY RAG.
SOMETIMES, THOUGH, IT HAS THE POWER TO SURPRISE YOU.

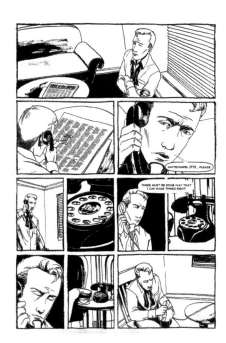

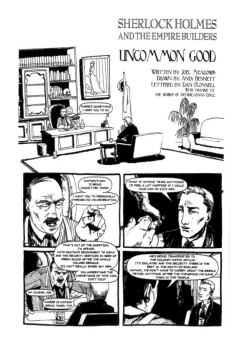

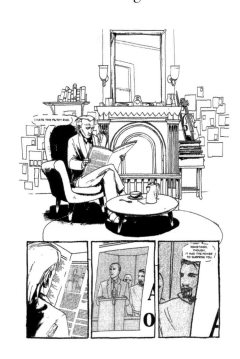

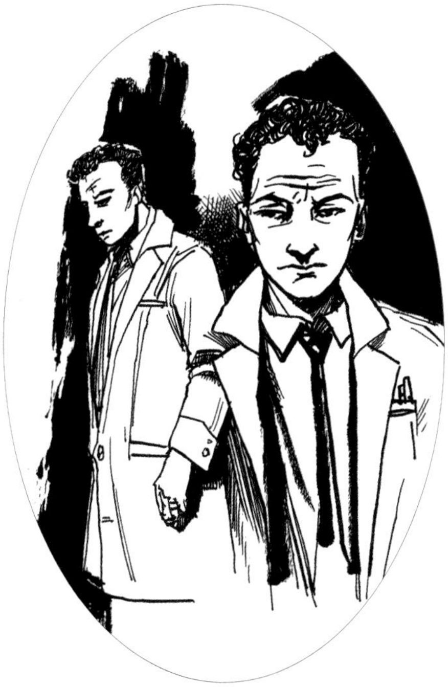
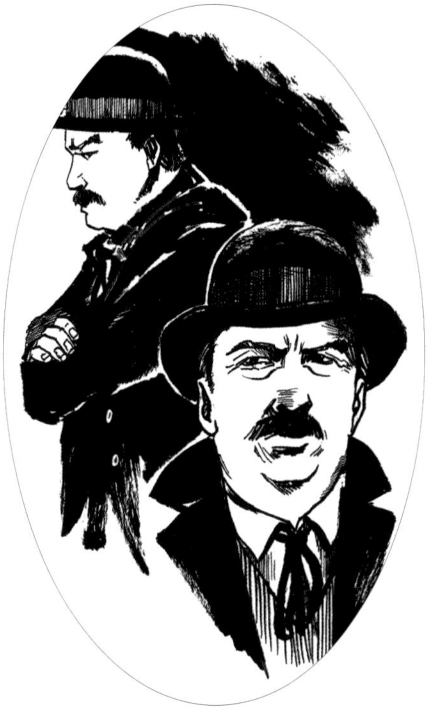
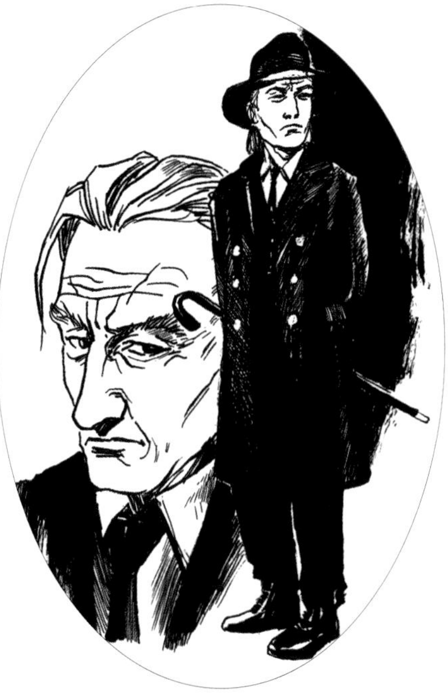

Holmes and The Empire Builders. After chatting to him I decided that it was time to have another go at getting this series out there. So in December 2020, we ran The House That Crime Built in our Tripwire winter 2020/2021 print special. It was very well-received so Prey followed in the print edition that was published in November 2021. This third short makes its debut here in our Tripwire 30 anniversary book.

I am very proud to see all three of the shorts together for the first time in print and Sherlock Holmes and The Empire Builders is my attempt to bring together everything that I enjoy in speculative fiction, all anchored by one of the most important, iconic fictional creations of all time. Andy Bennett's work continues to amaze me and one of the highlights of the past two difficult, strange years has been seeing new pages in from him. I am very lucky to have him as my artistic collaborator on this strip. His work on the third short is even better than its two predecessors.

The plan is to publish a full length graphic novel featuring Holmes and co next year and so these shorts have been a springboard to this. I only hope that we have been doing justice to Arthur Conan Doyle's richly realised world while bringing something new to proceedings. As Sherlock Holmes himself would say: The game's afoot again...

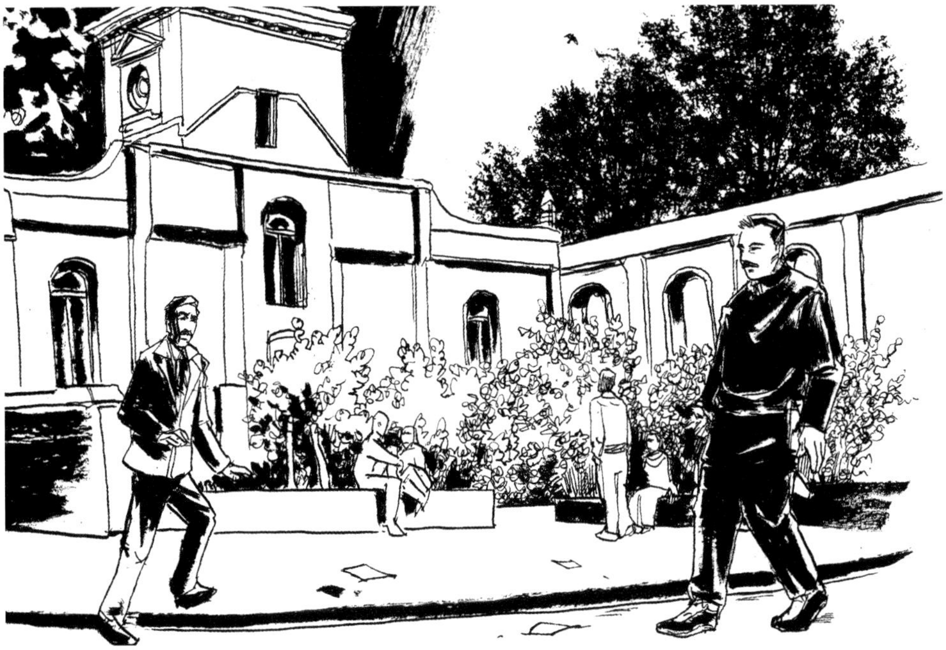
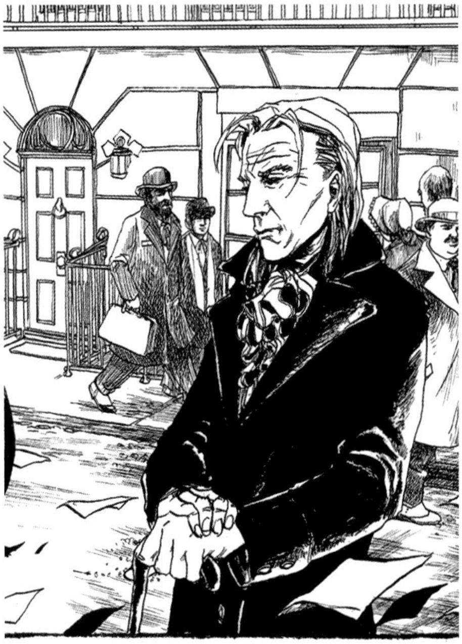

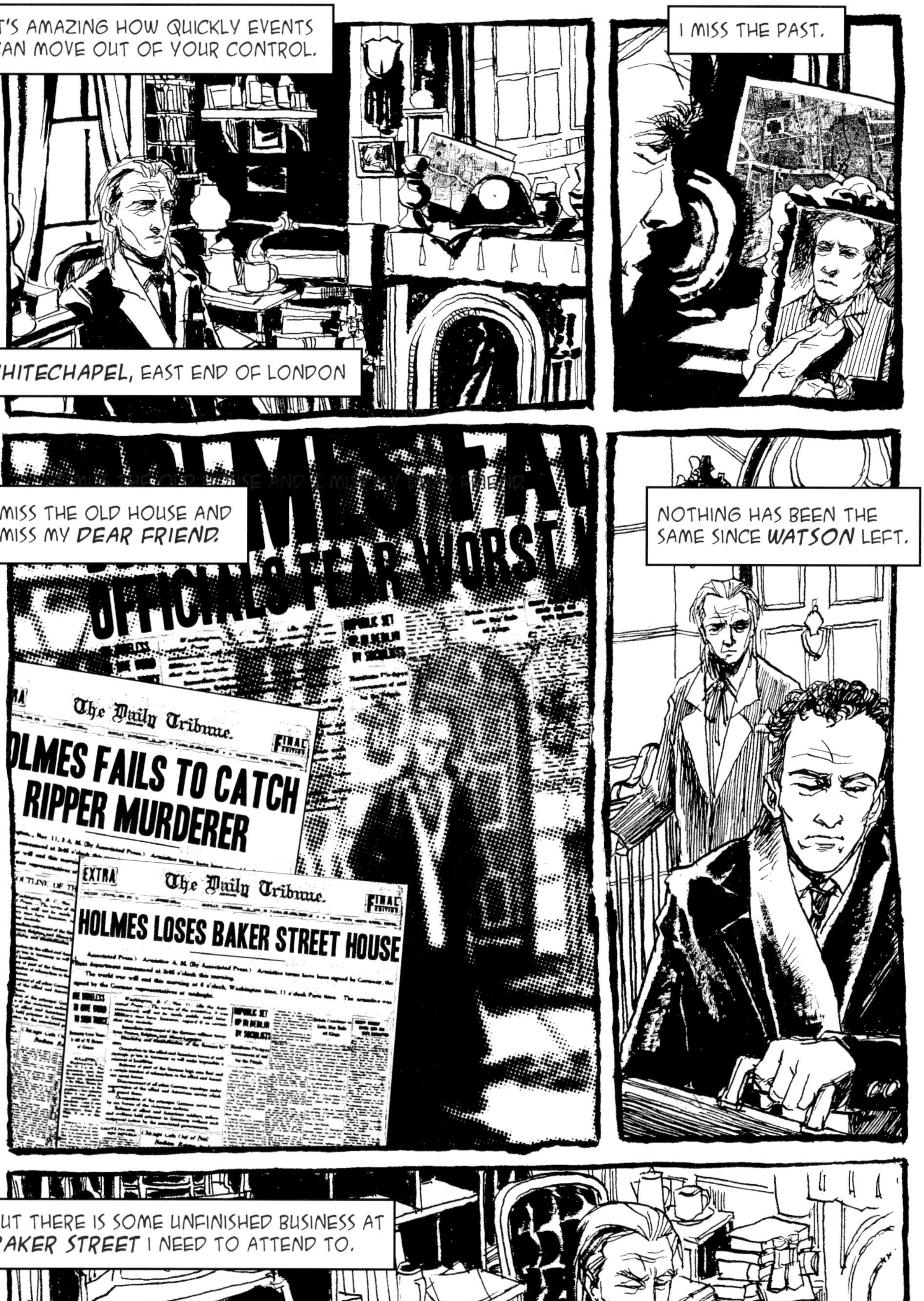
IT'S AMAZING HOW QUICKLY EVENTS CAN MOVE OUT OF YOUR CONTROL.
WHITECHAPEL, EAST END OF LONDON
I MISS THE PAST.
I MISS THE OLD HOUSE AND I MISS MY DEAR FRIEND.
OFFICIALS FEAR WORST
The Daily Tribune
OLMES FAILS TO CATCH RIPPER MURDERER
EXTRA
The Daily Tribune
HOLMES LOSES BAKER STREET HOUSE
NOTHING HAS BEEN THE SAME SINCE WATSON LEFT.
BUT THERE IS SOME UNFINISHED BUSINESS AT BAKER STREET I NEED TO ATTEND TO.

SHERLOCK HOLMES AND THE EMPIRE BUILDERS
THE HOUSE THAT CRIME BUILT

STORY BY JOEL MEADOWS ART BY ANDY BENNETT

WITH A TIP OF THE HAT TO THE WORK OF ARTHUR CONAN DOYLE

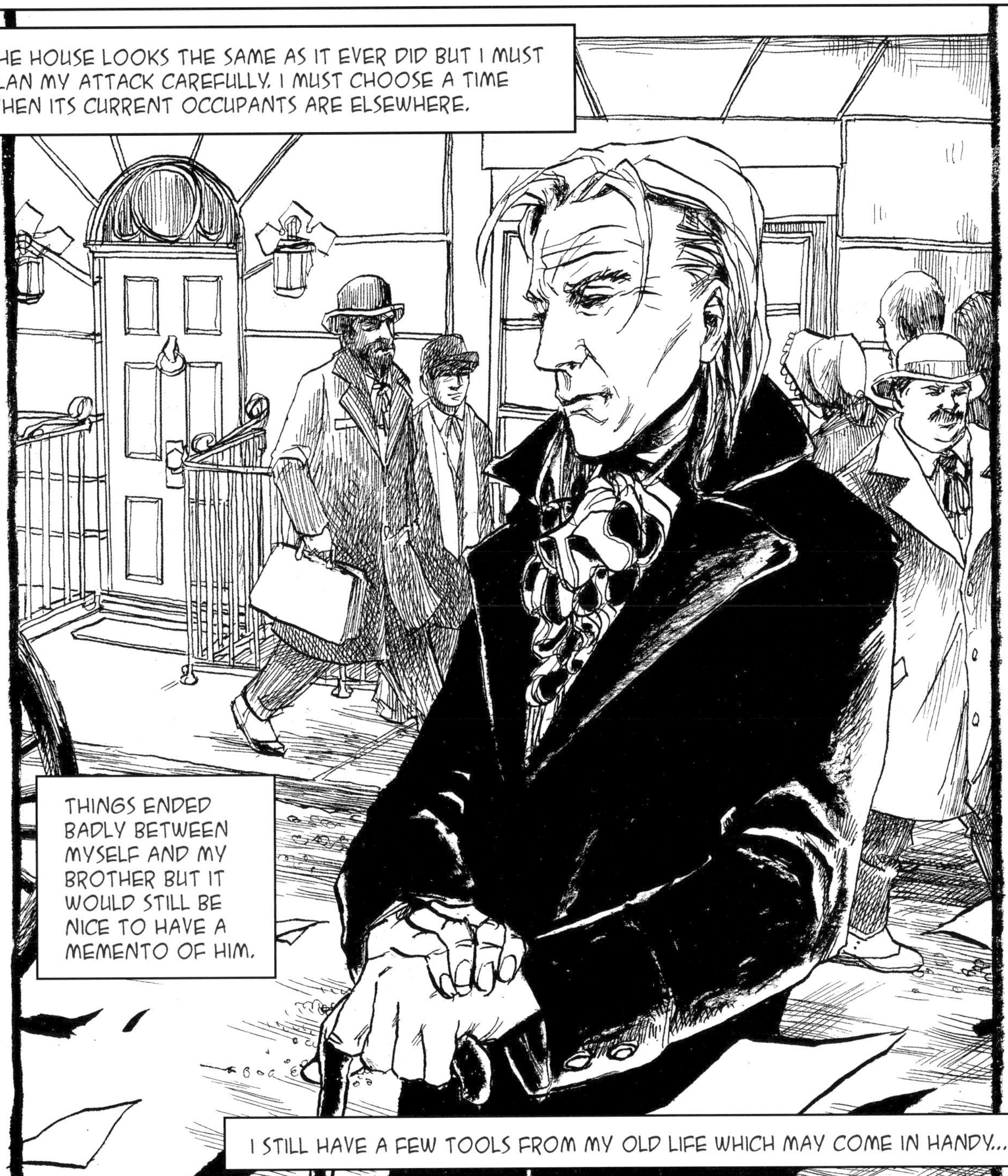
THE HOUSE LOOKS THE SAME AS IT EVER DID BUT I MUST PLAN MY ATTACK CAREFULLY. I MUST CHOOSE A TIME WHEN ITS CURRENT OCCUPANTS ARE ELSEWHERE.
THINGS ENDED BADLY BETWEEN MYSELF AND MY BROTHER BUT IT WOULD STILL BE NICE TO HAVE A MEMENTO OF HIM.
I STILL HAVE A FEW TOOLS FROM MY OLD LIFE WHICH MAY COME IN HANDY...

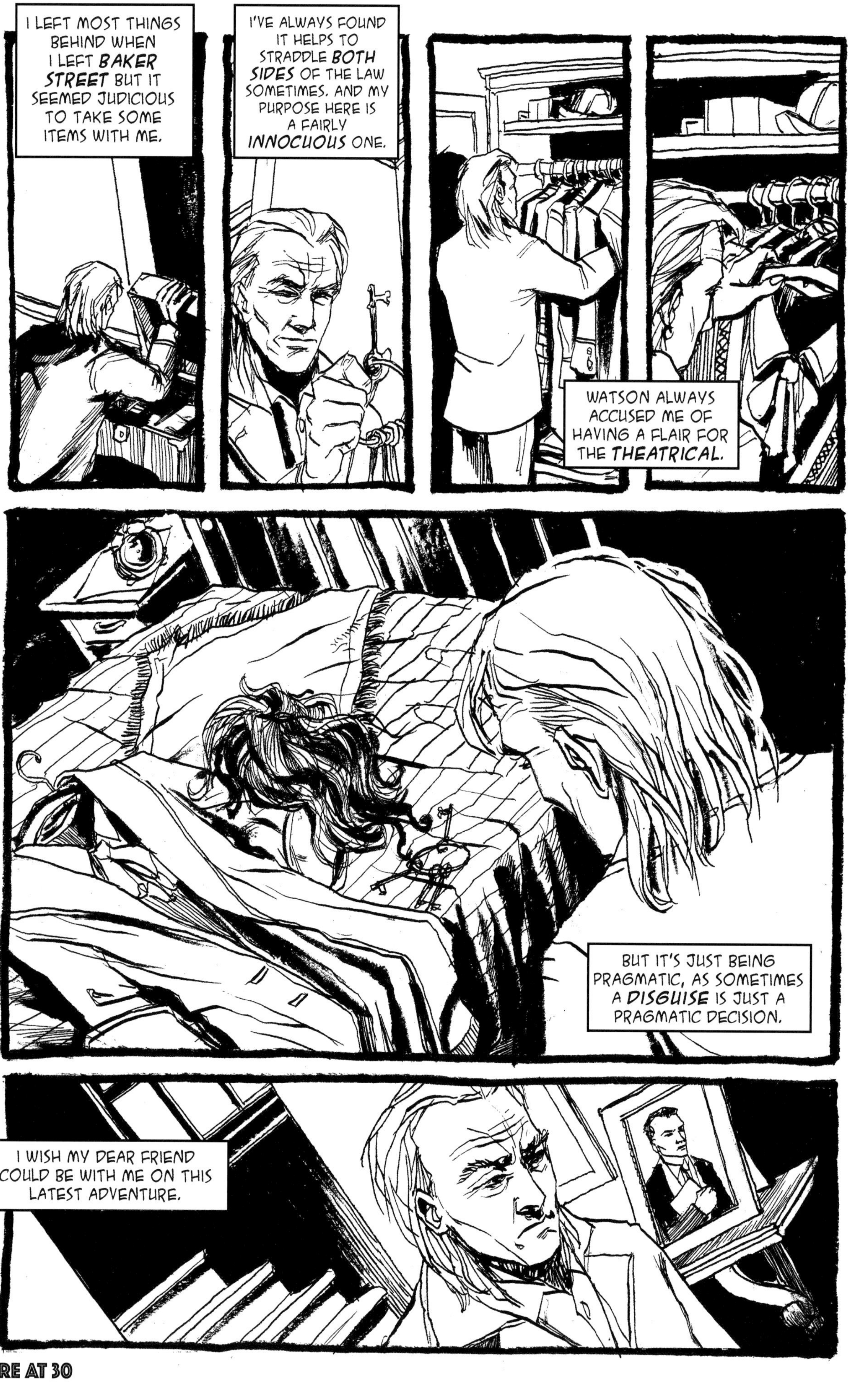
I LEFT MOST THINGS BEHIND WHEN I LEFT BAKER STREET BUT IT SEEMED JUDICIOUS TO TAKE SOME ITEMS WITH ME.
I'VE ALWAYS FOUND IT HELPS TO STRADDLE BOTH SIDES OF THE LAW SOMETIMES. AND MY PURPOSE HERE IS A FAIRLY INNOCUOUS ONE.
WATSON ALWAYS ACCUSED ME OF HAVING A FLAIR FOR THE THEATRICAL.
BUT IT'S JUST BEING PRAGMATIC, AS SOMETIMES A DISGUISE IS JUST A PRAGMATIC DECISION.
I WISH MY DEAR FRIEND COULD BE WITH ME ON THIS LATEST ADVENTURE.

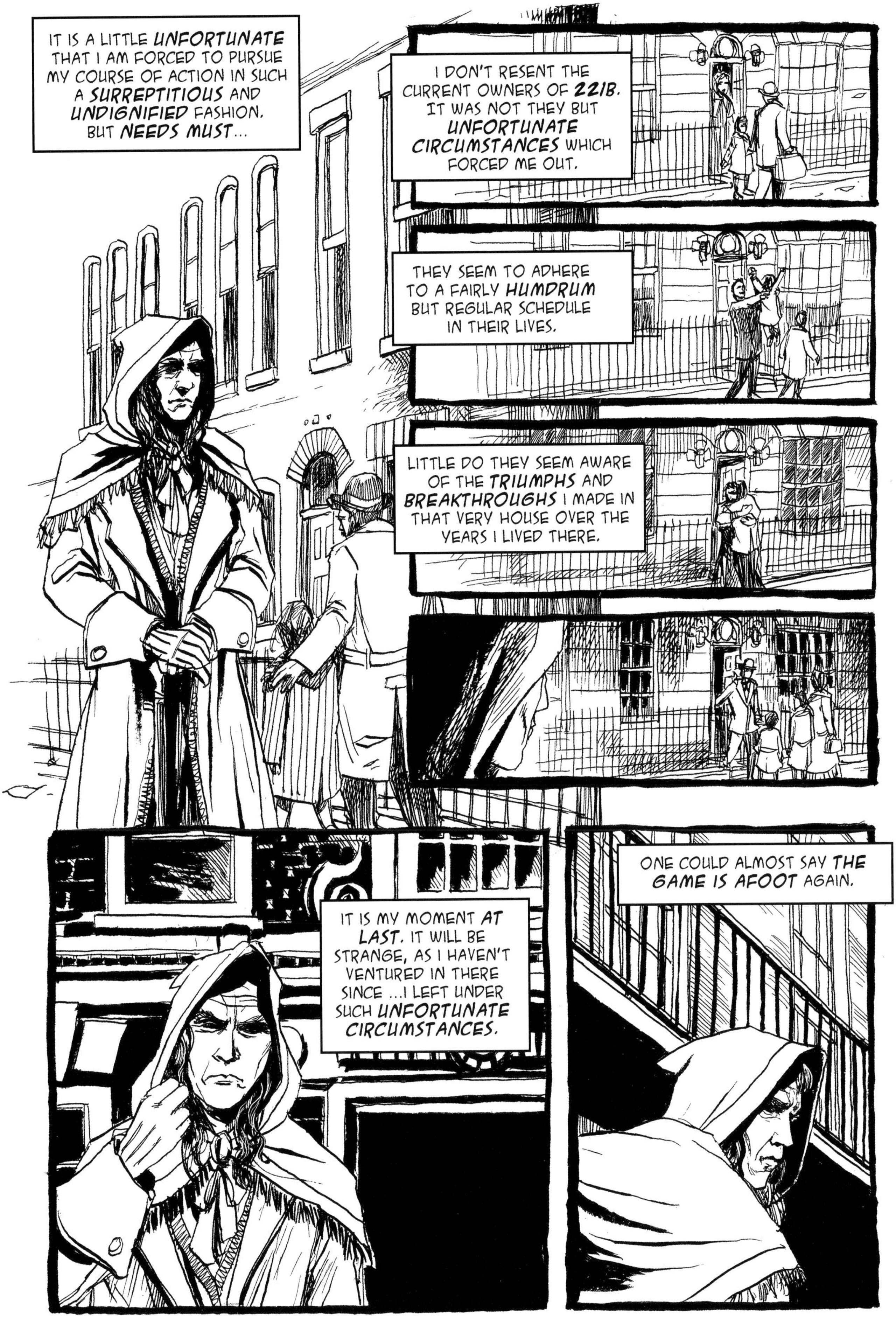
IT IS A LITTLE UNFORTUNATE THAT I AM FORCED TO PURSUE MY COURSE OF ACTION IN SUCH A SURREPTITIOUS AND UNDIGNIFIED FASHION. BUT NEEDS MUST...
I DON'T RESENT THE CURRENT OWNERS OF 221B. IT WAS NOT THEY BUT UNFORTUNATE CIRCUMSTANCES WHICH FORCED ME OUT.
THEY SEEM TO ADHERE TO A FAIRLY HUMDRUM BUT REGULAR SCHEDULE IN THEIR LIVES.
LITTLE DO THEY SEEM AWARE OF THE TRIUMPHS AND BREAKTHROUGHS I MADE IN THAT VERY HOUSE OVER THE YEARS I LIVED THERE.
IT IS MY MOMENT AT LAST. IT WILL BE STRANGE, AS I HAVEN'T VENTURED IN THERE SINCE ...I LEFT UNDER SUCH UNFORTUNATE CIRCUMSTANCES.
ONE COULD ALMOST SAY THE GAME IS AFOOT AGAIN.

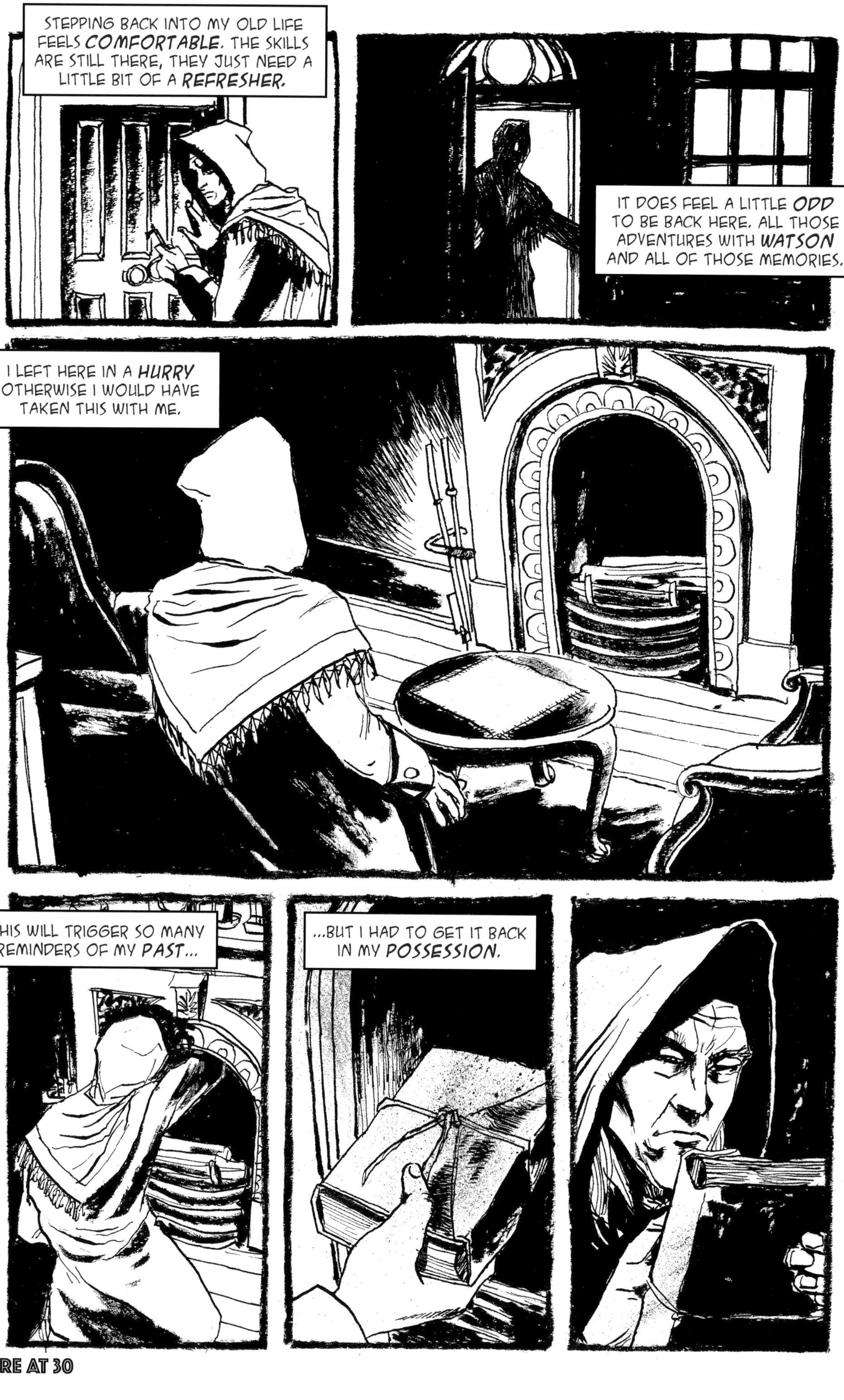
STEPPING BACK INTO MY OLD LIFE FEELS COMFORTABLE. THE SKILLS ARE STILL THERE, THEY JUST NEED A LITTLE BIT OF A REFRESHER.
IT DOES FEEL A LITTLE ODD TO BE BACK HERE. ALL THOSE ADVENTURES WITH WATSON AND ALL OF THOSE MEMORIES.
I LEFT HERE IN A HURRY OTHERWISE I WOULD HAVE TAKEN THIS WITH ME.
THIS WILL TRIGGER SO MANY REMINDERS OF MY PAST...
...BUT I HAD TO GET IT BACK IN MY POSSESSION.

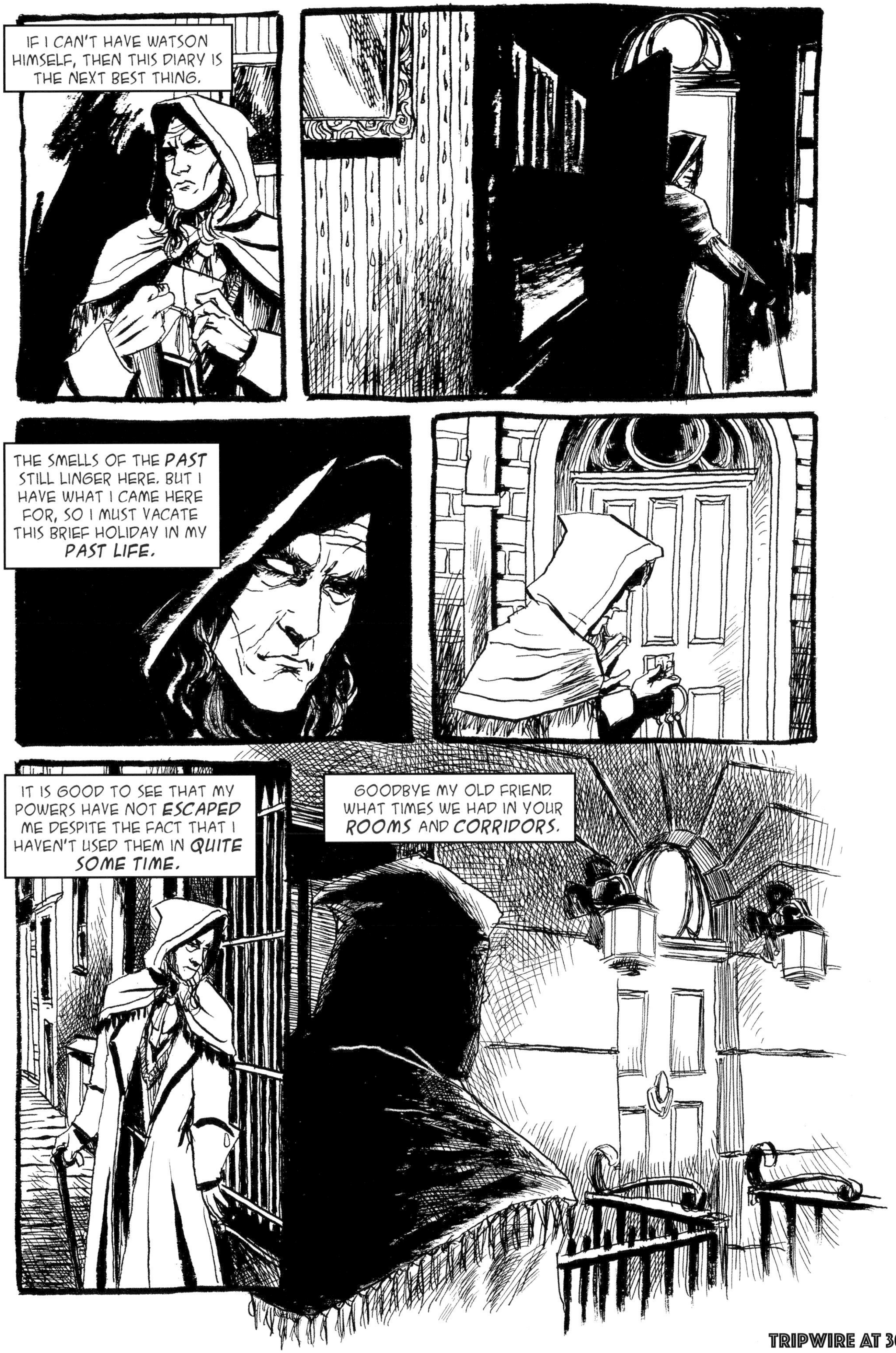
IF I CAN'T HAVE WATSON HIMSELF, THEN THIS DIARY IS THE NEXT BEST THING.
THE SMELLS OF THE PAST STILL LINGER HERE. BUT I HAVE WHAT I CAME HERE FOR, SO I MUST VACATE THIS BRIEF HOLIDAY IN MY PAST LIFE.
IT IS GOOD TO SEE THAT MY POWERS HAVE NOT ESCAPED ME DESPITE THE FACT THAT I HAVEN'T USED THEM IN QUITE SOME TIME.
GOODBYE MY OLD FRIEND. WHAT TIMES WE HAD IN YOUR ROOMS AND CORRIDORS.

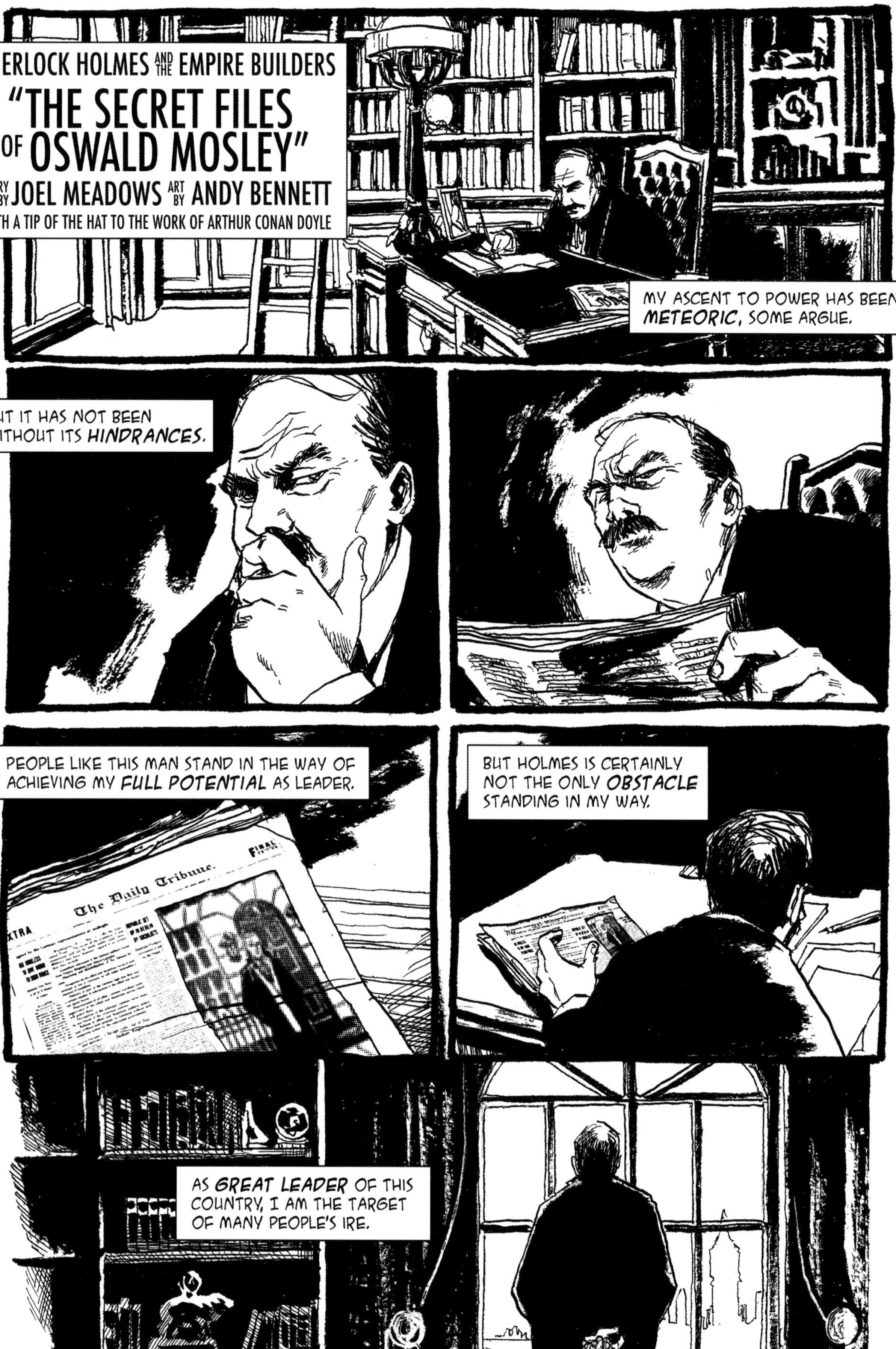
SHERLOCK HOLMES AND THE EMPIRE BUILDERS
"THE SECRET FILES OF OSWALD MOSLEY"
STORY BY JOEL MEADOWS ART BY ANDY BENNETT
WITH A TIP OF THE HAT TO THE WORK OF ARTHUR CONAN DOYLE
MY ASCENT TO POWER HAS BEEN METEORIC, SOME ARGUE.
BUT IT HAS NOT BEEN WITHOUT ITS HINDRANCES.
PEOPLE LIKE THIS MAN STAND IN THE WAY OF ACHIEVING MY FULL POTENTIAL AS LEADER.
The Daily Tribune.
BUT HOLMES IS CERTAINLY NOT THE ONLY OBSTACLE STANDING IN MY WAY.
AS GREAT LEADER OF THIS COUNTRY, I AM THE TARGET OF MANY PEOPLE'S IRE.

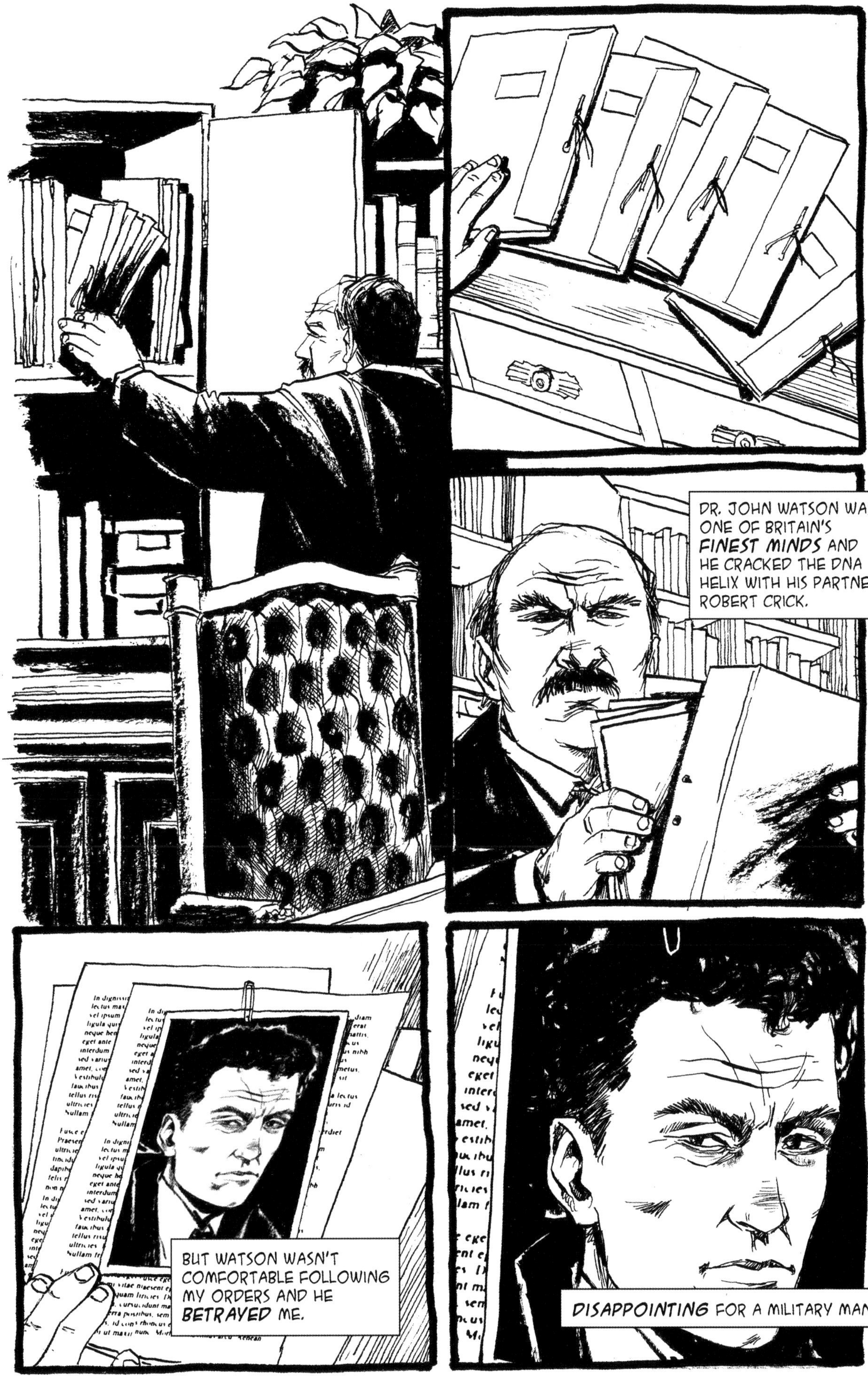
DR. JOHN WATSON WAS ONE OF BRITAIN'S FINEST MINDS AND HE CRACKED THE DNA HELIX WITH HIS PARTNER ROBERT CRICK.
BUT WATSON WASN'T COMFORTABLE FOLLOWING MY ORDERS AND HE BETRAYED ME.
DISAPPOINTING FOR A MILITARY MAN.

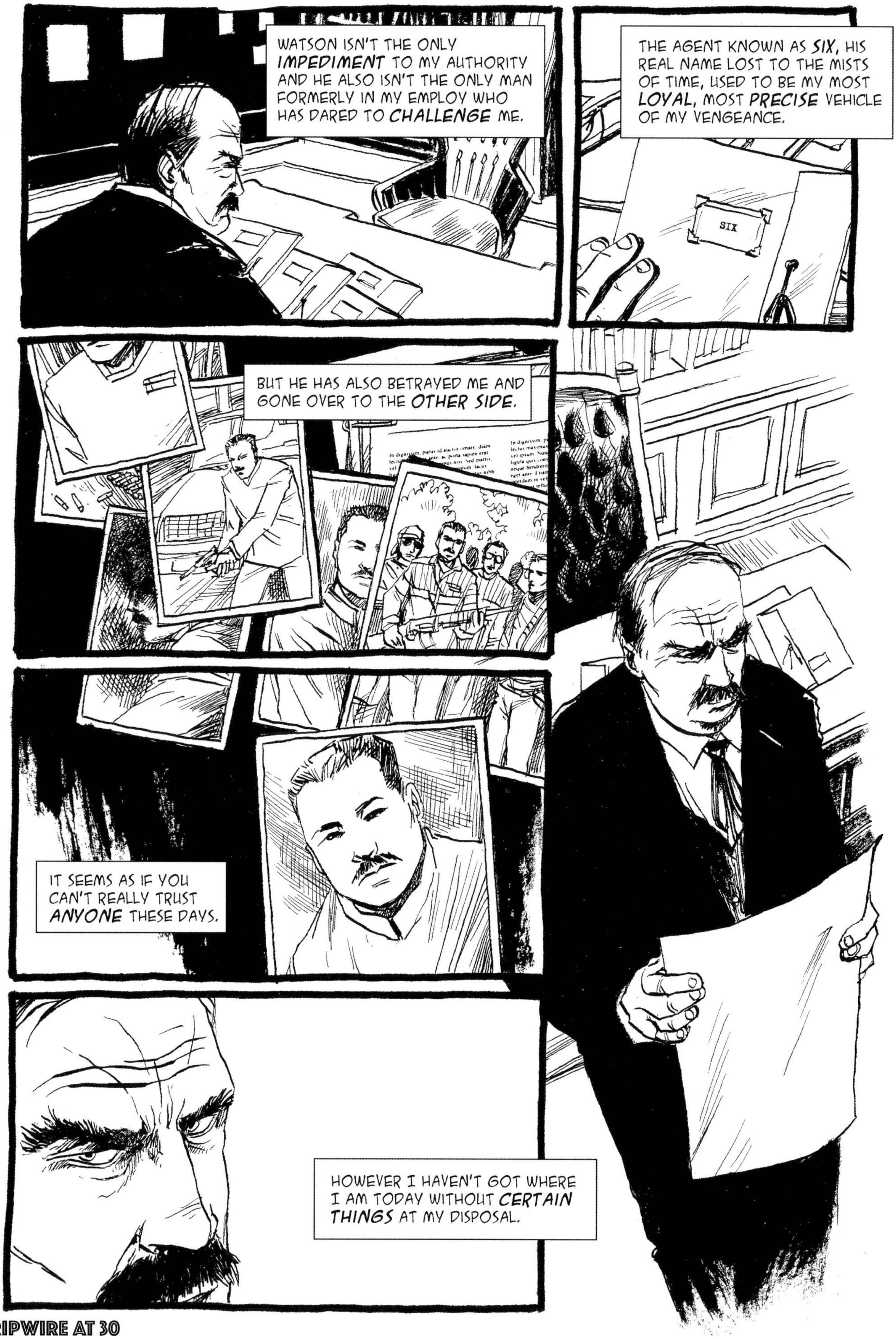
WATSON ISN'T THE ONLY IMPEDIMENT TO MY AUTHORITY AND HE ALSO ISN'T THE ONLY MAN FORMERLY IN MY EMPLOY WHO HAS DARED TO CHALLENGE ME.
THE AGENT KNOWN AS SIX, HIS REAL NAME LOST TO THE MISTS OF TIME, USED TO BE MY MOST LOYAL, MOST PRECISE VEHICLE OF MY VENGEANCE.
SIX
BUT HE HAS ALSO BETRAYED ME AND GONE OVER TO THE OTHER SIDE.
IT SEEMS AS IF YOU CAN'T REALLY TRUST ANYONE THESE DAYS.
HOWEVER I HAVEN'T GOT WHERE I AM TODAY WITHOUT CERTAIN THINGS AT MY DISPOSAL.

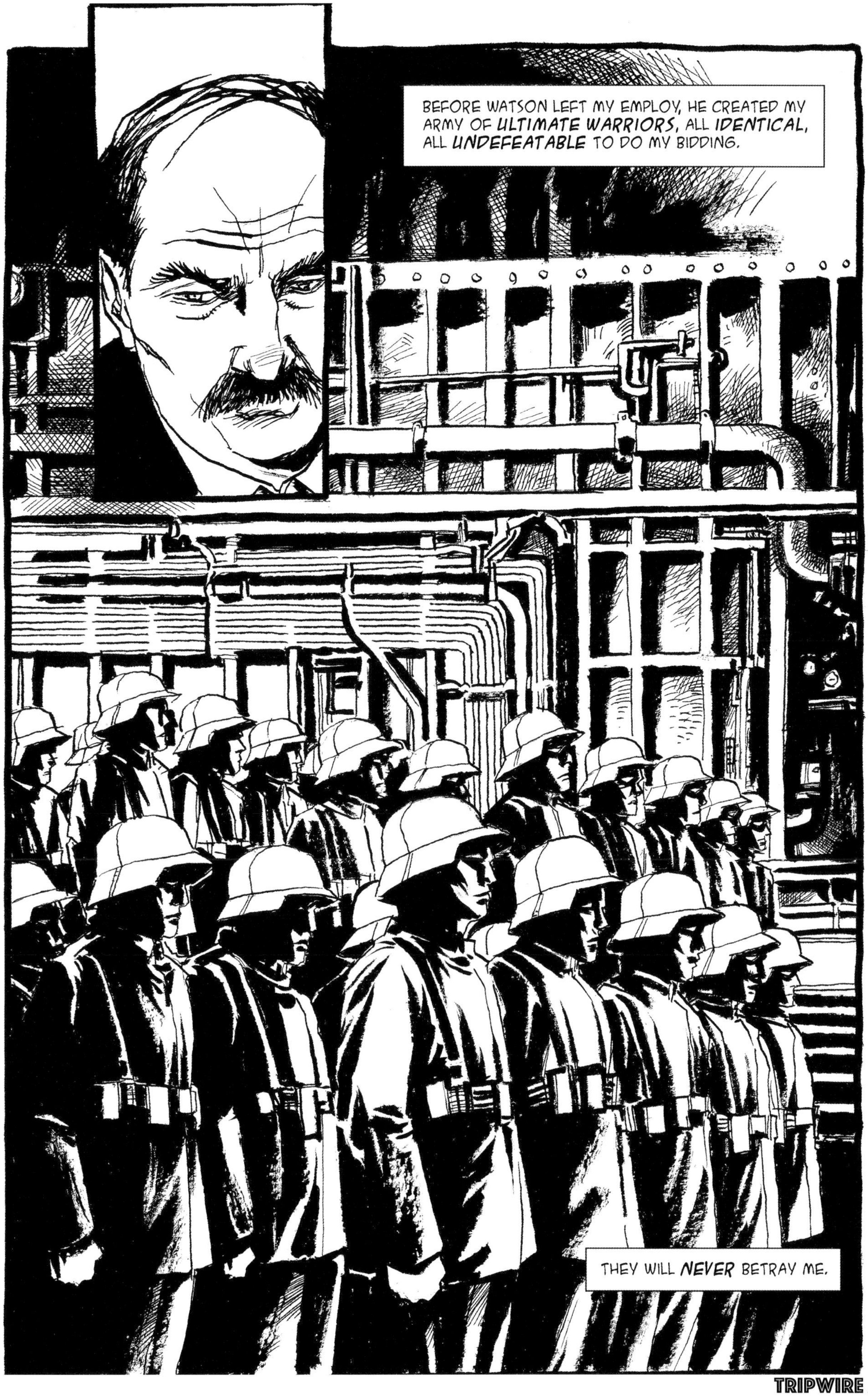
BEFORE WATSON LEFT MY EMPLOY, HE CREATED MY ARMY OF ULTIMATE WARRIORS, ALL IDENTICAL, ALL UNDEFEATABLE TO DO MY BIDDING.
THEY WILL NEVER BETRAY ME.

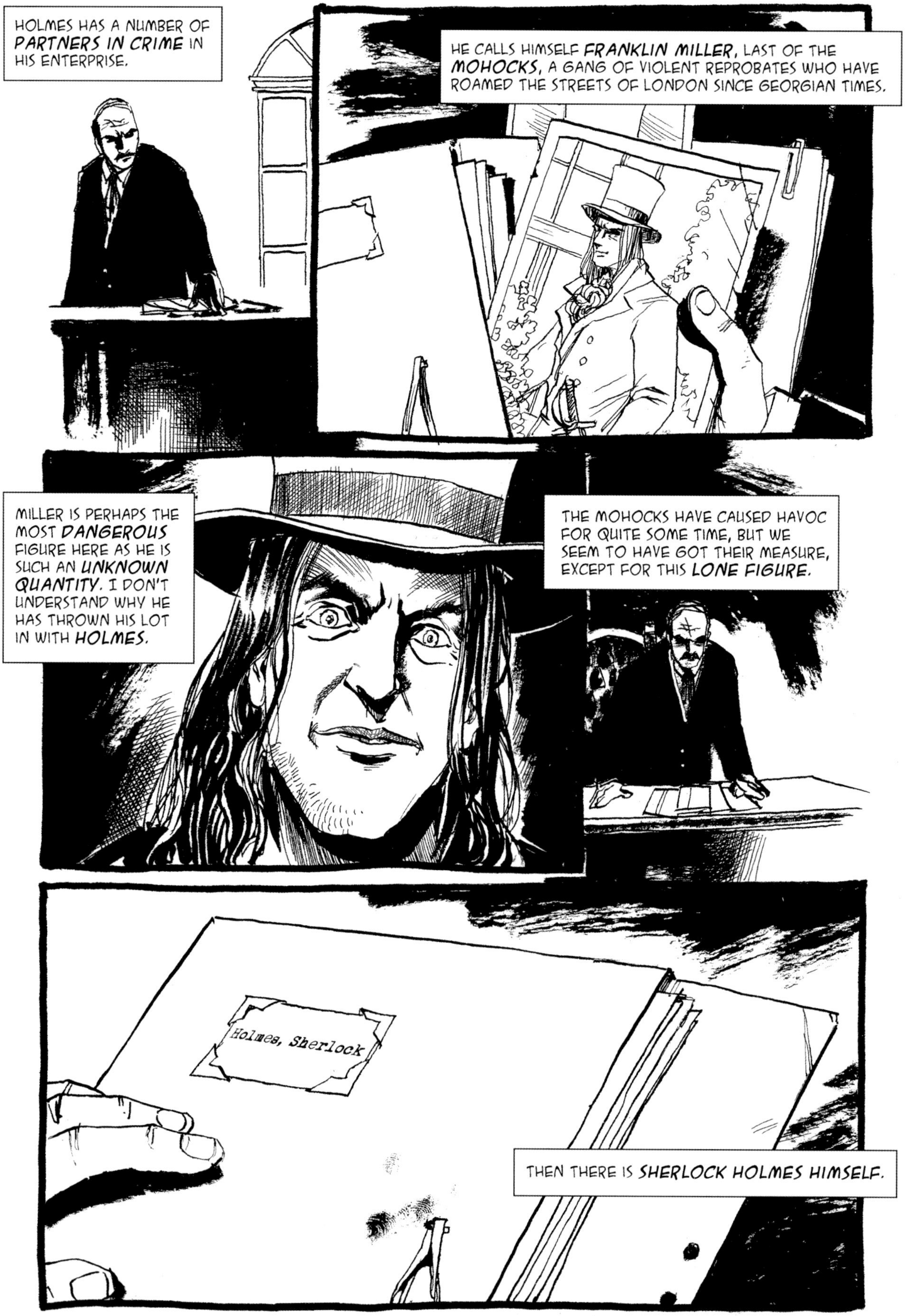
HOLMES HAS A NUMBER OF PARTNERS IN CRIME IN HIS ENTERPRISE.
HE CALLS HIMSELF FRANKLIN MILLER, LAST OF THE MOHOCKS, A GANG OF VIOLENT REPROBATES WHO HAVE ROAMED THE STREETS OF LONDON SINCE GEORGIAN TIMES.
MILLER IS PERHAPS THE MOST DANGEROUS FIGURE HERE AS HE IS SUCH AN UNKNOWN QUANTITY. I DON'T UNDERSTAND WHY HE HAS THROWN HIS LOT IN WITH HOLMES.
THE MOHOCKS HAVE CAUSED HAVOC FOR QUITE SOME TIME, BUT WE SEEM TO HAVE GOT THEIR MEASURE, EXCEPT FOR THIS LONE FIGURE.
Holmes, Sherlock
THEN THERE IS SHERLOCK HOLMES HIMSELF.

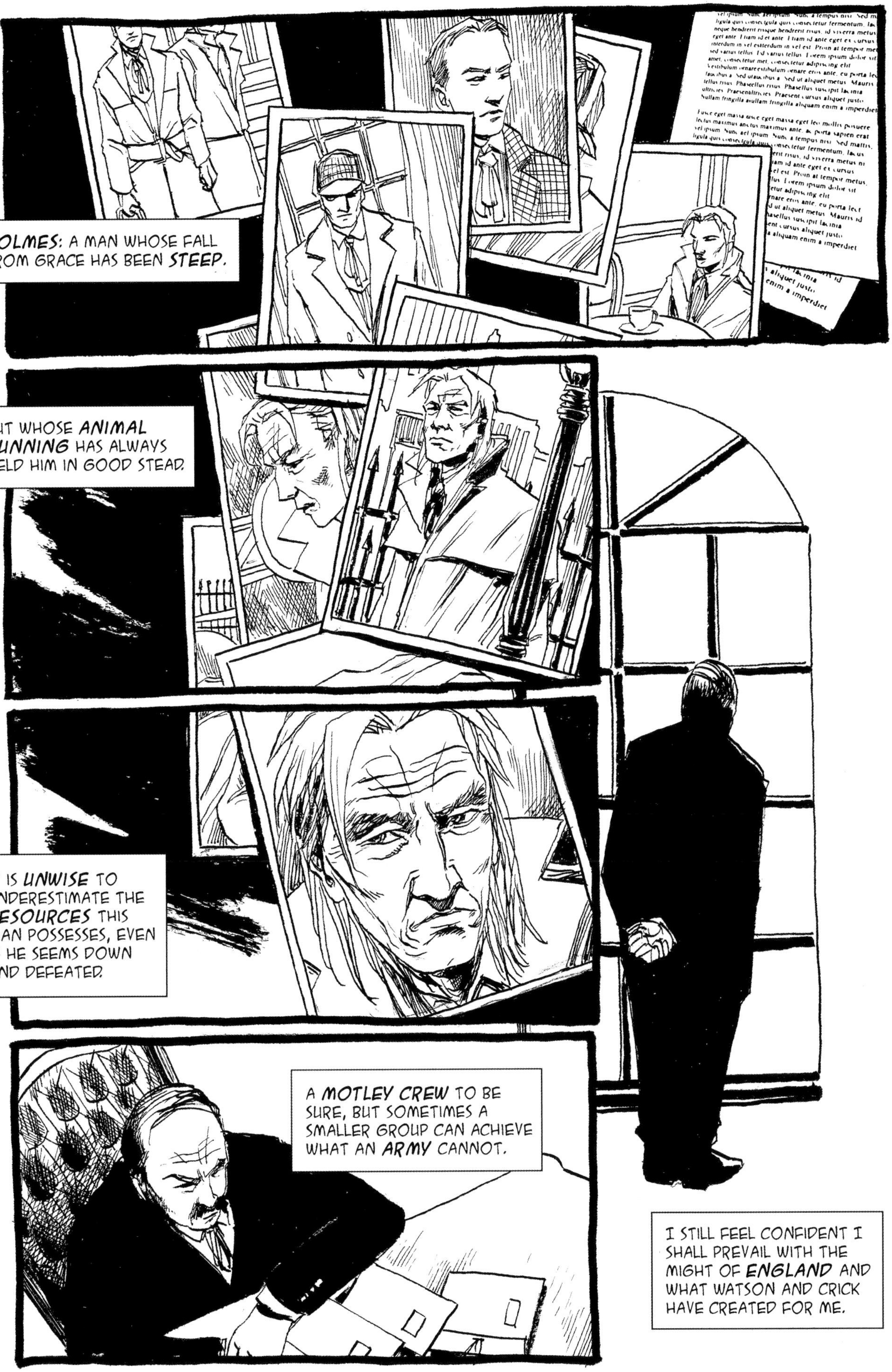
HOLMES: A MAN WHOSE FALL FROM GRACE HAS BEEN STEEP.
BUT WHOSE ANIMAL CUNNING HAS ALWAYS HELD HIM IN GOOD STEAD.
IT IS UNWISE TO UNDERESTIMATE THE RESOURCES THIS MAN POSSESSES, EVEN IF HE SEEMS DOWN AND DEFEATED.
A MOTLEY CREW TO BE SURE, BUT SOMETIMES A SMALLER GROUP CAN ACHIEVE WHAT AN ARMY CANNOT.
I STILL FEEL CONFIDENT I SHALL PREVAIL WITH THE MIGHT OF ENGLAND AND WHAT WATSON AND CRICK HAVE CREATED FOR ME.

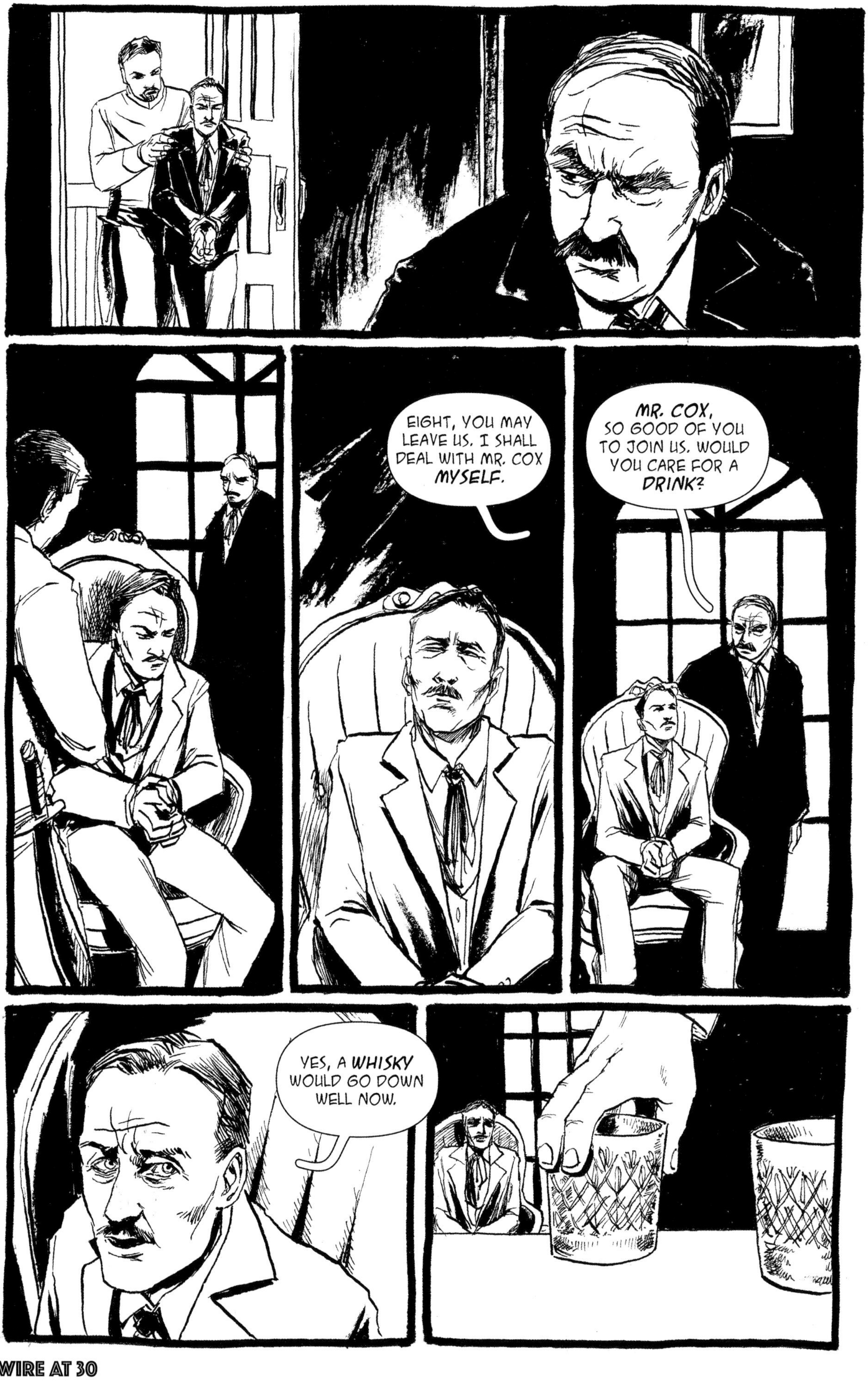
EIGHT, YOU MAY LEAVE US. I SHALL DEAL WITH MR. COX MYSELF.
MR. COX, SO GOOD OF YOU TO JOIN US. WOULD YOU CARE FOR A DRINK?
YES, A WHISKY WOULD GO DOWN WELL NOW.

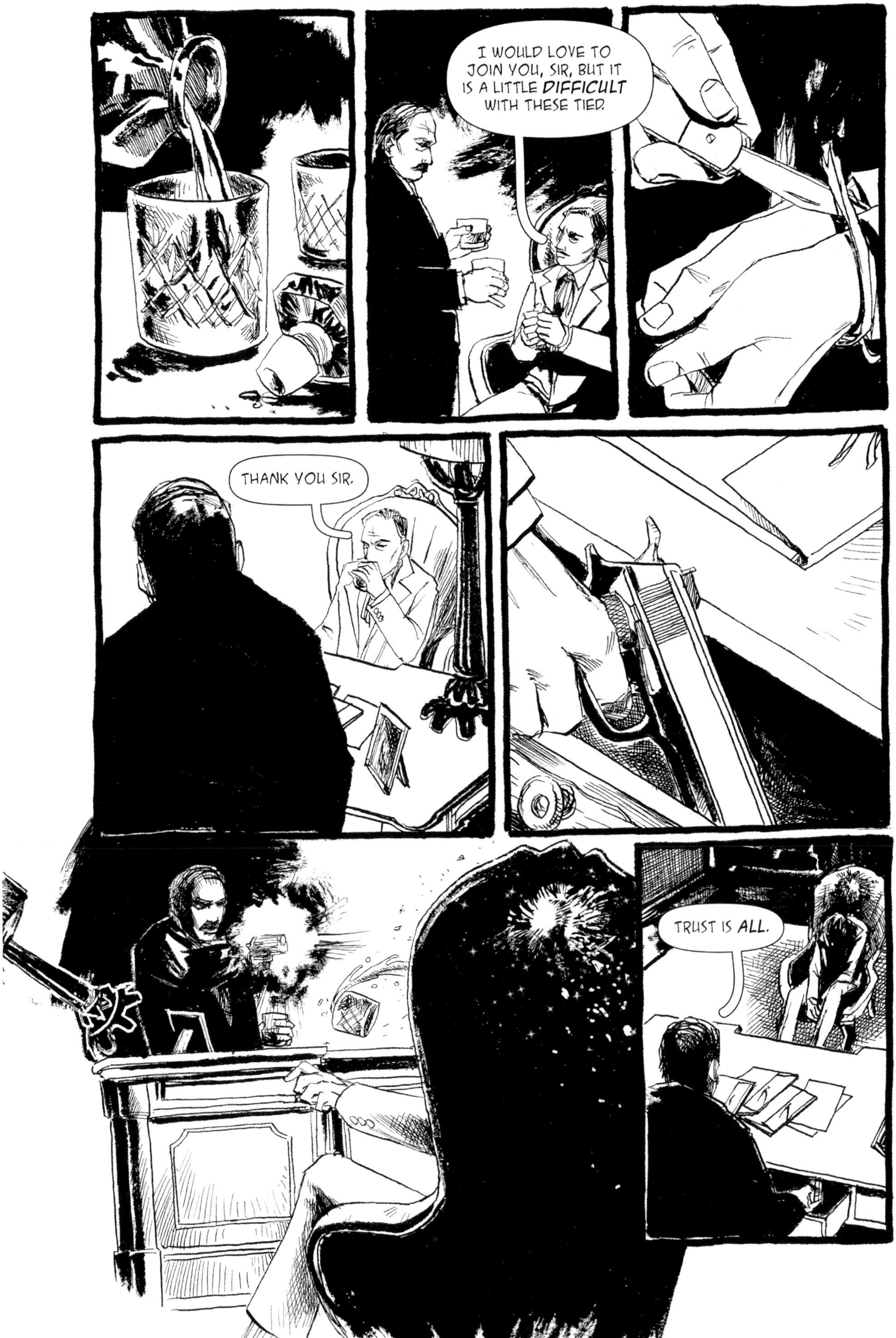
I WOULD LOVE TO JOIN YOU, SIR, BUT IT IS A LITTLE DIFFICULT WITH THESE TIED.
THANK YOU SIR.
TRUST IS ALL.

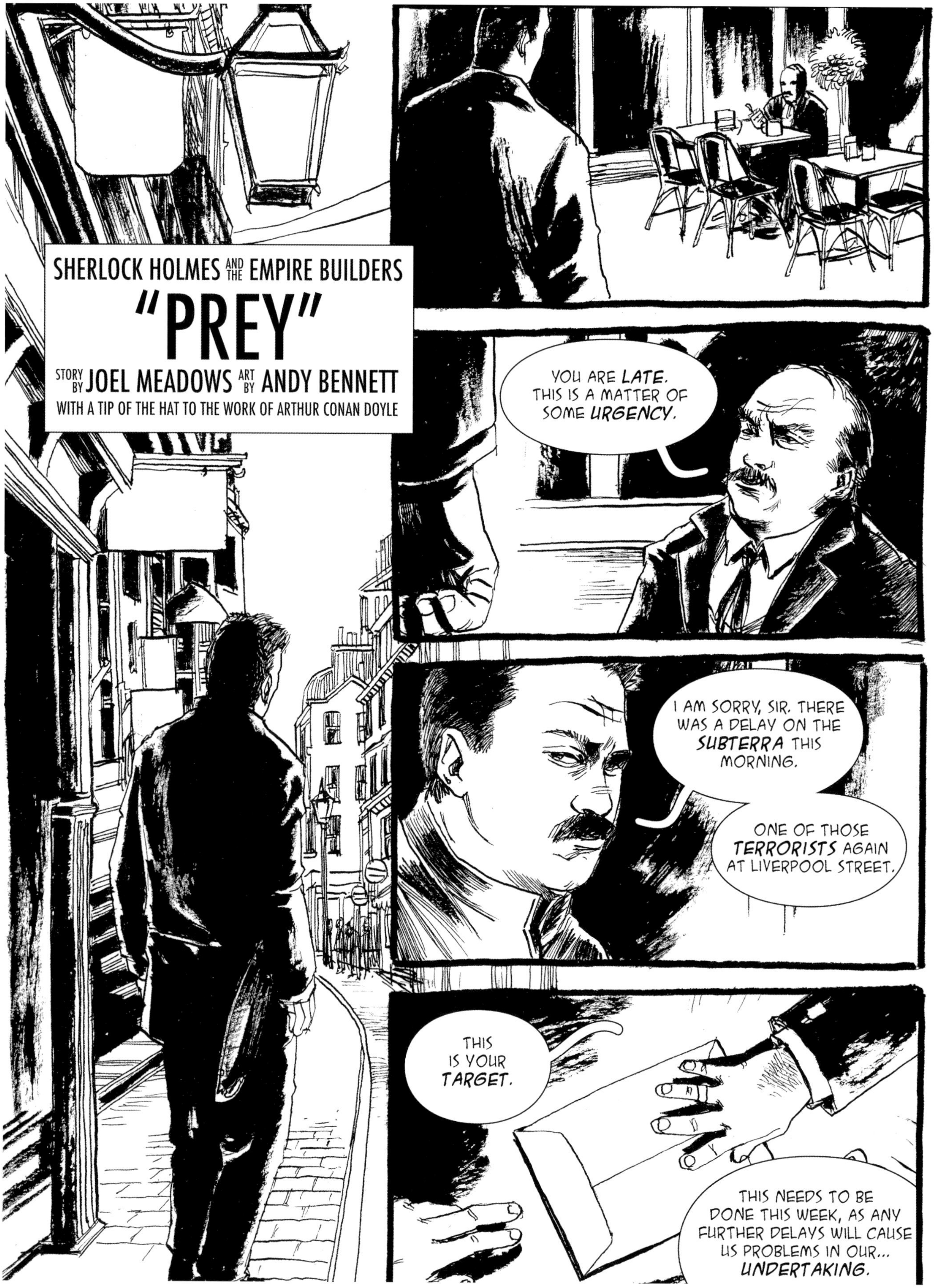
SHERLOCK HOLMES AND THE EMPIRE BUILDERS
"PREY"
STORY BY JOEL MEADOWS ART BY ANDY BENNETT
WITH A TIP OF THE HAT TO THE WORK OF ARTHUR CONAN DOYLE
YOU ARE LATE. THIS IS A MATTER OF SOME URGENCY.
I AM SORRY, SIR. THERE WAS A DELAY ON THE SUBTERRA THIS MORNING.
ONE OF THOSE TERRORISTS AGAIN AT LIVERPOOL STREET.
THIS IS YOUR TARGET.
THIS NEEDS TO BE DONE THIS WEEK, AS ANY FURTHER DELAYS WILL CAUSE US PROBLEMS IN OUR... UNDERTAKING.

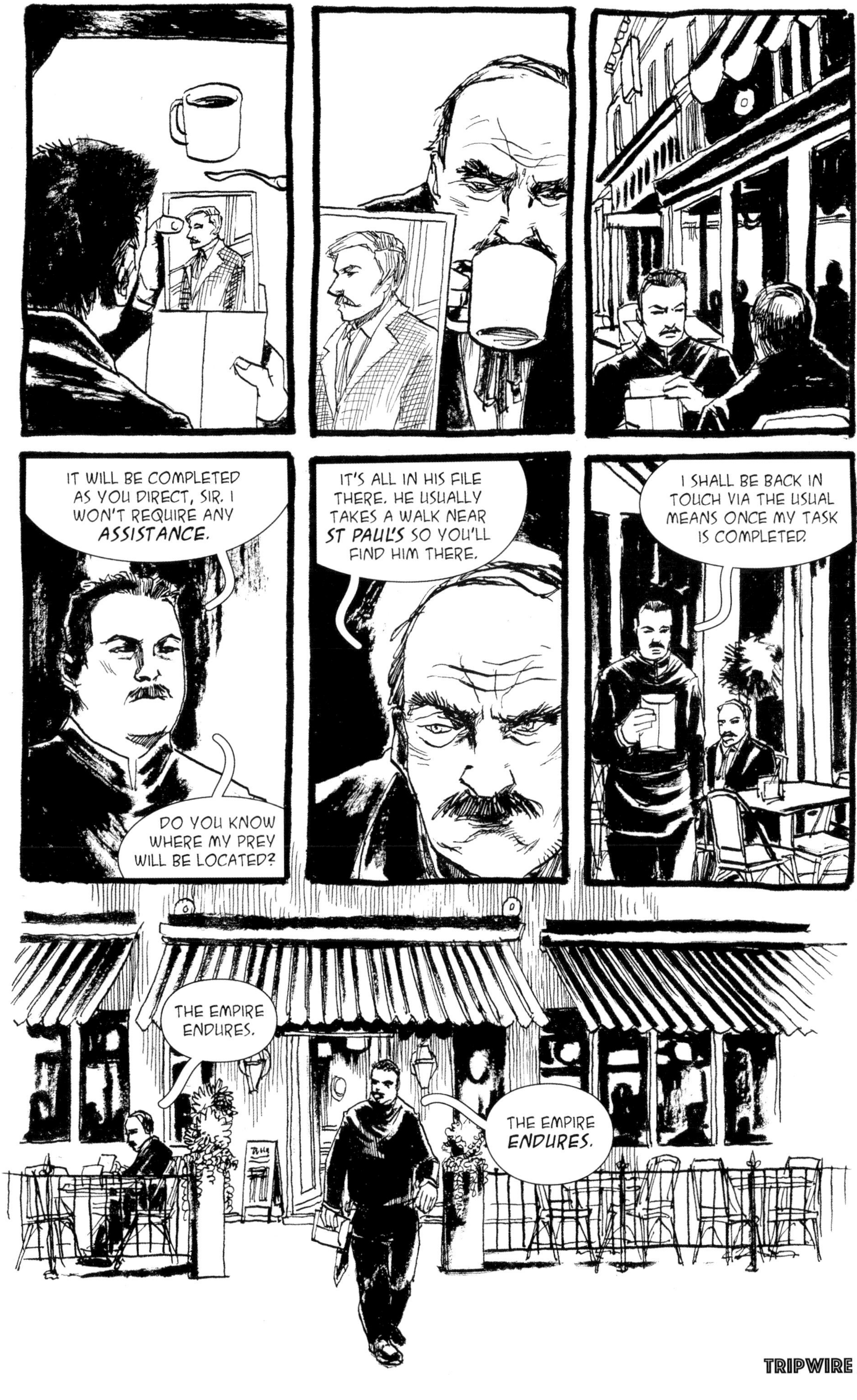
IT WILL BE COMPLETED AS YOU DIRECT, SIR. I WON'T REQUIRE ANY ASSISTANCE.
DO YOU KNOW WHERE MY PREY WILL BE LOCATED?
IT'S ALL IN HIS FILE THERE. HE USUALLY TAKES A WALK NEAR ST PAUL'S SO YOU'LL FIND HIM THERE.
I SHALL BE BACK IN TOUCH VIA THE USUAL MEANS ONCE MY TASK IS COMPLETED.
THE EMPIRE ENDURES.
THE EMPIRE ENDURES.

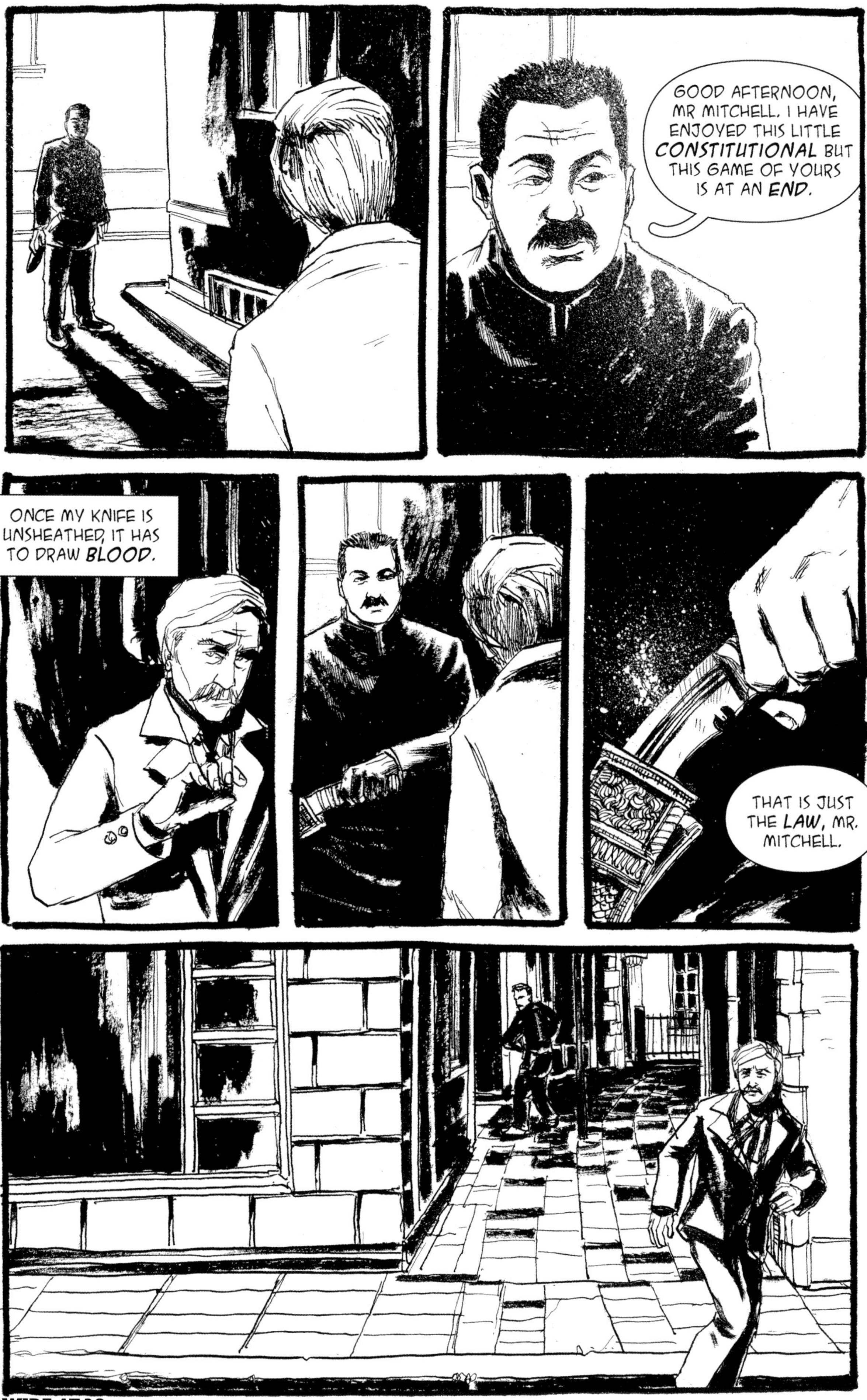
GOOD AFTERNOON, MR MITCHELL. I HAVE ENJOYED THIS LITTLE **CONSTITUTIONAL** BUT THIS GAME OF YOURS IS AT AN **END**.
ONCE MY KNIFE IS UNSHEATHED, IT HAS TO DRAW **BLOOD**.
THAT IS JUST THE **LAW**, MR. MITCHELL.

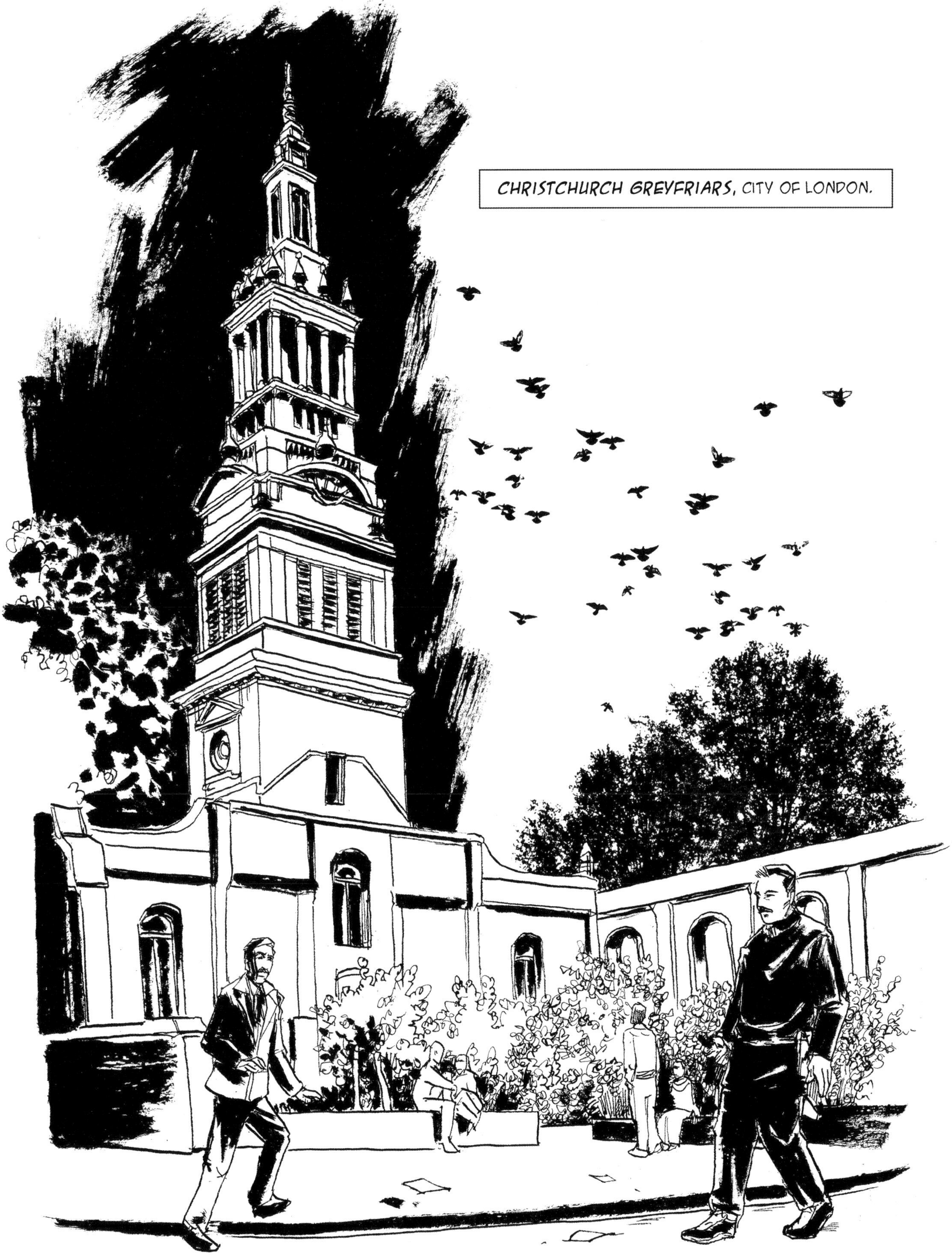
CHRISTCHURCH GREYFRIARS, CITY OF LONDON.

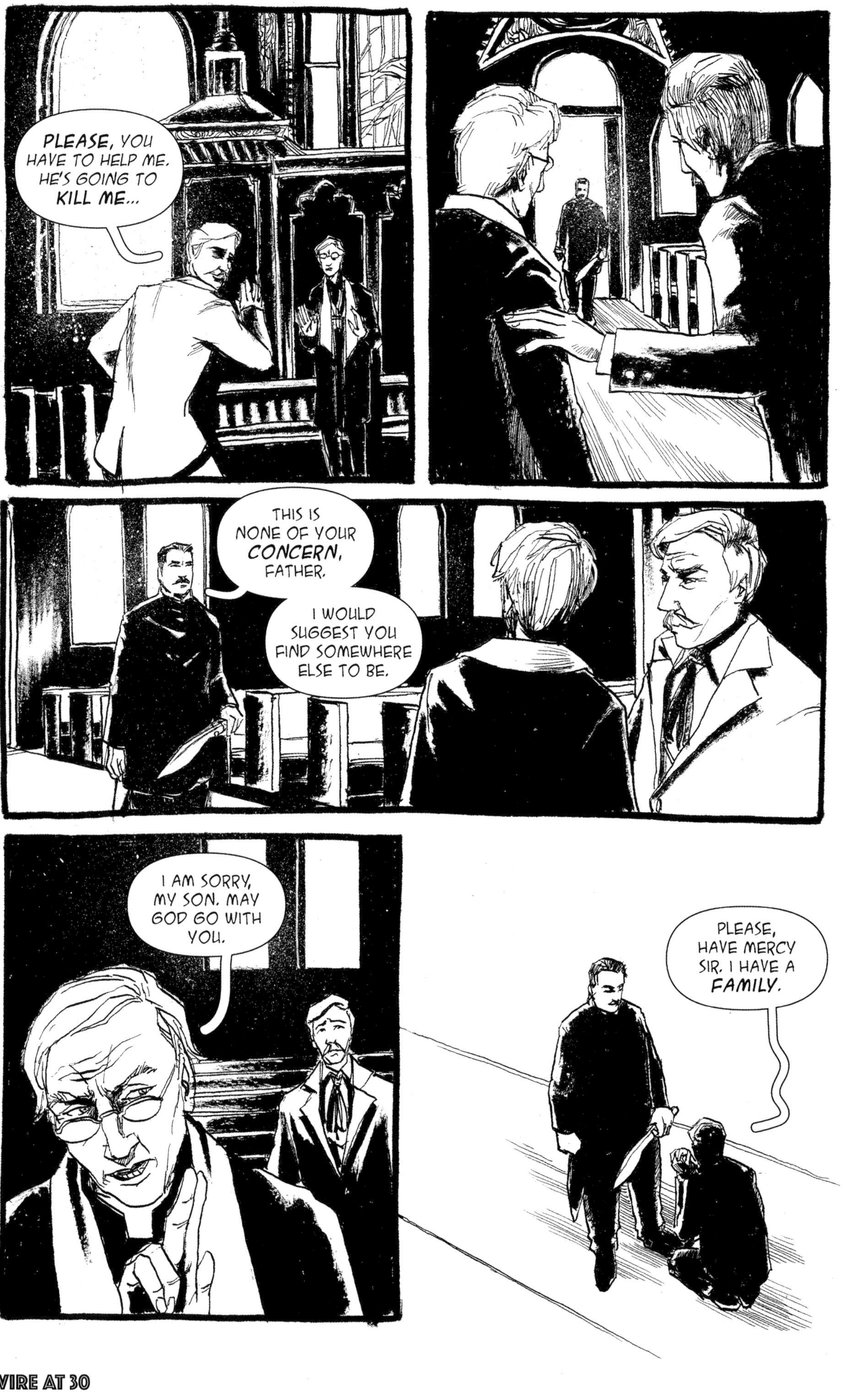
PLEASE, YOU HAVE TO HELP ME. HE'S GOING TO **KILL ME...**
THIS IS NONE OF YOUR ***CONCERN,*** FATHER.
I WOULD SUGGEST YOU FIND SOMEWHERE ELSE TO BE.
I AM SORRY, MY SON. MAY GOD GO WITH YOU.
PLEASE, HAVE MERCY SIR. I HAVE A ***FAMILY.***

IT SEEMS I DIDN'T NEED THIS TODAY.
IT SEEMS I AM TOO LATE. I SMELL *MOSLEY'S* FINGERPRINTS HERE.
IT SEEMS THE GAME IS *AFOOT*.

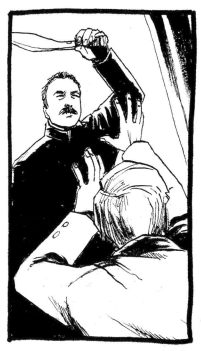

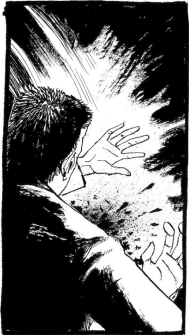

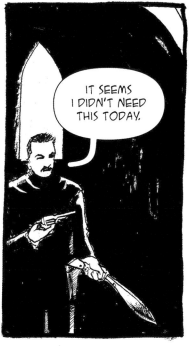

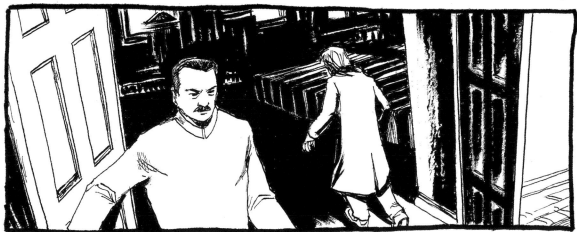

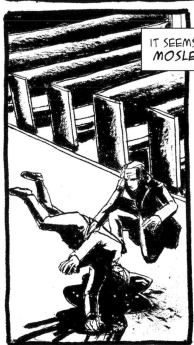

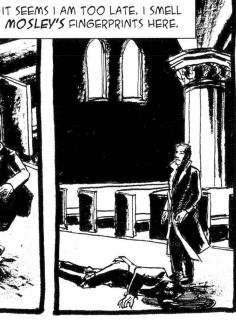

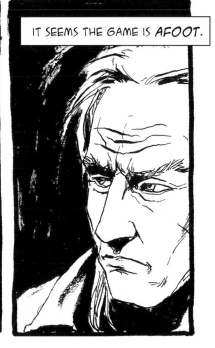

Sherlock Holmes will return in SHERLOCK HOLMES AND THE EMPIRE BUILDERS.

FRED the CLOWN in "TALENT NIGHT"

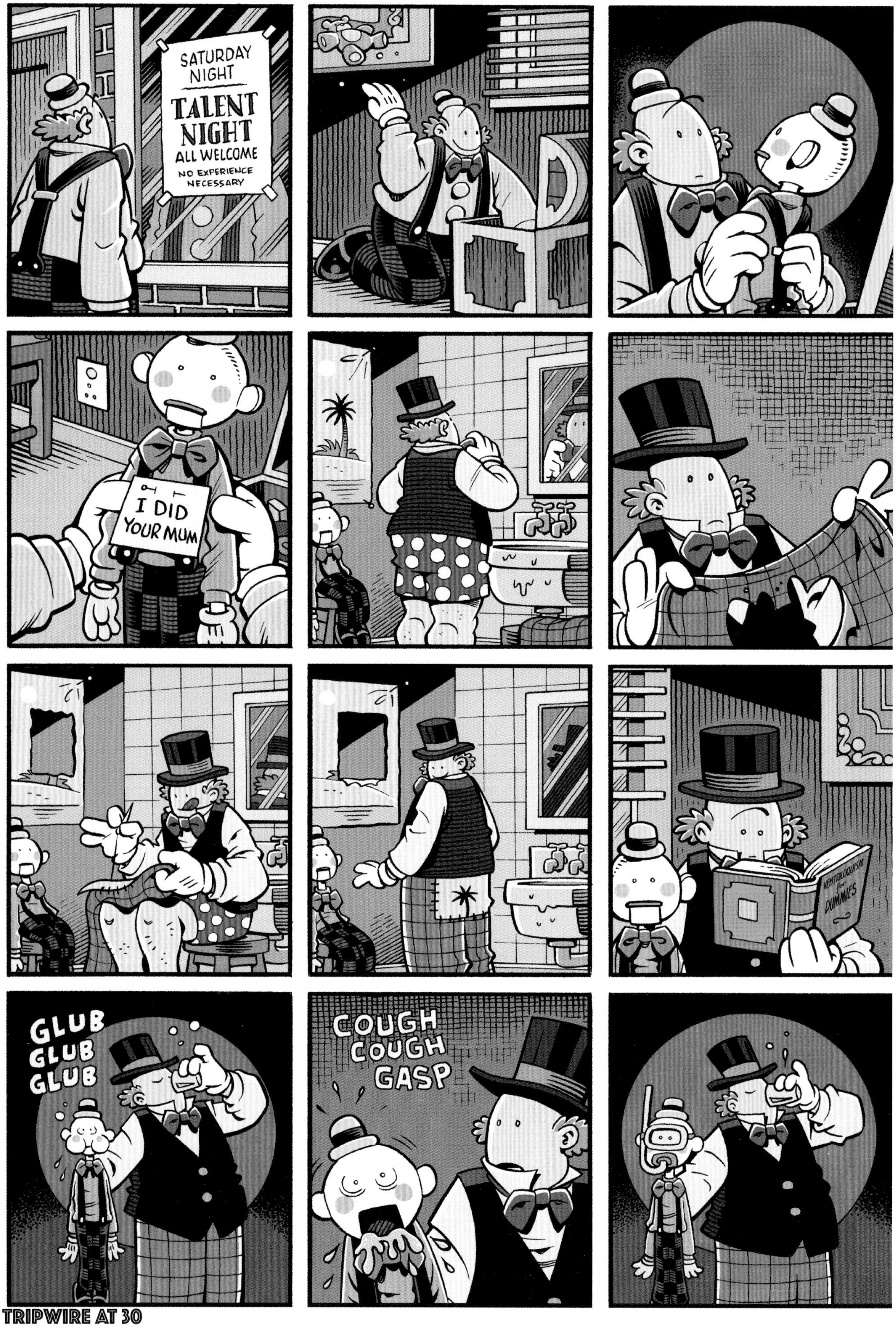
SATURDAY NIGHT
TALENT NIGHT
ALL WELCOME
NO EXPERIENCE NECESSARY
I DID YOUR MUM
VENTRILOQUISM for DUMMIES
GLUB GLUB GLUB
COUGH COUGH GASP

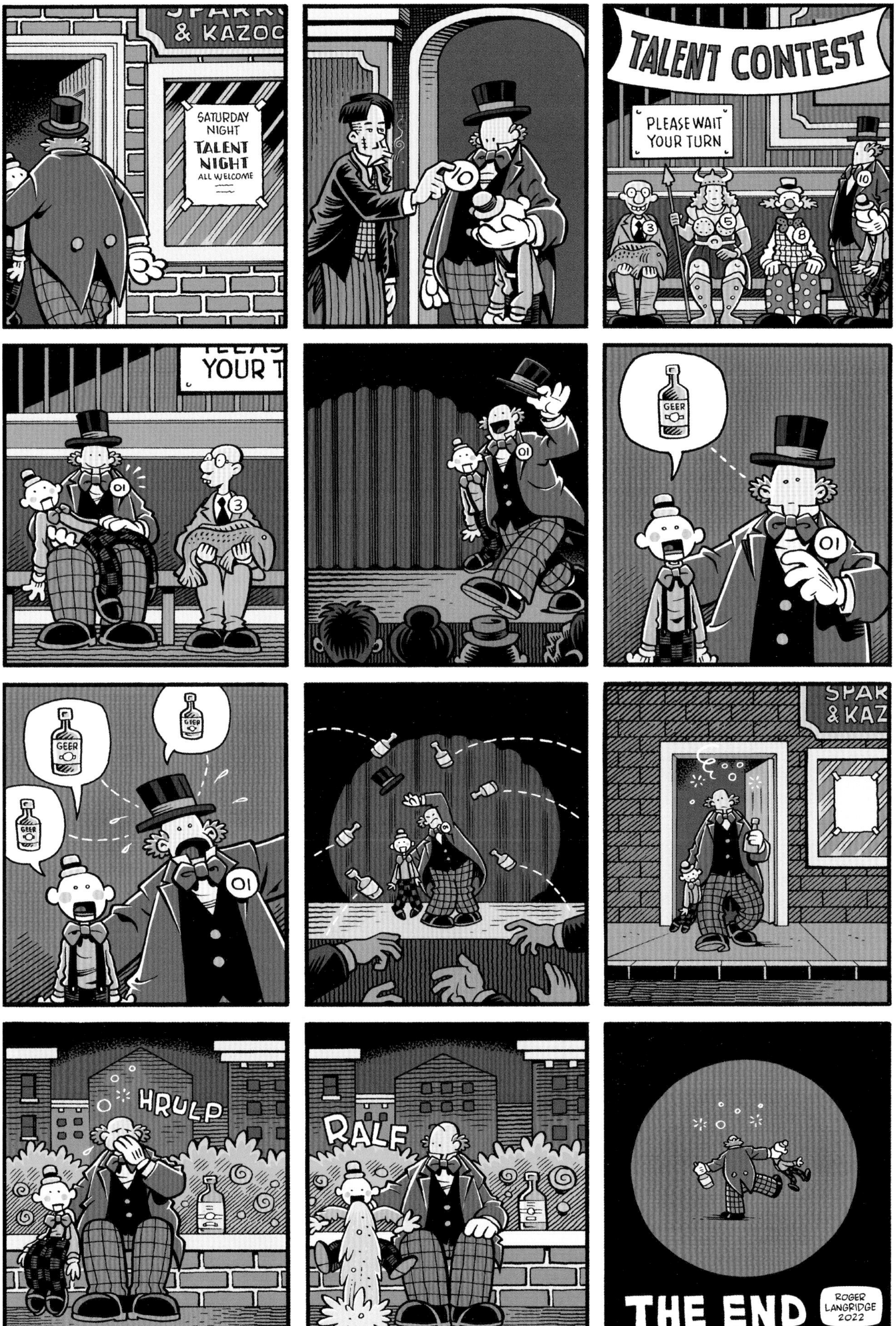
& KAZOO
SATURDAY NIGHT
TALENT NIGHT
ALL WELCOME
TALENT CONTEST
PLEASE WAIT YOUR TURN
GEER
GEER
GEER
GEER
HRULP
RALF
THE END
ROGER LANGRIDGE 2022

TRIPWIRE is many things to many people.

Wow, that is quite an epigram, isn't it? But honestly, it is also a true statement.

Huzzah!

For example, this book and the periodical it celebrates which you have in your hands right now is the leading genre magazine of popular culture worldwide. Again: A true statement. Writers and editors (me included) look at a variety of entertainment media and review, argue and preview them for the masses abroad. It is an honour. And, no matter what side of the Atlantic you find yourself on, TRIPWIRE will be covering some pop culture fixture that is of interest to you. And we have done it for three decades. Let's hear it for decades more, shall we.

TRIPWIRE is also its founder and owner, Joel Meadows. One of the toughest and most uncompromising editors in chief in comic books and beyond, he also has a smile that is genuine, his laughter is infectious, and his friendship and trust in you as a creator and collaborator is nothing less than lasting and beyond par. He's also a snappy dresser and a fine connoisseur of music and books, but that is beside the point.

Then, there is TRIPWIRE the publishing home itself. Of course, I view it in a far more personal manner. To me, it is a comic book Shangri-La amongst the rubble left after the "Four-Color Apocalypse of 1996." And, in considering where I am going to land mine and my co-creator Mike Malbrough's pride and joy – KENT MENACE – which was first reported on in this publication, as well as previewed within the pages of its most recent, now sought-after Winter Editions, all I have to say is that it's in the top running, mate! Like the much-beloved Doctor Who Holiday Specials, the Winter Editions are giant-sized mags which have been eagerly awaited by readers, and appreciated by fans across the planet. And besides that, Joel's word is his bond.

God bless TRIPWIRE and Joel Meadows for both these qualities. And, thank God we have something this good to read in our downtime.

Huzzah, indeed.

Scott Braden wrote this in August of 2022. A writer, editor and comic book creator, he really digs TRIPWIRE – and always will.

Scott Braden

consulting editor, Tripwire

co-creator Kent Menace

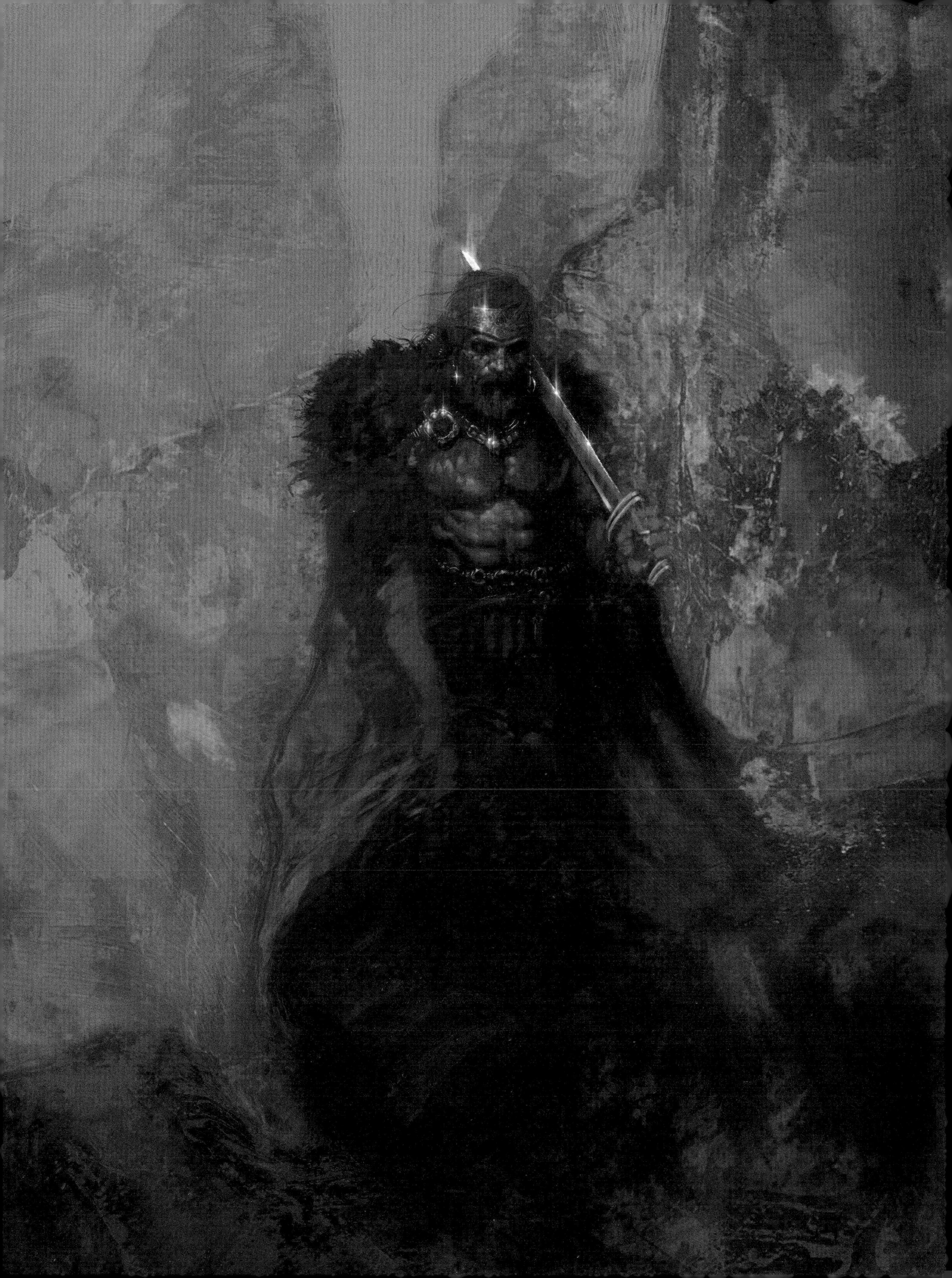

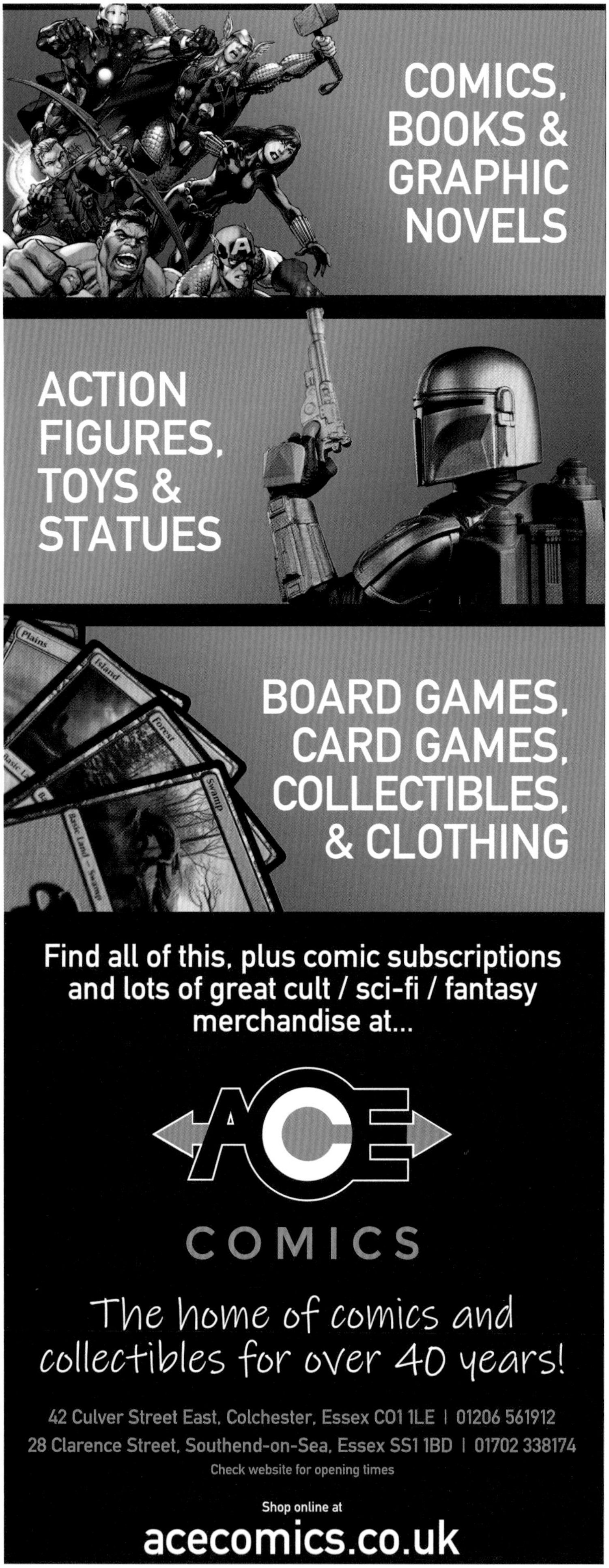

COMICS, BOOKS & GRAPHIC NOVELS
ACTION FIGURES, TOYS & STATUES
BOARD GAMES, CARD GAMES, COLLECTIBLES, & CLOTHING
Find all of this, plus comic subscriptions and lots of great cult / sci-fi / fantasy merchandise at...
ACE COMICS
The home of comics and collectibles for over 40 years!
42 Culver Street East, Colchester, Essex CO1 1LE | 01206 561912
28 Clarence Street, Southend-on-Sea, Essex SS1 1BD | 01702 338174
Check website for opening times
Shop online at
acecomics.co.uk

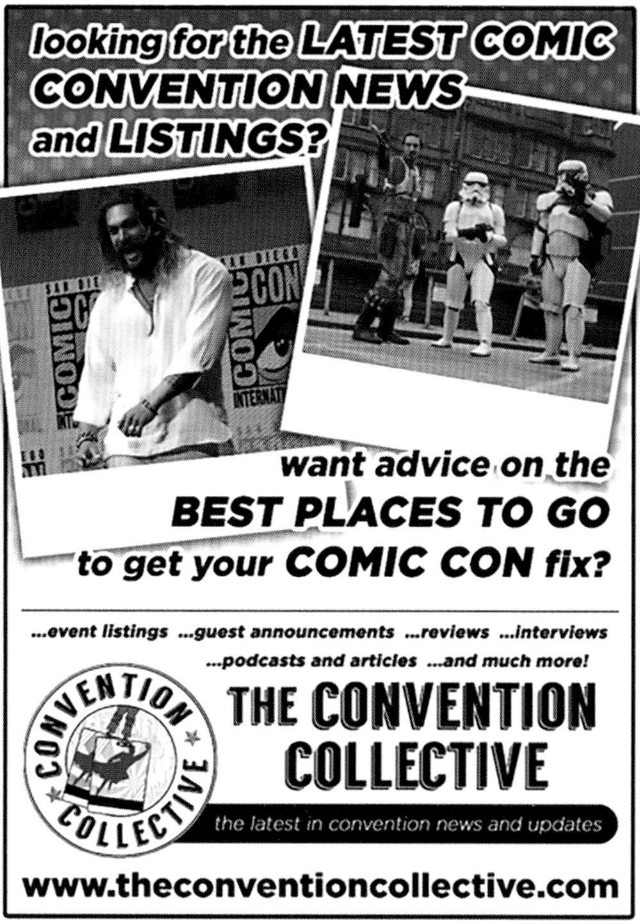

looking for the LATEST COMIC CONVENTION NEWS and LISTINGS?
want advice on the BEST PLACES TO GO to get your COMIC CON fix?
...event listings ...guest announcements ...reviews ...interviews
...podcasts and articles ...and much more!
CONVENTION COLLECTIVE
THE CONVENTION COLLECTIVE
the latest in convention news and updates
www.theconventioncollective.com

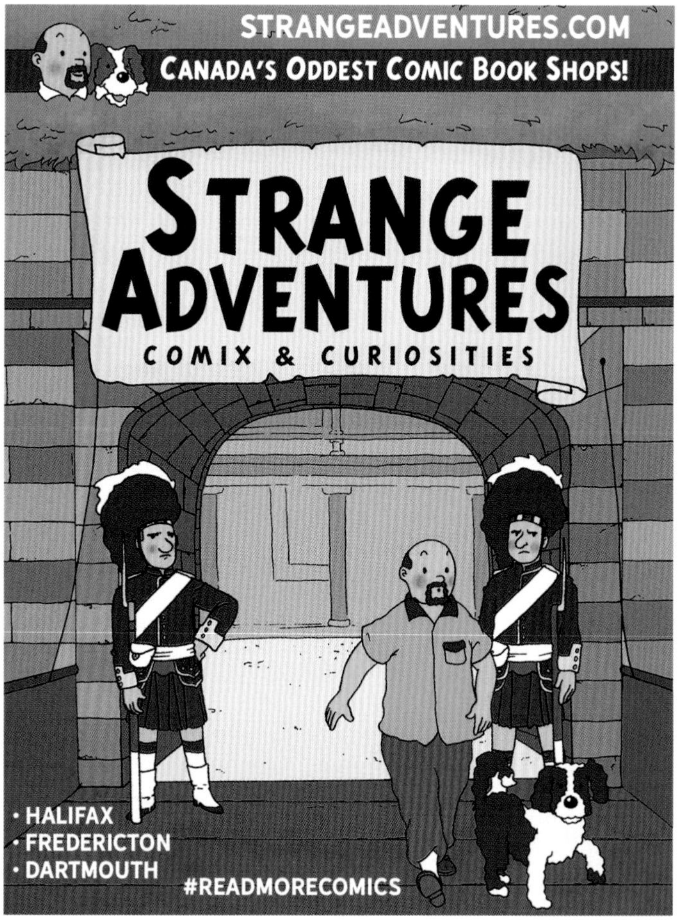

STRANGEADVENTURES.COM
CANADA'S ODDEST COMIC BOOK SHOPS!
STRANGE ADVENTURES
COMIX & CURIOSITIES
• HALIFAX
• FREDERICTON
• DARTMOUTH
#READMORECOMICS

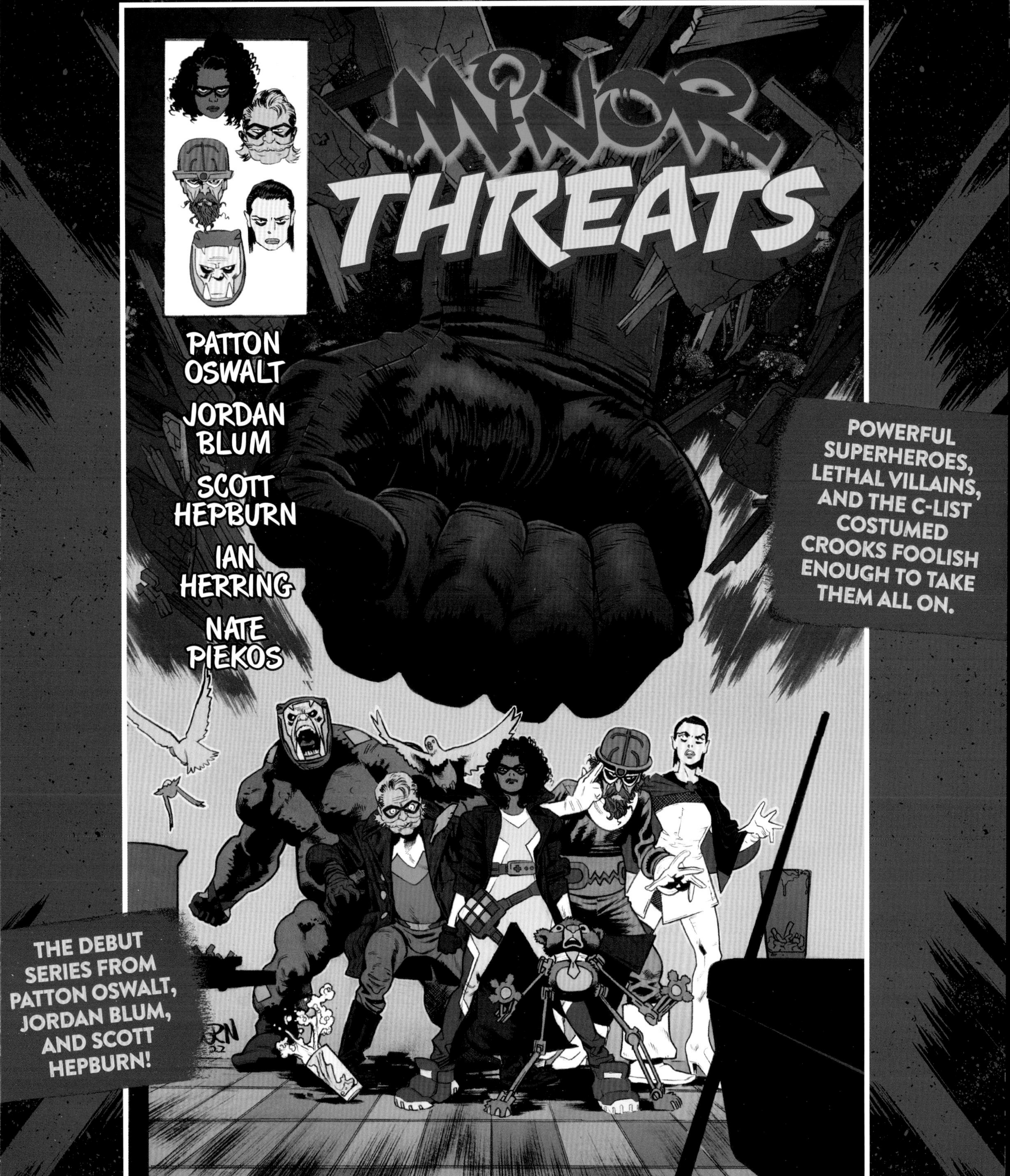
MINOR THREATS
PATTON OSWALT
JORDAN BLUM
SCOTT HEPBURN
IAN HERRING
NATE PIEKOS
POWERFUL SUPERHEROES, LETHAL VILLAINS, AND THE C-LIST COSTUMED CROOKS FOOLISH ENOUGH TO TAKE THEM ALL ON.
THE DEBUT SERIES FROM PATTON OSWALT, JORDAN BLUM, AND SCOTT HEPBURN!

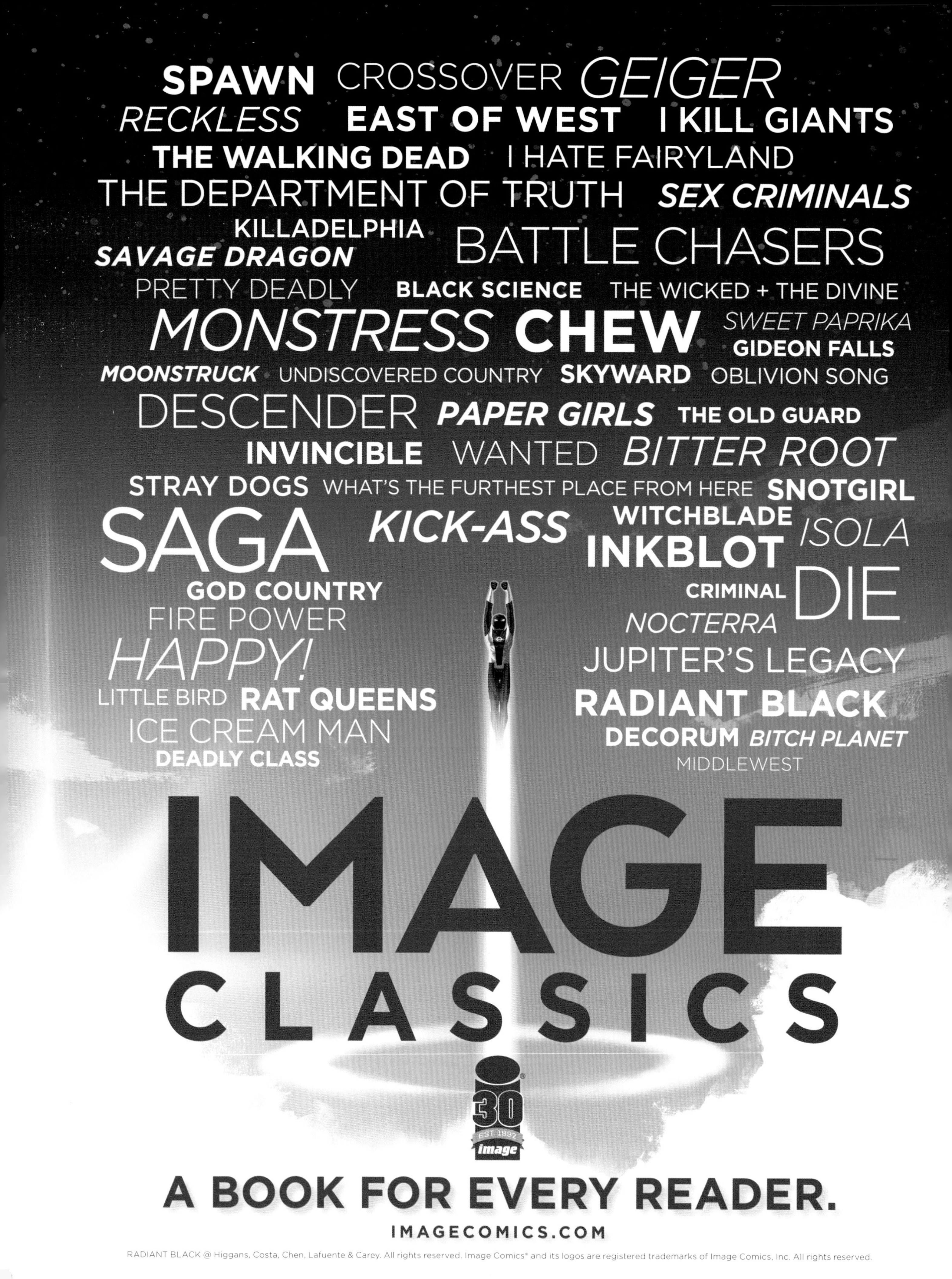
SPAWN CROSSOVER GEIGER
RECKLESS EAST OF WEST I KILL GIANTS
THE WALKING DEAD I HATE FAIRYLAND
THE DEPARTMENT OF TRUTH SEX CRIMINALS
KILLADELPHIA
SAVAGE DRAGON
BATTLE CHASERS
PRETTY DEADLY BLACK SCIENCE THE WICKED + THE DIVINE
MONSTRESS CHEW SWEET PAPRIKA
GIDEON FALLS
MOONSTRUCK UNDISCOVERED COUNTRY SKYWARD OBLIVION SONG
DESCENDER PAPER GIRLS THE OLD GUARD
INVINCIBLE WANTED BITTER ROOT
STRAY DOGS WHAT'S THE FURTHEST PLACE FROM HERE SNOTGIRL
SAGA
KICK-ASS
WITCHBLADE
INKBLOT
ISOLA
GOD COUNTRY
FIRE POWER
HAPPY!
LITTLE BIRD RAT QUEENS
ICE CREAM MAN
DEADLY CLASS
CRIMINAL
DIE
NOCTERRA
JUPITER'S LEGACY
RADIANT BLACK
DECORUM BITCH PLANET
MIDDLEWEST
IMAGE
CLASSICS
30
EST. 1992
image
A BOOK FOR EVERY READER.
IMAGECOMICS.COM
RADIANT BLACK © Higgans, Costa, Chen, Lafuente & Carey. All rights reserved. Image Comics® and its logos are registered trademarks of Image Comics, Inc. All rights reserved.

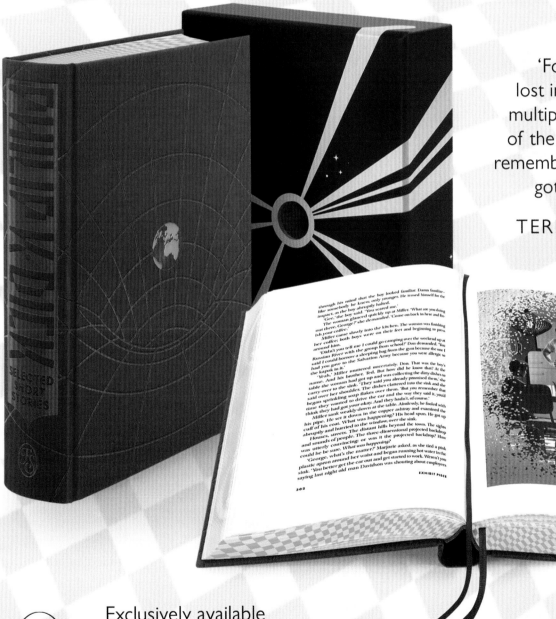

tripwire

"Tripwire is research done right celebrating and investigating the love of comic books." – **writer/ artist Jimmy Palmiotti (Harley Quinn, Jonah Hex, Pop Kill, Paper Films)**

"Tripwire is a vibrant part of entertainment coverage – specifically comics and geek culture. Supporting them, we support ourselves." – **writer Alex Segura (Pete Fernandez book series)**

"Tripwire is always well-researched and enthusiastic, by people who truly care about the importance of story. It's analytical without losing heart."–**JH Williams III (artist, Echolands, Promethea, Batwoman)**

"Tripwire covers such a wide variety of topics in the world of news, entertainment and the arts, and covers them so well, that it's pretty much become my go-to source for what's going on in media. I know if Tripwire is covering a subject, it's not only interesting, fun and informative, it's also legit." –**Bill Sienkiewicz (legendary artist and illustrator)**

"If you're a media fan, Tripwire has you covered. With articles and reviews full of insight covering the entire range of pop culture, and interviews with folks like Howard Chaykin, the Prince of Comics, Tripwire dissects, analyses, and reconstructs the world in which we all live."–**Walter Simonson (veteran writer and artist, Thor,Ragnarok, Manhunter)**

"In an industry and a world full of uncertainty, the constants that Tripwire offers in all its forms – great reporting, interesting information captivatingly presented, beautiful graphic design – are always a welcome thing.Joel Meadows and his team never fail to remind me why I love comics as much as I do, and why I feel the same about Tripwire, too." – **Chris Ryall (Szygy Publishing, Image Comics imprint, writer and former president, publisher and chief creative officer, IDW Publishing)**

Visit Tripwire's home on the web
https://tripwiremagazine.co.uk

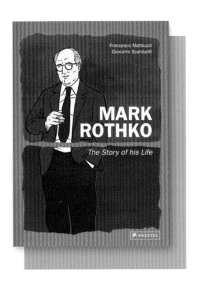
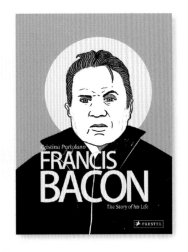
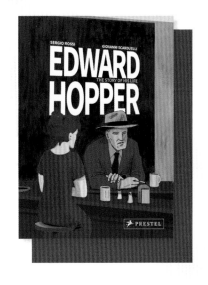
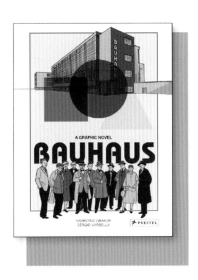
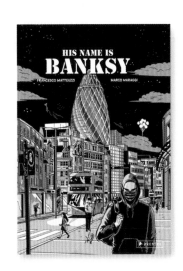

"Combining Archie-style teenage shenanigans and rivalries with a **Walking Dead** narrative arc is a stroke of genius, and the creative team give it their all, with lively animation-inspired visuals and densely designed backdrops. This rowdy volume delivers ample fun at the end of the world."
—PUBLISHERS WEEKLY

"Von Kummant's illustration is stunning and matches the lively tone of von Eckartsberg's script, which puts a new spin on dystopian survival tales in the Walking Dead vein by focusing the narrative around a teenage cast. A refreshingly original, promising start to the series."
—LIBRARY JOURNAL (STARRED REVIEW)

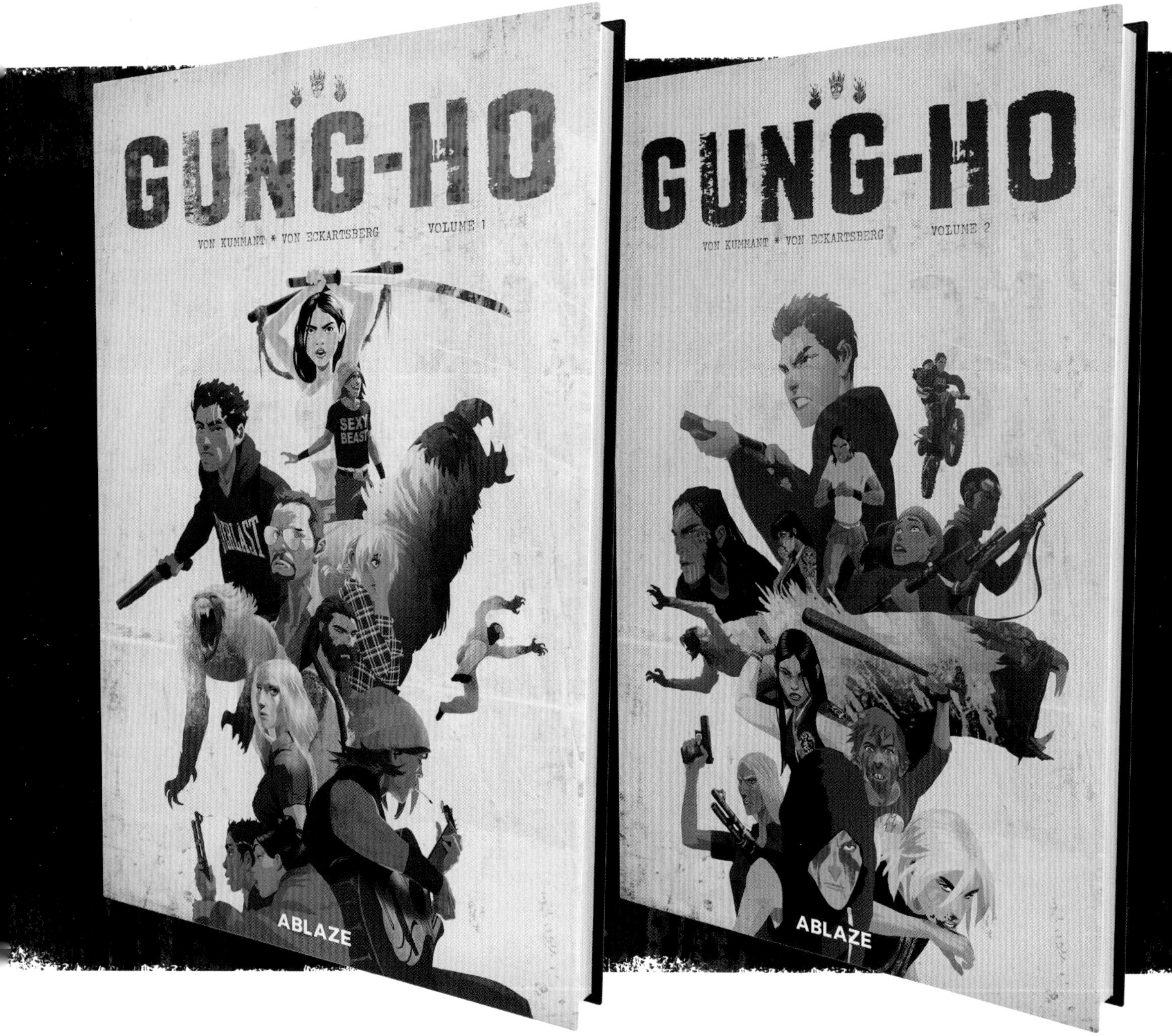
GUNG-HO
VON KUMMANT * VON ECKARTSBERG
VOLUME 1
ABLAZE
GUNG-HO
VON KUMMANT * VON ECKARTSBERG
VOLUME 2
ABLAZE

Creators **BENJAMIN VON ECKARTSBERG** and **THOMAS VON KUMMANT** deliver a creative and visual tour de force with jaw- dropping artwork that will transport you to a brand new post-apocalyptic world.

GUNG-HO Volume 1 HC collects the first two storylines of the series: **Black Sheep** and **Short Circuit**, along with a bonus cover gallery!

GUNG-HO Volume 2 HC collects the next two storylines of the series: **Sexy Beast** and **Anger**, also with a bonus cover gallery!

Available now!

GUNG-HO

ABLAZE
WWW.ABLAZE.NET

CONTRIBUTORS

Andy Bennett

Bennett was born in southern Ohio. He is a graduate of Shawnee State University in Portsmouth, and The Columbus College of Art & Design in Columbus. Today he serves as a digital media designer at Highlights for Children in Columbus, as well as offering freelance design and illustration work for a wide range of clients. He currently lives in Columbus with his wife Lisa. http://www.b3nn3tt.com/

Scott Braden

Having worked in the comics industry for more than a quarter century, Scott Braden has written articles about the four-color medium within the pages of Overstreet's Fan, Tripwire: The Genre Magazine, Comic Book Marketplace, the legendary Comics Buyers Guide, among others. His first comic book writing appeared in 1999's Galactica: The New Millennium for Realm Press – which was illustrated by Kent Menace co-creator Mike Malbrough. Besides focusing on chronicling the further adventures of Kent Menace, he also freelances for Gemstone Publishing, Tripwire and The Associated Press.

Laurence Campbell

Campbell is a comic artist who started his career at 2000AD, but quickly moved to Marvel to work on books like The Punisher Max and Deadpool Pulp. He finished a very long run on Dark Horse's BPRD series last year but has recently returned to the world of Hellboy with Hellboy and the BPRD: 1950s series. He teamed up again with regular collaborator Rob Williams on AWA's Old Haunts, with co-writer Ollie Masters, a series that is transferring to the big screen soon. Campbell also drew Hellboy miniseries The Sword Of Hyperborea with writer Rob Williams this year for Dark Horse.

Robert Cave

Cave is an experienced writer and editior whose work has been published in places like Guinness World Records Annual, Guinness Gamers Edition and also has contributed to Tripwire both in print and online for a number of years.

Andrew Colman

Senior editor Colman has worked on Tripwire both online and in print for over twenty years now, covering comics and film. He has also been involved with comic conventions in the UK and also contributed to Image Comics' Studio Space book in 2008.

Amanda Conner

Conner is an American comics artist and commercial art illustrator. She began her career in the late 1980s for Archie Comics and Marvel Comics, before moving on to contribute work for Claypool Comics' Soulsearchers and Company and Harris Comics' Vampirella in the 1990s. Her 2000s work includes MAD magazine, and such DC Comics characters as Harley Quinn and Power Girl. Her other published work includes illustrations for The New York Times and Revolver magazine.

Simon Davis

Davis is a British comic artist and painter who has worked extensively for 2000AD on strips like Slaine, Sinister Dexter and Thistlebone. He is also a painter of some repute, with his work being shortlisted in the prestigious BP Portrait Award at London's National Portrait Gallery on a number of occasions.

Lee Garbett

Garbett is the artist/co-creator of *Skyward* with writer Joe Henderson (showrunner of *Lucifer* on Netflix). Published by Image Comics, *Skyward* is currently

Jock

in development by Sony Pictures. He has worked for Marvel on *Loki: Agent Of Asgard*, *Spider-man*, *Defenders* and *Ghost Rider* and for DC on *Lucifer*, *Batman*, *Batgirl* and *The Outsiders*. Outside of comics, Lee designs posters, costumes and concept art for films.

Marty Grosser

Grosser is the editor of Diamond's Previews catalogue but he has a career in publishing that goes back to the 1980s. He also acts as editor on Scott Braden's Kent Menace series of comic strips and prose stories.

Tim Hayes

Tim Hayes is a UK-based freelance writer, critic, editor and technology reporter. He has written about comics, films, science and business in places like The Comics Journal, Sight & Sound, Tripwire, Little White Lies, and way back in the mists of time Comics International.

Frazer Irving

Irving is a British comic artist whose work has extensively appeared in *2000AD* but he has also collaborated with renowned Scottish comic writer Grant Morrison a number of times on books like *The Return Of Bruce Wayne*, *Batman and Robin* and *Klarion*. He has also worked with fellow British creator Si Spurrier on Image series *Gutsville* and his CV also includes work at Marvel on books like *Doctor Strange*, *Avengers* and *Thanos*.

Jock

Jock is the three times New York Times best-selling British artist best known for his comics work with writer Andy Diggle on DC/Vertigo's The Losers, the award-winning Batman: The Black Mirror, and Wytches with writer Scott Snyder, and the self penned Batman: One Dark Knight for DC Comics. Jock has also produced key art and concept design for every major Hollywood studio on films including Dredd, Annihilation, Star Wars: The Last Jedi, and the Oscar-winning Ex Machina. Born in Glasgow, Scotland, he now lives and works in Devon, England.

Roger Langridge

Roger Langridge is a New Zealand-born comics writer and artist who came to prominence with his work on Judge Dredd Megazine, The Straightjacket Fits with writer David Bishop. His creator-owned work on Fred The Clown has won him fans around the world and has been nominated for a number of awards including an Eisner. He has also worked on The Muppets comic and Snarked for Boom! Studios and is also a working illustrator. http://hotelfred.blogspot.com/

Shawn Martinbrough

Martinbrough is a professional illustrator and comic book artist. He began his career in 1992 working for Marvel Comics imprint Epic Comics on the title Clive Barker's Hellraiser. The next year he was hired by Milestone Media, a DC Comics imprint to work on the title Static. Later on he worked on Milestone titles such as Blood Syndicate and DC's own titles like Shadow Cabinet. His first "mainstream" work was in the beginning of the 2000's on the title Detective Comics, specifically in the storyline Batman: Evolution. Most recently, he worked as an artist designer in the movie The Dark Knight Rises and has also been working for Image Comics on the title Thief of Thieves.

Joel Meadows

Meadows is a journalist and writer with over three decades of experience on newspapers, magazines and books. His CV includes some of the world's most renowned publications including Time Magazine, The Times, The Sunday Times, The Guardian, Guinness World Records and The Observer. He has also written extensively about comics, film, TV and culture for publications like Playboy, Time Magazine, Esquire, Variety and Empire. He is also the editor-in-chief of Tripwire. He lives in London.

Frank Miller

Miller is a comic writer and artist responsible arguably for some of the most significant series in comics history. His work on Batman at DC and Daredevil at Marvel changed the industry forever. His cinematic approach to books like *Sin City*, Batman: The Dark Knight Returns, Batman: Year One and Daredevil: Born Again (the latter with artist David Mazzuchelli) has garnered him a reputation as one of the most influential creators of the past forty years.

Sedat Oezgen

Oezgen is a Turkish German comic book artist, who originated from Batman in south east Turkey. In 2007 Sedat released his first published work, which was a short comic about his family's story which revolves around his relationship to his grandfather. In 2009 Oezgen's first work in the US was published through Moonstone Books. In 2014 he decided to become a freelance comic book artist. Since then, Oezgen has worked for companies such as IDW, Valiant, Dynamite and Zenescope.

Sean Phillips

Phillips is a British comic artist with a career that has spanned over four decades, working on everything from *Hellblazer* at Vertigo to *WildCATS* and *Sleeper* at Wildstorm to *Marvel Zombies* at Marvel. Over the past twenty years he has teamed up with regular collaborator Ed Brubaker on series like Criminal, Reckless and Incognito.

Frank Quitely

Quitely is a Scottish comic artist and illustrator who has drawn every major comic character at DC and Marvel including Batman, Superman and X-Men. He has worked with renowned writer Grant Morrison on a number of books as well as collaborating with Mark Millar on *Jupiter's Legacy*. He has also created labels for Scottish whisky companies and a mural for a Scottish hotel.

Sean Phillips

Frank Quitely

Dan Schaffer

Schaffer is a London-based comic book writer, illustrator and screenwriter. Best known as the creator of the critically acclaimed comic series, *Dogwitch*, he has written and illustrated comics in multiple genres since 2002. Schaffer has most recently been working with Heavy Metal Magazine on the cyberpunk series *Wiremonkeys*. Dan's screenwriting credits to date include *Doghouse*, *The Scribbler* and *Peripheral*.

Bill Sienkiewicz

Sienkiewicz is a highly esteemed comics artist and illustrator whose career began in the 1980s. He has drawn every major icon at Marvel and DC including Batman, X-Men, Black Panther, Spider-man and others. He has also created a lot of movie posters for films including John Wick, Logan and Black Panther.

Martin Simmonds

Simmonds is a comic artist, and co-creator of *Dying is Easy* (with Joe Hill) for IDW and *Punks Not Dead* (with David Barnett) for Black Crown. He is also a contributing artist to Marvel's The Immortal Hulk by Al Ewing and Joe Bennett, and series cover artist for Marvel's Quicksilver: No Surrender and Jessica Jones. Most recently he has been working on Image's hit book *Department Of Truth* as its co-creator with writer James Tynion IV.

Walter Simonson

Simonson is a veteran comics writer and artist with a career that spans over six decades. He first came to prominence with *Manhunter* at DC with writer Archie Goodwin but it was his run on Marvel's Thor in the 1980s which really propelled him into fandom's consciousness. Most recently he has been working on creator-owned series *Ragnarok* for IDW.

Drew Struzan

Struzan is a legendary movie poster artist who has created posters for some of the most iconic films of the past forty years from *The Shawshank Redemption* to *Back To The Future*, *Indiana Jones and The Last Crusade* to *Blade Runner*. He is retired now but he leaves a huge body of work that spans modern cinema history.

Bryan Talbot

Talbot is an acclaimed British comic writer and artist whose career began in the 1970s in underground comics. In the late 1970s, Talbot's groundbreaking Luther Arkwright debuted, a series which he has returned to twice including the latest volume, *The Legend Of Luther Arkwright*, which came out this year. Talbot has also worked for US comic companies like DC and Dark Horse over the years.

Dirk Wood

Wood has worked in comics for decades now, first in retail and then at Dark Horse Comics in marketing. He moved onto working at IDW Publishing, where he ran imprint Wood Works. It was here where he acted as editor-in-chief of shortlived but well-received comics and journalism periodical *Full Bleed*. Currently he is Director of International Sales & Licensing at Image Comics.